ORIGIN AND SERVICES

OF

THE COLDSTREAM GUARDS.

VOL. II.

ORIGIN AND SERVICES

OF THE

COLDSTREAM GUARDS.

BY COLONEL MAC KINNON.

IN TWO VOLUMES.

VOL. II.

The Naval & Military Press Ltd

Reproduced by kind permission of the Central Library,
Royal Military Academy, Sandhurst

Published by
The Naval & Military Press Ltd
Unit 10, Ridgewood Industrial Park,
Uckfield, East Sussex,
TN22 5QE England
Tel: +44 (0) 1825 749494
Fax: +44 (0) 1825 765701
www.naval-military-press.com
www.military-genealogy.com
© The Naval & Military Press Ltd 2010

The Naval & Military Press ...

...offer specialist books for the serious student of conflict. The range of titles stocked covers the whole spectrum of military history with titles on uniforms, battles, official histories, specialist works containing Medal Rolls and Casualties Lists, and numismatic titles for medal collectors and researchers.

The innovative approach they have to military bookselling and their commitment to publishing have made them Britain's leading independent military bookseller.

In reprinting in facsimile from the original, any imperfections are inevitably reproduced and the quality may fall short of modern type and cartographic standards.

CONTENTS

OF

THE SECOND VOLUME.

CHAPTER I.

Clinton appointed Commander-in-Chief in America—British evacuate Philadelphia — Battle of Freehold Court-House — Clinton reaches Sandy Hook—Embarks for New York—Guards with other troops embark for the Capes of Virginia—Land at Glebe—Fort and ships destroyed—Stores and provisions taken from the enemy—Forces embark for New York—Guards, joined by troops from Virginia, sail up North River—Morgan lands—Clinton disembarks at Stoney Point —Fort La Fayette surrenders—Guards embark for Newhaven—Garth disembarks—Town taken—Vessels, artillery, and stores destroyed— Army marches through Fairfield—Shipping, stores, and town burnt —Troops re-embark—Land at Norwalk and Greenfield; both places destroyed—English return to New York—Guards formed part of the garrison during the winter—Clinton embarks at Sandy Hook to reduce South Carolina—Lord Stirling attempts to take Staten Island —Flank companies of the Guards, a few guns, some Hessians, and mounted Yagers, march for Young's house—Young's house taken— Arnold, the American General, carries on a secret correspondence— Major André tried as a spy and hanged—Army crosses the Catawba —Guards distinguish themselves—Americans return to North Carolina—Cornwallis attacks the enemy's lines at Guildford Court-House —Americans retreat in good order—British move towards Wilmington—Cornwallis reaches Petersburg, crosses the Roanoke, Meherrin, and Nottaway rivers—Army reinforced marches through Hanover country—Cornwallis defeats La Fayette—Crosses James River, and concentrates in York Town—Washington moves to White Plains—Joined by the French from Rhode Island—Arnold destroys New London—York Town invested—Cornwallis surrenders—Carleton succeeds Clinton in command—Ratification of peace—Thirteen provinces declared independent—Returns of the officers who served in America . . . . *page* 1

CHAPTER II.

Death of Waldegrave—Duke of York succeeds as Colonel of the Coldstream—Misunderstanding between Duke of York and Colonel Lennox—Murder of Lewis XVI.—England joins against the new Government of France—First battalions of the regiments of Guards embark for Holland—Clairfait obliges the French to retreat—Archduke Charles carries several batteries—Prince of Saxe-Coburg drives the French from Aix-la-Chapelle—Siege of Maestricht raised—Junction of Generals Miranda and Valence—Prussians, Hanoverians, and British advance by Bois-le-Duc—Grenadier battalion consists of five companies—Guards in quarters at Bergen-op-Zoom—Guards proceed by canal to Bruges—March through Tournay to Orcq—Coldstream attack the French near St. Amand—Duke of York's order dated Tournay—Condé blockaded—Investment of Valenciennes—Siege entrusted to the Duke of York—Capitulation—Condé surrenders—A reinforcement, including three light companies, one for each regiment of Guards, joins the army—Garrison of Valenciennes march out and lay down their arms—Cambray summoned—Duke of York's army separates from the Austrians—French defeated at Lincelles—Siege of Dunkirk—Houchard arrives with reinforcements—Attacks Freytag—Walmoden retreats—Duke of York abandons Dunkirk—Coldstream move towards Menin and encamp—Houchard arrested and sent to Paris—Quesnoy taken by the Austrians—French defeated at Villiers en Couche—Driven from Lannoy—Guards encamp on the plains of Cyscoigne—Coldstream go into St. Peter's barracks at Ghent—Duke of York returns to England 29

CHAPTER III.

Reinforcements for the brigade of Guards sent from England—Command of the army given to the Emperor—He reviews the different contingents above Cateau—Allies advance—Success of the two columns under the Duke of York—Siege of Landrecy—Duke of York drives the enemy from Cæsar's camp—French defeated near Cateau—Duke of York repulses the enemy near Tournay—Duke of York obliges the enemy to evacuate Lannoy—Guards, supported by the Seventh and Fifteenth Light Dragoons, drive the French from their intrenchments—Abercrombie obliged to retreat from the heights of Roubaix, round Lannoy, to Templeuve—Fox retreats, and joins Otto—Numerical superiority of the enemy—Pichegru commences operations with an army of two hundred thousand men—Pitt declared by French Jacobins an enemy to the human race—Decree forbidding quarter—Duke of York's order in consequence—Allies repulsed near Fleurus — Duke of York retreats to Romaux — Reinforcements land at Ostend—Light companies of the Guards at home embark—Moira joins the Duke of York—Tournay, Ghent, and Ostend fall into the hands of the French—Duke of York crosses the Maese—Enemy repulsed—Crosses the Maese—Takes Bommel—Pichegru attacks the Allies between Nimeguen and Arnheim—Duke of York returns to England—Walmoden succeeds in command—Allies abandon Heusden—Spirited stand made by the Guards at Rhenen—British retreat to Voorthuizen — Troops suffer great hardships in the retreat to Deventer — Retreat continues to Bremen — Coldstream embark at Bremenlee—Land at Greenwich, and march to London . . . . *page* 49

CHAPTER IV.

Light companies of the First, Coldstream, and Third Guards embark for Ostend—First battalions of the three regiments of Guards embark for Ireland—Expedition to Holland—Two brigades of Guards embark—Troops land near the Helder Point—Dutch driven back—Their fleet surrenders—French and Batavians repulsed—Duke of York takes command of the army—Battle of Bergen—Four thousand Russians land at the Helder—Battle of Alkmaar—Capitulation of the town — British and Russians re-embark — First battalion lands at Yarmouth 64

CHAPTER V.

First battalion joins the expedition under Abercrombie—British land in Aboukir Bay—Abercrombie attacks the French lines—Battle of Alexandria—Death of Abercrombie—Reinforcements arrive for the

Coldstream—Cavan appointed to command the brigade of Guards—Marabout capitulates — Alexandria surrenders — Army returns to England—First battalion lands—Marches through Winchester for London—Peace of Amiens—Buonaparte declared First Consul—War with France—First battalions of Coldstream and Third brigaded under Finch—Arrive at Chelmsford—Letter to Patriotic Fund from non-commissioned officers and soldiers of the Egyptian brigade of Guards—First battalion march for Cox-Heath Camp—In quarters at Chatham—George III. reviews his Guards at Wimbledon—Death of the Duke of Gloucester—Duke of York succeeds in command of the First Guards—Duke of Cambridge appointed Colonel of the Coldstream—Treaty of Petersburgh—First battalion embark under Lord Cathcart—Land at Cuxhaven—March to Bremen—Battle of Austerlitz—Expedition returns to England . . . . . *page* 74

CHAPTER VI.

Officers of the Coldstream address the Duke of York—Duke's reply — First battalion sails with the expedition for the Baltic — Investment of Copenhagen — Bombardment — Capitulation — Army re-embark — First battalion go into barracks at Chatham—Charles IV. abdicates in favour of Ferdinand—Napoleon arrives at Bayonne — Murat enters Madrid — Prince of Peace sent to Bayonne, followed by Charles and the Queen—Joseph Buonaparte proclaimed King of Spain—Insurrection at Oporto, which extends to Spain—French squadron at Cadiz capitulates—Dupont's army surrenders to Castanos—Spanish Patriots enter into a treaty with England — Expedition sails from Cork—Lands in Mondego Bay — Wellesley attacks the heights of Roliça, and defeats Junot at Vimeira—French quit Portugal—Napoleon returns to Paris—Troops from Sweden reinforce the British in Portugal—Napoleon arrives at Madrid—Junction of Moore and Baird—Moore retreats—French repulsed at Corunna—Death of Moore—Army returns to England—Second brigade of Guards embark at Ramsgate—Fleet arrives at Spithead—Sails—Dispersed by contrary and tempestuous winds—Transports find shelter in the Irish ports—Fleet sails from Cork for Cadiz—Supreme Junta refuses admittance—Fleet sails for the Tagus—Beresford appointed to command the Portuguese troops—Nine companies of the first battalion land at Lisbon—Cradock commands the army—Twenty thousand Portuguese troops taken into English pay—Soult defeats Romana, crosses the Minho, and carries Oporto—Silveira retakes

Chaves — Soult's communication with Spain intercepted — Guards march through Saccavem and Batalha to Lyria—Cradock resigns the command to Wellesley—General Orders—Guards march to Coimbra —Trant holds the line of the Vouga . . . . *page* 93

CHAPTER VII.

Wellesley arrives at Coimbra—Reviews the army—Advances— Attacks Oporto—Critical position of Soult's army—Rear-guard overtaken at Salamonde—Coldstream halt at Scavessa de Rio—Termination of the pursuit—Army returns to Oporto—Marches through Coimbra, Thomar, and concentrates at Abrantes—Stations of the corps under Victor, Sebastiani, Soult, and Mortier—Allies move on Placentia, form a junction with the Spaniards at Oropesa, and advance to Talavera de la Reyna—Troops suffer greatly from the want of provisions—Cuesta moves to St. Olalla, attacked, and retreats in disorder —Battle of Talavera—Light brigade arrives under Crauford—Soult forces the passes between Salamanca and Placentia—Wellesley returns to Oropesa—Cuesta quits the position at Talavera, and abandons the sick and wounded of the allied army—Two thousand sick and wounded soldiers proceed to Elvas—Allies cross the Tagus at Arzobispo— Spaniards left to defend the bridge—Surprised, and retreat with the loss of thirty guns and baggage—Cuesta retires to Deleytosa—Allies fall back to Zaraicejo—Brigade of Guards at Badajoz—General Order —War declared between France and Austria—Flank companies of second battalion embark for Flushing—British army crosses the Tagus —Brigade of Guards march to Vizeu—Hill's corps in the vicinity of Abrantes 109

CHAPTER VIII.

Wellington's communication to Colonel Stopford — Soult passes the Sierra Morena — Joseph Buonaparte enters Seville — Albuquerque barricades the bridge of Zuozo — Eleven companies of the Guards embark at Portsmouth for Cadiz—Allies collect a force at Cadiz— Wellington's head-quarters at Celerico—Army of Portugal assemble under Massena—Capture of Ciudad Rodrigo—Massena's proclamation — Ney attacks Crauford — Proclamation issued by Wellington— Massena enters Portugal—French concentrate at Vizeu—Battle of Busaco—Wellington retires to the lines of Torres Vedras—Romana joins from the Alentejo — Massena retreats — Wellington follows towards Santarem — Allies move into cantonments — Head-quarters and Guards at Cartaxo—Hill crosses the Tagus—Drouet reinforces Massena . . . . *page* 129

CHAPTER IX.

Seven thousand men arrive in the Tagus—French army retreat—Houghton's brigade crosses the Tagus—Skirmish at Pombal—After an obstinate resistance Ney retreats through Condeixa and Cazal Nova to Miranda de Corvo—Enemy retire in disorder from Foz d'Aronse—French retreat from their station behind the Alva—Wellington detained from want of provisions—Massena retreats from Guarda—Enemy defeated at Sabugal—French enter Spain—Termination of the third invasion by the French—Observation on the defence of Lisbon—Position of the Allies—Guards at Almadilla and Puebla—Troops embark at Cadiz—Confederates form a junction at Tarifa—Battle of Barrosa—Beresford lays siege to Badajoz—Almeida invested—Wellington visits the troops in the Alentejo—Returns to Villa Formosa—Position of the armies—Battle of Fuentes d'Honor—Massena recalled—Ragusa succeeds in command—Brennier escapes with the garrison of Almeida—Marmont retires on Salamanca—Guards return to the places occupied before the action—First division march to Penamacor—Guards ordered back to their former stations—Soult marches to relieve Badajoz—Battle of Albuera—Blockade of Badajoz—Guards with the corps under Spencer cross the Tagus—Encamp at St. Oloia—Soult returns to Seville—Marmont advances to Salamanca—Hill's corps remains in Alentejo—Wellington recrosses the Tagus—Head-quarters at Fuente Guinaldo—Graham succeeds Spencer—Blockade of Ciudad Rodrigo—Wellington retreats on the advance of Marmont—Allies go into winter quarters—Coldstream at Lagoisa, Valdozares, and afterwards at Pinhel—Hill surprises the post at Arroyo de Molinos 143

CHAPTER X.

Siege and capture of Ciudad Rodrigo—Army marches for the south—Siege of Badajoz—Town carried by assault—Hill left in the south—Wellington moves for the north—Marmont retires from Castello Branco—Head-quarters at Fuente Guinaldo—Troops cantoned between the Agueda and Coa—Hill carries the bridge of Almarez—Wellington fords the Tormes—Marmont advances—Allies in position on the heights of St. Christoval—Capture of the forts in Salamanca—French retreat and concentrate behind the Douro—Marmont reinforced attempts to cut off Wellington's communication with Salamanca and Ciudad Rodrigo — Battle of Salamanca — Marmont wounded—Command devolves on Clausel—French retreat on Valladolid—Wellington moves by Cuellar, through Segovia, to Madrid— The Isla opposite Cadiz abandoned by the French — First division leaves Madrid for the Escurial—King Joseph joins Suchet—Soult in Granada—Wellington enters Valladolid—Siege of Burgos—Siege raised — Reinforcements arrive under Dalhousie — Allies retreat— Head-quarters at Freynada—Hill returns to Estramadura—Troops go into cantonments for the winter—Coldstream at Musquetello *page* 168

CHAPTER XI.

French loss in Russia—Austria joins the Russians — Napoleon concentrates his force—Soult sets out with reinforcements for Germany—Graham crosses the Douro—The cavalry and Hill's corps reach Salamanca—Enemy retire from Valladolid to Burgos—Allies cross the Ebro—Attack at Osma—Battle of Vittoria—Retreat of the French—Left advance under Graham—Joseph makes a stand at Tolosa—Graham drives him beyond the frontier—Siege of St. Sebastian—Soult resumes the command in the south of France—Attacks Roncesvalles and Maya—Retreats—Wellington occupies the position he did previous to the advance of Soult — Capture of St. Sebastian —Left of the Allies cross the Bidassoa — Pampeluna surrenders — Position of the French on the Nivelle—Hope succeeds Graham as second in command—French lose their character for invincibility at Leipsic—Battle of Nivelle—Allies go into cantonments—Soult concentrates in front of Bayonne—Repulsed in his attacks on the left . 184

CHAPTER XII.

Hill moves to Hellete—French retire—Spaniards blockade St. Jean Pied de Port—Left wing invests Bayonne—Battle of Orthez—Soult retires—Beresford's corps marches for Bourdeaux—Great part of his force recalled—Battle of Toulouse—Sortie from Bayonne — Coldstream suffer severely — Coldstream in barracks at Bourdeaux — Hostilities close on land between England and France—Coldstream quit Bourdeaux for Pauliac—Conveyed by craft to the Stirling Castle — Arrive at Spithead — March to London — Six companies of the

xii   CONTENTS.

Coldstream embark for Holland—Inspected at Steenbergen—Failure of attack on Bergen-op-Zoom — Six companies go into quarters at Brussels—Six companies reinforced by four companies from England   .   .   .   .   *page* 199

CHAPTER XIII.

Napoleon escapes from Elba — Prince Regent determines to join the Allies—Reinforcements sent to Belgium—Position of the Allies —Napoleon heads the northern army—His proclamation—Coldstream march to Quatre Bras—Battle of Waterloo   .   .   .   208

APPENDIX.

NO.	DATE.	CONTENTS.	PAGE.
1	4 Sept. 1656	Cromwell's letter relative to the battle of Dunbar	229
2	4 Feb. 165⁰⁄₁	Cromwell's letter respecting the Medal of Dunbar	234
3	17 Nov. 1651	Ensign Wells's commission	235
4	24 Feb. 165⁸⁄₉	Letter from Monck to Lord Henry Cromwell	ib.
5	12 May, 1659	Letter from Monck and officers to Lord Fleetwood	236
6	10 Feb. 16⁵⁹⁄₆₀	Exchange of arms	238
7	14 Apr. 1660	Exchange of arms	ib.
8	26 June 1660	Lieutenant Pembruge's commission	ib.
9	3 Aug. 1660	Monck's commission as Captain-General	239
10	June, 1661	First appointment of Adjutants	250
11	5 May, 1663	Instructions to be observed by the Commissary-General of Musters	ib.
12	23 Jan. 166¾	Ensign Vincent's commission	252
13	May, 1664	Men sent to Guinea	253
14	24 Feb. 166⁴⁄₅	Arms to be delivered to Captain Huitson	ib.
15	15 Apr. 1667	Two companies added to the Coldstream	ib.
16	1 May, 1667	Firelocks lost during the Fire of London to be replaced	ib.
17	21 Feb. 16⁶⁸⁄₉	Men drafted to Sir Thomas Allen's squadron	254
18	2 Feb. 16⁶⁸⁄₉	Order for arms for drafts sent to Sir Thomas Allen	ib.
19	23 Mar. 16⁶⁹⁄₇₀	Order for powder to be issued to the regiment, and note from Mr. Hudson Gurney's M.S.	255
20	24 Mar. 16⁶⁹⁄₇₀	Stations of the army	256
21	11 Apr. 1670	Order for arms to Captain Kirkbye's company	258
22	11 Apr. 1670	Order for two drums to Captain Mutlowe's company	ib.
23	10 June, 1670	Arms furnished the regiment according to patterns	ib.
24	18 June, 1670	The Duke of York ordered to convene the Colonels of regiments on military affairs	ib.
25	19 Aug. 1670	One day's pay given to the Earl of Craven, and a certain number of men disbanded	259
26	22 Sept. 1670	Arms to be issued	260
27	23 Mar. 167⁰⁄₁	Quarters of the Colonel's company of the Coldstream	ib.
28	12 May, 1671	Pay of the Guards reduced when not in attendance on the King	ib.
29	16 Aug. 1671	Quarters of the Coldstream	ib.
30	3 Nov. 1671	Non-commissioned officers of the Guards not to keep alehouses, or marry without permission	261
31	18 Feb. 167¼	Draft from the Coldstream to the Duke of Monmouth's regt.	ib.
32	12 Mar. 167¼	Arms to supply those lost at Covent Garden fire	262
33	27 Mar. 1672	Detachments to be sent on board the Yaughs to do duty	ib.
34	13 Apr. 1672	Orders for colours for the Coldstream	ib.

xiv CONTENTS.

NO.	DATE.		PAGE.
35	3 May, 1672	Issue of arms	263
36	22 June, 1672	Order for court-martial on private Ellis of the Coldstream	ib.
37	3 July, 1672	Ensign Peryn's account, and warrant for payment	264
38	5 July, 1672	Arms to be issued for companies at sea	265
39	15 Nov. 1672	Order for a court-martial	266
40	23 Nov. 1672	Capt. Bevill Skelton to command the regiment sent to France	ib.
41	5 Dec. 1672	Order for a battalion to go to France	ib.
42	27 Feb. 167¾	Order for a guard to attend the theatre in Dorset Garden	267
43	22 Mar. 167¾	Statement of bandoleeres and drums delivered to six companies of the Coldstream	ib.
44	2 and 20 Apr. 1674	Court-martial to assemble on board the yacht, and sentence	268
45	29 Apr. 1674	Arms to be delivered in lieu of those taken by the men drafted to Churchill's regiment	ib.
46	8 May, 1674	Captain Huitson's company of the Coldstream to receive pay in England from the 8th of April	ib.
47	12 May, 1674	Orders for training and exercising on the new system	269
48	20 May, 1674	Grant of £200 to Captain Huitson	ib.
49	15 Sept. 1674	Guards to do duty over the Queen-Consort at Hampton-Court	ib.
50	19 Sept. 1674	Unserviceable arms of the Coldstream to be exchanged	ib.
51	23 and 29 Sept. 1674	One barrel of powder to be delivered to each company of the Coldstream every two months	270
52	3 Dec. 1674	Six musters instead of seven to take place annually	ib.
53	10 May, 1676	Penalties for drunkenness renewed	271
54	9 June, 1676	Reward to the Guards who assisted at the fire in Southwark	ib.
55	4 Oct. 1676	Draft of one company of the Coldstream sent to Virginia	ib.
56	19 May, 1677	Soldiers of the Guards first trained as grenadiers	ib.
57	11 and 12 Jan. 167⅞	Establishment of the regiment increased	272
58	14 Jan. 167⅞	Arms to be delivered to the 480 men added to the Coldstream	ib.
59	17 Jan. 167⅞	Order for the delivery of arms to the eight additional companies	ib.
60	1 Feb. 167⅞	For assuring payment for the clothing of new raised men	ib.
61	20 Mar. 167⅞	Order for Guards from Virginia to disembark at Gravesend	273
62	4 Apr. 1678	Warrant respecting the levy-money of the grenadier company	274
63	4 Apr. 1678	Levy-money for raising the grenadier company	ib.
64	9 Apr. 1678	Court-martial to assemble and inquire into a dispute among some officers of the Coldstream	275
65	13 Apr. 1678	Delivery of arms to the new-raised grenadier company	ib.
66	13 Apr. 1678	£100 to Major Mutlow for services performed	ib.
67	12 May, 1678	Leave for Ensign Clerke to return from Ostend	ib.
68	1 June, 1678	Ensign Clerke's prolongation of leave	ib.
69	3 June, 1678	Relating to the muster of the Coldstream in Flanders	276
70	22 June, 1678	A return of Captain Mutlow's company from Virginia	ib.
71	July, 1678	Payment for repairs of Major Mansfield's lodgings	ib.
72	18 July, 1678	Respite removed from the pay of three soldiers of Captain Wythe's company	ib.
73	28 July, 1678	State clothing from the King's wardrobe	277
74	7 Aug. 1678	Arms to be delivered in lieu of those sent with the drafts to Flanders	278
75	22 Aug. 1678	Arms to be issued to recruits	ib.
76	Sept. 1678	A letter from Monmouth to the Earl of Feversham	ib.
77	20 Sept. 1678	£92 19s. 11d. to Major Mansfield for clothing	279

CONTENTS.

NO.	DATE.		PAGE.
78	23 Sept. 1678	Ensign Troutbeck present at the musters in Flanders for March, May, and July	279
79	30 Sept. 1678	Two deserters from Captain O'Keover's company to be conducted to the guard of the Coldstream in St. James's Park	ib.
80	28 Oct. 1678	Fox-tail cravats for grenadiers	280
81	1 Nov. 1678	Dismissal of Popish recusants	ib.
82	2 Nov. 1678	Dismissal of Popish recusants	281
83	15 Nov. 1678	Reward for the invention of a new bayonet	ib.
84	7 Jan. 167$\frac{8}{9}$	Payment to Mons. Vannier for the gold and ivory sticks for the field-officers of the household troops	ib.
85	8 Mar. 167$\frac{8}{9}$	£105 to Capt. Wythe for bringing the companies of the Coldstream from Dover to London	282
86	10 Apr. 1679	£5 12s. to Drum-major-general Muwgridge, for impressing sixteen drummers for the Coldstream	ib.
87	25 Oct. 1679	Contingent account from 1675 to 1678	ib.
88	10 Dec. 1679	Powder expended at the fire at the Temple	284
89	2 June, 1680	A detachment of the Coldstream to embark for Tangiers	285
90	4 June, 1680	Precedency of regiments going to Tangiers	ib.
91	10 June, 1680	Order for a colour for the company going to Tangiers	ib.
92	19 July, 1680	£4 6s. 8d. to be paid to Captain Street, for sending the draft going to Tangiers from the companies at Windsor	ib.
93	10 Nov. 1680	Coldstream to recruit 120 men in lieu of those sent to Tangiers	286
94	19 Sept. 1683	Contingent account from April to September	ib.
95	7 Dec. 1683	Contingent account from September to November	287
96	26 Jan. 168$\frac{3}{4}$	Snaphance musquets of the latest pattern to be delivered to the Coldstream	288
97	27 Jan. 168$\frac{3}{4}$	Contingent bill from November to January following	ib.
98	28 Apr. 1684	Arms to be delivered to the new-raised grenadier companies	289
99	13 June, 1684	Contingent account from January to May	290
100	28 Nov. 1684	Contingent account from May to November	291
101	31 Oct. 1684	Grenade shells for the grenadier company	292
102	13 June, 1685	Coldstream to recruit to 100 men a company	ib.
103	9 July, 1685	Letter from Mr. Blathwayt to Colonel Mackay	ib.
104	12 July, 1685	A detachment to conduct prisoners concerned in the rebellion to Scotland	ib.
105	20 and 27 July, 1685	Warrant for reducing the Coldstream	ib.
106	15 Aug. 1685	Contingent account from November to June, 1685	293
107	7 Nov. 1685	Payment for waggons during Monmouth's rebellion	294
108	17 Dec. 1685	£288 to be paid to Mr. Holford for the colours for the Foot Guards for the Coronation	ib.
109	12 Feb. 168$\frac{5}{6}$	Contingent bill from July to December, 1685	ib.
110	22 Feb. 168$\frac{5}{6}$	Order for bayonets for the Coldstream	295
111	18 Mar. 168$\frac{5}{6}$	Remuneration to the men of the Guards employed in Hyde Park	296
112	15 Aug. 1686	Account of grenados furnished to the grenadier company	ib.
113	15 Aug. 1686	Contingent bill from January to June, 1686	297
114	11 Mar. 168$\frac{7}{8}$	Firelocks issued to the grenadier company	298
115	8 Mar. 168$\frac{7}{8}$	Order for the Coldstream and other troops to embark for Holland	ib.
116	17 Mar. 168$\frac{7}{8}$	Men of the First regiment of Guards, embarked for Holland, to be incorporated in the Coldstream	299
117	19 Mar. 168$\frac{7}{8}$	Men of the Prince of Denmark's regt., embarked for Holland, to e incorporated in the Coldstream	ib.

CONTENTS

NO.	DATE.		PAGE.
118	19 Mar. 1688/9	Extract of a Letter from Mr. Blathwayt respecting Dumbarton's regiment	300
119	21 Mar. 1688/9	Letter from Marshal Schomberg respecting Dumbarton's regt.	ib.
120	1 May, 1689	Two battalions in Holland to be reduced to 14 companies	ib.
121	27 Feb. 1690	Relating to debentures on the pay of the Coldstream	301
122	12 July, 1691	Notification to the Lieutenants of the Guards to assume the rank of Captains	ib.
123	19 Mar. 1691/2	Money due to the late Colonel Pope of the Coldstream to be paid to his executors	302
124	25 June, 1692	£100 to be paid to Colonel Bridgeman	ib.
125	5 June, and 1 Sept. 1693 &c. &c.	Pay to Colonel Skelton as Brigade-Major	ib.
126	1 July, 1693	Oath to prevent obtaining employment by bribery	303
127	17 Oct. 1694	£100 to be paid to Colonel Withers of the Coldstream as Adjutant-General	304
128	1 May, 1695	Fuzees for the grenadier company of the Coldstream	ib.
129	30 Dec. 1695	Relating to the caps, &c. pikes and arms of the Coldstream and other regiments	ib.
130	1 Jan. 1696/7	Retirement of Lt.-Col. and Adjutant Jones of the Coldstream	305
131	9 Oct. 1697	To prepare quarters for the Guards coming from Flanders	ib.
132	19 Oct. 1697	Route for the Coldstream to march to Deptford	306
133	17 Nov. 1697	Route for the Coldstream to march to London	307
134	26 Apr. 1698	Allowance for fuel, candles, and waggons on the march to Newmarket	ib.
135	3 Sept. 1698	A company to be formed of reduced officers to march at the head of the First Foot Guards	ib.
136	Dec. 1698	2000 fuzees delivered to the grenadier company of the Coldstream	308
137	2 July, 1700	Allowance for fuel and candle for the Guards kept by the Coldstream	ib.
138	Mar. 1701	Contingent account for 1700	ib.
139	Aug. 1702	Contingent account for 1701	309
140	14 Mar. 170½	Marlborough's commission as Captain-General	ib.
141	16 May, 1702	Route for a battalion of Guards to Portsmouth, and encamp in the Isle of Wight	311
142	22 May, 1702	Regiments to encamp in the Isle of Wight	ib.
143	8 June, 1702	Troops encamped in the Isle of Wight to embark	312
144	Oct. 1702	Hire of waggons, &c. from London to Bath	ib.
145	16 Dec. 1703	Contingent expences of the battalion to Portsmouth and Bath to be paid	313
146	8 Apr. 1704	Contingent expences to be paid for a detachment of the Coldstream to Dover and Southampton	ib.
147	June, 1704	Hire of waggons for the Coldstream to the Isle of Wight	ib.
148	7 July, 1704	Letter from Mr. Secretary Hedges to the Duke of Marlborough	314
149	10 July, 1704	Route of the battalion of Guards ordered to Portugal	315
150	July, 1704	Hire of waggons for the battalion sent to Portugal	316
151	29 May, 1705	Children's commissions restricted to two in each regiment	ib.
152	3 Nov. 1705	Petition of Hugh Baxter, Surgeon's-Mate to the Coldstream	ib.
153	22 Jan. 1705/6	Lieut.-Col. Morryson having come home on leave, another officer is to replace him	317
154	6 Feb. 1705/6	Lieut.-Col. Stevenage having come home sick, another officer is to replace him in Spain	ib.
155	8 Feb. 1705/6	310 men sent to Spain	ib.

CONTENTS. xvii

NO.	DATE.		PAGE.
156	12 Feb. 170⅝	Five officers and servants sent to Spain	317
157	18 & 23 Feb. & 2 Mar. 170⅝	} Extracts from letters relative to officers ordered to Spain	318
158	16 Mar. 170⅞	The pay of two men a company allowed the Coldstream to complete the expence of new arms in lieu of pikes	ib.
159	18 Apr. 1707	Standards, banners, &c. of the household troops to be altered on the occasion of the union with Scotland	ib.
160	28 Apr. 1707	Distribution of the Guards at home and abroad	ib.
161	30 June, 1707	Application for powder, and distribution of the Guards at home and abroad	319
162	15 Sep. 1707	Orders for the Guards to fill up the drafts sent to Spain	ib.
163	14 Jan. 170⅞	Relates to clothing of the army generally	ib.
164	2 Aug. 1708	Brevet officers to do duty according to their regimental rank	320
165	Feb. and June, 1709	} Description of deserters	ib.
166	16 Mar. 170⅞	Duke of Marlborough orders the regiments in Flanders to wear "black buttons and button-holes"	321
167	17 Sept. 1709	Letter describing the battle of Malplaquet, with a return and list of killed and wounded	ib.
168	19 Mar. 17¹⁰⁄₁₁	Guard sent to protect Covent-Garden Theatre	324
169	9 & 15 Aug. 1711	} A Field-Officer of the Foot Guards to be always in waiting on the Queen	325
170	12 Mar. 17¹¹⁄₁₂	Savoy barracks ordered to be fitted up for 500 men	ib.
171	19 Feb. 17¹²⁄₁₃	Quarters of the Coldstream	ib.
172	10 Apr. 1713	500 men of the Coldstream to be quartered at Hampton Court and Kensington till the Savoy barracks are completed	326
173	Dec. 1713	Contingent bill for the year 1713	ib.
174	25 Dec. 1713	Guards ordered to quell the mutiny in Will's marines	ib.
175	7 July, 1714	Detachment of the Guards to attend the Queen at Hampton Court and Windsor	327
176	3 Sept. 1714	Grenadiers ordered to Greenwich to receive George the First	328
177	27 Sept. 1714	Detachment of the Guards to relieve Lieutenant-General Webb's regiment at the Tower	ib.
178	12 Nov. 1714 2 & 7 Feb. & 10 Aug. 1715	} Quarters of the Coldstream	329
179	10 June, 1715	Guards posted about London to prevent white roses being worn	330
180	23 July, 1715	Four companies added to the Coldstream	ib.
181	July, 1717	Particulars of the state-clothing of the drummers and hautbois of the Guards	ib.
182	1717	A party of drummers of the Guards apprehended for beating a point of war at Lord Wexford's	332
183	27 Nov. 1718	A guard to attend the theatre in the Haymarket	ib.
184	9 Mar. 17¹⁸⁄₁₉	For hire of waggons, &c. on the march to Chippenham	333
185	28 May, 1719	Order for the Guards to salute the Lords Justices	ib.
186	4 June, 1719	Direction to the Colonels of the Guards for sending troops into the City	334
187	23 & 30 July, 1719	} Seven companies from each of the regiments of Guards ordered to encamp at the Isle of Wight	ib.
188	July, 1719	For hire of waggons, &c. for the Coldstream on the march to the Isle of Wight	335
189	14 Sept. 1719	One waggon "out of respect to the regiments of Guards" allowed to each company	ib.
190	Nov. 1719	For hire of waggons on the return of the Coldstream from the Isle of Wight to London	ib.

CONTENTS.

NO.	DATE.		PAGE.
191	20 Nov. 1719	A guard to attend the King's theatre, Haymarket	336
192	1 Apr. 1720	Order for a guard to do duty at the King's Theatre on opera nights	ib.
193	19 July, 1723	State of the Coldstream as it appeared at the review	337
194	15 Oct. 1723	Return of ale-houses, &c. in Southwark liable to quarter soldiers	ib.
195	20 Nov. 1729	Extract from warrant regulating clothing	338
196	13 June, 1735	Officers to appear with "twisted ramilyed wigs" according to pattern	ib.
197	18 June, 1735	How the soldiers are to appear at review on the 19th June	ib.
198	29 Oct. 1735	Officers to mount all guards in their regimentals and gaiters	ib.
199	1735	Prices fixed for soldiers to pay for their necessaries	ib.
200	11 Apr. 1736	Instructions for the duty of sentinels	ib.
201	6 July, 1737	Directions how to appear at the inspection by Col. Pulteney	339
202	25 July, 1737	Orders for officers named, to march in their blue frocks, hats, and wigs, with their divisions to Hampton Court	ib.
203	30 July, 1737	Instructions for the Hampton Court party	ib.
204	12 Sept. 1737	No compliments to be paid to the Prince or Princess of Wales till further orders	ib.
205	26 Nov. 1737	Order for the Coldstream to go into mourning for the late Queen Caroline	ib.
206	... 1742	Uniform of the Coldstream	340
207	3 Sept. 1745	Men to salute by touching their hats	341
208	9 Sept. 1745	No Irishmen or Papists to be enlisted	ib.
209	21 Sept. 1745	No Scotch, Irish, or vagabond, will be approved of as recruits	ib.
210	9 Oct. 1745	Usual compliments to be paid to the Venetian ambassador	ib.
211	25 Oct. 1745	The Guards not to laugh when the Militia are reviewed	ib.
212	21 and 23 Nov. 1745	Route for the Guards to march to Litchfield	ib.
213	24 Nov. 1745	Route for the first battalion of the Coldstream to march to Nottingham	342
214	26 Nov. 1745	Route of the Coldstream on reaching Nottingham altered to Litchfield	ib.
215	26 Nov. 1745	Route for an escort with the baggage to follow the first battalion to Litchfield	343
216	12 Jan. 1745/6	All officers to appear in "white gaiters and stiff-topt buff-coloured gloves"	ib.
217	24 June, 1746	A guard to be mounted over the rebels in Piccadilly	ib.
218	15 Aug. 1746	Detachments from the Guards to attend the execution of Lords Kilmarnock and Balmerino	ib.
219	Oct. 1746	Contingent account of the second battalion of the Coldstream under General Fuller	344
220	27 Nov. 1746	A detachment ordered to attend the execution of the rebels	345
221	3 Feb. 1746/7	No soldier will be permitted to wear a wig after 25th March	ib.
222	7 Apr. 1747	A detachment ordered to attend the execution of Lord Lovat	ib.
223	15 June, 1747	The men's hair to be tucked under their hats in future	ib.
224	25 May, 1748	The usual compliments to be paid to the Lords Justices	ib.
225	27 Feb. 1749	The soldiers of the Coldstream to be furnished with red breeches	ib.
226	10 Mar. 1749	Men to be provided with brown cloth gaiters	ib.
227	27 June, 1749	"Officers to wear boots when the men wear brown gaiters"	ib.
228	4 July, 1749	Officers on duty to wear buff-coloured waistcoats and breeches	ib.
229	1 July, 1751	Warrant for regulating the colours, clothing, &c. of the cavalry and infantry	346

CONTENTS.

NO.	DATE.		PAGE.
230	7 Nov. 1754	After Midsummer, Drum-majors not to pay for their clothes	356
231	15 Apr. 1758	Route for the first batt. of the Coldstream to the Isle of Wight	ib.
232	6 May, 1758	Fresh route for the Isle of Wight. Orders for the men to encamp each night on their march	ib.
233	8 Oct. 1758	Route for the first battalion of the Coldstream from the Isle of Wight to London	357
234	Oct. 1758	Contingent account of the first battalion from May to October	358
235	. . . 1758	Account of losses sustained by the first battalion of the Coldstream on the coast of France	359
236	22 Jan. 1759	The brown gaiters to be immediately blackened and tops put on them	360
237	23 July, 1760	Order for the second battalions of the three regiments of Guards to embark for Germany	ib.
238	24 July, 1760	Route for the second battalion of the Coldstream to march to Dartford prior to embarkation	ib.
239	21 June, 1761	Officers to attend the exercise of two guns attached to each battalion	ib.
240	27 Feb. 1763	Second battalion of the Coldstream to disembark and march to Sudbury, Lavenham, &c.	ib.
241	28 Feb. 1763	Second battalion of the Coldstream to march from Sudbury to London	ib.
242	25 May, 1772	Captain-Lieutenants of cavalry and infantry regiments " to bear and take the rank of Captain"	361
243	5 July, 1784	Report on the accoutrements of the Foot Guards and infantry	ib.
244	19 Apr. 1793	Light-infantry companies first appointed to the Guards	363
245	24 Aug. 1793	Letter from Mr. Long to the Secretary at War relative to the table at St. James's	364
246	4 Dec. 1793	Letter from Do. to Do. relative to Do.	ib.
247	23 Mar. 1794	Letter from Mr. Gorton to George Rose, Esq. relative to Do.	365
248	3 June, 1794	Letter from Mr. Long to the Secretary at War relative to Do.	ib.
249	. . .	Regulations for the table at St. James's	ib.
250	27 July, 1813	Appointment of Colour Serjeants from 25th June	367
250*	24 July, 1814	General Officers of the Guards removed from their regimental commissions	368
251	29 July, 1815	The Ensigns of the Foot Guards to have the rank of Lieuts.	ib.
252	. . .	Actual cost of the state-clothing of the band to 1815	ib.
253	. . .	Uniform of the Coldstream from 1793 to 1832	369
254	1792	Non-commissioned officers appointed to commissions	370
255	1797	Non-commissioned Officers' fund	372
256	1783	Nulli Secundus	373
257		Establishment of the regiment 23rd July, 1655	378
258		,, ,, ,, ,, 15th October, 1655	379
259		,, ,, ,, ,, 21st December, 1657	380
260		,, ,, ,, ,, 27th February, 16$\frac{58}{59}$	381
261		,, ,, ,, ,, 26th January, 16$\frac{60}{61}$	382
262		,, ,, ,, ,, 26th September, 1668	383
263		,, ,, ,, ,, 1st January, 16$\frac{13}{14}$	384
264		,, ,, ,, ,, 1st January, 168$\frac{2}{3}$	385
265		,, ,, ,, ,, 1st May, 1689	387
266		,, ,, ,, ,, 1695, and abstract of off-reckings	389
267		,, ,, ,, ,, 26th March, 1699	392
268		,, ,, ,, ,, 24th June, 1713	393
269		,, ,, ,, ,, 25th May, 1797	394
270		,, ,, ,, ,, 25th June, 1806	394

CONTENTS.

NO.		PAGE.
271	General Establishment from 1650 to 1833	398
272	Variations in the pay of the army from 1684	405
273	Stations from 1650 to 1832	412
274	List of Officers 1650 to 1651	451
275	,, ,, ,, 30th July, 1659	ib.
276	,, ,, ,, 18th August, 1660	ib.
277	,, ,, ,, .. . 1661	452
278	,, ,, ,, February, 168½	ib.
279	,, ,, ,, November, 1687	453
280	,, ,, ,, March, 1702	ib.
281	,, ,, ,, 11th January, 17½	454
282	,, ,, ,, 20th June, 1727	455
283	,, ,, ,, July, 1739	456
284	,, ,, ,, February, 1754	457
285	Coldstream roll	458

CORRIGENDA.

VOL. I.

Page 40, line 4, and p. 45, line 1,—for 'Mohum Castle' read 'Mochrum Castle.'

—— 325. The first battalion of the Guards do not appear to have sustained much loss at Malplaquet; the second battalion, in which were the six companies of the Coldstream, had the four officers named killed, and Capt. Borrett and Ensign Stocker wounded, as well as Captain Gould (First regiment) killed.

——, note.—For 'Serjeant Hall, of the battalion serving under the Duke of Marlborough,' read 'Serjeant Hall of the battalion of the Coldstream.'

—— 408, note.—Capt. Wynch died February 1762, in Germany.

VOL. II.

—— 391, Appendix.—The (0) where the asterisk is placed should have been a dot (.).

—— 419, Appendix. Stations.—April, 1709. Two companies of the Coldstream, Lieut.-Colonels Rivett's and Bethell's (former Grenadiers) ordered to join the detachment in Flanders. (Sailed from Harwich 6th, and disembarked at Ostend 7th May.)

—— 454, —— Sir Tristram Dillington, for 'Oct. 1709' read '. . 1710.'

—— —— Lieut. Thomas Serjeant, for ',, May 1713' read '. May 1713.'

—— 467, No. 189, 'Col. Stevenage died in October 1709.'

—— 480, No. 404, for 'Colquhon' read 'Colquhoun.'

—— 484, No. 480, Charles Rainsford, Lieut., for '29 June 1759' read '29 Jan. 1759.'

ORIGIN AND SERVICES

OF

THE COLDSTREAM GUARDS.

CHAPTER I.

Clinton appointed Commander-in-Chief in America — British evacuate Philadelphia—Battle of Freehold Court-House—Clinton reaches Sandy Hook—Embarks for New York—Guards with other troops embark for the Capes of Virginia—Land at Glebe—Fort and ships destroyed — Stores and provisions taken from the enemy — Forces embark for New York — Guards, joined by troops from Virginia, sail up North River—Morgan lands—Clinton disembarks at Stoney Point — Fort La Fayette surrenders — Guards embark for Newhaven — Garth disembarks—Town taken — Vessels, artillery, and stores destroyed — Army marches through Fairfield—Shipping, stores, and town burnt—Troops re-embark—Land at Norwalk and Greenfield; both places destroyed—English return to New York—Guards formed part of the garrison during the winter — Clinton embarks at Sandy Hook to reduce South Carolina — Lord Stirling attempts to take Staten Island — Flank companies of the Guards, a few guns, some Hessians, and mounted Yagers, march for Young's house — Young's house taken — Arnold, the American General, carries on a secret correspondence—Major André tried as a spy and hanged—Army crosses the Catawba—Guards distinguish themselves—Americans return to North Carolina—Cornwallis attacks the enemy's lines at Guildford Court-House — Americans retreat in good order—British move towards Wilmington—Cornwallis reaches Petersburg, crosses the Roanoke, Meherrin, and Nottaway rivers—Army reinforced marches through Hanover country—Cornwallis defeats La Fayette—Crosses James River, and concentrates in York Town — Washington moves to White Plains — Joined by the French from Rhode Island—Arnold destroys New London—York Town invested—Cornwallis surrenders—Carleton succeeds Clinton in command—Ratification of peace—Thirteen provinces declared independent—Returns of the officers who served in America.

1778. SIR HENRY CLINTON was now appointed to the chief command: this brave, zealous, and accomplished officer had gained great credit by his services during the seven years' war, and by his gallantry at Bunker's Hill: he, however, was so circumstanced in America, that he was able to add but little to his reputation by his efforts in that May 8th. country. He arrived at Philadelphia early in May. On his march through the Jerseys, the troops were encumbered with an enormous quantity of baggage; all the bridges were destroyed, and the enemy followed close in their rear.

June. The British army quitted Philadelphia on the eighteenth of June, and crossed the Delaware. Clinton approached the coast, to avoid crosing the Rariton. On the twenty-seventh he encamped near Freehold Court-house, in the June 28th. county of Monmouth. At eight o'clock next day he had descended from the adjoining heights, with the intention of continuing his retreat, when two columns of the enemy were seen moving on both his flanks. Clinton attempted to bring on a general action, and prepared for an immediate attack; but before it could be carried into execution, the Provincials retired, and posted themselves on a rising ground which they had previously occupied. They were now intrenched; and as the baggage obstructed the English, it became requisite that some decisive step should be taken to prevent its capture. Clinton quickly made his arrangements. The grenadiers with their left rested on the village of Freehold, the Guards were stationed on the right of the grenadiers, and commenced the attack with such spirit, that the enemy were put to flight. The Provincials were strongly posted in their second line. Notwithstanding the excessive heat and great fatigue the troops had already undergone, this second line was also attacked, and, after considerable resistance, broken by a steady and intrepid charge. The enemy, thrown into complete disorder, fled in all directions. At this moment Washington came up with fresh troops, whom he judiciously posted behind a ravine; and by his arrival probably saved his advanced corps from destruction.[1] The loss of the Americans, which exceeded that of the British, amounted to three hundred and sixty-one men, including officers. Colonel Trelawney of the Coldstream, and Captain Bellew of the First Guards, were wounded. No separate return was made of the loss in men. Sir Henry Clinton continued his march till the baggage reached

1778.
June 28th.

---

[1] " The British Grenadiers with their left to the village of
" Freehold, and the Guards on the right of the Grenadiers, be-
" gan the attack with such spirit that the enemy gave way im-
" mediately. The second line of the enemy stood the attack, and
" with greater obstinacy, but were completely routed. It would
" be sufficient honour to the troops barely to say, that they
" forced a corps, as I am informed, of near twelve thousand
" men from two strong positions; but it will, I doubt not, be
" considered as doubly creditable when I mention that they did it
" under such disadvantages of heat and fatigue, that a great
" part of those we lost fell dead as they advanced without a
" wound."—Sir William Clinton's Dispatch.

4 ORIGIN AND SERVICES OF

1778. Sandy Hook, when all apprehensions for its safety were at an end. At this place the army embarked, and landed the
July 5th. same day at New York.

1779. On the fifth of May the grenadiers and light infantry of
May. the Guards, commanded by Colonel Garth, the Forty-second, a Hessian regiment, the Royal Volunteers of Ireland, and detachments amounting to eighteen hundred men, sailed from New York under Brigadier-General Mathew,
May 8th. and entered the Capes of Virginia.

The government of Virginia had established a marine yard at Gosport, and a quantity of timber was collected for building ships. To defend the yard and docks adjoining, a fort was constructed on the banks of the river, half a mile below Portsmouth, which the commanders of the ex-
May 10th. pedition proposed to occupy. The troops landed at Glebe, three miles below the fort, with the intention of storming it next morning. The second division was put on shore in the evening; afterwards the troops advanced, when the enemy, to avoid being surrounded, retreated, leaving the fort to General Mathew, who posted his men in a strong position between Portsmouth and the south branch of Elizabeth River. The Guards took possession of Suffolk, the magazines, and stores. Detachments were sent to Norfolk and Gosport; all the vessels that remained in the river were taken, with naval and military stores, merchandise and provisions in great abundance. The fort was demolished, and the marine yard with all the timber burnt.
May 24th The troops re-embarked, and returned to New York. The
to
May 29th. loss of property sustained by the Provincials exceeded half a million. The vessels taken and destroyed amounted to one hundred and thirty-seven.

Preparations were made by Sir Henry Clinton, before the return of the expedition, to attack two forts sixty miles above New York, on Hudson's River. The Guards, with other detachments from the army, embarked, and were joined by the transports from Virginia. This force sailed up North River; part under Major-General Morgan landed a few miles below Fort La Fayette. Sir Henry Clinton proceeded to Stoney Point, where he disembarked: this was a position, from its elevation, of considerable strength; but being in an unfinished state, it was abandoned on the approach of the fleet. In the evening the troops were landed, with a few heavy guns, which were dragged up the hill during the night. About five o'clock next morning a fire opened from the top of Stoney Point on La Fayette, a small but strong fort on the opposite side of the river: this cannonade, the investment by land, and the attack from the vessels in the river, obliged the garrison to surrender. Orders were given to complete the fortifications at Stoney Point, troops were left for the defence of the forts, and the fleet dropped down to New York.

1779.
May 30th.

In July two thousand six hundred men under General Tryon, with the flank companies of the Guards, embarked for Newhaven, and sailed on the third. Before reaching that place, Brigadier-General Garth of the Guards disembarked with the first division of these troops. The inhabitants collected in great strength to oppose a march of seven miles, which he was obliged to make to avoid a creek. In defiance of an obstinate defence and increasing numbers, he forced his way and took possession of the town. Major-General Tryon with the remainder of the troops landed on the other side, to secure a fort on the high ground which commanded the harbour. Garth remained in Newhaven that night, and destroyed all the public stores and artillery in the town, and the vessels in the harbour; but, much to his credit, private property was far more respected than the towns-people had a right to expect,

July.

July 5th.

1779. after their irritating opposition on the preceding day, and their unwarrantable conduct during the time the troops had possession of the place. The casualties in the Guards were, Adjutant Campbell killed, Captain Parker wounded, one rank and file killed, one serjeant, nine rank and file wounded, and fourteen missing.

The army next proceeded to Fairfield, where the inhabitants proved even more hostile than at Newhaven.
July 8th. Here it was determined to make an example, forbearance at the latter place having produced no effect. The public stores of every description, the shipping, and even the town itself, were reduced to ashes.

The troops re-embarked; and the same scenes of devas-
July 11th. tation took place on their landing at Norwalk and Greenfield. The English, after this, fell down the river to New York.[1] The loss of the Guards at Fairfield was four rank and file killed, one serjeant, ten rank and file wounded, and two missing. At Norwalk they lost one rank and file wounded.

December. Sir Henry Clinton and a large force embarked at Sandy Hook on the twenty-sixth of December, with the intention of taking Charlestown and reducing the province of South Carolina; leaving in New York a garrison, of which the Guards formed a part, under the command of Lieutenant-General Knyphausen.

1780.
January. This winter, the severest ever remembered in America, passed without any event of importance, except an attempt made by Lord Stirling, the American General, about the middle of the month, to take Staten Island. After marching over the ice from the Jersey side, a small post was surprised by him, from which, however, he shortly retreated with some loss.

---

[1] The British lost in this short expedition, which lasted nine days, twenty killed, ninety-six wounded, and thirty-two missing.

At Young's House, in the vicinity of White Plains, the Americans had established a post, which intercepted the communication and the passage of cattle and provisions intended for the supply of New York. It was considered expedient to dislodge the enemy, who were there strongly fortified, and amounted to three hundred men. The post in question was not more than twenty miles from the advance of the Royal army. The rivers were all frozen. A communication was made through Major-General Mathew to the Honourable Lieutenant-Colonel Norton of the Coldstream, directing a detachment to be sent to Young's House on sledges; but Lieutenant-Colonel Norton having convinced General Mathew that the sledges would not answer, he was desired to proceed, or not, according to circumstances, and to use his own discretion.

1780.
January.

In the evening of the second of February, Colonel Norton set out with four flank companies of the Guards, two companies of Hessians, a few Yagers, some of them mounted, and two three-pounders. This detachment marched across the country by the most unfrequented tracts, to avoid the enemy's patroles; and at day-break their guides said they were still seven miles from Young's House. They were now much fatigued, having marched all night with the snow in many places two feet deep. The guns had been left behind, as the horses were unable to drag them on; the detachment was therefore unprovided with the proper requisites for forcing the doors: fortunately, however, they found on their way some axes, and an iron crow-bar. When within two miles the cavalry were ordered to be ready to cut off the retreat of the men in the house, and to intercept any reinforcements which might be sent to their relief; but, in consequence of the snow, they could only draw up on an eminence at some distance. As the flank companies of the Guards

February.

Feb. 3rd.

1780.
Feb. 3rd.

advanced, a detachment of the enemy was perceived marching to reinforce the post. Lieutenant-Colonel Hall's company ascended the hill on the right; some of the grenadiers inclined to their left, when a party of the enemy stationed in the orchard received them with great courage. Colonel Pennington[1] of the Coldstream came up with the rest of the grenadiers of the Guards, and succeeded in carrying the house. Forty men were found dead, and ninety made prisoners. The loss sustained by Lieutenant-Colonel Norton's detachment was two killed and twenty-five wounded.

Two days after this affair, it was thus noticed:—

" February 5th, 1780, Head Quarters, New York.

" His Excellency Lieutenant-General Knyphausen de-
" sires his thanks may be given in public orders to Lieu-
" tenant-Colonel Norton of the Guards, for his good con-
" duct and gallant behaviour in attacking and forcing a
" considerable body of rebels, advantageously posted at
" Young's House, in the neighbourhood of White Plains,

---

[1] In July, 1777, this officer embarked for America in the Scorpion sloop, commanded by his friend the Honourable John Tollemache. From some unaccountable caprice Pennington persisted in whistling as he walked the quarter-deck, notwithstanding the repeated remonstrances of the captain. On their landing at New York in September these officers fought a duel, when Tollemache was run through the body and killed. Pennington afterwards succeeded to the title of Muncaster. The following explanation is given in a note to Douglas's Peerage of Scotland, vol. I. page 488. " The quarrel originated in a sonnet written by Captain Penning-
" ton, which Captain Talmash took up as reflecting on the supposed
" wit of his lady. After firing a brace of pistols each without ef-
" fect, they drew their swords; Captain Talmash was run through
" the heart, and Captain Pennington received seven wounds, so
" severe, that his life was despaired of for some time."

" on the morning of the third instant. His Excellency 1780.
" returns his thanks to the officers and private soldiers of February.
" the different detachments employed on this service; and
" the General is particularly obliged to the officers and
" men of the West Chester Refugees for their very
" determined behaviour upon this as well as former oc-
" casions."

During the autumn the American General Arnold, who commanded a large force at West Point, on the North River, betrayed the confidence reposed in him by his party. The secret correspondence between Arnold and the British commander was carried on through the medium of Major André, an English officer, who was seized in disguise, when papers were found on his person which clearly proved every particular of the transaction. He was tried by a board of general officers, as a spy, and condemned to be hanged.[1] The American General has been censured for directing this ignominious sentence to be carried into execution; but doubtless Major André was well aware, when he undertook the negotiation, of the fate that awaited him should he fall into the hands of the enemy. The laws of war award to spies the punishment of death. It would therefore be difficult to assign a reason why Major André should have been exempted from that fate to which all others are doomed under similar circumstances, although the amiable qualities of the man rendered the individual case a subject of peculiar commiseration. The members of the court are said to have wept when they passed the sentence.

On the twenty-second of March a post of the insurgents   March.
was taken in the Jerseys: the expedition however was unsuccessful, as Lieutenant-Colonel Macpherson, who

---

[1] The sentence was carried into effect on the second of October.

ORIGIN AND SERVICES OF

1780. embarked at New York, and Lieutenant-Colonel Howard of the Guards, who embarked at Kingsbridge, did not arrive at the appointed time. Occasional incursions were
June. made by Lieutenant-General Knyphausen, who came in frequent contact with the advance of Washington's army, encamped at Morristown. The principal action occurred on the twenty-third of June, at Springfield, which place was destroyed.[1] The first battalion of the brigade of Guards was commanded by the Honourable Lieutenant-Colonel Cosmo Gordon of the third Guards; and the second battalion by Lieutenant-Colonel Schutz of the Coldstream. Owing to mismanagement, the affair did not terminate so favourably as was anticipated. The loss of the Guards was: "Killed, none; wounded, Colonel "Cosmo Gordon, slightly; four privates wounded."
July. Early in July the troops under Knyphausen returned to New York, and the Guards were stationed some time in that neighbourhood.
October. On the sixteenth of October, Major-General the Honour-

---

[1] On a report of this action reaching England, a Court-Martial was ordered to assemble at New York to inquire into the conduct of Lieutenant-Colonel Gordon, on an accusation made by Lieutenant-Colonel Thomas of the First Guards, for "not having "done his duty before the enemy on the twenty-third of June, 1780." He was tried in August, 1782, at New York, and "honourably ac- "quitted of the whole and every part of the charge exhibited "against him." Colonel Thomas had been previously tried at New York for "secretly aspersing the character" of Colonel Gordon on that occasion, and acquitted. "A mutual dislike and many acrimonious altercations" ensued in consequence, and the matter terminated in a fatal duel in Hyde Park, on the fourth of September, 1783, in which Colonel Thomas was mortally wounded, and died next day. Colonel Gordon was tried at the Old Bailey on the seventeenth of September, 1784, on a charge of wilful murder, and acquitted.

able Alexander Leslie, with the Guards and a force of three thousand men, sailed for the Chesapeak, and disembarked in Virginia. Visiting Suffolk, Hampton, Portsmouth, and other places adjacent, they destroyed every thing that came within their reach. 1780.

A detachment under the Honourable Lieutenant-Colonel Stewart and Captain Maitland of the First Guards, also Captains Schutz and Eld of the Coldstream, were engaged with " a party of Continentals and Militia at the Great Bridge," and defeated them, taking four pieces of cannon. Late in November the Guards and troops under Leslie re-embarked for Charlestown, at which place they arrived on the thirteenth of December, and found that orders had been left for them immediately to proceed up the country to join Lord Cornwallis. They began their march on the nineteenth, but did not effect their junction till the eighteenth of January.[1]

November.
December.
1781.
January.

On the first of February Lord Cornwallis forded the Catawba, a deep and rapid river, in face of the enemy. The passage was gallantly led by the brigade of Guards under Brigadier-General O'Hara of the Coldstream: these troops crossed with the greatest steadiness, and, although exposed to a galling fire, reserved theirs till they reached the opposite bank. The light infantry of the Guards, led by Lieutenant-Colonel Hall, first entered the water; they were successively followed by the grenadiers, February.

---

[1] Extract of a letter from Major-General the Honourable Alexander Leslie to Sir Henry Clinton, dated Camden, eighth of January, 1781. " I arrived here some days ago with the Guards, " regiment of Bose, and Yagers. I went to Wynnesborough to see " Lord Cornwallis; he moves this day, and I march to-mor-" row with the above troops and North Carolina regiment. I meet " his Lordship about seventy miles from hence."—American MSS. Royal Institution.

1781. the remainder of the battalion, and Lord Cornwallis's division. Lieutenant-Colonel Hall of the Third Guards, and seven rank and file, were killed; six serjeants, and fifty-seven rank and file, wounded.

The Americans returned to the province of North Carolina, and, having greatly augmented their forces,[1] took up a strong position.

Mar. 15th. At day-light on the fifteenth of March Lord Cornwallis with a very inferior force attacked the American army while drawn up within their lines at Guildford Court-House. After a sharp skirmish the advance, consisting of the cavalry, the light infantry of the Guards, and the Yagers under Lieutenant-Colonel Tarleton, obliged the enemy to retire. In the centre of their first line was an open space, both flanks extended to the woods, in which infantry were posted behind the fences. Their second line was about three hundred yards in rear of the first. Two brigades of the enemy also were formed in some open ground near the Court-House, about four hundred paces in rear of the second line. A corps of observation was posted on the right flank, under Colonel Washington, consisting of the First and Third Dragoons, a detachment of light infantry, and a corps of riflemen. Colonel Lee with a detachment was placed by the American commander for the protection of the left.

Whilst preparations were being made, a fire opened in

---

[1] " Exceeded seven thousand men."— Lord Cornwallis's Dispatch.

The British amounted to one thousand four hundred and forty-five, including cavalry.

In Gordon's History he makes from official documents, the number of the Americans amount to fourteen hundred and ninety continentals, two thousand seven hundred and fifty-three militia, and two hundred cavalry.

the centre from two of the enemy's guns[1] placed in the road. The attack on the right, under cover of a cannonade, was led by the Seventy-first, with the regiment of Bose, supported by the first battalion of the Guards. On the left the Twenty-third and Thirty-third regiments were supported by the grenadier and second battalion of Guards. The light infantry of the Guards and Yagers were posted in the wood on the left of the artillery, and behind them the cavalry were stationed, in order to take advantage of any circumstances that might occur. The troops advanced with steadiness and resolution across the plain. At about one hundred and forty yards the enemy opened their fire, but the British still moved on in perfect order, reserving theirs till the word of command was given; after which they charged. The enemy did not await the shock, but retreated behind the second line, which made more resistance, and kept up a brisk fire that did great execution; but this line at length gave way. Owing to the extent of the American position, the reserves were brought forward, and the first battalion of Guards[2] immediately formed on the right. The Thirty-third regiment being exposed to a galling fire, and outflanked, moved to the left, when the interval was immediately filled by the grenadiers, the second battalion of the Guards and Yagers. In consequence of this extension of the British front so much to the right and left, broken intervals appeared during the pursuit of the enemy's first and second lines. The whole, however, kept advancing, notwithstanding

1781.
Mar. 15th.

---

[1] "The cannon fired on us whilst we were forming, from the "centre of the line of militia, but were withdrawn by the Conti- "nentals before the attack."—Lord Cornwallis's Dispatch.

[2] "Were warmly engaged in front, flank, and rear, with "some of the enemy that had been routed on the first attack."— Lord Cornwallis's Dispatch.

1781.
Mar. 15th.

many impediments from the inequality of the ground, the thickness of the wood, and an obstinate resistance. The second battalion of Guards first gained the open space at Guildford Court-House, and " glowing with impatience to signalize themselves,"[1] attacked the Americans, though greatly superior to themselves in number, quickly routed them, and took two six-pounders. Unfortunately, however, whilst in the ardour of pursuit and in some consequent confusion, they received a destructive fire from a body of Provincials, and being charged by Washington's dragoons, were driven back with much slaughter, and lost the two guns which they had previously captured. The artillery then came up, and opened a fire which checked the pursuit of the Americans. The Seventy-first and Twenty-third regiments at the same time penetrated through the wood. General O'Hara quickly rallied the second battalion of Guards, when the enemy were again defeated and the two guns retaken.[2] The Americans then commenced their retreat; which was conducted with great regularity. Two regiments which, with the cavalry, had been sent in pursuit of the enemy, were recalled.

The casualties in the brigade of Guards were, the Honourable Lieutenant-Colonel Stewart, eight serjeants and twenty-eight rank and file, killed. Brigadier-Generals O'Hara and Howard, Captains Swanton, Schutz, Honourable William Maynard, Goodricke, Lord Dunglass,

---

[1] Lord Cornwallis's Dispatch.

[2] " The gallantry of Brigadier-General O'Hara merits my " highest commendation, for, after receiving two dangerous " wounds, he continued on the field while the action lasted; by " his earnest attention on all other occasions, seconded by the " officers and soldiers of his Majesty's Guards, who are no less " distinguished by their order and discipline than by their spirit " and valour."—Extract from Lord Cornwallis's Dispatch.

Maitland and Stuart, Adjutant Colquhoun; two serjeants, two drummers, one hundred and forty-three rank and file, wounded; twenty-two missing. Captains Schutz, the Honourable William Maynard and Lord Dunglass, of the Coldstream, and Captain Goodricke of the First, died of their wounds.

1781.
Mar. 15th.

General Green, the American commander, who had drawn off his army and retired in good order, took post behind a river three miles from the scene of action.

The English General was not in a condition to follow up his success, and was obliged to direct his march towards Wilmington, to supply his army with the requisite necessaries.[1]

April.

It having been determined to carry the war into the Southern Colonies, the troops under Lord Cornwallis arrived at Petersburg on the twentieth of May: they then crossed the Roanoke, Meherrin, and Nottaway rivers, on their route, with but little opposition. Here they found detachments under the command of Generals Phillips and Arnold, the latter having deserted the insurgents.

May.

Lord Cornwallis, being considerably reinforced, crossed James River at Westover on the twenty-fourth, and marched through Hanover County.

At Williamsburg he received dispatches from Sir Henry Clinton, acquainting him that New York was in great

---

[1] Extract of a letter from Lord Cornwallis to Sir Henry Clinton, dated Camp near Wilmington, tenth of April, 1781. At Guildford " our force was 1360 infantry rank and file, and about 200 " cavalry. A third of my army sick and wounded, which I was " obliged to carry in waggons or on horseback, the remainder " without shoes, and worn down with fatigue; I thought it was time " to look for some place of rest and refitment." — American MSS. Royal Institution.

1781.
May.

danger,[1] and desiring that part of his forces might be sent to join him without loss of time. Cornwallis prepared to comply with the order; and as it was impossible to remain

June.

longer at Williamsburg with so small a force, determined to pass James River and retire to Portsmouth. He there-

July 4th.

fore marched from Williamsburg, and took up a position which covered the ford to the island of James Town, where the Queen's Rangers, with the carriages and baggage, crossed. La Fayette, under the impression that the main body of the troops had passed, advanced by forced marches

July 6th.

in hopes of falling on his rear-guard. To strengthen this supposition, Cornwallis, already informed of his approach, ordered the piquets in case of attack to retire. La Fayette having crossed a morass with about fifteen hundred Americans and some artillery, formed in front of the British position. The English then advanced in two lines, and after a sharp contest succeeded in taking the enemy's cannon. The Americans fled in great confusion; and had not the day closed, probably the whole detachment would have been destroyed.

Cornwallis then passed James River, and forwarded the troops intended for embarkation to Portsmouth. On reaching that place it was found by no means a desirable post; he therefore left it, and on the twenty-second of

August.

August concentrated his force in York Town and Gloucester; which he fortified, being the only places capable of affording protection to ships of the line.

Washington had long projected an attack on New York, and Clinton had reason to suppose this plan was finally settled. In June Washington marched to White Plains,

---

[1] The information was discovered in an intercepted letter written by Washington to the Congress.

and was joined on the sixth of July by Count Rochambeau, with the French troops from Rhode Island. In the middle of August dispatches arrived from the Count de Grasse, which informed the two commanders that he should enter the Chesapeak with his fleet towards the end of the month. The American and French generals determined to attack Lord Cornwallis, and communicated their intentions to the Count de Grasse, that he might be aware of them on his passage. Every artifice was tried to deceive Sir Henry Clinton with regard to this project. 1781.

In the mean time Arnold had taken and destroyed New London, putting to death all the troops which had defended it. The attack on New London did not make any alteration in the plans of the combined French and American forces, who marched through Philadelphia, and proceeded to the Elk River, at the point of its confluence with the Chesapeak, where transports were waiting to receive them. On the twenty-fifth of September they landed at Williamsburg, and were joined by La Fayette and St. Simon. They left Williamsburg at the end of the month, and encamped near York Town. September. Sept. 28th.

Next day dispatches arrived from Sir Henry Clinton, dated the twenty-fourth of September, informing Lord Cornwallis that upwards of five thousand troops and a fleet of twenty-three sail of the line would leave New York by the fifth of October. Cornwallis, under the impression that he could hold both York Town and Gloucester till the promised reinforcements arrived, withdrew during the night from the out-works, which were occupied by the enemy, who proceeded regularly to invest York Town, and immediately broke ground. The first parallel was opened on the sixth of October, at the distance of about a quarter of a mile. From the ninth their batteries kept up a constant cannonade, which caused much damage to the un- Sept. 29th. Sept. 30th. October.

1781.
October.

finished works. During the night of the eleventh, a second parallel was opened by the enemy within three hundred yards of the works: to retard their progress the garrison kept up an incessant fire, and caused a severe loss. Two redoubts erected in front particularly annoyed the assailants; but on the night of the fourteenth they were carried by storm, one by the French, the other by the Americans, in the true spirit of emulation. Sickness, and the shot of the besiegers, caused the British to suffer much. A sortie was made with two hundred and fifty men under Lieutenant-Colonel Abercrombie, with the hope of impeding the formation of the second parallel, against which it was evident the new works on the left could not stand long, as the guns had been already silenced. This force, composed of detachments from the Guards and grenadiers of the Eightieth regiment, under Lieutenant-Colonel Lake of the Guards, with some light infantry under Major Armstrong, was ordered to carry the two batteries that appeared in the greatest state of forwardness. They suc-

Oct. 16th. ceeded in forcing the redoubts, spiked eleven heavy guns, killed and wounded about a hundred of the French troops who guarded them, and returned within their lines, having sustained only a trifling loss. The enemy, however, carried on their advances with such activity, that they mounted one hundred pieces of ordnance in battery, which effectually prevented the British from showing a single gun. Cornwallis, reduced to extremity, attempted to pass

Oct. 17th. the garrison over to Gloucester Point; for which purpose the greatest part of the Guards, and some of the Twenty-third regiment, were actually embarked and had reached the Gloucester side of the river; but a violent storm at midnight prevented this plan from being put into execution. From the dilapidated state of the works, little hopes of successful resistance could be entertained, and the only alternative then left to the English commander was to capitulate, or to consign the brave men that remained to inevitable destruction, should an assault take place.

1781.

Terms of capitulation were granted, on condition of his surrendering himself and the forces under his command prisoners of war. Next day York and Gloucester were taken possession of by General Washington.

Oct. 18th.

The hostile army consisted of seven thousand French, the same number of Continentals, and about five thousand militia.

During the siege the Guards had one serjeant, three rank and file killed, and the Honourable Major Cochrane, late of the First Guards, acting aid-de-camp to the Earl of Cornwallis; one serjeant, twenty-one rank and file wounded; three lieutenant-colonels, twelve captains, one ensign, two adjutants, one quarter-master, one surgeon, three mates, twenty-five serjeants, twelve drummers, four hundred and sixty-five rank and file surrendered prisoners, and were sent to Lancaster[1] in Pennsylvania.

The few men of the Guards who "escaped captivity" at York Town joined Major-General Leslie in South Carolina, under the command of Captain Swanton of the

---

[1] On the twenty-seventh of May, 1782, Captain Asgill of the First Guards was closely imprisoned, and removed from Lancaster to Chatham loaded with chains, and threatened with death, on the plea of retaliation for the recent execution of Captain Joshua Huddy, an American officer. A gallows of unusual height was erected in sight of his prison-window, placarded with these words —" For the execution of Captain Asgill." He continued in confinement till the thirteenth of November, when he was released by an order from the Congress at the request of Count Vergennes, the Minister of France. He made all haste to New York, but,

1781. Third Guards, and were afterwards sent by Sir Henry Clinton's orders from Charlestown to New York.

Clinton had made arrangements to embark with about seven thousand men, having previously sent to acquaint Lord Cornwallis that he hoped the fleet would leave New York on the fifth of October. Unfortunately it did not sail till the nineteenth, the day Lord Cornwallis surrendered. Clinton put to sea, determined to make the most vigorous efforts for the relief of Cornwallis, and was confident of success. The mortification he experienced on

Oct. 24th. arriving off the Capes of Virginia may be conceived, when he received intelligence which induced him to believe Cornwallis had capitulated. Convinced that his information was correct, and knowing the French [1] fleet exceeded the British, he decided on returning to New York, as the relief of York Town and Gloucester had been his only object.

1782. General Carleton succeeded Sir Henry Clinton in the

---

finding the Swallow packet had just sailed, got a boat and overtook her four leagues from the shore, having left his servant and all his property behind.

" Return of the Brigade of Guards prisoners with the enemy.
" New York, 4th December, 1782.

	Serjeants.	Drummers.	Rank and File.	Total.
First regiment	8	3	152	163
Coldstream do.	4	3	108	115
Third do.	2	2	103	107
Total	14	8	363	385

Jn. W. T. Watson,
Lt-Col. Coms Brigade of Guards.

[1] The British fleet consisted of twenty ships of the line, two fifty-gun ships, and eight frigates. The French amounted to thirty-six sail of the line, not including frigates.

chief command, from which time hostilities ceased, and no event worthy of notice occurred between the hostile armies in the vicinity of New York.

Negociations then terminated an ill-conducted and disastrous war, of which the entire odium was thrown on the Court by a faction that in this country excited and encouraged the Colonists to appeal to arms. Had the Administration of that day permitted the Provincials to work their way to independence by the sure but more insidious process of assembling a Parliament of their own, under the specious pretence of taxing themselves, there can be little doubt that the same faction would have ascribed the loss of America to a want of political foresight in the King and his advisers. Whenever a Colony has acquired sufficient strength to establish its independence, it may be expected to do so, as the grown-up son withdraws himself from the control of his father; but the period of colonial maturity is not easily defined, and the symptoms must be more strongly marked than they were in the instance of North America to justify a Government, bound to protect the rights of the mother country, in tamely relinquishing her dominion without a struggle. To judge fairly of the difficult and distressing situation in which the Court was placed, it is necessary to recollect that a strong opposing party at home was on the watch to attach blame, whatever course had been adopted; and that in point of fact the Colonists, far from presenting the means of successful insurrection, were only torn from England by the intervention of France, Holland, and Spain.

Conditional articles of peace were ratified between Great Britain, France, Spain, and America, when the thirteen provinces were declared independent.

On the twentieth of January the preliminary articles of

1783. peace with France were signed; those with America were to take effect from the same date.

The first detachment of the Guards arrived from North America in the Adamant, disembarked in January, and joined their respective regiments.

June 6th. The detachment of the Coldstream "which came from captivity" under Lord Cornwallis, embarked at New York on board the Jason and other vessels. They landed

July. at Portsmouth in the beginning of July, and marched to join their regiments in London.[1]

---

[1] Return of the Guards in America, consisting of ten companies in two battalions, from their embarkation in April, 1776, till their return in 1783.

		Officers.	Officers absent.	Non-comm'd Officers.	Rank and File.	Sick.	Wanting to complete.	Total.
Return dated 29th April, 1776	.	13		62	999	1		1105
,, ,, ,, Dec.	Under Sir Wm. Howe	40		56	900			996
,, ,, ,, Aug. 1777	,, ,, ,,	47		62	867	126	7	1109
,, ,, ,, Nov.	,, ,, ,,	41		62	924	69	7	1103
,, dated 1st Dec. 1779	Under Sir H. Clinton	38	16	62	786	168	38	1103
,, ,, ,, April, 1780	,, ,, ,,	31	18	62	777	120	95	1103
,, ,, ,, August	,, ,, ,,	23	18	62	795	85	120	1103
,, ,, ,, October	,, ,, ,,	23	18	62	773	93	134	1103
,, ,, 15th Nov.	,, ,, ,,	24	17	62	821	38	141	1103
,, ,, ,, Dec.	,, ,, ,,	26	15	62	816	40	144	1103
,, ,, ,, July, 1781	,, ,, ,,	17	24	62	748	148	104	1103
,, ,, 1st Oct.	,, ,, ,,	23	18	62	521	316	163	1103
,, ,, ,, ,, 1782	Under Sir Guy Carleton (including prisoners of war)	7		62	781		219	1069
,, of that part of the brigade of Guards remaining in America on the 1st of March, 1783	.	7		29	439			475

	Adjutant.	Quartermaster.	Surgeon.	Surgeon's Mate.	Serjeants.	Drummers.	Rank and File.
"Return of the brigade of Guards that came in from captivity between the 8th and 27th of May, 1783"	1	1	1	1	12	6	254

"Embarkation Return of the Guards, dated New York, 6th June, 1783."	Officers.	Staff.	Serjeants.	Drummers.	Rank and File.	Women.	Children.
First Foot Guards, embarked on board the Chatham		1	8	4	108	16	5
Coldstream ,, ,, ,, Jason and Chatham		1	3	4	70	3	1
Third ,, ,, ,, Jason					3		
Men ,, ,, on board the Lyon, by a return dated New York, 15th of June, 1783		2	3	2	79	2	2
Total		4	14	10	260	21	8

War-Office Returns.

OFFICERS OF THE FIRST FOOT GUARDS WHO SERVED IN NORTH AMERICA.

Rank	Name	From	To	Notes
Lt.-Col.	Thomas Howard	29 April, 1776	21 Sept. 1778	Killed on his passage home on board the Eagle Packet, in action with an American Privateer.
,,	West Hyde	,, ,, ,,	May, 1779	To England with Dispatches, dated 11th May, 1779.
,,	Sir John Wrottesley, Bart.	,, ,, ,,	March, 1778	Leave to England.
,,	Thomas Cox	,, ,, ,,	Sept. ,,	,, ,, ,,
Capt.	Thomas Gordon	,, ,, ,,	Sept. 1776	Promoted: leave to England.
,,	Robert Keith	,, ,, ,,	13 May, 1778	Promoted in Third Foot Guards: leave to England.
,,	Frederick Madan	,, ,, ,,	25 Dec. 1779	Died in America.
,,	Hon. John Thomas de Burgh	,, ,, ,,	Sept. 1776	Promoted: leave to England.
,,	Nicholas Bayley	,, ,, ,,	Jan. 1778	,, ,, ,,
,,	Charles Whitworth	,, ,, ,,	,, ,,	Leave to England.
,,	Hon. John Finch	,, ,, ,,	29 June, 1777	Wounded 26th, and died 29th of June, at Amboy.
,,	T. Dowdeswell	,, ,, ,,	July, 1777	Leave to England.
Ens.	Hon. W. H. Nassau	,, ,, ,,	,, ,,	,, ,, Sold out, 24th June, 1777.
,,	Thomas Glyn	,, ,, ,,	,, ,,	Promoted: leave to England.
,,	W. Colquhoun	July ,,	,, ,,	,, ,, ,,
,,	A. J. Drummond	,, ,,	,, ,,	
Capt.	A. Edmonstone		Oct. 1777	A.D.C. to Major-General Riedesel from Sept. 1776. Prisoner of war under the convention at Saratoga. To England on parole, Sept. 1779.
Lt.-Col.	George Garth	March, 1777	March, 1780	Leave to England.
Capt.	R. H. Pye	March, 1777	Aug. 1779	Promoted: leave to England.
,,	Hon. R. Fitzpatrick	,, ,,	May, 1778	,, ,, ,,
,,	Patrick Bellew	,, ,,	28 June, 1778	Wounded at the heights of Freehold: leave to England.
,,	Frederick Thomas	March, 1777 / March, 1781	14 Oct. 1780 / Sept. 1782	Leave to England. Returned. Commandant at James Island, Feb. 1782. Leave to England.
Ens.	E. S. Frazer	March, 1777	19 June, 1779	Exchanged to the 4th Foot. Arrived with Dispatches 9 July, 1779.
,,	John Jones	,, ,,	April, 1780	"Major of Brigade." "Prisoner with the French." "On Duty" at Home in March, 1782.
,,	George Parker	,, ,,	29 Dec. 1779	Wounded at Newhaven, 5 July, 1779. Leave to England.
,,	Francis Dundas	,, ,,	19 Oct. 1781	Surrendered prisoner of war at York Town.
Lt.-Col.	Lord T. Pelham Clinton, M. P., afterwards Earl of Lincoln, and Duke of Newcastle	May, 1777 / April, 1779 / Feb. 1781	18 Nov. 1777 / 15 May, 1780 / 17 Nov. 1781	A.D.C. to Sir Henry Clinton. Leave to England: arrived 24 Dec. 1777. Ditto Ditto. Arrived with Dispatches, 15 June, 1780. Returned as Brig.-Gen. Leave to Engd. Arrived 17 Dec. 1781.
Capt.	Thomas Colins	Aug. 1777	3 June, 1781	"Major of brigade to the Guards." Died in Virginia.

OFFICERS OF THE FIRST FOOT GUARDS WHO SERVED IN NORTH AMERICA.—Continued.

		From	To	
Capt.	Hon. Henry Phipps	March, 1778	Jan. 1779	Leave to England. Promoted to Major in 85th Foot.
Lt.-Col.	Edmond Stevens	15 May, 1778	Sept. 1778	From Lieutenant and Captain in Coldstream. Taken prisoner on board the Eagle Packet, 21 Sept. 1778, and landed at Corunna: to England on parole in Nov. following. Exchanged in Nov. 1780.
,,	John Howard, afterwards Earl of Suffolk	April, 1779	14 June, 1781	Commanding the Brigade of Guards from Feb. to Dec. 1780. Wounded at Guildford, 15 March, 1781. Arrived with Dispatches, 14 July, 1781.
,,	John Leland	,, ,,	27 May, 1781	Brigadier-Gen. Arrived with Dispatches, 23 June, 1781.
,,	Hon. James Stewart	,, ,,	15 March, 1781	Killed in action at Guildford.
Capt.	Hon. C. Cochrane	April, 1779 / March, 1781	2 Sept. 1780 / Oct. 1781	"Major in Lord Cathcart's Legion." Leave to England: arrived 14 Oct. 1780. Left the First Guards 25 Jan. 1781. Acting A.D.C. to Earl Cornwallis. Killed at York Town, Oct. 1781.
,,	Francis Richardson	April, 1779	19 Oct. 1781	A.D.C. to Major-Gen. Mathew. Brigade Major from June, 1781. Surrendered prisoner of war at York Town.
Ens.	Richard St. George	April, 1779 / March, 1781	16 Oct. 1780 / 20 Nov. 1782	A.D.C. to Sir Henry Clinton. Arrived with Dispatches 13 Nov. 1780. Appointed Deputy-Adjut. Gen. in North America 5 Dec. 1780. Promoted to Lieut.-Col. of 70th Foot 3 May, 1782: arrrived in England in Dec. following.
,,	Augustus Maitland	April, 1779	19 Oct. 1781	Wounded at Guildford, 15 March, 1781. Surrendered prisoner of war at York Town.
,,	John Goodricke	,, ,,	15 March, 1781	Killed in action at Guildford.
Lt.-Col.	Hon. Robert Seymour Conway	March, 1781	1 Oct. 1781	Arrived with Dispatches 3 Nov. 1781.
,,	Gerard Lake	,, ,,	19 Oct. 1781	Surrendered prisoner of war at York Town.
Ens.	Charles Asgill	,, ,,	,, ,, ,,	Ditto. Closely imprisoned from 27 May to 13 Nov. 1782, and threatened with execution. Arrived in England in Dec. following.
,,	James Perryn	,, ,,	,, ,, ,,	Surrendered prisoner of war at York Town. Exchanged in Oct. 1782, and embarked for England in Dec.
,,	Hon. G. Ludlow	,, ,,	,, ,, ,,	Surrendered prisoner of war at York Town. Sent by General Washington to New York with the account of Capt. Asgill's imprisonment. Embarked for England in Nov. 1782.

ORIGIN AND SERVICES OF
OFFICERS OF THE COLDSTREAM GUARDS WHO SERVED IN NORTH AMERICA.

		From	To	
Col.	Edward Mathew	29 Ap. 1776	2 Sept. 1780	Brig.-Gen. Commanding the Brigade of Guards from April, 1776, to Feb. 1780. Appointed Major-Gen. 19 Feb. 1779, and Col. of 62nd Foot 17 Nov. following. Arrived in England 14 Oct. 1780. General and Com.-in-Chief of the Leeward Islands, 26 Oct. 1781.
Lt.-Col.	Harry Trelawney	,, ,, ,,	Oct. 1778	Commanded the First Battalion. Wounded at the Heights of Freehold, 28 June, 1778. Leave to England.
,,	A. G. Martin	,, ,, ,,	Jan. 1780	Promoted: leave to England.
,,	Richard Grenville	,, ,, ,,	July, 1777	Leave to England: arrived 16 Aug.
Capt.	J. S. Dyer, afterwards Sir John Dyer, Bt.	,, ,, ,,	April, 1778	,, ,, Promoted in First Foot Guards.
,,	G. S. Bourne	,, ,, ,,	Dec. 1776	Died at New York.
,,	Edmond Stevens	,, ,, ,,	14 May, 1778	Major of Brigade to the Guards. Promoted in First Foot Guards.
,,	William Bosville	,, ,, ,,	May, 1777	Sick leave to England.
Ens.	Thomas Thoroton	,, ,, ,,	July ,,	Promoted: leave to England.
,,	Charles Trelawney	,, ,, ,,	,, ,,	,, ,, ,,
,,	Nicholas Boscawen	,, ,, ,,	,, ,,	
Deputy Marshal	Robert Wilson	,, ,, ,,	Jan. ,,	Appointed Adjutant to the Brigade of Guards.
Lt.-Col.	Charles O'Hara	Mar. 1777 / Oct. 1780	Feb. 1779 / 19 Oct. 1781	Leave to England: returned to take the command of the Brig. of Guards. Wounded at Guildford 15 Mar. 1781. Surrendered prisoner of war at York Town. Exchanged 9 Feb. 1782. Promoted to Major-Gen., and sent from New York to the relief of Jamaica in May following.
Capt.	James Hamilton	March, 1777	2 Sept. 1780	Leave to England: arrived 14 Oct.
,,	H. De la Douespe	,, ,,	Dec. 1777	Promoted: leave to England: arrived 18 Jan. 1778.
Ens.	John Byron	,, ,,	Feb. 1778	Promoted: leave to England.
,,	Hon. W. Maynard	,, ,,	17 April, 1781	Wounded at Guildford, 15 Mar. and died on 17 April.
,,	W. A. Visc^t. Cantilupe, afterwds. E. of Delaware	,, ,,	April, 1778	Promoted: leave to England.
Capt.	L. Pennington	July, 1777	Nov. 1781	Leave to go from Suffolk to New York, 16 July, and from thence to England.
Ens.	W. Lord Dunglass	,, ,,	12 Dec. 1781	Wounded at Guildford, 15 Mar. and died in Dec.
Lt.-Col.	William Schutz	April, 1779	Jan. ,,	Leave to England.
,,	Hon. C. Norton	,, ,,	March ,,	,, ,,
Capt.	Robert Lovelace	,, ,,	1 Feb. ,,	Retired from the service.
Ens.	William Schutz	,, ,,	21 March ,,	Wounded at Guildford, 15th, and died 21st March.
,,	George Mathew	,, ,,	Dec. 1780	Leave to England.
,,	George Eld	,, ,,	19 Oct. 1781	Surrendered prisoner of war at York Town. Embarked for England in Oct. 1782.
Lt.-Col.	George Morgan	March, 1781	,, ,,	Surrendered prisoner of war at York Town.
Capt.	Henry Greville	,, ,,	,, ,,	Surrendered prisoner of war at York Town. Embarked for England on parole in Sept. 1782.
,,	Charles Gould, afterwards Sir C. Morgan, Bt.	,, ,,	,, ,,	Surrendered prisoner of war at York Town. Embarked fo England in June, 1782.

OFFICERS OF THE THIRD FOOT GUARDS WHO SERVED IN NORTH AMERICA.

		From	To	
Lt.-Col.	George Ogilvie	29 April, 1776	July, 1777	Promoted: leave to England: arrived 16 Aug.
,,	Sir G. Osborn, Bt.	,, ,, ,,	,, ,,	Muster-Master-General in America. Ditto.
,,	T. Twisleton, afterwards Lord Saye and Sele	,, ,, ,,	Dec. ,,	Leave to England.
Capt.	Cavendish Lister	,, ,, ,,	July ,,	Quarter-Master. Promoted: leave to England.
,,	Charles Leigh	,, ,, ,,	,, ,,	Promoted: leave to England.
,,	D. D'Anvers Rich	,, ,, ,,	April, 1778	,, ,,
,,	Edward Archer	,, ,, ,,	June, 1777	Sold out. Leave to England.
Ens.	W. D. Faucitt	,, ,, ,,	9 May ,,	Exchanged to 44th Foot.
,,	Robert Johnstone	,, ,, ,,	July ,,	Promoted: leave to England.
Capt.	William Faucitt		2 Sept. 1780	A.D.C. to Lieut.-Gen. de Heister, from May, 1776, and afterwards to Major-General Knyphausen. Promoted: leave to England.
,,	George, Viscount Chewton		Dec. 1777	A.D.C. to Earl Cornwallis, from Dec. 1775. Arrived in England 18 Jan. 1778. Promoted in the Coldstream.
Lt.-Col.	H. Stephens	March, 1777	March, 1779	Leave to England.
,,	James Murray	,, ,,	May, 1778	Appointed Colonel of the 77th Foot: leave to England.
Capt.	J. W. T. Watson	,, ,,	Dec. 1782	A.D.C. to Sir Henry Clinton: afterwards Commandant of the "Provincial Light Infantry:" latterly commanding the Brigade of Guards. Ordered home.
,,	Charles Horneck	,, ,,	19 Oct. 1781	Surrendered prisoner of war at York Town. To England on parole in Aug. 1782.
Ens.	George Watkins	,, ,,	29 Dec. 1779	Leave to England.
,,	William Stead	,, ,,	July, 1777	Promoted: leave to England.
,,	F. Boscawen	,, ,,	April, 1782	Died at sea 18 April.
Capt.	Sir Francis Carr Clerke, Bart.	April	7 Oct. 1777	A.D.C. to Major-General Burgoyne. Killed at Saratoga.
,,	Thomas Swanton	May	Sept. 1782	Wounded at Guildford 15 March, 1781. Embarked for England.
Ens.	George Beauclerk	May, 1777 / April, 1779	Aug. 1778 / 24 Aug.1780	On leave: rejoined: leave to England.
Lt.-Col.	Hon. C. Gordon	Sept. 1777	Dec. 1782	On leave at New York, from 14 Oct. 1780. Embarked for England.
Capt.	Charles Rooke	,, ,,	Jan. 1779	A.D.C. to Major-General Daniel Jones. Leave to England.
Lt.-Col.	G. Guydickens	April, 1779	Nov. 1780	Leave to England.
,,	Francis Hall	,, ,,	1 Feb. 1781	Killed in action crossing the Catawba.
Ens.	N. Christie, afterwards N. C. Burton	,, ,,	19 Oct. 1781	Surrendered prisoner of war at York Town. To England Dec. 1782.
,,	John Stuart	Aug. 1780	March ,,	Wounded at Guildford, 15 Mar.: leave to England.
Lt.-Col.	William Grinfield	March, 1781	19 Oct. ,,	Went to America on leave in June, 1777, and ordered to take the command of a draft from the Guards: returned in Jan. 1778. Surrendered prisoner of war at York Town. To England, Dec. 1782.
Capt.	John Grimston	,, ,,	,, ,, ,,	Surrendered prisoner of war at York Town. To England on parole in Aug. 1782.

STAFF OFFICERS APPOINTED TO THE BRIGADE OF GUARDS FOR SERVICE IN NORTH AMERICA.

		From	To	
Brigade Major	E. Stevens	12 Mar. 1776	14 May, 1778	Coldstream. Promoted in First Foot Guards.
,,	Thomas Colins	. . 1778	3 June, 1781	First regiment. Died in Virginia.
,,	F. Richardson	June, 1781	1782	,, ,, Prisoner of war, Oct. 19, 1781.
Adjutant	Michael Cox	12 Mar. 1776	25 April, 1776	First regiment. Promoted to a Company. (Did not go to America.)
,,	Hon. J. Finch	April, 1776	29 June, 1777	First regiment. Died of his wounds.
,,	Robert Wilson	January, 1777	July, 1781	From Deputy-Marshal, Coldstream. Leave to England. Promoted to Lieutenant in an independent company, July 11, 1782.
,,	W. Campbell	29 Aug. ,,	5 July, 1779	From Serjeant, Third Guards. Killed in action at Newhaven.
,,	J. Colquhoun	1780	1782	Ditto. Wounded in action at Guildford, March 15, 1781.
,,	Thomas Alkins	July, 1781	June, 1783	From Serjeant, Coldstream. Prisoner of war, Oct. 19, 1781. To England with the last detachment of Guards.
Quart.-master	Cavendish Lister	12 Mar. 1776	July, 1777	Third Guards. Leave to England on promotion.
,,	Thomas Furnival	19 Mar. 1779	1782	From Serjeant, Coldstream.
,,	John Hill	1780	June, 1783	Ditto, First Guards. Prisoner of war, Oct. 19, 1781. To England with the last detachment.
Surgeon	—— Smithies	28 Feb. 1776	. . .	New appointment.
,,	John Rush	. . .	3 May, 1782	Ditto. Prisoner of war, Oct. 19, 1781. Appointed "Apothecary to the General Hospital in North America," May 4.
Mate	Joseph Hopkins	. . .	Nov. 1782	New appointment. Prisoner of war, Oct. 19, 1781. Embarked for England.
,,	—— Gordon	. . .	June, 1783	New appointment. Prisoner of war, Oct. 19, 1781. To England with the last detachment.
,,	Js. Keir	. . .	,, ,,	New appointment. Prisoner of war, Oct. 19, 1781. To England with the last detachment.
Chaplain	Rev. S. Cooke	28 Feb. 1776	Nov. 1782	New appointment. On leave at New York, from Oct. 1780. Embarked for England.

CHAPTER II.

Death of Waldegrave—Duke of York succeeds as Colonel of the Coldstream—Misunderstanding between Duke of York and Colonel Lennox—Murder of Lewis XVI.—England joins against the new Government of France—First battalions of the regiments of Guards embark for Holland — Clairfait obliges the French to retreat—Archduke Charles carries several batteries—Prince of Saxe-Coburg drives the French from Aix-la-Chapelle—Siege of Maestricht raised—Junction of Generals Miranda and Valence—Prussians, Hanoverians, and British advance by Bois-le-Duc—Grenadier battalion consists of five companies—Guards in quarters at Bergen-op-Zoom—Guards proceed by canal to Bruges — March through Tournay to Orcq — Coldstream attack the French near St. Amand — Duke of York's order dated Tournay—Condé blockaded — Investment of Valenciennes—Siege entrusted to the Duke of York—Capitulation—Condé surrenders — A reinforcement, including three light companies, one for each regiment of Guards, joins the army—Garrison of Valenciennes march out and lay down their arms — Cambray summoned — Duke of York's army separates from the Austrians — French defeated at Lincelles — Siege of Dunkirk — Houchard arrives with reinforcements — Attacks Freytag — Walmoden retreats—Duke of York abandons Dunkirk—Coldstream move towards Menin and encamp — Houchard arrested and sent to Paris — Quesnoy taken by the Austrians — French defeated at Villiers en Couche—Driven from Lannoy—Guards encamp on the plains of Gascogne — Coldstream go into St. Peter's barracks at Ghent—Duke of York returns to England.

The Nulli Secundus Club was instituted on the fourth of March, 1783. The propriety of establishing a club in a regiment has been questioned. As a general observation, it may be admitted that clubs are not in unison with military discipline. In the present case, however, the objection does not apply, the Coldstream being always so officered, that they have been equally remarkable for gentlemanly cordiality at table, and soldierlike obedience on parade.[1]

1784.
Oct. 22nd.

Lord Waldegrave died about this period, and was succeeded in the command of the Coldstream by his Royal Highness Frederick Duke of York.

John Earl of Waldegrave was born in 1718. He entered the First regiment of Guards on the thirteenth of May, 1735. In January, 1751, he was appointed Colonel of the Ninth regiment of Foot, and afterwards successively to the Eighth Dragoons, Fifth Dragoon guards, and Second or Queen's regiment of Dragoon Guards. He had also the rank of General, and was Master of the Horse to the Queen.

1786.
April 11th.

1789.
May 17th.

An order[2] from the King, at this time, directed that the battalion officers should use swords instead of espontoons. A misunderstanding took place between his Royal Highness the Duke of York and Lieutenant-Colonel Lennox, which terminated in a duel. The dispute ori-

---

[1] See Appendix, No. 256, for List of Members, Rules of Club, &c.
[2] " April 11th 1786.—His Majesty has been pleased to order that " the espontoon shall be laid aside, and that in lieu thereof " the battalion officers for the future are to make use of " swords."—Coldstream Orderly-Room.

ginated in an observation made by His Royal Highness, that Colonel Lennox had been addressed by an individual at the club at Daubigney's in a manner that no gentleman ought to permit. The observation being reported to Colonel Lennox, he took the opportunity on parade to inquire of his Royal Highness what were the words which he had submitted to hear, and by whom they were spoken: to this his Royal Highness gave no other answer than by ordering the Colonel to his post. The parade being over, his Royal Highness went into the orderly-room and sent for Colonel Lennox, when he intimated to him, in the presence of the officers of the Coldstream, that he desired to derive no protection either from his rank as a Prince, or his situation as Commanding-officer; and that when off duty he wore a brown coat, and was ready as a private individual to give Colonel Lennox the satisfaction required by one gentleman from another. After this declaration, Colonel Lennox wrote a circular to every member of Daubigney's Club, requesting them to inform him whether the words, as stated, had been addressed to him, and desiring an answer from each member by the following morning; adding, that he should consider their silence on the subject as an acknowledgment that no such words could be recollected. After the time named for an answer to his circular letter, Colonel Lennox sent a written message to the following purport:—" That not being able to recollect any occasion on which words were used towards him at Daubigney's, that ought not to be addressed to a gentleman, he had taken the step which appeared most likely to gain information on the subject to which his Royal Highness had made allusion, and of the party by whom they had been used:—that none of the members of the club had afforded him any information, and

1789.
May.

1789.
May.

consequently, that no such insult had been offered him to their knowledge; and therefore he expected, in justice to his character, that his Royal Highness would contradict the report as publicly as it had been asserted by his Royal Highness." This letter was delivered to the Duke of York the same day by the Earl of Winchelsea. His Royal Highness's answer not proving satisfactory, a message was sent by Colonel Lennox to appoint a meeting; the time and place were then settled.

The following is the account given by the seconds of the affair. In consequence of this misunderstanding, his Royal Highness the Duke of York, attended by Lord Rawdon, and Lieutenant-Colonel Lennox, accompanied by the Earl of Winchelsea, met at Wimbledon Common. The ground was measured twelve paces, and both parties were to fire together. Lieutenant-Colonel Lennox's ball grazed his Royal Highness's curl, but the Duke of York did not fire. Lord Rawdon then interfered, and said " he thought enough had been done;" when Colonel Lennox observed, " that his Royal Highness had not fired :" Lord Rawdon replied, " it was not the intention of the Duke of York to fire; his Royal Highness entertained no animosity against Lieutenant-Colonel Lennox, and had only come out on his invitation to give him satisfaction." Colonel Lennox wished the Duke to fire, which was declined, with a repetition of the reason. Lord Winchelsea then expressed a hope that his Royal Highness would not object to say he considered Colonel Lennox a man of courage and honour. His Royal Highness replied, that he should say no such thing: he had come out with the intention of giving Colonel Lennox the satisfaction he demanded, but did not mean to fire at him; if Colonel Lennox was not satisfied, he might have another shot. Colonel Lennox declared that he could not possibly fire again, as his Royal Highness did not mean to return it. The seconds signed a paper stating that "both parties behaved with the most perfect coolness and intrepidity."

1789.
May.

Lieutenant-Colonel Lennox called a meeting of the officers of the Coldstream, to deliberate and give their opinion whether in the late dispute he behaved as became an officer and a gentleman. After much discussion, they came to the following resolution: " It is the opinion of the Coldstream regiment, that subsequently to the fifteenth of May, the day of the meeting at the orderly-room, Lieutenant-Colonel Lennox has behaved with courage; but, from the peculiar difficulty of his situation, not with judgment."

The unusual, if not unprecedented, occurrence of a Prince of the Blood, and one so near the throne, voluntarily placing his life in such imminent peril, created at the time a strong sensation. The House of Brunswick is remarkable for courage; and bravery is so much the characteristic of this family, that there certainly was no necessity for his Royal Highness to have met Colonel Lennox. He went there, however, from pure gallantry, to give his antagonist satisfaction, by permitting him to have his fire, but with the determination not to return it.

At this period Necker's folly or treachery in giving the democratic party a double representation among the assembled states of France brought about the revolution, and involved all the great European Powers in a succession of destructive wars. The Court, feeble, dissipated, and alarmed, was unable to withstand its new and violent opponents, whose encroachments were at length consummated by the unjustifiable trial and death of an amiable and innocent king.

On the eventful murder of Lewis the Sixteenth, England

1793.
Jan. 21st.

1793. declared war, and joined the confederacy formed against the regicide government of France.

The first battalions of the three regiments of Guards received orders to prepare for embarkation, and all their companies were completed.[1] The grenadiers were formed into a separate battalion under Colonel Leigh of the Third Guards, and Major-General Lake was appointed to command the brigade.

Feb. 24th.

Feb. 25th. Previous to their departure they were inspected by his Majesty King George the Third. From the parade they marched to Greenwich, where their embarkation was witnessed by the Royal Family. After anchoring at the Nore, the convoy sailed for Helvoetsluys; on landing, the

Mar. 3rd. troops were placed in schuyts and sent to Dort.

The Prussian troops were advancing by Bois-le-Duc, while a corresponding movement was made by the Hanoverians, who had been joined by the British under the Duke of York.

At Dort, a light company was formed from the brigade of Guards, and attached to the grenadier battalion, which now consisted of five companies under Lieutenant-Colonel James Perrin of the First Guards.

April. The Guards embarked for Bergen-op-Zoom on the first of April, at which place they were quartered some days; thence they proceeded by the canal through Antwerp and Ghent, and on the nineteenth landed at Bruges. They afterwards marched through Thielt, Courtray, and Tournay, and reached the village of Orcq on the twenty-fifth.

Two light companies were formed at home and added to the establishment of the regiment under a warrant dated nineteenth of April.[2]

A great deal of skirmishing, and some sharp affairs had

---

[1] To four serjeants, four corporals, and two drummers.
[2] See Appendix, No. 244.

taken place between the armies, previous to the arrival of the brigade of Guards.

In consequence of General Dampierre's repeated attacks on the Prussians, the Guards were greatly harassed, and constantly kept under arms in readiness to move. At midnight, on the seventh, they left their cantonments at Orcq, near Tournay, and proceeded to the camp of Maulde, where they halted at day-light, and joined the Austrian and Prussian infantry; the former were ordered to dislodge the enemy from St. Amand, and also to drive them from the wood. In the afternoon the Duke of York marched through St. Amand, which place had been obstinately maintained, as appeared from the ruined and dilapidated state of the buildings and the dead lying in all directions. The Coldstream Guards advanced to the forest, where they halted till the arrival of the Prussian General Knobelsdorf, who rode up, and, with a smile, said in broken English, " that he had reserved for the Coldstream Guards the " honour, the special glory of dislodging the French from " their intrenchments in the forest; that the British troops " need only show themselves in the wood, and the French " would retire." He however omitted to state, that the Austrians had been three times successively repulsed, with the loss of one thousand seven hundred men, and General Knobelsdorf proposed for the Coldstream the honour of performing with six hundred rank and file what five thousand Austrians had not been able to accomplish. The fact was, that on the failure of the Austrians, application had been made to General Knobelsdorf for some fresh battalions from the Prussian army, which requisition he immediately made over to the Duke of York. The Coldstream, under Colonel Pennington, was moved towards the wood of Vicogne, the Prussian General accompanying them himself along the chaussée. On arriving at the skirts of the wood, he pointed to the entrance and gal-

1793.

May.

May 8th.

1793.
May 8th.

loped off. The enemy's redoubts commanded the chaussée leading to the wood of St. Amand, and on the approach of the right companies of the Coldstream, who had nearly closed on the flying enemy, a tremendous fire was opened within pistol-shot by guns wheeled from a battery concealed in the bushes and underwood of the forest. On passing a temporary bridge over a broad ditch, the two right companies under Colonels Bosville and Gascoyne lost, in ten minutes, more than half their numbers, and retired to the skirt of the wood. So sudden was their onset that the last division had scarcely crossed the hedge-row, separating the chaussée from the wood, when the two leading companies found themselves under a destructive fire. The left wing did not lose a man.

In this action the French General Dampierre lost his thigh by a cannon-ball, and died next day. Ensign Howard of the Coldstream, who carried the colours, the serjeant-major,[1] two serjeants, and seventy-three rank and file were killed, wounded, or missing.

May 10th.

The conduct of the Coldstream was thus noticed in a

---

[1] " The Serjeant-Major of the Coldstream regiment, by name
" Darley, was amongst the wounded in the action of the 8th.
" He performed prodigies of valour; he had his arm broke and
" shattered by a ball, but yet continued to fight with the most
" animated and determined bravery for near two hours. He put
" to death a French officer who made an attack upon him, but
" at length had his leg broke by another cannon shot, in conse-
" quence of which he fell into the hands of the French.

" The Duke of York sent a trumpet on the morning of the 9th, to say
" that the surgeon who attended him should be liberally rewarded
" for his trouble, and to request that no expence should be spared
" in procuring him every comfort that his situation would admit
" of.

" The following letter was written by Captain Hewgill of
" the Coldstream, and Secretary to His Royal Highness, to Ser-
" jeant-Major Coleman of the battalion of the Coldstream here :

letter written by the Adjutant-General, Colonel Sir James Murray,[1] dated the tenth of May.

1793. May 10th.

" The attack commenced about seven o'clock. It was
" directed against the posts occupied by General Clairfait,
" which extend from the Scheld to the Abbaye de Vicogne,
" and the Prussian corps which defends the wood in the
" front of the high-road, leading from that place to
" St. Amand.

" To these points were directed the whole efforts of the
" French army, which had been previously reinforced by
" all they could bring together from every quarter. Ge-

" Head-Quarters, May 10, Tournay.
" SERJEANT-MAJOR COLEMAN,
" I write to you by desire of His Royal Highness the Duke
" of York to acquaint you, for the information of Mrs. Darley,
" that her husband is alive, and, though in custody of the enemy,
" has written a few lines to say he is well treated and taken care of.

" The Duke feels much for his unfortunate situation, and has
" given orders that a trumpeter shall be sent to-morrow to him
" with whatever he wants, and a letter to acquaint the French sur-
" geon attending him that he will pay all the expenses of his cure.

" He has one arm and his thigh broke, besides two other
" wounds: there may therefore be some doubt of his recovery,
" which I think you should take an opportunity of communicating
" to your daughter.

" His Royal Highness, as well as every officer and soldier of
" the Coldstream, can bear witness to his good conduct and
" gallantry in the action of the 8th.

" Brave as a lion, he fought with his broken arm till a
" second shot brought him to the ground; and since his con-
" finement he has dictated a letter, wherein he explains his money
" concerns with an incredible degree of accuracy and honesty.

" In short, all our prayers attend this valuable man, and I
" have authority to say from the Commander-in-Chief that he will
" never forget him. " E. HEWGILL."
—*European Magazine*, 1793, page 395.

[1] Adjutant-General to the forces under the Duke of York.

1793.
May 10th.

"neral Knobelsdorf having been under the necessity of
"sending a considerable part of his troops to support the
"Austrians at the Abbaye de Vicogne, his Royal Highness
"about five o'clock left two battalions in the camp at
"Maulde, and marched with the Coldstream, the flank
"battalion, and that of the Third regiment, to his sup-
"port. When the battalion of the Coldstream, which was
"upon the left, arrived, the enemy had nearly reached the
"road; they already commanded it to a great degree by
"their fire: the guns attached to the battalion were
"placed upon it, and, by a well-directed and well-sup-
"ported fire, kept the battery which was opposed to them
"in check, and did considerable execution.

"The battalion advanced into the wood, attacked and
"drove the enemy before them: in going forward they be-
"came unfortunately opposed to the fire of a battery, from
"which they suffered severely. They fell back to their
"position at the edge of the wood, which they maintained
"for the rest of the day, notwithstanding a heavy can-
"nonade. The enemy made no attempt to approach them.

"Nothing can exceed the spirit and bravery displayed
"by the men and officers of the battalion upon this oc-
"casion."

On the eleventh of May the following General Order
was issued :—

"Head-Quarters, Tournay.

"His Royal Highness the Duke of York returns his
"warmest thanks to the officers and privates who were en-
"gaged on the eighth instant, and particularly to those of
"the Coldstream Guards, who bore the brunt of the attack.

"The Hanoverians to relieve the brigade of Guards in
"all their posts to-morrow, in order to ease those troops
"who have undergone so much fatigue."[1]

---

[1] On the twelfth of May a feu-de-joie was fired in celebration of the victory.

Condé was now blockaded; and previous to the investment of Valenciennes, it was necessary to attack the fortified camp of Famars.

On the twenty-third of May the Duke of York led the first column, consisting of sixteen battalions of English, with some Hanoverian and Austrian troops. After a cannonade, the hussars crossed the Roxelle, without opposition, at the village of Mershe, and on the advance of a body of infantry, which would have turned the batteries, the enemy retreated to a redoubt they had constructed behind the village of Famars. General Clairfait also attacked the French stationed on the heights of Auzain, which were obstinately defended; but at length the Austrians gained the post. This success enabled the Prince of Cobourg to complete the investment of Valenciennes; the camp of Famars being occupied by the English and Hanoverians. The redoubt behind Famars was held till night, when the enemy abandoned it and retired across the Scheld.

The siege of Valenciennes was entrusted to the Duke of York, who carried it on with great vigour.[1]

---

[1] " About ten o'clock on the night of the 2d of June, a working party of the Guards, and the brigade of the line, consisting of about 300 men, and a strong covering party under the engineer, began the intrenchments. July the 3d, the Earl of Cavan was wounded in the head by a piece of shell. On the 9th a soldier of the Coldstream was killed by a shell in the trenches. 12th of July, one of the Coldstream was dangerously wounded by a shell. 18th, four men were wounded by a shell. On the 25th the first mine was sprung, then a second and third within the space of a few minutes; after the third mine was sprung, the troops, being in readiness, rushed with the greatest impetuosity and jumped over the palisadoes, carrying all before them at the point of the bayonet; the enemy, after a stout resistance, left the works in possession of the victors."—*Extracts from the Journal of Corporal Robert Brown of the Coldstream Guards,* p. 74.

1793.
July 25th.

After a practicable breach was effected, the Duke ordered the English and Austrians to make a general assault: the storming party consisted of one hundred and fifty men of the Guards,[1] and the same number from the line, under Major-General Abercrombie: they succeeded and carried the out-works. The loss in the battalion companies of the Coldstream during the siege was two rank and file killed; one captain (Earl of Cavan), one serjeant, thirteen rank and file, wounded; one rank and file died of his wounds. The flank battalion lost four rank and file killed; two serjeants, eighteen rank and file, wounded: three rank and file died afterwards. The town capitulated on the twenty-eighth, and was taken possession of by the Duke of York, in the name of the Emperor of Germany: this political error rallied into unanimity the hitherto hesitating inclinations of the French people. A detachment of the Guards occupied the gate of Cambray.

July 29th.

Condé had already surrendered, and the garrison were made prisoners of war, after a siege of three months, during which they had been much reduced by famine and disease.

On the twenty-ninth a reinforcement of about six hundred men under Lieutenant-Colonel Tad Watson of the Third Guards joined the brigade; amongst them were three light infantry companies, one for each of the regiments of Guards: the company belonging to the First regiment was commanded by Lieutenant-Colonel Ludlow, that of the Coldstream by Lieutenant-Colonel Eld, and that of the Third Guards by Lieutenant-Colonel Campbell; these companies joined the flank battalion, and completed it to eight companies.

---

[1] On the twenty-sixth of July the following General Order was issued:—" His Royal Highness the Commander-in-Chief returns " his thanks to Major-General Abercrombie, Colonel Leigh, and " Lieutenant-Colonel Doyle, for the gallantry they showed on the " attack last night.'

The flank companies of the Guards and light infantry, with the men who had composed the storming party on the twenty-fifth instant, lined the road from the Cambray gate to Briquet, when the garrison of Valenciennes marched out for the purpose of laying down their arms.

On the sixth of August the Coldstream proceeded towards Cambray, and encamped about two leagues to the westward of that fortress. Some days after the Austrians had taken possession of Valenciennes the French were obliged to quit their strong position behind the Scheld; and Cambray was summoned.[1]

At a council of war it was agreed, in opposition to the opinion of the Prince of Cobourg and of General Clairfait, that the army under the Duke of York should separate from the Austrians. The British, in consequence, broke up, and marched on the fourteenth of August on their route to Dunkirk, the siege of that fortress having been determined on for the purpose of replacing it under the dominion of England. The Guards passed Tournay on the fifteenth, Lannoy on the sixteenth, and halted next day, with the exception of the flank battalion, which encamped near a village called Ghelins. On the eighteenth his Royal Highness proceeded from Turcoin to Menin.

The French had driven the Dutch troops from Lincelles, which they had occupied by an order from the Prince of Orange. Major-General Lake was directed, with three battalions, consisting of the First, Coldstream, and Third Guards, to assist the Dutch troops in recapturing that

---

[1] It was reported in Paris that Cambray had been summoned to surrender on the 8th by General Boros, and that the Commandant returned the following answer: "I have received "your letter, General, and have no other answer to return than "that I know not how to surrender, but I know how to fight."— National Convention, Aug. 16. Declay.

1793.
Aug. 18th.

place; but the latter had retreated by a different road from that taken by the Guards in their advance.[1] Notwithstanding this circumstance, and the decided superiority on the part of the enemy, Lake made his preparations, and formed under a heavy fire, when he attacked a redoubt of unusual size and strength, situated on high ground in front of Lincelles. The woods were strongly defended by the enemy, and their flanks were covered by ditches. The column was led by the First Guards, which deployed with great celerity, the Coldstream forming on the left. The line then advanced amidst a shower of grape, and after two volleys made a furious charge, accompanied by loud huzzas,[2] stormed the works, and dispersed the

---

[1] General Lake had despatched an aid-de-camp to the headquarters of his Royal Highness the Commander-in-Chief at Menin, informing him of the flight of the Dutch, and the perilous situation of the Guards; the second brigade, as well as some battalions of Hessians, were consequently ordered to support them; but could not possibly arrive till the affair was terminated. The Dutch troops having been also ordered to re-occupy their former position, the Guards were permitted to march back to their camp, and the redoubts having been levelled with the ground, the post was early the next morning abandoned as untenable, being only two leagues and a half distant (above seven miles and a half) from Lisle. The Dutch were so thoroughly ashamed of their behaviour, and so crest-fallen, that they slunk about, avoiding as much as possible the British soldiers; and the Prince of Waldeck, who commanded the garrison of Menin, the next morning, in a very noble manner, caught the first officer of the Guards he met with by the hand, and after extolling the gallantry of the British soldiers (when surrounded by his own officers), exclaimed, "Your " glory is our shame."—*Campaign of* 1793, 1794, *and Retreat through Holland to Westphalia*, vol. I. page 90.

[2] " The French, who had been accustomed to the cold, lifeless " attacks of the Dutch, were amazed at the spirit and intrepidity " of the British, and not much relishing the manner of our

enemy, who vainly attempted to rally.¹ At ten o'clock p. m. the pursuit was discontinued, when the Fourteenth and Fifty-third regiments with some Hessian infantry relieved the Guards, who returned to their former ground near Menin, where they arrived, after undergoing great fatigue, about three o'clock in the morning.

1793.
Aug. 18th.

In this action the Coldstream lost Lieutenant-Colonel Bosville,² and eight rank and file killed. Lieutenant-Colonel Gascoyne, Ensign Bayly, two serjeants, and forty-five rank and file were wounded.³

The following order appeared on the nineteenth of August:—

" His Royal Highness the Commander-in-Chief returns
" his warmest thanks to Major-General Lake, Colonels
" Hulse, Greenfield, Pennington, Major Wright, and the
" officers and men belonging to the brigade of Guards and
" artillery under his command, for the gallantry and in-

" salute, immediately gave way, abandoning all that was in the
" place, and, in their flight, threw away both arms and accoutre-
" ments. We took one stand of colours, two pieces of cannon,
" with two pieces they had taken from the Dutch."—*Journal of Corporal Robert Brown of the Coldstream Guards.*

¹ The Adjutant-General, in his dispatch, says, " The battalions
" were instantly formed, and advanced, under a heavy fire, with
" an order and intrepidity, for which no praise can be too high.
" After firing three or four rounds they rushed on with their
" bayonets."

" The enemy amounted to about five thousand men, and lost
" eleven guns and about three hundred men."

² It is said that Lieutenant-Colonel Bosville's death was in consequence of his extraordinary height, being six feet four inches high: he was shot in the forehead.

³ Three hundred and forty-six rank and file of the Coldstream were engaged on the 18th of August, 1793.

1793.
Aug. 18th.
"trepidity they so evidently showed in the attack of the "French redoubts at the village of Lincelles yesterday "afternoon."

On the twentieth the Guards passed through Ypres, and encamped next day near Furnes; from whence the Duke of York proceeded on the twenty-second in pursuit of the enemy to Ghievelde: on his approach they abandoned their position, and his Royal Highness was enabled at once to take up the ground which he intended to occupy during the siege of Dunkirk. The Guards encamped to the left of the canal, the flank battalion on the right.

Aug. 24th.
A general attack was made on the out-posts between the canal of Furnes and the sea. The flank battalion forced their way through deep ditches full of water, and strong double hedges, driving the enemy into the town.

Among the killed was Lieutenant-Colonel Eld of the light company of the Coldstream, with eight rank and file: one lieutenant, twenty-five rank and file, were wounded.

The Hanoverians, meanwhile, under Marshal Freytag, with an army of observation of twelve thousand men, kept in awe the garrison of Bergnes and the camp at Mont-Cassel.

When the committee of public safety heard of the separation of the Duke of York's army from the Austrians, they lost no time in sending Generals Souham and Hoche with fresh troops to the assistance of Dunkirk.

O'Moran, a supposed spy, was seized by the orders of Hoche, and sent to Paris.[1]

---

[1] O'Moran was supposed to keep up a treasonable correspondence with the British, as will be seen by the following extract of a letter from General Hoche to the War Department:—

"Je suis arrivé ici avec le Général Souham, qui est un

On the evening of the sixth the enemy made a sortie from Dunkirk; their attack was principally directed against the right, but was gallantly sustained by the first brigade: the Fourteenth regiment suffered severely. 1793. September.

Houchard had arrived with strong reinforcements for the relief of Dunkirk: he attacked Freytag's position, by whom a partial retreat was effected. The following day the attack was renewed, and General Walmoden was obliged to give way, with the loss of three hundred men and three guns. In this action his Royal Highness Prince Adolphus, since Duke of Cambridge, and Marshal Freytag were wounded, and for a short time made prisoners.

The loss of the battle of Hendtschoote obliged the Duke of York, after some sharp out-post fighting, to abandon the siege, leaving from forty to fifty pieces of heavy cannon, baggage, and military stores behind.

The Coldstream marched through Aven Capelle, Dixmuyde, and Rousselaer, towards Menin, when the troops encamped. Sept. 12th, 14th, & 15th.

Houchard was arrested by order of the French republican government, and sent to Paris. The charges preferred against him were—First, that after defeating the English he did not drive them into the sea. Secondly, that he sent no succours to the troops butchered at Cambray. Thirdly, that he abandoned Menin, and in his retreat exposed his army to considerable danger. Hou-

---

" vrai sans-culotte. Enfin, à force de travail, nous commençons à
" nous reconnoître. Pitt avait ici des agens. Des papiers incen-
" diaires ont été répandus, des signaux donnés à la flotte ennemie,
" mouillée à trois quarts de lieue de la ville, et les matelots, frappés
" d'une terreur panique, et probablement travaillés par l'aristo-
" cratie, s'étaient insurgés."

chard was found guilty on these charges, and guillotined at Paris, November fifteenth, 1793.

There is no reason to suppose that Houchard was deficient in fidelity to his employers, or zeal for the cause in which he was embarked; this commander seems to have been the victim of low cruelty and ignorance. At that period the French armies were numerous, but badly organized, and without generals of experience. Houchard's troops had repeatedly been defeated; and when the loss of the battle of Hendtschoote induced the British to relinquish the siege of Dunkirk, it did not by any means follow that they were unable to make good their retreat. Napoleon, it is true, delighting to play the Jupiter-Scapin in public, instructed his Marshals to drive the English into the sea; and often told his soldiers, that no such word as *impossible* existed in the French language: but that accurate judge of military affairs never put his generals to death for not accomplishing what he knew to be impracticable. The uninstructed and atrocious Jacobins in France, who had possessed themselves of the powers of government when Houchard was sent to the relief of Dunkirk, little qualified to distinguish between a retiring and a ruined army, conceived that because the Duke of York abandoned the siege, nothing remained for the French general but to destroy him. Whether the second and third charges against Houchard were better founded cannot now be ascertained with certainty; at the utmost, they rather afford evidence of incapacity than of treachery and cowardice. Allowing them to be established, it must be admitted that the French commander was unfit for his situation, and that the interests of the cause he had undertaken to uphold required his dismissal: few persons however are forward in discovering their own deficiencies; and to a dispassionate mind the question naturally pre-

sents itself, how far those who employ a general of doubt- 1793.
ful efficiency are less culpable than the individual they
send forth at a venture to risk the lives of thousands in
his probation. If the emigration had left the Jacobins no
tried commanders at their disposal, the fact may perhaps
be pleaded to excuse their making the hazardous selection,
but will hardly justify the condemnation of Houchard to
the guillotine for not being a man of intuitive genius.

On the seventeenth of September the following order
was issued:—
"The Commander-in-Chief thanks the troops for the
"spirit with which they have gone through their late
"fatigues and distresses occasioned by long and rapid
"marches."

Quesnoy was taken by the Austrians, and the enemy
defeated at Villiers en Couche. The Prince of Cobourg
crossed the Sambre, and drove the French into their
intrenchments at Maubeuge; while Marshal Clairfait
threatened Cambray and Bouchain.

The Brigade of Guards marched through Menin and Oct. 10th.
Courtray to Peck, a village near Tournay, where they
halted two days; they then proceeded to St. Amand, and
encamped between Quesnoy and Landrecy. The troops
returned on the twenty-third by the same roads they had
before passed.

About the end of October the Third Guards with a de- Oct. 28th.
tachment of the Fifteenth Light Dragoons attacked the
enemy at Lannoy, and after two hours' fighting, succeeded
in driving them from the village. From the twenty-ninth
of this month to the eighth of November, the Coldstream
was encamped on the plains of Gascogne; on the following day the campaign ended, and the Guards marched
into barracks at Tournay. In December the brigade of Dec. 14th.

1793. Guards moved to Ghent, where the Coldstream[1] occupied St. Peter's barracks.

On the thirteenth his Royal Highness thanked the army for their conduct during the campaign.

1794. Feb. 6th. The Duke of York quitted the army for London; Sir William Erskine was left in command during his absence.

---

[1] Return of Officers of the First battalion of the Coldstream on the Continent.

Comps.	Captains.	Lieutenants.	Ensigns.
Grenadier	Lieut.-Col. Wm. Morshead	Capt. Harry Calvert (Aid-de-camp to the Duke of York) ,, Richard Gregory ,, Charles Hotham, vice Calvert, appointed A.D.C.	
Colonel's Company.	H.R.H. the Duke of York's company	Capt. Lieut. Earl of Cavan	Richard Hulse Sir J. Shelly, vice Hulse promoted
2d Major's Company	Col. Lowther Pennington	Capt. Wm. De Visme ,, John Calcraft, vice De Visme ,, J. Forbes, vice Calcraft	Wm. Lemon K. A. Howard Henry Bayly, vice Howard
	Lieut.-Col. George Fitz Roy	,, Charles Hotham ,, Roger Morris, vice Hotham	K. A. Howard Wm. Lemon, vice Howard
	Lieut.-Col. Tho. B. Bosville	,, John Calcraft ,, Hon. George Pomeroy, vice Calcraft	Hon. W. Fitz Roy
	Lieut.-Col. George Nugent	,, Wm. Wynyard	George H. Dyke
	Lieut-Col. T. E. Freemantle	,, Lord Say and Sele (to the Light Inf. Company)	Samuel Ongley
	Lieut.-Col. Hon. Edward Finch	,, Wm. Buller	Wm. Templetown Thomas Stibbert, vice Templetown
	Lieut.-Col. Isaac Gascoyne	,, Hon. George Pomeroy ,, Wm. De Visme, vice Pomeroy	Richard Hulse Joseph Fuller, vice Hulse
Light Inf. company *	Lieut.-Col. George Eld	,, Lord Say and Sele ,, Charles Hotham	

Adjutant, Captain William Wynyard.
Quarter-Master, Samuel Lunt.
Surgeon's Mate, T. B. Hugo.
,, Edw. Alexis Giraud.

Camp at Menin, September 29th, 1793.

* The light infantry company, ordered to be raised by a King's warrant, dated April 19th, 1793, and added to the establishment from 5th of June, embarked July 9th, 1793.

CHAPTER III.

Reinforcements for the brigade of Guards sent from England—Command of the army given to the Emperor—He reviews the different contingents above Cateau—Allies advance—Success of the two columns under the Duke of York—Siege of Landrecy—Duke of York drives the enemy from Cæsar's camp—French defeated near Cateau—Duke of York repulses the enemy near Tournay—Duke of York obliges the enemy to evacuate Lannoy—Guards, supported by the Seventh and Fifteenth Light Dragoons, drive the French from their intrenchments—Abercrombie obliged to retreat from the heights of Roubaix, round Lannoy, to Templeuve—Fox retreats, and joins Otto—Numerical superiority of the enemy—Pichegru commences operations with an army of two hundred thousand men — Pitt declared by French Jacobins an enemy to the human race—Decree forbidding quarter — Duke of York's order in consequence — Allies repulsed near Fleurus—Duke of York retreats to Romaux—Reinforcements land at Ostend — Light companies of the Guards at home embark—Moira joins the Duke of York—Tournay, Ghent, and Ostend, fall into the hands of the French—Duke of York crosses the Maese — Enemy repulsed — Crosses the Maese—Takes Bommel—Pichegru attacks the Allies between Nimeguen and Arnheim—Duke of York returns to England—Walmoden succeeds in command—Allies abandon Heusden—Spirited stand made by the Guards at Rhenen—British retreat to Voorthuizen—Troops suffer great hardships in the retreat to Deventer—Retreat continues to Bremen—Coldstream embark at Bremenlee—Land at Greenwich, and march to London.

1794. March.

On the first of March reinforcements embarked from England, amounting to eight hundred men for the brigade, of which two hundred were for the Coldstream.

A council of war assembled at Ath. It was proposed that Marshal Clairfait should take the command of all the auxiliary forces, and that the Duke of York should act under his orders.[1] After a month's delay, it was decided that the command should be given to the Emperor, April 9th. who arrived at Brussels.

A general movement was made throughout the army; the brigade of Guards marched by St. Leger to Vendegies

---

[1] The following statement was published by the Convention early in 1794.*

REPUBLICAN ARMIES.		ARMIES OF THE COALESCED POWERS.	
Army of the North	222,000	Army of the Prince of Coburg	140,000
United Armies of the Rhine and the Moselle	280,000	Army of the Duke of York	40,000
Army of the Alps	60,000	Army appertaining to Holland	20,000
Army of the Oriental Pyrenees	*80,000	Austrian Army on the Rhine	60,000
Army of the South	60,000	Prussian Army	64,000
Army of the West	80,000	Army of the Empire	20,000
		Army of Condé	12,000
Total	780,000	Total	356,000

* May be considered as exaggerated.

sur l'Ecaillon. The Emperor proceeded to Valenciennes, where, on the heights above Cateau, he reviewed the whole army, amounting to one hundred and eighty-seven thousand men, consisting of Austrians, British, Dutch, Hanoverians, and Hessians. At the conclusion of the review, the Guards pitched their tents for the first time this year.[1] *1794. April 16th.*

On the following day, as the enemy were in force about Cambray, the army advanced in eight columns. The fourth and fifth were under the Duke of York. One of the columns under the immediate command of his Royal Highness was intended to carry the village of Vaux. Major-General Abercrombie commenced the attack, sup- ported by the grenadier companies of the First Guards under Colonel Stanhope, who stormed and gallantly took a battery. At the same moment three battalions of Austrian grenadiers occupied the wood, and made themselves masters of the works which had been constructed. Nine cannon were taken during the day by the column under the Duke of York. Sir William Erskine was also successful with the troops under his orders, and gained possession of the redoubts and two pieces of cannon. The Coldstream lost four men killed, and one wounded. The village of Vaux having been plundered, was set on fire: the Duke of York was obliged to move to the battery that had been taken. *April 17th.*

The Coldstream and Third Guards marched through the *April 18th.*

---

[1] "April 14.—The troops were furnished with straps for the "purpose of carrying our great-coats slung across the shoulders "neatly rolled up. This in all sorts of weather was part of our "equipment." — *Journal of Corporal Robert Brown of the Coldstream Guards*, page 108.

1794.
April 19th.

wood of Leisse, but afterwards returned to Vaux. When relieved by General Abercrombie's corps, they continued their route through Cateau, and were posted on the Cambray road.

It being determined to lay siege to Landrecy, the direction of it was given to the Prince of Orange, whilst the Emperor with his army protected the operations on the side of Guise, and the troops under the Duke of York covered Cambray. General Worms was stationed near Douay and Bouchain. Count Kaunitz defended the Sambre, and Clairfait held Flanders from Tournay to the sea.

On the twenty-third the Duke of York drove the enemy from Cæsar's camp near Cambray. Some days after this the heights of Cateau,[2] which the British occupied, were attacked; but the enemy were repulsed with the loss of thirty-five pieces of cannon, and three hundred officers and men taken prisoners.[3]

---

[1] The following order was issued by his Royal Highness the Duke of York, April 19th, 1794:

"An officer and forty men of the Guards to be immediately sent to Basuyaux, to enforce the order for preventing pillaging and burning houses, and the officer to inform General Otto of his arrival."

[2] April 26th.—The enemy was repulsed in an attempt to raise the siege of Landrecy, and pursued by the cavalry to the gates of Cambray. On this occasion the Blues, 1st, 3rd, 5th Dragoon Guards, the Royals, 7th, 11th, and 16th Dragoons greatly distinguished themselves.

[3] Extract from the General Order dated 12th of May, 1794.

"All pieces of ordnance, colours, tumbrels, and horses taken from the enemy are to be delivered to the British artillery, and receipts taken for the same; application from the officer commanding the regiment who took them are, within three days, to be sent to Mr Commissary Williamson, who, by order of his

THE COLDSTREAM GUARDS.

A large body of the enemy who attacked the Duke of York near Tournay was defeated. On this occasion General Harcourt, Major-General Dundas and Sir Robert Laurie distinguished themselves. _{1794. May 3rd.}

The Emperor at length determined on making a general and simultaneous effort to drive the French out of the Low Countries. For this purpose five columns of troops were ordered to advance; two of them were unable from fatigue to arrive in time;[1] the others on reaching Moucron found the enemy too strong to be attacked, and retreated to Turcoin. The column led by the Duke of York,[2] composed of seven English, five Austrian, and two Hessian battalions, with ten squadrons of cavalry, forced the enemy to evacuate Lannoy; the troops then halted. They afterwards proceeded to Roubaix. General Abercrombie pushed on with the four battalions of Guards, and found the enemy strongly intrenched; they were cannonaded for some time. The flank battalion of Guards then advanced with the greatest regularity to storm, supported by the Seventh and Fifteenth Light Dragoons, who gallantly _{May 16th.}

" Royal Highness the Commander-in-Chief, will pay the following " rewards, viz.—

	£.
" For each cannon or howitzer	20
" For each pair of colours	10
" For each tumbrel	10
" For each horse	12

[1] Here we find the solution of Buonaparte's Italian victories; his columns always arrived at the time indicated. Activity and combination could not fail to defeat superior forces under Generals who seem to have planned simultaneous movements without knowing their ground, their distances, or what their troops could accomplish.

[2] His Royal Highness accompanied the centre column, consisting of the brigade of Guards, first brigade of the line, and the free corps of O'Donnell.

1794.
May.

drove the French before them and took three guns. On the morning of the seventeenth the enemy attacked Turcoin; the same day a column from Lisle, and another corps, forced their way through General Otto's position at Waterloo, and assailed the rear of the British. When the advance parties from Lisle showed themselves between Roubaix and Mouveaux, it was impossible for the Duke of York to join the brigade of Guards. Abercrombie was directed to retreat by Roubaix, at which place the troops were to assemble, and the Coldstream had been posted to cover the communication. On reaching the heights of Roubaix, his Royal Highness was beset on all sides for three miles by repeated attacks of the enemy's artillery and cavalry; he therefore continued his retreat to Lannoy. Finding that place in possession of the French, he went round the town under a heavy fire, and made his way

May 17th.

through the fields to Templeuve. Major-General Fox was attacked by the Lisle column, and also retreated; but as his communication with the brigade of Guards and Lannoy was cut off, he joined General Otto. In this action Lieutenant-Colonel Gascoyne was wounded. The Coldstream lost one drummer, and fifteen rank and file killed, wounded, and missing.

During the conflict at Turcoin,[1] the brigade of Guards and the heavy cavalry remained as a reserve in the camp at Templeuve, and continued under arms all night.

The position occupied by the British extended from the Scheld to the Orchies Road, and was secured by redoubts covering the front and flanks.

The Prince of Orange drove the enemy from Charleroi, before which town they had broken ground.

---

[1] The French have given a very exaggerated account of the action of Turcoin, and estimate the loss of the British at two thousand prisoners and sixty pieces of cannon.

Such was the numerical superiority of the French, arising from their compulsatory system, that when one corps of troops was beaten, its place was immediately occupied by another.

At day-break on the twenty-second of May, Pichegru with two hundred thousand men commenced a series of attacks on the position of the Allies: his troops advanced under a heavy fire of artillery; and after many unsuccessful efforts, having made no impression on the line, he was obliged, late in the evening, to retire. Major-General Fox and the second brigade made themselves conspicuous by the spirited manner in which they stormed and carried the village of Pontechin.

The sentiments of hostility entertained by the ruling party in the enemy's Government against this country were so ferocious, as almost to exceed belief in the present day. The French Jacobins declared Mr. Pitt, the British Prime Minister, an enemy to the human race. They issued an order to their armies that no quarter should be given to the English or Hanoverians; an injunction scarcely to be paralleled in the darkest and most barbarous days of ancient warfare. This order was received with merited contempt by the brave men who composed the French armies; it was sent to the Republican troops with the following address:—

"England is capable of every outrage on humanity, "and every crime towards the Republic. She attacks the "rights of nations, and threatens to annihilate liberty. "How long will you suffer the slaves of George to con- "tinue on your frontiers, the soldiers of the most atro- "cious of tyrants? He formed the Congress of Pilnitz, "and brought about the disgraceful surrender of Toulon. "He massacred our cities, and endeavoured to destroy "the national representation. He starved your plains.

1794.
May.

"and purchased treasons on the frontiers. When the events of battle should place in your power either English or Hanoverians, bring to remembrance the vast tracts of country English slaves have laid waste. Carry your views to La Vendée, Toulon, Lyons, Landrecy, Martinico, and St. Domingo; places still reeking with blood, which the atrocious policy of the English has shed. Do not trust to their artful language, which is an additional crime, worthy of their perfidious character and Machiavelian government. Those who boast that they abhor the tyranny of George, say, can they fight him? No! no! Republican soldiers: you ought, therefore, when victory shall put in your power either Englishmen or Hanoverians, to strike; not one of them ought to return to the traitorous territory of England, or to be brought into France. Let the British slaves perish, and Europe be free!"

The Duke of York immediately noticed the sanguinary decree in terms worthy of his character and his country.

"General Orders, June 7th.

June 7th.

"His Royal Highness the Duke of York thinks it incumbent on him to announce to the British and Hanoverian troops under his command, that the National Convention of France, pursuing that gradation of crimes and horrors, which has distinguished the periods of its government as the most calamitous of any that has yet occurred in the history of the world, has just passed a decree that their soldiers shall give no quarter to the British or Hanoverian troops. His Royal Highness anticipates the indignation and horror which has naturally arisen in the minds of the brave troops whom he addresses, upon receiving this information. His Royal Highness desires, however, to remind them, that mercy

"to the vanquished is the brightest gem in a soldier's
"character; and exhorts them not to suffer their resent-
"ment to lead them to any precipitate act of cruelty on
"their part, which may sully the reputation they have
"acquired in the world. His Royal Highness believes
"that it would be difficult for brave men to conceive that
"any set of men, who are themselves exempt from sha-
"ring in the dangers of war, should be so base and
"cowardly as to seek to aggravate the calamities of
"it upon the unfortunate people who are subject to their
"orders.

1794.
June 7th.

"It was indeed reserved for the present times to pro-
"duce to the world the proof of the possibility of the
"existence of such atrocity and infamy. The pretence
"for issuing this decree, even if founded in truth, would
"justify it only to minds similar to those of the members
"of the National Convention. It is, in fact, too absurd
"to be noticed, and still less to be refuted. The French
"must themselves see through the flimsy artifice of an
"intended assassination, by which Robespierre has suc-
"ceeded in procuring that military guard, which has at
"once established him the successor of the unfortunate
"Louis, by whatever name he may choose to dignify his
"future reign. In all the wars which from the earliest
"times have existed between the English and the French
"nations, they have been accustomed to consider each
"other in the light of generous as well as brave enemies,
"while the Hanoverians, for a century the allies of the
"former, have shared in this reciprocal esteem. Huma-
"nity and kindness have at all times taken place the
"instant that opposition ceased; and the same cloak has
"been frequently seen covering those who were wounded,
"and enemies, whilst indiscriminately conveying to the
"hospitals of the conquerors.

1794.
June 7th.

"The British and Hanoverian armies will not believe that the French nation, even under their present infatuation, can so far forget their characters as soldiers, as to pay any attention to a decree, as injurious to themselves as it is disgraceful to the persons who passed it: on this confidence his Royal Highness trusts that the soldiers of both nations will confine their sentiments of resentment and abhorrence to the National Convention alone; persuaded that they will be joined in them by every Frenchman who possesses one spark of honour, or one principle of a soldier: and his Royal Highness is confident that it will only be on finding, contrary to every expectation, that the French army has relinquished every title to the fair character of soldiers and of men, by submitting to, and obeying so atrocious an order, that the brave troops under his command will think themselves justified, and indeed under the necessity of adopting a species of warfare, for which they will stand acquitted to their own conscience, to their country, and the world: in such an event the French army alone will be answerable for the tenfold vengeance which will fall upon themselves, their wives and their children, and their unfortunate country, already groaning under every calamity which the accumulated crimes of unprincipled ambition and avarice can heap upon their devoted victims.

"His Royal Highness desires these orders may be read and explained to the men at their successive roll-callings."

To the credit of the French troops, neither officers nor soldiers carried the brutal commands of the Convention into execution; many of the superior officers positively refused to enforce the decree, and it was generally disregarded by their army.

THE COLDSTREAM GUARDS. 59

The Princes of Cobourg and Orange, with General Beaulieu, attacked General Jourdan, who was strongly posted near Fleurus. This action continued till nearly the close of the day, when the Allied army was repulsed at all points. They took advantage of the night and retreated on Marbois and Nivelle, in the hope of reaching Namur. 1794.
June 7th.

The Duke of York, finding it impossible to form a junction with Clairfait, retreated through Tournay to Romaux, where the troops under his command encamped till the third of July, when reinforcements arrived from England and landed at Ostend. June 26th.

July.

The four light infantry companies of the battalions of Guards at home embarked for the Continent on the fifth of July. The light infantry of the second battalion of the Coldstream consisted of Captain and Lieutenant-Colonel John Calcraft, Lieutenants and Captains John S. Stewart, and George Hart Dyke, five serjeants, five corporals, two buglers, and one hundred and fifty-four privates.[1]

As the French occupied the country about Ostend, it was necessary for Lord Moira, who led the reinforcements, to make his way through all opposition and endeavour to join the Duke of York: this, by a rapid movement, he effected at Malines. July 9th.

Tournay, Ghent, and Ostend, all fell nearly at the same time into the hands of the French.

The light companies of the Guards, with a detachment for the Coldstream, arrived on the seventeenth: the light companies joined the flank battalion, now increased to twelve companies.

The troops marched through West Wesel towards Ro- July 23rd.

---

[1] The establishment at this time was only ninety-five privates: the fifty-nine supernumeraries might have been to recruit the battalion.

60   ORIGIN AND SERVICES OF

1794. Aug. 24th. sendale; passed Breda, and encamped near Osterhout, at which place head-quarters were established. On the
September. first of September they moved to Berlicom. On the fourteenth the out-posts were attacked along the Dourmel, and the troops of Hesse Darmstadt were forced with considerable loss.

Sept. 16th. The Duke of York at length thought it prudent to cross the Maese, and encamped at Wichen.

The enemy were repulsed in their attempts to advance on the twenty-first and twenty-second of September.

October. Early in October the Duke of York concentrated his army about Nimeguen. On the twentieth a general at-
Oct. 24th. tack was made on all the out-posts. A few days after the enemy advanced towards Nimeguen. A change of position took place during the night of the thirtieth, when the
Oct. 31st. Coldstream moved through Yoondon by Eelst, and arrived on the sixth of November at Sandyke.

The winter[1] was unusually severe; before Christmas the Maese and Waal were frozen. The enemy crossed the Maese, and another corps marched over the ice and took possession of the island of Bommel.

1795. January. In January Pichegru passed the Waal at several points, and made a general attack on the Allies, whose line extended between Nimeguen and Arnheim.

---

[1] A committee was formed at the Crown and Anchor in the Strand for supplying the army in Flanders with extra clothing: during the year the Coldstream was furnished with eight hundred and seven flannel waistcoats, and one hundred and fifty-nine pairs of shoes. A letter from his Royal Highness the Duke of York to William Devaynes, Esq. the Chairman, says, "his Royal Highness "is fully sensible how much is due to the activity and spirit that "have actuated the committee at which you preside, in forward- "ing what will tend so materially to preserve the health of the "British soldiers in their present situation; and their grateful "acknowledgements cannot be wanting to their country for the "liberal provision it has made them."

The Duke of York had previously returned[1] to England, in consequence of which the command devolved on General Walmoden, who had to contend with a victorious army greatly superior in numbers.

The brigade of Guards passed the Leck a second time on the tenth, and moved next day to the right of Rhenen.

The Allies were attacked and forced, and the Austrians abandoned Huessen, while the Hanoverians retired across the Lingen. At Rhenen the French were kept in check for a considerable time, and subsequently repulsed by the brilliant and spirited stand made by the brigade of Guards in conjunction with the infantry of the Prince of Salm. During the night the English retreated to Voorthuizen, taking with them their sick and wounded, with the exception of three hundred, who were left behind and treated by the French with great humanity.

The sufferings of the army during this retreat, in the severest part of one of the coldest winters known for some years in Holland, were of the most serious nature; the state of the sick and wounded was dreadful; many were frozen in the waggons and perished. The sixteenth of January was a day peculiarly memorable for the hardship and distress endured by the troops on their retreat to Deventer. The men had marched at the usual hour, and about three in the afternoon reached Welaw, where it was intended to halt for the night, but circumstances were such as to make it necessary to prolong the march fifteen miles further. The troops, besides suffering from the severity of the weather and from fatigue, had obtained no rations during the day. The march was continued for about four miles over a sandy desert. The wind being excessively high, carried with it drifted snow and sand

---

[1] Left the army on the sixth of December.

1795.
January.

with such violence that the human frame could hardly resist its power; the cold was intense; the water collected in the eyes of the men congealed as it fell, and hung in icicles from their eye-lashes; the breath froze and lodged in incrustations of ice about the face, and on the blankets and coats wrapped round the soldiers. Numbers of men and women after dark lost sight of the column, and slept to wake no more. The troops reached Brickborge between ten and eleven at night, where the houses were already filled with Hessian soldiers, who opposed their admission in almost every instance; and it was only obtained at last by force or stealth.[1]

Notwithstanding one of the most fatiguing and distressing marches ever experienced, the retreating army succeeded in conveying to Deventer all their ammunition, artillery, and military stores of every description. Fifty thousand French were eager in pursuit; and the English

Jan. 27th. quitted Deventer only two days before it was entered by the enemy. Almost all the marches during this distressing retreat were made through roads covered with ice or snow,

Feb. 10th. mud or water. The British crossed the Vecht and the river Ems. On the twenty-fourth of February they were overtaken by a portion of the French troops; but they displayed such courage and firmness that the efforts of the enemy to interrupt them were unavailing. The army therefore continued to retreat till it reached Bremen on the twenty-eighth of March, where it was joined by the two

---

[1] On the nineteenth of January the Prince of Orange embarked in an open boat at Scheveling: an immense crowd assembled at the Hague on the morning of his departure, and insisted on his being brought to trial for the part he had taken in favour of the English. His Guards however protected him from all violence, and conducted him to the water-side, when he was again in danger till they dispersed the populace.

flank battalions. At this place head-quarters and the brigade of Guards were stationed.

1795.

In taking a retrospective view of the campaign, the British troops will not be found deficient in their accustomed steadiness in the field, and habits of subordination and military discipline. From their manner of living, and the abundant supplies furnished by the commissariat department, they are seldom exposed to great privations. But when the want of food or clothing is experienced, as it was in this campaign, or when the men, without sufficient shelter, are subject to hardships from the inclemency of the seasons, those evils are usually borne by them in a manner that evinces the superiority of the British soldier. The troops behaved, throughout the campaigns of 1793 and 1794,[1] with a spirit that did them infinite credit, and especially during this arduous retreat.

The Coldstream left Bremen on the eleventh of April, arrived at Willsdorf on the thirteenth, and embarked at Bremenlee next day on board the Bellona and Loyal Briton transports. After a tedious voyage, the first battalion was landed at Greenwich, and marched to their quarters in London. The men had eight days' leave granted them to see their friends.

May 9th.

---

[1] " Soon after the commencement of the war with France it was
" resolved to detach a body of troops for the protection of Holland.
" Eighteen hundred Guards were accordingly embarked for that
" service in presence of the King and Royal Family at Greenwich.
" They soon reached the place of destination, and their arrival,
" small as their numbers were, fortunately turned the tide of suc-
" cess against the French.

" In the course of two campaigns they distinguished themselves
" in Flanders on various occasions, particularly at Lincelles,
" where all the three battalions behaved to admiration."—*Grose's Military Antiquities*, vol. II. page 208.

CHAPTER IV.

Light companies of the First, Coldstream, and Third Guards embark for Ostend—First battalions of the three regiments of Guards embark for Ireland—Expedition to Holland—Two brigades of Guards embark—Troops land near the Helder Point—Dutch driven back — Their fleet surrenders — French and Batavians repulsed—Duke of York takes command of the army—Battle of Bergen—Four thousand Russians land at the Helder—Battle of Alkmaar — Capitulation of the town — British and Russians re-embark—First battalion lands at Yarmouth.

1798.
May.

AN expedition to Ostend, under General Coote, composed of about twelve hundred men, and the eight light companies of the First,[1] Coldstream, and Third Guards, was fitted out for the purpose of destroying the basin, gates, and sluices of the Bruges canal, and intercepting the navigation between Ostend and Holland.

The command of the light infantry battalion devolved on Colonel Calcraft of the Coldstream, captain of the light company of the second battalion, Colonel the Honourable Edward Finch, who commanded the light company of the first battalion, having been accidentally wounded at a field-day on Barham Downs previous to the embarkation.

The transports sailed from Margate on the fourteenth of May, and as early as five o'clock on the morning of the nineteenth the troops, with artillery, miners, and every requisite, were on shore. About ten o'clock the sluice-gates and works were imperfectly blown up,[2] and the men

---

[1] The four light companies of the First Guards did not disembark, having separated at sea.

[2] " His Majesty's Guards were conspicuous on all occasions on " this service, and have added to their former laurels."

ordered to re-embark; but the surf and wind had so much increased, that to leave the shore became impracticable. General Coote, under these circumstances, thought fit to summon Ostend[1] to surrender, and received for answer "That the garrison must be first buried under the ruins." Coote then attempted to intrench himself on some sandhills near the coast. Early on the morning of the twentieth he was attacked by several columns of the enemy; and after some ineffectual endeavours to contend against superior numbers, the troops surrendered as prisoners of war, when they were marched from Ostend through Lille into the citadel. The officers belonging to the two companies of the Coldstream taken were Lieutenant-Colonel John Calcraft, Captains Thomas Armstrong and Willoughby Beane, and Assistant-Surgeon Fullelove.[2] Several of the officers obtained leave to return to England the sooner to effect their exchange.[3]

1798.

This expedition may be added to the list of injudicious attempts made at various times by England on the Continent, without any object of importance, or national advantage, to be attained. Whatever damage was done to the sluices or canals between Bruges and Ostend could not be of material benefit to Great Britain, or of any great public injury to France. This petty, vexatious, and buccaneering

---

[1] General Coote, in his dispatches, says "a feint."

[2] Loss of the Coldstream on the 20th of May: 4 rank and file killed, 2 drummers missing. Surrendered prisoners in the four companies of the Coldstream and Third, 2 Captains and Lieutenant-Colonels, 5 Lieutenants and Captains, 1 Quarter-Master, 1 Assistant-Surgeon, 16 serjeants, 9 drummers, and 260 rank and file. Lieutenant-Colonel Campbell of the Third Guards not included, having died of his wounds.

[3] After being detained prisoners nine months the two companies were exchanged, and on their return landed at Dover, whence they marched to their quarters in London.

1798.

system of warfare has been much practised by the English, though it could only tend to keep up the flame of discord between hostile countries by adding the irritation of private injury to national conflict. It is to be hoped that civilization is too far advanced, and the mutual interest of nations too well understood, to permit the recurrence of such acts of folly, inhumanity, and wasteful expenditure.

June 12th. The first battalions of the three regiments of Guards embarked at Portsmouth, and sailed for Ireland, where disturbances had broken out; the Coldstream were on board the Queen Charlotte and Repulse. Two battalions from the First and Third regiments of Guards were quartered at Waterford; the first battalion of the Coldstream, under Lieutenant-Colonel Gascoyne, at Ross. The brigade was under the command of Major-General Stanwix.[1]

[1] Strength of the three battalions of Guards, August 1st, 1798.

Officers.	Officers absent.	Non-Com. Officers.	Rank & File.	Sick.	Total.	Wanting to complete.	Total establishment.
62	25	135	1747	130	2099	523	2622

OFFICERS OF THE COLDSTREAM GUARDS IN IRELAND FROM JUNE, 1798.

Major-Gen. Slaughter Stanwix.
Colonel Andrew Cowell.
  ,,   Hon. Edward Finch.
  ,,   Isaac Gascoyne.
Lt.-Col. C. Howard Bulkely.
  ,,   Arthur Brice.
  ,,   Edm. Lord Dungarvon.
Lt. & Capt. K. A. Howard.
  ,,   ,,   H. Bayly.
  ,,   ,,   Hilton Jolliffe.
  ,,   ,,   Hon. C.G. M'Lellan.
  ,,   ,,   Tho. Stibbert.
  ,,   ,,   Jas. Phillips.
  ,,   ,,   Rich. Boulton.
  ,,   ,,   J. Allen Lloyd.
  ,,   ,,   R. D. Jackson.

Ensign Montagu Wynyard.
  ,,   George Morgan.
  ,,   Gilbert Stirling.
  ,,   Charles Phillips.
  ,,   Charles Vis^t. Petersham.
  ,,   Lord Charles Bentinck.
  ,,   George Sidley.
  ,,   John Thompson.
  ,,   Hon. A. Duncan.
  ,,   Matthew Onslow.
  ,,   John Frederick.
Quarter-Master John Holmes.
Surgeon George Rose.
Assistant do. John Simpson.
  ,,   ,,   John Gilham.

At this time the grenadier battalion, composed of eight companies, four from the First, two from the Coldstream, and the same number from the Third Guards, with the third battalion of the First Guards, formed the first brigade of Guards under Major-General D'Oyley. The first battalion of the Coldstream and that of the Third Guards under Major-General Burrard formed the second brigade.

In July, by the military arrangements entered into between the Confederate Courts and Great Britain, it was agreed that a diversion should be attempted by sending an expedition to invade Holland, in conjunction with twenty thousand auxiliaries to be furnished by Russia. Early in August twelve thousand men assembled on the coast of Kent, and an equal number were preparing to meet at the same point.

The brigade of Guards under Major-General Burrard left the camp at Barham Downs for Sandwich. They embarked at Ramsgate on the twelfth, and sailed with the first division under Sir Ralph Abercrombie. Contrary winds prevented the English fleet, commanded by Lord Duncan, from reaching the Texel till the twenty-seventh. The disembarkation, which was covered by Vice-Admiral Mitchell, took place near the Helder Point. The troops had scarcely begun to move forward when the right was briskly attacked by a considerable Dutch force under General Daendels: the attack was repeated with fresh troops, but the enemy were repulsed after a severe contest, and retired to a position two leagues further in the rear. Towards the close of the day Major-General D'Oyley's brigade of Guards was brought into action, and suffered some loss. The Coldstream lost seven rank and file wounded, one missing. The casualties among the men of the two grenadier companies are necessarily omitted during the campaign, as they were not separately stated

1799.
August.

from that of the battalion of grenadiers. Late at night the garrison of a fort at the Helder Point, consisting of nearly two thousand national troops, withdrew. Next morning the works were occupied by the British.

The passage of the Texel being opened, the Dutch fleet lying near the Vlieter surrendered to Admiral Mitchell. In the mean time, till the expected reinforcements should arrive from England, Sir Ralph Abercrombie intrenched

Sept. 1st. his troops in the peninsula of the Helder. The British were in position along the Groot Sluys of the Zype, with Oude Sluys on Zuider Zee on the left, and Petten on the North Sea on their right. Abercrombie, apprised of the enemy's intention, took the necessary precautions.

Sept. 10th. At day-break the French and Batavians attacked the intrenchments in three columns, on the right and centre. One of the enemy's columns, composed of Dutch, commanded by General Daendels, moved on the village of St. Martin; a second under General de Monceau, also composed of Dutch, moved on Crabbendam and Zyper Sluys; the French left assailed that part of the position occupied by the brigade of Guards under Major-General Burrard. They were received with determined courage, and every where driven back. About ten o'clock the enemy retreated towards Alkmaar, leaving many killed and wounded, one gun and a number of waggons and pontoons.

Sir Ralph Abercrombie in his dispatch says, " It is im-
" possible for me to do full justice to the conduct of the
" troops. The two brigades of Guards repulsed with
" with great vigour the column of French which had
" advanced to attack them, and where the slaughter of the
" enemy was great."[1]

---

[1] Sir Ralph Abercrombie's dispatch—London Gazette Extraordinary, Sept. 16, 1799. No. 15182.

This affair cost the enemy one thousand killed and wounded, and the Allies about two hundred. 1799.

The loss of the Coldstream was one rank and file killed, eight wounded. After the action the army re-occupied its position.

The Duke of York landed in Holland, and took the command of the army. Soon after the Russian contingent and all the forces destined for the expedition arrived, when it was determined to commence offensive operations. Sept. 13th.

Two hours before day-break on the nineteenth all were in readiness to attack the lines of General Brune in front of Alkmaar. The right column consisted of twelve Russian battalions, the Seventh Light Dragoons, and General Manners's brigade under the Russian General d'Herman, extending to the sand-hills on the coast near Camperdown, where part of the enemy had posted themselves most advantageously. The next column was commanded by Lieutenant-General Dundas, and consisted of two squadrons of the Eleventh Light Dragoons, the two brigades of Guards, and Prince William of Gloucester's brigade. Two squadrons of the Eleventh Light Dragoons and the brigades of Major-Generals Don and Coote formed the third column, under Sir James Pulteney. The left column, under Lieutenant-General Sir Ralph Abercrombie, was composed of two squadrons of the Eighteenth Dragoons, and the brigades of the Earl of Chatham, Major-General Moore, and the Earl of Cavan; besides four battalions, one of grenadiers, and one of light infantry of the line, and the Twenty-third and Fifty-fifth regiments under Colonel Mac Donald. The intention was to outflank both wings of the enemy. Sir Ralph Abercrombie was detached to Hoorn in rear of the Dutch, who formed the enemy's right. The first brigade of Guards moved from Tatenhoorn and Krabendaw, on the left of the Alkmaar canal, to co-operate with the corps under Major-General Sedmorab- Sept. 19th.

1799.
Sept. 19th.

zen in attacking Schoreldam. The second brigade of Guards, under Major-General Burrard, was to keep up the communication with the column under Sir James Pulteney. General Herman attacked the front and left of the enemy's line, which gave way; the Russian column, however, was placed in a critical position. From having advanced too far, they were nearly surrounded, and the village of Bergen, which had been for some time in their occupation, was retaken by General Vandamme at the point of the bayonet. The Russians had given themselves up to plunder, and being unsupported, were, after a gallant contest, almost destroyed. Had they shown on this occasion as much discipline as intrepidity, they might have retained the ground they had gained. General Herman was made prisoner, and General Esseu dangerously wounded.

The right wing of the Batavian army under General Daendels was opposed to the British, who maintained their position till past twelve P. M., when they retired in consequence of the defeat of the Russian column. The Duke of York endeavoured to repair the disorder occasioned by their misconduct, and immediately attacked the village of Schorel with General Manners's brigade, supported by three Russian battalions, the brigade of Guards, and the Thirty-fifth regiment, commanded by Prince William. As all attempts to retrieve the disaster at Bergen proved ineffectual, after carrying Schorel, the Commander-in-Chief withdrew his left. Sir Ralph Abercrombie also quitted the post of Hoorn during the night, and the two armies resumed their former positions.

The British in this encounter lost one hundred and twenty killed, four hundred wounded, and five hundred missing. The French stated their loss to be one hundred and fifty killed, and three hundred wounded. That of the Russians was considerable.

The casualties in the Coldstream were, Lieutenant-

Colonel Morris of the grenadier battalion of Guards killed, 1799. one serjeant, nine rank and file killed; Lieutenant-Colonel Cunynghame, one serjeant, and twenty-one rank and file wounded; one serjeant and thirteen rank and file missing.

Reinforcements of upwards of four thousand Russians landed at the Helder on the twenty-sixth, and marched to join their main body.

The inclemency of the weather compelled the contending armies to remain opposite each other till the second of October. October, when the Duke of York attacked the enemy's lines. "The points where this well-fought battle was "principally contested, were from the sea-shore in front of "Egmont, extending along the sandy desert, or height, "above Bergen:"[1] the contest was severe, and continued from six o'clock A. M. till the same hour in the evening. Sir Ralph Abercrombie commanded the right, Lieutenant-General Dundas the centre, and Major-General Burrard the left. After a gallant resistance the enemy were totally defeated, and retired in the night from their ground on the Lange Dyke, the Koe Dyke at Bergen, and from their extensive range of sand-hills between the latter place and Egmont-op-Zee to a still stronger position at Beverwick, three leagues from Haarlem.

The victory was attended with a loss of more than two thousand men; that of the enemy exceeded four thousand killed, three hundred prisoners, seven pieces of cannon, and many tumbrels.

The British took possession of Alkmaar; and on the sixth Oct. 3rd. the Duke of York, knowing the enemy expected reinforcements, thought it expedient again to attack, and, if possible, to force them to retire "before they had an oppor-

---

[1] The Duke of York's dispatch—London Gazette Extraordinary, Oct. 8, 1799. No. 15190.

1799.
October.

tunity of strengthening by works the short and very defensible line which they occupied." The British and Russians first gained possession of the villages of Limmen and Baccum. The enemy advanced, and the action became general along the whole line from Limmen to the sea, and continued with great obstinacy on both sides till dark, when they retreated, leaving the Confederates masters of the field.

The following is an extract from his Royal Highness the Duke of York's dispatch, dated " Head-Quarters, Alkmaar, October 7th, 1799 :—

" Nor ought I to omit the praise due to Colonel Clephane, " commanding four companies of the Third, and one com- " pany of the Coldstream regiment of Guards, who by a spi- " rited charge drove two battalions of the enemy from the " post of Archer Sloot, making two hundred prisoners."

The loss of the Allies was two thousand five hundred and fifty-five killed, wounded, and prisoners. The Coldstream lost one man killed, thirteen wounded, and three rank and file missing.

The Duke of York ascertained that since the second, the enemy had been reinforced by six thousand infantry, and their position at Beverwick considerably improved. These were obstacles which it would be necessary to remove previous to making any attempt on Haarlem. The enemy had also detached a strong force to Purmirind, which, if the Duke of York's army advanced, would be left in his rear. His Royal Highness, therefore, taking these circumstances into consideration, together with the want of supplies of every description and the impracticable state of the roads, judged it advisable to withdraw from his advanced position, and wait for further instructions from England.

Subsequently the Allies concentrated in their intrenchments within the Helder Point. Alkmaar and Hoorn were again occupied by the enemy, who nearly surrounded the Allied camp. In face of the French army it would have been dangerous to attempt to re-embark: on the other hand, the English had it in their power to cut the dykes, which would devastate the country. A convention was therefore signed on the eighteenth of October, which provided that the British and Russian army should embark as soon as possible without committing any injury, and that eight thousand French and Dutch prisoners of war, then detained in England, should be restored unconditionally to their respective countries.

The army commenced their re-embarkation on the twenty-second. The first battalion of the Coldstream landed at Yarmouth on the thirty-first, and marched to their quarters in Upper Westminster. The grenadier battalion, in which were the grenadier companies of the Coldstream, disembarked at Ramsgate.

OFFICERS OF THE COLDSTREAM GUARDS IN HOLLAND, 1799.

Colonel Hon. Edward Finch.
Lt.-Col. C. Howard Bulkely.
,, Hon. James Forbes.
,, Roger Morris.
,, Arthur Brice.
,, Edmund Earl of Cork.
,, John Leveson Gower.
,, Francis Cunynghame.
,, K. A. Howard.
Capt.-Lieut. Thos. Armstrong.
Captain Henry Bayly.
,, Henry MacKinnon.
,, M. Warren Peacocke.
,, Hilton Jolliffe.
,, Hon. C. Grey M'Lellan.
,, Thomas Stibbert.
,, Hon. John Wingfield.
,, William Sheridan.

Captain James Phillips.
,, Richard Boulton.
,, John Allen Lloyd.
,, Rich. Downes Jackson.
Ensign Sir John Gordon, Bart.
,, George Morgan.
,, Gilbert Sterling.
,, Charles Phillips.
,, Richard Beadon.
,, John Thompson.
,, John Frederick.
,, W. T. Myers.
,, L. F. Adams.
Quarter-Master John Holmes.
Surgeon George Rose.
Assistant do. John T. Simpson.
,, John Gilham.

CHAPTER V.

First battalion joins the expedition under Abercrombie—British land in Aboukir Bay — Abercrombie attacks the French lines—Battle of Alexandria—Death of Abercrombie—Reinforcements arrive for the Coldstream — Cavan appointed to command the brigade of Guards—Marabout capitulates—Alexandria surrenders — Army returns to England — First battalion lands — Marches through Winchester for London — Peace of Amiens — Buonaparte declared First Consul — War with France — First battalions of Coldstream and Third brigaded under Finch — Arrive at Chelmsford—Letter to Patriotic Fund from non-commissioned officers and soldiers of the Egyptian brigade of Guards —First battalion march for Cox-Heath Camp—In quarters at Chatham — George III. reviews his Guards at Wimbledon—Death of the Duke of Gloucester—Duke of York succeeds in command of the First Guards — Duke of Cambridge appointed Colonel of the Coldstream—Treaty of Petersburgh—First battalion embark under Lord Cathcart — Land at Cuxhaven—March to Bremen—Battle of Austerlitz—Expedition returns to England.

IN May, 1798, General Buonaparte had sailed from Toulon for Egypt with a large force, and the French continued to hold possession of that country.

1800. On the eighteenth of August, 1800, eight companies of the first battalion of the Coldstream embarked at the Cove of Cork on board two sixty-four gun ships, the Dictator and Delft, and joined an expedition under Sir James Pulteney, against Vigo, which produced no result. They then proceeded from Vigo to the Mediterranean, where they united with the army under Sir Ralph Abercrombie, which after some delay reached Marmorice Bay.

THE COLDSTREAM GUARDS. 75

The second division also arrived in a few days. The cavalry and sick were put on shore, and the regiments landed in succession.

The expedition remained some time on the coast of Asia Minor, and sailed on the twenty-second of February from Marmorice with the daring purpose of wresting Egypt from the grasp of that celebrated army of Italy, whose achievements in Europe had filled the civilized world with admiration and astonishment. The veteran comrades of Buonaparte, notwithstanding the losses they had sustained in their contests with the Turks and Mamelukes, were still greatly superior in numbers to the troops[1]

1800.

FORCE OF THE BRITISH ARMY,
Including 1000 sick, and 500 Maltese.

Guards . { Major-Gen. Hon. George J. Ludlow

1st or Roy^{ls}
Two bat^{ns} of } Major-Gen. Coote
the 54th
92d

8th
13th
19th } Maj.-Gen. Cradock
90th

2d
50th } Major-Gen. Lord Cavan
79th

18th
30th
44th } Brigadier-General John Doyle
89th

Minorca
De Rolle's } Major-General John Stuart
Dillon's

RESERVE.

40th Flank companies
23d
28th
42d
58th
Corsican Rangers
Detachment 11th Dragoons
Do. Hompesch's Dragoons } Maj.-Gen. Moore

12th Dragoons
26th Do. } Brigadier-Gen. Finch

Artillery and Pioneers } Brigadier-Gen. Lawson

1800. under Abercrombie; they were besides in possession of the resources of the country and of all its strong-holds, which had been fortified with the utmost skill and care. Eighteen months' occupation had inured the French to the burning suns of Egypt, which had become their adopted country, and they confidently prepared to repel the meditated attack. The British were strangers to that ungenial climate, and laboured under all the debilitating consequences of a protracted voyage and long confinement on ship-board: but without pausing to calculate disadvantages, they cheerfully proceeded to accomplish their country's errand.

1801. Mar. 1st. The day previous to anchoring in Aboukir Bay it was given out that the brigade of Guards was to be in the first line.

The following order was issued on the fourth of March:—

" The troops will hold themselves in readiness to land " as soon as the weather permits. The first division that " disembarks, consisting of the brigade of Guards, re-" serve, 2ᵈ battalions of the Royals, and 54ᵗʰ regiments, " will carry their blankets and three days' provisions, and " will leave their knapsacks on board."

Mar. 8th. The weather was unfavourable; but becoming more moderate at two o'clock on the morning of the eighth, the first division, consisting of the reserve under Major-General Moore, the brigade of Guards under Major-General the Honourable James Ludlow, the Royals, the first battalion of the Fifty-fourth regiment, and part of the second battalion, with some other detachments, the whole being under the command of Major-General Coote, got into the boats and pushed off for their rendezvous, some hundred paces from the shore. Each flank was protected by light armed vessels, and several bombs and gun-brigs were moored with their broadsides to the beach. At nine o'clock the signal was given. About two thousand French were advantageously posted on the top of some sand-hills; the centre of their position was nearly two hundred feet above the level of the sea, on which were planted twelve pieces of cannon. These guns, as well as the castle of Aboukir, commanded the landing. When the boats approached, they were assailed with grape and musketry from the shore. The reserve jumped out of their boats, formed, and pushed forward: the Twenty-third and Fortieth regiments gallantly charged the height, and kept advancing to the two hills in the rear. The Forty-second regiment gained the summit, notwithstanding a heavy discharge of grape-shot, and the opposition of a considerable force of infantry: on reaching the top, they were charged by a body of dragoons, who were however repulsed. On landing, the Guards were suddenly attacked by the same dragoons, who had rallied. The Fifty-eighth regiment, which had already formed on the right, opened a fire, under cover of which the Guards were enabled to show front, when the enemy's cavalry suffered greatly. The Fifty-fourth regiment and Royals reached the shore at the moment when a hostile column was advancing against the left of the Guards: on perceiving them, the French gave one discharge and retired. The heights were then occupied by the British, and, General Coote with the Guards coming up, the French retired behind the sand-hills.

1801.
Mar. 8th.

The loss of the enemy amounted to nearly four hundred; that of the British to seven hundred and forty-two men. In the Coldstream the casualties were, Ensign Warren and seventeen rank and file killed; Captains Plunkett, Frederick, Beadon, and Myers, Surgeon Rose, eleven serjeants, one drummer, and fifty-seven rank and file

1801. wounded. Captain Frederick and Surgeon Rose died of their wounds.

Aboukir Castle[1] still held out: it was blockaded by the Queen's regiment and the Twenty-sixth dismounted Dragoons.

Mar. 9th. The British troops were ordered to make a movement in advance: the next day they approached the enemy, when some skirmishing took place. On the eleventh the following General Order was issued:—

"The army will advance to-morrow; the brigade of "Guards marching from the right will lead the first co-"lumn: they will proceed along the road near the sea-"beach, facing the redoubts of Mandora to the left."

Mar. 12th. Sir Ralph Abercrombie next day moved to Mandora Tower, where the army encamped. The light troops of the enemy engaged the piquets nearly the whole march, which did not exceed four miles. The French, having received reinforcements from Cairo and Rosetta, had increased their strength to about thirty guns and six thousand men, including cavalry.

Mar. 13th. On the thirteenth the enemy occupied a strong position on a rising ground, the ascent to which was gradual; their right extended towards the canal of Alexandria, their left to the sea. Abercrombie, whose troops were in two lines, formed them into columns of battalions, left in front, with the intention of attacking the enemy's right. When the British advanced, the French moved down from their position, and directed a spirited fire of musketry and artillery on the Ninety-second regiment. The enemy's cavalry at the same time charged the extreme right, and came in contact with the Ninetieth regiment, commanded

---

[1] Surrendered on the thirteenth.

by Colonel Graham, since created Lord Lynedoch. This corps with undaunted courage awaited their approach, and at the exact moment threw in a volley, which obliged the French cavalry to swerve to the right previous to their flight. The English formed in two lines, the reserve in column on the right. The Guards supported the centre. General John Stuart's and Doyle's brigades moved in column in rear of the left. All preserving the greatest order steadily advanced under a heavy fire of artillery and musketry. The French were forced to retire through a plain of three miles to their lines in front of Alexandria.

1801.
Mar. 13th.

The English lost twelve hundred and eighty-four killed and wounded; the French about five hundred, with four guns. Ensign Jenkinson of the Coldstream was killed, and Captain Beadon wounded; two rank and file killed, and four wounded. Major-General Cradock distinguished himself; it was principally owing to his excellent arrangements that the enemy's cavalry was repulsed. The French Colonel Latour Maubourg was dangerously wounded.

Lieutenant-Colonel Brice of the Coldstream Guards commanded the piquets on the fourteenth, when he was attracted by some firing, and, proceeding to the spot, was wounded and taken prisoner,[1] and died two days after.

The British troops in every encounter from the time of their landing had shown themselves decidedly superior to the French. Their position was about four miles from Alexandria, with the sea on their right flank, and the Lake of Aboukir on the left. In front of the centre a considerable plain extended as far as the elevated ground

---

[1] Sir Robert Wilson, in his Expedition to Egypt, says, "he "missed his way when going his rounds, which it was almost im- "possible to prevent." Walsh, in his Campaign, also gives the same account.

1801.
March.

on which the enemy had intrenched themselves. The Twenty-eighth and Fifty-eighth regiments were posted among some ancient ruins and redoubts on the right, supported by the Twenty-third, Fortieth, Forty-second, and the Corsican Rangers. Between the right and the right centre, occupied by the Guards on a rising ground, was a flat, on which there were some cavalry. From the hill where the Guards stood the line ran obliquely to the left, at the end of which two batteries were intended to be constructed, and were in a state of forwardness. On the left of the Guards the Ninety-second, Second, Fifty-fourth, First, Eighth, Eighteenth, Ninetieth, and Thirteenth regiments were stationed in échelon, ready if necessary to form on the Guards. The second line was composed of the regiments of Minorca, De Rolle's, Dillon's, the Queen's, Forty-fourth, Eighty-ninth, Twelfth, and the Twenty-sixth dragoons.

The troops under the French General Menou, recently arrived from Grand Cairo, occupied a strong defensive position on some steep hills. In front of their right ran a strip of land joining the canal, which occasioned the left of the English to stand in the oblique position before described.[1]

Mar. 21st.

An hour before day on the morning of the twenty-first of March, General Menou, with his army increased to thirteen thousand men, and about equal to the English, made a false attack on the left; but the report of musketry soon announced that the right was the point he really intended to assault. The British awaited the enemy's approach with great composure: the latter ad-

---

[1] The City and Pharos of Alexandria, with Pompey's Pillar and Cleopatra's Needle, were distinctly to be seen from the English camp.

vanced with loud huzzas and drums beating; Colonels Paget and Houstoun, however, whose regiments held the key of the position, would not permit a shot to be fired till they were close at hand, when the troops were ordered to open their fire, which obliged the French to retreat. The enemy then wheeled to their right for the purpose of surrounding a redoubt; a second column attacked in front, and a third penetrated the ruins before mentioned. At this moment Colonel Crowdjye with the Fifty-eighth, after two or three rounds, rushed on them with the bayonet; this charge was supported by the Twenty-third. The Forty-second seized the opportunity, and advanced in the most gallant manner to cover the open space at which the column had entered, who after great loss surrendered. The Twenty-eighth, the Forty-second, and Fifty-eighth regiments, and the flank companies of the Twenty-third and Fortieth under Colonel Spencer, greatly distinguished themselves. General Stuart came up with his brigade, which quickly threw the enemy into disorder, and at length forced them to a precipitate flight. It was at this critical moment that Sir Ralph Abercrombie received his mortal wound.[1]

1801.
Mar. 21st.

At day-break a strong column of French grenadiers, supported by a line of infantry, attacked the position occupied by the Guards, whose skirmishers were driven in. The enemy's intention was to turn the left flank of the brigade, all the troops being placed in échelon. On the near approach of the French, several companies of the left battalion were thrown back. By a steady and incessant fire, together with the advance of General Coote's brigade, they completed the confusion of the enemy, who had already

---

[1] Sir Ralph Abercrombie died on board the Foudroyant on the 28th of March.

shown an inclination to waver. The attack was principally confined to the right and centre. General Menou, finding all his attempts unsuccessful, retreated, after a last effort to carry the position by a charge of cavalry under Brigadier-General Roize,[1] supported by General Regnier with the divisions under Lanusse, Rampon, and Friant.

The loss of the English was fourteen hundred and sixty-four men. Between three and four thousand French were left on the field of battle. The casualties in the Coldstream Guards were, seven rank and file killed, one serjeant, fifty-two rank and file wounded.

The following General Orders were given out by Lord Hutchinson. "Major-General Ludlow and the brigade "of Guards will accept the thanks of his Excellency the "Commander-in-Chief for the cool, steady, and soldier- "like manner in which they repulsed the attack of the "enemy's column."

The Coldstream remained in camp before Alexandria.[2] On the eighth of July a reinforcement for the regiment of one hundred and fifty men arrived in the Active frigate; they were conveyed across the Lake in boats belonging to the fleet, and landed at the depôt. On the ninth of August Major-General the Earl of Cavan was appointed to take command of the brigade of Guards.

A corps under General Coote, including the Guards, was embarked on the Lake Mareotis, and sent to the westward. Three battalions of Brigadier-General Finch's brigade had been previously despatched in a number of

---

[1] General Roize was killed with many distinguished officers, and the French cavalry completely broken and almost destroyed.—*General Regnier's State of Egypt*, pages 270, 271.

[2] State of the first battalion Coldstream Guards in camp, four miles from Alexandria, March 30th. Two captains, eleven lieutenants, four ensigns, thirty-two serjeants, twelve drummers, six hundred and forty-seven rank and file, two hundred and three sick.

barks:[1] these had drifted to leeward during the night, and considerably retarded the landing. When the troops were on shore, a position was taken along a ridge of quarries about half a mile broad, at the foot of which was a sandy plain that extended to the sea; the breadth of this peninsula did not exceed two miles. There was a small island opposite the western division, on which stood Fort Marabout. On the evening of the eighteenth, General Coote advanced about two miles and occupied a position, the Guards extending across the quarries; the rest of the troops formed en potence, facing the sea. 1801. Aug. 16th.

At six o'clock P. M., after the guns of Marabout had been dismounted by the batteries, the garrison capitulated. The Coldstream had two rank and file wounded, Aug. 21st.

General Coote marched at day-light in three columns. The Coldstream and Third Guards under Lord Cavan formed two columns on the right, and General Ludlow's brigade the third. Major-General Finch's brigade was in reserve: the advanced guard, consisting of the Twenty-seventh, with some of Lowenstein's riflemen, and two hundred of the Guards, were under Lieutenant-Colonel Jolliffe of the Coldstream. Next morning, at four o'clock, the British piquets fell in with and drove in the French out-posts. The columns entered the plain at day-light, and kept gallantly moving on under a sharp cannonade.[2] The Turks took possession of Sugar-loaf Hill on the right. The Coldstream had two wounded. Aug. 22nd.

---

[1] Walsh's Egypt, vol. II. page 200. About four hundred.

[2] " The Guards on the right had continued their march in-
" different to the grape which played upon them, forcing, by their
" steady progress, the French to evacuate the battery opposed to
" them."—*Sir Robert Wilson's Egypt*, vol. II. page 22.

Sir Robert Wilson also mentions a singular escape of General Coote and a company of Guards, who were passing under a heavy fire of grape, which struck off several of the men's caps without doing any injury.

1801.
August.

On the twenty-fourth General Spencer landed with Brigadier-General Blake's brigade, and some Mamelukes also joined General Coote's division, besides about seven hundred Turks. Several ships of war entered the harbour for the purpose of protecting the left of the line. Next day a battery opened from eight heavy guns and mortars against the redoute des Bains. After dark Lieutenant-Colonel Smith with the Twenty-sixth regiment and some dragoons, supported by Lieutenant-Colonel Layard, attacked and drove in the left of the enemy's piquets in the most spirited manner with the bayonet, the men not having even loaded their muskets. The batteries continued firing on the eastern side of the town till twelve, when the enemy's fire ceased; it was soon discovered that they had withdrawn their guns. In the evening an aid-de-camp of General Menou presented a letter at the advanced posts, proposing a suspension of hostilities for three days, with a view to settle terms. An answer in the affirmative was returned, and all hostilities were to cease, on the French firing three guns loaded with blank cartridge, to be answered in the same manner by the English, when the standards of both armies were to be lowered. On the evening of the twenty-ninth, Menou sent by his aid-de-camp to request a prolongation of the truce for thirty-six hours, which was rejected. The French General begged to be allowed till two o'clock the following day. The capitulation was concluded without further delay by Brigadier-General Hope, who was received by the French General with great politeness, and invited to dine: the dinner consisted entirely of horse-flesh.

September.

The garrison of Alexandria, which surrendered on the first of September, amounted to nearly twelve thousand, including five thousand nine hundred and sixty-five soldiers of artillery, cavalry, and infantry, besides marine artillery, sappers, miners, and seamen doing garrison-duty, &c. &c.

The other division of the French army having surrendered at Cairo, the enemy were no longer in possession of any part of Egypt; and the object of the expedition being attained, Lord Cavan delivered to the Captain Pacha the keys of the city of Alexandria. The army shortly after prepared for embarkation. *1801. September. Sept. 26th.*

Blame has been attached by some French writers to General Menou, for not opposing the invaders with his whole force. It may also have accorded with the selfish policy of Buonaparte, that the odium of an unsatisfactory termination to an enterprise planned by himself, should be ascribed to mismanagement after his departure. But threatened by the approach of the Indian army under Sir David Baird, and embarrassed by the questionable fidelity of the Egyptian population, Menou doubtless felt the necessity of leaving a considerable force at Cairo. Well aware that the British on their debarkation must enter the field subject to many disadvantages, he met them with an army equal in numbers, and superior in artillery and cavalry. Such comparative means Buonaparte himself would have deemed sufficient to face and overthrow the veterans of Austria in his Italian campaigns; nor, had he been in Egypt at the period of the battle of Alexandria, would he have allowed it to be said, that to enable his boasted invincibles to attack the Islanders with success, it was necessary to bring against them an overwhelming superiority of twice their numbers. Menou at that period, like his great master in the art of war, had no conception of the qualities of British troops; but he knew that he had under his command the celebrated army of Italy, which had victoriously contended against the finest armies of the European Continent. With this experience of Austrian warfare, and with a well-founded confidence in his men, Menou challenged his antagonists to a combat on nearly equal terms, and was, to his great surprise, defeated.

1801.
September. He found, when too late, that he had miscalculated the prowess of the British soldiery. A few years after, the same rough lesson was taught Napoleon.

October. The first battalion of the Coldstream arrived at Malta on the seventeenth of October, landed the next day, and went into barracks, where they remained three weeks. Afterwards they re-embarked, landed in separate divisions between the sixth and twenty-ninth of December at Portsmouth, and marched from Winchester on Friday the eighth
1802. of January. In a few days they reached London.[1]

---

[1] Return of the Officers of the first battalion of the Coldstream in the expedition to Egypt:—

	Captains.	Lieutenants.	Ensigns.
Gren^r. Comp^y.	At home		
	H. R. H. the Duke of York's company	Capt. Lt. H. F. Bouverie Capt. F. Adam	G. T. B. Warren
1st Maj.	Maj.-Gen. Earl of Cavan	,, Hon. Ed. Plunkett ,, T. L. Campbell	John Hamilton
	Col. Hon. Edward Finch	,, John Thompson ,, James Philips	George Collier
	,, Brice	,, Sir I. Gordon	Richard Beckett
	,, Earl of Cork	,, Sir Gilbert Stirling ,, Chs. Philips	Thos. Roberts
	Lt.-Col. H. MacKinnon	,, Rich^d. Beadon ,, John Frederick	T. W. Brotherton
	,, ,, Hilton Jolliffe	,, Thos. Stibbert ,, Chs. Fane	Lord Delvin
	,, ,, W. M. Peacock	,, Ed^d. Dalling ,, W. Myers	Jenkinson
Light Comp^y.	At home		

Adjutant, Sir Gilbert Stirling.
Quarter-Master, John Holmes.
Surgeon, George Rose.
Assistant Surgeon, John Gilham.
    ,,   ,,   H. Fearon.
Drum-Major, William Lamb.
Deputy-Marshall, William Alpe.

Changes that took place.
Ensigns Warren and Jenkinson killed; Col. Brice, Capt. Frederick, and Surgeon Rose, died of their wounds.

Joined.
Capt. Geo. Sedley
Ensign, Hon. Ed^d. Acheson
Lieut.-Col. G. H. Dyke

Returned to England.
Capt. Hon. Ed^d. Plunkett
,,   Sir Gilbert Stirling
,,   ,,   ,,   Sedley
,,   H. F. Bouverie
Surgeon, John Gilham
Lt.-Col. H. MacKinnon, via Germany, &c.

THE COLDSTREAM GUARDS. 87

The treaty of Amiens put an end to hostilities in March. During this peace Buonaparte was made President of the Cisalpine Republic. Louisiana, the Duchy of Parma, and the Island of Elba, were ceded to France by the private treaty with Spain. An amnesty was granted to all emigrants who had not borne arms against the revolutionists; Buonaparte had been declared First Consul for life, and was empowered to appoint his successor. The Legion of Honour was instituted by him for the encouragement of military, naval, and scientific men, and also of those most eminent in the administration of affairs. 1802. Mar. 25th.

On the twelfth of May the English Ambassador quitted France, and hostilities between England and the French Government recommenced. The First Consul threatened to invade England, which created considerable alarm, and the nation was placed in a state of defence. The British Government seized all the French ships they could find, making the crews prisoners. Sixty thousand seamen were voted by Parliament, and the army was increased to one hundred and twenty-nine thousand men. An army of Reserve was raised, and volunteer corps were formed throughout the country. May.
May 18th.

The first battalion marched to Chelmsford, when they were brigaded with the first battalion of the Third Guards, under the command of Major-General the Honourable Edward Finch. On the tenth of August the brigade was inspected by his Royal Highness the Duke of York, in the main street at Chelmsford. 1803.
June 27th.

August.

It was from this place that the subjoined letter, so highly creditable to the brigade, was addressed to the Secretary of the Patriotic Fund:—

" Chelmsford New Barracks, August 19, 1803.

' GENTLEMEN, Aug. 19th.

" Impressed with a due sense of the cause for

1803. "which we are about to contend, and equally anxious with "the rest of our fellow-subjects to promote that zeal "which animates the breast of every Englishman to the "preservation and defence of blessings that ought not to "be lost but with existence, the non-commissioned offi- "cers and private soldiers of his Majesty's Egyptian "brigade of Foot Guards, consisting of the first battalion "of the Coldstream and the first battalion of the Third "regiment, commanded by the Honourable Major-Gene- "ral Edward Finch, are desirous to subscribe from their "weekly subsistence as follows, viz. : from the serjeants "two full days' pay each; and from the corporals, drum- "mers, and privates, one full day's pay each, amounting "to £111. 5s. 7d., towards the support of the Patriotic "Fund, now established for the relief of those who "may eventually suffer in the prosecution of a con- "test, as glorious as it will no doubt be honourable, "should the implacable enemy of our country invade "her shores."

"In the name of the non-commissioned officers, drum-
"mers, and privates of the Egyptian brigade of Foot
"Guards,

"HENRY SELWAY, Serjeant-Major 1st Battⁿ Cold-
"stream Guards.

"ALEXANDER ADAMS, Serjeant-Major 1st Battⁿ
"Third Guards."

1804. In May, Cambaceres acquainted Buonaparte that it was the wish of the senate and of the people that he should accept the imperial dignity. Buonaparte consented to an arrangement which was so "essential to the welfare of the state," and was declared Emperor on the twentieth of

August. In the following December he was crowned by Pope Pius at Paris. — 1804.

The first battalions of the Coldstream and Third Guards marched from Chelmsford for Cox-Heath, where they encamped with several regiments of militia, under the Earl of Chatham.[1] — July 24th.

On the first and second of November they went into barracks at Chatham, and remained there during the winter. — November.

The four flank companies from the second brigade of Guards at Chatham, and the six flank companies of the third brigade in London, marched to Windsor to attend the installation of the Garter. — 1805. April.

In May the first battalion marched from Chatham to London, and was reviewed at Wimbledon by his Majesty George the Third.[2] — May 27th, 28th, 29th.

On the death of the Duke of Gloucester, the Duke of York succeeded him in the command of the First regiment — June 14th.

---

[1] The corps encamped at Cox-Heath on the first of August, 1804.
    23d Light Dragoons.
    Coldstream Guards . 1st Battalion.
    Third Guards . . 1st Battalion.
    West York Militia . (First.)
      Do.   Do. . (Third.)
    East York Do.
    East Norfolk Do.
    West Do. Do.
    Bucks Do.
—Quarter-Master General's Office.

[2] Troops reviewed at Wimbledon by his Majesty King George the Third, June 14th, 1805:

The brigade of Life Guards, one troop of Horse Artillery, one car-brigade of Artillery, right brigade of Foot Guards, left brigade of Foot Guards, a battalion of Light Infantry of Foot Guards, one

1805
Sept. 5th.

of Guards, and the Duke of Cambridge was appointed Colonel of the Coldstream.

The Emperor of Austria had acceded to the treaty of Petersburgh on the ninth of August. Napoleon's plans for the invasion of England were consequently at an end, and the encampment of one hundred thousand men on the French coast was broken up. He declared to the senate his determination of immediately placing himself at the head of his army.

The French at this time were on the Rhine, and consisted of seven corps, independent of the cavalry under the direction of Marshal Murat. The different corps were commanded by the following Marshals: Bernadotte, Davoust, Soult, Lannes, Ney, Augereau, and General Marmont. Marshal Massena, with sixty thousand men under his orders, was in Italy, and, on reaching the Adige, had his forces increased by twenty thousand French under General Gouvion St. Cyr. The army of the Emperor of Germany consisted of three hundred thousand men in the most efficient state. The preparations of Russia were also on a great scale; her army amounted to upwards of one hundred and eighteen thousand men.

The English, by way of a diversion in favour of Austria, equipped a force of twenty-six thousand men under Lord Cathcart.

The first battalion of the Coldstream, commanded by Lieutenant-Colonel Thomas Armstrong, marched from Chatham on the thirtieth of August to Deal, and after-

Oct. 9th. wards to Dover, from which place they proceeded to Rams-

---

car-brigade of Artillery, one troop of Horse Artillery, five squadrons of the Ninth Light Dragoons, five squadrons of the Fourteenth Light Dragoons.

gate, when they embarked.[1] They sailed from the Downs on the fourth of November, and, having landed at Cuxhaven, marched to Bremen.

1805.
Oct. 23rd.
Nov. 20th.

Napoleon crossed the Rhine, and by the rapidity of his

---

[1] Return of Officers of the 1st battalion Coldstream Guards. October 23d, 1805.

Comps.	Captains.		Lieutenants.	Ensigns.
Grens.	Lieut.-Col. Henry MacKinnon	Capts.	J. Thompson Henry Sullivan Chas. Maitland Christie	
	[1] Brig.-Gen. W. Wynyard	,,	Chas. Philips	Charles Doyle [2] Matt. Fortescue
	Lt.-Col. T. Armstrong	,,	Lord A. Gordon	Thomas Wood John Freemantle
	,, ,, W. M. Peacocke	[1] ,,	Edwd. Dalling	[3] Hon. G. Pelham George Bowles
	[1] Brig.-Gen. Wm. P. Acland	,,	Sir I. L. Johnstone	Dan. MacKinnon Hon. Francis Hay Drummond
	Lt.-Col. W. H. Pringle	[1] ,,	R. Beckett	Hon. John Walpole Hon. Edward Boscawen
	,, ,, Matthew Lord Aylmer	,,	W. H. Raikes	Thomas Thoroton Thos. Barrow
	,, ,, Thos. Stibbert	,,	F. M. Sutton	H. W. Vachell W. Fairfield
	,, ,, Sir W. Sheridan	,,	George Smyth	Edd. Jenkinson G. T. Baldwin
Light Infantry	,, ,, Richard Hulse	,, ,, ,,	Thos. Braddyll George Collier Charles Parker	

Adjutant, Captain Montague Wynyard.
Quarter-Master, John Holmes.
Surgeon, Charles Combe.
Assistant Surgeon, I. G. MacKenzie.
   ,,   ,,   Thomas Rose.

[1] Absent on the Staff.
Brigadier-General Wm. Wynyard.
   ,,   ,,   Wm. P. Acland.
Captain Edwd. Dalling.
  ,,   Ricd. Beckett.
[2] Absent. Recruiting.
[3] Do. Sick.

1805. movements obliged the Austrians to act on the defensive. General Mack was hemmed in at Ulm and obliged to capitulate. Murat came up with General Werneck on the nineteenth of October, and after an engagement at Trachtelfingen the Austrian General capitulated. Marshal Massena, after a bloody contest at Coldiero, was beaten by the Archduke Charles.

Early in November, General Hillinger with an Austrian corps of five thousand men capitulated near Verona; he was made prisoner soon after the Archduke commenced his retreat.

The French troops entered Vienna on the thirteenth of November. The Allies were forced by Napoleon to risk a general action, much against their own interest, as in a few days the third Russian army was expected to join them.

Dec. 2nd. The battle of Austerlitz commenced at the dawn of day and ended at night. The result of this action baffled the hopes of Austria, Russia, and England. In consequence of the victory gained by the French, the British troops returned from Bremen.

1806.
Feb. 23rd. The first battalion of the Coldstream disembarked at Ramsgate, and marched to Deal barracks.

CHAPTER VI.

Officers of the Coldstream address the Duke of York—Duke's reply—First battalion sails with the expedition for the Baltic—Investment of Copenhagen—Bombardment—Capitulation—Army re-embark — First battalion go into barracks at Chatham — Charles IV. abdicates in favour of Ferdinand—Napoleon arrives at Bayonne—Murat enters Madrid—Prince of Peace sent to Bayonne, followed by Charles and the Queen—Joseph Buonaparte proclaimed King of Spain — Insurrection at Oporto, which extends to Spain—French squadron at Cadiz capitulates—Dupont's army surrenders to Castanos — Spanish Patriots enter into a treaty with England — Expedition sails from Cork — Lands in Mondego Bay—Wellesley attacks the heights of Roliça, and defeats Junot at Vimeira—French quit Portugal—Napoleon returns to Paris—Troops from Sweden reinforce the British in Portugal—Napoleon arrives at Madrid—Junction of Moore and Baird—Moore retreats—French repulsed at Corunna—Death of Moore—Army returns to England—Second brigade of Guards embark at Ramsgate — Fleet arrives at Spithead — Sails — Dispersed by contrary and tempestuous winds—Transports find shelter in the Irish ports — Fleet sails from Cork for Cadiz — Supreme Junta refuses admittance — Fleet sails for the Tagus — Beresford appointed to command the Portuguese troops—Nine companies of the first battalion land at Lisbon—Cradock commands the army—Twenty thousand Portuguese troops taken into English pay—Soult defeats Romana, crosses the Minho, and carries Oporto—Silveira retakes Chaves—Soult's communication with Spain intercepted—Guards march through Saccavem and Batalha to Lyria—Cradock resigns the command to Wellesley—General Orders—Guards march to Coimbra—Trant holds the line of the Vouga.

The Duke of York gave up the command of the regiment: at this period the officers of the Coldstream presented

1807.
May.

1807.   a vase to his Royal Highness as a testimony of their gratitude and attachment, which occasioned the following address, and reply:

"Sir,

"We the Officers of his Majesty's Coldstream
"Guards, impressed with the greatest respect and affec-
"tion, beg leave to present to your Royal Highness this
"Vase, as a tribute of gratitude for the unremitted kind-
"ness and various instances of consideration and regard
"with which we have been favoured by your Royal High-
"ness during the long period we had the honour of serving
"under your immediate command as Colonel of the Regi-
"ment. Our fervent prayers are, that your Royal High-
"ness may long enjoy every happiness and blessing of
"life; and, as Officers zealously devoted to our Sovereign,
"and most affectionately to you, Sir, we trust our future
"services will ensure to us a continuance of those favour-
"able sentiments, and of that protection, which it has so
"long a period been our pride and happiness to ex-
"perience from your Royal Highness.

"To Field-Marshal
"His Royal Highness the Duke of York."

Horse-Guards, 6th May, 1807.

May 6th.   "Gentlemen,

"I receive with sentiments of the most heartfelt satis-
"faction this token of regard from the Officers of the
"Coldstream Guards, and feel much indebted for the
"kindness with which you have expressed yourselves
"towards me.

"I avail myself with great pleasure of this opportunity
"to assure you, that no Colonel had ever greater induce-
"ments to be partial to a corps than I had during the
"long period I had the command of the regiment; as it

"was my happiness to find myself associated with men who equally claimed my esteem and affection in the civil capacities, as they were uniformly entitled to my approbation as officers.

"Though not in the immediate command of the regiment, you may be assured, Gentlemen, that the Coldstream will ever retain my most ardent wishes for its honour and welfare. I am attached to the regiment by ties and considerations, the force of which no time can lessen; and in your happiness, individually and collectively, I shall ever feel the most lively interest.

"I am, &c.
"FREDERICK."

Although the Duke of York quitted the command, he constantly entertained a strong predilection for the Coldstream, and continued through life to watch over its welfare with the greatest interest. Future historians will record the unwearied and successful efforts of his Royal Highness as Commander-in-Chief to ameliorate the character and condition of the British soldier; but in giving an account of the services of the Coldstream, it may be permitted here to remark, that the internal regulations, the discipline, and the respectability, for which it has been so much and so justly extolled, emanated in a great measure from this illustrious Prince and amiable man.

The government of Denmark, which had hitherto observed a strict neutrality, influenced by France, prohibited all commerce with Great Britain; and an expedition, under Lord Cathcart and Admiral Gambier, was fitted out to prevent the Danish navy from passing into the hands of the French.

The brigade of Guards, under Major-General the Honourable Edward Finch, consisting of the first battalion of

1807.
August.

the Coldstream and first battalion of the Third Guards, embarked at Chatham, and arrived in Elsinore Roads on the ninth of August.[1]

All arrangements being completed for putting the men on shore, and the wind not allowing the transports to sail towards Copenhagen, it was determined to land half way

---

[1] Return of the Officers of the 1st battalion of the Coldstream at Copenhagen, 1807.

	Captains.	Lieutenants.	Ensigns.
Gren[r]. Comp[y].	Lieut.-Col. H. Mac Kinnon	Capt. T. Thompson ,, Sir H. Sullivan, "aid-de-camp to Major-Gen. the Hon. Ed[d]. Finch" Capt. C. M. Christie	
	Major-General Lord Forbes, absent on the Staff at home	Capt. Chas. Philips	N. Dickenson Hon. T. Ashburnham
	Lieut.-Col. Thomas Armstrong	,, Thos. Wood	Wm. Lord Alvanley Ed[d]. Noel Long
	Brig.-Gen. W. P. Acland, absent on the Staff at home	,, Hon. G. Pelham	Hon. F. H. Drummond George Bowles
	Lt.-Col. M. W. Peacocke	,, Thos. Braddyll, on the Staff	Hon. I. Walpole Peter Gaussen
	,, ,, William H. Pringle	George Smyth, on the Staff	Hon. W. G. Crofton Edwd. Harvey
	,, ,, Lord Aylmer	,, Edward Jenkinson	Wm. Burroughs Hon. Edwd. Boscawen
	,, ,, T. Stibbert	,, Edwd. Dalling	Dan. Mac Kinnon Chs. Gregory
	,, ,, Sir William Sheridan	,, Richard Beckett, Brigade-Major	Mat. Fortescue W. L. Walton
Light Comp[y].	,, ,, R. Hulse	,, Sir Gilbert Stirling ,, G. Collier ,, Thos. T. Barrow	

Adjutant, W. H. Raikes.
Quarter-Master, T. Holmes.
Battalion-Surgeon, C. Coombe.
Assistant, T. Mackenzie.
         ,,   T. Rose.

between Elsinore and that capital, at a village called Welbeck. At five o'clock on the morning of the sixteenth of August the troops got into the boats, and remained on the beach; towards the evening they commenced their march in three columns till night, when they halted till day-break, and again marched for the purpose of investing the capital. 1807.
August.

General Peyman, the Danish Commander-in-Chief, had previously sent to request passports for the King's nieces to proceed to Colding in Holstein. Soon after the brigade of Guards had entered the road to Copenhagen they were formed into line, and received the Princesses with the honours due to their rank.

Lord Rosslyn with six thousand men from the Isle of Rugen joined the army, which now amounted to about twenty-seven thousand.

The Guards occupied the suburbs between Fredericksberg and the city; in their advance they were opposed by a piquet of the enemy, which they dislodged.

The British broke ground before Copenhagen on the eighteenth of August; after which the operations continued, notwithstanding frequent efforts to interrupt them on the part of the Danes. On the twenty-fourth the town was more closely invested; a summons was sent on the first of September, which not being complied with, the batteries opened next morning, and after a bombardment of three days, an armistice of twenty-four hours was proposed by the enemy for the purpose of preparing articles of capitulation. This delay was thought unnecessary; Lieutenant-Colonel Murray was instructed to intimate that no proposal could be listened to, unless accompanied by the unconditional surrender of the fleet. It was then agreed that the whole of the Danish navy September.

1807.
September.

should be delivered up, and Zealand evacuated by the English within six weeks, or sooner if possible.

At four o'clock on the evening of the seventh the citadel was entered by Major-General Spencer's brigade.

No Englishman can desire to perpetuate the remembrance of this expedition, which laid the capital of a neutral state in ruins, and carried war and desolation among an innocent people. Its policy was doubtful, and its morality more than questionable. England indeed had reason to suspect, that the intention of Buonaparte was to compel the unfortunate Danes to unite their ships with his, as the price of their exemption from the ravages of his victorious troops, already threatening them. If ever nation deserved commiseration, the Danes deserved it at that period: had they complied with the request of the English government, and voluntarily given up their fleet to be carried to England for safe custody, the certain consequence would have been the subjugation of their country by the French armies. In this disastrous predicament, an unoffending but feeble community were only allowed to choose between their political annihilation, and the bombardment of their chief city. They preferred the latter, were overpowered, and England carried off their ships in triumph; but they saved their national independence. Napoleon, had he retained his Imperial crown, would probably have thrown on England the onus of showing that he ever contemplated the appropriation of the Danish fleet to his own purposes. Unfortunately, the proofs of England's injustice are recorded in characters of blood: she was frightened for her safety, her magnanimity forsook her, and her fears made her cruel. There is no reason to suppose that the addition of a few sail of the line would have transferred the superiority on the ocean to the fleets of the enemy, or that the expenses of the expe-

dition might not have been better bestowed on the aug- 1807.
mentation of the naval power of Great Britain, to enable
her, after her suspicions were realized by the junction
of the Danish men-of-war with those of France, to do
that with honour which could only be dishonourably done
while they remained dismantled in their own peaceful
harbours. If the principle of making war by anticipation,
without waiting for an overt act of hostility, be once
admitted, there can be no repose or security among the
nations of Europe; the existence of the false principle of
anticipatory warfare will generate and justify fear, and
fear will magnify danger. It is far from the interest of
the civilized world to multiply the causes of war, or that
neutral nations should be subjected to fire and sword,
their ships seized, their towns destroyed, their fields ra-
vaged, and their crops annihilated by one belligerent
to prevent the other from making use of them. The bombardment of Copenhagen, and the seizure of the Danish
ships, were contrary to the most obvious principles of
justice, and cannot even be vindicated on the treacherous
plea of necessity; for at sea England ruled supreme: it
was a fierce imitation of the ruthless, unhesitating policy
of Napoleon.

The army began to re-embark on the thirteenth of October.
October, and by the twentieth all had got on board; the
Guards and the Fourth regiment being the last that
remained on shore.

The first battalion anchored in Yarmouth Roads, and
then proceeded to Chatham, where they went into
barracks.

In March Charles the Fourth abdicated the throne of 1808.
Spain in favour of his son Ferdinand; but soon after, in a Mar. 19th.
letter to the French Emperor, he declared that it had been
compulsory. In April Napoleon arrived at Bayonne, April 15th.

1808.
April 20th.
April 30th.
June.

ostensibly for the purpose of settling the differences among the Royal Family of Spain. Ferdinand, at the suggestion of the French ambassador, was induced, in opposition to the advice of his councillors, to meet him. In Ferdinand's absence Murat entered Madrid at the head of a French army: Godoy, Prince of Peace, who had been imprisoned, was released and sent under an escort to Bayonne. Charles the Fourth, with the Queen, also repaired thither. Napoleon had an interview with Charles, at which the Queen of Spain and Ferdinand were present. After Charles had accused Ferdinand of usurpation, and lavished on him the grossest abuse, and the Queen had declared his illegitimacy, he was by threats and promises at last induced to sign a document renouncing all right and claim to the throne; and the other branches of the royal family were prevailed on to resign their pretensions in a similar manner. Charles the Fourth then ceded his claims in favour of Napoleon. Ferdinand, Don Antonio, his uncle, and his brother Don Carlos, fixed their residence at Valency. Charles, the Queen, and the Prince of Peace, retired to Rome.

Joseph Buonaparte was proclaimed King of Spain by an Imperial decree issued at Bayonne on the sixth of June. Ten days after this extraordinary event an insurrection broke out at Oporto, which spread with such rapidity through the northern provinces of Portugal that the French, who had taken possession of that country, were quickly expelled from it. The insurrection extended to Spain; and the French squadron at Cadiz was compelled to capitulate. Dupont's army of fifteen thousand men surrendered to the Spanish General Castanos. The Patriots entered into a treaty with England. The Spanish troops in Denmark under the Marquis de la Romana succeeded in getting on board the British fleet, and were conveyed to the Peninsula to assist their fellow-country men in opposing the usurpations of Napoleon.

On the twelfth of July a force of nine thousand three hundred and ninety-four men, commanded by Sir Arthur Wellesley, sailed from Cork: on clearing the coast the frigate in which he embarked left the fleet and steered for Corunna, where he had an interview with the provincial authorities, to whom he offered his co-operation. This was declined, on the ground that there was no immediate necessity for it in that quarter. Sir Arthur consequently sailed for Oporto, and held a conference with the Bishop and other functionaries. From Oporto he proceeded off Lisbon: after communicating with Sir Charles Cotton, he returned, and commenced landing his troops in Mondego Bay on the first of August. General Spencer arrived on the sixth with reinforcements. The army then advanced.

On the seventeenth Sir Arthur Wellesley attacked the heights of Roliça with complete success, and on the twenty-first defeated the French under the Duke d'Abrantes at the battle of Vimeira,[1] which led to the evacuation of Portugal by the troops of Napoleon.

The French Emperor returned to Paris on the eighteenth of October, and made known to the legislative body his determination to proceed in a few days for Madrid to place his brother Joseph on the Spanish throne. An army exceeding one hundred thousand men had already reinforced the French in that country.

The British troops in Sweden returned unexpectedly

---

[1] The enemy lost nearly three thousand men. Generals Foy and Thiebault, however, state the loss under two thousand.

1808. under Sir John Moore, and were sent without delay to reinforce the army of Portugal.

December. Napoleon entered Madrid on the fourth of December, and issued a proclamation on the seventh, in which he declared that should the Spaniards prove themselves unworthy of his confidence, and resist his wishes, he had determined to treat them as a conquered province, give his brother another kingdom, and place the crown of Spain on his own head.

Napoleon quitted Madrid on the nineteenth, and put himself at the head of his troops for the purpose, as he boasted, of driving the British into the sea.

On the twentieth the troops under Sir John Moore and Sir David Baird formed a junction at Mayorga; four days after, that army commenced its disastrous retreat. This retrograde movement, necessary perhaps from circumstances, but rendered calamitous by insubordination and mismanagement, ended in the battle of Corunna.[1] The British, on coming in contact with the enemy, recovered their discipline, and vigorously repulsed the French, who attacked in great force. But the triumph was clouded by the death of Sir John Moore, who was killed in the action.

This army embarked for England in the course of the night and following morning.

In the mean time another expedition was prepared; and the brigade quartered at Chatham, under Brigadier-General Henry Campbell, composed of the first battalions of the Coldstream and Third Guards, marched to Ramsgate,

Dec. 27-30. where they went on board. During the night they anchored in the Downs, and proceeded next morning with

---

[1] January 16th, 1809.

other troops for Spithead. Major-General Sherbrooke was appointed to the command.[1]

1809.
Jan. 1st.

The fleet sailed on the fifteenth of January, and encountered a series of contrary and tempestuous winds. On the thirtieth the ships were dispersed in a tremendous gale, when most of the transports took shelter in the Cove of Cork. The expedition sailed again on the twenty-fifth of February, and proceeded direct for Cadiz, in the hope of securing that important sea-port. The Supreme Junta, however, refused the troops admittance, stating as an excuse, that the confidence of the Spaniards in their allies was at an end. General Sherbrooke perceiving that further negociation would only be attended with loss of time,[2] proceeded for the Tagus, and the defence of Portugal then became the primary object of Great Britain.

March.

---

[1] Force which sailed under Major-General Sherbrooke:

	Lt.-Col.	Capt.	Sub.	Staff.	Rk. & File.	Wom.	Commanded.
1st Bat. Colds. Gds.	7	7	14	5	1120	17	Lt.-Col. Hulse
1st Bat. 3d Guards	7	14	16	3	1361	19	Col. Hon. E. Stopford
	14	21	30	8	2481	36	Brig.-Gen. Campbell
	Major.						
87th Foot	2	6	23	6	791	15	Major Gough
88th Foot	2	8	25	6	842	22	Lt.-Col. Duff
	4	14	48	12	1633	37	Major-Gen. Tilson
Total	14 5	34	78	20	4114	73	

Lt.-Col. Lord Aylmer, Dy.-Adj. General.
Col. Burke, Dy.-Qr. Mas.-General.
Mr. Boys, Pay-Master-General.
Dr. Somers, Principal Medical Officer.

[2] During the night of the ninth of March the Prince George transport, head-quarter ship of the Coldstream Guards, ran down an American brig, the crew of which, with the exception of one man, was saved; when the Isis, of fifty guns, coming to their assistance, got foul of the Prince George, whose mizen-mast was carried away; and it being supposed the transport must sink, the Captain and forty men got on board the Isis. Unfortunately Ensign Edward Noel Long, one drummer, and one private, were lost.

1809.   Major-General Beresford was appointed Commander-in-Chief of the Portuguese levies, with the rank of Marshal in their service. He was perfectly qualified for the situation, and employed himself with the greatest zeal and activity in re-modelling the Portuguese army, which, previous to his command, had been in the lowest state of degradation. This General introduced subordination, and convinced them of the advantages arising from discipline. English officers were placed in command of regiments, and a regular organization established.

Mar. 13th. Nine companies of the first battalion of the Coldstream, after landing, occupied the barracks at Belem, and on the twenty-second marched to Saccavem, where they remained till April.[1]

April.   The British force in Portugal, under the command of Lieutenant-General Sir J. Cradock, amounted to about eighteen thousand men, besides twenty thousand native troops taken into British pay. In addition to these, fresh levies were raised in all parts, and the inhabitants now looked forward with confidence to the successful defence of their country.

Soult had crossed the Minho on the twenty-seventh of February, and shortly after completely defeated the Spaniards under the Marquis de la Romana, near Monterry. The French Marshal after this exploit crossed the Minho, and marched on Oporto,[2] which was carried by

---

[1] The light company of the Coldstream had been driven into the Waterford River by the gales which occurred at the end of January; from Waterford they proceeded to the Cove of Cork, and joined the expedition under Major-General Hill, and only landed at Belem (under the command of Lieut.-Colonel Fuller) on the sixth of April: they marched next day for the purpose of joining the first battalion.

[2] The French bulletins announced Soult's army would reach

assault,[1] although defended by a force of twenty thousand irregular troops, and a line of works extending from the Douro to the sea, on which were mounted two hundred guns. At the capture of this place a dreadful scene of carnage ensued.

The Portuguese General Silveira retook Chaves,[2] and also rendered an essential service in cutting off Soult's communication with Spain, and securing the bridge of Amarante.

The Guards marched from Saccavem, through Batalha, to Lyria, where Sir John Cradock resigned the command of the army to Sir Arthur Wellesley, who arrived at Lisbon on the twenty-second of April.

" Adjutant-General's Office,
" Lisbon, 27th April, 1809.

" GENERAL ORDER,

" His Majesty has been pleased to appoint Lieutenant-
" General Sir Arthur Wellesley, K.B. to be Commander
" of his Forces in Portugal; and his Excellency having
" arrived in this country to assume the command, all re-
" ports, applications, &c. are henceforward to be ad-
" dressed to him through the usual channels.

" His Excellency having appointed the following officers
" to be his Aides-de-Camp, they are to be obeyed ac-
" cordingly."

Oporto on the twentieth of March, and arrive at Lisbon by the end of the month.

[1] Capturing nearly fifteen hundred prisoners.

[2] March 29th. The Portuguese are said to have lost ten thousand.

1809. Lieut.-Col. Bathurst, 60th Foot, Military Secretary.

Captain the Hon. Fitzroy Stanhope, 1st Guards,
  „ Lord Fitzroy Somerset, 43d Foot,
  „ Henry Bouverie, Cold^m Guards,
  „ George Canning, 3d Guards,
} Aides-de-Camp.

STAFF OF THE FORCES IN PORTUGAL.

Lieut.-Gen. Sir Arthur Wellesley, K.B. Commander of the Forces.

Major-Gen. Sherbrooke,
  „ Payne,
  „ Lord W. Bentinck
  „ Paget,
} With the local rank of Lieut.-Generals in Portugal during the continuance of this service.

Major-Gen. Cotton.
  „ Hill.
  „ Murray.
Brig.-Gen. A. Campbell.
  „ H. Campbell.
  „ R. Stewart.
  „ A. Cameron.

Major-Gen. Erskine.
  „ McKenzie.
  „ Tilson.
Brig.-Gen. H. Fane.
  „ Drieberg.
  „ Langworth.

Colonel Donkin, Colonel on the Staff.

ADJUTANT GENERAL'S DEPARTMENT.

Brigadier-Genl. the Hon. Charles Stewart, Adjutant-General.

Lieut.-Col. Darrock, 36th Regiment,
  „ „ Lord Aylmer, Cold^m. Guards,
Bt.-Lt.-Col. Hinuber, 68th Foot,
Lt.-Col. John Elley, R. Reg^t. Horse Guards,
Major F. S. Tidy, 14th Foot,
Bt.-Major Williamson, 30th do.
Major Geo. Berkeley, 35th do.
Major Colin Campbell, 70th do.
} Assis^t.-Adjutant-Generals.

Captain Willoughby Cotton, 3rd Guards,
  „ John Elliott, 48th Foot,
  „ Charles Dashwood, 3rd Guards,
  „ Francis Cockburn, 60th Foot,
  „ Vernon Graham, 26th do.
  „ Henry Mellish, 87th do.
} Deputy-Ass^t.-Adj^t.-Generals.

Lieut. George During, 1st Battⁿ K. G. L. is attached to this Department until further orders.

THE COLDSTREAM GUARDS.

QUARTER-MASTER-GENERAL'S DEPARTMENT. 1809.

Colonel George Murray, 3rd Guards, Quarter-Master-General.

Lieut.-Colonel Wm. Delancey, Perm. Staff,
,, ,, James Bathurst, 60th Foot,
,, ,, R. Bourke, Perm. Staff,
Major George de Blaquiere, do.
,, Augustus Northey, do.
} Assistant-Quarter-Master-Generals.

Captain Matthew Sutton, 97th Foot,
,, Algernon Langton, 61st do.
,, Dawson Kelly, 27th do.
,, J. Haverfield, 48th do.
,, George Scovell, 57th do.
,, Robert Waller, 103rd do.
,, William Beresford, 8th Gn. Bn.
} Deputy-Ass^t.-Quarter-Master-Generals.

MEDICAL DEPARTMENT.

A. Thompson, Inspector of Hospitals.

——— Bolton, Deputy Inspector of Hospitals.

C. Larchin
E. Somers
} Physicians { ——— Buchan.

J. F. Nicholay
——— Morrel
J. Forbes
L. Kraziesur
} Staff Surgeons {
A. Bole
S. Higgins
H. Irwin
J. Cooke.

William Williams
William Graham
} Apothecaries.

R. Matthews, Acting Apothecary.
W. H. O'Reily, Deputy Purveyor.
24 Hospital Mates.

COMMISSARIAT DEPARTMENT.

John Murray, Esq. Commissary-General.
Charles Dalrymple, Deputy-Commissary-General.

Rawlings
Boys
Dunmore
} Acting Deputy-Commissary-General.

Honeyman
O'Meara
Pratt
Murray
Gauntlett
} Assistant Commissary {
Young
Dillon
Grieve
Aylmer
McKenzie.

1809.

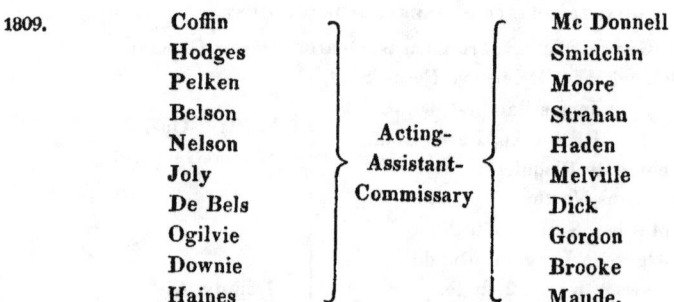

Previous to this time Marshals Soult and Victor had agreed to proceed to Lisbon, the former by Coimbra, the latter by Abrantes; but this plan was not carried into execution.

May.   The brigade of Guards marched into Coimbra on the first of May, where they were received with shouts of joy; the balconies were filled with females; embroidered and damask cloths, as is customary in Catholic countries on great festivals, were suspended from the windows; sweetmeats, sugar-plums, and orange flowers, were showered on the soldiers in great profusion during their passage through the town: in the evening the city was illuminated.

Colonel Trant was stationed in front, holding the line of the Vouga with two thousand irregular troops, of which three hundred were students from the University. This position he kept against the enemy until the advance of the British on the tenth.

CHAPTER VII.

Wellesley arrives at Coimbra—Reviews the army—Advances—Attacks Oporto—Critical position of Soult's army—Rear-guard overtaken at Salamonde—Coldstream halt at Scavessa de Rio—Termination of the pursuit—Army returns to Oporto—Marches through Coimbra, Thomar, and concentrates at Abrantes—Stations of the corps under Victor, Sebastiani, Soult, and Mortier—Allies move on Placentia, form a junction with the Spaniards at Oropesa, and advance to Talavera de la Reyna—Troops suffer greatly from the want of provisions—Cuesta moves to St. Olalla, attacked, and retreats in disorder — Battle of Talavera — Light brigade arrives under Crauford—Soult forces the passes between Salamanca and Placentia — Wellesley returns to Oropesa —Cuesta quits the position at Talavera, and abandons the sick and wounded of the allied army — Two thousand sick and wounded soldiers proceed to Elvas—Allies cross the Tagus at Arzobispo—Spaniards left to defend the bridge—Surprised, and retreat with the loss of thirty guns and baggage — Cuesta retires to Deleytosa—Allies fall back to Zaraicejo—Brigade of Guards at Badajoz — General Order — War declared between France and Austria—Flank companies of second battalion embark for Flushing—British army crosses the Tagus—Brigade of Guards march to Vizeu—Hill's corps in the vicinity of Abrantes.

SIR ARTHUR WELLESLEY arrived on the second of May at Coimbra, and advanced against Oporto after reviewing his army, which consisted of twenty-five thousand

1809.
May 6th.

1809. men, including three thousand Germans and nine thousand Portuguese.

Beresford was ordered with the Portuguese to intercept Soult if he should attempt to retreat by Amarante. General Hill with his division embarked on the ninth at Aveiro to turn the enemy's right. The rest of the army under Sir Arthur moved by the direct road to Oporto. On the eleventh the French were dislodged from a range of hills on which they were strongly posted at Grijon. They retreated and entered Oporto during the night, after which the bridge of boats was removed, being the only bridge over the Douro at that place.

May 12th. Soon after seven A.M. on the twelfth the British marched through Villa Nova, and halted on the heights opposite Oporto, which was effected without their columns being exposed to view. The enemy had neglected to guard the river above the town, not expecting any attempt would be made in that direction. After a few boats were collected higher up, at a bend in the Douro, out of sight of the enemy's piquets, Major-General Paget crossed with the Buffs, and was followed by the rest of Major-General Hill's brigade. They took possession of a building which was maintained in spite of every effort of the French to dislodge them; here General Paget lost his arm. Several guns were planted near the convent of Sarea in Villa Nova to support the attack. Major-General Murray with his brigade and some cavalry crossed at Barca d'Avintas, a few miles higher up. The Guards then advanced to the water-side through Villa Nova, where the river was upwards of three hundred yards broad, very deep, and extremely rapid. They crossed at two o'clock P.M. in boats at the spot where the bridge, prior to its removal, had been placed;[1] and, on landing, were immediately sent in pursuit. They charged the right of the French, and drove them through the principal streets, taking many prisoners and baggage. The enemy's left was endangered by the appearance of the brigade under Major-General Murray. The rest of the British crossed as quickly as the boats could convey them. The Guards, while driving the French through the streets, were every where received by the inhabitants in the same manner as at Coimbra. Amidst the conflict the soldiers were encouraged with enthusiastic cheers; " Viva os Inglezes," " Viva Grand Britania," " Viva O Grand Wellington," resounded on all sides. Hogsheads of wine were brought into the streets and given to the troops, and blessings were universally bestowed by the inhabitants on the brave English who had so gallantly relieved them from their cruel oppressors.

Soult's loss must have been very considerable: his army left the place in complete disorder: they were undoubtedly surprised, and, according to the statements of the inhabitants, had thought themselves perfectly secure.

The passage of the Douro was one of the most gallant and brilliant exploits that had taken place for a series of years. The English General crossed this broad and rapid river at mid-day, with only a few boats, in the face of an active and skilful enemy. Although the city of Oporto was defended by one of the ablest Marshals of France, commanding troops unused to defeat, this victory was achieved with a loss on the part of the British not exceeding one hundred and twenty-five killed and wounded.

---

[1] The light infantry of the Coldstream were the first that passed over to the town.

1809.
May 12th.

When the pursuit was over the brigade of Guards returned to Oporto, and were quartered in the Rue d'Almeida.

After congratulating the army on their success, Sir Arthur Wellesley thus alludes to the conduct of the Guards in the General Order.

" Oporto, 12 May, 1809. — The timely passage of the
" Douro, and subsequent movement on the enemy's
" flank by Lieutenant-General Sherbrooke with the bri-
" gade of Guards and 29th regiment, and the bravery of
" the two squadrons of the 14th Light Dragoons under
" the command of Major Harvey, and led by Brigadier-
" General Charles Stewart, obtained the victory which
" has contributed so much to the honour of the troops on
" this day."

The situation of Soult's army was critical; having learnt at Penafiel that Beresford had obliged Loison to quit the ground he occupied on the Tamega, Soult determined to march on Guimaraens; to effect which he abandoned his guns, ammunition, military chest, baggage, and took to the paths across the mountains, leaving Braga[1] on the left. By this manœuvre he gained a day in advance.

Sir Arthur left Oporto on the fourteenth, and arrived at Braga next day, where the troops were received with the same enthusiasm as at Coimbra and Oporto. On the sixteenth the British moved from Braga, and came on the rear-guard of the French army, which was strongly

---

[1] This fine city had been plundered, and every thing valuable or ornamental had been destroyed. The retreat of the French was every where marked by burning villages, and inconceivable wretchedness of the inhabitants.

posted at Salamonde. The enemy's right was protected by a deep ravine; the road as far as the village was exposed to the fire of their position: their left was covered by an extremely high hill. Two companies of the Coldstream under Colonel Henry Mac Kinnon crowned the height, for the purpose of turning the enemy's left: on their appearance the brigade of Guards was ordered to advance. This attack was led by the light companies of the Coldstream and Third Guards, with the Sixtieth rifles, under the command of Lieutenant-Colonel Fuller of the Coldstream. After firing a volley the enemy fled in great confusion. Two or three guns were brought to bear on the bridge of Ponte Nova, over which they endeavoured to escape, though not in the direct road of retreat; and at this spot great numbers were killed, many were crushed, others fell over the bridge, which had no parapet, and were drowned.

1809. May.

Sir Arthur Wellesley, in his dispatch, dated Monte Alegre, May the eighteenth, 1809, says, " The brigade of " Guards were at the head of the column, and set a lau- " dable example; and in the affair with the enemy's rear- " guard on the evening of the sixteenth they conducted " themselves remarkably well."

The French continued their retreat, and on the eighteenth the Coldstream crossed the bridge at Ruvaens, and halted, after a long march, at Scavessa de Rio, in the Sierra Gerres, where they remained the next day, and the pursuit terminated.

The British returned through Braga to Oporto, which they reached on the twenty-fourth. This town they left on the twenty-eighth, and arrived at Coimbra on the third of June; they then continued their route through Lyria and Thomar to Abrantes, near which place the army was concentrated.

June.

1809.
June.

The arrangements of the army were as follows on quitting Abrantes:

CAVALRY.	COMMANDING OFFICERS.		
3d Dragoon Guards,	Sir Granby Calcraft	} Brig.-Gen. Fane	} Lt.-Gen. Payne.
4th Dragoons,	Lord Ed. Somerset		
14th Lt. Dragoons,	Lt.-Col. Hawker	} Maj.-Gen. Cotton	
16th do.	Maj.-Hon. L. Stanhope		
23d do.	Col. Seymour	} Maj.-Gen. Erskine	
1st do. K. G. Leg.	Baron Alten		

Artillery	{ Col. Robe „ Framingham }	Maj.-Gen. Howarth.

1st batt. Coldst. Gds.	Lt.-Col. Hulse	} Brig.-Gen. Campbell	} 1st Division, Maj.-Gen. Sherbrooke.
1st batt. 3d Gds.	Col. Hon. E. Stopford		
40th regiment		} Brig.-Gen. Cameron	
83d do.	Lt.-Col. Gordon		
60th, one company			
1st reg. K. G. Legion,	Major Bodecker	} Brig.-Gen. Langworth	
2d do. do.			
Light inf. five comps.			
5th reg. K. G. Legion,	Major Gerber	} Brig.-Gen. Lowe	
7th do. do.	Major Berger		
Light inf. five comps.			
3d reg. Buffs,	Lt.-Col. Muter	} Brig.-Gen. Tilson	} 2d Division, Maj.-Gen. Hill.
66th do. 2d batt.	Capt. Kelley		
60th, one company			
1st batt. detachments,	Lt.-Col. Bunbury	} Brig.-Gen. R. Stewart	
29th reg.	„ White		
45th reg. 1st batt.	Lt.-Col. Guard	} Maj.-Gen. McKenzie	} 3d Division.
24th do.	Col. Drummond		
60th, one company		} Colonel Donkin	
87th, 2d batt.	Major Rose		
88th, 1st batt.	Major Vandeleur		

				1809. June.
7th reg. 2d batt. 53d do. do. 60th, one company	Sir Wm. Myers	} Brig.-Gen. Campbell	} 4th Division	
2d batt. detachments, 97th reg. ,, 60th, one company	Lt.-Col. Copson Lt.-Col. Lyon	} Brig.-Gen. Anson		

STAFF.

Major-General Sherbrooke
,, ,, Payne
,, ,, Lord Wm. Bentinck
,, ,, ,, Paget

} Local rank of Lieutenant-Generals.

Major-Gen. Cotton.   Brig.-Gen. A. Campbell.
,, Hill.   ,, H. Campbell.
,, Erskine.   ,, R. Stewart.
,, McKenzie.   ,, Cameron.
,, Tilson.   ,, Fane.
                ,, Anson.
                ,, Langworth, K. G. L.
                ,, Lowe, K. G. L.

Col. Donkin on the Staff.
Adj^t-Genl Hon. C. Stewart.
Q^r-Master-Genl Col. George Murray.

The Ninety-fifth, Fifty-second, and Forty-third regiments, under General Crauford, from England, and the Forty-eighth and Sixty-first regiments from Gibraltar, were at Lisbon on their way to join the army. Sir Arthur Wellesley now determined to commence operations in Spain.[1]

---

[1] The British troops under Sir Arthur Wellesley amounted to about nineteen thousand infantry and one thousand five hundred cavalry. Romana with fifteen thousand men was in Gallicia; and Blake with about twenty thousand was in Valencia; Beresford, with twelve thousand Portuguese and ten thousand Spaniards, under the Duke del Parque, was to watch Soult; and the pass of

1809. The French under Victor, amounting to upwards of twenty thousand men, were on the Tagus: Sebastiani's corps, not quite so numerous, were in La Mancha: several thousand men were quartered in and about Madrid. Marshals Soult, Ney, and Mortier, with a large force, were in Old Castile, Gallicia, and Leon: besides which there were a division of cavalry, and forty thousand men stationed in Arragon, Catalonia, and the adjacent country.

June 27th. The allies marched from Abrantes, by Salvatierra,
July 12th. on Placentia. They left Placentia on the seventeenth of July, formed a junction with General Cuesta's army at Oropesa, and moved in two columns on Talavera de la Reyna; from whence Marshal Victor, after making a slight resistance, retired across the Alberche.

The most positive assurances had been given by the Spanish Government to Sir Arthur Wellesley that his army should be regularly supplied with provisions and means of transport during his advance; but, either from neglect on the part of the proper authorities, or from the exhausted state of the country, these promises were not fulfilled. In consequence the troops underwent great privations.[1] Sir Arthur refused to move, and even threatened to return to Portugal if the rations and means of conveyance so frequently demanded and promised were not forthcoming.

The Spanish General Cuesta advanced to Santa Olalla: he was there attacked, and retreated in great disorder to the Alberche, where his troops joined the British. The

---

Banos was to be guarded to prevent Soult's advancing to Placentia.

[1] An officer of the Coldstream gave a dollar for a small loaf on the day preceding the battle of Talavera.

position of the Allies occupied nearly two miles. The
Spaniards were strongly posted on the right in front of
Talavera, extending to the Tagus; here they were sheltered
from the fire of the French guns, and the space was in-
tersected with ditches, mud enclosures, olive trees, and
vineyards. The centre of the line was more open. The
left was on a lofty ascent, and a ravine ran along the
front. The communication from the hill with the rest of
the English line was of easy and gradual descent. This
height was at first occupied only by Colonel Donkin's
brigade, who, being unable to defend so large a space, had
his left turned: he was reinforced by General Hill, when
the enemy were driven from the summit. Soon after dark
an attempt was made to dislodge the German Legion,
which however maintained its ground. About the same
time a fire commenced from the left of the British line,
which was taken up by the Guards, and partially went
down the brigade: from this unfortunate occurrence,
Lieutenant-Colonel Ross, Captain Bryan, and two men
were killed. In this conflict the British loss amounted to
eight hundred; that of the French was estimated at one
thousand.

<small>1809. July 27th.</small>

At day-light two strong columns, supported by a third, <small>July 28th.</small>
under a discharge of artillery, advanced against the left of
the British position. This attack was conducted with great
order; the French moved on at a quick pace, crossed the
ravine, and mounted the ascent, where they were received
by the brigades of Tilson and Richard Stewart. A destructive fire of musketry was well kept up on both sides;
but the assailants were at length thrown into disorder,
and retired to their original ground. During the attack General Hill, who commanded on the left, was
wounded.

The roll of the French drums was distinctly heard at one

1809.
July 28th.

o'clock, and the enemy were again seen in motion through clouds of dust. About two the French light troops advanced; four dense columns followed them, covered by eighty guns. The English, notwithstanding the heavy loss they sustained from the cannonade, patiently reserved their fire till the near approach of the enemy.

General Sebastiani almost reached the redoubt on the right of the British; but the troops commanded by Brigadier-General Alexander Campbell, with two Spanish battalions, drove them back with great slaughter, taking thirteen pieces of cannon.

On the left, Brigadier-General Anson with the Twenty-third, and First German hussars, was ordered to charge the head of Villatte's column. When at the gallop, the brigade was suddenly checked by a deep ravine. The Twenty-third light dragoons, in defiance of the fire from the squares, dashed heedlessly on, passed between the divisions of Ruffin and Villatte, and charged a brigade of chasseurs. A body of cavalry sent by Marshal Victor coming up, the regiment was surrounded, broken, and nearly annihilated.

The centre, occupied by Sherbrooke's division, on the approach of the column under Lapisse was in readiness to charge. The French advanced with great resolution under the protection of their numerous artillery. They were received with calm intrepidity by the first division, who discharged a volley, and rushed on them with irresistible impetuosity. The brigade of Guards pursued the enemy so far as to expose itself to be attacked by the reserve columns, and taken in flank by the fire of the artillery. The French cavalry also advanced, and the brigade suffered very severely: about six hundred in a few minutes were killed and wounded, and its entire destruction appeared inevitable. The first battalion of the Forty-eighth regiment,[1] and Major-General Cotton's cavalry, were ordered to their support, when the Guards rallied, and again heroically advanced with renewed huzzas to the aid of the gallant Forty-eighth. These cheers were echoed along the whole of the British line! It was the shout of triumph! The French were beaten; and although some skirmishing was kept up by the light troops, and occasionally a heavy cannonade, they retired to their original position.[2]

1809.
July 28th.

In the evening of the twenty-eighth the grass, which was very long and dry, ignited, and the fire spread with such rapidity, that several of the wounded were burnt to death. During the night the men lay on their arms, and suffered greatly from the want of provisions. Next morning a rear guard of cavalry was all that was visible of the French army.

July 29th.

---

[1] "Commanded by two gallant officers, Lieutenant-Colonel Donelan and Major Middlemore, the latter taking the command when the former fell."

[2] The British lost about five thousand three hundred and sixty-seven men, amongst whom were Major-Generals McKenzie and Langworth. The loss of the French may be calculated at between eight and ten thousand. The loss of the Spaniards, according to their own statement, was twelve hundred. Seventeen guns were captured by the English.

List of officers of the Coldstream Guards killed and wounded at Talavera, 27th and 28th July, 1809:

Lieutenant-Colonel Ross, Captain Beckett, and Ensign Parker, killed: Lieutenant-Colonels Stibbert, Sir W. Sheridan, Captains Bouverie, Collier, Milman, Christie, Wood, Jenkinson, Bryan, and Ensign Sandilands, wounded.

Captains Jenkinson and Bryan (Adjutant) died of wounds.

Killed { 3 officers / 33 rank and file

Wounded { 10 officers / 11 serjeants / 1 drummer / 241 rank and file.

1809.
July.

The following appeared in General Orders, dated Talavera de la Reyna, July twenty-ninth, 1809.

" The charge made by the brigade of Guards under the " command of Brigadier-General Henry Campbell, on the " enemy's attacking column, was a most gallant one."

The light brigade, consisting of a troop of horse-artillery, the Forty-third, Fifty-second, and Ninety-fifth rifles, under Major-General Robert Crauford, joined, after marching sixty-two miles in twenty-six hours in the hottest weather, leaving only seventeen stragglers on the road.

Soult having forced the strong passes between Salamanca and Placentia, Sir Arthur Wellesley resolved that
Aug. 3rd. the British army should immediately march to Oropesa, leaving the Spanish General Cuesta to remain in position at Talavera.

Notwithstanding this arrangement, Cuesta left his position without the knowledge of Sir Arthur Wellesley, and joined him with his army at day-light on the fourth, having marched all night. In so doing Cuesta abandoned the sick and wounded of the British army, amounting to five thousand men, who had been left at Talavera under the command of Colonel Henry Mac Kinnon of the Coldstream Guards. As Marshal Victor was only a few leagues distant, Colonel Mac Kinnon had received instructions in case of necessity to make the best of his way to Merida by the bridge of Arzobispo. When he saw Cuesta marching away, he applied to that General for transport, and it was with great difficulty he could procure half a dozen bullock cars. Colonel H. Mac Kinnon, who wrote and spoke the French language remarkably well, obtained for those unfortunate men, whom there was no possibility of removing, the most humane and honourable treatment.[1] After pa-

---

[1] Marshal Victor arrived at Talavera on the seventh. His ad-

rading all those that were able to move, at three o'clock in the afternoon of the third he set out on his march to Calera. The following day he joined the British at Arzobispo, and forty more cars were added to his means of transport; but these were in so bad a state, that having to cross the worst roads in the world, only eleven of them reached Deleytosa. Colonel H. MacKinnon nevertheless marched about two thousand sick and wounded soldiers from Talavera to Elvas, a distance of fifty-one leagues, without any assistance from the local authorities, and with only one commissary's clerk to furnish them with food. During his march, the inhabitants frequently evinced feelings of hostility, and he was compelled to resort to coercive measures to preserve his men from starvation.[1]

Sir Arthur Wellesley crossed the Tagus at Arzobispo; Cuesta followed, leaving the Duke del Albuquerque with a considerable force to defend the bridge, and withdrawing the remainder of his army to Paraleda de Garben. The French having succeeded in fording the river, not more than two hundred yards above the bridge, surprised the Spaniards, and took their works in rear. On this occasion Albuquerque charged with great determination; but fresh troops came up, which obliged the Spaniards to retreat, with the loss of thirty guns, ammunition, and baggage. Cuesta retired to Deleytosa, and the British fell back from that place to Zaraicejo.

1809.

Aug. 4th.

---

vance (Fifth chasseurs) took possession of Talavera on the sixth. The following officers of the Coldstream were taken prisoners:— Lieutenant-Colonel Sir William Sheridan, Captains Christie, Milman, and Bryan; Ensign Sandilands, and Assistant-Surgeon Whymper.

[1] The wounded taken prisoners in the hospitals of Talavera were six lieutenant-colonels, three majors, sixteen captains, thirty-two lieutenants, eleven ensigns, two thousand rank and file; all in charge of one staff-surgeon and twenty-one assistant-surgeons.

1809.
August.

It was found impossible to supply the troops with provisions; and as all concert between Cuesta and Sir Arthur was at an end, the latter resolved to establish his head-quarters at Badajoz.

The brigade of Guards reached Merida on the twenty-fourth of August, and remained there till the beginning of September; they afterwards marched towards Talavera

Sept. 3rd. Real. Whilst they were in this neighbourhood huts were constructed to protect the men from the heat, which was excessive. The brigade entered Badajoz on the tenth of October.

General Order, dated Badajoz, September 24, 1809.

" The Commander of the Forces deems it but justice to
" the two battalions of Guards to state, that their returns
" have in every respect been as accurate as the conduct of
" those excellent corps has been regular and exemplary
" in every other respect."

War had been declared on the sixth of April between France and Austria. Napoleon quitted Paris in that month to take the field. Marshal Davoust was with a French corps at Ratisbon, Massena at Ulm, Oudinot at Augsburg. Head-quarters at Strasburg.

The Bavarians, under Le Fevre, Generals Roy and Wrede, were at Munich, Landshut, and Staubing. A division of Wirtemburgers was at Hydenheim. The Saxons were encamped at Dresden, and Poniatowski's corps was under the walls of Warsaw.

Napoleon gained the battle of Abensberg on the twentieth, where he overthrew two corps commanded by the Archduke Lewis and General Hillier; the day after, he gained another victory at Landshut. On the twenty-second he attacked the Archduke Charles at Eckmuhl, and forced the latter to retire behind the Danube with great loss.[1]

To create a diversion in favour of Austria, a formidable expedition was prepared by England for invading the French dominions. About the end of July forty thousand men were collected: a fleet of thirty-nine sail of the line, with thirty-six frigates, besides a vast number of gunboats, bomb-vessels, and other small craft, was fitted out. The object of this armament was the occupation of Flushing, and the destruction of the French ships, arsenals, and dock-yards at Antwerp. The command of the expedition was entrusted to Lord Chatham. The fleet was under Sir Richard Strachan, and sailed in two divisions for the island of Walcheren on the twenty-eighth and twenty-ninth of July.

The flank companies[2] of the second battalion of the

---

[1] The Austrians lost about two thousand prisoners, with part of their artillery. According to the French accounts, forty thousand were taken prisoners, besides one hundred pieces of cannon.

[2] Return of the Grenadier and Light Infantry companies of the Coldstream, forming part of the Grenadier and Light Infantry battalions on service at Walcheren:—

The five companies forming the Grenadier battalion, commanded by Lieut-Colonel P. Cocks, consisted of 5 captains and lieut.-colonels, 1 lieutenant and major, 14 lieutenants and captains, 1 adjutant, 1 quarter-master, 1 surgeon, 1 assistant-surgeon, 34 serjeants, 34 corporals, 19 drummers, 542 private men.

OFFICERS OF THE COLDSTREAM.
Lieut.-Colonel George Smyth.
Captain Thomas Thoroton.
  „   Hon. Wm G. Crofton.
  „   H. Wm Vachell.
Quarter-Master B. Selway.

Strength of the Grenadier company of the Coldstream:—
6 serjeants, 4 drummers, and 120 rank and file.

Head-quarters, Fort de Batz, 24th Aug^t, 1809.

The five companies forming the Light Infantry battalion, com-

1809. Coldstream embarked at Chatham, proceeded to the Nore, and were put on board ships of war.

The troops landed on the first of August, and invested Flushing. After a bombardment by sea and land, from which the town suffered greatly, General Monnet the governor demanded a suspension of hostilities, which terminated in the surrender of the town: the garrison, amounting to nearly six thousand men, were made prisoners of war.[1] The force opposed to the British on the island rather exceeded nine thousand men.

Lord Chatham, whose army, long detained among unwholesome marches, began to suffer severely from fever, having ascertained that the enemy had availed themselves of the slowness of his proceedings to improve their means of defence, relinquished his intention of attacking Antwerp, and the greater part of the troops in consequence re-embarked on the fourteenth of September for England.

When Cromwell had achieved one of his greatest victories, he called it his "crowning mercy." The attempt

---

manded by Lieut.-Colonel John Lambert, consisted of 5 captains and lieut.-colonels, 13 lieutenants and captains, 1 adjutant, 1 quarter-master, 1 surgeon, 1 assistant-surgeon, 35 serjeants, 35 corporals, 10 buglers, 545 private men.

OFFICERS OF THE COLDSTREAM.
Lieut.-Colonel Thomas Braddyll.
Captain Thomas Barrow.
,, Newton Dickenson.
,, Lord Alvanley.
Assistant-Surgeon John Crake.

Strength of the Light Infantry company of the Coldstream :—7 serjeants, 2 buglers, and 121 rank and file.

Head-quarters, Reyland, 24th Aug^t, 1809.

[1] The London Gazette of Tuesday, August 22nd, states that the garrison of Flushing amounted to 200 officers, 4985 rank and file, and 618 sick.

against Antwerp, better known as the Walcheren expedition from having got no further, may be termed by England her "crowning absurdity," whether the magnitude and expense of the preparations are considered, or the original conception of the plan those splendid preparations were expected to realise. All former disastrous and ill-considered debarkations on the enemy's coast are thrown into shade when compared with this memorable scheme for surprising an important fortress belonging to the most powerful monarch and most active warrior of the period; care being first taken to give him due notice of the approaching surprise by the preparatory siege of Flushing. After lingering for weeks together in the pestilent islands of the Scheld, the English General, to his apparent astonishment, discovered that Napoleon, whose resources and energy were known to the whole world, had contrived in the interval to render a coup-de-main on Antwerp altogether impracticable. Much has been said of the inefficiency of the British commander on that occasion; and it was strongly urged by the opponents of the then existing administration, that an officer should not have been selected whose habitual dilatoriness had previously acquired for him the appellation of "the late" Lord Chatham. But as his inglorious return was not attended with any personal consequences, there is reason to suppose that the fault rested elsewhere, and that the General's course had been marked out for him before he left England. Tardiness of movement is at all times a very questionable evidence of military talent; but in the case of a coup-de-main, the application of the maxim "slow and sure" can only mean, sure not to succeed. The sufferings of the troops, and the cost to the country of twenty millions sterling, are yet remembered with indignant sorrow: it is to be hoped that future British Cabinets will at length learn from so many repeated lessons, that although such enterprises may

1809. succeed against detached islands cut off from all assistance, they cannot with prudence be adventured on the Continent, with the inadequate force that a maritime power can suddenly and secretly convey on ship-board to the territories of a powerful enemy, whose troops may in a few hours be collected from every quarter in overwhelming numbers. Although Napoleon had carried with him to the open field his strongest and most disciplined soldiers, it was pure infatuation to suppose that he had not left in France thousands who were fully competent for garrison duty; or that, having left them, they should be so placed as not to be within reach of his most important fortresses. Nothing happened which might not have been foretold, except the wonderment of the English Ministers on finding that failure is the attendant of folly. Walcheren was retained till the twenty-third of December, when it was evacuated.

A battle was fought by the Spaniards on the nineteenth of November at Ocana, where their best troops were destroyed.[1] Napoleon considered this victory as the conclusion of the war, and exultingly exclaimed, in his speech to the Senate, " I shall show myself beyond the Pyrenees, " when the frightened Leopard will fly to the sea to avoid " shame, defeat, and death: my Imperial Eagles shall be " planted on the ramparts of Cadiz, and be seen on the " towers of Lisbon."

In this state of affairs Sir Arthur Wellesley, created Viscount Wellington, deemed it expedient to confine himself to the defence of Portugal: the army in consequence crossed the Tagus.

The brigade of Guards marched through Portalegre, Abrantes, Coimbra, and arrived at Vizeu on the thirtieth

---

[1] By the French account four thousand men were killed, twenty-six thousand taken prisoners, the remainder dispersed. The French admit their loss to have been one thousand seven hundred.

of December, where they were stationed.[1] This place was also fixed on as the head-quarters.

1809.

[1] Return of the officers of the 1st battalion Coldstream that embarked 31st of December, 1808, for the Peninsula.

Comps.	Captains.	Lieutenants.	Ensigns.
Gren.	Lt.-Col. John Ross	Capt. L. F. Adams ,, C. M. Christie ,, E. Jenkinson	
	,, ,, Rich. Hulse commanding the Bat.	,, Thos. Wood	Lord Kilcoursie E. N. Long
	,, ,,H. MacKinnon acting Major	[1] ,, R. Beckett	John Boswell Hon. J. Ashburnham
	Col. W. M. Peacocke	,, Hon. G. Pelham	Thomas Steele P. Sandilands
	[1] Brig.-Gen. W. P. Acland	,, Sir H. Sullivan	George Bowles Hon. F. H. Drummond
	Lt.-Col. T. Stibbert	,, F. M. Sutton	Thos. Sowerby John Prince
	,, Sir. W. Sheridan	[1] ,, H. F. Bouverie	E. Harvey Harry Parker
	,, Hon. H. Brand	[1] ,, H. F. Cooke	W. L. Walton
	,, ,, Js. Philips	,, F. M. Milman	W. Burroughs [1] E. Lascelles
Light Inf.	,, ,, Jos. Fuller	,, G. Collier ,, W. H. Raikes ,, D. MacKinnon	

Adjutant, Captain Geo. Bryan.
Quarter-Master, John Holmes.
Battalion Surgeon, Charles Coombe.
Assistant-Surgeon, Thos. Rose.
 ,, ,, Wm. Whymper.

[1] On the Staff.

The following changes had taken place in December, 1809.

Joined.

Capt. Gore, Lt. James V. Harvey, Ensigns Lockwood, Hon. John Wingfield, Mildmay, Wedderburn, and White, Ensign Freemantle, Acting Adjutant 1st battalion.

Absent.

Col. Peacocke, Commandant at Lisbon, Brig.-Gen. Acland, Staff, Lieut.-Col. Sir W. Sheridan, Capt. F. M. Milman, and Assistant-Surgeon Whymper, prisoners of war. Capt. C. M. Christie, from prisoner of war, to 2d bat. in England. Capt. Thos. Steele, Capt. Harvey, and Capt. Burroughs, to 2d bat. at home on promotion. Ensign E. N. Long, drowned 9 March, Ensign Sandilands, from prisoner of war and sick to England. Ensign Freemantle, Adjutant to 2d bat. at home, Lt.-Col. J. Ross, Capt. R. Beckett, and Ensign H. Parker, killed July, 1809. Capt. E. Jenkinson, and Capt. and Adjutant Bryan, died of their wounds. Ensign Hon. John Ashburnham, supposed to be lost on passage home in Dec.

1809. General Hill's corps was placed in and about Abrantes. The remainder of the army occupied Guarda, Celerico, Pinhel, and places in the neighbourhood. The river Cea ran along the front of the line.

The confident expectation expressed by the Emperor of France at this period, that " the Leopard would fly to the sea," was not the result of a too sanguine temperament fondly bent on giving reality to its own unfounded wishes; the anticipation was that of a skilful soldier, founding his calculations on the ordinary rules of military science, and allowing his adversary, whose future movements he sought to divine, a fair portion of courage and talent. The Spanish army was annihilated; the spirit of that people appeared crushed; and no adequate force remained in Spain to impede the successful progress of the Emperor's legions. Wellington, outnumbered by the French, retired through Portugal, a country deemed indefensible against the power of Napoleon. Every thing seemed to indicate that the Peninsula would become the prey of the invader, and that the British were making for Lisbon to repeat the embarkation of Corunna: but the mind of their General rose above the difficulties of his situation; the Leopard did not fly to the sea; he only drew back and took a more deadly spring.

CHAPTER VIII.

Wellington's communication to Colonel Stopford — Soult passes the Sierra Morena — Joseph Buonaparte enters Seville — Albuquerque barricades the bridge of Zuozo — Eleven companies of the Guards embark at Portsmouth for Cadiz — Allies collect a force at Cadiz — Wellington's head-quarters at Celerico — Army of Portugal assemble under Massena — Capture of Ciudad Rodrigo — Massena's proclamation — Ney attacks Crauford — Proclamation issued by Wellington — Massena enters Portugal — French concentrate at Vizeu — Battle of Busaco — Wellington retires to the lines of Torres Vedras — Romana joins from the Alentejo — Massena retreats — Wellington follows towards Santarem — Allies move into cantonments — Head-quarters and Guards at Cartaxo — Hill crosses the Tagus — Drouet reinforces Massena.

On the thirteenth of January the following letter appeared in Brigade Orders, directed to Colonel the Honourable Edward Stopford:

1810.
January.

"Vizeu, 13 January, 1810.

" Sir,

"I have taken frequent occasions of stating pub-
" licly the great satisfaction which the conduct of the
" Guards has invariably given me; which satisfaction has
" been renewed on the recent march through Portugal;
" in which, as they were the head of the column, they set
" the example to the other troops, of the most orderly and
" regular behaviour. I am anxious to testify this satis-
" faction in a manner which shall prove to them that the
" attention which they pay to their duty is not unob-

1810.
January.

"served by their superiors; and if the commanding
"officers of the two battalions will be so kind as to recom-
"mend a serjeant each, I will recommend them to vacant
"ensigncies in the army.

(Signed) "WELLINGTON.
" Honble Col. Stopford,
" Commanding 2ᵈ Brigade of Guards."

Jan. 20th. Soult, with little opposition, forced the passes of the Sierra Morena, which had been fortified, overthrowing twenty thousand men intended for their defence, and advanced into Andalusia. On the twenty-first of January he reached Baylen. Seven days after, Victor joined him before Seville, which place opened its gates on the thirty-first, and Joseph Buonaparte entered the city in triumph.

February. Mortier was sent into Estramadura, and Victor marched for Cadiz, which was unprepared for defence. Vanegos, the governor, was much disliked, and resigned. A Junta was then elected by ballot.

The Duke of Albuquerque, in opposition to the orders he had received to march on Cordova, hastened in this extremity with all speed to Cadiz, and by the rapidity of

Feb. 4th. his march arrived just in time to barricade the bridge of Zuozo in the Isla de Leon. The French were therefore disappointed in their expectations of entering the place.

Mar. 7th. Six companies of the First Guards,[1] two companies of the

---

[1] Return of two companies of the Second battalion of the Coldstream, at Isla de Leon, Tarifa, &c., from March 1810, to May 1811.

	Capt and Lt.-Col.	Lts. and Capts.	Ensigns.	Quarter Master.	Assist. Surg.	Serjeants.	Drumrs.	Rank and File.	Total.
Consisting of	1	3	4	1	1	12	3	224	249
Joined from England 1st and 8th April, 1811	.	.	.	.	1	1	.	42	44

THE COLDSTREAM GUARDS.

second battalion of the Coldstream, commanded by Lieutenant-Colonel Jackson, and three from the Third Guards

1810.
Mar. 7th.

		Present.		
		From	To	
Capⁿ and Lt Cl	R. D. Jackson	Mar. 1810	March, 1811	Appointed Assist.-Quar.-Mast. Gen. in Portugal in March, 1811.
Lt.& Capⁿ	J. Hamilton	,,	Remained on Staff	Appointed Deputy-Assist.-Quar.-Mast. Gen., Isla de Leon, in April, 1810
,,	W.C. Wynyard	Nov. ,,	Ditto	Joined and appointed Brig.-Major to Maj.-Gen. Dilkes in Nov. 1810. Do. to Col. Coote in May, 1811, and Dep.-Assist.-Adj-General in July, 1811, Isla de Leon.
,,	Hon. J. Walpole	March ,,	May, 1811	In command of Lt.-Col. Woodford's Company. On leave from Oct. 1810 to Jan. 1811. Left the Station 24th May, and joined the 1st Battalion.
,,	M. Fortescue	,, ,,	23 June, 1810	"Leave to proceed to England, 23rd June, retiring from the Service."
Ens.	G. H. M. Greville	,, ,,	May, 1811	Left the Station 24th May, and joined the 1st Batt.
,,	M. Watts	,, ,,	5 March	Killed at Barrosa, 5th March.
,,	C.A.F. Bentinck	,, ,,	April	Wounded at do. Leave to England.
,,	John Talbot	,, ,,	May	Wounded at Barrosa, 5th March. Embarked with the detachment for England.
As^t. Sur.	C. Herbert	,, ,,	Oct. 1810	Leave to England in Oct.: retired from the Service.
,,	W. Whymper	April, 1811	May, 1811	Joined from England 1st April, 1811, and embarked for England on 4th May.
Qu^r. Mr.	Serj. B. Selway (actg)	Mar. 1810	,, ,,	Embarked with the detachment for England on 4 May.

	Lieut. and Captain.	Ensigns.	Staff.	Serjeants.	Drums.	Rank and File.
Left the Station at Isla de Leon, 4th and 24th May, 1811	1	2	2	12	3	243
Embarked for England 4th May	.	1	2	9	3	145
Joined the 1st Battalion at camp near St. Olaia, 25th June	1	1	.	3	.	98

Alex. Woodford promoted to Captain and Lieut.-Col. to one of these Companies, dated 8th March, 1810; "on the Staff in Sicily" to May, and "doing duty in London" from June, 1810.

1810.

under Brigadier-General Dilkes, marched from London to embark at Portsmouth for Cadiz, from whence they proceeded to the Isle of Leon.

April.

A force of between five and six thousand British and Portuguese was there collected under Lieutenant-General Graham. Both sides exerted themselves in constructing fortifications. The French strengthened Rota, Puerto Real, Puerto Santa Maria, and Chiclona. They formed intrenched camps between these places and at Trocadero; and established batteries, whence they threw enormous shells half filled with lead into the town. The English restored the old works and erected new ones along the Santa Petri river; they also cut a canal across the isthmus, near the Corta Dura, between the Isla and Cadiz. The Allies were considerably augmented. Strong reinforcements also arrived for the French in Spain, who had upwards of three hundred thousand men in different parts of the Peninsula.

Towards the end of April[1] Lord Wellington moved from Vizeu to Celerico, at which place the brigade of Guards was quartered.

For some time a powerful army had been assembling, which consisted of the Second, Sixth, and Eighth corps under Marshal Massena. This was denominated " the army of Portugal."

May.

Almeida was strengthened, and hopes were entertained that it would detain the enemy some time, should Ciudad Rodrigo fall.

Massena commenced the siege of Ciudad Rodrigo in

June 15th. June, but the garrison did not capitulate till the tenth of

---

[1] The Coldstream marched on the twenty-seventh, and reached Celerico next day. Part of the regiment were quartered in the neighbouring villages.

July, after a siege of twenty-five days with open trenches. This General addressed a proclamation from Ciudad Rodrigo, in which he stated that the Emperor of the French had put under his orders an army of one hundred thousand men[1] to take possession of Portugal, and to expel the English, the pretended friends of the Portuguese, whose purposes were insidious and selfish: he added, that in opposing the Emperor they opposed their true friend, who was governed by principles of universal philanthropy; that the English had put arms into their hands which would prove instruments of annihilation to them. " Can the feeble army," he asked, " of " the British General expect to oppose the victorious " legions of the Emperor? Already a force is collected " sufficient to overwhelm your country. Snatch the mo- " ment that mercy and generosity offer! As friends you " may respect us, and be respected in return; as foes " you must dread us, and in the conflict must be sub- " dued. The choice is your own, either to meet the

1810. July.

---

[1] British, Spanish, and Portuguese Armies:

With Lord Wellington, thirty thousand; with Lieutenant-General Hill, fourteen thousand; Reserve with Major-General Leith, ten thousand. There was also in co-operation a corps of Portuguese militia consisting of ten thousand, besides ten thousand Spanish troops under Romana; making a total of seventy-four thousand.

French Army under Massena:

The Infantry of the Second, Sixth, and Eighth corps, sixty-two thousand; the Cavalry six thousand; Artillery, &c. four thousand. Besides which he was afterwards joined by two divisions of the Ninth corps under Drouet, consisting of ten thousand, as well as the remainder of the corps under General Claperede, eight thousand. A corps of thirteeen thousand, under Mortier, was in co-operation on the south of the Tagus; making a total of one hundred and three thousand.

1810.
July.

"horrors of a bloody war, and see your country de-
"solated, your villages in flames, your cities plundered;
"or to accept an honourable peace, which will obtain for
"you blessings that a vain resistance would deprive you
"of for ever."

Ney with his corps attacked General Crauford on the morning of the twenty-fourth, who was obliged to retreat behind the Coa; Crauford, however, succeeded in maintaining the bridge till evening, notwithstanding the repeated attempts made by the enemy with a very superior force.

Previous to the investment of Almeida, Wellington took the precaution to withdraw his troops from Pinhel and Trancoso to the valley of the Mondego, behind Celerico, that he might retire leisurely if Massena advanced without waiting the surrender of that fortress. Almeida was invested by Massena: the batteries of the besiegers were

August. not opened till towards the end of August, but the town unexpectedly surrendered on the twenty-seventh, owing to the explosion of the magazines in the citadel, by which calamity a great number of inhabitants and houses were destroyed.

On the fourth the following proclamation was issued by Lord Wellington:

"The Portuguese must now perceive that no other
"means remain to avoid the evils with which they are
"threatened, but a determined and vigorous resistance,
"and a firm resolution to obstruct as much as possible the
"advance of the enemy into the interior of the kingdom,
"by removing out of his reach every thing that may con-
"tribute to his subsistence, or facilitate his progress. The
"army under my command will protect as large a portion
"of the country as is possible; but it is obvious that the

"people alone can deliver themselves by a vigorous re- sistance, and preserve their goods by removing them beyond the reach of the enemy. The duties, therefore, that bind me to his Royal Highness the Prince Regent of Portugal, and to the Portuguese nation, oblige me to make use of the power and authority with which I am intrusted to compel the careless and indolent to make the necessary efforts to preserve themselves from the dangers which threaten them, and to save their country. I therefore make known and declare, that all magistrates, and persons in authority, who shall remain in the villages and towns, after having received orders from the military officers to remove from them, and all persons, of whatsoever class they may be, who shall maintain the least communication with, or aid and assist the enemy in any manner, shall be considered as traitors to the state, and tried and punished as an offence so heinous requires."

Massena's army entered Portugal in three columns, headed by Junot, Ney, and Regnier.

The Allies retreated in the finest order by the road on the left bank of the Mondego, leaving the other through Vizeu to Coimbra open.

The French army concentrated at Vizeu; but their junction was retarded by a well-planned attack made by Colonel Trant on a convoy of the enemy near Togal, within half a day's march of Vizeu. The Colonel captured two officers and one hundred men, and caused the artillery under their convoy to fall back on Trancoso, which occasioned a delay of five days to the French General, as it obliged him to wait its arrival.[1] By this occurrence

---

[1] In an intercepted dispatch Massena says, "being obliged to wait five days at Vizeu for my artillery."

1810. Wellington gained time to execute one of the most brilliant manœuvres of this brilliant campaign. At Ponte de Murcella, the day after Massena had reached Vizeu, the bridge was destroyed.

Sept. 26th. On the twenty-sixth Generals Hill and Leith joined the Allies, now in position on the heights of Busaco. The troops were ordered to conceal themselves as much as possible behind the brow of the hill. The French, placed immediately below, were distinctly seen from every part of the high ground, extending nearly eight miles from the Mondego in a northerly direction. A convent crowned the summit of Busaco, surrounded by extensive woods; this point was nearly three hundred feet high, but its elevation varied considerably in different places: two roads crossed the hill, one near the convent, the other more to the south. Sir Brent Spencer with the first division occupied the centre, on the right of which were the Guards; the Coldstream extended to Picton's division, which joined with Leith's; General Hill was on the extreme right; General Cole's division occupied the left. The light division was in advance, in front of the left and left centre. The cavalry under Sir Stapleton Cotton formed in the rear. General Fane's brigade was on the left of the Mondego.

Sept. 27th. Before day on the morning of the twenty-seventh, the British, who had been ordered on the previous evening to stand to their arms, were in readiness to receive the enemy. Ney's corps, formed in three masses, approached the convent; Junot was at some distance in the rear, and with him the greater part of the cavalry. Regnier attacked in two columns, and ascended a part of the hill, where he was opposed by the piquets and light troops of the third division, assisted by a flank fire of grape from some guns: notwithstanding this resistance he succeeded in gaining the summit in great force. The French 1810. Sept. 27th. had at first only to contend with the Eighty-eighth regiment, belonging to part of Colonel Henry MacKinnon's brigade; but it was soon after reinforced by the Forty-fifth and Eighth Portuguese regiments, also under his orders. The brigade thus united poured in a destructive fire of musketry, and furiously charged; in doing which they were joined by a brigade from Leith's division. They then drove the enemy with great impetuosity before them, who left upwards of seven hundred dead.

Marshal Ney was equally unsuccessful in his attack on the light division under Major-General Crauford, who had judiciously formed behind the hill; so that on crowning the height, Ney's column had unexpectedly to encounter the effects of the artillery and musketry, followed by a charge. His column was not only routed, but the leading regiments were totally destroyed. The loss of the British and Portuguese did not much exceed twelve hundred; that of the French, on a moderate calculation, was supposed to be about five thousand.

Animated by the example of the British officers employed under Beresford in the organization of their army, and now associated with them in the field, the Portuguese, in many respects, did honour to the character recorded of them in the historical annals of that country.

Had Massena followed Ney's advice and attacked Busaco on the twenty-fifth, there would have been more chance of success, as it was at that time only partially occupied. On the twenty-seventh the issue of the attempt was at no time doubtful. His only alternative when he failed was to retire on Spain, or to turn the position, which he might equally have done on the preceding day.

After the battle a Portuguese peasant was taken, and informed the enemy that the heights extending

1810.
Sept. 27th.

northwards from Busaco, called the Sierra de Carmula, were practicable for cavalry, and presented good roads to Coimbra and Oporto.[1] Massena then determined to turn the left of the Allied army.

Wellington intended that Colonel Trant's division of militia, consisting of about two thousand men, which from the commencement of the campaign had been employed in harassing the enemy's rear, should march to Sardaõ, a few miles distant from Busaco. But as the order was conveyed through General Barcellar, who commanded in the north, that officer conceived that the movement was for the protection of Oporto, and with that belief sent Trant round by that city. After forced marches of two hundred miles, Trant at length reached Sardaõ on the twenty-eighth, previous to the crossing of the Carmula by the French. His men, diminished by fatigue to about twelve hundred, were inadequate to resist an army headed by a numerous cavalry, marching in one column, especially as there were several passes, each of which required a more effective force than the armed peasantry under Trant to defend them. Being informed on the thirtieth that the army had evacuated Busaco, Trant took post behind the Vouga. On his retreat he was charged by the enemy's cavalry and lost some men. Massena cleared the passes without difficulty during the twenty-

---

[1] Extract from Pampalona's " Aperçu Nouveau des Campagnes en Portugal," page 153.

" Le Général La Croix, en battant la campagne sur la droite " de l'armée, ramassa un paysan qui lui indiqua la route de Bo- " yalva à Sardaõ: il s'en approcha avec précaution, et hâta d'en " instruire Massena, qui, sur ce rapport, se décida à tourner la " position de l'ennemi. C'est cette circonstance qui fit dire au " Maréchal Ney, que c'était la manœuvre du paysan; il ne quali- " fiait jamais cette manœuvre autrement."

eighth and twenty-ninth and marched for Coimbra, where he established his head-quarters on the first of October. Leaving his hospital stores, and about five thousand sick and wounded under a guard, he advanced by Condexia, in expectation of falling in with the rear of Wellington's army, which during the night withdrew from the position and fell back to the south of the Mondego. The army then retired in the finest order towards their lines by the two parallel routes of Thomar and Lyria, occasionally halting to preserve the relative connexion of the two columns: that on the Thomar road was commanded by General Hill.

<small>1810.
October.</small>

On the morning of the fifth of October Wellington continued his retreat, when the enemy advanced in great force, but were kept in check, with a trifling loss, which enabled the Allies to retire leisurely, the right by Thomar and Santarem, the centre through Batalha and Rio Mayor, and the left by Alcobaça and Obidos. The weather at this time was cold, and the rain fell in torrents. Massena continued to follow by the Rio Mayor road, and in the afternoon of the tenth drove the Allies out of the village of Sobral. On the same day the British troops were concentrated within their lines. Lord Wellington's foresight in the formation of these extensive works was worthy of his fame and extraordinary talents; they were begun and completed without attracting any particular notice. The British troops were as much surprised at finding themselves in their strongly-fortified and impregnable position, as the French commander was astonished and confounded when he saw that the further progress of his overwhelming force was effectually arrested. Next day six thousand Spaniards, under the Marquis de la Romana, joined Wellington from the Alentejo.

<small>Oct. 10th.</small>

The lines of Torres Vedras extended from the Tagus on

1810.
November.

the right, or east, to the sea on the west. General Hill's division occupied the village of Alhandra on the right, which was flanked by a number of gun-boats; Crauford's division joined their left. On the mountain which overhung Sobral, and completely commanded the great road to Lisbon, was a strong redoubt, occupied by a brigade of Portuguese commanded by General Pack. The first division under Lieutenant-General Spencer, including the brigade of Guards, was stationed in the centre. Picton's division communicated with Spencer's on the right, and with General Cole's on the left, which last carried on the line of defence to the sea.

Whilst affairs were in this state south of the Mondego, Trant, having taken up a position on the Vouga to cover Oporto after the retreat of the armies from Busaco, had resolved to surprise whatever force Massena might have left in Coimbra, and accordingly reached Mealhada in the night of the sixth of October. From thence he advanced next day to Coimbra, in front of which, at the village of Fernos, he came suddenly on one of the enemy's advanced posts. He entered the gates unobserved, and after an hour's resistance the French, to the number of five thousand, chiefly sick and wounded, surrendered. Trant's loss did not exceed twenty-five or thirty men. A company of the Imperial Marine Guards fell into his hands, with the hospital stores and medical staff of the enemy. By this movement of Trant's, Massena was left to the scanty resources of his immediate vicinity, being deprived from that time of all communication beyond his own patroles in the direction of the rivers Zezere and Mondego.

The French army suffered greatly from want of supplies and exposure to the weather. Marshal Massena, who could no longer conceal from himself the hopelessness of the task he had undertaken, after remaining inactive upwards of a month, retreated on the night of the fourteenth of November, for the purpose of taking up a line of cantonments in the vicinity of Thomar.

1810. November.

The Allied army followed the enemy towards Santarem, when the Guards passed through Alenquer and Cartaxo. Wellington made a demonstration for an attack. The Guards were to cross the causeway; but the guns not arriving, the advance was postponed until the following day. At six o'clock A.M. on the twentieth the brigade of Guards assembled at their alarm-post; but in consequence of the rain that had fallen during the night, the low country in front of the enemy's position was so flooded as to render any attempt at passing dangerous and uncertain.

On the enemy being discovered in great force, the troops were withdrawn, and the army went into cantonments. The Guards returned to Cartaxo, at which place head-quarters were established: the remainder of the army were cantoned at Alcoentre, Rio Mayor, Azembuja, Alenquer, and Villa Franca. Hill's corps crossed the Tagus, and went into quarters at Barcos, Chamusca, and Caregiro.

At the end of December General Drouet with ten thousand men reinforced Massena's army: this corps went into cantonments in and about Lyria.

December.

142   ORIGIN AND SERVICES OF

RETURN OF OFFICERS OF THE FIRST BATTALION OF THE COLDSTREAM FOR THE YEAR 1810.

	Officers present in the Peninsula.	From	To		Officers absent.	Cause of absence.	From	To
Col.	Richard Hulse	1 Jan.	Nov.	Lt.-G.	John Calcraft (1st Major)	Leave	1 Jan.	31 Dec.
,,	H. Mac Kinnon	,,	Feb.	Col.	Richard Hulse	Commanding a Brigade	Dec.	,,
Lt.-C.	Joseph Fuller	,,	June	Col.	H. Mac Kinnon	Commanding a Brigade	March	,,
,,	Thomas Stibbert	,,	31 May	,,	W. M. Peacocke	Commandant at Lisbon	1 Jan.	,,
,,	Hon. H. Brand	,,	31 Dec.	Br.-G.	Wroth P. Acland	Staff at home	,,	,,
,,	James Philips	,,	,,	Lt.-C.	Joseph Fuller	Posted to 2d Battⁿ.	June	,,
,,	Sir G. Stirling, Bart.	Feb.	,,	,,	M. Lord Aylmer	Asst. Adj^t. Genl.	1 Jan.	,,
,,	George Smyth	Oct.	,,	,,	Thomas Stibbert	Leave to England. Retired	1 June	27 June
Capt.	E. Dalling (Major)	Feb.	,,	,,	Sir W. Sheridan	Prisoner of war	1 Jan.	31 Dec.
,,	Lucius F. Adams	1 Jun.	,,	Capt.	H. F. Bouverie	Staff (Acting Mily. Secy.)	,,	—
,,	George Collier	,,	,,	,,	Henry F. Cooke	Staff (Deputy Ass^t.Adjutant General)	,,	31 Dec.
,,	Sir H. Sullivan, Bart.	,,	,,	,,	John Hamilton	Depy. Assitant Qu^r. Master Genl. Cadiz	April	,,
,,	Francis Sutton	,,	23 Nov.	,,	Francis Sutton	Sick leave to Eng^d.	24 Nov.	,,
,,	W. H. Raikes	,,	31 Dec.	,,	F. M. Milman	Prisoner of war	1 Jan.	,,
,,	Thomas Gore	,,	24 Oct.	,,	Thomas Gore	Sick leave to Eng^d.	25 Oct.	,,
,,	H. W. Vachell	Feb.	31 Dec.	,,	Thomas Wood	Leave to Eng^d. on resignation	29 Nov.	,,
,,	Thomas Wood	1 Jan.	28 Nov.	,,	Hon. G. Pelham	A. D. C. to B^r. Genl. Campbell.	1 Jan.	—
,,	Thomas Barrow	Sept.	31 Dec.	,,	Hon. W. G. Crofton	On his way to join	Dec.	—
,,	D. Mac Kinnon	1 Jan.	,,	,,	Henry Dawkins	Brig^r. Major to Hon. E. Stopford	June	31 Dec.
Ens.	George Bowles	,,	Feb.	,,	Thomas Steele	On his way to join	Dec.	,,
,,	John Boswell	,,	March	,,	George Bowles	Prom^d. in 2d Batt.	Feb.	—
,,	Hon. Francis Drummond	,,	22 July	,,	John Boswell	Ditto.	March	—
,,	Thomas Sowerby	,,	7 Sept.	,,	Hon. F. Drummond	Ditto.	23 July	,,
,,	E. Lascelles	,,	,,	,,	Thomas Sowerby	Ditto.	8 Sept.	,,
,,	John Prince	,,	April	,,	Edwd. Lascelles	Ditto.	,, ,,	,,
,,	G. F. A. Lord Kilcoursie	,,	11 Sept.	,,	P. Sandilands	Sick in England	1 Jan.	,,
,,	J. V. Harvey, (Lieut.)	,,	31 Dec.	Ens.	John Prince	Ditto. Posted to 2d Battⁿ.	April	,,
,,	W. L. Walton	,,	,,	,,	Lord Kilcoursie	Leave to England	12 Sept.	,,
,,	W. Lockwood	,,	,,	,,	Hon. J. Ashburnham	Supposed to be drowned on passage to England	Jan.	—
,,	Hon. John Wingfield	,,	,,	,,	G. H. Percival	Sick in England	,,	Sept.
,,	Paulet St. John Mildmay	,,	,,	As^t. Sur.	W. Whymper	Taken prisoner 6 Aug. 1809: Made his escape 20 Dec. 1809.	1 Jan.	25 Feb.
,,	A. Wedderburn	,,	,,			Sick leave to England	10 Nov.	31 Dec.
,,	Charles White	,,	,,	Ens.	John Mills	On his way to join	Dec.	,,
,,	Thomas Bligh	Feb.	,,					
,,	Charles Shawe	,,	,,					
,,	G. H. Percival	Oct.	,,					
,,	William Stothert	,,	,,					
,,	W. G. Baynes	Sept.	,,					
,,	John S. Cowell	Oct.	,,					
Adjut.	H. Dawkins (Capt.)	Feb.	June					
,,	J. Freemantle (Capt.)	Oct.	31 Dec.					
Q.-Mr.	John Holmes	1 Jan.	,,					
Surgⁿ.	Charles Coombe	,,	,,					
Ast. Sur.	Thomas Rose	,,	,,					
,,	W. Whymper	26 Feb.	9 Nov.					

CHAPTER IX.

Seven thousand men arrive in the Tagus—French army retreat—Houghton's brigade crosses the Tagus—Skirmish at Pombal—After an obstinate resistance Ney retreats through Condeixa and Cazal Nova to Miranda de Corvo—Enemy retire in disorder from Foz d'Aronse—French retreat from their station behind the Alva—Wellington detained from want of provisions—Massena retreats from Guarda—Enemy defeated at Sabugal—French enter Spain—Termination of the third invasion by the French—Observation on the defence of Lisbon—Position of the Allies—Guards at Almadilla and Puebla—Troops embark at Cadiz—Confederates form a junction at Tarifa—Battle of Barrosa—Beresford lays siege to Badajoz—Almeida invested—Wellington visits the troops in the Alentejo—Returns to Villa Formosa—Position of the armies—Battle of Fuentes d'Honor—Massena recalled—Ragusa succeeds in command—Brennier escapes with the garrison of Almeida—Marmont retires on Salamanca—Guards return to the places occupied before the action—First division march to Penamacor—Guards ordered back to their former stations—Soult marches to relieve Badajoz—Battle of Albuera—Blockade of Badajoz—Guards with the corps under Spencer cross the Tagus—Encamp at St. Oloia—Soult returns to Seville—Marmont advances to Salamanca—Hill's corps remains in Alentejo—Wellington recrosses the Tagus—Head-quarters at Fuente Guinaldo—Graham succeeds Spencer—Blockade of Ciudad Rodrigo—Wellington retreats on the advance of Marmont—Allies go into winter-quarters—Coldstream at Lagoisa, Valdozares, and afterwards at Pinhel—Hill surprises the post at Arroyo de Molinos.

SEVEN thousand men for the army under Wellington arrived in the Tagus on the fourth of March. 1811. March.

1811.
March.

The following General Order was issued at Cartaxo:

"Adjutant-General's Office, Cartaxo, 4 March, 1811.
"GENERAL ORDER:

"1. As the object in assembling the troops in any station to witness a punishment is to deter others from the commission of the crime for which the criminal is about to suffer, the Commander of the Forces requests that upon every occasion on which the troops are assembled for this purpose, the order may be distinctly read and explained to them, and that every man may understand the reason for which the punishment is to be inflicted.

"2. As during the two years, during which the brigade of Guards have been under the command of the Commander of the Forces, not only no soldier has been brought to trial before a general court-martial, but no one has been confined in a public guard, the Commander of the Forces desires, that the attendance of this brigade at the execution to-morrow may be dispensed with."

On the night of the fifth the French retreated, and head-quarters removed to Santarem, where the Guards were stationed.

Mar. 6th. General Houghton's brigade crossed the Tagus. The light division, followed by the rest of the army, advanced; on their approach the enemy retired from Thomar, and concentrated at Pombal. The Allied army came up with them on the evening of the eleventh, too late, however, for a general attack: the day closed with a smart skirmish, when the enemy were so vigorously driven out of the town that they had not time to blow up the bridge which had been previously mined. Massena retreated in the night; but before quitting Pombal he set it on fire.

Ney was found posted with a strong force in front of Redinha: the masses deployed, and the British moved in three lines across the plain: the enemy's rear-guard, after an obstinate resistance, hastily retired on Condeixa. 1811. Mar. 6th.

On this occasion the loss was nearly equal, not exceeding altogether four hundred men.

Massena's object was to retard the advance of the Allies, and in this he succeeded, as the positions on which his rear was generally posted required a march of several hours to turn their flank.

General Montbrun with a force of cavalry and a few guns summoned Coimbra. The place was saved by the firm reply and admirable conduct of Trant, although he had only two hundred of his Militia with him, having received orders from General Barcellar on the eleventh instant to withdraw the greater part of his force to cover Oporto. The French General, under the impression that a British detachment had landed at Figuiera to reinforce that officer, then gave up all idea of crossing the Mondego.

The enemy occupied strong ground at Condeixa, and appeared determined to continue stationary; but this short halt was only intended by Massena to give time for his baggage to precede him on the Ponte de Marcella road. This being ascertained by Lord Wellington, he resolved to frustrate the plan, and instantly despatched Picton's division, with orders to make a circuit of some miles, and turn the enemy's left. About three o'clock Picton was discovered by the French rear-guard, and his appearance occasioned great confusion among them. The enemy fired the town, and their columns fell back on Cazal Nova, at which place Ney halted in so formidable a position that it was again found necessary to turn his flank: on this being done, he fell back on another. In short, the country presented a succession of favourable positions adapted to Mar. 13th.

1811.
Mar. 14th. check pursuit, by which the French rear-guard was enabled to retire in good order on Miranda de Corvo. From this place Wellington once more obliged the enemy to retreat, which caused them to destroy the greater part of their stores, ammunition, and baggage, as they were deficient in the means of transport.

Mar. 15th. Next day the Allies were detained several hours by a thick fog, which cleared about nine, when the troops continued the pursuit of the French through Miranda de Corvo. This place having been burnt, was a heap of smoking ruins.

Ney was strongly posted in the afternoon of the fifteenth with his right on a wood, and his left resting on the village of Foz d'Aronse. A false attack was made on his right; at the same moment his left was surprised by Picton, and an advantageous position being selected for the horse artillery, the French were thrown into disorder, which was increased by the darkness that so soon follows sun-set in Portugal. Numbers of the enemy were trampled to death. In their confusion they also fired on each other; and the bridge was so crowded from their anxiety to cross the river, that no less than two hundred and fifty were drowned.

At half-past seven o'clock next morning the Coldstream advanced from the low ground to crown the height previously occupied by General Picton's division.

After halting a day to enable the commissariat to forward supplies, of which the Allied troops were in great want, the light division forded the Ceira on the seventeenth of March, and the remainder of the army crossed over a bridge constructed during the night. The enemy stationed themselves behind the Alva, having destroyed the bridge near Pombeira and Marcella. Wellington ordered two divisions to ford the river near Pombeira, which movement threatened to cut off the enemy's communication with
Mar. 18th. Celerico, and compelled Massena to retire in great haste,

leaving the foragers he had sent out to their fate: nearly a thousand of them were taken. And here the French again destroyed their baggage and ammunition.

About one o'clock P. M. the Guards left the heights above Pombeira; the first division forded the Alba at Sarsedas.

From the deficiency of supplies Wellington found it impossible to proceed; he was therefore obliged to wait for the arrival of provisions, and in consequence Massena on the twenty-first reached Celerico unmolested.

The army having halted a few days, marched on Celerico, where the brigade of Guards arrived on the twenty-ninth.

Massena occupied Guarda, a town built on the top of a steep hill, forming part of the Estrella range of mountains: the place commanded from its position the whole surrounding country. Thus situated, he conceived himself secure from any attack. Wellington, nevertheless, determined to make the attempt. His arrangements were so skilful, that on the morning of the twenty-ninth the Allied columns were not discerned by the enemy until they had nearly gained the summit; the French, surprised and confounded, retreated without firing a shot, from perhaps the strongest ground they could have occupied.

Massena, however, still felt anxious to make it appear that he could maintain himself in Portugal: for this purpose he took a position along the Coa; his right, extending to Ruivina, protected the ford of Rapoulha de Coa; his left reached to Sabugal, and a corps was stationed at Alfayates.

Trant and Wilson had crossed the Coa near Almeida to threaten the enemy's communication with Spain. The right of the Allies was opposite Sabugal, the left at the bridge of Ferreras. At day-break on the third of April

1811.
April 3rd.

the cavalry forded the Coa on the right. The light division passed three miles above Sabugal; the fifth was to cross the bridge; and the third division forded at a short distance above. The bridge of Ferreras was observed by the seventh division, and the sixth was stationed opposite Ruivina. The morning was dark, with thick fog accompanied by storms of rain. The action was commenced by a battalion of the Rifle brigade, who after being charged, got possession of an enclosure, which they retained against the efforts of the whole of Regnier's corps until the remainder of the light division came to their assistance. The contest was then carried on with great vigour; but on the approach of the fifth division, the French retired on Rendo, leaving three hundred dead, and a howitzer on the field, besides twelve hundred prisoners. The loss of the Allies did not exceed one hundred and seventy killed and wounded.[1] The pursuit continued to Alfayates, when the French entered Spain. Portugal, with the exception of the garrison of Almeida, was now entirely freed from their troops.

Thus ended the third French invasion of Portugal under Massena, "l'enfant gâté de la Fortune." Napoleon had sent with him to that devoted country the chosen veterans of France; men who had conquered at Marengo, at Austerlitz, and Jena. At first the French army imagined the lines of Torres Vedras might be easily forced, and considered the entire subjugation of Portugal, the plunder of Lisbon, and the favourite idea of sending the British to their ships, objects of easy accomplishment. Such were the "Châteaux en Espagne" built by the French when this memorable invasion was undertaken; nor were

---

[1] The French had intended to fire a feu-de-joie for the birth of the King of Rome.

their illusive hopes destroyed until they had approached those lines. When, however, Massena found himself unable to make any impression on them, and that neither forage, provisions, nor any other necessary for an army, could be obtained, he, with bitter conviction, saw that the superior foresight and skill of Wellington had destroyed all his hopes of aggrandizement, of glory, of the crown of Portugal, and of additional trophies for the troops of Napoleon!

It is impossible for an Englishman and a soldier not to exult in the recollection of this glorious campaign. But the writer forbears to enlarge on the subject: the facts speak for themselves, and the indignant reprimand which Massena received from Napoleon through his Minister-at-War, alike expressive of the surprise and disappointment of that excellent judge of military operations, is the proper commentary on the successful defence of Portugal under circumstances originally so unpromising. In his address to the Portuguese, Massena had announced that he entered their country at the head of one hundred thousand men, and asked, with no small appearance of reason, whether the feeble army of the British General could reasonably expect to oppose the victorious legions of France? The Marshal answered his own question when he was at length compelled to declare in his justification to his angry master, that the principles of military science did not permit him to attempt the lines of Torres Vedras.

It is no reproach to Sir John Moore, who ranked among the bravest and most intelligent British generals of his time, to say, that what all men but Wellington thought impossible, appeared impossible to him.

The letter of that general to Lord Castlereagh, written at no very long period before Sir Arthur Wellesley directed the lines of Torres Vedras to be constructed, will prove how far even Sir John Moore was from supposing it to be within the reach of human ability to check an enemy at Lisbon, and to baffle any attempt on that capital.

"Salamanca, Novem^r 25, 1808.

" I am not prepared at this moment to answer mi-
" nutely your Lordship's question respecting the defence
" of Portugal; but I can say generally that the frontier
" of Portugal is not defensible against a superior force.
" It is an open frontier—all equally rugged, but all
" equally to be penetrated. If the French succeed in
" Spain, it will be vain to attempt to resist them in Portu-
" gal. The Portuguese are without military force; and,
" from the experience of their conduct under Sir Arthur
" Wellesley, no dependance is to be placed on any
" aid they can give. The British must, in that event, I
" conceive, immediately take steps to evacuate the
" country. Lisbon is the port, and therefore the only
" place from whence the army with its stores can embark.
" Elvas and Almeida are the only fortresses on the fron-
" tier. The first is, I am told, a respectable work. Al-
" meida is defective, and could not hold out ten days
" against a regular attack. I have ordered a depôt
" of provisions for a short consumption to be formed there,
" in case this army should be obliged to fall back; per-
" haps the same should be done at Elvas. In this
" case we might check the progress of the enemy whilst
" the stores are embarking and arrangements are made for
" taking off the army. *Beyond this the defence of Lisbon*
" *or Portugal is not to be thought of.*

" I have the honor to be, &c.

" JOHN MOORE."[1]

---

[1] See Appendix to a Narrative of the Campaign under Sir John Moore. By James Moore, Esq. Page 48.

The French generals, to whom every inch of ground in the Peninsula was known, held the same opinion. 1811.

Napoleon, determined to bring the whole of the Peninsula under the sway of France, had formed the plan of placing his brother Joseph on the throne of Spain, and one of his generals, either Junot or Massena, on that of Portugal. The success which had hitherto attended the French arms, the ignorance of military affairs, and the want of every requisite for the formation of an army, either among the Spaniards or Portuguese, were such — the imbecility of their governments, the superstition, it may be added, the state of degradation into which the population of both countries had sunk, were so notorious, that neither the Emperor of the French, nor any of his Marshals, imagined that serious opposition to his schemes would be attempted. He boldly proclaimed to France and to Europe that he would plant his eagles on the towers of Lisbon! and when Napoleon uttered a prophecy, he had prepared what he deemed ample means for its accomplishment. No sooner did he find himself unexpectedly opposed in the Peninsula, than he became fully aware of the importance of carrying his point; not so much from the vanity of disposing of the thrones of two such kingdoms, as from the conviction, that if he failed in his attempt, the character he had acquired and wished to confirm, of invincibility, would be lost; and that the effect on France, his army, and Europe, would prove highly injurious to his hitherto admitted supremacy. He therefore poured his legions into Spain; determined by force, or, if necessary, by extermination, to obtain that which the good-will of the people would not grant.

The amount of the French troops in Spain and Portugal

1811. was nearly three hundred thousand men;[1] and the only obstacle to the entire subjugation of the Peninsula was the force under Wellington, consisting of forty-eight thousand eight hundred and fifty-seven;[2] not more than one-sixth of the number of the French.

Napoleon's orders to his commanders were to expel the English; and indeed the execution of these orders, after the retreat of Sir John Moore, was considered by the French generals by no means difficult.

Wellington, conscious that his handful of men would have to contend against the whole French power in the Peninsula, which sooner or later would be brought to bear against him; knowing also the little reliance that could be placed either on the Spanish Junta or on the Spanish generals who commanded their troops, conceived the idea of fortifying the passes in front of Lisbon; and with the Tagus on one flank, and the sea on the other, to make a stand, and there to decide whether the conquest of the Peninsula by Napoleon, or its liberation by himself, should be achieved. This plan was not a conception of the moment; it was deliberately adopted after

---

[1] General state of the French army in the Peninsula. From the Imperial Muster-Rolls, January 15th, 1811.

KING JOSEPH Commanding.

Present under arms.		Detached.		Absent.	Effective.	Horses.	
Men.	Horses.	Men.	Horses.	Hospital.	Men.	Cavalry.	Draught.
295,227	52,462	17,780	4714	48,831	361,838	41,189	15,987

—From Col. Napier's Appendix, page 667.

In 1810 the grand total of effective men in Spain amounted to 369,924 men, 43,574 horses, and 17,145 draught horses.—From Col. Napier's Appendix, page 667.

[2] Adjutant-General's Returns, January, 1811. Out of which 9298 were in hospital.

the maturest calculation of its practicability and attendant difficulties.

Wellington saw that Portugal might be defended by lines drawn so as to cover Lisbon, and secure to the protecting force supplies from the Tagus on one side and the sea on the other.[1] The successful result of his measures, and the ignorant declamations uttered against them in Parliament, are now matter of history.

At Torres Vedras the French met with a complete check; their plan of operations was entirely broken; and they were obliged to retreat, discomfited and disheartened, into Spain, whither they were followed by the British, flushed with the anticipation of success, and with a confidence in their leader which was the pledge of victory.

The political influence of this retreat can scarcely be appreciated: it proved to Europe that the French were not invincible; it evinced the good effects of a determined op-

---

[1] The following is the substance of the Duke of Wellington's observations on the defence of Lisbon:

"The Tagus cannot be passed but at a certain point; you "have therefore only to rest one flank of the army on that river, "and, having a naval superiority, you may defy any attack, and "are perfectly secure on that side. The sea covers the other "flank, the distance of which from the river is not more than "twenty miles. An army therefore of forty or fifty thousand "men may resist, in a mountainous and difficult country, any "force which an enemy could bring into the field, even without "intrenchments." As the British army consisted of a great proportion of militia and Portuguese troops, in whom at one time not much confidence could be placed, the Duke thought it a necessary security to cause works to be erected; and, having plenty of time, they were prepared accordingly. Had the Allies been less ably commanded, those lines would never have been constructed, and the troops must have embarked, leaving Portugal to its fate.

1811. position to the ambitious projects of Napoleon, and encouraged Russia in withstanding his outrageous demand, that British commerce should be excluded from her ports. The lines of Torres Vedras broke the wand of the enchanter, and led to that resistance by the Northern States of Europe, which ended in the downfall of French dominion, and of a man as remarkable for the great powers of his mind as for his inordinate ambition; whose activity and military talents were commensurate with his anxiety to extend his sway over mankind, and with his indifference to the evils he inflicted on his fellow-creatures in pursuing that object.

The desolation in Portugal occasioned by Massena's invading army can scarcely be conceived: not an article of subsistence [1] was to be found; every town and village was deserted; the wine that could not be consumed was left running in the gutters; the corn-stacks burnt; in the houses, which from want of means or time were not destroyed, all the furniture was broken; neither horse, mule, cow, nor ass, not even a goat, could be seen. The women captured by the French in their marauding excursions were brought in as to a market and sold for the benefit of the captors; many of these unfortunate females were left to perish by famine and disease remote from their native villages. Lord Wellington in his dispatch says: " The conduct of the French army, throughout this retreat, " has been marked by a barbarity seldom equalled, " and never surpassed. Even in the towns of Torres " Novas, Thomar, and Pernes, in which head-quarters of " some of the corps had been for some months, and " in which the inhabitants were induced by promises of " good treatment to remain, they were plundered and

---

[1] See Moniteur.

" many of their houses destroyed on the night the
" enemy withdrew from their position; and they have
" since burned every town and village through which they
" passed."

After the enemy quitted Portugal, the Allies were stationed near the Duas Casas, the out-posts at Gallegos and on the Agueda. All communication between the garrison of Almeida and the French was cut off.

The brigade of Guards halted on the ninth at Almadilla, having forded the Coa above Sabugal, and passing through Aldea Velha. On the seventeenth the Coldstream moved, for the convenience of quarters, to Puebla.

Badajoz had surrendered to Soult on the eleventh of March, when the garrison laid down their arms; and on the twenty-first of February ten thousand infantry and six hundred cavalry had been embarked at Cadiz for Tarifa, to make a diversion by attacking the enemy's rear at Chiclana. The tempestuous state of the weather forced them into Algesiras, where they landed and marched the following day for Tarifa. There they were joined by the Twenty-eighth regiment, the flank companies of the Ninth and Eighty-second regiments, amounting to about four thousand five hundred men, including two companies of Portuguese and some German hussars, under General Graham. On the twenty-seventh of February General La Pena with about seven thousand Spaniards arrived; and next day the troops were re-organized, and Graham, taking command of the British, consented to act under the Spanish General. The vanguard was given to Lardizabel, and the cavalry were commanded by Colonel Whittingham, Marescal del Campo in the service of Spain.

In the nights of the third and fourth of March the

1811. enemy attacked the Spanish force, and were repulsed. Next day a detachment from St. Roque joined the Allies under General Bejines, but retired after some skirmishing. La Pena then opened his communication with the Isla de Leon, and ordered his troops to crown the heights of Bermeja, having directed Graham to support him. The General obeyed; but no sooner had he entered the wood than the Spanish commander withdrew, giving orders that his cavalry should follow him. La Pena then marched to the river Santi Petri, leaving the heights of Barrosa, which were covered with baggage, to be protected by only five battalions and four guns.

During Graham's advance two divisions of the enemy were discovered; one of them made for the heights of Barrosa, the other marched on his flank.

The Duke of Belluno had under his command nine thousand men belonging to the divisions of Laval, Ruffin, and Villatte, with fourteen guns: about two thousand five hundred belonging to the division of the latter had orders to watch the Spaniards at the Santi Petri and Bermeja.

The ground was an extensive plain, nearly surrounded by a pine forest, and crossed by uneven sandy heights, which rose from the shore. The hill of Barrosa was about a mile from the mouth of the Santi Petri.

The French General perceiving Graham's situation, and aware of the relative position of the Spanish troops, immediately ordered Laval to attack him, whilst he attempted to cut off the detachment on the road to Medina; for which purpose he ascended the opposite side of the hill, where the five battalions, with the guns, baggage, &c. had been left by La Pena. The enemy succeeded in taking three of the guns; on which the Spanish troops immediately dispersed.

Graham, finding it impossible to retreat without giving his adversary a decided advantage, at once determined on becoming the assailant.

The British column had been marching, right in front, for an hour and a half through the wood, when Major Brown told General Graham that the enemy were formed on a rising ground which the column had recently quitted. The troops in consequence countermarched under a heavy fire of artillery, and formed in two masses. The right column, led by Brigadier-General Dilkes, moved against Ruffin, who had crowned the summit of Barrosa: at the same time Colonel Wheatly attacked the right of the enemy, and, after a sharp contested fire, continued to advance. The Eighty-seventh regiment, and two companies of the Coldstream Guards under Lieutenant-Colonel Jackson, made an intrepid charge, which threw the enemy back in great disorder. Ruffin's troops on the hill manfully contested the height; but, notwithstanding all their efforts, the English drove the French from the position, on which they left three guns, after a severe loss.

General Graham was unable to follow up his success, as his men had been under arms for twenty-four hours, during which time they received no supply of rations.

The attack on Barrosa, which did not continue more than two hours, reflects great credit on the troops engaged.

The enemy suffered severely, and lost two Generals, Ruffin and Rousseau, the latter being mortally wounded; one eagle, six guns, and upwards of two thousand five hundred men killed, wounded, and prisoners. The British loss amounted to eleven hundred and sixty-nine. The following is a copy of General Graham's dispatch:

"Where all have so distinguished themselves, it is

1811. "scarcely possible to discriminate any as the most deserv-
"ing of praise. Your Lordship will, however, observe
"how gloriously the brigade of Guards, under Brigadier-
"General Dilkes, with the commanders of battalions, Co-
"lonel Honourable C. Onslow and Lieutenant-Colonel
"Sebright, (wounded,) as well as the three separated
"companies under Colonel Jackson, maintained the high
"character of his Majesty's household troops."

The casualties of the detachment of the Coldstream Guards engaged were:—one ensign, eight rank and file killed; two ensigns, one sergeant, forty-five rank and file wounded. Killed, Ensign Watts; wounded, Ensigns Bentinck and Talbot.

Marshal Beresford, who was in the Alentejo, received orders early in March to invest Badajoz without delay, that the garrison might not have sufficient time allowed them to repair the damage done to the fortifications during the last siege.

April. Almeida was now closely blockaded; Massena had retired on Salamanca, for the purpose of restoring to his troops that confidence, order, and discipline, which they had lost in his hasty retreat. After this he advanced, having been considerably reinforced, and reached Ciudad Rodrigo on the twenty-fifth of April.

Wellington took advantage of the enemy's absence to visit the troops in the Alentejo under Beresford, and, having made all the necessary preparations in conjunction with him, returned to his head-quarters at Villa Formosa on the twenty-eighth.

May. Massena on the second of May crossed the frontier with about forty thousand men and five thousand cavalry. The British were reduced to about thirty-two thousand infantry and twelve hundred cavalry.

May 2nd. At twelve o'clock the same day the Coldstream received orders to march by the left of Almadilla, where they remained till late in the evening. During the night the brigade of Guards moved to Nava d'Aver, and on the third the army was placed in position.

1811.
May 3rd.

The river Coa runs in a northerly direction; its banks are very steep, and render the passage very difficult for an army, except at some few places, which are at the bridges of Almeida and Castello Bom, about seven miles above and at the ford of St. Roque, near Freynada. Almeida is situated on the right of the Coa; consequently Wellington had no option but to engage with the river in his rear.

The British commander, on changing his position, found it necessary to extend it to the right, as in case of disaster the bridge of Sabugal was the only place where the army could cross the Coa; the right wing was therefore extended to Nava d'Aver, which was occupied by Julian Sanchez, and supported by the seventh division. Wellington took up his ground behind the river of Duas Casas: the first, third, and seventh divisions were strongly posted in rear of Fuentes d'Honor; the sixth and light divisions watched the bridge of Almeida across the Duas Casas: and the fifth division the fords across that river at Fort Conception and Aldea d'Obispo. Trant's and Wilson's militia had been in observation on Almeida, and were relieved by Pack's brigade on the sixteenth of April. The investment of Almeida was placed under the direction of General Alexander Campbell.

The enemy formed, on the third, behind the Duas Casas: their left overlooked the village of Fuentes; their right extended about two miles, running nearly in a parallel direction to the position of the Allies. The same afternoon the French resolutely attacked the village of Fuentes, where a most gallant resistance was made; fresh troops were constantly supplied by both parties: the contest

1811.
May.

continued till night, when the assailants were finally driven back across the Duas Casas.

The French Marshal was occupied on the fourth in reconnoitring the position. During the night the Duke d'Abrantes' corps with the cavalry from Almeida moved May 5th. to the left. About six o'clock next morning Massena carried the village of Porço Velho: the light division and cavalry were sent to support General Houston; at the same time the first and third divisions moved to their right. The Guards were thrown back *en potence*. The enemy's cavalry, supported by the infantry and artillery, drove in part of the seventh division. Don Julian Sanchez left Nava d'Aver with his men, and placed himself immediately in front of the Guards: here his lieutenant was unfortunately shot by a soldier of the Coldstream, who mistook him for a Frenchman. Some advantageous ground on which the English cavalry were stationed being abandoned, was instantly seized by the French. The light division then advanced to support the cavalry, but, finding the height occupied, formed into squares, and retired in good order, repelling all the efforts of the hostile cavalry to force them; the Chasseurs Britanniques under Lieutenant-Colonel Eustace, also distinguished themselves by the steady manner in which they repulsed the enemy's dragoons. The Allies were concentrated towards the left, on the seventh, the light divisions and cavalry moving on Fuentes d'Honor. The two remaining divisions followed in succession. Wellington now found himself obliged to abandon his communication across the Coa by the bridge of Sabugal. The position extended along the height from Turon to the Duas Casas. The first division was on the right, in two lines; Colonel Ashworth's brigade in the centre; and the third division, also in two lines, on the left. The village of Fuentes d'Honor, in their front, was occupied by the light troops. The light division and cavalry were in reserve. The infantry of Don Julian joined the seventh division in Freynada. The French cavalry advanced in mass under a heavy cannonade to within a short distance of the line where the Guards were formed, when the brigade of nine-pounders under Captain Lawson opened, and obliged the enemy to halt. After a few rounds of grape, they went about in great confusion. The piquets of the first division, under Lieutenant-Colonel Hill of the Third Guards, succeeded in repulsing a charge of the enemy's cavalry; but in making their way to the cover of the army they were again attacked and broken before any force could be sent to their assistance. Lieutenant-Colonel Hill was taken prisoner, others were wounded, and the party was overpowered. The French throughout the day were unremitting in their attacks on Fuentes d'Honor, where several regiments and officers greatly distinguished themselves. On one occasion the Seventy-first, Seventy-ninth, and Eighty-eighth regiments, belonging to Colonel Henry Mac Kinnon's brigade, were ordered up. Led by that officer, they gallantly charged a heavy mass of infantry that had gained the chapel eminence, and drove the French through the village with great slaughter. The contest lasted till night, when the fire gradually slackened; the upper part of the village was retained by the British, and the enemy made no further attempt.[1] The casualties in the Coldstream were, four rank and file killed; Captain Harvey, two ser-

1811.
May 5th.

---

[1] The Ninety-second regiment arrived on the position at Fuentes d'Honor much distressed from want of provisions; which circumstance being made known to the brigade of Guards, they volunteered giving up a ration of biscuit, then in their haversacks, which was received by the gallant Highlanders with three hearty cheers.

1811.
May 5th. jeants, and forty-nine rank and file wounded; Ensign Stothert and seven rank and file taken.¹

Massena was recalled to France, and the Duke of Ragusa, who had been appointed to the command of the army of Portugal in his stead, arrived from Paris on the seventh of May. On the same day the French retreated.

A loud explosion was heard at twelve o'clock on the night of the eleventh, General Brennier the Commandant of Almeida having sprung a mine in order to facilitate his escape with the garrison, consisting of about fifteen hundred men. This he accomplished by a sudden and well-conducted movement. General Pack, who commanded the investing piquets, hastily collected some troops and followed, keeping up a constant fire on the rear of the French, which was not returned; neither did they slacken their pace, but marched across the country, protected by the darkness of the night, and descended the valley of Barba del Puerco. They lost many men, but their main body succeeded in reaching the bridge on the Coa, where they found the second French corps drawn up in order of battle to cover them.²

May 7th. Having assumed the command, Marmont retired towards Salamanca, in the neighbourhood of which town his army was placed in cantonments.

On the eleventh the Guards returned to the places they had occupied previous to the action. The fifth, sixth, and light divisions were left on the Agueda and Coa. The first division moved from their cantonments and marched in the evening of the twenty-fifth through Soita to Pena-

---

¹ The loss of the Allies amounted to about fifteen hundred; three hundred of whom were made prisoners. The enemy's loss greatly exceeded that of their opponents.

² The French lost three hundred men, killed, wounded, and taken.

THE COLDSTREAM GUARDS. 163

macor, whence the Guards were ordered to go back to their former stations, part of the division only being required in the south. The Guards returned through Sabugal, and arrived at Almadilla and Puebla.

1811.

May 27th.
May 29th.

Beresford had on the eighth of May completely invested Badajoz.

Marshal Soult left Seville with the intention of succouring the town; on his march he was reinforced with fresh troops.

Beresford in consequence raised the siege and advanced to meet him, when it was agreed with Blake, who commanded the Spaniards in this direction, that the Allied army should take up a position at the village of Albuera, and Beresford, though junior, was allowed to take the command-in-chief pro tempore. They occupied the position with nearly thirty thousand infantry, of which seven thousand only were British, two thousand cavalry, and thirty-eight pieces of artillery.

May 15th.

Soult's force consisted of twenty thousand infantry, three thousand cavalry, and forty guns. The Allies remained masters of the field. As the Guards took no part at Albuera, a description of that battle is not here inserted. It may, however, be remarked, that Lord Beresford's conduct throughout the day proved him to merit that character and consideration in the army, which he has always maintained.

The intrepidity of the British infantry, on whom the brunt of the battle fell, was conspicuously displayed in this action. Fifteen hundred men only remained out of seven thousand. The loss of the French was also very considerable.

Wellington learnt, by an intercepted letter, on the tenth of June, that Marmont intended to unite with Soult in the Alentejo. The siege of Badajoz, which had been renewed

June.

1811.
June.

after the battle of Albuera, was in consequence of this information converted into a blockade.

The Coldstream left Puebla on the fifth for Almadilla; next day the brigade of Guards marched from that place with the corps under Spencer, and moved from the north in a parallel direction with Marmont, passing Sabugal and Castello Branco. They then crossed the Tagus and proceeded to Portalegre, where the Coldstream halted three days. On the twenty-third of June they encamped near St. Oloia, when, to protect them from the great heat, the troops were hutted. A draft joined the regiment from Cadiz on the twenty-fifth, consisting of Captain the Honourable John Walpole, Ensign Greville, three serjeants, and ninety-eight rank and file; soon after the first division was reviewed by Lord Wellington, accompanied by the Prince of Orange.

Soult returned to Seville, and Marmont advanced to Salamanca, being unable to provide supplies for their army when together.

July 22nd.

Hill's corps remained in the Alentejo. The brigade of Guards left St. Oloia, reached Portalegre the twenty-third, and on the thirty-first received orders to return to the north. Lord Wellington recrossed the Tagus with the rest of the army, and fixed his head-quarters at Fuente Guinaldo.

Sept. 6th.

On the sixth of September, General Graham succeeded Sir Brent Spencer in the command of the first division.

Lord Wellington blockaded Ciudad Rodrigo: on the approach of Marmont he retired, and occupied a defensive position. The British general was not prepared to besiege the place; his object being to oblige the enemy to withdraw from Galicia and Navarre, and thus give relief to those oppressed provinces.

General Picton was in advance on the height of El

Bodon, between Fuente Guinaldo and Pastores. The light division was near Martiago. The left wing, in which were the Guards, was in the lower Azava. Sir Stapleton Cotton with the cavalry was in the centre.

1811.

Marmont joined his forces with General Dorsenne on the twenty-second of September, and relieved Ciudad Rodrigo: he entered the place with a large convoy on the twenty-fourth. The French advanced two days after in great force, and obliged the Allies to retreat. Next day the village of Aldea de Ponte was attacked by the enemy, and gallantly contested by the fourth division. After dark the British again retreated, and took up a strong position behind the Soito. Here Wellington offered the enemy battle, but Marmont fell back on Ciudad Rodrigo; and Dorsenne returned to the north. The Allied army then went into cantonments. The brigade of Guards was stationed in front of Celerico; the Coldstream at Lagoisa, Valdozares, and afterwards at Pinhel. The head-quarters were at Freynada.

October.

General Hill left Portalegre on the twenty-second of October, and after three days reached Malpartida. The next evening he made a forced march to Acuesa, and silently waited till morning, when he surprised a post under General Girard at Arroyo de Molinos, which was carried at the point of the bayonet. Many men were killed, and fifteen hundred taken, besides General Brun and the Duke d'Aremberg, with all their artillery, stores, and baggage.

This was a brilliant exploit, and in itself of sufficient moment to establish a claim to military eminence. The reputation of Hill, however, does not rest on a solitary act of courage or skilful generalship: his name will descend to posterity interwoven with the triumphs of Wellington.

RETURN OF OFFICERS OF THE FIRST BATTALION OF THE COLDSTREAM FOR THE YEAR 1811.

	Officers present in the Peninsula.	From	To		Officers absent.	Cause of absence.	From	To
Lt.-C.	Joseph Fuller	March	31 Dec.	Lt.-G.	John Calcraft, 1st Major	Leave	1 Jan.	31 Dec.
,,	Hon. H. Brand	1 Jan.	April					
,,	James Philips	,,	31 Dec.	Col.	Richard Hulse	Commanding a Brigade	,,	,,
,,	Sir G. Stirling, Bart.	,,	,,	,,	H. Mac Kinnon	Do. Sick leave	,,	3 July
,,	George Smyth		3 July				4 July	Dec.
,,	Thomas Braddyl	Oct.	3 Dec.	,,	W. M. Peacocke	Commandant at Lisbon	1 Jan.	31 Dec.
Capt.	E. Dalling, (Maj.)	1 Jan.	31 July					
,,	L. F. Adams, (Major)	,,	31 Dec.	M.-G.	W. P. Acland	On the Staff at home.	,,	,,
,,	George Collier	,,	3 Dec.			Asst. Adjt. Genl. Portugal.		11 July
,,	Sir H. Sullivan, Bart.	,,	Nov.	Col.	M. Lord Aylmer	Sick leave to England	12 July	Dec.
,,	W. H. Raikes	,,	31 Dec.					
,,	H. W. Vachell	,,	Sept.	Lt. Cl.	Hon. H. Brand	Posted to 2d Battn.	April	
,,	Thomas Barrow	,,	31 Dec.			Leave to England on resignation.		
,,	Hon. W. Geo. Crofton	Feb.	,,	,,	George Smyth		4 July	
,,	D. Mac Kinnon	1 Jan.	15 Aug.			Asst. Qur. Mr. Genl. Portugal		
,,	Hon. J. Walpole	25 June	31 Dec.	,,	R. D. Jackson		March	31 Dec.
,,	Thomas Steele	Feb.	,,			Leave to England on resignation		
,,	Edward Harvey	March	,,	,,	Thos. Braddyl		4 Dec.	
,,	George Bowles	Oct.	,,					
,,	Thomas Sowerby	Nov.	,,	,,	H. F. Bouverie	Acting Mily. Secy. Portugal	Jan.	31 Dec.
,,	James V. Harvey	1 Jan.	30 Mar.					
Ens.	W. L. Walton	,,	23 April	Capt.	Edward Dalling	Died 31st July		
,,	W. Lockwood	,,	22 May	,,	George Collier	Promoted in 2d Battn.	4 Dec.	
,,	Hon. J. Wingfield	,,	4 May					
,,	Paulet St. John Mildmay	,,	30 Nov.			Deputy Asst. Adjt. Genl. Portugal	1 Jan.	17 Sept.
,,	A. Wedderburn	,,	Dec.	,,	H. F. Cooke			
,,	Charles White	,,	31 Dec.			Leave to England	18 Sept.	31 Dec.
,,	Thomas Bligh	,,	,,					
,,	Charles Shawe	,,	,,	,,	Sir H. Sullivan, Bart.	Sick leave to Lisbon	Nov.	,,
,,	G. H. M. Greville	25 June	,,					
,,	John Talbot	Oct.	,,	,,	H. W. Vachell	Promoted in 2d Battn.	Sept.	
,,	G. H. Percival	1 Jan.	,,					
,,	William Stothert	,,	5 May			A.D.C. to Hon. E. Stopford	June	15 Aug.
,,	W. G. Baynes	,,	31 Dec.	,,	D. Mac Kinnon	Sick leave to England	16 Aug.	31 Dec.
,,	John S. Cowell	,,	,,					
,,	W. N. Burgess	Feb.	,,					
,,	John Mills	Jan.	,,	,,	Henry Dawkins	Brigade Major Portugal	1 Jan.	31 Dec.
,,	James Bradshaw	March	,,					
,,	F. L. Beckford	Oct.	,,	,,	J. V. Harvey	Promoted in 2d Battn.	1 April	,,
,,	Fred. Vachell	,,	,,					
Adjt.	J. Freemantle (Capt.)	1 Jan.	,,	,,	W. L. Walton	Ditto.	24 ,,	,,
Q-Mr.	John Holmes	,,	,,	Ens.	W. Lockwood	Leave to England. Resigned	23 May	
Surgn.	Charles Coombe	,,	,,	,,	Hon. J. Wingfield	Died 4th May		
Asst Sur.	Thomas Rose	,,	,,	Capt.	P. St. J. Mildmay	Promoted in 2d Battn.	1 Dec.	,,
,,	Edward Nixon	March	,,	,,	A. Wedderburn	Ditto ,,	Dec.	,,
				Ens.	W. Stothert	Taken prisoner at Fuentes d'Honor	5 May	,,

THE COLDSTREAM GUARDS.

STRENGTH OF THE FIRST BATTALION OF THE COLDSTREAM AT PINHEL, 25th December, 1811.

Capts. and Lieut.-Cols.	Lieutenants and Capts.	Ensigns.	Adjutant.	Q.-Master.	Surgeon.	Assistant Surgeons.	Staff employ and otherwise absent.			Absent without leave.	Commission vacant.	Serjeants.	Drummers.	Rank and File.	Sick.	On Command.	Total.
							Capts. and Lt.-Cols.	Lieuts. and Capts.	Ensigns.								
4	11	13	1	1	1	2	6	3	2	One Sub.	One Ens.	69	22	744	144	61	1086

	Officers present.		Officers absent.	Cause of absence.
Col.	1. J. Fuller	M.-Gen.	R. Hulse	1. Staff, Portugal
Lt.-Col.	2. J. Philips	,,	H. Mac Kinnon	2. Ditto
,,	3. Sir G. Stirling		W. M. Peacocke	3. Ditto
Capt.	4. L. F. Adams, (Major)	Col.	M. Lord Aylmer	4. Asst. Adjt.-Gen. ditto
		Lt.-Col.	R. D. Jackson	5. Asst. Q.-Master-Gen. ditto
,,	6. Hon. J. Walpole	,,	4. A. Woodford	On the march from Lisbon to join
,,	7. T. Steele	,,	H. F. Bouverie	6. Taken on from 2d battalion
,,	8. E. Harvey	Capt.	F. Sutton	1. Taken on from 2d battalion
,,	9. G. Bowles	,,	E. Lascelles	3. With 2d battalion
,,	10. T. Sowerby	,,	3. W. H. Raikes	Sick at Val dos Ayres
Ensign	1. C. White	,,	D. Mac Kinnon	In England
,,	3. C. Shawe	,,	H. Dawkins	2. Brigade-Major, Portugal
,,	4. G. H. M. Greville	,,	11. A. Wedderburn	On duty at Lisbon: belonging to 2d battalion
,,	5. J. Talbot			
,,	6. G. H. Percival	,,	4. T. Barrow	On the road to join from sick, absent
,,	8. J. S. Cowell	,,	2. Sir H. Sullivan	Leave for 6 weeks to Lisbon
,,	9. W. N. Burgess	,,	5. Hon. W. G. Crofton	Leave for 6 weeks to Lisbon
,,	10. J. Mills			
,,	11. J. Bradshaw	Ensign	2. T. Bligh	On the road to join from sick, absent
,,	12. F. L. Beckford	,,	7. W. G. Baynes	On duty at Coimbra
Adjutant	J. Freemantle, (Capt.)	,,	13. F. Vachell	Leave for 1 month to Lisbon
Q.-Mastr.	J. Holmes	,,	J. L. Blackman	1. With 2d. bat.
Asst. Surg.	T. Rose		W. Stothert	2. Prisoner of war
,,	E. Nixon	Surgeon	C. Coombe	Sick at Val dos Ayres
		Capt.	P. St. J. Mildmay	To join 2d battalion
		Lt.-Col.	G. Collier	To England on promotion
		,,	T. Braddyll	To England on resignation.

(Signed)   CHARLES STEWART,
M.-G. and A.-G.

CHAPTER X.

Siege and capture of Ciudad Rodrigo — Army marches for the south—Siege of Badajoz—Town carried by assault—Hill left in the south — Wellington moves for the north — Marmont retires from Castello Branco — Head-quarters at Fuente Guinaldo—Troops cantoned between the Agueda and Coa—Hill carries the bridge of Almarez — Wellington fords the Tormes — Marmont advances—Allies in position on the heights of St. Christoval—Capture of the forts in Salamanca — French retreat and concentrate behind the Douro—Marmont reinforced attempts to cut off Wellington's communication with Salamanca and Ciudad Rodrigo—Battle of Salamanca—Marmont wounded—Command devolves on Clausel—French retreat on Valladolid—Wellington moves by Cuellar, through Segovia, to Madrid — The Isla opposite Cadiz abandoned by the French — First division leaves Madrid for the Escurial — King Joseph joins Suchet — Soult in Granada — Wellington enters Valladolid — Siege of Burgos — Siege raised — Reinforcements arrive under Dalhousie — Allies retreat — Head-quarters at Freynada — Hill returns to Estramadura—Troops go into cantonments for the winter—Coldstream at Musquetello.

1812.
January.

MARMONT having detached four divisions of his army, besides the one under General Dubreton, stationed in the province of Las Montanas, Wellington determined at once to lay siege to Ciudad Rodrigo.

On the sixth, head-quarters were transferred to Gallegos; but from a fall of snow and the inclemency of the weather, the army did not move till the eighth, when General Crauford's division crossed the Agueda, and invested the town. After dark Lieutenant-Colonel Colborne with a detachment of the light division stormed and carried an advanced redoubt on the great Teson. Sir Thomas Graham was intrusted with the direction of the siege. From the eighth instant the Coldstream was quartered at Espeja. The brigade of Guards formed the working party in the trenches on the ninth, on which night the first parallel was established and the several batteries marked out. The Guards were also in the trenches on the thirteenth, when a fortified convent, situated on the right of the redoubt before taken, was carried by the light infantry companies, supported by Lord Blantyre's brigade.

1812. January.

The garrison made a sortie on the fourteenth, and were repulsed without effecting any injury except filling in a part of the sap. In the evening the batteries opened, and the convent of St. Francisco, which flanked the approaches on the left, was escaladed and carried by the Fortieth regiment.

On the seventeenth the Guards again took their turn in the trenches.

The second parallel was completed; but Wellington determined to order an assault the moment the breaches were deemed practicable, without waiting for the opening of the sap to blow in the counterscarp; and as every exertion was made, two breaches were completed on the nineteenth. General Picton's division was directed to storm the greater breach, and General Crauford's the smaller. After dark the columns moved forward, and in less than an hour the British were formed on the ramparts.

General Crauford was mortally wounded whilst leading his division up the glacis. General MacKinnon was killed, with many others, by the unfortunate explosion of an expense magazine after a shower of grape and mus-

1812.
January.

ketry, and just as the troops had pushed on and cleared the breach.

The Allies lost during the siege and in the storming about one thousand three hundred men. Seventy-eight officers and seventeen hundred men of the French were made prisoners, besides a heavy loss in killed and wounded.

The capture of a complete battering train, with magazines filled with shot, shells, muskets, cartridges, and other ammunition, was the result of this success.

As soon as Ciudad Rodrigo was again placed in a state of defence and supplied with stores and provisions, Wellington planned his arrangements for the reduction of

February. Badajoz. The army in consequence was put in movement for the south: in February no British troops remained on the Agueda or at any point north of the Tagus. Trant occupied the line of the Coa and its vicinity; his orders were to watch Marmont on the frontier, and also to cover the magazines at Celerico.

The first division left their quarters and passed through Sabugal to Castello Branco. The Coldstream, after halting one day, continued their route by Abrantes to Elvas. At the latter place the division encamped close to the town, when tents were furnished the men for the first time. On the sixteenth they broke up, and the brigade of Guards crossed the Guadiana over a pontoon bridge below the town of Badajoz, which was thus invested by the third, fourth, and light divisions, under Beresford. General Graham advanced with the first, sixth, and seventh divisions, and two brigades of cavalry, towards Llerena; whilst General Hill's corps moved from their cantonments near Albuquerque to Merida: the enemy on their approach retired to Cordova.

March. The siege of Badajoz was prosecuted without intermis-

sion, although torrents of rain had swept away the pontoon bridge; and from the rapidity of the current, the flying-bridges could only be worked with great difficulty. These obstacles occasioned supplies of all descriptions to be kept back; and the trenches on the low ground were filled with water. 1812.
Mar. 21st.

Soult advanced with a large force to the relief of the town. Graham and Hill then retired on Albuera.

The second parallel was formed; enfilading and breaching batteries had been erected; and on the sixth of April, after the firing had been kept up seven days, three breaches were deemed practicable. At ten o'clock P.M. simultaneous attacks were made; the first that succeeded was that of Picton's division, led by General Kemp. General Walker, with his brigade, also entered by escalade on the Olivença road. General Philippon, the commandant, escaped to St. Christoval, a fort on the opposite side of the Guadiana, which shortly after surrendered. The number of prisoners taken in Badajoz amounted to nearly four thousand: the loss of the Allies from the commencement of the siege was about five thousand men. April.

Wellington left Hill's corps on the south of the Tagus, and put his army in motion for the north.

During the siege of Badajoz, Marmont had advanced as far as Castello Branco; but, informed of Wellington's movement, he retreated towards Ciudad Rodrigo, and having raised the blockade of that place, retired on Salamanca.

Head-quarters were again established at Fuente Guinaldo, and the troops cantoned between the Agueda and Coa. May.

Previous to entering Spain, Lord Wellington had ordered General Hill to move by Zaraceijo, for the purpose May 12th.

1812.
May 12th.

of destroying the bridge of boats across the Tagus, at Almarez, which, if effected, would render the communication between the enemy's armies on the north and south of the Tagus more difficult. All the permanent bridges had been destroyed during the war by one or other of the belligerent powers. The bridge at Almarez was covered at each extremity by strong works, besides being protected on the south by the castle and redoubts of Miravete. From the difficulty of approach, it was not till day-break

May 19th. on the nineteenth of May that an attack could be made. The right column then moved to the assault of Fort Napoleon, on the left bank of the river. The British rushed on with fixed bayonets, and drove the enemy over the bridge: so great was the panic, that the troops in Fort Ragusa, on the right bank, abandoned their works, and fled in disorder. Eighteen guns, and two hundred and fifty men, were taken. The British loss was under two hundred. Hill afterwards returned to Almandrelejo.

June 17th. The army left their cantonments on the Agueda, and forded the Tormes above and below Salamanca. Two forts, constructed by the enemy, could only be reduced by a regular attack: the sixth division, under Major-General Clinton, was therefore selected for this duty; and the rest of the army was kept in readiness to check the enemy, who were anxious to hold a communication with the forts. An attempt to carry the principal fort, St. Vincente, failed. Major-General Bowes, and one hundred and twenty men, were killed.

Marmont made a forward movement on the twentieth, and found the Allies posted on the height of St. Christoval; their right resting on the Tormes near Carbrerizos, their left near Villares de la Reyna: a skirmish took place with the cavalry. During the night of the twenty-first the enemy established themselves on the right flank of the position; from which they were afterwards dislodged by the seventh division. On the night of the twenty-third Marmont crossed the Tormes in great force; but finding that the first, sixth, and seventh divisions, under Graham, had also forded the river with some cavalry and artillery, he returned and re-occupied his former ground. 1812.
June 17th.

A few days after, the largest of the forts, which had been battered with red-hot shot, was seen to be on fire. June 27th.

The men were formed ready for an assault, when a proposition was made to capitulate in three hours; in reply to which Wellington gave them five minutes to march out, promising them their baggage. The garrison not taking advantage of the offer, the storming party advanced, under Lieutenant-Colonel Davies of the Thirty-sixth regiment: the small fort was carried, and the attack on St. Vincente had commenced, when the commandant accepted the proposed terms. About seven hundred men were made prisoners, the works blown up, and the captured guns, with the stores, given to the Spaniards. The Allies lost four hundred and fifty men killed and wounded.

After the capture of these forts Marmont retreated behind the Douro, where he concentrated his forces, his centre resting on Tordesillas. July.

Wellington established his head-quarters at Rueda, and his line extended from La Seca to Pollos.

The French had been reinforced on the seventh by General Bonnet, with eight thousand men; and their present position being most advantageous, Marmont resolved on becoming the assailant. On the sixteenth large bodies crossed the river at Toro: the same evening the British troops moved to Fuente la Peña and Carnizal, on the Guarena. The next day it was ascertained that the enemy had recrossed the Douro, and were again concentrated at Tordesillas, at which place their army

1821.

crossed the river, and assembled at Nave del Rey and Castrejon.

July 18th.

Marmont had now opened his communication with the army of the centre, which was on its march from Madrid to support him: his present object was to prevent the Allies from having any intercourse with Salamanca and Ciudad Rodrigo.

On the twenty-first the Allies concentrated on the Tormes, having repulsed the enemy on the eighteenth, who had attempted to turn their left and gain the valley of Carnizal.

Between Huerta and Alba de Tormes the French crossed the river, pressing forward their left to gain the Ciudad Rodrigo road. Wellington also crossed by the bridge at Salamanca, and before day-light next morning both armies were in position; the right of the Allies extending nearly to the steep heights called the Sister Arapiles; their left resting on the Tormes. The enemy's front was covered by a wood.

July 22nd.

At day-break on the twenty-second much skirmishing took place. A French column advanced about eight o'clock, and seized the farthest and most extensive height. The British troops immediately took possession of the other. Some changes were then made in the arrangements of the Allied army, and a succession of manœuvres on the part of the enemy showed that it was Marmont's intention to turn the right of the Allies. Probably against a less skilful general than Wellington he might have succeeded. But in making this attempt, which was covered by a constant skirmish and cannonade along the whole front, he pushed his left too far, and weakened his centre; the moment was seized by Wellington, who instantly determined to attack. At this time the first and light divisions formed the left, the fourth and fifth were drawn up in two lines behind the village of Arapiles; the sixth and seventh, and the Spaniards under Don Carlos de España, were in column for their support. On the right was the division of Major-General Pakenham, with the greater part of the cavalry. The village of Arapiles, which the enemy made repeated efforts to carry, was situated between the two armies, and was occupied by the light companies of the Guards under Lieutenant-Colonel Woodford of the Coldstream. Pakenham advanced to the attack with the third division in columns of battalions, when they wheeled to the left, supported by General D'Urban's brigade of Portuguese cavalry: on reaching the height General Pakenham deployed, his right outflanking the enemy's left. He then advanced, and carried every thing at the point of the bayonet. The cavalry made a successful charge in front; during which General Le Marchant was killed. General Pack, with the Portuguese brigade, failed more than once to carry the Arapiles; the enemy, after repulsing them, advanced from the height, and suddenly attacked the left of the fourth division; the disorder this occasioned was checked by the advance of part of the fifth. The third and fourth divisions then moved forward, and crowned the height. The last stand was made by the enemy on their right, who attempted to rally, their troops having retired in good order from the Arapiles. Clinton's division was ordered to attack in front, supported by the third and fifth divisions; the fourth making at the same time a flank movement on the left. Clinton, in this advance, suffered severely from the fire of the artillery and musketry; but he steadily persevered till within a short distance of the enemy, on whom his troops rushed with the bayonet, when the fourth division appearing, the French quitted their position in great disorder. The first and light divi-

1812.
July 22nd.

1812.
July 22nd.

sions followed in pursuit from sun-set till the troops halted from fatigue. The French crossed the Tormes the same night at Alba. Their loss must have been very great; besides killed and wounded, seven thousand were made prisoners. Lord Wellington, in his dispatch, states that eleven guns were left in possession of the Allies: several others were afterwards found, making a total of not less than twenty. The loss on the part of the Allies was five thousand two hundred. In the Coldstream the casualties were principally from the light company. Ensign Hotham was wounded; one serjeant, two corporals, and four privates were killed; three serjeants, one corporal, one drummer, and seventeen privates were wounded; eight men also were missing.

The following is an extract from Lord Wellington's dispatch:—

"I must also mention Lieutenant-Colonel Woodford, "commanding the light battalion of the brigade of "Guards, who, supported by two companies of the Fusi-"liers, under the command of Captain Crowder, main-"tained the village of Arapiles against all the efforts of "the enemy."

At this time the colossal power of Napoleon had brought half the population of Christendom under his sway. He now resolved to undertake an expedition into Russia. The French army marched in ten corps, under Davoust, Oudinot, Ney, Eugene Beauharnais, Poniatowski, Gouvion St. Cyr, Regnier, Junot, Victor, and Macdonald. The body guard was under Le Fevre, and the young guard under Mortier. The reserve of the cavalry, commanded by the King of Naples, was in four bodies, under Nansouty, Montbrun, Grouchy, and Latour Maubourg. The cavalry of the Guard, as well as the Austrian force, acted separately. This army is said to have exceeded four hundred and seventy-five thousand men, besides one hundred thousand auxiliaries. It perished miserably among the snows of Russia.

1812. July.

The Duke of Ragusa having been wounded, the command devolved on General Clausel, who retreated to Valladolid, followed by the British, which town the latter entered on the thirteenth; but as the French General continued his retreat to Burgos, Wellington determined to march against the army of the centre, and for this purpose repassed the Douro. After remaining some days at Cuellar, he moved by Segovia to Madrid, leaving some troops under General Paget near the Douro.

Aug. 7th.

King Joseph had quitted Madrid on the twenty-first of July to unite with Marmont; but hearing of that General's defeat on the twenty-fifth near Airivole, he retreated on Segovia, with the expectation that Wellington would follow, hoping to draw his attention from Clausel. On the first of August Joseph fell back, leaving behind him some dragoons, who were defeated by General D'Urban's Portuguese brigade of cavalry.

The Allies entered Madrid on the twelfth, and were received with great enthusiasm by the population.

Joseph, with the army of the centre, had retired from the Capital on the preceding evening, taking the road to Toledo, leaving about seventeen hundred men at Fort La China, in the palace of the Retiro, who surrendered next day.

On the twenty-fifth the French abandoned their works opposite Cadiz and the Isla. Two days afterwards the combined force, under General La Cruza and Colonel Skerret, entered Seville. Here the enemy attempted to defend the bridge, but the grenadiers of the First Guards charged with the bayonet, and put them to flight; several of their number were left dead in the streets, and more

1812.
August.

than two hundred prisoners were taken, with a quantity of baggage, horses, and money.

The first division of the Allied army left Madrid, and was quartered in the palace of the Escurial with the fourth, fifth, and sixth divisions.

King Joseph joined Suchet in Valencia; Soult was in Granada.

With the exception of one battalion, all the English had marched from Cadiz. General Hill, who was at Truxillo, intended to advance on Oropesa, to act in concert with the army under Wellington.

September.

On the first of September Wellington left Madrid, and entered Valladólid, where the Guards remained a few days, and marched to Burgos, the castle of which, strongly defended by field-works bristled with cannon, commanded the river. The place was invested on the night of the nineteenth, and the siege intrusted to the first and sixth divisions. During the night a detachment from the Forty-second regiment stormed and carried a horn-work on the hill of St. Michael, which covered the lower wall of the castle. Next day batteries were erected on this hill. In the night of the twenty-second the besiegers endeavoured to escalade and establish themselves on the outer wall and first line of field-works; they failed however in the attempt, and retired with considerable loss. A week after a mine was exploded: working parties had been constantly in the trenches constructing batteries, but the breach was not deemed practicable.

Sept. 29th.

October.

Early in October, the Commander of the Forces had occasion to notice in Orders the misconduct of several of these working parties, but at the same time observed, that " he was happy to make an exception in favour of the " Guards, who, he is informed, have invariably performed " this duty, as they have every other in this army, in the " most exemplary manner."

THE COLDSTREAM GUARDS. 179

1812.
October.

A second breach was made on the evening of the fourth, and a lodgement effected between the outer wall and the first line of field-works; but the garrison drove back the British, who however, on being reinforced, obliged the French to retire behind their defences. Before day-light on the eighth the garrison made a rush, overthrew the guard, and destroyed all the works between the second line and outer wall. Another and last attempt was made on the eighteenth, but the heavy fire from the garrison rendered it impossible for the assailants to maintain their ground.

The loss of the Allies during the siege exceeded two thousand, which was about equal to that of the garrison.[1]

The following is an extract of a dispatch, dated "Cabeçon, October 26th, 1812," detailing the operations against the castle of Burgos on the eighteenth of October:

" It is impossible to represent in adequate terms my
" sense of the conduct of the Guards and German Legion

---

[1] CASUALTIES IN THE COLDSTREAM.

Killed, &c. in the assault and capture of Fort St. Michael on the 19th of September, 1812; wounded, 1 serjeant, 2 rank and file.

Killed, &c. in the siege of the Castle of Burgos, from the 20th to the 26th of September inclusive.—Killed, 13 rank and file; wounded, 1 captain, 2 serjeants, 39 rank and file. Wounded, Capt. Fraser.

From 27th Sept. to 3rd October.—Killed, 1 serjeant, 2 rank and file; wounded, 8 rank and file.

From 4th to 5th Oct.—Killed, 1 rank and file; wounded, 6 do.

From 6th to 10th Oct.—Killed, 1 Ensign, 11 rank and file; wounded, 27 rank and file, and one missing. Killed, Ensign Buckeridge.

From 11th to 17th Oct.—Killed, 3 rank and file; wounded, 1 do.

From 18th to 21st Oct.—Killed, 1 captain, 1 ensign, 1 serjeant, 22 rank and file; wounded, 2 captains, 1 serjeant, 32 rank and file. Capt. Edward Harvey killed; Ensign Burgess killed; Hon. W. G. Crofton and Hon. John Walpole wounded.

1812.
October.

" upon this occasion; and I am quite satisfied, that if it had been possible to maintain the posts which they had gained with so much gallantry, these troops would have maintained them. Some of the men stormed even the third line, and one was killed in one of the embrasures of that line.

" I had reason to be satisfied with the conduct of the officers and troops during the siege of Burgos, particularly with the brigade of Guards."

The siege of Burgos[1] was raised on the twenty-first: during the night the army filed under the walls of the castle, and crossed the bridge of the Arlanzon, which, although enfiladed by the artillery, was accomplished with scarcely any loss. By crossing this bridge, a march was gained on the enemy, who followed.

Oct. 24th. Reinforcements which had disembarked at Corunna under the Earl of Dalhousie, composed principally of the first brigade of Guards, joined the army in position behind
Oct. 25th. the Carrion. Next day the bridges over the Carrion and Pisuerga were blown up to arrest the progress of the
Oct. 29th. enemy.

After the Allies left Cabeçon they destroyed the bridge, and crossed the Douro at Tudela and Puente del Duero. These bridges were also blown up; but in the evening the French passed in considerable force, by swimming the river near the bridge of Tordesillas. They then attacked and carried the ruins of the bridge, which was defended by a German battalion, and restored their communications.

---

[1] The name of the French officer who commanded in Burgos was Colonel Le Breton. After the restoration of the Bourbons this officer held the rank of Lieutenant-General, and whilst commanding in Strasburg, had an opportunity of paying military honours with that garrison to the Duke of Wellington, who was then on an inspection of the frontiers.

Wellington, the next morning, moved to the left, and occupied nearly the same ground which the Allies had quitted previous to their former retreat on Salamanca. In this position the troops remained till the sixth, when they retired to Torrecilla del Ordem, and three days afterwards found themselves once more on the heights of St. Christoval, in front of Salamanca. Wellington broke up from the position and retired on Ciudad Rodrigo, which town he reached on the eighteenth. During the march from St. Christoval to Ciudad Rodrigo, the weather was extremely inclement, and the troops suffered severely from heavy roads, cold, and constant rain, which made it even difficult for them to light their fires; the supply of rations was also irregular.

1812.

November.

The army crossed the Agueda, and on the twenty-fourth of November head-quarters were once more established at Freynada.

Nov. 19th and 20th.

General Hill returned to Estramadura.

The troops went into cantonments for the winter. The Coldstream reached Musquetello on the sixth of December, where they were quartered.

Dec.

ORIGIN AND SERVICES OF

RETURN OF OFFICERS OF THE FIRST BATTALION OF THE COLDSTREAM FOR THE YEAR 1812.

	Officers present in the Peninsula.	From	To		Officers absent.	Cause of absence.	From	To
Col.	Joseph Fuller	1 Jan.	31 May	M. Gl.	K. H. Howard, (2nd Major)	Commanding a brigade	1 Jan.	31 Dec.
Lt.-Cl.	Hon. H. Brand	June	6 Oct.	,,	Richard Hulse	Ditto. Died	,,	7 Sept.
,,	James Philips	1 Jan.	Dec.	,,	H. Mac Kinnon	Ditto. Killed at Ciudad Rodrigo.	,,	19 Jan.
,,	Sir G. Stirling, Bart.	,,	28 Feb.	,,	W. M. Peacocke	Commandant at Lisbon	,,	31 Dec.
,,	A. Woodford	,,	31 Dec.	Col.	Joseph Fuller	Posted to 2d Battn.	1 June	,,
,,	J. Macdonell	May	,,	,,	Matthew Lord Aylmer	Asst. Adjutant Genl. Portugal	1 Jan.	,,
Capt.	L. F. Adams, (Major)	1 Jan.	April	Lt.-Cl.	Sir W. Sheridan	Prisoner of war	,,	,,
,,	W. H. Raikes	{ 1 Jan. / Aug.	26 Jan. / 31 Dec.	,,	Hon. H. Brand	Sick. In England	7 Oct.	,,
,,	Tho. Barrow	{ 1 Jan. / July	9 Feb. / 31 Dec.	,,	James Philips	Ordered to join 2d Battalion	Dec.	,,
,,	Hon. W. Geo. Crofton	1 Jan.	31 Dec.	,,	Sir G. Stirling	Retired by the sale of his commission	1 Mar.	,,
,,	D. MacKinnon	June	Sept.	,,	R. D. Jackson	Qur. Mr. Genl. Dept. Portugal	1 Jan.	,,
,,	Hon. J. Walpole	1 Jan.	19 Nov.					
,,	Thomas Steele	,,	31 Dec.	,,	H. F. Bouverie	Asst. Adjutant Genl. Portugal	,,	,,
,,	Edward Harvey	,,	18 Oct.	,,	Lucius F. Adams	To join 2d Battalion on promotion	April	,,
,,	W. Burroughs	July	31 Dec.					
,,	George Bowles	1 Jan.	,,	Capt.	John Hamilton	Qr. Mr. Genl. Dept. Leave to Engd	{ 1 Jan. / Mar.	Feb. / 31 Dec.
,,	Thomas Sowerby	,,	,,	,,	Sir H. Sullivan	Sick leave in England. Posted to 2d Battalion	Jan.	31 Dec.
,,	Ed. Lascelles, (appointed Adjut. vice Freemantle)	April	,,	,,	F. Miles Milman	Prisoner of war	1 ,,	,,
,,	P. Sandilands	,,	,,	,,	W. H. Raikes	Sick. Leave to England	27 ,,	Aug.
,,	C. MacKenzie Fraser	May	5 Oct.	,,	Thomas Barrow	Leave to England	10 Feb.	July
Ens.	Charles White	1 Jan.	April	,,	W. C. Wynyard	Adjt. Genl. Dept. Cadiz	1 Jan.	31 Dec.
,,	Thomas Bligh	,,	,,	,,	D. MacKinnon	In England Ditto. Sent recruiting	{ 1 Jan. / Sept.	May / 31 Dec.
,,	Charles Shawe	,,	3 June	,,	Hon. J. Walpole	Sick, wounded. Leave to England	20 Nov.	,,
,,	George H. M. Greville	,,	1 Nov.	,,	Henry Dawkins	Brigade Major, Portugal	1 Jan.	,,
,,	John Talbot	,,	Dec.	,,	Edward Harvey	Killed before Burgos	18 Oct.	,,
,,	G. H. Percival	,,	31 ,,	,,	John Freemantle	A.D.C. to the Marquis of Wellington	Nov.	,,
,,	W. Geo. Baynes	,,	,,	,,	C. M. Fraser	Sick, wounded. Leave to England	6 Oct.	,,
,,	John S. Cowell	,,	,,	,,	Charles White	To join 2d Bat. on promotion	April	,,
,,	W. N. Burgess	,,	18 Oct.					
,,	John Mills	,,	31 Dec.					
,,	James Bradshaw	,,	28 Oct.					
,,	F. L. Beckford	,,	3 Oct.					
,,	J. C. Buckeridge	May	7 Oct.					
,,	J. L. Blackman	April	31 Dec.					
,,	Will. Grimsted	,,	3 Oct.					
,,	Beaumont Ld. Hotham	{ April / 30 Nr.	22 July / 31 Dec.					
,,	Hon. John Rous	July	31 Dec.					
,,	W. Anstruther	June	,,					
,,	Charles Shirley	Dec.	,,					
,,	Fred. Vachell	1 Jan.	,,					
Adjut.	J. Freemantle, (Capt.)	,,	Nov.					
Qu.Mr	John Holmes	,,	8 May					
Ast. Sur.	Thomas Rose	,,	5 Oct.					

THE COLDSTREAM GUARDS.

RETURN OF OFFICERS OF THE FIRST BATTALION OF THE COLDSTREAM FOR THE YEAR 1812.—Continued.

	Officers present in the Peninsula.	From	To		Officers absent.	Cause of absence.	From	To
Ast. Sur.	Edward Nixon	1 Jan.	3 Dec.	Capt.	Thomas Bligh	To join 2d Bat. on promotion	April	31 Dec.
,,	Thomas Maynard	Oct.	31 ,,	,,	Charles Shawe	Ditto.	4 June	,,
				,,	G. H. M. Greville	Ditto.	2 Nov.	,,
				,,	John Talbot	Ditto.	Dec.	,,
Qu.Mr	Tho. Dwelly, (date of appointment)	15 Oct.	27 ,,	Ens.	William Stothert	Prisoner of war	1 Jan.	,,
				,,	W. N. Burgess	Killed before Burgos	18 Oct.	,,
				,,	James Bradshaw	Leave. Joined 2d Battalion	29 Oct.	,,
				,,	F. L. Beckford	Sick leave. In England	4 Oct.	,,
				,,	J. C. Buckeridge	Killed before Burgos	7 Oct.	,,
				,,	Will. Grimsted	Leave to England	4 Oct.	,,
				,,	Beaumont Ld. Hotham	Sick absent, wounded	23 July	29 Nov.
				Qu.Mr	John Holmes	To join 2d Bat. in England	9 May	31 Dec.
				Bat. Sur.	Charles Coombe	Sick absent. To England	1 Jan. Feb.	Feb. 31 Dec.
				Ast Sur.	Thomas Rose	Leave to England	6 Oct.	31 Dec.
				,,	Edward Nixon	Ditto.	4 Dec.	,,
				Qu.Mr	Thomas Dwelly	To join 2d Bat. in England	28 ,,	,,

CHAPTER XI.

French loss in Russia—Austria joins the Russians — Napoleon concentrates his force — Soult sets out with reinforcements for Germany — Graham crosses the Douro — The cavalry and Hill's corps reach Salamanca — Enemy retire from Valladolid to Burgos—Allies cross the Ebro—Attack at Osma—Battle of Vittoria—Retreat of the French—Left advance under Graham—Joseph makes a stand at Tolosa — Graham drives him beyond the frontier—Siege of St. Sebastian—Soult resumes the command in the south of France—Attacks Roncesvalles and Maya—Retreats—Wellington occupies the position he did previous to the advance of Soult—Capture of St. Sebastian—Left of the Allies cross the Bidassoa — Pampeluna surrenders — Position of the French on the Nivelle— Hope succeeds Graham as second in command—French lose their character for invincibility at Leipsic Battle of Nivelle—Allies go into cantonments—Soult concentrates in front of Bayonne—Repulsed in his attacks on the left.

1813. The loss sustained by Napoleon in Russia caused the defection of Prussia. The Crown Prince of Sweden called on the Germans to aid in the great work of restoring liberty to Europe. After the negociations at Prague, Austria united with Russia, and Bavaria followed the example. The Russians advanced to the Elbe, and forced the French troops to retreat before them. The hostility of their former allies made the French suspicious of those that remained; and Napoleon thought it prudent to concentrate, that his communication with France might not be interrupted.

Soult, with a considerable portion of his troops, had been ordered to join the grand army in Germany: but notwithstanding this diminution, the force left in Spain amounted to upwards of one hundred and fifty thousand men; part of whom were in Catalonia and Valencia, the remainder spread over Castille, Leon, and the northern provinces. *1813.*

All the requisite preparations for opening the campaign being completed, on the sixteenth of May five divisions under Graham crossed the Douro in boats, with orders to march on Zamora. Wellington, with the cavalry under General Fane, and a corps of Spaniards, reached Salamanca towards the end of the month. Sir Rowland Hill also arrived there from Estramadura. *May.*

The divisions under Graham first came up with the enemy on the Esla, who offered no opposition, but retired, destroying the bridges of Zamora and Toro. Pontoons were laid down and formed a bridge, over which the Allies crossed, and halted near Zamora.

The French who occupied Madrid, and those on the Tagus, passed the Douro. Valladolid was evacuated, and the enemy retired to Burgos, a strong post. *June.*

After a reconnoissance under Sir Rowland Hill, General Reille was dislodged from the heights of Hormaza. The French army retired on Vittoria during the night of the twelfth of June, after having blown up about four hundred of their men in destroying the castle of Burgos. The Allies then moved to the left and crossed the Ebro near its source by the bridges of St. Martin and Fuentes de Arenas. *June 11th.*

On the eighteenth the light division was successful against a body of infantry. The enemy at Osma made a sharp attack on the first and fifth divisions under Graham, and although much superior in numbers, were repulsed

1813.

and followed to Espejo. In this affair four men of the Coldstream were wounded.

June 19th.

In the night of the twelfth, the French, commanded by King Joseph, Marshal Jourdan acting as his Major-General, concentrated in front of Vittoria; their right was stationed near that town, and extended across the Zadora on high ground covered by field-works; their left ran behind the river to the village of Subijana d'Alava, with an advance-post resting on the height in front, which terminated at Puebla d'Arlanzon; and the centre occupied a hill commanding the valley of Zadora. In this position their right covered the road from Bilboa, their left that from Logrono, and their centre the great road from Madrid.

June 21st.

Wellington reconnoitred the enemy's position on the twentieth. Next morning he advanced in three corps; the right, composed of the second division, with a division of Portuguese under the Conde de Amarante, and Morillo's Spanish corps, commanded by Hill. The centre consisted of the fourth and light divisions. The left, comprising the first and fifth divisions with a body of cavalry, was under Graham. To this force was attached a division of Spaniards, who were ordered to make a wide movement, cross the Zadora, and enter the great road from Valladolid to Bayonne, and intercept the enemy in their retreat.

The right of the Allies first engaged above Puebla, and drove the enemy from the heights: reinforcements were sent from both sides; and after some severe fighting the hill was taken, retaken, and taken again; when it remained in possession of General Hill's corps, who followed up his success. The centre divisions passed the Zadora over some bridges intended for foot-passengers. Picton's and the seventh division crossed the bridge on the Mendonza road, and drove the enemy before them, with the loss of twenty-eight guns. The French retired in good order on Vittoria.

1813.
June 21st.

Graham, whose column on the previous evening had been sent to Margiana, advanced by the road from Bilboa to Vittoria: he attacked the front and flank of the right, and succeeded in driving the French from their position above Abechuco. Every exertion was then made by the enemy to regain Gamorra-Major; and although they failed, they prevented General Oswald's division from profiting by the advantage first gained. The entrance of the centre division into Vittoria obliged the enemy to retire, that they might avoid being taken in rear. The division then crossed the river and posted themselves on the high road to Bayonne, driving back the French on the road leading to Pampeluna, the only one left open to them. Confusion and dismay spread among the enemy's ranks, who were pressed on all sides; and had it not been for the local impediments which opposed the progress of the artillery and cavalry, the French army would have been annihilated. One hundred and fifty-one guns were taken, besides vast quantities of ammunition, caissons, and baggage, together with Marshal Jourdan's baton. The loss of the enemy is pretended by their own historians not to have exceeded six thousand men: that of the Allies was under five thousand.

After this battle the left, under Graham, advanced on Bilboa, in hopes of intercepting General Foy, who on receiving the account of Joseph's defeat retired on Bayonne. At Tolosa he made a stand; but Graham attacked and drove him beyond the frontier. The left wing kept advancing towards Bayonne, forcing the enemy from every position where they attempted any resistance.

1813.
June 25th.   At this period colour-serjeants were first introduced, in the proportion of one to each company.¹

Wellington decided on besieging St. Sebastian; a desirable point for establishing the communication with

July 1st.   England. Sir Thomas Graham invested that place with the first and fifth divisions. To save time batteries were erected on the sand-hills. The convent of St. Bartholomew was carried on the seventeenth. Two breaches were deemed practicable on the twenty-fifth. A mine sprung under the glacis of the front line was the signal for a party of two thousand men, who were in readiness at day-break, to rush forward. This unexpected explosion created so much alarm, that it enabled the assailants to reach the breach with little loss; but in their attempt to ascend they were checked by a front and flank fire, which destroyed five hundred; when the remainder fell back on their trenches. The same day the garrison made a sortie, and succeeded in taking many Portuguese prisoners.

Soult returned from Germany to command the French force in the south. His first object was to relieve Pampeluna, which had been invested by a corps of Spaniards: after various conflicts, he advanced in two columns, amounting to thirty-five thousand men, against the passes of Roncesvalles and Maya, near the mountain Cubiry. He was, however, repulsed in his attacks, and retreated with his army early on the thirty-first, in three columns, by St. Jean Pied de Port, Echalar, Sarré, and Maya. The Allied army followed and came up with the enemy's rear-guard, strongly posted in the pass of Donna Maria, from whence they were driven by the brigade under General Barnes.

The loss of the French since Soult had resumed the

---

¹ See Appendix, No. 250.

command was upwards of eight thousand men, and greatly exceeded that of the Allies. _{1813.}

Lord Wellington in the beginning of August returned to the position occupied by his army previous to the advance of Soult. _{August.}

Supplies of stores and a battering train arrived from England, and were landed on the eighteenth of August.

Towards the end of the month the Allies had placed nearly eighty guns in battery before St. Sebastian, whose fire on the town continued without intermission during the day from their first opening. On the night of the twenty-ninth the garrison attempted another sortie, and were repulsed. _{Aug. 28th.}

The storming party, which formed early on the thirty-first, consisted of seven hundred and fifty volunteers, two hundred of whom were supplied by the Guards. The detachment from the Coldstream consisted of one lieutenant, one ensign, two serjeants, one drummer, and fifty men, under Captain Barrow and Ensign Chaplin. _{Aug. 31st.}

The column, after many desperate attempts, found itself, on reaching the summit, assailed by a heavy fire from the place, that destroyed all in the advance. In the words of General Graham, "no man outlived the attempt to gain the ridge."

" Notwithstanding the great extent of the breach,
" there was but one point where it was possible to enter,
" and there by files. All the inside of the wall to the
" right of the curtain formed a perpendicular scarp of at
" least twenty feet to the level of the streets, so that the
" narrow ridge of the curtain itself, formed by the breach-
" ing of its end and front, was the only accessible point.
" During the suspension of the operations of the siege,
" the enemy had prepared every means of defence which
" art could devise."

1813.
Aug. 31st.

It was not till the attack was renewed, and after a most determined assault, that the besieged were driven from their defences. The Allies then succeeded in forcing the barricades, and pushed forward into the town, with a loss of about two thousand three hundred killed and wounded. The enemy retired to the castle, leaving about seven hundred prisoners.

The casualties in the Coldstream were, five rank and file killed, Ensign Thomas Chaplin and twenty-seven rank and file wounded, and one missing.

September.

On the ninth, fifty heavy guns and mortars opened on the castle of St. Sebastian; which, after a bombardment of two hours, surrendered. The garrison amounted to upwards of two thousand, including about five hundred sick.

October.

On the seventh of October, the first and fifth divisions, with General Wilson's Portuguese brigade, forded the Bidassoa at low water, for the purpose of driving the enemy from the mountain of La Rhune. A corps of Spaniards crossed the river higher up, with the intention of attacking the works on the Montagne Vert. General Alten with the light division, and the Spaniards under Longa, were to attack the pass of Bera. General Giron with the army of Andalusia was to march against the intrenchments of La Rhune. The fifth division crossed the river, followed by the first, and advanced against the French, who had scarcely formed in line before they were driven from their works, with the loss of several guns.

At Bera the attack of the light division was particularly successful. General Giron carried the lower slopes of La Rhune; the enemy, however, crowned the heights, when
Oct. 7. the close of day put an end to further efforts.

Next day the Spaniards carried an intrenched line beyond the mountain with little opposition. These advantages were gained with a loss of about sixteen hundred men. In the Coldstream the casualties were, two rank and file killed, and ten wounded.

<small>1813. Oct. 7th.</small>

On the eighteenth the Coldstream moved to the camp near St. Jean de Luz.

On the thirty-first, after a blockade of four months, the garrison of Pampeluna surrendered prisoners of war.

The enemy from the beginning of August had been in possession of a formidable line of works on the Nivelle; their right rested on the sea, covered the town of St. Jean de Luz, and extended twelve miles in a direct line; their centre occupied the village of Sarré and the adjacent rising ground; their left, covered by the river Ainhoe, rested on a height, which was defended by several works that added to the strength of their position. A mountain protected the approach to the village, the extremity of which was also fortified. In the progress of these works no labour or expense had been spared.

The incessant rain and snow in the mountains greatly retarded Lord Wellington.

On crossing the Bidassoa, Graham, who had been appointed to head the force in Holland, was succeeded in command of the left wing of the army by Sir John Hope. It consisted of the first division under Major-General Howard, with the fifth division, the independent, and two Portuguese brigades. The centre was formed in two columns, the right of which comprised the third, fourth, and seventh divisions under Marshal Beresford; and the left, the light division, with the Spanish army of reserve, supported by a brigade of cavalry. The sixth and Portuguese division under Sir John Hamilton, and the Spanish division commanded by Morillo, formed the right wing.

<small>November.</small>

In Germany the French lost their character for invincibility, and were deserted by their auxiliaries; the results of which were apparent in the subsequent victories of the Confederates and the ultimate downfall of Napoleon's power. He could no longer send reinforcements to recover the ground lost in Spain; and Wellington resolved to pass into France.

Previous to entering that country, the British Commander issued the following humane and generous proclamation:

" Officers and soldiers must recollect, that their nations
" are at war with France, solely because the ruler of the
" French nation will not allow them to be at peace, and is
" desirous of forcing them to submit to his yoke; and
" they must not forget, that the worst of the evils suffered
" by the enemy, in his profligate invasion of Spain and
" Portugal, [have been occasioned by the irregularities
" of his soldiers, and their cruelties, authorised and en-
" couraged by their chiefs, toward the unfortunate and
" peaceful inhabitants of the country. To avenge this
" conduct on the peaceable inhabitants of France, would
" be unmanly and unworthy of the nations to which the
" Commander of the Forces now addresses himself."

Calm and confident, Wellington, from the heights of the Pyrenees, looked down on the well-guarded territories of the great enemy of his country, and, with steady purpose, prepared to tame the pride of a mighty Prince who, while he carried war and misery into almost every capital of Europe, made it his haughty boast that the women of the great nation had never seen the smoke of an enemy's camp. The Herculean task of the British General was accomplished; he had chased the far-famed legions of Napoleon from the gates of Lisbon to the utmost limits of the Spanish boundary, and had restored the affrighted inhabitants of the Peninsula to their native towns and villages in peace and safety. His was no selfish triumph, destined only to convey to future ages the name of a successful conqueror. Wellington stood before the world at once a hero and a benefactor; and the shouts of his exulting soldiers were mingled with the blessings of rescued millions, whom his genius and courage had delivered from the grasp of the oppressor. It was his high and peculiar glory that the brilliant achievements in Spain and Portugal, which secured him an imperishable reputation as a commander, gave repose to unoffending nations, and had no object but to foil a military chief whose restless unscrupulous ambition rendered murder, conflagration, and pillage familiar to the sight of every neighbouring kingdom that dared to resist his usurpations. After long and carefully perusing the living map that lay spread out beneath his feet, Wellington ordered his army to advance; and on the tenth of November the troops descended from the Pyrenees through the mountain passes by moon-light, to transfer to France the calamities of domestic war, and teach the admirers of splendid but unprincipled aggression, that there is at length a day of retribution.

The Allies on reaching the line of piquets halted, preparatory to the attack, which was to commence at daylight; they were so placed as to be concealed from the enemy.

At the dawn of day a cannonade was commenced against some redoubts in front of Sarré, after which the infantry rushed to the assault and carried the works and the village. The light division forced the lines on Petite la Rhune. The enemy having abandoned the redoubts, General Alten formed on the summit of the hill they had quitted. The army then advanced, covered by skirmishers towards the heights behind Sarré, when the French successively abandoned their intrenchments, and

1813.
Nov. 10th.
fled in great disorder down the hill with a view to reach the bridges over the Nivelle.

Whilst the light division was proceeding to assault a redoubt, the garrison endeavoured to escape; Beresford, however, intercepted them and made about six hundred prisoners.

Clinton received orders to ford the Nivelle, and attack the heights of Ainhoe, supported by General Hamilton's division placed in échelon. He marched directly on the right to attack the enemy in front, who, being driven back, left the redoubts on the heights of Ainhoe unprotected. The French detachments by which they were occupied hastily retreated, and caused a body of their troops on the left to recede. The British divisions then advanced, when the French quitted the line in front of Ainhoe and retired towards Cambo.

The enemy, driven from the centre of their line, concentrated on the heights above St. Pé; whence they were dislodged whilst forming, by a flank movement of the third and seventh divisions on the left, in conjunction with the sixth division which marched in the opposite direction. The centre of the Allies was established in rear of the enemy's right. The close of day put an end to the operations, and Soult, under cover of the night, withdrew, and retired to Bayonne.

During these movements the enemy lost fifty guns, two thousand men, fifteen hundred prisoners, and great quantities of stores and ammunition.

The loss of the Allies was under six hundred killed, and two thousand wounded.

Ensign Anstruther and thirteen rank and file of the light company of the Coldstream were wounded.

The Allies went into cantonments between the ridge of Nivelle and the sea.

Soult concentrated his army in an intrenched camp in front of Bayonne. _{1813. November.}

The distance between the contending armies did not exceed two miles at the nearest point, which induced Wellington to construct a defensive line for the protection of his front against any sudden attack.

The Coldstream advanced on the ninth beyond Bidart, within three miles of Bayonne, encountered the enemy, and returned at night to their quarters at St. Jean de Luz.[1] _{December.}

The allied army advanced on the ninth of December, and the left wing, under Hope, closely reconnoitred the enemy's intrenchments at Bayonne, with little opposition. Hill passed the Nive by the fords at Cambo. Clinton's division crossed by the bridge of boats at Ustariz.

The French made a stand at Ville Franque; but were dislodged by the light infantry of Clinton's division. In the night the enemy withdrew all their posts into the town of Bayonne.

Next day Hill's corps took post with their right on the Adour, the left reaching to Ville Franque, and their centre across the road from Bayonne to St. Jean Pied de Port; some cavalry were also sent to Urcuray to watch a division of the enemy posted near St. Palais. Sir John Hope returned to his former cantonment, and Beresford retired to the left bank of the Nive, keeping up his communication with General Hill by a bridge of boats. _{Dec. 10th.}

Soult left Bayonne early on the morning of the tenth, and advanced with the determination of attacking the left under Hope.

The road to St. Jean de Luz was defended by the fifth division and two Portuguese brigades. The light division

---

[1] Head-quarters.

1813.
Dec. 10th.
was placed about two miles to the right, and separated from the left corps by a range of hills, too steep to enable a body of troops to occupy them.

The French attacked and drove the light division within the village of Arcanques, where they were strongly intrenched, and afterwards established themselves on the hills. This being effected, the enemy attacked the left, consisting of the fifth division, which received them with great gallantry: General Robinson was wounded; and the French having advanced in front of Barouillet through some wood, compelled Major-General Campbell's Portuguese brigade, and General Robinson's brigade which supported it, to retire, and thereby they forced the position.

A Portuguese battalion moved forward on the road, and went into the rear of the wood: the Ninth regiment on the extreme right wheeled round and charged with the Portuguese, by which the enemy were driven back and suffered severely. The French, however, again renewed the attempt to dislodge the fifth division, when the remainder of the left wing, consisting of the brigade of Guards, brought up from their cantonments under Major-General Howard, opportunely arrived: the enemy's attacking columns were then repulsed; and night closed on the combatants.

Soult, having failed in his efforts to destroy the left of the Allies, retired with part of his force during the night from the position in front of Sir John Hope.

Dec. 11th. This General next day sent some of his troops to the support of the light division; and being thus weakened, he was again attacked by the enemy, whom he repulsed.

On the same day the Coldstream moved to the outposts, whence they afterwards returned to their quarters at St. Jean de Luz; but were occasionally sent to the out-post near Bidart.

The French still continued in front of the left, and on the afternoon of the twelfth there was some sharp skirmishing,[1] but no alteration took place in the position of either army. Little else of interest occurred pending these operations, with the exception of some unsuccessful attacks made by Soult on the corps of Sir Rowland Hill, which commenced on the ninth and ended on the thirteenth of December. Although Soult from his position was enabled to direct his whole force against any given point of the extended line of the Allies with a great superiority in numbers, yet he made no impression by these attacks. The loss of life on both sides was, however, considerable.

1813.
Dec. 11th.

---

[1] The Coldstream had three men wounded.

RETURN OF THE OFFICERS OF THE FIRST BATTALION OF THE COLDSTREAM FOR THE YEAR 1813.

	Officers present in the Peninsula.	From	To		Officers absent.	Cause of absence.	From	To
Lt. Cl.	A. Woodford	1 Jan.	31 Dec.	Lt.-G.	J. Calcraft, 1st Major	Leave	1 Jan.	31 Dec.
,,	J. Macdonell	,,	,,	M.-G.	K. A. Howard, 2d Maj.	Commanding a Brigade	,,	,,
,,	G. Collier	Jan.	,,	,,	W. M. Peacocke	Commandant at Lisbon	,,	,,
,,	J. Hamilton	July	,,					
Capt.	W. H. Raikes	1 Jan.	16 May			Ast Adjt. Gen. Portugal	Jan.	June
,,	Thomas Gore	March	31 Dec.	,,	M. Lord Aylmer	Commanding a Brigade	July	31 Dec.
,,	T. Barrow, (Major)	1 Jan.	22 ,,					
,,	Hon. W. G. Crofton	,,	31 ,,	Lt. Cl.	Sir W. Sheridan	Prisoner of war	1 Jan.	,,
,,	Thomas Steele	,,	,,					
,,	W. Burroughs	,,	,,			In England.		
,,	G. Bowles	,,	,,	,,	Hon. H. Brand	Posted to 2d battalion	,,	,,
,,	T. Sowerby	,,	,,					
,,	P. Sandilands	,,	,,			Asst. Q.-Mr.	1 Jan.	April
,,	John Prince	Jan.	,,	,,	R. D. Jackson	Gl. Portugal		
,,	J. V. Harvey	July	,,			Leave to Engd Returned	Oct.	31 Dec.
Ens.	G. H. Percival	1 Jan.	14 Mar.			Ast Adjt. Gen.	1 Jan.	,,
,,	W. G. Baynes	,,	21 July	,,	H. F. Bouverie	Peninsula		
,,	J. S. Cowell	,,	Oct.			Sick leave to	18 May	June
,,	John Mills	,,	Jan.	,,	W. H. Raikes	England		
,,	J. L. Blackman	,,	31 Dec.			Posted to 2d battalion	July	31 Dec.
,,	B. Lord Hotham	,,	,,	Major	T. Barrow	Leave to England	23 Dec.	,,
,,	Hon. J. Rous	,,	,,			Adjutt. Gen.	1 Jan.	July
,,	W. Anstruther	,,	,,	Capt.	W. C. Wynyard	Dept. Cadiz		
,,	C. Shirley	,,	,,			On Staff at home	Aug.	31 Dec.
,,	J. Drummond	Jan.	,,			Sick, wounded, England		
,,	Hon. R. Moore	,,	,,	,,	Hon. J. Walpole	On Staff, Kent district	1 Jan.	,,
,,	C. A. Girardot	,,	,,					
,,	T. Chaplin	May	26 Sept.			Brig.-Major,		
,,	E. Clifton	July	31 Dec.	,,	H. Dawkins	Sec. Brigade of Guards	,,	,,
,,	Henry Salwey	Sept.	,,					
,,	G. G. Morgan	,,	,,			A. D. C. to		
,,	F. Vachell	1 Jan.	,,	,,	J. Freemantle	Marquis of Wellington	,,	,,
,,	W. Kortright	,,	,,			A. D. C. to		
Adjt.	E. Lascelles, (Capt.)	1 ,,	,,	,,	A. Wedderburn	Lt.-Gen. Sir John Hope	,,	,,
Q. Mr.	B. Selway	,,	,,	,,	W. G. Baynes	To England on promotion	22 July	,,
Surg.	Thomas Rose	July	,,	,,	J. S. Cowell	To England on promotion	Oct.	,,
Ast. Sur.	W. Whymper	June	,,	Ens.	G. H. Percival	To join 2d batt.	15 Mar.	,,
,,	T. Maynard	1 Jan.	,,	,,	W. Stothert	Prisoner of war	1 Jan.	,,
				,,	John Mills	Leave to England	Feb.	,,
				,,	F. L. Beckford	Sick, England Recruiting	1 Jan.	,,
				,,	W. Grimstead	Leave in England	,,	,,
				,,	T. Chaplin	Sick, wounded: to England	27 Sept.	,,

CHAPTER XII.

Hill moves to Hellete—French retire—Spaniards blockade St. Jean Pied de Port — Left wing invests Bayonne—Battle of Orthez—Soult retires — Beresford's corps marches for Bourdeaux—Great part of his force recalled—Battle of Toulouse —Sortie from Bayonne — Coldstream suffer severely — Coldstream in barracks at Bourdeaux—Hostilities close on land between England and France—Coldstream quit Bourdeaux for Pauliac—Conveyed by craft to the Stirling Castle — Arrive at Spithead — March to London — Six companies of the Coldstream embark for Holland — Inspected at Steenbergen — Failure of attack on Bergen-op-Zoom—Six companies go into quarters at Brussels—Six companies reinforced by four companies from England.

THE severity of the season obliged the Allies to keep in their cantonments, and consequently nothing of moment occurred until about the middle of February, when Wellington endeavoured to draw Soult from his position near Bayonne.

On the fourteenth of February Hill's corps broke up from Urcuray and moved to Hellete, from whence they obliged the enemy's troops to retire on St. Palais. General Harispe left a garrison at St. Jean Pied de Port, which was blockaded by the Spanish corps under Mina, and, being joined by other troops, made a stand on the height of La Montagne, whence he was driven, and crossed the Bidassoa. The left wing of the Allies, intended for the investment of Bayonne, moved forward at one

1814.

February.

1814.
Feb. 23rd.

o'clock A.M. on the morning of the twenty-third, driving the enemy's out-posts before them: the heavy guns were then brought up and placed in battery. The river Adour was to be crossed by means of pontoon rafts, which could only be worked during slack tide. In the evening, when two light companies of the Coldstream and Third Guards, with four battalion companies of the latter regiment, had passed, two columns of the enemy deployed, fired a volley, and rushed on them with the bayonet. The Guards, however, being most judiciously posted by Major-General Stopford on a ridge of sand, with their right resting on the river, their left towards the sea, the allied artillery on the other side flanking the ground in their front, and assisted by a discharge of Congreve rockets, threw the enemy into confusion and forced them to retire. In the night pontoons, used as row-boats, were substituted for the rafts; and, as only fifteen men passed over each turn, it was not until the evening of the next day that the first division and some cavalry were on the right bank. By the twenty-sixth a bridge was constructed below the town, which during the remainder of the war served as the regular communication between

Feb. 27th. St. Jean de Luz and Spain. The following evening, after a sharp skirmish, Bayonne was blockaded. Sir John Hope with the left wing was intrusted with the siege. The direct road to Bourdeaux was now open by the bridge thrown across the Adour.

Wellington on the twenty-seventh of February attacked Soult, whose army, strongly posted near Orthez, had successfully resisted the repeated efforts of the Allies to gain the heights. But the British commander determined to change his plan; the result was the brilliant, rapid, and total defeat of the French, who sustained a loss of three thousand men and six pieces of artillery. The casualties on the part of the Allies did not exceed two thousand five hundred. 1814.

Soult retired towards Tarbes by the road to Toulouse: in consequence of the heavy rains and the destruction of the bridges the French were not closely pursued in their retreat.

Wellington had been informed that, although favourable to the Bourbon cause, the inhabitants of Bourdeaux were prevented from giving vent to their feelings by a small garrison which kept them in awe. Soult probably supposed that Wellington would not advance on this town while the garrison of Bayonne held out. Marshal Beresford, having with him the Duc d'Angoulême, was however ordered to march with his corps to expel the French troops from Bourdeaux; but they immediately retired on his approach, and the English General was met by the entire population, who instantly destroyed all the emblems of Napoleon. Wellington, considering that so large a force was unnecessary for the defence of Bourdeaux, recalled Beresford, leaving Lord Dalhousie there with about five thousand men.

On the tenth of April the battle of Toulouse was gained, though not without great loss. The British and Portuguese had five thousand killed and wounded, and the Spaniards nearly three thousand; but, in estimating this fatal result, it must be remembered that the attack continued during the entire day, and was directed against intrenchments of a most formidable description. The loss of the French was three thousand six hundred. April.

Wellington closely pressed the siege of Toulouse, and on the night of the twelfth Soult retired, leaving three Generals and one thousand six hundred prisoners.

Early on the morning of the fourteenth, and after the intelligence of the event which had occurred at Paris on April 14th.

1814.
April 14th.

the seventh [1] was known, a desperate sortie was made from the French camp in front of the citadel of Bayonne, directed principally against the position occupied by the second brigade of Guards at St. Etienne, opposite to the citadel. Major-General Hay was killed at the first onset, and the enemy gained temporary possession of the village of St. Etienne. The centre of the British was also driven in, and General Stopford was wounded. General Hope, on coming up with some troops in the dark, encountered the enemy, by whom he was wounded and taken prisoner, his horse having been shot under him. Reinforcements were quickly brought up, the lost ground recovered, and the assailants driven back with great slaughter: but this was a lamentable and useless waste of lives, as Napoleon had already abdicated.

The Allies lost more than eight hundred men in killed, wounded, and prisoners.

The casualties of the Coldstream in consequence of this sortie from Bayonne were, one captain, one lieutenant, one serjeant, one drummer, and thirty rank and file killed; one captain, three lieutenants, two ensigns, eleven serjeants, and one hundred and eleven rank and file wounded; two serjeants and eighty-two rank and file missing.

Lieutenant-Colonel Sir Henry Sullivan and Captain the Honourable W. G. Crofton were killed. Lieutenant-Colonel Collier, who died, having had both his thighs am-

---

[1] On the eleventh of April, 1814, the treaty of Paris was ratified by Marshals Ney, Macdonald, and Caulaincourt, on the part of Napoleon; and by the Ministers of Austria, Russia, and Prussia. By the convention, Napoleon renounced all sovereignty over France and Italy; stipulating that the Island of Elba should be his domain and residence during life: the abdication was signed at Fontainbleau.

putated; Captain Burroughs, Ensigns Vachell and Pitt died of their wounds. Captains James Vigors Harvey and Henry Dawkins were wounded.   1814. April 14th.

Thus closed hostilities on land between two nations who had been engaged in an incessant warfare, with only one year's interruption, from 1793.

The Coldstream left their ground near Bayonne on the second of May: after being encamped some time they marched to Bourdeaux, where the men went into barracks, and the officers were billeted on the inhabitants till the twenty-third of July; the first battalion then quitted the town for Pauliac, a village on the Garonne, whence they were conveyed in large craft to the Stirling Castle of seventy-four guns, at the mouth of the river, on board of which they embarked, and arrived at Spithead on the twenty-eighth; they then marched to Portman-Street barracks.   May.

RETURN OF THE OFFICERS OF THE FIRST BATTALION OF THE COLDSTREAM, FROM JANUARY TO JULY, 1814.

	Present.	From.	To		Absent.	Cause of absence.	From	To
Lt.Cl.	A. Woodford	1 Jan.	July	Lt.-G.	J. Calcraft, (1st Major)	Leave	1 Jan.	July
,,	J. Macdonell	,,	31 Jan.	M.-G.	Harry Chester	Ditto	,,	,,
,,	George Collier	,,	10 May	,,	Warren M. Peacocke	Commandant at Lisbon	,,	,,
,,	John Hamilton	,,	July	,,	Joseph Fuller	Staff, at home	,,	,,
,,	Sir H. Sullivan, Bt.	March	14 Apr.	,,	Matth. Lord Aylmer	Com^g. a Brigade in France	,,	,,
,,	Thomas Gore	1 Jan.	11 Feb.	Lt.Cl.	Sir W. Sheridan	Prisoner of war	,,	—
Capt.	Hon. W. G. Crofton	,,	14 Apr.	,,	R. D. Jackson	Ast. Qur. Mr. Gl. in France	,,	,,
,,	Thomas Steele	,,	July	,,	H. F. Bouverie	Ast. Adjt. Gl. in France	,,	,,
,,	W. Burroughs	,,	26 Apr.	,,	J. Macdonell	Ordered to join Detacht in Holland	1 Feb.	—
,,	George Bowles	,,	July	,,	George Collier	Died of his wounds	10 May	—
,,	Tho. Sowerby	,,	,,	,,	Sir H. Sullivan	Killed at Bayonne	14 Apr.	—
,,	P. Sandilands	,,	,,	,,	Thomas Gore	To join 2d Bn. on promn.	12 Feb.	—
,,	John Prince	,,	9 Jan.	Capt.	Th. Barrow, (Maj.)	Leave in England	1 Jan.	July
,,	J. V. Harvey	,,	June	,,	W. Clinton Wynyard	A.D.C. to Maj. Gl. Acland: died	,,	27 Apr.
Ens.	J. L. Blackman	,,	4 April	,,	Hon. W. G. Crofton	Killed at Bayonne	14 Apr.	—
,,	Beaumont Ld. Hotham	,,	Feb.	,,	D. Mac Kinnon	Recruiting in England	1 Jan.	July
,,	Hon. J. Rous	,,	May	,,	Hon. J. Walpole	Staff, at home	,,	,,
,,	W. Anstruther	,,	13 Feb.	,,	Hen. Dawkins	Brig. Maj. to 2d brigade of Guards.	,,	8 June
,,	Chas. Shirley	,,	8 June	,,	W. Burroughs	Sick, wounded, to Engd.	9 June	July
,,	J. Drummond	,,	July	,,		Died of his wounds	26 Apr.	—
,,	Hon. R. Moore	,,	,,	,,	J. Freemantle, (Maj.)	A.D.C. to Marquis of Wellington	1 Jan.	July
,,	C. A. Girardot	,,	,,	,,	John Prince	Leave to England	10 ,,	,,
,,	Edw. Clifton	,,	,,	,,	Js. V. Harvey	Sick, wounded, to Engd.	June	,,
,,	Henry Salwey	,,		,,	A. Wedderburn	A.D.C. to Sir J. Hope	1 Jan.	,,
,,	G. G. Morgan	,,	,,	,,	Charles White	A.D.C. to the Duke of Cambridge	,, ,,	,,
,,	Fred. Vachell	,,	13 May	,,	W. Stothert	Prisoner of war	,, ,,	—
,,	Hon. J. Forbes	March	July	,,	J. L. Blackman	To join 2d Bn. on promn.	5 Apr.	,,
,,	William Pitt	,,	24 Apr.	,,	Beaumont Ld. Hotham	Ditto do.	Feb.	,,
,,	Wm. Kortright	1 Jan.	July	,,	W. Anstruther	Sick, wounded, to Engd.	14 ,,	,,
,,	H. Armytage	March	,,	,,	Hon. J. Rous	To join 2d Bn. on promn.	June	,,
,,	Hon. Wm. Rufus Rous	,,	,,	,,	Charles Shirley	Ditto do.	9 June	,,
,,	Henry J. W. Bentinck	April	,,	Ens.	Fred. Vachell	Died of his wounds	13 May	,,
Adjut.	E. Lascelles, (Capt.)	1 Jan.	,,	,,	Hon. J. Forbes	With 2d battalion	1 Jan.	Feb.
Q.Mr.	Benj. Selway	,,	,,	,,		Ditto	,, ,,	,, ,,
Surg.	Thomas Rose	,,	June	,,	William Pitt	Died of his wounds	24 Apr.	—
Ast. Sur.	W. Whymper	,,	4 Jan.	Surg.	Thomas Rose	To England in charge of sick	June	July
,,	Thos. Maynard	,,	July	Ast. Sur.	W. Whymper	Leave to England	5 Jan.	—

While the first battalion was engaged in driving the French out of Spain, six companies of the second battalion of the Coldstream had embarked at Greenwich for Holland, under Lieutenant-Colonel Adams, on the twenty-fourth of November, 1813, and landed at Scheveling on the sixth of December, from which place they marched to the Hague, and thence to Delft and Helvoet Sluys. On the sixteenth they embarked and sailed to Williamstadt, and went to Steenbergen, then moved into cantonments near Bergen-op-Zoom, and returned to Steenbergen on the ninth of January, where they were inspected on the twenty-first by his Royal Highness the Duke of Clarence. They passed through Esschen, West Wesel, and continued their route through Rosendale, Staebroeck, to Santvliet, for the purpose of attacking the fortress of Bergen-op-Zoom.

Sir Thomas Graham had collected about four thousand British bayonets to carry this strong fortress by a coup-de-main; for which purpose the troops were formed in four columns: two were to attack at different points; the third was to make a false attack; while the fourth attempted the entrance of the harbour, which was fordable at low water. Major-General Cooke led the left, and met with some impediments from the ice in crossing the ditch, but succeeded in gaining the rampart. The right column, under Major-General Skerret, forced itself into the town; but that officer being wounded, and great loss sustained, much confusion prevailed. The centre column, which was driven back, formed again, and advanced to effect a junction with the left column on the ramparts. At day-light the besieged turned the guns on the British, who were without protection on the out-works. General Cooke at length ordered the Guards to retreat, which was conducted in the steadiest and most soldier-like manner.

1814. General Bizanet, the governor of the fortress, agreed to a suspension of hostilities.

The loss of the British amounted to about three hundred killed, and one thousand eight hundred prisoners, amongst whom were many wounded.

The casualties in the Coldstream, during the eighth and ninth of March, were, Captain Shawe, severely wounded; one rank and file killed, and about thirty taken prisoners.

The following is an extract from the Brigade Order:—

"Hogerhyde, March 10, 1814.

" Colonel Lord Proby returns his best thanks to the
" officers, non-commissioned officers, and privates of the
" detachment from the third brigade of Guards who were
" engaged in the attack upon Bergen-op-Zoom: he
" feels equally satisfied with the gallantry which they
" displayed in the assault; with their steady conduct
" during the many hours they maintained their position
" upon the ramparts; and with the soldierly and orderly
" manner in which they effected the retreat.

" Lord Proby particularly remarked the excellent con-
" duct of the officers who commanded the advanced
" party, and that which carried the ladders: Captain
" Rodney, Ensign Gooch, and Ensign Pardoe."

The six companies of the second battalion of the Coldstream were successively quartered at West Wesel, Mechlin, Lippelo, and Dendermonde. They afterwards crossed the Scheld and took possession of Antwerp. On the third of August they moved to Mechlin, and entered Brussels next day. On the second of September the colours and four companies joined from England, completing the detachment to ten companies.

THE COLDSTREAM GUARDS.

OFFICERS OF THE SIX COMPANIES OF THE SECOND BATTALION OF THE COLDSTREAM WHO EMBARKED FOR HOLLAND, 24th Nov. 1813.

	Present.	From	To		Present.	From	To		Present.	From	To
		1813.	1814.			1813.	1814.			1813.	1814.
Lt. Cl.	L.F.Adams	Nov.	Sept.	Capt.	W.L.Walton, Acting Adjt.	Nov.	31 Dec.	Ens.	J. Mills	Nov.	Feb.
,,	H. Loftus	,,	June	,,	Thomas Bligh	,,	Sept.	,,	T. S. Duncombe	,,	Sept.
				,,	Charles Shawe	,,	,,	,,	F. Eyre	,,	,,
				,,	John Talbot	,,	,,	,,	T. Powys	,,	,,
				,,	G. H. Percival	,,	,,	,,	H Gooch	,,	31 Dec.
				,,	W. G. Baynes	,,	31 Dec.	,,	A. Cuyler	,,	,,

Adjutant, Capt. C.A.F.Bentinck — Nov. — Sept.
Actg. Adjt. ,, W. L. Walton — Sept. — 31 Dec.
Ast. Surg. ,, George Smith — ,, — ,,
,, ,, ,, Sept. Worrell — ,, — March.

	Officers joined.	Present.		Officers absent.	Cause of absence.	Absent.	
		From	To			From	To
		1814.	1814.			1814.	1814.
Ens.	M. Beaufoy	Jan. Dec.	Oct. 31 Dec.	Capt. John Mills	Leave to England	Feb.	31 Dec.
Lt.-Col.	J. Macdonell	May	Sept.	Ast. Sur. S. Worrell	Ordered to England	April	,,
Bn.Surg.	W. Whymper	March	31 Dec.	Lt. Cl. Henry Loftus	Leave. To 1st bat.	July	,,
	The remaining companies of the second battalion embarked for Holland 27 Aug. 1814.			,, J. Macdonell	Ordered to join 1st bat.	Sept.	,,
				,, L. F. Adams	Ditto	,,	,,
				Capt. Thomas Bligh	Ditto	,,	,,
Col.	H. F. Bouverie	Aug.	31 Dec.	,, Charles Shawe	Ditto	,,	,,
Lt.-Col.	D. MacKinnon	,,	. Dec.	,, John Talbot	Ditto	,,	,,
,,	Hon. J. Walpole	,,	31 ,,	,, G. H. Percival	Ditto	,,	,,
Capt.	E. Sumner	,,	31 Dec.	,, C. Shirley	Ditto	,,	,,
,,	J. L. Blackman	,,	. Dec.	Ens. T. S. Duncombe	Ditto	,,	,,
,,	W. Grimstead	,,	31 ,,				
,,	Hon. J. Rous	,,	Oct.	,, Francis Eyre	Ditto	,,	,,
,,	C. Shirley	,,	Sept.	,, Thomas Powys	Ditto	,,	,,
,,	J. Drummond	,,	31 Dec.				
,,	Hon. R. Moore	,,	,,	Adjt. C.A.F.Bentinck	Dep. Assist. Adjt.-Gen.	,,	,,
Ens.	H. F. Griffiths	,,	,,				
,,	J. F. Buller	,,	,,	Capt. Hon. J. Rous	Leave of absence	Oct.	,,
,,	John Montagu	,,	,,	Ens. Mark Beaufoy	Ditto	,,	Nov.
,,	G. R. Buckley	,,	,,	,, F. I. Douglas	Ditto	,,	31 Dec.
,,	James Hervey	,,	,,	,, Robert Bowen	Ditto	,,	Nov.
,,	Henry Vane	,,	,,	Lt. Cl. D. MacKinnon	Ditto	Dec.	31 Dec.
,,	F. I. Douglas	,,	Oct.	,, W. Gomm	Ditto	,,	,,
,,	R. Bowen	Dec.	Oct. 31 Dec.	Capt. J. L. Blackman	Ditto	,,	,,
,,	A. Gordon	Aug.	,,				
Qur. Mr.	B. Selway	,,	,,				
Ast Surg.	W. Hunter	,,	,,				
Col.	Hon. Alex. Abercromby	Oct.	,,				
Lt.-Col.	W. Gomm	Nov.	. Dec.				
,,	H. Wyndham	,,	31 ,,				
Capt.	G. Bowles	Oct.	,,				
,,	T. Sowerby	Nov.	,,				
,,	B. Lord Hotham	,,	,,				

CHAPTER XIII.

Napoleon escapes from Elba—Prince Regent determines to join the Allies — Reinforcements sent to Belgium — Position of the Allies—Napoleon heads the northern army—His proclamation—Coldstream march to Quatre Bras—Battle of Waterloo.

1815. AT the Congress of Vienna it was made a question, whether St. Helena should be selected as the place of Napoleon's future residence; the Duke of Wellington opposed the measure, and it was given up. Napoleon, who had been informed that the Allied Monarchs had it in contemplation to send him to that remote island, escaped from Elba in a brig, accompanied by three small vessels containing about eleven hundred men, among whom were one hundred dismounted Polish cavalry. On the first of March he landed near Cannes, in the Gulf of Juan, reached Lyons on the tenth, and ten days after made his triumphal entry into Paris, Louis the Eighteenth having fled to Ghent.

A message was delivered to both Houses from the Prince Regent, declaring his intention to join the Allies.

Austria, Russia, Prussia, and England[1] entered into an agreement not to lay down their arms till Napoleon was again deprived of the supreme power in France.

The Coldstream left Brussels on the twenty-fourth of

---

[1] The expenditure of England during the year 1815 amounted to upwards of one hundred and sixteen millions!

March for Ath. The Prince of Orange at one time had determined to attack Lille; but this scheme was overruled, and the Guards returned to Enghien.

Reinforcements were almost daily sent from England; all the troops that could be spared were hurried to the Low Countries; even those on their return from America were forwarded without disembarking: the exertions on the part of government were unremitting.

At this period the Duke of Wellington was at Brussels: the right wing of his army in and about Ath was commanded by Lord Hill; the left, in the vicinity of Braine le Comte and Nivelle, was under the Prince of Orange; the Earl of Uxbridge, with the cavalry, was stationed about Grammont; the reserve was in the town and neighbourhood of Brussels. The forces under the Duke of Wellington amounted to seventy-eight thousand five hundred and five men, but the actual number in the field did not exceed sixty-four thousand, with one hundred and twenty guns,[1] including twelve with the reserve.

Napoleon quitted Paris on the twelfth, and on the fourteenth he placed himself at the head of his troops, to whom he addressed the following proclamation:—

"Avesnes, June 14th.

"SOLDIERS!

"This day is the anniversary of Marengo and Fried-
" land, which twice decided the destiny of Europe. Then,
" as after the battles of Austerlitz and Wagram, we
" were too generous. We believed in the protestations
" and oaths of princes, to whom we left their thrones.
" Now however, leagued together, they strike at the in-
" dependence and sacred rights of France. They have
" committed unjust aggressions. Let us march forward and

---

[1] The Belgians had also forty guns.

1815.
June.
"meet them. Are we not still the same men? Soldiers! at Jena, these Prussians, now so arrogant, were three to one; at Montmirail six to one. Let those who have been captives to the English describe the nature of their prison-ships, and the sufferings they endured. The Saxons, the Belgians, the Hanoverians, the soldiers of the Confederation of the Rhine, lament that they are obliged to use their arms in the cause of princes, who are the enemies of justice, and destroyers of the rights of nations. They well know the coalition to be insatiable. After having swallowed up twelve millions of Poles, twelve millions of Italians, one million of Saxons, and six millions of Belgians, they now wish to devour the states of the second order among the Germans. Madmen! one moment of prosperity has bewildered them. To oppress and humble the people of France is out of their power; once entering our territory, there they will find their doom. Soldiers! we have forced marches before us, battles to fight, and dangers to encounter; but firm in resolution, victory must be ours. The honour and happiness of our country are at stake! and, in short, Frenchmen, the moment is arrived when we must conquer or die!"

The French army of Flanders was composed of nearly twenty thousand men of the Imperial Guard, and five corps d'armée, besides a force of about twelve thousand cavalry under Grouchy, and the Young Guard, which made, at a moderate calculation, a total of one hundred and fifty thousand men, with two hundred and ninety-six pieces of artillery.

June 15th. During the night of the fifteenth, Wellington obtained information that the enemy had crossed the Sambre, and were marching in force on Charleroi and Fleurus; the troops in their different cantonments received orders to move on Nivelle, where the Prince of Orange was stationed.   1815. June 16th.

The Coldstream left Enghien at three o'clock in the morning of the sixteenth, and, after resting about four hours at Braine le Comte, pushed on to Quatre Bras, where only a small portion of the army was assembled. The division of Guards thus made a march of twenty-five miles. When the second brigade halted, the light companies were sent round on the left of the Bois de Bossu, in rear of the Brunswickers.

The Coldstream did not reach the position until about four o'clock in the afternoon; and notwithstanding their fatigue, immediately deployed in support of the First Guards. That brigade was at the time engaged with the enemy, and greatly distinguished itself, though not without suffering severely. After clearing the wood, they retired, and the light companies of the second brigade under Lieutenant-Colonel Macdonell took the advance; on his right were detachments from the battalion companies of the Third Guards under Lieutenant-Colonel Home, which communicated with the Brunswickers. Lieutenant-Colonel Daniel MacKinnon, with four companies, went in support. The troops maintained their ground with firm intrepidity, and repulsed at all points the repeated efforts of a large body of cavalry under Kellerman, who made frequent and desperate charges, seconded by two corps d'armée and a considerable preponderance in artillery. At the close of day the firing ceased. Marshal Ney then rallied on the height of Frasnes. The loss of the Allies amounted to about four thousand men; that of the French to rather more.

The British cavalry and the remainder of the army came up during the night.

While Ney was endeavouring to force the position at Quatre Bras, in which he was unsuccessful, Napoleon attacked and defeated the Prussians at St. Amand and

1815.
June 16th. Ligny. During the night, Marshal Blucher, who found himself, after the loss of fifteen thousand men, too weak to retain his position at Sombreff, retired to concentrate on Wavre. It was not till the morning of the seventeenth
June 17th. that the disaster of the Prussians was known at Quatre Bras.

Wellington in consequence made a corresponding movement: at ten o'clock his army fell back in perfect order through Genappe on Waterloo. The two light companies of the second brigade of Guards, being ordered to mask the retreat on the right, did not leave the ground till past two o'clock.

A body of the enemy's Lancers, supported by masses of cavalry, attempted to harass the rear: they were bravely attacked on their advance from Genappe by the Seventh Hussars, who failed, after a gallant effort. Colonel Elley had however taken the precaution to order the First Life Guards to be prepared: that celebrated body of men then charged with the most determined impetuosity, and overthrew the French cavalry. About five P. M. the allied army had taken up its position, which crossed the roads from Nivelle and Charleroi. In front of the Nivelle road was the chateau and garden of Hugomont; fronting the left centre was the farm of La Haye Sainte.

The enemy, with the exception of Marshal Grouchy's corps, detached for the purpose of observing the Prussians, were on the opposite heights: the space between was open, and the two armies were not more than three quarters of a mile from each other; in some places nearer. Before the position was a gentle descent. The second brigade of Guards was situated on the right of the centre, and crowned the slope above Hugomont. The chateau of Hugomont faced the enemy without any external fence in its front. Behind it was the farm-yard, protected on the left and rear by a wall, and on the right by farm buildings.

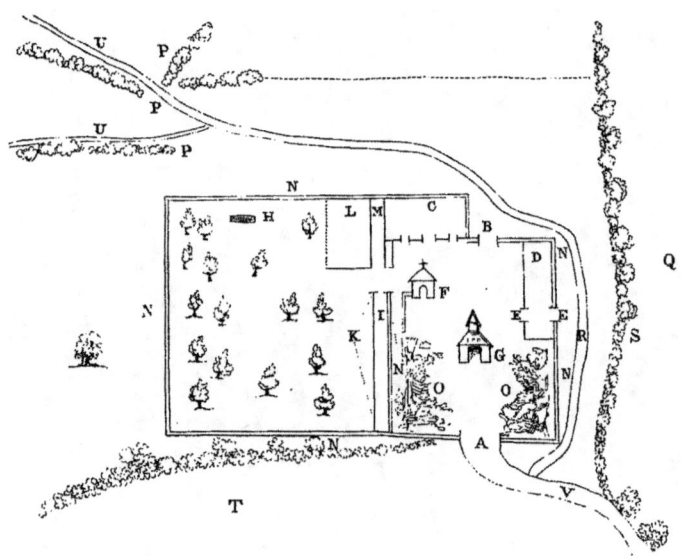

A Great Gate.	N Walls separating the Garden from the Orchard, &c.
B Arched Gate.	
C Farm House.	O Ruins.
D Barn.	P Gaps into the Orchard and Fields.
E Barn-doors.	Q Field leading to Mon Plaisir, where Jerome Buonaparte was.
F Chapel.	
G Pigeon-house.	
H Blackman's Tomb.	R Lane.
I Little Garden.	S High Hedge.
K Wood Pales.	T Hollow Way.
L Vegetable Garden.	U Pathways.
M Garden.	V Lane leading to Nivelle Road.

To the left of the house and yard was a garden surrounded by a wall, and to the left of that, but adjoining, there was an orchard inclosed by a hedge and ditch. A large gate in the rear led into the yard, and through that supplies were received during the action; two other entrances to the yard were closed up. Outside of the buildings on the right there was a road and a high hedge. A wood in front, which stretched some distance to the right, covered this post.[1]

1815.
June 17th.

Although the number of disposable troops under Wellington at the opening of the campaign has been stated at sixty-four thousand, yet, after deducting the corps of observation, which consisted of five thousand men, under Prince Frederick of Orange at Halle, and the four thousand lost at Quatre Bras, the Duke's force at Waterloo cannot be rated at more than fifty-five thousand.

The army under Napoleon has always been estimated at one hundred and fifty thousand men. Supposing he lost twelve thousand at Ligny, Quatre Bras, and on the seventeenth; allowing also for the corps with Grouchy, which might amount to forty-five thousand, there remains a numerical superiority of at least thirty-eight thousand.

The battle of Waterloo has been so often described, that it is proposed to confine the narrative as much as possible to those particulars which strictly relate to the part taken in the conflict by the second brigade of Guards and the light companies of the first brigade.

Soon after the Guards reached the position, the light companies[2] were sent to the post of Hugomont. The

---

[1] See plan of Hugomont.

[2] The first brigade of Guards was composed of the second and third battalions of the First Guards, under Major-General Maitland; the second brigade, of the second battalion of the Coldstream, and the second battalion of the Third Guards, under Major-General Byng.

1815.
June 17th.

light companies of the second brigade took possession of the orchard for a short time, after which they were placed in the wood; the two light companies of the first brigade under Lieutenant-Colonel Lord Saltoun then occupied the orchard. The enemy had also despatched a party to the chateau, who, on perceiving the advance of the detachment, made a rush to get first into the place: the two parties came in contact: after an exchange of shots Saltoun secured the post. He was reinforced by three companies of Hanoverian Yagers; these men joined the advance piquet under Captain Evelyn and Ensign Standen of the Third Guards.

The light companies of the second brigade, composed of the light infantry of the Coldstream under Lieutenant-Colonel Henry Wyndham, and that of the Third under Lieutenant-Colonel Charles Dashwood, covered the right of the chateau. Those of the first brigade communicated from the orchard with the wood. These companies therefore during the night acted as piquets to the force under Lieutenant-Colonel Macdonell in the chateau, who had been detached with the light companies of the second brigade, and on whom, as senior officer, the command devolved. He reached Hugomont about seven in the evening, and was unceasingly employed in preparing for its defence.

After the brigade had taken up their ground, heavy rain fell, accompanied by wind, lightning, and loud thunder: the position was chiefly covered with standing corn, but the Coldstream occupied a bean-field bearing a young crop a few inches high, which soon became knee deep in mire, and every vestige of vegetation disappeared. A recollection of the recent unexpected attack on the Prussians, the proximity of the enemy, the fury of the storm, and the darkness of the night, kept the battalion on the alert till dawn appeared.

On the morning of the eighteenth, as additional means

of strengthening the place, loop-holes were made in the building and garden-walls of Hugomont. Platforms were also erected, and the gates barricaded, with the exception of one in the rear, which was left open intentionally: these precautions assisted materially in making good the most memorable defence perhaps recorded in the annals of modern warfare.[1]

Previous to the battle, the Duke of Wellington, attended by his staff, rode through the wood of Hugomont, where he saw Lieutenant-Colonel Macdonell, told him he would be immediately attacked, and gave orders to "defend the post to the last extremity."

At ten o'clock the light companies of the Guards were relieved by a battalion of eight hundred Nassau light troops: part of this corps was stationed in the lofts, buildings, yards, and out-offices; the remainder, with the Hanoverian Yagers, were distributed in the orchard and wood. Lord Saltoun then joined the second brigade on the position. Lieutenant-Colonel Macdonell with his companies moved to the right of the chateau.

At twenty minutes past eleven o'clock, the first gun was fired from a battery in front of the second brigade of Guards; it made a gap for a moment in the head of the column commanded by Prince Jerome Buonaparte, as it

---

[1] A truly characteristic trait of the Duke of Wellington occurred on the morning of the battle of Waterloo.

General Alava went from Brussels to join his Grace, and found him in a tree observing the movements of the French army. On the Duke turning round and seeing General Alava, he called out, "How are you, Alava? Buonaparte shall see to-day how a General of Sepoys can defend a position!"—a remark which showed at once his contempt for an opinion given of him by Buonaparte, and a confidence in himself and in his troops, accompanied with a degree of cheerfulness almost amounting to an assurance of victory.

1815.
June 18th.

moved to the attack on Hugomont.[1] The advance of the enemy was covered by a "tremendous cannonade" on the whole line from upwards of two hundred guns.

Shortly after the action had commenced, the tirailleurs drove the Nassau battalion and the company of Hanoverian Yagers through the wood to the rear of the chateau. This attack was repulsed by the two companies of the second brigade. The French were fast closing round, when Macdonell charged and drove them back on their advancing columns. These attempts were vigorously repeated for an hour and a half, but each time they failed.

About one o'clock a cart of ammunition, which had been sent for early in the day, was brought into the farmyard of Hugomont, and proved most seasonable. The men had only time to fill their pouches, when a discharge of artillery suddenly burst upon them, mingled with the shouts of a column rushing on to a fresh attack. A cloud of tirailleurs pushed through the wood and corn-fields: they were aimed at with fatal certainty from the loopholes, windows, and summit of the building. But the enemy eventually compelled the few men that remained outside to withdraw into the chateau by the rear gate. In the mean time, the French redoubled their efforts against it, and the fire of the immediate defenders of that point for a moment ceased. The gate was then forced. At

---

[1] "About ten o'clock he commenced a furious attack upon "our post at Hugomont. I had occupied that post with a detach-"ment from General Byng's brigade of Guards, which was in po-"sition in its rear; and it was for some time under the command "of Lieutenant-Colonel Macdonell, and afterwards of Colonel "Home; and I am happy to add that it was maintained throughout "with the utmost gallantry by those brave troops, notwithstanding "the repeated efforts of large bodies of the enemy to obtain posses-"sion of it."—Duke of Wellington's Dispatch. Waterloo, July 19th, 1815.

this critical moment, Macdonell rushed to the spot with the officers and men nearest at hand, and not only expelled the assailants, but reclosed the gate. The enemy from their overwhelming numbers again entered the yard, when the Guards retired to the house, and kept up from the windows such a destructive fire, that the French were driven out, and the gate once more was closed.

1815.
June 18th.

General Foy having chased the Nassau troops before him, passed through the wood and surrounded the chateau: all attempts to rally these men proving fruitless, Lieutenant-Colonel MacKinnon with the Grenadiers and first company moved to the support of the place, and the enemy were forced back. Lieutenant-Colonel Acheson then joined: the whole followed in pursuit and entered the wood, where they were received with an incessant discharge of small arms. Colonel Woodford left the seventh and eighth companies in the position for the protection of the colours, and brought down the rest of the battalion. The third and fourth companies of the Third Guards were also sent to Hugomont under Lieutenant-Colonel Home, and occupied the hollow way near the entrance of the wood; these were succeeded by other detachments of equal strength from the same regiment.

On the retreat of the Nassau troops, Lord Saltoun with the light companies of the first brigade was again ordered to Hugomont, and recovered the orchard, and also part of the wood in its front; the latter, however, there was no possibility of holding in opposition to the vast superiority of the enemy. Lord Saltoun therefore made occasional sallies from the orchard: his orders were, in the event of its being forced, to retire into the chateau; but he defended it against every attempt.

The entrance of the wood was attacked in the most gallant manner by the Coldstream. The companies under

1815.
June 18th.

Colonel Woodford cheered, and after charging, opened a fire, but the powerful resistance they met with could not be overcome. This officer therefore retired, and entered Hugomont.

Afterwards the enemy exerted themselves to carry the orchard. They twice got possession of the hedge, but gained no further ground, as the defenders were firm, and the troops on the garden wall which overlooked the orchard poured in a cross fire and occasioned them severe loss.

A detachment from the Third Guards, and the grenadiers of that corps, with fifty Hanoverian riflemen under Lord Saltoun, bravely charged a howitzer, but did not succeed. This, however, had the effect of stopping any thing further on that side, and the enemy contented themselves with firing from behind a ditch which ran nearly parallel to the hedge and ditch in front of the orchard.

At two o'clock, Lord Saltoun was relieved by Lieutenant-Colonel Mercer of the Third Guards, who arrived with reinforcements. The Third Guards had been moved for the purpose of support by detachments of two companies at intervals, and after Colonel Woodford entered Hugomont with the Coldstream, they occupied the orchard, under Colonel Hepburn.

The enemy were undaunted in their attacks; but Hugomont was defended with a calm and stubborn gallantry, that alone could have enabled so small a force to resist the repeated and fierce assaults of nearly thirty thousand men, of whom the second French corps was composed. The cross discharge from the artillery was incessant: the bursting of shells set part of the building in flames, and as the fire extended to the chapel and stables, many of the wounded soldiers of the Coldstream perished. The Guards, nevertheless, at no time exceeding two thousand

THE COLDSTREAM GUARDS. 219

men,[1] maintained the post amidst the terrible confla- 1815.
June 18th.
gration within, and the murderous fire of the enemy from
without. When the contention terminated, the French
dead lay piled round the chateau, in the wood, and
every avenue leading to it.[2]

> " Farewell, sad Field! whose blighted face
> Wears desolation's withering trace;
> Long shall my memory retain
> Thy shatter'd huts and tramped grain,
> With every mark of martial wrong,
> That scathe thy towers, fair Hugomont!
> Yet though thy garden's green arcade
> The marksman's fatal post was made;
> Though on thy shatter'd beeches fell
> The blended rage of shot and shell;
> Though from thy blacken'd portals torn,
> Their fall thy blighted fruit-trees mourn,
> Has not such havock brought a name
> Immortal in the rolls of fame?
> Yes,—Agincourt may be forgot,
> And Cressy be an unknown spot,
>   And Blenheim's name be new;
> But still in story and in song,
> For many an age remember'd long,
> Shall live the towers of Hugomont
>   And field of Waterloo."[3]

---

[1] Exclusive of the eight hundred Nassau light troops and three companies of Hanoverian riflemen.

[2] The following is an extract from the Duke of Wellington's dispatch:—" It gives me the greatest satisfaction to assure your " lordship that the army never upon any occasion conducted itself " better. The division of Guards under Lieutenant-General Cooke, " who is severely wounded, Major-General Maitland, and Major- " General Byng, set an example which was followed by all."

Silver medals were given to every officer and soldier present during the sixteenth, seventeenth, and eighteenth. See medal.

[3] Walter Scott.

LIST OF KILLED AND WOUNDED IN THE SECOND BRIGADE OF GUARDS, INCLUDING THE LIGHT COMPANIES OF THE FIRST BRIGADE.

FIRST REGIMENT OF FOOT GUARDS.
OFFICERS PRESENT AT THE BATTLE OF WATERLOO.

Company.	Rank.	Names.	Remarks.	Company.	Rank.	Names.	Remarks.
Light Company, 2d Bat.	Lt.-Col.	W. H. Milne	Killed.	Light Company, 3d Bat.	Lt.-Col.	Lord Saltoun	Commanding.
	Capt.	T. Brown			Capt.	Ed. Grose	
	,,	F. F. Luttrell	Wounded.		,,	C. P. Ellis	Wounded.
	Ensign	A. Greville					

Grenadier Guards Orderly-Room.

COLDSTREAM GUARDS.
OFFICERS PRESENT AT THE BATTLE OF WATERLOO.

Company.	Rank.	Names.	Remarks.	Company.	Rank.	Names.	Remarks.
Grenadier	Colonel	A. Woodford	Commands. the battⁿ.	Fourth	Lt.-Col.	Hon. E. Acheson	
	Lt.-Col.	D. MacKinnon	Wounded. Acting 2nd Major.		Capt.	J. L. Blackman	Killed.
	Capt.	E. Sumner	Died of his wounds, 26 June.		Ensign	A. Gordon	
				Fifth	Ensign	R. Bowen	
					,,	J. F. Douglas	
	Ensign	H. F. Griffiths	Wounded.		,,	C. Short	
First	Lt.-Col.	J. Macdonell	Actg. 1st Maj. Detached to Hugomont.	Sixth	Lt.-Col.	H. Wyndham	Wounded.
	Capt.	T Sowerby			Capt.	Lord Hotham	
	Ensign	I. Montagu	Wounded.	Seventh	Capt.	G. Bowles	
					Ensign	J. Hervey	
Second	Colonel	Hon. A. Abercrombie	Assist. Qur.-Mar.-Genl.	Eighth	Lt.-Col.	H. Dawkins	
					Ensign	M. Beaufoy	
	Ensign	Hon. J. Forbes		Light Infantry	Capt.	W. L. Walton	Actg. Adjutant.
	,,	A. Cuyler	Staff.		,,	Hon. R. Moore	Wounded.
					Ensign	H. Gooch	
Third	Lt.-Col.	Sir W. Gomm	Staff.	Staff	Adjut. Capt.	A. F. Bentinck	D. A. Adj. Genl.
	Capt.	T. S. Cowell	Taken sick evening of 17th, went to Brussels.		Qu^r. M^r.	B. Selway	
					Surgeon	W. Whymper	
	Ensign	H. Vane	Wounded.		Asst. Surg.	George Smith	
	,,	Hon. W. Forbes			,, ,,	W. Hunter	
				1st Bat.	Lt.-Col.	Freemantle	Staff.

Coldstream Orderly-Room.

THE COLDSTREAM GUARDS.

THIRD REGIMENT OF FOOT GUARDS.
OFFICERS PRESENT AT THE BATTLE OF WATERLOO.

Company.	Rank.	Names.	Remarks.	Company.	Rank.	Names.	Remarks.
Grenadiers	Colonel	F. Hepburn	Commands the battⁿ.	Seventh	Lt.-Col.	Hon. Sir A. Gordon	Killed. (A.D.C. to Com. of the Forces.)
	Lt.-Col.	F. Home	Act^g. 2nd Maj.		Capt.	Hon. H. Forbes	Killed.
	Capt.	R. B. Hesketh	Wounded.		,,	R. H. Wigston	On guard at Waterloo.
	,,	John Ashton	Killed.		Ensign	Charles Lake	Wounded.
First	Lt.-Col.	E. Bowater	Wounded.		,,	David Baird	Wounded.
	Capt.	T. Crawford	Killed.	Eighth	Lt.-Col.	Charles West	Wounded.
	Ensign	B. Drummond	Acting Adjut.		Capt.	Montgomerie	Wounded.
	,,	H. S. Blane			Ensign	I. Prendergast	
Second	Capt.	H. Hawkins			,,	H. B. Montagu	
	Ensign	W. James	BaggageGuard.	Light Infantry	Lt.-Col.	C. Dashwood	Wounded.
	,,	W. F. Hamilton			Capt.	G. Evelyn	Wounded.
Third	Lt.-Col.	D. Mercer	Act^g. 1st Maj.		,,	John Elrington	
	Capt.	C. J. Barnett			Ensign	G. D. Standen	
	Ensign	W. Butler		Staff	Adjut.	W. Stothert	Killed. (Brig.-Maj. to 2nd Brig. of Guards.)
Fourth	Capt.	B. Drummond			Qu^r. M^r.	J. Skuce	
	Ensign	Simpson	Killed.		Surgeon	S. Good	
Fifth	Lt.-Col.	C. F. Canning	Killed. (A.D.C. to Com. of the Forces.)		Ass^t. Surg.	F. G. Hanrott	
	Capt.	E. B. Fairfield			,, ,,	J. R. Ward	
	Ensign	T. Wedgwood					
	,,	A. C. Cochrane					
Sixth	Lt.-Col.	H. W. Rooke	Ass^t. A. Genl. 1st Division.				
	Capt.	J. W. Moorhouse					
	Ensign	Hon. E. Stopford	A.D.C. to Maj.-Genl. Sir J. Byng.				
	,,	Hon. G. Anson	On guard in the village of Waterloo.				

Scots Fusilier Guards Orderly-Room.

RETURN OF KILLED, WOUNDED, AND MISSING, ON THE 18th OF JUNE, 1815

	Capts.	Lieuts.	Ensigns.	Serjts.	Drumrs.	Rank and file.
Second Battalion, Coldstream Guards, killed	,,	1	,,	1	,,	53
wounded *	,,	2	3	13	,,	229
missing	,,	,,	,,	,,	1	3
Second Battalion, Third Guards, killed	,,	3	,,	2	,,	37
wounded †	,,	3	3	10	,,	178

—London Gazette, 8th July, 1815.

* Died of their wounds, 1 Lieutenant, 1 serjeant, 27 rank and file.
† Died of their wounds, 3 serjeants, 3 corporals, 41 rank and file.

The loss of the two light companies of the second and third battalions of the First Guards is included in the returns of their respective battalions.

1815. Waterloo exemplifies in a high degree that obstinate and determined courage under fire which the troops of Great Britain had attained in the school of Wellington. In giving some account of this battle as far as the Guards were concerned, the writer has had the gratification of concluding his work by exhibiting the part taken by them in that memorable conflict.

The state of Europe at that time is well known. The policy of Wellington was to act on the defensive, not to seek an action, nor yet to retreat before Napoleon. A million of bayonets were advancing from all parts of the Continent to put down his newly-resumed power; but they were not yet all assembled. The scheme of the Emperor was to attack and defeat in detail the several armies by which he was to be opposed. The French were sufficiently powerful to justify such an expectation. The Prussians, overthrown on the sixteenth of June, had retired in disorder. The next and most important object of Napoleon was the destruction of the English: this completed, the other armies might be panic-struck, and the confederacy against France dissolved. The Belgians detested the Dutch connexion, and the Russians being paralysed, the Emperor of Austria, finding the scale of chances balanced, was not unlikely to declare for his son-in-law. Had these events taken place, France no longer checked, and the star of Napoleon regaining the ascendant, the liberties of Europe would once more have been trampled under the feet of his victorious legions. Such were the natural anticipations of the French, should they triumph. The struggle, therefore, with the English was not one of common occurrence; the contest was for supremacy, for glory, for every thing held most dear by the gallant and chivalrous troops of France.

The enemy chose his ground, his time, and mode of

attack; his troops were far more numerous, and were animated by their recent victory over the veteran Blucher.

1815.

To insure success, the energies and experience of the great and comprehensive mind of Napoleon were concentrated. The recollections of the rivalship of the two nations, of their military predominance in Europe, of soldiers raised to the rank of Generals and afterwards to thrones, were revived in the French army, by all those arts, the practice of which, a long and intimate acquaintance with the French character had taught Napoleon. He called on his veterans to conquer, and told them the day was arrived for retrieving the disasters of the Russian campaign, of Dresden, Leipsic, Montmartre, and Paris. The Emperor called not in vain; promotion, pillage, and revenge flashed before the ardent and inflamed imaginations of the French soldiery. The triumphs of Marengo and Austerlitz animated them with hope; their former conquests, their valour, their numbers, and the well-known talents of their chief, made them feel secure of victory. Every soldier in the Imperial army was sensible of the importance of the day: Napoleon took advantage of their enthusiasm, and with infinite skill made his preparations.

The advance of the French at Waterloo was covered by an immense artillery; their native courage was heightened by every sentiment that can stimulate the human breast.

Wellington, aware of the enemy with whom he had to contend, was also well acquainted with the quality of his own troops, and relied on their cool and steady bravery. He baffled throughout the day the repeated attacks of the French cavalry and infantry. His right was thrown back on a ravine near Merke Braine; on the left his communication with Marshal Blucher at Wavre was open through Ohaine.

1815.   The French columns rushed on, supported by their splendid cavalry; the Imperial Guard being in reserve. Their numbers and the renown of their Emperor gave a vigour to their movements, not easy to be withstood.

After many severe repulses, Napoleon thought the moment had arrived to throw in his reserve and decide the day; a manœuvre by which he had so often triumphed over his opponents. His Imperial Guards were ordered to advance and charge the British squares. Labedoyere flew to the front, exclaiming, " *Courage, mes enfans!* the English waver, and will give way! charge those squares, and the day is ours!" The bullets of the hitherto invincible Imperial Guard whistled through the British ranks, and the French cavalry charged with the determination of men accustomed to vanquish. After heroic deeds had been performed by the Imperial Guard, these fine troops, the first soldiers of the European Continent, remained on the field, a monument of their desperate valour and of the futility of their attempts to shake the impenetrable battalions opposed to them.[1]

---

[1] " Nous les avons vus, au jour de notre désastre, ces enfans " d'Albion, formés en bataillons carrés dans la plaine entre le " bois d'Hougoumont et le village de Mont Saint-Jean. Ils " avaient, pour arriver à cette formation compacte, doublé et re- " doublé leurs rangs à plusieurs reprises. La cavalerie qui les ap- " puyait fut taillée en pièces, le feu de leur artillerie fut éteint. " Les officiers-généraux et d'état-major galopaient d'un carré à " l'autre, incertains où ils trouveraient un abri: chariots, blessés, " parcs de réserve, troupes auxiliaires fuyaient à la débandade " vers Bruxelles. La mort était devant eux et dans leurs rangs; " la honte derrière. En cette terrible occurrence, les boulets de " la Garde Impériale, lancés à brûle-pourpoint, et la cavalerie de " France victorieuse, ne purent pas entamer l'immobile infanterie " Britannique. On eût été tenté de croire qu'elle avait pris racine " dans la terre, si ses bataillons ne se fussent ébranlés majestu-

Then it was that Wellington ordered the line of infantry to advance, and instantly the immoveable British squares that had stood firm as their native rocks, insensible to bullets, to charges of cavalry, and to death, insensible to every thing but their duty, moved forward, driving the enemy before them with all the attendant consequences of panic, confusion, and irretrievable ruin.

In other battles, positions have been selected with judgment, and defended with courage; but the strong intrenchments at Genappe were carried by the French levies under Dumourier, and the redoubts of Borodino were insufficient to stop the advance of Napoleon on the ancient capital of the Czars. At Waterloo there were no works of military art to cover the British army. They had, and required no protection but their arms, nor any shelter but their matchless discipline, to enable them to repel the furious assaults of an enemy bent on forcing their position. Their unflinching resistance at first perplexed the scientific calculations of the Emperor, then changed his confidence into anxiety, and finally drove him to that state of desperation which flies to a last great effort as its only hope. He had promised victory to his soldiers; he threw his veterans forward, and failed. Up to this period a large

---

" eusement quelques minutes après le coucher du soleil, alors que " l'arrivée de l'armée Prussienne apprit à Wellington que, grâces " au nombre, grâces à la force d'inertie, et pour prix d'avoir su " ranger de braves gens en bataille, il venait de remporter la " victoire la plus décisive de notre âge."—*Histoire de la Guerre de la Péninsule sous Napoléon; par le Général Foy.* Vol. I. page 322.

Napoleon said, " Even the Old Guard could make no impression on them: their fire was dreadful; and, as to charging, you might as well charge stone walls."

" La gloire de l'armée Britannique lui vient avant tout de son " excellente discipline, et de la bravoure calme et franche de la " nation."—*General Foy*, vol. I. page 259.

1815. and well-earned portion of the glories of the strife must be given to the brave men who for so many successive hours beat off the attacks of their opponents. Their conduct is beyond all praise, and the merit was their own. But the master-mind that ruled the fight throughout the day, the eagle glance that at its close converted a well-sustained defence into an irresistible charge on the assailing columns and swept them from the ground on which they stood, belonged exclusively to Wellington. He closed on his adversary, and broke the Imperial Sceptre for ever.

Thus was the battle of Waterloo gained; the most important in its results of ancient or modern times. Here the two greatest captains of this or any other age were opposed to each other: here they were fairly matched, and ample opportunity was afforded for a trial of generalship and military skill. The best troops of France were in the field, and the result is decisive of the superiority of Wellington over his great competitor, while it affords another instance of the unequalled steadiness, perseverance, and courage of the British soldier.

HUGOMONT.

APPENDIX.

APPENDIX.

No. 1.

For the Honourable William Lenthal, Esquire, Speaker of the Parliament of England.[1]

Sir,

I hope it is not ill taken, that I make no more frequent addresses to the Parliament; things that are of trouble in point of provision for your army, and of ordinary direction, I have, as I could, often presented to the Council of State, together with such occurrences as have happened, who I am sure, as they have not been wanting in their extraordinary care, and provision for us, so neither what they judge fit and necessary to represent the same to you; and this I thought to be a sufficient discharge of my duty on that behalf.

It hath now pleased God to bestow a mercy upon you, worthy your knowledge, and of the utmost praise and thanks of all that fear and love his name, yea, the mercy is far above all praise, which that you may the better perceive, I shall take the boldness to tender unto you some circumstances accompanying this great business, which will manifest the greatness and seasonableness of this mercy. We having tried what we could to engage the enemy three or four miles west of Edinburgh, that proving ineffectual, and our victual failing, we marched towards our ships for a recruit of our want, the enemy did not at all trouble us in our rear, but marched the direct way towards Edinburgh, and partly in the night and morning, slips through his whole army, and quarters himself in a posture easy to interpose between us and our victual, but the Lord made him lose the opportunity, and the morning proving exceeding wet and dark, we recovered by

---

[1] Geo. IIId's collection of Pamphlets, vol. 478.—British Museum.

that time it was light, into a ground where they could not hinder us from our victual; which was a high act of the Lord's providence to us. We being come into the said ground, the enemy marched into the ground we were last upon, having no mind either to strive to interpose between us and our victual, or to fight, being indeed upon this lock, hoping that the sickness of your army would render their work more easy by the gaining of time; whereupon we marched to Mussleburgh to victual, and to ship away our sick men, where we sent aboard near five hundred sick and wounded soldiers; and upon serious consideration finding our weakness so to increase, and the enemy lying upon his advantages, at a general council it was thought fit to march to Dunbar, and there to fortify the town, which we thought, if any thing, would provoke them to engage, as also that the having of a garrison there, would furnish us with accommodation for our sick men, would be a place for a good magazin (which we exceedingly wanted), being put to depend upon the uncertainty of weather for landing provisions, which many times cannot be done, though the being of the whole army lay upon it, all the coast from Leith to Berwick not having one good harbour; as also to lie more conveniently to receive our recruits of horse and foot from Berwick.

Having these considerations, upon Saturday the thirtieth of August, we marched from Mussleburgh to Haddington, where by that time we had got the van brigade of our horse, and our foot and train into their quarters, the enemy was marched with that exceeding expedition, that they fell upon the rear forlorn of our horse, and put it in some disorder, and indeed had like to have engaged our rear brigade of horse with their whole army, had not the Lord by his providence put a cloud over the moon, thereby giving us opportunity to draw off those horse to the rest of the army, which accordingly was done without any loss, save of three or four of our aforementioned forlorn, wherein the enemy (as we believe) received more loss. The army being put into a reasonable secure posture, towards midnight the enemy attempted our quarters on the west end of Haddington, but (through the goodness of God) we repulsed them. The next morning we drew into an open field, on the south side of Haddington, we not judging it safe for us to draw to the enemy upon his own ground, he being prepossessed thereof, but rather drew back to give him way to come to us, if he had so thought fit. And having waited about the space of four or five hours, to see if he would come to us; and not finding any inclination in the enemy so to do, we resolved to go according to our first intendment to Dunbar. By that time we had marched three or four miles, we saw some bodies of the enemy's horse draw out of their quarters, and by that time our carriages were gotten near Dunbar, their whole army was upon their march after us; and indeed our drawing back in this manner, with the addition of three new regiments added to them, did much heighten their confidence, if not presumption and arrogancy. The enemy that night, we perceived, gathered towards the hills, labouring to make a perfect interposition between us and Berwick; and having in this posture a great advantage, through his better knowledge of the country, which he effected by sending a considerable party to the strait pass at Copperspeth, where ten men to hinder, are better than forty to make their way. And truly this was an exigent to us, wherewith the enemy reproached us with that condition the Parliament's army was in, when it made its hard conditions with the King in Cornwall; by some reports that have come to us, they had disposed of us, and of their business, in sufficient revenge and wrath towards our persons and had swallowed up the poor interest of England, believing that their army and their King would have marched to London without any interruption; it being told us, we know not how truly, by a prisoner we took the night before the flight, that their King was very suddenly to come amongst them with those English they allowed to be about him; but in what they were thus lifted up, the Lord was above them. The enemy lying in the posture before mentioned, having those advantages, we lay very near him, being sensible of our disadvantage, having some weakness of flesh, but yet consolation and support from the Lord himself to our poor weak faith, wherein I believe not a few amongst us shared, that because of their numbers, because of their advantages, because of their confidence, because of our weakness, because of our strait, we were in the mount, and in the mount the Lord would be seen, and that he would find out a way of deliverance and salvation for us; and, indeed, we had our consolations and our hopes. Upon Monday evening the enemy, whose numbers were very great, as we hear about six thousand horse and sixteen thousand foot at least, ours drawn down, as to sound men, to about seven thousand five hundred foot, and three thousand five hundred horse; the enemy drew down to their right wing about two-thirds of their left wing of horse, to the right wing shogging also their foot and train much to the right, causing their right wing of horse to edge down towards the sea. We could not well imagine, but that the enemy intended to attempt upon us, or to place themselves in a more exact condition of interposition. The Major-General and myself coming to the Earl of Roxborough's house and observing this posture, I told him, I thought it did give us an opportunity and advantage to attempt upon the enemy, to which he immediately replied, that he had thought to have said the same thing to me, so that it pleased the Lord to set this apprehension upon both of our hearts at the same instant. We called for Colonel Monk, and shewed him the thing, and coming to our quarter at night, on demonstrating our apprehensions to some of the colonels, they also cheerfully concurred; we resolved therefore to put our business into this position, that six regiments of horse and three regiments and a half of foot should march in the van, and that the Major-General, the Lieutenant-General of the horse, and the Commissary-General and Colonel Monk, to command the brigade of foot, should lead on the business; and that Colonel Pride's brigade, Colonel Overton's brigade, and the remaining two regiments of horse, should bring up the cannon and rear; the time of falling on to be by break of day, but through some delays it proved not to be so till six o'clock in the morning: the enemies word was "The Covenant," which it had been for divers days; ours "The Lord of Hosts." The Major-General, Lieutenant-General Fleetwood, and Commissary-General Whaley, and Colonel Twisleton gave the onset, the enemy being in very good posture to receive them, having the advantage of their cannon and foot against our horse; before our foot could come up, the enemy made a gallant resistance, and there was a very hot dispute at swords point between our horse and theirs. Our first foot, after they had discharged their duty, being overpowered with the enemy, received some repulse, which they soon recovered; but my own regiment, under the command of Lieutenant-Colonel Goff, and my Major White, did come seasonably in, and at the push of pike did repel the stoutest regiment the enemy had there, merely with the courage the Lord was pleased to give, which proved a great amazement to the residue of their foot, this being the first action between the foot. The horse in the mean time did with a great deal of courage and spirit beat back all opposition, charging through the bodies of the enemies horse and their foot, who were after the first repulse given, made by the Lord of Hosts as stubble to their swords. Indeed I believe I may speak it without partiality, both your chief commanders, and others in their several places, and soldiers also, were acted with as much courage as ever hath been seen in any action since this war. I know they look not to be named, and therefore I forbear particulars.

The best of the enemy's horse and foot being broken through and through in less than an hour's dispute, their whole army being put into confusion, it became a total rout, our men having the chase and execution of them near eight miles; we believe that upon the place and near about it, were about three thousand slain, prisoners taken of their officers you have this enclosed list, of private soldiers near ten thousand, the whole baggage, and train taken, wherein was good store of match, powder and bullet, all their artillery great and small, thirty guns. We are confident they have left behind them not less than fifteen thousand arms. I have already brought in to me near two hundred colours, which I herewith send you. What officers of quality of theirs are killed, we yet cannot learn; but yet surely divers are, and many men of quality are mortally wounded, as Colonel Lumsdel, the Lord Liberton, and others; and that which is no small addition, I do not believe we have lost twenty men; not one commissioned officer slain that I hear of, save one cornet, and Major Rooksby, since dead of his wounds; and not many mortally wounded, Colonel Whaley only, cut in the hand-wrist, and his horse twice shot and killed under him, but he well recovered another horse and went on in the chase. Thus you have the prospect of one of the most signal mercys God hath done for England and his people this war. And now may it please you to give me the leave of a few words. It is easy to say, The Lord hath done this! It would do you good to see and hear our poor foot go up and down, making their boast of God; but, Sir, it is in your hands to give glory to him, to improve your power and his blessings to his praise. We that serve you, beg of you not to own us, but God alone; we pray you own his people more and more, for they are the chariots and horsemen of Israel; disown yourselves, but own your authority and improve it, to curb the proud and the insolent, such as would disturb the tranquillity of England, though under what specious pretences soever; relieve the oppressed, hear the groans of poor prisoners in England: be pleased to reform the abuses of all professions, and if there be any one that makes many poor to make a few rich, that suits not a Commonwealth. If he that strengthens your servants to fight, pleases to give you hearts to set upon these things in order to his glory, and the glory of your Commonwealth, besides the benefit England shall feel thereby, you shall shine forth to other nations, who shall emulate the glory of such a pattern, and through the power of God turn into the like. These are our desires, and that you may have liberty and opportunity to do these things and not be hindred, we have been and shall be (by God's assistance) willing to venture our lives, and not desire that you should be precipitated by importunities from your care of safety and preservation, but that the doing of these good things may have their place amongst those which concern well-being, and so be wrought in their time and order. Since we came in Scotland, it hath been our desire and longing to have avoided blood in this business, by reason that God hath a people here fearing his name, though deceived, and to that end have we offered much love unto such in the bowels of Christ, and concerning the truth of our hearts therein have we appealed unto the Lord. The ministers of Scotland have hindered the passage of these things to the hearts of those to whom we intended them; and now we hear, that not only the deceived people, but some of the ministers, are also fallen in this battle. This is the great hand of the Lord, and worthy of the consideration of all those, who, taking into their hands the instruments of a foolish shepherd, to wit, meddling with worldly policies, and mixtures of earthly power, to set up that which they call the Kingdom of Christ, which is neither it, nor if it were, would such means be found effectual to that end, and neglect, or trust not to the word of God, the sword of the Spirit, which is alone powerful and able for the setting up of that kingdom, and, when trusted to, will be found effectually able to that end, and will also do it. This is humbly offered for their sakes, who having lately turned too much aside, that they might turn again to preach Jesus Christ, according to the simplicity of the Gospel; and then no doubt they will discern and find your protection and encouragement. Beseeching you to pardon this length, I humbly take leave, and rest,

Sir, your most humble servant,
O. CROMWELL.

Dunbar, September 4, 1650.

2.

Dr. Harris, in the Appendix to his "Historical and Critical Account of O. Cromwell," page 538, printed an original letter of Cromwell's to the Parliament, (then in the possession of James Lamb, Esq. of Fairford in Gloucestershire, and subsequently of John Raymond Barker of the same place,) on their sending Symonds (*Simon*) to Edinburgh, for his orders about the famous medal struck in memory of the victory at Dunbar :—

For ye Honble the Comittee for the Army, these.

Gentl., It was not a little wonder to me to see that you should send Mr. Symonds so great a journey about a business importinge so little, as far as it relates to me, when, as if my poore opinion may not be rejected by you, I have to offer to that wch I thinke the most noble end, to witt, the commemoracon of that great mercie at Dunbar, and the gratuitie to the army, wch might better be expressed upon the meddal by engraving as on the one side the Parliam^t, wch I heare was intended, and will do singularly well; so, on the other side, an army wth this inscription over the head of it, THE LORD OF HOSTS, wch was o^r word that day : wherefore, if I may begg it as a favo^r from you, I most earnestly beseech you, if I may do it wthout offence, that it may be soe; and if you thinke not fitt to have it as I offer, you may alter it as you see cause, only I doe thinke I may truely say it will be verie thankfully acknowledged by me, if you will spare the having my effigies in it.

The gentlemans paynes and trouble hither have been verie great, and I shall make it my second suite unto you that you will please to conferr upon him that imploym^t in y^r service wch Nicholas Briott[1] had

---

[1] In the original this name is inserted in another hand.

before him; indeed, the man is ingenious and worthie of encouragem^t. I may not presume much, but if at my request and for my sake he may obteyne this favo^r, I shall putt it upon the accompt of my obligacons, wch are not a few, and I hope shal be found readie gratefully to acknowledge and to approve myself, Gentl.,

Yo^r most reall servant,   O. CROMWELL.

Edinburgh, 4th of Feb. 1650.

3.

MS. Harleian. 7502.—(Original).

A Commission from Oliver Cromwell, appointing John Wells, Ensign, Nov. 17, 1651. Presented by Mr. Hatsell, 1760, to the Museum :—

Oliver Cromwell, Esqr, Captaine Generall and Comand^r in Chiefe of the Armies and Forces raised and to be raised by authority of Parliament within ye Comonwealth of England.

To John Wells, Ensigne.

By virtue of the power and authority to me derived from ye Parliam^t of England, I doe hereby constitute and appointe you Ensigne of y^t comp^y of foote whereof Captaine Ethilbert Morgan is Capt^e, raised and to be raised under my comand for ye service of the Comonwealth, in the reg^t whereof Lieu^t Gen^{ll} George Monck is Collonell. These are therefore to require yo^u to make yor psent repaire unto the same comp^y, and, taking charge thereof as Ensigne, duly to exercise the inferio^r offic^{rs} and sould^{rs} of the s^d comp^y in armes, and to use yor best care and endeavo^r to keepe them in good ord^r and discipline, comanding them to obey you as theire Ensigne. And you are likewise to observe and follow any orders and direcõns as you shall from tyme to tyme receive from myselfe and y^r superio^r offic^{rs} of the s^d regim^t and army, according to the discipline of warr. Given under my hand and seale, the 17th November, 1651.   O. CROMWELL.

4.

For the Right Ho^{ble} the Lord Henry Cromwell, these.
Att Dublin.

May itt please yor Ex^{cie};—Having the opportunitie of this bearer, I make bold to acquaint yor Ex^{cie} with what newes I heare, wch is, that Charles Stuart intends this sumer (if monies doe nott fayle him) to give vs some trouble both in Ireland and Scotland; and I heare the Earle of Ormond is to come over into Ireland, and alsoe Inchiqueene if they can pswade him, and Middleton hither; and Mr. Secretary Thurloe writes worde to mee, that they intend likewiss to give them

trouble in England, butt itt is nott visible to mee by their preparations wch way they are able to doe itt. I have a great ambition to bee a planter vnder yor Ex^cle, if I could gett butt libertie to bee loose from my comand heere, wch I hope in a short time I shall have. I have nothing else to trouble yor Lo^slpe withall, but to lett you know that I I am, yor Ex^cies most humble servant, GEORGE MONCK.
Dalkeith, 24° Febr., 165⅞.

5.

(Additional MS., Birch's Collection, No. 4165, fol. 19.)

For his Ex^cie the Lord Fleetwood. To be comunicated to the Geñall Councell of Officers att Wallingford House.

Right ho^ble and worthy friends;—Having, through the rich mercies of our most gracious God, lived to see a revive of that glorious cause in y^r hearts which hath bin sealed with soe much precious bloud, attested with soe many glorious and signall providences of God, and purchased with soe vast a treasure of these nations, wee cannot butt (with the greatest demonstrations of joy and gladnesse) owne yor late proceedings in pursuance of those blessed ends wee have for soe many yeares been contending for; and that God hath att last, after soe many yeares declining and deferred from his and his people's cause and interest turned backe yor eyes vppon yor former vowes and engagements made in the day of yor espousalls, and begotten in you a livelie sense both of yor past faylinges and p̃sent duty, wee cannot butt looke vppon as the greatest and happiest prognostick of our future peace and establishment that ever our eyes yett beheld, and accordingly doe with humbled hearts both reverence and embrace this dispensation of Divine Providence as that wherby a passage is made for our enjoying those good thinges soe longe since hoped for. That God hath hitherto indulged vs whilest every one was following after his idoll and advancing his p̃ticular interest above that of God and his people, deserves to bee for ever had in remembrance, as that whereby wee are kept alive vnto this day. Certainly, had hee nott bin a longe suffering God, and exceeding slow to wrath, hee had longe ere now given vs the dregs of his indignation to drinke, and made vs a reproach and hissing to the adversaries of his truth, making vs to reele and stagger, and dash one against another, till wee had accomplish't that on our selves which the bloudiest of our adversaries could nott have beheld without horror and amazement. Butt now, since we hope the sence of these thinges lies as heavy on yor spiritts as on our owne, wee shall cease to bee yor remembrancers of what hath bin left vndone, or done amisse, and putt you in minde of what in this great day of the Lord's appearing you ought to doe; and in this we shall bee very brief, intending to bee more pticular as occasion may offer.

In the first place, therfore, wee earnestlie entreate you, that in the worke you have vndertaken, as you would lay aside the interest of any private pson, soe that yor eye may nott bee fastened vppon the interest of any pticular ptie whatsoever, as itt is distinct or subdevided from the whole interest of God, and of those that professe his name in sinceritie and truth, butt that you would earnestly study and endeavour to advance such in whose hearts the power of godlinesse shall bee made manifest, through holy, strict, and religious conversation, although they may bee of different mindes in the more externall and lesse necessary parts of religion.

2. That seeing his late Highnesse hath bin pleased to manifest soe much self-deniall and love to his country, in appearing for the interest thereof against his owne, in this great day of change, that you will vse yor indeavours with all affecc̄onate care and industry, that himself and family (together with her Highnesse Dowager) may have soe honourable a provision settled vppon them, and such other dignities, as are suitable to the former great services of that familie to these nations.

3. That as you are of the freeborne people of England, and nott mercinaries, you will in yor places, and according to the duty of yor callinges, maintaine the just liberties of the whole people, their good lawes and righte, and remove all oppression and every heavy and intolerable yoake from off their neckes.

4. That you would assert the freedome and priviledges of their representatives, duly assembled and consisting of psons rightly qualified as being the basis and ffoundation of the Governem^t of this Com̄onwealth.

And lastly; that as the best expedient for the curing our distemps, wee heartily rejoice that you have anticipated our desires in inviting the Members of the Longe Parliam^t to reassemble, and carry on the worke of the nation under a Com̄onwealth Governem^t; and wee desire that you would owne them, and stand by them as those by whome God hath formerlie done glorious thinges for his people's libertie, and that some effectuall course bee taken for begetting a good vnderstanding, and mutuall correspondency betwixt the Parliam^t and army, that soe there may bee noe more dashing in pieces, nor dissolvings of them, butt such as are regular and according to the established forme of Governem^t. And wee doe assure you, that as in what you have already done in order to these thinges you have our hearty and affectionate concurrence, soe our constant purpose and resolution is hereafter to stand by you and all the people of God, in the maintenance of them against all oppressers whatsoever. And that this good cause may prosper in yor and our hearts and hands, is and shall bee the dayly prayer of yor most affecc͠onate friends and humble servants,[1]

Dalkeith, 12th May, 1659.   GEORGE MONCK.

ROBERT READE	RALPH COBBETT	THOMAS READE
HEN. DORNEY	JOHN CLOBERY	TIMO. WILKES
DAN. DAVISON	ABRA. HOLMES[3]	JERE SMYTH[2]
P. CRISPE	M. RICHARDSON	HEN. BRIGHTMAN
RICH. HEATH	JO. HUBBELTHORNE	PH. WATSON
THO. JOHNSON[2]	THOMAS DEANE	JOHN PADDON.
JAMES WRIGHT	WILL. DAVIS	
JOSEPH WALLINGTON	ETHELBERT MORGAN[3]	
WILL. HELLIN	RT. WINTER[3]	

6.

To the Officers of the Ordnance in the Tower of London.

I desire you to exchange the old musquets, and deliver new arms in their stead to my regiment.

Given under my hand, February 10th, 16$\frac{59}{60}$.

GEORGE MONCK.

7.

To the Officers of the Ordnance in the Tower of London.

You are, upon sight hereof, to receive from Major Nicholls all the match-lock musquets of the four companies of my regiment, now lying in the Tower of London, and deliver so many snaphance musquets to him, or whom he shall appoint; and in so doing this shall be your warrant.

Given under my hand at St. James's, April 14th, 1660.

GEORGE MONCK.

8.

(MS. Sloan. 3299.)

Sr George Monck, Capt Gen^ll and Com͠ander in Chiefe of all his Maties Forces in England, Scotland, and Ireland, Master of his Maties Horse, Knight of the most noble Order of the Garter, and one of his Maties most hono^ble Privy Councill.

To James Pembruge, Lieutenant.

By virtue of the power and authority to mee given by his most excellent Matie Charles the Second, by the grace of God King of

---

[1] In the Mercurius Politicus, No. 568, this letter is printed without the signatures; and in that journal is headed "A Letter from the Lord General Monck, "and the Council of Officers in Scotland to his Excellency the Lord Fleetwood, "and the General Council of Officers in England."

[2] Officers of Monck's regiment of Horse.
[3] Ditto   ditto   ditto   Foot.

APPENDIX. 239

England, Scotland, ffrance, and Ireland, Defender of the ffaith, &c. I doe hereby constitute and appoint yo^u, James Pembruge, to bee Lieutenant to Captaine Annesley his company of ffoote, in Colonel Allsop his regiment, under my comand for the service of his Matie. You are therefore to take into your charge and care the said company as Lieutenant thereof, and duly exercise the officers and soldiers of the same in armes; and alsoe to use your best care and endeavo^r to keepe them in good order and discipline, comanding them to obey yo^u as their Lieutenn^t: and yo^u are likewise to followe and observe such orders and direcõns as yo^u shall from time to time receive from his Matie, the Parliament, Privy Councill, or my selfe: and alsoe yo^u are to obey the superiour officers of the regiment and army, according to the discipline of warr, in pursuance of the trust reposed in yo^u and your duty to his Matie.

Given under my hand and seale, at the Cockpitt, the 26th day of June, 1660, and in the 12th yeare of his Maties raigne.

GEORGE MONCK.

9.

Commission of George Monck, Duke of Albemarle, as Captain-General.[1] (MS. Harleian. 3319. fol. 7.)

Charles [the Second], by the grace of God [King of England, Scotland, France, and Ireland, Defender of the Faith,] &c. To our right trusty and right well-beloved cousin and counsello^r, George, Duke of Albemarle, Ma^r of our Horse, and Knight of the most noble Order of the Garter, greeting. Know yee, that wee, reposeing speciall trust and confidence in yor approved wisdome, fidelity, valour, and great abillityes, have assigned, made, constituted, and ordained, and by these our letters-pattent doe assigne, make, constitute, and ordaine you to be our Captaine-Gen^{ll} of all our armyes and land forces, and men whatsoever, now leavyed or raised, or which hereafter shall be raised and [or] levyed, in or out of our realmes of England, Scotland, and Ireland, or dominion of Wales, or any of them, or any other our dominions or territoryes whatsoever, and assembled or to be assembled into an army or armyes.

With them both to resist and withstand all invasions, tumults, sediciõns, conspiracyes, and attempts, that may happen within our said realmes, dominions, and territoryes, or any of them, to be made ag^t

---

[1] This Commission is entered on the Rolls, at the Rolls Chapel Office, Chancery Lane.

The words between brackets have been supplied from a copy printed in "A Collection of Private Papers, 8vo. London, 1703, stated to have been" found among the Manuscripts of the late famous M—— of H—— (Marquis of Halifax).

our person, state, safety, crowne, and dignity, and to be lead into any of our said realmes, dominions, and territoryes, or any of them.

And there to invade, assault, repell, resist, fight with, subdue, slay and kill, all, every, or any enemyes or rebells ag^t us, of what nacōn soever, that in our said kingdomes, dominions, and territoryes, or any of them, or any part or partes thereof, shall raise, make, cause, adhere to, or be part of any insurreccōn, commocōn, tumult, sedicōn, conspiracy, or attempt whatsoever ag^t our person, state, safety, crowne, and dignity.

And wee further have assigned, made, constituted, and ordained, and by these our letters-pattents doe assigne, make, constitute, and ordaine you the said armyes and land forces, and every part thereof, and all officers and others whatsoever, imployed or to be imployed in or concerning the same, with all such other forces, of what nacōn soever, as shall be hereafter joyned to the said armyes and land forces, or any part thereof, to rule, governe, command, dispose, and imploy, in, for, or about such defences, offences, invasions, execucōns, and other military and hostile acts and services, as are or shall be by us, from time to time, and att any time, respectively directed, limitted, or appointed, in or by these our letters-pattents, or by our instruccōns which wee have delivered unto you under our signe manuall, or which shall hereafter be dirrected, limitted, or appointed, by any instruccōns under our signe manuall, signett, privy seale, or great seale, delivered or to be delivered unto you, or sent and received, or to be sent and received by you.

And further, wee have given and graunted unto you full power and authority, and hereby doe give and graunt to you full power and authority, the same armyes and land forces, and every or any p^t thereof, and the men soe levyed, raised, or assembled, or to be levyed or assembled, or sent, conducted, or brought, or that otherwise shall come to you either by any other speciall order and comaund, or by any other comission whatsoever, given and graunted by us or by authority of this comission, and according to the intent thereof as aforesaid, by yo^{r}self, or by yor deputy or deputyes, comand^r, captaines, or other officer or officers as to you shall seem meet, to try, exercise, arraye, and putt in readiness, and them and every of them after their abillityes, degrees, and facultyes, or according to the provision of armes appointed for them, well and sufficiently to cause to be weaponed and armed.

And to take or cause to be taken the musters of them by the comissary-gen^{ll}, or other comissaryes or officers whom you shall assigne as often as you shall see cause, as alsoe of any of our trayned bandes within our said kingdomes, dominions, and territoryes, or any of them, and in all and every other place or places into which, by vertue of this our comission, or by vertue of any other comission or warrant from us, you shall lead or send, or in which you shall, according to the purport of this comission, finde any part of the said army or armyes, or men as aforesaid.

And alsoe the same [said] army or armyes, men and persons, so arrayed, tryed, exercised, and armed, as well horsemen as footmen, of all kindes and degrees, to governe, leade, and conduct, against all and singular enemyes, rebells, traitors, and all and every other person or persons attempting any thing against our person, state, safety, crowne, and dignity, within our said kingdomes, dominions, and territoryes, every or any of them.

And our said armye and land forces, and the men aforesaid, from time to time, and att any time, to divide, distribute, and dispose into parts, regiments, troopes, and companyes, or otherwise att your discrecōn; and the same army or armyes, and the said partes, regiments, troops, or companyes, or any of them, to convey or send, or cause to be conveyed or sent, by land or by sea, or other passage by water, to any place or places, for the service aforesaid respectively, according to yor discrecōn.

And with the said enemyes, rebells, traytors, and other person and [or] persons so attempting as aforesaid, to fight, and them to invade, resist, represse, pursue, and follow, in and unto any part of our said kingdomes, dominions, and territoryes, every or any of them, [and them] to subdue, slay, and kill, and to doe, fulfill, and execute all and singular other acts, matters, and things whatsoever respectively, which shall be in yor discrecōn requisite either for leading, conducting, government, order, and rule of our said armyes and land forces, and men, and every part of them, or for the conservacōn of us, our state, and safety, and for the suppression and subdueing of such enemyes, rebells, trayto^{rs}, or other offenders as aforesaid.

And further, to doe, use, and execute against and upon the said enemyes, rebells, traytors, and others as aforesaid, and their adherents, and every of them, as occasion shall require, by yor discrecōn, the law martiall, or law marshall, as our Captaine-Generall.

And of such enemyes, rebells, trayto^{rs}, and other offenders as aforesaid, taken, or apprehended, or being brought into subjeccōn, to save from death or other punishment whom you shall thinke fitt to be soe saved, and to slay, destroy, and putt to execucōn of death, or otherwise to punish such or soe many of them as you shall think meet by yor discrecōn to be putt to death, or otherwise punished respectively, by any maner of meanes, according to the law martiall or law marshall, to the terror of all other offend^{rs}.

[Power of Pardoning.]

And wee doe further, by these our letters-pattents, give and graunt to you our Captaine-Gen^{ll}, full power and authority for us and in our name, as occasion shall require, according to yor discrecōn, by publique proclamation or otherwise, to make tender of our regall grace [mercy] and pardon to all such enemyes, rebells, or traytors, as shall in our said kingdomes, dominions, and territoryes, or any of them, submitt themselves to us, and desire to be received to our grace, mercy, and pardon, and according to yor discrecõn to receive to our grace and mercy, and to pardon all and every such person and persons as shall soe submitt and desire to be received to our grace, mercy, and pardon as aforesaid.

And we doe hereby graunt for us, our heires and successors, that every such person and persons soe submitting and desiring, and soe admitted by you unto our grace and mercy, and pardoned by you as aforesaid, shall be by us pardoned, and shall and may have and sue out pdons accordingly.

And further our will and pleasure is, and by these presents we doe give and graunt you full power and authority, that in case any invasion of enemyes, insurrecõn, comocõn, or rebellion, shall happen to be, increase, or beginne to arise within our said kingdomes, dominions, and territoryes, or any of them, that then from time to time, and att all times when any such shall be, increase, or beginne to arise, you may with such power and forces as you shall think fitt, either by yo^{r}selfe, or by others deputed and comaunded by you, resist, represse, and reforme the same by battaile, or other kinde of force; or at yor discrecõn, by such other proceedings as by the laws of our said realmes respectively, or the law martial, or lawes marshall, or by the intent and purport of this comission may otherwise be used.

[Power to command forces from the Deputy-Lieutenants of Countyes.]

And for the better execucõn of this our comission, we doe further give and graunt to you full power and authority from time to time, and att all times, att yor discrecõn, to comaund and require of and from all or any of our lieuetenants speciall, and their deputye leiuetenants of our severall countyes [of and] within our said kingdomes dominions and territoryes, and of and from every or any of them, to send to you, or to such place or places as you shall appoint, such number of able men for the warres, as well horsemen as foot-men of the Trayned Bandes in the said countyes respectively, or others sufficiently armed and furnished, at such time and times, and from time to time, as you in yor discrecõn shall appoint and require.

[Power of graunting comissions to levy and rayse forces.]

And further also, from time to time and att all times, at yor discrecõn, to give and graunt to any person or persons as to you it shall seem meet, any comission or comissions, warrant, and authority for the leavying or raiseing of any troopes or companyes of [any] horsemen or footmen in any place whatsoever within our said kingdomes, dominions, and territoryes, [or any of them,] and for the bringing or conducting of them to you, or to such place or places as you shall from time to time, or att any time, in yor discrecōn assigne and appoint.

[Power of constituting Deputyes.]

And further also, wee doe give and graunt to you, o^r Captaine-Gen^{ll}, full power and authority from time to time, and att all times by writeing under yor hands and seale, to appoint, ordain and constitute, one or more deputy or deputyes, of what quality or condicōn [what] soever, or by what name or names soever you shall think fitt, under you and in yor stead, to doe and execute all and every, or any, the powers and authority whatsoever by these presents graunted by us unto you.

[Power to appoint officers in chief or superior officers.]

And also, wee give you full power and authority to appoint all and every, or any superior officer or officers, or officer or officers in chief, of what quality or dignity soever respectively, as well of the horsemen as of the footmen, and of the ordnance, artillery, or amunicōn, of or belonging to, or that shall hereafter in any wise belong to the said army or armyes, or land-forces, and all and every Collo^{ll}, Captaines, and other inferior officers, and all and every other Comaunder and Comaund^{rs}, officer and officers whatsoever, which shall by you att any time, and from time [to time] be thought fitt or requisite for the better government of the said army or armyes, or land-forces, or any part thereof, and for the execuciōn of the intent and purport of these our letters-pattents.

[Power to appoint a Provost-Marshall.]

And further, wee doe give and graunt unto you full power and authority to appoint within our said army or armyes one Provost-Marshall, or more Provost Marshalls, according to yor discrecōn, to use and exercise that office in such case as you shall thinke requisite, And for the execucōn of the law-martiall or law-marshall according to your discrecōn and warrant given to him or them, and the intent and purport of these our letters-pattents, and as the law-marshall or martiall requireth.

[Power to hold Courts-Marshall.]

And further alsoe wee doe give and graunt to you full power and authority to hold, or cause to be held within the said army or armyes, or any part thereof, one or more military or martial, or marshall court or courtes, from time to time, and att all times, according to your discrecōn or comaund. And also in the same court or courtes, or otherwise, by y^rselfe or by yor deputy or deputyes, or by or in your counsel of warre, or by any other ways, and [proceedings,] or course as to you shall seem meetest, to heare, examine, determine, and punish all mutinyes, disobediences, deptures from Captaines, Comand^{rs}, and Governo^{rs}, and all capital and criminall offences whatsoever.

And wee further give and graunt to all and every such deputy and deputyes, or superior officer and officers, and officer and officers in chiefe, and all and every other comaunder or officer, so as aforesaid by you appointed, ordained, or constituted, or otherwise, according to the purport and intent of these ꝑsents appointed, ordained, or constituted, full power and authority to doe and execute whatsoever he or they respectively shall be by you soe ordained or appointed, to doe according to the tenour of these ꝑsents.

[Power of making laws for government of the Army.]

And also wee give and graunt unto you full power and authority, att yor discrecõn, from time to time, and att all times, to make, constitute, and ordaine, lawes, statutes, and ordinances for the government, ordering, ruleing, and military discipline of our said army or armyes, and every or any ꝑt thereof, and of all and every officer and officers, ꝑson and persons, of, in, and belonging to the same, and for touching and concerning all and every the prisoners, goodes, booty, or spoile that shall or may happen to be att any time by you, or any officer, or any other person of the said armye or armyes, or any part thereof, taken and concerning all other matters whatsoever in any wise to the said army, or this yor imployment belonging.

And the same lawes, statutes, ordinances, and every of them, to cause to be ꝑclaimed in such places, and att such times as to you shall seem meet, and the same and every of them to put in execucõn, and to appoint and ordaine such pains and penaltyes, either by losse of life, or member, place, office, money or goods, or otherwise, in the said lawes, ordinances, and statutes, and every or any of them, as in yor discrecõn you shall think meet, and to cause to be attached, apprehended, and imprisoned, or pardoned, or left or sett att liberty att yor discrecõn, all and every, or any ꝑson or ꝑsons offending against any of the said statutes, lawes and ordinances, and against or concerning such person or persons, to comaund such ꝑceeding, and to use either such justice, or such mercy, as to you shall seem most meet.

And wee doe hereby graunt and ordaine that all and every the statutes, lawes, and ordinances, soe from time to time and at any time to be made, constituted, or ordained by you, shall have full power and force, and remaine, and be in the said army and armyes, and every part thereof respectively, in full power and force, according as you shall make, constitute, or ordaine.

[Power to Pardon.]

And further, that you shall have from time to time, and at all times during the force of this our comission, full power to pardon and remitt all and every crimes and offences whatsoever comitted against the said lawes, statutes or ordinances, or any of them, or against the laws martial or law marshall in the said army, or any part thereof, or by any officer, souldier, or other, being part thereof, or belonging thereunto.

And wee further, for us, our heires and successors, doe graunt by these our letters pattent, that no person or persons whatsoever shall be proceded against, molested, sued, or in any wise impeached in any court whatsoever, or otherwise, for any crime or offence whatsoever, soe as aforesaid by you pardoned or remitted, nor sued, impeached, or molested in any court whatsoever, or otherwise, for or by reason of any matter or cause whatsoever, being finally determined and sentenced according to the power and jurisdiccōn by these presents given and graunted by us as aforesaid.

[Liberty of staying about the King.]

And further wee give and graunt unto you power, liberty, and authority upon all occasions, when to you it shall seem meet and necessary, if you be not by us otherwise expressly comanded, to come and repair to our person, wheresoever we shall be, and there, or att, in, neer, or about our court and household to remaine untill we shall signifye to you our expresse pleasure for your departure or returne.

[Of constituting Comissarys.]

And further alsoe wee give and graunt to you full power and authority from time to time, and at all times, to appoint and constitute one or more comissary or comissaryes, and any other officer or officers as to you shall seem meetest, for the providing and taking upp of victualls, and all or any other provision for the said army or armyes, or any part thereof, and to give him or them respectively power and warrant soe to doe from time to time and at all times, within any p̄t of our said kingdomes, dominions, and territoryes, or any of them.

[To take up Carriages, Vessels, Boats, &c.]

And further alsoe by yourselfe, or others deputed or authorized by you, to take up and use such carriages, horses, boates, or other vessels as in yor discrecōn, and as often as you shall think meet, shall bee needful for the conveying or conducting of the said army or armyes, or any part thereof, or for bringing or carryiug ammunicōn, ordnance, artillery, victualls, and all or any other provisions necessary or requisite for the said army or armyes, or any part thereof, to or from any place or places, according to the intent of these [presents.] And to that intent and purpose to depute and authorize, and give warrant or warrants to any person or persons whatsoever for such taking upp and use as aforesaid.

[Power of graunting warrants to the Treasurers of the Armyes.]

And further, from time to time to give warrant and authority to our treasurer or treasurers of the said army or armyes for the time being, for the issueing and paying of all and every such sumes of money as are or shall be from time to time payable to any person or persons whatsoever in the said army or armyes, or any part thereof, or due to any person or persons whatsoever, by reason of the same respectively.

[Power of graunting Safe-conducts.]

And wee doe further hereby give power and authority to you our Captaine-Gen^ll, for causes especially moveing you, by yor letters under yor seale, from time to time, [when and] as often as to you its hall seem meet, to graunt safe-conducts, as well general [as] speciall, in all places by land or by water, to any person or persons whatsoever, generally to doe and execute all and every thing and things which to the office of a Captaine-Generall of an army under us doth belong, and which for the good and safety of us and our state and the government and discipline of our said army shall be by you thought expedient and necessary.

[Comaunde of all Garrisons and Forts and Castles, and to displace or continue the Governors, Captaines, &c.]

And for the better execucōn of this our service, wee doe further give unto you our Captaine-Gen^ll full power and authority, as you in yor discrecōn shall think meet, and for the advancem^t of this our service, to comaund all our garrisons and our forts and castles, now fortifyed or hereafter to be fortifyed, and to amove, displace, or continue the governo^rs, captaines, or other inferior officers, souldyers, and garrisons, as to yor discrecōn shall seem meet, and the occasion of the service shall require, and to furnish the same garrisons, castles, and fortes, with other governo^rs, comaund^rs, and souldiers, as you shall think meet for the safety and good of our armyes and the advancement of our service.

To have, hold, exercise, and injoy, all and every the powers and authorityes aforesaid, by you our said Captaine-Generall, and by yor deputy and deputyes as aforesaid, during our will and pleasure.

And wee will and comaund you our Captaine-Gen^ll, that with all speed you doe execute the premisses with effect.

Wherefore wee will and comaund all and singular leivetenants of our countyes and leiveten^ts speciall, dukes, marquesses, earles, viscountes, barons, barron^ts, knights, sheriffes, treasurer or treasurers of our said army, mayo^rs, bayliffes, constables, captaines, and all other officers and souldiers, ministers, and all and every our loveing subjects, of what estate, degree, or condition soever he or they shall be, that they and every of them respectively, with their power and serv^ts, from time to time, [and] according as they shall be comaunded by you, or authorized according to the purport and intent of these our letters-pattents and the authority and power to you herein given, be obedient to you, and attendant, aiding, assisting, counselling, and helpeing you, and ready at yor comaundem^t in the due execucōn hereof, as they and every of them tender our displeasure, and will answeare to the contrary att their perills.

And further, our pleasure is, and wee doe hereby give and graunt for us, our heires, and successo^rs, that whatsoever either you or any other person or persons, of what degree, office, state, or condicōn soever, upon or by yor comission, warrant, or comaund, shall doe by virtue or authority of this our comission or letters-patents, or according to our instruccōns aforesaid, or according to the tenour, effect, or purport of this our comission, touching the execucōn of the premisses or any part thereof, both you and the said other person or persons, upon the shewing forth of these our letters-patents, or the constat or the inrollment thereof, shall be in all and every [of] our courts, and elsewhere in our dominions, discharged and acquitted in that behalfe, against us, our heires and successo^{rs}, and free from all impeachm^t and other molestation for the same.

   In witness, &c.   Witnesse ourself, &c.

[In witness whereof we have caused these our letters to be made patents. Witness ourself, at Westminster, the third day of August, in the twelfth year of our reign.
      By the King. Barker.]

Charles, by the grace of God, King of England, Scotland, France, and Ireland, Defendo^r of the Faith, &c. To our trusty and well-beloved Generall George Monk, greeting. Upon the great confidence wee repose in your courage, conduct, fidelity, and affeccōn to us and the good of our kingdomes, wee, by these p^{e}sents, constitute and appoint you to be Captaine-Generall and Comaunder-in-Chiefe of all forces which are or shall be raised for our service within our kingdomes of England, Scotland, and Ireland, and the territoryes thereunto belonging, giveing you full power and authority to order, conduct, and comaund the same in all things, accordeing to the lawes and customes of warre, and therewith to fight, kill, and destroy all who are or shall be in armes against us, and to seize on any forts or places in rebellion against our authority, and to keep and defend the same for us and in our name, and to doe and execute all acts and powers belonging to the duety and office of a Captaine-Generall and Comaunder-in-Chiefe; and wee hereby require all major-generalls, collonells, and other inferior officers and soldiers under you, to obey you in all things as Captaine-Generall and Comaunder-in-Chiefe of all our forces within our said kingdomes and dominions; and you are to be obedient to such orders as you shall from time to time receive from us; for all which, this our comission shall be your sufficient warrant. Given at our Court at, &c.

Endorsed "Heads of the late Lord-General's function, &c."
 endorsed by Sir Joseph Williamson.—State-Paper Office.
 (1678.)

His Maties establishment comprizes all military officers in his Maties guards, forces, and guarrissons, wth the number of eache troope, regiment, and company, and their paye respectively. The officers' commissions are all entered in the office of the commissary-generall of the musters, by wch they know the names of the persons commissioned for the said military offices, and by the establishm^t it appears what numbers of soldiers are allowed to bee under their respective comands. The comissaryes-generall (thus governed in the business of the musters) doe muster the forces and garrisons seaven times in every yeare; that is to saye, twoe musters of forty-twoe days each, in summer, when the days are long, and five musters of fifty-six dayes eache for the rest of the yeare. Of every muster of a troope or company, three rolles are sign'd by ye comissaryes of ye officers, one of wch rolls, written in parchem^t, is carried to the paymaster-generall, who thereuppon audits the accompt of what is due uppon eache muster to the troops, regim^{ts}, and companyes respectively, and sent certificates or debentures for the same to the late Lord Generall, uppon wch hee gave warr^{ts} to Sr Stephen ffox to paye the monies due to them accordingly, soone after the expiration of every muster. One other of the said muster rolles was still kept by ye comissaryes, and the third roll was kept by ye officers of the respective troops, regim^{ts}, and companyes.

In garrissons and quarters where noe allowances was settled for fire and candle for the guards kept by them in his Maties establishment, the late Lord Generall gave warr^{ts} to the paymaster-gen^{ll} for twelvepence a day for fire and candle for the guards kept by eache company; and the late Lord Gen^{ll} likewise gave warr^{ts} to the paymaster-generall for the paym^t of all others needfull contingent charges of his Maties forces and garrissons, all wch allowances and payments were assigned to bee paide out of the moneis allowed and designed (in his Maties establishm^t) for contingent charges, the same (in the present establishment) being thirteen hundred pounds per annum.

Noe troops or companyes removed or changed their quarters but by warrant from the Lord-Gen^{ll}, who (but uppon abslut necessity) would not appoint the same unless it were soone after ye expiration of a muster, because at these times they were usually furnish'd wth moneis to paye their quart^{rs} at the places from whence they removed. Armes and amunition for the guards, forces, and garrissons was issued out by order from the Lo:-Gen^{ll}, directed to the Com^{rs} of his Maties Ordin^{ce}; but where great supplyes were desired of stores for garrissons, it was first brought to his Maties or the Councells consideration, unless it were for the changeing of new armes for ould unserviceable armes spent or spoiled in his Maties service. In all orders for partyes to marche, the constables were required to bee assisting for the quartering of them uppon their marche in innes, victualing-howses, and ale-howses.

All orders for convoyes of his Maties treasure, directed that the officers comanding those convoyes should observe such orders as should bee given them by the conducto^r or other civill officer who had the charge of the treasure, (whose names were usually sent from the com^{rs} of the Treasury-Chamber or the Navy-Office, and were inserted in the orders,) untill the treasure were safely lodged at the place of its designacion.

Upon information of disobedience of inferior officers towards their superior officers or of soldiers to their officers, or other great offences, the Lord-Generall gave commissions to court-martialls to examin such offences, and to bring such offenders to their tryall, and condigne punishm^t, provided that the same extended not to the taking away of life or limbe, lesser offences being punish'd by regimental court-martiall or court-martialls of the garrissons.

Complaints of creditors of officers or soldiers were usually referr'd to their superior officers to examine and compose the differences, or report the cases to the Lo:-Gen^{ll}. After reports that the debts were just, if the debto^r being an officer did not satisfy his creditor by payment or security within a time limited, the Gen^{ll} then left him to the lawe; and if it were the case of a privat soldier, the Gen^{ll} ordered his Cap^{ne} to discharge him, and to entertain another into his place. In the orders leaveing officers to the lawe, there was a restriction that their persons should not bee arrested.

Whensoever his Ma^{ty} gave order for the raiseing of any forces, and had given commissions to the officers, the Generall gave orders to them for the raiseing of their men by beate of drum for the armeing, quartering, and for the mustering of eache troope and company, (as soone as halfe the numbers established for them should bee brought to bee mustered,) and likewise for the paying of them from the day of their first muster (as soone as conveniently might be) to the day of the then next generall muster of the forces, that all the musters might comence together.

When his Ma^{ty} gave orders for the disbanding or reducing of any of the forces, the Generall sent ord^s to the troopes, regim^{ts}, or companyes, for the disbanding or reducing of them accordingly, (by a day limited in the ord^{rs}, from which time their paye is determined,) and for the delivering upp of their armes into his Maj^{ties} stoares, and sending the Generall a receipt for the same, wch receipts the Generall sent to the Com^{rs} of the Ordin^{ce}. Noe addition was made to the establishm^t but by additionall establishments prepared by the Gen^{ll}, who sent, und^r his hand (at the bottome) five duplicats of them to his Maties Principall Secretary of State, to be humbly presented to his Ma^{ty}. After his Ma^{ty} signed them, they were distributed as followeth, to wit, one of them to the Gen^{ll}, one of them to his Maties Principall Secretary, one of them to the Paym^r-Gen^{ll}, another to the Comissary-Gen^{ll}, and one of them to the Com^{rs} of the Treasury; and the like course was taken about all generall establishm^{ts}.

The forces in towne quarter in the Citty and Libertyes of Westm^r, and in the outletts of the Citty of London without the walls; the justices of peace direct therein, and the quarter-m^rs and constables signed the billets they are all uppon innes, victualing-howses, taverns, and ale-houses; complaints of quarters, or of differences betweene soldiers and townesmen, were by the Generall still referr'd to the Earle of Craven, whose influence with the civill magistrats allwayes tended to the composure or according of those differencies, and was allwayes effectual in that behalfe.

10.

Charles R.—Our will and pleasure is, that the severall officers hereafter named, and under the salaries and entertainmente herein expressed, be added to our establishment of the forces lately by us raised for the defence of our person and governm^t, and continued in our pay from the day of their respective constitutions, untill further order to the contrary, signified by us, or our right trusty and right intirely beloved couzen and counsello^r, George Duke of Albemarle, Capt.-Gen^all of our forces; and the Comissary-Gen^rall of the musters, paym^r, and all other officers and persons concern'd, are to take notice hereof. Given under our signe manuell att Whitehall, this . . . . . . [1]

P. Mensem.

	£	s	d
One adjutant to his Ma^te regiment of ffoote, att 4s. p. diem	5	12	0
One adjutant to his Grace George Duke of Albemarle's reg^t of ffoote att 4s. p. diem	5	12	0
One quarter-m^r to his Ma^te regiment of Horse at 5s. p. diem	7	0	0
One kettle-drum for the Kinges R^t of Horse att 3s. p. diem	4	4	0
	22	8	0

Col. Russell[2] desires their may be eadded

	s.	d.
one serg^t to ye Kinges company att	1	6 p. diem.
A drum-major att	1	6
A marshall att	4	0

[1] Endorsed.   [2] The Colonel of the 1st Foot Guards.

"June, 1661.
"Order for adjutants &c. to bee added to the establishm^t."

11.

Military Papers—Charles II. State-Paper Office.

Ord^rs and Instruccõns to be observed by our Commissary-Generall of ye Musters and his Dep^ty, and by the officers and souldiers of our respective Guards of Horse and Foot, and our severall garrisons in our pay and entertainment.

1. None shall be allowed upon any muster, who by losse of limbes

or otherwaies is unable for our service, but by ord^r from us or our Generall.

2. Noe officer or souldier shall be allowed or passed the muster that diligently attends not his duty, and is not present at the muster, except absent by permission of us, or our Grãll, or the cheife officer cõmanding the regiment, troope, or garrison to which he belonges, and none to be absent more then two monthes in a yeare, except such as are members of Parliament, and them dureing their sitting in Parliament.

3. All passes or lycences for being absent shall be p^{r}sented to the muster-master, who is required to enter the same in a booke, fairely written, to prevent collusion; and who ever exceeds ye time limited by his passe for his absence shall be respited, and not to be allowed the muster without ord^r of our Generall.

4. None shall p^{r}sent himself or be p^{r}sented to be mustered by a counterfeit name or surname, thereby to defraud us of our pay, or upon any other accompt, and that officer or souldier offending herein, upon complaint thereof to our Generall, shall be cashiered, and also loose his pay for such musters.

5. No housekeeper in the usuall quarters of our Guards of Horse or Foot, or our other regim^{ts}, or in any garrison, shall be received and entertained into our service and pay, and mustered as a private souldier without ord^r of our Generall; nor shall any officer demand or receive, directly or indirectly, any sume of money whatsoever, of or from any non-commission officer or private souldier, for admitting and entertaineing him into any of our troopes, companyes, or guarrisons und^r his comand.

6. All comiss^{us} granted by us or our Generall to any officer in our pay, shall be p^{r}sented to ye muster-master, who is to enter the same in a booke, fairely written; and no commission officer shall be allowed in musters, who is not comissioned by us or our Generall, or that refuseth or neglects to enter the same with our Commissary-Gra^{ll} of the Musters, or his dep^{ty}.

7. None shall be mustered but such as are compleatly armed, viz. Each horseman to have for his defensive armes, back, breast, and pot, and for his offensive armes, a sword, a case of pistolls, the barrells whereof are not to be und^r fourteen inches in length, and each trooper of our Guards to have a carbine, besides the aforesaid armes. And the Foot to have each souldier a sword, and each pikeman a pike of 16 foote long, and not und^r; and each musqueteer a musquet, with a collar of bandaliers, the barrell of wch musket to be about foore foot long, and to conteine a bullet foureteen of which shall weigh a pound weight.

8. No souldier shall depart from his colours wthout lycence of his cheife officer of ye troope, company, or garrison to wch he belongs, it being felony by the statute of ye 18th of Henry ye 6th, chap. 19. Nor

shall any non-comiss[n] officer or private souldier, after enrollment and being mustered, be dismissed or cashiered by any officer w[th]out ord[r] of our Gra[ll], or a regimentall court-marshall; and in case such non-comiss[n] officer or private souldier be of our troopes of Horse Guards, by a court consisting of the then p[r]sent comission officers of the three troopes of Horse Guards, nor out of any garrison, but by a court-marshall as our Gra[ll] shall direct, or by his ord[r].

9. The muster-master shall allwayes give convenient notice to y[e] officer in cheif comanding the regiment, troope, company, or garrison, before the muster-day, of the time and place for y[e] muster, that the officers and souldiers may have time to make ready for the muster, and that three muster-rolls may be p[r]pared of their respective troopes and companyes; in w[ch] rolls the names of all the private souldiers are to be written alphabetically; one of w[ch] rolls is to be in parchement for y[e] paymaster, and to be subscribed (w[th] one also w[ch] y[e] muster-master is to keepe) by two comission officers at least of their respective troopes and companyes, together wth the muster-master, and the other muster-roll to be subscribed onely by the muster-master, w[ch] the officer is to keepe, and noe roll to be received and allowed by the muster-master and paymaster otherwaies, and the said muster-rolls to be perfected forthwith after the muster.

10. Noe officer or souldier shall be mustered and paid in a double capacity, except a generall officer or feild officer in the same regiment whereof he is a feild officer, or governo[r] of a guarrison haveing comand of horse and foote for our service in the same, except by our speciall warrant or order of our Generall; w[ch] warrant or ord[r] shall bee also registred w[th] our Comiss[ry]-generall of musters in a booke.

11. All officers and souldiers, together w[th] the muster-masters, not duely observeing these ord[rs] and instrucc[o]ns, or any of them respectively, shall be cashiered. Whitehall, May 5[th], 1663.

To our Commissary-Generall of y[e] Musters and his dep[tyes],
and to all officers and souldiers of our respective Guards
of Horse and Foote, and our severall garrisons in our pay
and entertainement.

By his Ma[ties] comand,
(Signed) HENRY BENNET.

12.

George Duke of Albemarle, Earl of Torrington, Baron Monk of Potheridge, Beauchamp and Tees, Captain-General and Commander-in-Chief of all his Majesty's Forces, Knight of the Most Noble Order of the Garter, Master of his Majesty's Horse, and one of his Majesty's most Hon[ble] Privy Council.

By virtue of the power and authority to me given by his most excellent Majesty, Charles 2nd, &c., I do hereby constitute and appoint you, Anthony Vincent, to be Ensign to my own company of foot, in my own regiment, under my command, for the service of his Majesty; you are therefore to take into your charge and care the said company as Ensign thereof, and duly to exercise the officers and soldiers of the same in arms, and use your best care and endeavour to keep them in good order and discipline, hereby commanding them to obey you as their Ensign; and you are likewise to follow and observe such orders and directions as you shall from time to time receive from his Majesty or myself; and also you are to obey the superior officers of the said company, regiment, and army, according to the discipline of war, in pursuance of the trust reposed in you, and your duty to his Majesty. Given under my hand and seal, at the Cock-pit, the 23^d day of January, 166$\frac{3}{4}$, and in the 15th year of his Majesty's reign.

ALBEMARLE.

13.

May, 1664.

Fifty men were drafted from the regiment for the expedition to Guinea, and a like number for sea-service, under the command of the Duke of Yorke.

14.

To the Right Honble John Lord Berkley, and the rest of the Commissioners for managing the office of his Majesty's Ordnance.

These are to desire you to cause to be delivered out of his Majesty's stores in the Tower of London unto Captain John Huitson, 500 matchlocks, with 500 collars of bandeliers, for the use of 500 men, which are to be raised by his Majesty's order, and added to my regiment of Foot Guards for sea-service.

Given under my hand, this 24th day of Febr^y, 16$\frac{63}{64}$.

ALBEMARLE.

15.

Two companies were added, April 15th, 1667; commanded by Sir Robert Holmes, Kn^t, and Captn Robert Coke; each company armed with 30 pikes, 60 musquets, with collars of bandeliers, 13 firelocks, 103 swords, 2 halberds, 1 partizan, 2 drums.

16.

A warrant, dated 1st of May, 1667, to replace 120 firelocks lost by the regiment during the "Fire of London."

17.

Charles R.—Right trusty and right welbeloved cousin and councellor, wee greete you well. Whereas wee have thought fit, for the better carrying on of our service in the Streights, to send some partyes of land-soldiers, to bee distributed into such of our men-of-warr in those parts as have neede of them, our will and pleasure is, that you give order for one comission-officer, one serjeant, or one corporall, with fifty musketeeres, under their com̃and, to bee drawne (as proportionably as you can) out of the respective companyes of your regiment of our Foote Guards, and to bee delivered over to such officer or officers as shall bee appointed to receive them by our dearest brother, the Duke of Yorke, our Highe-Admirall of England, in order to their imbarqueing in the shipps now preparing to passe into the Streights, to bee there distributed as aforesaid. The said comission-officer and serjeant, or corporall, are to imbarque, goe along with, and com̃and the said party of your regiment, in their voyage, and to bee carefull to observe such orders as they shall receive from the com̃ander of the shipp in which they passe, untill they shall deliver their men aboard with our Admirall Sr Thomas Allen, who will afford accomodation to the officers for their returne; and then they are to come back to the regiment againe. You are to send an officer to apply to our Paymaster-Generall of our land-forces for three months' advance of paye uppon account for the twoe officers who goe to com̃and the said party, which money is to bee paide unto them to fit them for their voyage, and is to bee defalked from the regiment uppon paying off the musters, for which the same is, or shall become due to the said officers. And when the said com̃anded party shall bee aboard, you are to give orders to your captaines to recruite and fill upp their companyes complete againe, which the Comissaryes-Generall of the musters are to allowe of accordingly. For which this shall bee sufficient warrant. Given at our Court at Whitehall, the 21st day of February, 1669, and in the 22^d yeare of his Maties reigne.

By his Maties com̃and,

ARLINGTON.

To our right trusty and right welbeloved Cousin and Councellor, William Earle of Craven.

"The like letter, (mutatis mutandis,) dated and signed ut supra, to Col. John Russell, for the drawing out and sending a comission-officer, a serjeant, or corporall, and fifty sold^{rs} out of his 14 companyes of the ffoote Guards about the towne."

18.

Charles R.—Right trusty and welbeloved, wee greete you well. Whereas we have thought fit for the better carrying on of our service in the Streights to send some partyes of land-soldiers out of our Foote Guards, and the Admirall's regiment, to bee putt aboard such of our men-of-warr in those parts as have neede of them, and it being necessary that there bee a supply of fire-armes, powder, matche, and bullet sent along with them, our will and pleasure therefore is, that you give order for one hundred, thirty-six fire-armes, eleaven barels of powder, eleaven hundred pound waight of matche, with bullet proportionable, and one hundred thirty-six collars of bandaleeres, (a third part of which said fire-armes are to bee snaphances,) to bee delivered unto such officer or officers as shall bee appointed to receive them by our dearest brother the Duke of Yorke, our Highe-Admirall of England, in order to the imbarqueing the same with the said soldiers in the shipps now preparing to passe into the Streights, to bee distributed (with the said soldiers) according to such orders as shall bee given by our Admirall, Sr Thomas Allen, in that behalfe. Given at our Court at Whitehall, the 21st day of ffebruary, 1669, and in the 22^d yeare of our reigne.

By his Maties comand,
ARLINGTON.

To our right trusty and welbeloved, our
Comissioners of the Ordinance.

19.

Charles R.—Our will and pleasure is, that out of our stoares you cause twelve barrells of powder,[1] with bullet proportionable, and a double proportion of matche, to be delivered unto Captaine Thomas Mansfield, for the use of the twelve companies of the regiment of our Foote Guards, under the command of our right trusty and right welbeloved cousin and councellour, William Earle of Craven. Given at our Court at Whitehall, the 23rd day of March, 16$\frac{69}{70}$, and in the two-and-twentieth yeare of our reigne.

By his Maties command,
ARLINGTON.

To our right trusty and welbeloved, our
Commissioners of the Ordnance.

---

[1] In a MS. belonging to Hudson Gurney, Esq., will be found a receipt to make gunpowder, written by an English scribe about the year 1300, in very precise terms; viz. saltpetre, quick sulphur, and charcoal from willows. It is termed a powder "ad faciendum le Crake."

Guns are called crakeys of war in Gawin Douglas's Translation of the Eneid.—Folio. Edinburgh, 1810.

20.

Quarters of the Forces. 24th March, 16⁶⁹⁄₇₀.

His Maties three troopes of Guards
Fourteene companies (part) of his Maties regiment of Foote, under the command of Collonell John Russell
Twelve companies of Foote, being the regiment commanded by the late Lord Generall, now under the command of the Right Hono^ble William Earle of Craven
} All quartered in and aboute the citties of London and Westminster.

His Maties regiment of Horse Gds., commanded by the Right Hono^ble Aubrey Earle of Oxford {
- His Maties troope, commanded by the Lord Hawley . . . att Canterbury
- Earle of Oxford, Colonell, his troope at Reading
- Major ffrancis Windham's troope at Salisbury
- Sr Edward Brett's troope, at Watford and Rickmundsworth; ordered to Hamersmith
- Lord Freschevill's troope . at York
- S^r ffrancis Compton's troope . at Uxbridge and Colebrook
- Sr Henry Jones's troope, at Sennock and Bromley; ordered to . . Highgate and Islington
- Sr Thomas Armestrong's troope at Farneham.

Ten companies, being the remain^g part of his Maties owne regiment of Foote Gds., under the command of Coll. John Russell {
- Captaine Wyan's companie . at Berwick
- Captaine Stradling's companie at Berwick
- Captaine Musgrave's companie, at Berwick; ordered to . . . . Carlisle
- Captaine John Walter's companie at Berwick
- Captaine John Strode's companie at Dover Castle
- Captaine Osborn's companie . at Portesmouth
- Captaine Eaton's companie . at Tinmouth Castle
- Captaine Herbert Jeffery's
- Captaine Skelton's, and
- Captaine Sr Phillip Moncketon's } at York.

APPENDIX. 257

Twelve companies, being the Lord High Admirall's regim^t of Foote, under Sr Chas Littleton's command	Collonell Sr Chas Littleton's ⎫ Captaine Anthony Buller's ⎬ comp^s at Harwich Liet^t-Coll. Sr John Griffith's ⎫ Captaine Bennett's, and ⎬ comp^s at Hull Captaine Middleton's ⎭	
	Major Nathan^l Dorrell's companie	at Land-Guard Fort
	Captaine Cartwright's company	at Gravesend
	Captaine Bromley's company	at Plymouth
	Captain Titus' companie	at Deal and Walmer
	Captain Vaughan's company	at Chepstow Castle
	Captain Herbert's company	at Guernsey
	Capt. Sr Bourchier Wrey's companie	at Sheerness.
Ten companies, being the Holland regiment, commanded by Sr Walter Vane	Collonel Sr Walter Vane's ⎫ Capt. Sr Tho. Woodcock's ⎬ comp^s at Windsor Castle Lt.-Coll. Sr Tho. Howard's ⎫ Major Sr Tho. Ogle's, and ⎬ comp^s at Plymouth Capt. Henery Pomeroy's ⎭ Capt. Sr Herb^t Lundsford's ⎫ Captaine Baptist Alcock's ⎬ comp^s at Berwick	
	Captaine Henry Sidney's companie	at Carlisle
	Captaine William Cownley's company at Carlisle; ordered to	Berwick
	Captaine Manley's company	at Jersey.

Here followeth severall Guarrison companies not regimented.

    One company at Berwick
    One companie at Carlisle
    One companie at Chester
    One companie at Guernsey
    Three companies at Hull
    Two companies at Jersey
    One companie at Pendennis
    Two companies at Plymouth
    Six companies at Portesmouth
    Two companies at Scilly
    One companie at Isle of Wight
    Governour and thirty soldiers, at Sandon Fort, in the island
    One companie at Scarborough Castle
    Three companies at Tower of London
    One companie at Tinmouth Castle
    A lieutenant and thirty soldiers at Upnor Castle
    One companie at Windsor Castle.

21.

Two halberts, foure firelocks, six muskets, and foure pikes, broken in the last Easter holidayes by Cap^{ne} Richard Kirkbye's company of the Coldstream, to be exchanged from the stores of the Ordnance.

Dated 11th April, 1670.

22.

Two ould unserviceable drums of Cap^{ne} John Mutlowe's company of the Coldstream, to be exchanged for two drums, with drumsticks, out of the stoares of the Ordnance.

Dated 11th April, 1670.

23.

Charles R.—Whereas wee are given to understand, that by directions of our late Generall deceased, foure hundred new pikes, and six hundred new collars of bandeleere, were contracted for to bee made (according to patternes), and to bee delivered into the office of our ordinance, which were intended for the use of the regiment of our ffoot Guards, now under the command of our right trusty and right welbeloved cousin and councellour, William Earle of Craven, in regard that the pikes and collars of bandeleeres, which they now have, being long, and still used for their ordinary duty, and mounting the Guards, were not judged soe usefull as these new ones, which are to bee reserved for any extraordinary occasion of our service: We have therefore thought fitt, and doe hereby signify unto you our will and pleasure, that you cause the said foure hundred pikes, and six hundred collars of bandeleeres, to be delivered out of our stoares, unto our trusty and welbeloved John Miller, Esq^e, major of the said regiment, for their use, as an additionall supply of armes, to bee reserved as aforesaid, hee giving an indenture or receipt under his hand for the same. And for soe doeing this shall bee your warrant. Given at our Court at Whitehall, the tenth day of June, 1670, in the 22^d yeare of our reigne.

By his Maties command,
ARLINGTON.

To our right trusty and welbeloved
Sr Thomas Chichely, Master of our Ordinance.

24.

The Duke of York to convene the Colonels of regiments to consider of military affairs, unregulated since my Lord General's death.

Dated 18th June, 1670.

25.

Charles R.—Whereas wee have beene graciously pleased to grant unto you, our right trusty and right welbeloved cousin and councellour, William Earle of Craven, Collonell of a regiment of our ffoot Guards, one private soldier's pay out of each company of the twelve companies of the said regiment under your command, You are therefore to give order to the respective Captaines, or other officers-in-chiefe, with the said twelve companies, by the next muster, to disband one soldier out of each company in the said regiment; And that at the said next muster, the said Captaines, or other officers respectively, shall enter the names hereon indorsed in their muster-rolles, (being the names to bee mustered in the said twelve companies respectively,) in the places of the soldiers soe to bee disbanded to the end that the pay for the names soe entered may bee allowed to you the said Earle of Craven; of which our Commissaries-Generall of the Musters are hereby required to take notice, and to pass and continue the said twelve names in the muster-rolles of the said companies, in the ensueing musters; that is to say, one of them in each company, untill further order, wee haveing given order to our Paymaster-Generall of our fforces to stop that soldiers pay in his hands, from each of the said companies, to the end that the same may bee from time to time paid unto you. And for soe doeing this shall bee your warrant. Given at our Court at Whitehall, the 19th day of August, 1670.

By his Ma[ties] command,
ARLINGTON.

To our right trusty and right welbeloved
Cousin and Councellour, William Earle of Craven.

Here followeth the twelve names indorsed on the back of the foregoing order.

In the Earle of Craven, Collonel, his owne company	Rowland Starkey.
In Lieut-Coll. Sr James Smith's company	Samuell Parry.
In Major John Miller's company	Paul Mercer.
In Captaine Winter's company	John Thomas.
In Captaine Mansfield's company	Nicholas Cholmley.
In Captaine Peter's company	Lancelot Lowther.
In Captaine Mutlowe's company	Edward Barford.
In Captaine Clarke's company	Richard Collinson.
In Captaine Coke's company	Peter Johnson.
In Captaine Bertye's company	Hugh Guilliame.
In Captaine Huitson's company	Robert Peterson.
In Captaine Kirkbye's company	William Jameson.

26.

4 partizans, 11 halberts, 27 pikes, 35 matchlocks, 32 firelocks, and 3 drums, to be delivered out of the Ordnance stores, in lieu of those broken at several times in dispersing of Conventicles, and at the fire in Southwark, as certified by Major John Miller, 16th Sept., 1670.
Dated 22d Sept., 1670.

27.

Charles R.—We being given to understand that the Colonels comp^y of the Coldstream reg^t of our Foot Guards, under the command of our right trusty and right welbeloved cousin and councillor, William Earl of Craven, had formerly set out to them for their quarters in the precincts following, to wit, from the Castle Tavern on Snow Hill, to Holborne Conduit, and so on to Holborne Bridge, and all Holborne below bar, except Elye Rents, part of Field Lane from Holborne to the sign of the George; part of Shoe Lane from Holborne to the sign of the George; part of Fetter Lane from Holborne to the sign of the Three Horse Shoes and Castle Yard; part of the east side of Gray's Inn Lane from Holborne to Baldwin's Gardens, and Baldwin's Gardens and St Dunstan's in the West, as much as is standing since the conflagration, we have thought fit to continue these quarters of the said company. You are therefore to quarter the said company in inns, victualling-houses, taverns, and alehouses, with all equality and indifferency within the limits and bounds aforesaid, until further orders. Wherein we require all our officers and constables whom it may concern to be assisting unto you; and you are to be careful that your soldiers carry themselves civilly, and duly pay for what they shall receive at their quarters. Given at our Court at Whitehall, the 23d day of March, 167¾.

By his Majesty's command,

ARLINGTON.

To our trusty and well-beloved Capt. Saunders,
Captain-Lieutenant of the company above mentioned.

28.

The pay of the soldiers of the Foot Guards "which usually attends our person" to be reduced to 8^d a day, the same as the line, when on duty at Rochester, &c., until they shall return to attend us.
Dated 12th May, 1671.

29.

Charles R.—Our will and pleasure is, that for the contiguous quartering of the Coldstream regiment of our Foot Guards, under the command of our right trusty and right welbeloved cousin and councillor, William Earl of Craven, they continue and re-assume their quarters in the respective parishes, places, and precincts following, vizt; that part of the parish of St Giles's in the Fields not taken up by our own regiment of Foot Guards, under Colonel Russell's command, the parishes of St Andrew's Holborn, St Dunstan's in the West, St Bridgett's, the precincts of Bridewell, the parishes of Great St Bartholemew, and St Bartholemew's the Less, St Sepulchre's, St James's Clerkenwell, St Botolph's Aldersgate, St Giles's Cripplegate, St Leonard Shoreditch, St Mary Islington, and Moorfields, being part of St Botolph's Bishopsgate: In all which places you are, with all equality, to take up quarters for the said regiment in inns, victualling-houses, taverns, and alehouses, until further orders. Wherein all our officers, justices of peace, and constables, whom it may concern, are hereby required to be assisting unto you; and you are to be careful that the soldiers carry themselves civilly, and duly pay their quarters.

And it is nevertheless our will and pleasure that two companies (removable from time to time out of the said regiment) be continued to quarter and do duty in our Borough of Southwark until further orders; for all which this shall be sufficient warrant. Given at our Court at Whitehall, the 16th day of August, 1671.

By his Majesty's command,

ARLINGTON.

To our trusty and well-beloved John Miller, Esqr, Major of
the Coldstream regiment above mentioned.[1]

30.

No serjeant or corporal of the two regiments of Guards to continue to keep any victualling or ale house: nor any soldier to marry without the consent of his Captain, upon pain of being cashiered, and losing the pay that might be due.

Dated 3^d Nov., 1671.

31.

Charles R.—Right trusty and right welbeloved cousin and councellour, wee greet you well. Our will and pleasure is, that you give orders for drawing out of tenn soldiers (without theire armes) out of each of the twelve companies of the Coldstreame regiment of our ffoote Guards under your command, who are to be cleared with for their pay, and to be delivered unto such officer or officers as our most deare and intirely beloved sonne, James Duke of Monmouth, shall appoint to receive them; to the end that they may be entertayned in a regiment of ffoote, which wee have give order to our said sonne to

---

[1] The warrants, extracts from them, and other documents for which no authority is given, were obtained at the War-Office.

raise and command: And you are, after the said men shall be drawne out and delivered as aforesaid, to give order to the captaines to recruite their companies; for which this shall be sufficient warrant. Given at our Court at Whitehall, the 18th day of February, 167½, and in the 24th yeare of our reigne.

By his Maties command,

ARLINGTON.

To our right trusty and right welbeloved cousin and councellour, William Earle of Craven, or in his absence, to the officer-in-cheife commanding the Coldstreame regiment of our Foot Guards under his command.

32.

Six snaphance musketts, and six collars of bandeleers, to Captain Bertye's comp^y; and four snaphance musketts, and four collars of bandeleers to Captⁿ Huitson's comp^y, in lieu of so many lost and destroyed in the late fire in Covent Garden.

Dated 12th March, 167¼.

33.

It being frequently necessary to send yaughs or advice-boats downe the river into the Downs, or upon the coast, the King's regiment of Guards and the Coldstream are to send alternately ten or eleven men, with their arms, on board, upon this service, as often as the Duke of York shall appoint.

Dated 27th March, 1672.

34.

Charles R.—Right trusty and welbeloved councellour, wee greet you well. Wee are graciously pleased to grant that twelve colours, with staves and tassells to them respectively, be forthwith provided and made, according to the modell and distinctions of the last colours made and provided in our wardrobe for the use of the Coldstreame regiment of our Foot Guards, under the command of our right trusty and right welbeloved cousin and councellour, William Earle of Vacat. Craven, of which our trusty and welbeloved Major John Miller will give you the modell. Our will and pleasure therefore is, that you cause the said twelve colours, with staves and tassells to them as aforesaid, to be made and fitted, and that you cause them to be delivered unto the said Major John Miller for the use of the twelve companies of the said regiment. And for soe doing, this, with his receipt for the same, shall be your warrant and discharge. Given at our Court at Whitehall, the 13th day of April, 1672.

By his Maties command,

ARLINGTON.

To our right trusty and welbeloved councellour, Ralph Montague, Esqr, master of our wardrobe.

35.

Charles R.—Upon consideration of the annexed certificate of Major John Miller, it is our will and pleasure, that out of the stores of our office of the Ordnance you cause ninety-one snaphance musketts, ninety-one matchlock musketts, one hundred eighty-two collars of bandileers, (suitable to the rest of their bandeleers,) nyne halberts, one drumm, twelve barrells of powder, with a double proportion of match, to be delivered to such officer as the said Major Miller shall appoint, for the use of the nyne companies heere in towne (as they are now to be recruited) of the Coldstreame regiment of our Guards, under the command of our right trusty and right welbeloved cousin and councellour, William Earle of Craven, except the said drumm, which is for the use of Captaine John Huitson's company, now in our ffleete, for which this, with the indenture or receipt for them, shall be your warrant and discharge. Given at our Court at Whitehall, the 3^d of May, 1672.

By his Maties command,

ARLINGTON.

To our right trusty and welbeloved councellour, Sr Thomas
Chichely, Kn^t, our Master-Generall of our Ordnance.

"For recruites to Captaine Coke's company when hee went
"to sea:—10 firelock musketts, 10 match locks, 20 collars of
"bandeleeres.

"ffor recruiting nyne companies—81 ffire lock musketts,
"81 match locks, 162 collars of bandeleeres, broad belts, and
"covered with leather.

"One halbert for each company—9 halberts.

"Captain Huitson, one drumm, broaken on shipp board.

"Twelve barrells of powder, with a double proportion of
"match.

"These I doe hereby certifie, under my hand, this
"1st of May, 1672.

"JO. MILLER."

36.

Charles R.—Whereas Alexander Ellis, a soldier of Captn John Peters's comp^y in the Colds^m reg^t of our Guards, under the command of our trusty and right welbeloved cousin and councillor, William Earl of Craven, is now in the custody of the martial of the said regiment for mutinous and offensive words and demeanour towards his captain, the said Ellis pretending some of his pay to be due unto him. Our will and pleasure therefore is, that there be a court-martial, to consist of six captains of our reg^t of Guards, under the command of our trusty and welbeloved Colonel John Russell,[1] and of six captains

---

[1] First regiment of Foot Guards.

of the said Colds^m reg^t, (of which court-martial Lt Col. Edward Gray[1] is to be president,) to hear and examine the business aforesaid. You are therefore to give directions to the martial of our said reg^t of Guards to attend the said colonels respectively, to nominate the captains for the said court-martial, and to summons the said president and twelve captains to meet and hold the said court-martial for this business, and to give notice to the parties concerned of the time and place of such court-martial; the martiall of our said regiment being hereby required to observe your directions therein, and to attend the said court-martial. And we do hereby require and authorise the said court-martial to hear and examine the business aforesaid, and (after full examination and hearing thereof) to give judgement and sentence therein, according to military discipline, or according to such rules as we have given in matters of that nature, which they are hereby authorised to cause to be put in execution. For which this shall be sufficient warrant. Given at our Court at Whitehall, 22nd June, 1672.

By his Majesty's command,

To our trusty and welbeloved Dr Samuel Barrow,   ARLINGTON.
Judge-Advocate to our Forces.

37.

The Accompt of Ensign Peryn's Charges of the Right Hon^e the Earl of Craven's Colds^m reg^t of his Majesty's Foot Guards, being commanded to conduct neer 300 men from the fleet, and afterwards by post to Portsmouth to conduct 30 soldiers, by orders from his Majesty.

	£.	s.	d.
Impri^s, for a boat to Gravesend	0	10	0
My expenses at Gravesend till commanded to London	1	11	0
For a boat to London	0	10	0
For a boat to Gravesend a 2nd time	0	10	0
My expenses there till commanded to the fleet	1	5	0
For post-horses to Rochester	0	4	0
For a boat to the fleet	1	7	0
For a boat to attend me to get the soldiers from aboard the fleet and carry them aboard several ketches	1	15	6
For a boat from fleet to Queenborough	0	7	0
For post-horses to Gravesend and my expenses on the road	1	11	0
For a boat to London	0	10	0
For post-horses to Portsmouth and my expenses on the road	2	11	6
My expenses in getting the soldiers ashore at Portsmouth, and on my march from thence to London	2	13	6
For a horse from Portsmouth	0	12	0
Dated the 21st June, 1672.	15	17	6

JO. PERYN.

---

[1] First regiment of Foot Guards.

I have perused this bill of disbursements, and do think the same reasonable to be allowed and paid off to Ensign John Peryn, who by order lately conducted the parties of soldiers abovementioned, from his Majesty's fleet to the Colds^m reg^t of his Majesty's Guards.

Jo. MILLER,
(Major of the Colds^m reg^t).

Charles R.—Warrant dated 3rd July, 1672, directing payment of £15 17s. 6d. to Ensign Peryn, for conducting from the fleet 300 soldiers of the Colds. reg^t of the Foot G^{ds}, as appears by the annexed accompt attested by the major of the said regiment.

By his Majesty's command,

To Sir Stephen Fox, K^t, CLIFFORD.
Paym. Genl of our Forces.

38.

Charles R.—Warrant dated Whitehall, 5 July, 1672.—Nine comp^s of the Colds^m reg^t herein ment^d, that of the arms of their comp^s respectively, so many are lost and spoiled as is herein ment^d, at sea, on board our shipps: our will and pleasure is, that you cause forty-nine snaphance musketts, fifty matchlock muskets, three halberts, thirty-three collars of bandeleers, and nine pykes, to be delivered, &c.

To Sir Thomas Chicheley, K^t, CLIFFORD.
our Master-Genl of our Ordnance.

A List of Arms lost and broken at Sea belonging to the Coldstream regiment, certified by Captⁿ Sanders and all the Captains.

My Lord Craven's company; firelocks 2, matchlocks 3, collars of bandeleers 1.

Major Miller's company; firelocks 2, matchlocks 1, collars of bandeleers 3.

Capt. Mansfield's company; firelocks 7, matchlocks 8.

Captⁿ Mutlowe's comp^y; firelocks 6, matchlocks 9, halberts 1.

Captⁿ Kirkby's comp^y; firelocks 1, matchlocks 1, bandeleers 1.

Lt-Col. Sir James Smith's comp^y; firelocks 8, collars of bandeleers 12, halberts 1.

Captⁿ Winter's comp^y; firelocks 6, matchlocks 10, halberts 1.

Captⁿ Peter's comp^y; firelocks 8, matchlocks 12, pikes 4, collars of bandeleers 16.

Captⁿ Clark's comp^y; firelocks 9, matchlocks 6, pikes 5, collars of bandeleers 5.

In all, firelocks 49, matchlocks 50, halberts 3, bandeleers 33, pikes 9.

These arms being certified to me by the captains of each company to have been lost and broken at sea, I do hereby humbly certify that I have received the particulars from each of them under their hands. As witness my hand, this 5th day of July, 1672.   Jo. MILLER.

39.

Charles R.—Some quarrell or misdemeanours having lately happened betweene Lieutent George Lascells and Ensigne Robert (Roger) Kirkby, two officers of the Coldstreame regiment of our Foot Guards, under the command of our right trusty and welbeloved cousin and councellour William Earle of Craven, at the Foot Guards of the said regiment, our will and pleasure is, that there be a court-martiall, to consist of six captaines of our regiment of Guards under the command of our right trusty and welbeloved Colonell John Russell, and of six captaines of the said Coldstreame regiment, (of which court-martiall Lieutenant-Colonell Edward Grey is to be president,) to heare and examine the businesse aforesaid. You are therefore to give directions to the martiall of our said regiment of Guards to attend the said colonells respectively, for their nominations of the captaines of their regiments respectively, to sitt at the said court-martiall, and to summon the said president and twelve captaines to meet and hold the said court-martiall for this businesse, and to give notice to the parties concerned for the time and place of such court-martiall, the martiall of the said regiment being hereby required to observe such directions therein, and to attend the said court-martiall. And wee doe hereby authorize and require the said court-martiall to heare and examine the aforesaid matter, and (after full examination and hearing thereof) to give judgement and sentence therein according to military discipline, or according to such rules as wee have given in matters of that nature, which they are hereby authorized to cause to be put in execution. For which this shall be sufficient warrant. Given at our Court at Whitehall, the 15th day of November, 1672.

By his Maties command,

To our trusty and welbeloved   ARLINGTON.
Doctor Samuell Barrowe,
Judge-Advocate to our Forces.

40.

Captain Bevill Skelton, of 1st Foot Guards, as eldest captain, is to command the eight companies drawn out of several regiments for service in France, and is to receive his pay during his absence.

Dated 25th November, 1672.

41.

Order for stating and certifying what is due upon the last Muster to the 8 Companies designed for France.

Charles R.—Our will and pleasure is, that according to the muster-rolls you audit the accompts of what pay will be due to the eight companies of Foot, which we have ordered to expect our further orders at Canterbury, for fifty-six days' pay, commencing on the day of the last general muster commencing on the sixteenth of November last; to wit, to Capt. Bevill Skelton's and Capt. Edward Sackville's companies of our own regiment of Guards, to Capt. John Huitson's company of the Coldstream regiment, to Capt. Churchill's of our High Admiral's regiment, to Capt. John Howard's of the Holland regiment, to Captain John Trelawney's of Colonel Fitz-Gerald's regiment, to Capt. John Pigot's of our right trusty and right entirely beloved cousin and councillor George Duke of Buckingham's regiment, and to Capt. Ashburnham's company of the Lord le Power's regiment: and when you have audited the said accompts respectively, you are to give one or more debentures or certificates under your hand for the pay due to each of the said companies for the muster aforesaid, upon which we will give warrants for the payment thereof, to enable them to pay their quarters already due, and for their subsistence and payment of their quarters, that they may be in readiness to observe our further orders; for which this shall be your warrant. Given at our Court at Whitehall, 5th December, 1672.

By his Majesty's command,

ARLINGTON.

To our trusty and well-beloved servant, Sir Stephen Fox,
Knt., our Paymaster-General of our Forces and Garrisons.

Endorsed, "Warrant for payment of 8 companies designed for France; mustered 16 Nov^r, 1672."

(Additional MS., British Museum, 5752, folio 204.)

42.

Charles R.—Right trusty and right welbeloved cousin and councellour, wee greet you well. Wee have thought fitt and doe hereby signify unto you our will and pleasure, that you give order for continuing or sending a careful officer, with such number of soldiers as (upon the request of Mr Thomas Betterton) you shall thinke reasonable, from time to time, out of the Coldstreame regiment of our ffoot Guards, under your command, to the theatre in Dorset Garden, to keepe the peace there, att and about the times of the publicque representations, soe that noe offense may be given to the spectators, nor noe affront given to the actors. And soe wee bid you very heartily farewell. Given at our Court at Whitehall, the 27th day of ffebruary, 167⅔. By his Maties command,

To our right trusty and right welbeloved ARLINGTON.
cousin and councelo^r William Earle of Craven.

43.

An accompt of what drums and collars of bandeleeres are wanting to the six companies that were not at sea the last summer

APPENDIX.

in his Majesty's Coldstream regiment of Foot Guards, with an addition of a drummer for his Lordship's own company.

Sir James Smith's company	48 collars of bandeleeres.		2 drummes.
Major Winter's	48 Do.	Do.	2 Do.
Captain Mansfield's	48 Do.	Do.	2 Do.
,, Mutlowe's	48 Do.	Do.	2 Do.
,, Coke's	48 Do.	Do.	2 Do.
,, Wythe's	48 Do.	Do.	2 Do.
The Lord of Craven's company			1 drumme.

Soe there is wanting in all 288 collars of bandeleeres, 12 drums.

ROBERT WINTER.

Usual warrant to deliver the same " from the stores within the Office of Ordnance."

Dated 22ᵈ March, 167¾.

44.

A General court-martial to assemble to try five soldiers of the Coldstream regiment for mutinous conduct against their officers on board the yacht proceeding to the Downs.

Dated 2ⁿᵈ April, 1674.

The above five sold" to be put on board the Cambridge in the Downs.

Dated 20ᵗʰ April, 1674.

45.

In regard that 50 soldiers a piece of the three companies of the King's regiment and Coldstream regiment of Foot Guards, which were in the service of the King of France, together with their arms, were delivered for the recruiting of Colonel John Churchill's regiment; our will and pleasure is that out of the stores of the Ordnance you cause 150 soldiers arms, in the usual proportion of matchlock and snaphance musketts and pikes, with collars of bandeleeres to the fire arms, to be delivered in lieu of so many left with the soldiers aforesaid, and further to exchange for serviceable arms 34 armes of Captaine Skelton's company, 38 of Captaine Sackville's, and 40 of Captaine Huitson's.

Dated 29ᵗʰ April, 1674.

46.

Captain Huitson's company of the Coldstream regiment lately arrived (14ᵗʰ April, mustered 20ᵗʰ April) from foreign service, consisting

of 48 men, " to be mustered from 8th April" (" the date to which paid aboard") at 60 soldiers, besides officers, being completed to that number on the muster of the 2d of May.
Dated 8th May, 1674.

47.

Circular addressed to the Guards and the Governours of the Guarrisons.

Sr,—In regard his Majesty would have the established fforces of ffoot trained and exercised in the use of their armes in a manner different from that which they have been accustomed to, it is his Majesties pleasure that the same be put in practice; in order whereunto, if there be any officers of the guarrison of Dover, or other persons there, who may understand that way of training and exerciseing, when it shall be shewen to them, I desire you would be pleased to send one or two such officers or persons to mee, that I may take order for his or their seeing it, soe as to give you an accompt thereof, that you may give it in Order to be observed in the exercises of the company quartered there, soe to prevent the trouble of any officers comeing up from that guarrison hither for that occasion, which, by his Majesties command, is thus signified to you by,   Sr,

Your affectionate ffriend and servant,

Whitehall,   MONMOUTH.
12th May, 1674.

To Coll. John Strode, (the King's regt of Foot Guards,)
     Governour of Dover.

48.

£200 granted to Captain Huitson of the Coldstm as " of his Majesties gracious bounty and reward."
Dated 20th May, 1674.

49.

So long as the Queen Consort shall keep her Court at Hampton one company (by turns) of the King's regiment of Guards and the Coldstream to do duty there, and to commence from the 17th September, and to be relieved every forty-eight hours.
Dated 15th September, 1674.

50.

The following unserviceable arms of the Coldstream regiment of Foot Guards to be exchanged from out of the stores of the

APPENDIX.

Office of Ordnance, and delivered to Richard Washbourne, quartermaster.

Dated 19th September, 1674.

	Partizans.	Halberts.	Drums.	Musquetts.	Pikes.	Collars of bandileers.
The colonel's company		2			12	9
Lieut.-Col. Sir James Smith's		1		8 Firelocks / 4 Matchlocks	12	3
Major Robert Winter's	1		2	7 Firelocks / 3 Matchlocks	10	6
Captain Thomas Mansfield's		2			6	10
,, John Mutlowe's		1		12 Matchlocks	12	8
,, John Clarke's					4	7
,, Robert Coke's				3 Firelocks / 2 Matchlocks	5	20
,, Richard Kirkbye's					4	7
,, John Huitson's		1	1			
,, John Saunder's					11	18	20
,, John Miller's		1	2		23	25	18
,, Robert Wythe's		2	1	8 Firelocks / 16 Matchlocks	24	18	12
Totall	1	10	6		123	131	50

ROBERT WINTER, Major.

51.

Fourteen barrells of powder, with a double proportion of match, to be delivered for the use of the 14 companies of the King's regiment of Foot Guards attending the Court, and twelve barrels, with a double proportion of match for the use of the 12 companies of the Coldstream; and from henceforth, at the end of every two months, the same proportions of such ammunition for the several companies attending the King, until further order.

Dated 23rd September, 1674.

The same proportion of powder and match (one barrel each company) to be delivered to the companies of Guards doing duty at Rochester, and from the 23rd of September, at the end of every two months, the same proportion to be supplied; also for the use of the companies of the Coldstream who shall next relieve at Rochester and other places.

Dated 29th September, 1674.

52.

Six musters instead of seven a year to take place from 1st January next in each regiment.

Dated 3rd December, 1674.

APPENDIX.

53.

"Our orders for regulating our established forces in the year 1660," authorising penalties to be inflicted, and punishment awarded, by sentence of court-martials on any officer or soldier for drunkeness, renewed.

Dated 10th May, 1676.

54.

The sum of £25 to be distributed, as of his Majesties gracious bounty, to the inferior officers and soldiers, being 191 persons, drawn out of both the regiments of Foot Guards, to work, assist, and hinder the spreading of the fire in Southwark, on the 26th May last.

Dated 9th June, 1676.

55.

My Lord,—It is his Majesties pleasure that your Lordship forthwith give orders for the drawing out of seaven men a piece out of the twelve companies of the Coldstreame regiment of the Foot Guards under your Lordship's command, being in all fourescore and foure soldiers with their armes, in the usuall proportions of pikes and musketts, to be imbarqued for his Majesties service. And that Capt John Mutlow, with the eldest lieutenant and ensigne that may be sent out of that regiment, (without sending two commissioned officers out of a company,) and the two eldest serjeants, be sent from that regiment as officers for one company ; and that, after the soldiers shall be shipp'd, the companies shall be recruited againe to their former numbers. Your Lordship is to take care that the officers respectively doe cleere with, and pay off the soldiers soe drawne out, without deducting any money for their cloathes ; and that you cause them to be sent from the severall places where they are quartered aboard such vessells as the principall officers and commissioners of the navy shall appoint to receive them, in which the said officers and these men are to imbarque themselves for Virginia ; and the officers are to send your Lordship the shipp commander's receipts for the said men.

Your Lordship's most humble servant,

4th October, 1676.   MONMOUTH.

To the Rt Honble William Earle of Craven, or other
the officer-in-chiefe commanding the Coldstreame
regiment of his Maties Foote Guards under his
Lordship's command—These.

56.

Charles R.—Whereas we have thought fit that two soldiers of each company, now in the Tower, of the two regiments of Foot Guards, shall be trained and exercised by our trusty & well beloved Captⁿ Charles Lloyd for the duty of granadiers; our will and pleasure is, that out of the stores within the Office of our Ordnance you cause to be delivered unto the said Captⁿ Charles Lloyd 20 granadier pouches, 20 fuzees, 20 hatchets and girdles for the use of the 20 soldiers out of the 10 companies in the Coldstream regiment, and for so doing this shall be your warrant. Given at our Court at Whitehall, 19th May, 1677.

By his Majesty's command,

WILLIAMSON.

57.

The establishment of the Coldstream reg^t to be increased from 60 to 100 men a company.

Dated 11th January, 167$\frac{6}{7}$.

To be raised by beat of drum, and to show the warrant to the Lord Mayor before beating in the city.

Dated 12th January, 167$\frac{6}{7}$.

58.

King's warrant, dated January 14th, 16$\frac{77}{78}$, for adding 480 men to the regiment, so as to complete each of the twelve companies to one hundred rank and file, and arms to be issued from the Ordnance, vizt. 320 musketts, 160 pikes, 320 collars of bandileeres, and 12 halberts.

59.

Charles R.—Whereas we have thought fit (for the occasion of our services) to raise and establish eight companies to be added to the twelve companies of our Coldstream regiment of Foot Guards, so as to consist of 20 companies of 100 men in each company, besides officers; that is to say, one captain, one lieut^t, one ensign, three serj^{ts}, three corporals, and two drummers. Our will and pleasure is, that out of the stores within the Office of our Ordnance, you cause to be delivered to the regiment eight partizans, 24 halberts, 16 drums with sticks, 550 musketts, 274 pikes, and 550 collars of bandileers, and for so doing this shall be your warrant. Given at our Court at Whitehall, the 17th day of January, 167$\frac{6}{7}$.

By his Majesty's command,

J. WILLIAMSON.

60.

For assuring payment for cloathes for all the new raised soldiers and recruits in the present conjuncture.

Charles R. — For the new cloathing with a cloath coat lyned with bayes, one paire of kearsey breeches lyn'd with pocketts, two shirts, two crevats, one pair of shoes, one pair of yarne hoes, one hatt edg'd & hattband, one sash, and also one sword and belt, the non-com^d officers and sold^{rs} of the new comp^s and recruits that shall be raised in pursuance of our respective add^l estab^{ts}, dated 10th and 14th of January, 167$\frac{7}{8}$. Our W. & P. is, that the s^d cloathing be satisfied for out of the off-reckonings of their pay, over and above their weekly subsistence money from time to time. And in case the said new raised forces be disbanded before the off reck^{gs} reserved shall be sufficient to pay for the above cloathing, what they fall short shall be paid out of our treasure then remaining, or to come into your hands, provided that the particulars before mentioned do not exceed fifty-three shillings in the whole for each man. Dated Whitehall, 1st Feby 167$\frac{7}{8}$.

To Lemuele Kingdon, Esq. Paym. of the Forces.

61.

Charles R.—Trusty and welbeloved, wee greet you well. Understanding that five companies, which were in our service at Virginia, namely, Colonel Herbert Jeffrey's, Lieut.-Col. Edward Picke's, Major John Mutlow's, and Captaine Charles Middleton's companies, and Capt. William Meoles, deceased, his late company, are come in the ship Unitie, of which Captaine Bartholemew Ketcher is commander, into the Hope; Our will and pleasure is, that you stop the said ship at Gravesend, and cause the said companies to come a shore there, being 375 soldiers besides officers, whereupon you are to discharge the said ship, and to quarter the said companies at Gravesend, and the townes and places adjacent, in inns, &c^a, and you and the officers are to take care, &c^a, and to keep the soldiers thereabouts untill we shall send further orders for the disposing of them. And soe wee bid you heartily farewell. Given at our Court at Whitehall, the 20th day of March, 167$\frac{7}{8}$.

By his Majesties command,
J. WILLIAMSON.

To our trusty and welbeloved Sir ffrancis Leeke, Kn^t,
and Barr^t, Govr of our Guarrisons of Gravesend
and Tilbury, or, in his absence, to the officer-
in-chiefe commanding there.

Officers and soldiers of the Guards landed and mustered at Gravesend, March 23^d, 167^7, from Virginia.

In Colonel Jefferye's company—Lieutenant, 3 serjeants, 3 corporalls, 1 drummer, 69 private soldiers.

Capt. Picke's company— captain, ensigne, 3 serjeants, 3 corporalls, 1 drummer, 67 private soldiers.

Capt. Mutlow's company—captain, lieutenant, 3 serjeants, 3 corporalls, 1 drummer, 69 private soldiers.

Ex^d J. BAYNES, (Dep^y Comm^y of Musters.)

62.

Charles R. — We having thought fit, and accordingly ordered, that there shall be one hundred men raised, besides officers, to serve as a company of granadiers under Captain William Rigg's command; which company we have thought fit to add to the Coldstream regiment of our Foot Guards under your command; and we having allowed the sum of one hundred pounds to be put into your hands as levy money for the raising of the said company; we do hereby declare that the said levy money is to be paid unto you, upon condition that you shall be answerable unto us for the making and completing of the said levy of the said company within six weeks next after that you shall have received the said levy money, in order to the paying of it to the said Captain Rigg. Given at our Court at Whitehall, the 4th day of April, 1678.

By his Majesty's command,

J. WILLIAMSON.

To our right trusty and right well beloved cousin
and councillor William Earl of Craven, Colonel of
the Coldstream reg^t of our Foot Guards.

63.

GRENADIER COMPANY.

Memo. A printed order was filled up and directed to Captn Wm Rigg (dated 30th March, 1678) for raising his company of granadiers added to the Colds^m reg^t of Foot Guards.[1]

Capt. W. Rigg's Comm^n as Capt. of the Granadier Comp^y,
dated 1 March, 167$\frac{7}{8}$.

Charles R.—Our will and pleasure is, that out of such monies as are, or shall come to your hands, for the use and service of a war against the French King, you pay unto our right trusty and right well beloved cousin and councillor William Earl of Craven, or whom he shall appoint, the sum of one hundred pounds as levy money for the raising of one hundred men, besides officers, to serve as a company of granadiers under Capt. William Rigg's command, which we have thought fit to add to the Coldstream reg^t of our Foot Guards under the said Earl of Craven's command, for the use and service of a war against the French King; and for so doing, this our warrant, together with the acquittance of the said Earl of Craven or his assign confessing the receipt thereof, shall be your discharge. Given at our Court at Whitehall, the 4th day of April, 1678.

By his Majesty's command,

J. WILLIAMSON.

To our trusty and well beloved servant,
Lemuel Kingdon, Esqr.

---

[1] At this time the grenadier companies were generally added to all regiments.

APPENDIX. 275

64.

A court-martial to assemble to enquire into the dispute amongst the following officers, viz. Captain Eastland, Lieutenant Sandys, and Lieutenant Dallison of the Coldstream Guards. Sir James Smith, or in case of his bodily indisposition, Major Thomas Mansfield to be president.

Dated 9th April, 1678.

65.

Extract from a warrant dated April 13th, 1678.

The following arms to be delivered to the company of granadiers of the Coldstream Guards, consisting of one captain, two lieutenants, three serjeants, three corporals, and one hundred soldiers, viz.:— 103 fuzees, with slings to each; 103 cartridge boxes, with girdles; 103 granadoe pouches; 103 bayonets; 103 hatchets, with girdles to them; 3 halberds; 2 partizans.

66.

£100 to be paid to Major John Mutlow of the Colds^m, as of his Majesties gracious bounty for service performed, for the use and service of a war against the French King.

Dated 13th April, 1678.

67.

To Lord Howard, of Escrick, com^g at Ostend.

Ensign John Clerke, of Capt. Clerke's comp^y of the Coldstream reg^t, to be allowed to come over from Ostend for fourteen days, " in order to the acknowledging and passing of a fine and recovery this present terme."

Dated 12th May, 1678.

68.

James Duke of Monmouth and Buccleugh, Earle of Doncaster and Dalkeith, Lord Scott of Askdale, Tindale and Whitchester, and Captain-Generall of his Majesties Land Forces, &c^a.

Having by letter bearing date the 12th of May last to the Right Honble Thomas Lord Howard of Escrick, commander of his Majesties forces in Ostend, given leave to Ensigne John Clerke, Ensigne of Captaine John Clerke's company of the Coldstreame regiment of his Majesties Foot Guards (now in Flanders) to come over into England for the space of fourteene dayes, I doe hereby continue the lycence soe granted to the said Ensigne Clerke for his continuance here for fourteene dayes more next after the date hereof, hereby requiring the commissaryes-generall of the musters to allow and pass him upon the musters, notwithstanding his absence from the said company in Flanders for the time aforesaid. Given under my hand the first day of June, 1678. MONMOUTH.

To Henry Howard, Esqr and Sr Cecill Howard, Kn^t, Commissaryes-Generall of the Musters, their Deputy and Deputyes.

69.

The muster-rolls of the companies of the Coldstream reg^t in Flanders, commencing the 1st March and the 1st May, 1678, should have been two each; one before the increase, and one after the late increase to the establishment. Distinct muster-rolls to be made of the said comp^s, and Major Mansfield is to sign them instead of the officers of those comp^s, and the commissaries of the musters are then to pass them.

Dated 3^d June, 1678.

70.

Part of Capt. Mutlowe's company of the Coldstream Guards put on board ship and mustered by me at Virginia, the 2nd day of April, 1678: Ensign Thomas Seymour, Serjeant Lodov. Carlisle, Corporal James Edge, Privates John Cox, Saml Jones, Thomas Stafford, Willm Tohams, Thomas Booker, Thomas Peters, John Bragg, John Hume, Willm Morris, Robert Linley, John Smith.

Part of do. put on board and do. the 19th April, 1678: Lieut. John Tonge, Serjeants Roger Walker, Willm Cooper, Corporals Saml Hostin, Gervis Crump, Drum^r Jonas Atkins, George Dance, Privates Charles Brown, Richd Beasley, Thos Britton, Willm Butler, Willm Barrington, John Elmeston, James Harlow, John Hange, Thos Hichman, George Guy, Saml Lewis, Nicholas Parsons, Wm Quartermaine, John Rack, Henry Rakestraw, John Severne, Humphry Smallwood, John Tompson, Richard Tyler, Sampson Whyte, Richd Winwood, Thomas Wittehall, John Whiting, Thomas Whitehead; Chirurgeon's Mate, Thomas Bochan; Quarter-M^r and Martiall, John Tonge.

These are humbly to certify that the above-named officers and soldiers, now mustered on ship-board at Virginia by me on the respective days above mentioned in order to their transportation for England, some of which landed in England the latter end of May, and the rest about the 10th June instant.

GEORGE WACOPE,

June 22nd, 1678. Commissary of the Musters.

[2 officers and 24 men of the 1st Foot Guards, and 6 men of the Holland regiment (now the 3^d Foot) embarked and arrived at the same time. They formed part of the regiment under Lt-Colonel Herbert Jeffrey, of the 1st Foot Guards, sent to Virginia in October, 1676.]

71.

Payment to be made for the repairs, &c. of Major Mansfield's (of the Coldstream) "Lodgings at the Foot Guard by Goring House," from 1st April, 1677, to 1st July, 1678.

72.

Respite removed from the pay of Phillip Gubb, Willm Ward, and John Washborne, private soldiers in Captn Wythe's comp^y of the

APPENDIX. 277

Coldstream Guards, absent from the muster on the 1st of March last, but since appeared.

Dated 18th July, 1678.

73.

Provisions furnished out of his Majesty's great Wardrobe for a war against France, by virtue of his Majesty's warrant, under his signet and sign manual, directed to the Right Hon. Ralph Montagu, Master of the said Wardrobe, being the particulars hereafter mentioned, as appears by the bills signed by the several officers belonging to the aforesaid great wardrobe.

Velvet coats and cloth cloaks trimmed with silver and silk lace, and silver and silk buttons and loops, the coats embroidered with his Majesty's Lrēs,[1] and crowns on backs and breasts, for several trumpeters and kettle-drummers.

Also rich embroidered banners trimmed with gold and silver fringes, and painted banners trimmed with silk fringes, with boots, stockings, hats, gloves, swords, bands, cuffs, and shirts for them.

Also velvet coats trimmed with silver and silk buttons and loops, embroidered with his Majesty's Lrēs, and crowns on backs and breasts, for ten hautboys and four drummers; with cloth cloaks, breeches, hatts, and stockings, and two standards for the detached party to be drawn out of the Horse Guards.

Colours for the King's royal regiment of Dragoons, and for the Queen's regiment of Horse, all richly embroidered with his Majesty's distinctions, and trimmed with gold and silver fringes and strings, and tassells suitable.

Ensigns for the Foot Guards, with staves to the standards, colours, and ensigns.

	£.	s.	d.		£.	s.	d.
1. William Edwards	36	16	0	10. Thomas Mason	5	0	0
2. Thomas Hawley	151	1	4	11. Thomas Templer	5	0	0
3. Nicholas Fownes	340	6	10½	12. Lawrence Verrier	0	12	6
4. James Smithsby	67	19	9	13. Margaret Marshall	56	0	0
5. William Tostin	352	5	0¾	14. Edward Younger	5	15	0
6. Benjamin Shute	16	18	8	15. John Paudevin	14	14	6
7. Daniel Denie	70	4	0	16. John Allan .	44	15	6
8. William Terry	14	0	0	17. Daniel Deine .	43	5	6
9. Wm. Rutlish & Geo. Pinckney	414	0	0	Total	1638	14	8¼

ROBERT NOTT,
(Depy to the Master of the Great Wardrobe).

Charles R.—Our will and pleasure is, that of such monies as are

---

[1] Letters.

or shall come to your hands for the use and service of a war against the French King, you pay unto our trusty and welbeloved Ralph Montagu, Esqr, Master of our great Wardrobe, or whom he shall appoint, the sum of one thousand six hundred and thirty-eight pounds fourteen shillings and eightpence farthing, to be paid to the several persons, and in the respective proportions within mentioned, for the particulars and work within expressed, for the use and service of a war against the French King, according to the within accompt thereof, under the hand of Robert Nott, Esqr, Deputy to the Master of our said great Wardrobe, in full discharge of the said accompt. And for so doing, this our warrant, together with the acquittance of the said Ralph Montagu, or his assign, confessing the receipt thereof, shall be your discharge. Given at our Court at Whitehall, the 28th day of July, 1678.

By his Majesty's command,

J. WILLIAMSON.

To our trusty and welbeloved servant, Lemuel Kingdon, Esqr.

74.

Eightscore of arms in the usual proportion of pikes and musketts, with collars of bandeleers to the musketts, to be delivered in the room of the like number, taken by the drafted men from the Coldstream to Flanders.

Dated 7th August, 1678.

75.

78 musquets, with collars of bandeleeres and 3 pikes, to be delivered to Quarter-Master Richd Washbourne, of Colds. Guards, for recruits raised in lieu of those sent with their arms into Flanders.

Dated 22nd August, 1678.

76.

The following is a copy of a Letter from the Duke of Monmouth to the Earl of Feversham.

(September, 1678.)

" My Lord,—I have received your L^{pps} of the 6th & 9th. The King
" doth not think fitt to make any alterations in the commissions of the
" officers of the Guards, but they must stand as they now are
" to content themselves with a precedency before all others of the
" same degree. As to the march of the Guards, it is my opi-
" nion that they should always march in the center of the brigade
" they are in, and camp there too. The King is not yet come to any
" resolution concerning the quantity of bread to be allowed to the
" officers, for which reason their hath been none ordered them as

" yet. As to their subalterns who have taken care of the sick att
" Bruxells, the King is pleased to consider their extraordinary
" charge in that place as your L^{pp} represents it, & would have
" an account kept of those that have done duty their, to whome there
" will bee something ordered as a gratuity. Yo^r L^{pp} will likewise
" order exact account to be kept of what is due for bread more
" then the styver p^r diem ordered to bee stopt, from the time of the
" first delivery to the time you had notice to make the deduction
" according to the contract, which overplus the King will have payd
" by easy deductions from the sould^{rs} when they are out of the field
" and have noe bread furnished them; and in making up the said ac-
" count it is to be remembered, the bread given att first was onely rye-
" bread for some days, and was to be payd for att the Hollanders'
" price, which is I suppose less then a styver a ration. I don't think
" necessary to make any order concerning the payment of the subal-
" terns sooner then the end of the muster, but the paymaster being
" allways wth the troops and the treasure with him, it can bee noe in-
" conveniency to him to assist some times an officer with the advance
" of his pay, and therefore I believe hee will not refuse it, especially
" upon your intimation to him that you think it fit to be done. I am
" Y^r L^{pps} humble ser^t,
" To the Earl of Feversham." "MONMOUTH."

Original "Book of Entryes of the Duke of Monmouth's, when General of the Army."—State-Paper Office.

77.

Warrant for paying £92. 19s. 11d. to Major Thos Mansfield for clothes distributed to eighty men of the Coldstream reg^t last ordered to Flanders under Captain Tonge of that reg^t.

Dated 20th Sept. 1678.

78.

Ensign Thomas Troutbeck, of Captain Herbert Price's late comp^y of the Coldstream reg^t in Flanders, passed the musters of March, May, and July, 1678, although respited in the former rolls.

Dated 23d Sept. 1678.

79.

John Rymer, now in gaol at Derby, and Richd Carr, in gaol at Stafford, deserters from Capt. O'Keover's comp^y of the Coldstream reg^t, and lately apprehended, to be conducted to the guard of the Colds, reg^t in St. James's Park.

Dated 30th Sept. 1678.

80.

	£.	s.	d.
Furnisht by your Grace's order 70 crevatts of ffox tailes, at three shillings and sixpence a peece	12	5	0
For two peeces of scarlett ribbon	3	12	0
Summe	15	17	0
Poundage	0	16	0
In all	16	13	0

James, Duke of Monmouth and Buccleugh, Earle of Doncaster and Dalkeith, Lord Scott of Askdale, Tindall, and Whitchester, and Captain-Generall of his Majesties Land Forces, &c^a.

These are to require you, out of such monies as are or shall come to your hands, to and for the speedy and compleate paying and disbanding the fforces, officers, and soldiers, raised since the 29th of September, 1677, to pay unto Monsr St. Gilles, or whom hee shall appoint, the summe of sixteene pounds thirteene shillings, the same being due unto him for furnishing the granadeeres of his Majesties owne regiment of Guards with seaventy crevatts of ffox tailes at three shillings and six pence a peece, and with ribbon for them, to and for the speedy and compleate paying and disbanding the forces, officers, and soldiers raised since the 29th of September, 1677. And for soe doing, this, together with the acquittance of the said Monsr St. Gilles, or his assignee, confessing the receipt thereof, shall be your warrant and discharge. Given under my hand the 28th day of October, 1678.

MONMOUTH.

To Lemuell Kingdon, Esqr. (Paymaster of the Forces).

81.

Charles R.—Most dear and most entirely beloved Son, we greet you well. We have thought fit and do hereby signify unto you our will and pleasure, that you forthwith give orders for the displacing and turning out of their respective employments, not only out of our Guards of Horse and Foot, but also out of other our established land forces as well regimented as not regimented in this our kingdom and in our isles of Guernsey and Jersey, and town of Berwick-upon-Tweed respectively, all and every such officers and soldiers as are Popish recusants, or have not returned such certificates as the law requires of such officers and soldiers within the time limited for the same. And so we bid you most heartily farewell. Given at our Court at Whitehall, the 1st day of November, 1678.

By his Majesty's command,
J. WILLIAMSON.

To our most dear and most entirely beloved son,
James Duke of Monmouth, Captain-General, &c.

82.

"At the Court of Whitehall, the second of November, 1678. By
"the King's most excellent Majesty and the Lords of his Majesties
"most honourable Privy Council. His Majesty was this day pleased
"to declare in Council, that whomsoever shall make discovery of any
"officers or souldiers of his Majesties Horse or Foot Guards, who
"having formerly taken the Oaths of Allegiance and Supremacy, and
"the Test, enjoined by the late Act of Parliament, for preventing dan-
"gers which may happen from Popish recusants, hath since been
"perverted or hereafter shall be perverted to the Romish religion, or
"hear mass; such discoverer, upon information thereof given to
"his Grace the Duke of Monmouth, Lord-General of his Majesties
"Forces, shall have a reward of twenty pounds for every officer or
"souldier so discovered as aforesaid. And to the end his Majesties
"pleasure herein may be fully known, his Majesty doth command that
"the Order be forthwith printed and published."—London Gazette,
No. 1353.

In pursuance of the above,
Order sent to the Commissary Generals, Henry Howard, Esq. and Sir Cecil Howard, Knt., not to muster any Popish recusant. Dated 2nd November, 1678.   MONMOUTH.

Order to the Earl of Craven (and all the other Colonels of regiments) to forthwith dismiss out of the companies in England all and every such officers and soldiers as are Popish recusants. Dated 2nd Nov. 1678.   MONMOUTH.

83.

James Duke of Monmouth, &c.

These are to require you, out of such monies as are or shall come to your hands, to pay unto John Gibbons, or whom hee shall appoint, the summe of eight pounds eight shillings, the same being due to Phillip Russell, as of his Majesties gracious bounty to him for his invention of a new sort of Bayonett. And for soe doing, this, together with the acquittance of the said John Gibbons, or his assignee, confessing the receipt thereof, shall be your warrant and discharge. Given under my hand the 15th day of November, 1678.

MONMOUTH.

To Lemuell Kingdon, Esqr.

84.

Monsr St. Gille Vannier to be paid his bill for a gold stick for the Captain of the Horse Guards, which he carries when he waites upon his Majesty, £22. 7s. 0d.; for three sticks more with ivory heads for other officers, £2. Dated 7th Jany 167$\frac{8}{9}$.

85.

James Duke of Monmouth, &c.

These are to require you, out of such monies as are or shall come to your hands, to pay unto Captn Robert Wyeth, or whom he shall appoint, the sum of one hundred and five pounds, in full satisfaction of his disbursements for boates hired to bring the soldiers of the five companies of the battalion of the Coldstream regiment of his Majesties Foot Guards, that lately came from Flanders, from on board his Majesties shipps to Dover; for waggons to carry the sick men, tents, ammunition, and armes of those companies from Dover to Gravesend, and for barges for bringing those sick men, tents, ammunition, and armes from Gravesend to London; and for soe doing, &c^a.

Given under my hand and seale the 8th day of March, 167$\frac{8}{9}$.

MONMOUTH.

To Lemuell Kingdon, Esqr.

86.

Order to pay Drum-Major-General John Mawgridge, for " impresting and furnishing 16 drummers for the eight companies added to the Coldstream Guards in 1678," £5. 12s. 0d.

Dated 10th April, 1679.

87.

An Accompt of Disbursements made by Quarter-Master Richard Washbourne for the use and service of his Majesties Coldstreame regiment of Foot Guards, commanded by the Right Honble William Earle of Craven, from the 17th of June, 1675, to which tyme his former bill was drawne and paid, to the 21st day of October, 1678.

1675.			£.	s.	d.
June 22. For bringing from the Tower to the Tilt Yard 15 barrells of powder and 2400 wt. of match, and charges thereon			1	12	6
Aug. 31.	Ditto	12 barrells of powder and 2400 wt. of match	1	12	6
Nov. 2.	Do.	12 barrells of powder and 2400 wt. of match	1	12	6
1676.					
Ap. 20.	Do.	10 barrells of powder and 2000 wt. of match	1	12	6
Oct. 17.	Do.	20 barrells of powder and 2000 wt. of match	3	5	0
Jan. 25.	Do.	20 barrells of powder and 2000 wt. of match	3	5	0
1677.					
Ap. 24.	Do.	20 barrells of powder and 2000 wt. of match	3	5	0
Oct. 9.	Do.	20 barrells of powder and 2000 wt. of match	3	5	0
			19	10	0

APPENDIX. 283

| | | £. | s. | d. |

1677/8.   Brought forward   19 10 0
Jan. 18. For bringing from the Tower to the severall companyes, armes for the recruites of six companyes of the said regiment 2 0 0
Jan. 22. Do. do. of the six other companyes . . 2 0 0
Ditto. Charges for takeing out the armes for two of the additionall companyes, Capt. Sinkeclar's and Capt. Eastland's 2 0 0
Jan. 29. Ditto for two other of the add^l comp^s, Capt. Parry's and Capt. Sullyard's 2 0 0
June 30. Ditto for one other add^l comp^y, Capt. Newporte's . 1 0 0
Feb. 2. Ditto do. Capt. Talmache's . 1 0 0
Feb. 4. Ditto do. Capt. Oakeover . 1 0 0
Feb. 9. Ditto do. Capt. Brett's . 1 0 0
Feb. 20. For bringing from the Tower to the Tilt Yard 20 barrells of powder and 2000 wt. of match . . 3 5 0
1678.
  For locks and keys for the sev^{ll} Guard doores and the waggons for the said tymes, as appeares by bill 2 0 0
  For scoureing of the carpetts for both Guards severall tymes 3 0 0
  For mending the Guard windowes severall tymes . 2 10 0
  For tarpolling the waggons, &c. severall tymes and charges thereon 3 0 0
  For clensing within the pallisade where the waggons stand sev^{ll} tymes 0 18 0
  For bellowes for all the Guards, severall tymes . 0 15 0
  For broomes and cleaneing the Guards at 3^d p. diem. being 1222 dayes 15 5 6
  For cleareing the dunghills at severall tymes . 1 12 0
  For mending the tables and chaires in the officers roomes 0 13 6
  In charges for conducting a party of soldiers with serjeants sent on board the Forsight at Sheerness, and for boates to put them on board the yatch at Sheerness, and returneing with the 3 serjeants from thence 4 12 0
  For mending the centry gownes severall tymes . 0 15 6
  Charges on sending to the Tower and returning back to the Tilt Yard 4 waggons and two tumbrills that were exchanged, and hyreing horses for the same 1 15
June 27. For straw at the campe at Hounslow Heath, and expences therein for cartts, &c. 10 0 0

                                                                      81 11 6

	£.	s.	d.
1678. Brought forward	81	11	6
June 27. For shypping off of soldiers severall tymes at Tower Hill	3	0	0
Paid to Adjutant Edgerton for money by him disburst at sev^{ll} tymes for the regim^t	6	2	6
Tot.	90	14	0
Poundage	4	10	0
	95	4	0

"The Major of his Majesties Coldstreame regiment of Guards hath "perused this bill and seene the vouchers, and doe believe the "things therein to bee necessary for his Majesties service.
"T. MANSFIELD, Major."

James Duke of Monmouth, &c.

These are to require you, out of such moneyes as are or shall come to your hands, to pay unto Richard Washbourne, Quarter-Master of his Majesties Coldstreame regiment of Foot Guards under the Earle of Craven's command, or whom hee shall appoint, the sum of nynety-five pounds foure shillings, the same being due to him for soe much disbursed by him for the service of his Majesties said Coldstreame regiment of Foot Guards from the 17th day of June, 1675, to the one and twentieth of October, 1678, according to the within accompt thereof, certified under the hands of Thomas Mansfield, Esq. Major of the said Coldstreame regiment of Foot Guards, in full discharge of the said accompt. And for soe doing, this, together with the acquittance of the said Richard Washbourne or his assignee, confessing the receipt thereof, shall bee your warrant and discharge. Given under my hand and seale the 25th day of October, 1679.

To Lemuel Kingdon, Esq. MONMOUTH.

88.

"These are to certify that there is expended 14 barrells of powder "out of the stoares of his Majesties Coldstreame regiment at the fire "at the Temple. T. MANSFIELD."

Charles R. — Our will and pleasure is, that out of our stores, belonging to the Office of Ordnance, you cause 14 barrels of powder to be delivered unto our trusty and wellbeloved Major Mansfield, being for so many expended by our Coldstream regiment of Foot Guards at the fire at the Temple; and for so doing this shall be your warrant. Given at our Court at Whitehall, the 10th day of December, 1679.

By his Majesty's command,
SUNDERLAND.

APPENDIX. 285

89.

For ye commanded party of the Coldstream regm^t of Guards to ship in the Thames.

Charles R.—Our will and pleasure is, that (notwithstanding our former orders) you give order for the captaine, two lieutenants, one ensigne, four serjeants, six corporalls, two drummers, and one hundred and twenty soldiers, drawne out of the Coldstreame regiment of our Foot Guards under your command, with their armes, to imbarque and ship in such vessells as our commissioners of our Admiralty or Navy shall appoint to receive them in our river of Thames, and so to transport themselves (observing in their passage the orders of the shipp commanders with whom they imbarque) to our garrison of Tangiere, where they are to land and to observe such orders as they shall receive from our Governour or other the officer in chief commanding there. Given at our Court at Whitehall, the second day of June, 1680.

By his Majesties command,

SUNDERLAND.

To our right trusty and right well-beloved cousin William
Earle of Craven, Colonell of the Coldstreame regiment of
our Foot Guards.

Original Entry Book, State-Paper Office.

90.

The comp^s and commanded men for Tangier to serve in battalions; that the five comp^s now going out of this kingdom under the command of John Earle of Mulgrave shall have the first place as a battⁿ of Guards; that the four comp^s of the Scotch reg^t with the four other comp^s from Ireland make one battⁿ, and take the rank of the said Scotch reg^t, that is to say, next after the battⁿ of Guards; that when the rest of the said Scotch reg^t arrive there (with the four Scotch & four Irish comp^s, already ment^d) make two batt^{ns} and take rank after the battⁿ of Guards; that the 12 comp^s of the garrⁿ reg^t (Tangier) & the four English comp^s sent thither last year make two batt^{ns}, and take rank after those of the Guards and Scotch regiment.

Dated (4th) June, 1680.

91.

Order for one colour for the company of the Coldstream, forming part of the battalion of Guards, proceeding to Tangier.

Dated 10th June, 1680.

92.

The] sum of £4. 6s. 8d. to be paid to Capt. John Street of Colds^m for so much disbursed for boat-hire for conveying the men going to Tangier, drawn out of the Earl of Craven's and his own comp^y, quartered at Maidenhead, from Wyndsor to London on the 1st of June.

Dated Whitehall, 19th July, 1680.

93.

The Coldstream reg^t to recruit 120 men in lieu of like number drawn out for Tangier.

Dated 10th Nov. 1680.

94.

An Accompt of Contingent Disbursm^ts made by Lieutenant Matthew Ingram for the use and service of his Maj^ties Coldstream regim^t of ffoot Guards, commanded by the right Honble William Earle of Craven, from the last of April, 1683, to the first of September following, being one hundred and twenty-three days, by the said Colonell's command.

	£.	s.	d.
For bringing from the Tower to the Tylt Yard 10 barrells of powder and 200 wt. of match, and charges thereon	1	12	6
Paid for cleanseing the ground where the ammunition waggons stand in the Park	0	2	0
Paid for removing the match out of the stow-room to make roome for armes	0	3	6
For making up another stow-room for it	0	4	6
The carpenter's bill for making a new stow-room fited for coles for the officers' roome in the Mewes, &c.	2	10	8
The bricklayer's bill for the same	1	4	6
For lockes and keys for the same, and for the Parke Gate	0	7	0
For mending the windowes and tyleing the officers' roomes	0	13	6
For bringing from the Tower to the Tilt Yard 10 barrells of powder, &c.	1	12	6
For horse hire to Maidenhead to recall 2 companies there	0	18	6
For caryeing of powder to the ffire at the Temple and back againe	0	3	0
For candle and oyle for the lamps for 3 companies at the Mewes from the said last of April, 1683, being 123 dayes at 2s. 6d. per diem	15	7	6
For sweepeing all the Guards, at 4d. per diem for 120 dayes	2	1	0
Totall is	27	0	8

JOHN HUITSON, Major.

Charles R.—Our will and pleasure is, that of such moneys as are or shall come to your hands for contingent uses for our Guards and Guarisons, you pay to Lieutenant Matthew Ingram, Quarter-Master of the Coldstream regiment of our Foot Guards under the command of our right trusty and right welbeloved cousin and councellour William Earle of Craven, the sume of twenty-seaven pounds and eight pence for ffire, oyle, and candle, and other necessaryes for the use of six companies of the said regiment upon duty in our Mewes from the last of April, 1683, to the first of September following, being one hundred twenty-three days, according to the within accompt thereof, subscribed by our trusty and welbeloved John Huitson, Esq. Major of the said regiment, in full discharge of the said accompt. And for soe doing, &c. Given at our Court at Winchester, the 19th day of September, 1683.

By his Maties command,
WILLIAM BLATHWAYT.

To our trusty and welbeloved servant Charles Fox, Esq. our Paymaster-Gen^{ll} of our Guards and Guarrisons.

95.

An Acc^t of Contingencies disburst by Lieut. Matthew Ingram for the use and service of his Maties Coldstream regim^t of Foot Guards, commanded by the Right Honble William Earle of Craven, from the 1st of September, 1683 inclusive, to the first of November following, being 61 dayes, by his said Colonell's command.

	£.	s.	d.
For bringing from the Tower to the Tilt Yard 10 barrells of powder and 2000 wt. of match, and charges thereon .	1	12	6
For carpenters' worke done in the stow-roome in ye Mewes .	0	18	0
For cole basketts, broomes, &c. for the Mewes . .	0	3	0
For mending all the lanthorns and sconces in the Mewes .	0	9	6
For scouring and mending the carpetts of the Guards .	0	9	0
For oyle and candle for 3 companies in the Mewes Guard, and officers, from ye 1st of September to the 28th instant, at 2s. 6d. p. diem	3	10	0
For fire, candle, and oyle for the lamps for the same, from the 29th of September to the 1st November following, at 3s. p. diem	13	4	0
For sweeping all the Guards, at 4s. per diem . .	1	0	4
For boat hire to carry the two companies to relieve at Tilbury	6	0	0
For 2 fire pans and tongs for the officers' roome and guard at St. James's	0	7	6
Paid by Capt. Markham for part of a waggon to Winchester and back, with sick men and amunition by ye Coll^s order .	2	12	0
Paid by Capt. Pope for the same, his part . .	2	5	6
	32	11	4

	£.	s.	d.
Brought forward	32	11	4
For sweeping the chimneys in the barracks, guard and officers roomes in the Mewes	0	10	6
For scouring and mending all the centinells gownes	0	9	6
	*33	9	10

JOHN HUITSON, Major.

(* Error 33 11 4)

Charles R.—Our will and pleasure is, that out of such moneys as are or shall come to your hands for contingent uses for our guards and guarisons, you pay to Lieutenant Matthew Ingram the sume of thirty-three pounds nine shillings and ten pence for fire, oyle, and candle, and other necessaryes for the use of six companies of the said regiment from the first of September, 1683, to the first of November following, being sixty-one dayes, according to the within accompt thereof, subscribed by John Huitson, Esq. Major of our Coldstream regim^t in full discharge of the said accompt. And for soe doeing, &c. Given at our Court at Whitehall, the 7th day of December, 1683.

By his Maties command,
WILLIAM BLATHWAYT.

To our trusty and welbeloved servant, Charles Fox, Esq. our Paymaster-Gen^{ll} of our Guards and Guarisons.

96.

A warrant of Charles the 2d, dated Jan. 26, 168¾, ordering the arms of 12 companies to be exchanged, each company to have 43 snaphance musquets of the latest pattern, 20 pikes, and two halberds.

97.

An Accompt of Contingent Disbursem^{ts} made by Lieut. Matthew Ingram, for the use and service of his Maties Coldstream regim^t of ffoot Guards, commanded by the Right Honble William Earle of Craven, from the last day of October, 1683, to the 1st January following, being 61 dayes, by his Colonell's command.

	£.	s.	d.
For bringing from the Tower to the Tilt Yard 10 barrells of powder and 2000 wt. of match, and carriage thereon	1	12	6
For empting ye house of office in the Mewes	4	10	0
For tarras and tiles to make up the wall and foundation against the house of office, and workmen	1	19	6
	8	2	0

APPENDIX 289

	£.	s.	d.
Brought forward	8	2	0
For fire, oyle, and candle for the lamps for the officers upon the guard in the Mewes for 61 dayes, at 8s. per diem	24	8	0
For carrying of powder and bringing it to ye fire in Swallow-Street	0	3	6
For sweeping all the Guards, at 4d. p. diem	1	0	4
	33	13	10

JOHN HUITSON, Major.

Charles R.—Our will and pleasure is, that out of such moneys as are or shall come to your hands for contingent uses for our Guards and Guarisons, you pay to Lieut. Matthew Ingram, Quarter-Master of our Coldstream regim^t of ffoot Guards, the sum of thirty-three pounds thirteen shillings and tenn pence for fire and candle for four companies of our Guards upon duty in the Mewes, and other necessaries, for the use of the said regim^t, according to the within accompt thereof subscribed by our trusty and welbeloved John Huitson, Esq. Major of the said regiment. And for so doing, &c. Given at our Court at Whitehall, the 27th day of January, 168$_\frac{1}{7}$.

By his Maties command,

WILLIAM BLATHWAYT.

To our trusty and welbeloved servant, Charles Fox, Esq. &c.

98.

Charles R.—Right trusty and well-beloved Counsellor, we greet you well. Having thought fit to establish two companies of grenadiers on foot to be establisht to our two regiments of Guards, consisting of one captaine, two lieut^{ts}, 3 serjeants, 3 corp^{ls}, and 50 private soldiers in each of them; our will and pleasure is, that out of our stores remaining in the Office of our Ordnance, you cause to be delivered to such officer or officers as the respective colonels or chief officers of the said regiments shall appoint to receive the same, 2 drums, 53 light fuzees with slings, 53 cartouch boxes with girdles, 3 halberds, 2 partizans, 53 grenado pouches, 53 bayonets, 53 hatchets with girdles, for each of the two companies, as soon as they shall have delivered their present arms into the Office of Ordnance. And for so doing, this, together with the respective receipts of the colonel or chief officer, shall be your discharge. Given at our Court at Windsor, this 28th day of April, 1684.

By his Majesty's command,

SUNDERLAND.

99.

An Accompt of Contingent Disbursments laid out by Lieut Matthew Ingram, for the use and service of his Maties Coldstream Regim^t of Foot Guards, commanded by the Right Honble William Earle of Craven, from the last of December, 1683, to first May, 1684, being 121 days, by his said Colonel's command.

	£.	s.	d.
Jan. 10. For bringing amunition from ye Tower to the Tilt-Yard, and charges thereon	1	12	6
For carryage of powder to the fire at Greys Inn	0	3	6
For mending all ye centinells' gownes, and new makeing one	0	10	6
For mending glass windows of ye barracks in ye Mews	0	13	6
For mending the roof and tyleing the officers roome	0	14	10
For mending the back and chimney in ye guard at the Mews	0	6	6
For sweeping the chimneys there	0	4	6
For coach hire and boat hire to Long Reach, to meet the Battalion from Tangier	0	15	6
For barges to bring the said Battalion from thence to Lambeth	10	10	6
For fetching out all the armes of the regiment at several times out of the Tower	2	6	0
For tilt boates for the 2 compa^s from Tilbury	3	0	0
For sweeping all the guards, at 4d. per diem	2	0	4
For locks and keys for St. James's Guard and the Mews	0	3	8
For charges laid out by Lt Bridgeman and Ens^n Shenton, in boat hire, &c. in moving the Battalion from Tangier	0	19	6
For bringing amunition from the Tower	1	12	6

Sum̃e is 25 13 10

JOHN HUITSON, Major.

Charles R.—Our will and pleasure is, that out of such moneys as are or shall come to your hands for the pay of our Guards and Guarisons, you pay to Matthew Ingram, Gentleman, Quarter-Master to the Coldstream regiment of our Foot Guards, under the command of our right trusty and right welbeloved cousin and councilor William Earl of Craven, the summe of twenty-five pounds thirteen shillings and tenpence, for so much disbursed by him for the use of the said regim^t from the last day of December, 1683, to the first of May following, according to an accompt thereof, hereunto annexed, attested under the

APPENDIX. 291

hand of John Huitson, Esq., Major of the said regim^t, in full discharge of the said accompt. And for so doing, this, together with the acquitance of the said Matthew Ingram, confessing the receipt thereof, shall be your warrant and discharge. Given at our Court at Windsor, the 13th day of June, 1684.

By his Maties command,

WILLIAM BLATHWAYT.

To our trusty and welbeloved servant, Charles Fox, Esq., our Pay-Master-Gen^{ll} of our Guards and Guarisons.

100.

An Accompt of Contingent Disbursm^{ts} laid out by Lt Matthew Ingram, for the use and service of His Maties Coldstream reg^t of Foot Guards, commanded by the Right Honble William Earle of Craven, from the first of May, 1684, to the first of November following, by his Colonell's command.

May the 8th, 1684.

	£.	s.	d.
For bringing amunition from the Tower to the Tilt-Yard	1	12	6
For cutting down the weeds and cleansing the waggon place	0	3	6
For cloath to mend the beds in the Mews, and thread and workmanship	0	12	6
For carriage of powder to ye fire in York Buildings	0	7	6
For carrying into the Tower the broken arms and partizans in the regiment at several times	0	18	6
For sweeping all the chimneys in the barracks, guard and officers houses in the Mews	0	11	6
For a new sconce and two new lanthornes, and mending all the old ones	0	15	6
For a shovell, coale basketts, and brooms, &c. in the Mews	0	5	6
For carpenters worke and timber to mend the formes, benches and bedsteads in ye barracks	0	9	0
For bricklayers worke and bricks to mend the tyleing and plaistering in the officers houses and guards in the Mews	0	17	6
For making new backs, and bricks, in all the barracks and guard in the Mews	0	19	6
For glazing all the windows in the officers houses and barracks in the Mews	0	12	6
For emptying the house of office in the Mews	4	10	0
For sweeping all the guards, at 4d. p. diem	3	1	4

October the 4th, 1684.

For bringing amunition from the Tower	1	12	6
For locks and keys for the Mews, &c.	0	6	6

17 15. 10

APPENDIX.

	£.	s.	d.
Brought forward	17	15	10
For thirty-six new centinell gowns, at 18s. a-piece	32	8	0
For mending the chairs in the guards, &c.	0	15	6
For carriage of powder to the fire in Lincoln's Inn Fields	0	5	6
Paid as a guift to my Lord Mayor's bargemen for the barge ferrying over the regiment at ye review at Putney Heath	21	1	0
Totall	72	5	10

JOHN HUITSON, Major.

Charles R.—Usual warrant to pay the amount,
dated Whitehall, the 28th of November, 1684.

W^M BLATHWAYT.

101.

A warrant authorizing the issue to the Grenadier company of 106 grenade shells, with 6 fuzees to each.

Dated October 31st, 1684.

102.

The Coldstream reg^t to recruit to 100 men a company, and one serjeant more to be added to each company, except the Grenadier company.

Dated 13th June, 1685.

103.

Whitehall, 9th July, 1685.

Sir,—I have presented your letter of the 8th instant to his Majesty, who is very well satisfied with what you had done and intended in relation to the forces under your command. The occasion of the enclosed orders is the taking of the late Duke of Monmouth by the militia of Dorset; the King had the news last night, and commands this express to find you out, that you may distribute with all speed the enclosed orders to the respective troops.

To Colonel Mackay.   W^M BLATHWAYT.

104.

100 men with officers to conduct the prisoners concerned in the rebellion to Salisbury, and deliver them over to the gaol; afterwards to proceed to London.

Dated 12th July, 1685.

105.

A warrant, dated 20th July, 1685, for reducing each company to 80 rank and file.

A warrant, dated 27th July, for a further reduction; each company to consist of 2 serjeants, 3 corporals, 2 drummers, and 60 privates.

APPENDIX.

106.

An Accompt of Disbursements made by Lieut. Ingram, for the use and service of his Ma^ts Second regiment of Foot Guards, commanded by the Rt. Honble William Earle of Craven, from the first of November 1684, to the 30th day of June, 1685, inclusive, by the command of his said Colonell.

	£.	s.	d.
For bringing from the Tower to the Tilt Yard amunition for the said regiment	1	12	6
For brickwork in the cellar in the officers house in the Mews	1	8	4
For mending two broken lanthornes	0	2	4
For bringing granadoes and fuzees for the two regim^ts from the Tower to the Tilt Yard	1	4	6
For extraordinary fire and candle in the Mews when the late King lay sick	2	16	0
For 10 p^r of sheets for the barracks	5	0	0
For carrying of amunition for the regiment from the Tower to the Tilt Yard and charges	1	12	6
For sweeping all the guards, at 4*d*. p. diem	4	0	0
For mending locks, keys, &c. as p. a bill laid out by the sutler	0	15	6
For clamps and mending all the chaires on the guards	1	2	6
For carrying of amunition for the regiment from the Tower to the Tilt Yard and charges	1	12	6
For locks and keys for the doores under the Parliament-house	0	10	6
For candles and fire, and things to burn under the Parliament-house	2	5	0
For carrying broken armes into the Tower, and taking out others in their places	1	5	0
For shifting of the waggons of powder 5 times	0	7	6
For locks and keys for the amunition waggons	0	5	6
For carriage of the bandaliers and amunition, and taking out new armes for the recruites	1	16	6
For emptying the house of office in ye Mews	4	10	0
For a tumbrill to carry powder to the fires	9	15	0
For horse hire, &c. wth an order to Brandford	0	7	6
For carrying powder to the fire near Gerrard Street	0	5	6
Summe*	42	15	4
	42	14	8
* Over-added	0	0	8

JOHN HUITSON, Major.

James R.—Usual warrant to pay the amount,
Dated Windsor, the 15th of August, 1685.
WM. BLATHWAYT.

107.

James R.—Our will and pleasure is, that out of such monies as are or shall come to your hands for the contingent uses of our guards, guarisons, and land forces, you pay unto our trusty and welbeloved Edward Sackville, Esq., one of the brigadiers of our forces, and Lieuten^t-Colon^{ll} of our Coldstream regiment of Foot Guards, or whom he shall appoint, the summe of one hundred and fifteen pounds eight shillings and sixpence; the same being expended for waggons and other contingent disbursements for the use of seaven companies in our said regiment, from the time of their marching out of London to the west, in the late rebellion, to the time of their return to the quarters of that regiment, which is to be distributed by the said Lieutenant-Colonell Sackville, according to the disbursements of the captains or commanders-in-chief of the respective companies aforesaid. And for so doing, this, together with the acquittance of the said Lieutenant-Colonell Sackville or his assignee, shall be your warrant and discharge. Given at our Court at Whitehall, the 7th day of November, 1685, in the first year of our reign.

By his Ma^{ts} command,

WILLIAM BLATHWAYT.

To our trusty and welbeloved Charles Fox, Esq.,
Paymaster-General of our Guards, &c.

108.

The sum of £288 to be paid to Thomas Holford, Portcullis, Pursuivant at Arms, for thirty-six colours for the two regiments of Foot Guards, at £8 each, made and provided against his Majesty's Royal Coronation.

Dated 17th December, 1685.

109.

Disbursements made by L^t. Matthew Ingram for the use of his Ma^{ts} Coldstream regiment of Foot Guards, from the first July, 1685, to first January 168⅚.

	£.	s.	d.
Aug. 20. For the carriage of amunition from the Tower to the Tilt Yard, &c.	1	12	6
For boat-hire to put 10 men and a sarg^t on board the kitchin yatch	0	15	6
23. For carriages and exp. in taking out drums and haltberts for the regiment	0	12	6
For straw and use of a house for 4 comp^{as} at Hammersmith as they marched to Hounslow Heath, having no quarters	2	5	6
	5	6	0

APPENDIX. 295

	£.	s.	d.
Brought forward	5	6	0
Aug. 29. For shifting the powder waggons and cutting down the weeds	0	5	6
Sept. 5. To Mr. Wheatley for two hand-barrows	0	13	4
For glazeing all the windows in all the barracks and officers house in the Mews	1	10	6
For mending the cole-cellers and making of little store-roomes in the barracks for coales	1	9	6
For cleansing and washing the barracks with vinegar and stuff to burn in them	0	12	6
For sweeping the chimneys there	0	7	6
Oct. 18. For carriage of amunition from the Tower to the Tilt Yard	1	12	6
19. For levelling the ground in Hyde Parke	0	5	6
For boat-hire &c. for 10 men and return	0	6	6
For boat-hire and exp. to put on board 12 men and a sarjeant for Flanders	0	15	6
For boat-hire, &c. in their return	0	6	6
For mending the lanthornes and sconces, and a new one for the guard in the Mews	0	8	6
For basketts and broomes	0	4	0
For vinegar and stuff to burn under the Parliament-house	0	3	6
For coales and candles there, at 2s. per diem	1	4	0
For sweeping all the guards, at 4d. per diem	3	1	4
For mending of chaires and several other things, laid out by the sutler per order	0	17	6
For harness for two horses for the tumbrill	3	10	0
Dec. 8. For carriage of amunition as before	1	12	6
JOHN HUITSON, Major.			
Totall	24	12	8

James R.—Usual warrant to pay the amount,
Dated Whitehall, the 12th of February, 168$\frac{5}{6}$.
WM. BLATHWAYT.

110.

James R.—Right trusty and well-beloved Counsiller, we greet you well. It being necessary that all the musquetteers in our two regiments of Guards should for their more complete arming, be furnished with bayonets; Our will and pleasure is, that you cause to be delivered to the respective officers of our said regiments the number of such bayonets as our said stores afford, proportionable to the said musquetteers in each of them; And for so doing this shall be your warrant. Given at our Court at Whitehall, this 22d day of February, 168⅚. By his Majesty's command,

SUNDERLAND.

To our trusty and welbeloved cousin Lord Dartmouth.

111.

James R.—Our will and pleasure is, that out of the monies appointed for the contingent use of our guards, guarisons, and land-forces, you pay unto the persons hereafter mentioned the summe of one hundred and sixteen pounds eleven shillings and six pence, which we are graciously pleased to allow for the work done in Hyde Parke, after the rate of sixpence per diem to every non-commission officer and soldier employed therein; vizt. unto Major Eyton the summe of seaventy-nine pounds fifteen shillings and sixpence, for the labour of three thousand one hundred ninety-one men of our First regiment of Foot Guards; to Captain John Miller the summe of thirty-five pounds eight shillings, for the labour of fourteen hundred and sixteen men of our Coldstream regiment of Foot Guards; and to Thomas Richers the summe of eight-and-twenty shillings, for the labour of fifty-six men of our Royall regiment of Fuziliers. Which summes are to be paid without deduction, and to be distributed to the respective non-commissioned officers and soldiers employed as aforesaid, by the persons aforenamed, whose several acquitances shall be your discharge. Given, &c. 18th March, 168⅚, &c.

By his Ma^{ts} commands,

WM. BLATHWAYT.

To our r^t trusty and r^t welbeloved cousin and counc^{llr} Richard Earl of Ranelagh, Paymaster, &c.

112.

An Accompt of Disbursements made by Thomas Silver, Fire-Master, for the use of Captn Bridgman's comp^a of Granadiers (Coldstream) for fixing of granados, from the first of January, 1685, to the last of June following.

	£.	s.	d.
For fuzees for exercise and service, 900, at nine shillings p. hundred	4	1	0
For compositions to make them up	3	15	0
For workmen to assist	3	3	6
	10	19	6

I have examined this bill and believe the same to be true,

JOHN HUITSON, Major.

James R.—Usual warrant to pay the amount,
Dated Windsor, the 15th August, 1686.

WM. BLATHWAYT.

APPENDIX. 297

113.

An Accompt of Contingent Disbursements made by Quar^r-Ma^r Ingram, for the use and service of His Ma^{ts} Coldstream regiment of Foot Guards, from the first day of January, 168$\frac{5}{6}$, to the first day of July, 1686, exclusive.

		£.	s.	d.
Jan. 7.	For six p^r of new sheets for the barracks in the Mews	2	14	0
	For carriage of amunition from the Tower to the Tilt Yard	1	12	6
	For carrying of powder to the fire at Montague House	0	6	6
Mar. 20.	For carrying of powder from the Tower to the Tilt Yard	1	12	6
	For a survey on the bedding in the Mews, and expended	0	7	6
April 1.	For carrying in and exchanging and bringing home the armes of the recruits	1	8	6
17.	For glazeing the windows of St. James's Guards, and officers roomes	1	9	0
19.	For taking out and carrying of amunition and armes to the Royall Hospitall at Chelsea	0	10	6
May 1.	For three waggons to New-Hall and back again with the Battalion	4	10	0
21.	For taking out and carrying of the Bagonets for the regiment	0	14	6
	For emptying the house of office in the Mews	4	10	0
	For mending the Tilt-Yard gate, and caseing up a window	0	5	6
June 8.	For carriage of amunition from the Tower to the Tilt Yard	1	12	0
	For sweeping all the guards, at 4d. p. diem	3	0	4
25.	For carrying of powder to the fire at St. James's	0	7	6
	Given the gunners, &c. p. His Ma^{ts} order to the Earle of Craven	3	10	0
	For taking out of bedding at the Mews, and beating, cleaning, and airing it severall days	2	6	0
	For sweeping down the roofe of the Barn Barracks	0	12	0
	For washing, sweeping and cleaning the barracks, stow-roomes, and officers house	2	16	0
	For vinegar, brimstone, pitch, and rozin, to wash and burn	0	8	6
	For locks and keys to the barracks and stow-roomes	0	14	8
		35	8	0

	£.	s.	d.
Brought forward	35	8	0
For sweeping all the chimneys	0	7	6
For six new lanthornes and four new sconces for the barracks	1	18	0
The carpenter's bill for mending the bedsteads, tables, formes and doors in the barracks, and iron worke	1	13	4
The glazier's bill for all the windows in the barracks and officers house	1	18	9
For carrying of bedding from the Tower to the Mews, and carrying of old sheets back again .	1	15	10
For fire panns, tongs, and fork	0	11	6
	* 43	3	5
* Undercast	0	9	6

JOHN HUITSON, Major.

James R.—Usual warrant to pay the amount,
Dated Windsor, the 15th of August, 1686.
WM. BLATHWAYT.

114.

A Warrant from King James 2d, dated White Hall,
11th March, 168⅞.

Authorizing the issue to Lieutenant-Colonel James Bridgeman, Captain of the company of Grenadiers belonging to our Coldstream reg^t of Foot Guards, of the following arms in exchange:—

83 firelocks slunge.[1]   83 daggers.

115.

William R.—Whereas we have ordered the several battalions and regiments following, viz. two batt^{ns}[2] of 1st regiment of Guards, two batt^{ns} of Coldstream reg^t of Guards, the Royal regiment of Foot,[3]

---

[1] The musquet slings were of dromedary leather, 4 inches wide, with large iron buckles and tin clasps.

[2] Appear to have been counter-ordered, as all the twenty-eight companies of the regiment were ordered to march to Windsor and the towns adjacent in April (1689) following. Two battalions were ordered to embark for Ireland in July 1690. One battalion embarked for Flanders in January 169¾, and another battalion in January 169½.

[3] This regiment (the present First Foot or Royals) revolted, and refused to

Prince George Hereditary Prince of Denmark's regiment, the reg^t commanded by Colonel Charles Churchill, the Royal regiment of Fusiliers, the regiment commanded by Colonel Hodges, to embark for Holland, in pursuance of the treaty of alliance with the States General of the United Provinces: We do hereby charge and require you to take care that the said regiments be forthwith embarked accordingly; and that you give order that such regiments as are at any distance from the place or places of shipping, do march thither at such time and in such manner as you shall think fit; and that you do, or cause to be done, all and every thing and things, which to the better performance of this service shall be requisite. And for so doing this shall be your warrant. Given at our Court at Whitehall, the 8th day of March, 168$\frac{8}{9}$. By, &c.

WILLIAM BLATHWAYT.

To our right trusty and welbeloved councillor,
  John Lord Churchill, Lieut.-General of our Forces.

116.

William R.—Our will and pleasure is, that the several private soldiers and non-commissioned officers of our First regiment of Foot Guards, now on board the ships bound for Holland, be incorporated, as they are hereby incorporated, in the Coldstream regiment of our Foot Guards; and all officers, and others to whom it may belong are to take notice of our pleasure signified in this behalf. Given at our Court at Hampton Court, the 17th day of March, 168$\frac{8}{9}$.

By, &c.

WILLIAM BLATHWAYT.

117.

William R.—Our will and pleasure is, that the several private soldiers and non-commissioned officers of Prince George hereditary prince of Denmark's regiment of Foot, now at Gravesend, be forth-

---

embark, and marched off with their arms and two or three guns from Ipswich to the Isle of Ely, and the County of Lincoln, (intending to make their way to Scotland,) where Lt.-Gen. Ginckle obliged them to submit. Lieut. Alexander Gawen, the ringleader, and the rebellious soldiers, consisting of 500 men, and 20 officers, (the remainder having previously returned to their colours) were ordered to be escorted to London; and the regiment was subsequently sent to its destination. In October, 1689, another battalion of the regiment was ordered from Scotland to join this battalion, then in Holland. In consequence of this revolt, it is said, King William caused the first Mutiny Act to be framed, which passed both Houses of Parliament, and is dated 3rd April, 1689.

with put on board the ships bound for Holland, and incorporated, as they are hereby incorporated, in the Coldstream regiment of our Foot Guards. Given at our Court at Whitehall, the 19th day of March, 168$\frac{8}{9}$. By, &c.

WILLIAM BLATHWAYT.

To our right trusty and welbeloved councillor John Lord
Churchill, Lieut.-General of our Forces.

118.

Extract. "Whitehall, 19 March, 168$\frac{8}{9}$.

" I have had no news as yet of the regiment of Dunbarton, only that
" they are all returned (except 400) to their colours, who will be
" certainly cut off by the troops that are sent in pursuit of them, or
" by the country people, in virtue of the enclosed proclamation, which
" is already dispersed in all places."

"WM. BLATHWAYT."

To Major Maitland, Scots Guards, on march to Ipswich.

119.

Whitehall, March 21, 168$\frac{8}{9}$.

My Lord,—It is necessary that your Lordship do forthwith send some person with subsistence for five hundred men and twenty officers of the Royall reg^t of Foot, lately seized in Lincolnshire by his Majesty's order, to suffice until their being brought to London, whither they are now marching under the command of Lt.-General Ginkell, from whom the person appointed by your Lordship is to receive orders.

Le M^{al} DE SCHOMBERG.

These prisoners with Lieut.-Gen^{ll} Ginkell will be found between
Royston and Rumford.

To my Lord Ranelagh.

120.

William R.—Our will and pleasure is, that upon your arrival in Holland you cause three companies to be drawn out of our Coldstream regiment of Foot Guards, two whereof are to be incorporated into our First regiment of Foot Guards under the command of our right trusty and welbeloved councillor Henry Lord Sydney, and the other company to be disposed of as we shall direct.[1] Given at our Court at Hampton Court, the first day of May, 1689, in the first year of our reign.

By his Majesty's command.

To our right trusty and right welbeloved cousin and councillor
John Earl of Marlborough, Lieut.-Genl of our Forces.

---

[1] The two battalions in Holland, in consequence of this order, were reduced from seventeen to fourteen companies. In January following, seven fresh com-

APPENDIX. 301

121.
(British Museum, Add¹ MS. 5752. fol. 206.)

William R.—Our will and pleasure is, and we doe hereby authorize and direct, that you send us debentures for the pay of our Coldstream regiment of Foot Guards, from the 1st November, 1688, to the last of April, 1689, inclusive, according to the compleat numbers allowed on their establishments, notwithstanding any defect in or want of muster-rolls for the said time, deducting thereout the pay of soe many non-commission officers and soldiers for the months of March and April, 168$\frac{8}{9}$, as were wanting upon the musters of the said regiment for the month of May following: and in making out the said debentures you are to take care not to include the pay of any Roman Catholicque officers belonging to the said regiment for the months of November and December, 1688, except the ordinary subsistence to lieutenants and ensigns; and except also such whose pay was advanced by order of the late King, before the time of his abdication; according to the rules you were, by warrant of the 25th of January, 1689, directed to observe in making out debentures for such other of our forces as were employed in our service in Flanders. And for soe doing, this shall be your warrant. Given at our Court at Whitehall, this 27th day of February, 1690, in the third year of our reign.

By his Majesty's command.

122.
Signification to the Lieutenants of the 1st Foot Guards and Coldstream Guards, by command of His Majesty King William.

Henry Viscount Sidney, one of the lords of their Majesty's most Honᵉ Privy Council, Principal Secretary of State, &c.

Whereas, by his Majesty's warrant under his royal sign manual, bearing date at Gemblours the $\frac{5}{15}$ day of July, 1691, in the third year of his reign, giving for the time to come the rank and command of captains of foot to the lieutenants of his First and Second regiments of Foot Guards, and has thereby directed and authorised one of his principal secretarys of state to issue out, under his hand and seal, particular significations of his pleasure therein, to all and every of the present lieutenants of the said regiments, thereby authorising and empowering them to take their rank and command as captains of foot accordingly; these are therefore, by virtue of the authority aforesaid, to authorise and empower you to take your rank and command as captain of foot; and hereof all officers and soldiers whom it may concern,

---

panies were ordered to be recruited and assemble at Colchester, from whence they marched to Windsor as a battalion for home duty; and one battalion only continued on the establishment in the Low Countries.

are required to take due notice and pay obedience to his Majesty's pleasure accordingly. Given at the camp at Gerpines the 12/22 day of July, 1691. SYDNEY.

This signification addressed to " John Delavell, Esq., Lieut. of the comp^y commanded by Sir Charles Hara, in their Majesty's First reg^t of Foot Guards."

The like signification to the other Lieutenants of the Foot Guards.

123.

The sum of £628 19s. 0d. to be stopped from the next payment made to the Coldstream Guards, and paid to Lt.-Col. Wm Wakelyn and Walter Shaw, executors of Richard Pope, deceased, late Lieut^t-Colonel and Captain in the Coldstream.

Dated 19th March, 169½.

124.

William R.—Our will and pleasure is, that out of such moneys as are or shall come to your hands for the contingent uses of our forces, you pay unto our trusty and welbeloved James Bridgman, Esq., Lieutenant-Colonel of our Coldstream regiment of Foot Guards, the summe of one hundred pounds, as of our royal bounty. And for so doing this, together with the acquittances of the said Colonel Bridgman or of his assign, shall be your warrant and discharge. Given at our camp at Melé, the 25th day of June, 1692, in the fourth year of our reign. By his Majesty's command,

WM. BLATHWAYT.

To our trusty and right welbeloved cousin and councillor, Richard Earl of Ranelagh, Paymaster-General of our Forces.

125.

William R.—Our will and pleasure is, that out of any moneys now in your hands, not appropriated to the subsistance of our forces, you pay unto Lieut.-Coll. Skelton (Coldstream) the summ of seventy-six pounds ten shillings for his pay as Major to the brigade of our Foot Guards in the Low-Contrys, from the first day of June to the thirty-first day of October last inclusive, being one hundred fifty-three days, at the rate of tenn shillings a day: and for so doing, this, together with the acquittance of the said Lt.-Colonel Skelton, or of his assign, shall be your warrant and discharge. Given at our camp at Perk, the 5th day of June, 1693, in the fifth year of our reign.

By his Majesty's command,

WM. BLATHWAYT.

To the Earl of Ranelagh, &c. &c. or to his deputy in the Low-Countrys.

APPENDIX. 303

William R.—Our will and pleasure is, that out of any moneys now in your hands you pay unto Lt.-Coll. John Skelton (Coldstream) the summ of ninety pounds ten shillings, which we are pleased to allow him for his pay as Major of Brigade, from the first of November to the 30th of April last, the Duke of Wirtemberg having certified that he did that duty within the garrison of Ghendt during the said time; and for so doing, &c. St. Quintin Linnick, the 1st of September, 1693, &c.

By his Majesty's command,

To the Earl of Ranelagh, &c. &c. &c.   WM. BLATHWAYT.

Do. £92 to Lt.-Col. Skelton, as Major of Brigade to the Foot Guards, from 1st May to 1st November, 1693. Dated Ninove, 14 Sept. 1693.

Do. £92 to Lt.-Col. Skelton as Major of Brigade to the Foot Guards, from 1st May to 31st October, 1694. Dated Rouselaer, $\frac{11}{21}$ Sept. 1694.

Do. £90 10s. 0d. to Lt.-Col. Skelton as Major of Brigade to the Foot Guards, from 1st November, 1694, to 30th April, 1695. Dated Lembeck, 13 Sept. 1695.

Do. £92 to Lt.-Col. Skelton as Major of Brigade to the Foot Guards, from 1st May, to 31st October, 1695. Dated Lembeck, 13 Sept. 1695.

126.
(MS. Harl. 1250, fol. 181.)

" The oath to be taken by all officers commission'd in the army, 1 July,
" 1693.—This oath was to prevent their obtaining their employments
" by bribery."

William R.—Our will and pleasure is, that you do not allow upon the musters any person who shall be hereafter commissioned by us, our Generall, or the Commander-in-Chief of our Forces, until he shall, besides the oath of fidelity to be taken by every officer and soldier in our army, have first taken and subscribed an oath in the words following, viz.:

" I, A. B., do swear, that I have not made any present or gratuity
" for the obtaining the employment of   ; neither will I, nor
" shall any person for me, with my knowledge att any time hereafter,
" directly or indirectly make any present or reward for the same to
" any person whatsoever. And I do further swear, that if att any time
" hereafter it shall come to my knowledge that any guift, present, or
" reward, has been made by any friend, either before or after my ob-
" taining this employment, that I will immediately discover the same
" to his Majesty or the Commander-in-Chief.

" And for so doing this shall be your warrant. Given att our camp
" at Perk, this 1st July, 1693; in ye fifth year of our reign.

" By his Maj^{tys} command,

" WILLIAM BLATHWAYT."

" To our r^t trusty and r^t welbeloved cousin Henry Earle of
" Suffolk, Commissary-Generall of ye musters, and to his
" deputy or deputys."

127.

Hague, the 17/27 October, 1694.

Sir,—I desire you will supply Colonel Withers (Coldstream) with the summ of one hundred pounds, in part of what is due to him, as Adjutant-Generall of the Forces, since the first of January last, and to certify the same to the Earl of Ranelagh, to be deducted by him out of the warrant to be issued in England in that behalf. So hereby you will oblige,

Sir, your, &c.

WM. BLATHWAYT.

To Mr. Robert Hill, (Deputy Paymaster in the Low Countries.)

128.

Disbursements made by Thomas Silver for fixing granadoes for exercise and service of the granadiers of the Coldstream regiment of Foot Guards, from the 1st of January, 169¾, to the 31st of December following:

For 3700 fuzees to the granadiers belonging to the Coldstream regiment of Foot Guards	16 13 0
For composition to make up the said ffuzees	14 15 0
For workmen who assisted in making up the said ffuzees	14 0 0
	£45 8 0

William R.

Usual warrant to pay the amount. Dated Kensington, the 1st May, 1695.

129.

William R.—For the better regulating several particulars, wherein alterations have been introduced in our army contrary to our royal intentions, we do hereby declare our will and pleasure to be,

1st, That none of our regiments or companys of foot do wear capps, excepting only the royal regiment of Fuziliers, the regiment of Scots Fuziliers, and the granadiers of each respective regiment.

2nd, That there be fourteen pikemen in each company of 60 men, excepting the two regiments afore-mentioned and the granadiers; and that each company of our Foot Guards have likewise a proportionable number of pikes.

3rd, That each captain of foot, while he is upon duty, do carry a pike, the lieutenant a partizan, and every ensign a half-pike, when he does not carry his colours.

And the respective colonels and commanders of any of our regiments and battalions, and all others whom it may concern, are hereby strictly required to take care that our directions hereby signified, be forthwith complied with and duly observed for the future. Given at our Court at Kensington, this 30th day of December, 1695, in the seventh year of our reign.

By his Majesty's command,
WM. BLATHWAYT.

Addressed to the Earl of Romney, Lord Cutts, Sir H. Belasyse, Maj.-Gen. Churchill, Brigadier Steuart, Brigadier Erle, Col. Robert McKay, Col. Fred. Hamilton, Col. Ingoldsby, Major-Gen. La Meloniere, Col. Coote.

130.

William R.—Whereas in consideration of the long and faithful services of Lieut.-Coll. Edward Jones, late Captain-Lieutenant and Adjutant to our Coldstream regiment of Foot Guards, we are pleased to continue unto him his pay as Captain-Lieutenant, and likewise one half of the pay of Adjutant of the second battalion of our said regiment; our will and pleasure is, that you pay unto the said Lieut.-Coll. Edward Jones, from time to time, the pay of Captain-Lieutenant of our Coldstream regiment of Guards and one half of the Adjutant's pay accordingly; and that the youngest lieutenant of our said regiment for the time being, do serve upon ensign's pay, and the youngest ensign without pay, and the adjutant of the second battalion upon half-pay, untill further order. And for so doing this shall be your warrant. Given at our Court at Kensington, this 1st day of January, 169$\frac{6}{7}$, in the eighth year of our reign.

By his Majesty's command,
WM. BLATHWAYT.

To our right trusty and welbeloved John Lord Cutts, Major-Generall of our Forces, and Colonel of our Coldstream regiment of Foot Guards; or to the Colonel or officer-in-chief with our said regiment for the time being.

131.

Horse Guards, October 9th, 1697.

Sir,—The King having ordered the three troops of horse, one troop of Gren^r Guards, and four B^{ns} of Foot Guards, to come over from Flanders with the first opportunity, and be quartered in and about London, in the usual quarters of the guards, I desire you will acquaint the bench of justices with it; that they may order a review to be made of all the quarters as soon as possible, and there shall be an officer of each of the regiments of foot to go along with the constables, or such other person as the justices shall appoint. You will press to have this done as soon as possible, to avoid the confusion that may otherwise happen, if the troops should come over before this matter is settled.

The number of troops that are to come over you will see by the enclosed. I am, Sir, your ob^t humble servant,

GEORGE CLARK,
To Mr. Crawford, (Secretary at war in the absence
(Comm^y of Musters.) of Mr. Blathwayt.)

Including the Companies in England.

Total Men.

Troops of Horse Guards :—3 troops, each consisting of, trumpeters 4, kettle drum^r 1, private men 200,=205, besides officers 615
One troop of Grenadier Guards : — serjeants 3, corporals 6, drummers 4, hautboys 4, troopers 180,=197, besides officers   197
First Regiment of Foot Guards:—24 companies, each consisting of, serjeants 3, corporals 3, drummers 2, private men 80,=88, besides officers, 2112; 4 companies of grenadiers of like numbers, 352 2464
Coldstream Regiment of Foot Guards : — 12 companies, each consisting of, serjeants 3, corporals 3, drummers 2, private men 80,=88, besides officers, 1056; 2 companies of grenadiers of like numbers, 176 1232
Regiment of Dutch Foot Guards:—25 companies, each consisting of, serjeants 3, corporals 3, drummers 2, private men 91,=99, besides officers 2475
One company of Cadees, consisting of, serjeants 3, capt^n of arms 1, corporals 3, drummers 2, cadees 86,=95 . . . 95

Total 7078

In England already:—of the First regiment of Foot Guards, 20 companies; of the Coldstream regiment, 6 ditto; of the Dutch Foot Guards, 8 ditto; total, 34 companies.

132.

By the Lord Justices:—Tho. Cantuar. I. Somers, Sunderland, Dorset, Romney, Orford.

We do hereby direct, that upon the arrival from Flanders of the Battalion of his Majesty's Coldstream regiment of Foot Guards under your command, you cause them forthwith to be quartered in Deptford, Greenwich, and Woolwich, where they are to remain until further orders, and the officers are to take care, &c. Given, &c. this 19th day of October, 1697. By, &c.

GEORGE CLARK.
To the Right Hon. the Lord Cutts, Colonel of his Majesty's Cold^m reg^t of Foot Guards, or to the officer-in-chief with the said regiment.

Route for the Battalion of his Majesty's Coldstream regiment of Foot Guards from their landing at Harwich to Deptford, Greenwich, and Woolwich.

1st day, Harwich; 2nd do. Manningtree; 3d do. Colchester; 4th do. Witham; 5th do. Chelmsford; 6th do. Brentwood; 7th do. Barking; 8th do. Deptford, Greenwich, and Woolwich.

To march in such parties and rest on such days as the officer-in-chief shall see cause.

133.

William R.—Our will and pleasure is, that you cause the Battalion of our Coldstream reg^t of Foot Guards under your command, now at Deptford, Greenwich, &c., to march forthwith into the Hamlets of our Tower of London, where they are to remain until further orders. And the officers are to take care, &c. Given, &c. 17 November, 1697.

By, &c.

Wm. Blathwayt.

To our right trusty and welbeloved John Lord Cutts, Major-General of our Forces, and Colonel of our Coldstream reg^t of Foot Guards, or to the officer-in-chief with the 2 Batt^n above mentioned.

134.

Colonel William Mathews, Major of the Coldstream, to be paid an allowance of £66 4s. 10d., for the hire of seven waggons, and for fuel and candle, &c.; with a Battalion of seven companies of the Coldstream from London to Newmarket, between the 30th March and 22nd April, 1698. The Battalion encamped every night on the march.

Dated 26th April, 1698.

135.

September 3rd, 1698.

Sir,—His Majesty having been pleased to order, that a comp^s be formed out of the officers of the regiments that have lately been broke, which are to march at the head of the 1st regiment of Foot Guards, if any of the officers are willing to enter into this service, you will send them to Colonel Shrimpton, Major of the said regiment, as soon as may be convenient. I am, &c.

George Clark,
(Secretary at War in the absence
To Major-General Earle.[1]   of Mr. Blathwayt.)

" Like letter of the same date, sent to his Grace the Duke of Bolton,

---

[1] Earle's regiment was incorporated with Colonel Lutterell's, the present Nineteenth Foot.—War-Office Records.

"Colonel Gibson, Colonel Northcott, Colonel Farrington, Colonel Coote, Colonel Brudenall, Colonel Saunderson." (Regiments lately disbanded.)

136.

Received 2000 fuzees, &c. for the use of the Grenadier companies of the Coldstream, from 1st January, 169$\frac{7}{8}$, to 31st December following.

(S.)   WM. MATTHEWS, Major.

137.

The sum of £289 6s. 8d. to be paid to Colonel Wm Matthews of the Coldstream, for fire and candle for the guards kept by the Coldstream, at Kensington, Hyde Park, Acton Road, Arlington Gate, Tilt Yard, St. James's, Whitehall, Somerset House, the Savoy, Hampton Court, and Windsor, from 1st of April, 1699, to 24 April, 1700.

Dated 2nd July, 1700.

138.

An Acco^t of the Conting^t Charges of the Coldstream reg^t of Guards for the year 1700, given in by Quarter-Mr Wakelin.

"Qua^r-Mas^r Wakelin's bill of disbursm^{ts} for the Coldstream reg^t of Guards, one year, ending Lady-day, 1701."

	£.	s.	d.
Paid for fetching ammunition for the Guards	7	0	0
for labourers to load and unload	0	7	6
for 2 new centinel boxes in St. James's Park	6	15	0
for carriage of them thither	0	4	6
for new boarding 5 centinel boxes in the Park, at St. James's, and mending those in Hyde Park	4	10	0
for mending the door at the Tilt Yard	0	3	0
for standish, pens and ink	0	6	0
for mending the wooden bed at the Tilt Yard	1	10	0
for a wooden horse	0	17	6
for fetching the colours	0	1	0
The totall summ is	21	14	6

The aforesaid summs have been disbursed for his Majesty's service, and it's reasonable this bill should be paid.

WM. MATHEW.

139.

Account of the Conting^t Charges of the Coldstream Reg^t of Guards, for the year 1701, given by Qua^r-Mast^r Wakelin.

"Capt. Charles Wakelin's bill for the year 1701."

	£.	s.	d.
For mending the centinel boxes in Hyde Park, St. James's Park, and St. James's House	6	8	0
For removing the centinel boxes in winter	0	18	0
For fetching ammunition for the Guards	7	0	0
For labourers to load and unload	0	9	0
For standish, pens, ink, and paper	0	6	0
For locks to the powder waggons	0	3	0
For a wooden horse	1	8	9
	£16	12	9

It is reasonable this bill shou'd be paid, August ye 20th, 1702.

WM. MATHEW, (Major.)

140.

By the Queen.—Trusty and welbeloved, we greet you well; and will and command you that under our privy seal (remaining in your custody) you cause our letters to be directed to the Keeper of our Great Seal of England, commanding him, that under our Great Seal of England (in his custody being) he cause our letters to be made forth patent in form following:

Anne, by the grace of God, &c.[1] To our right trusty and right welbeloved cousin and councillor John Earl of Marlborough, greeting. Whereas we have thought it necessary for our service to appoint and constitute a captain-general for the commanding, regulating, and keeping in discipline our troops and land forces which are or shall be allowed by Act of Parliament to be raised and kept on foot; know ye therefore that we, reposing especial trust and confidence to the approved wisdom, fidelity, valour, great experience, and abilities of you the said John Earl of Marlborough, have constituted and appointed, and by these presents do constitute and appoint you to be captain-general of all our troops and land forces already raised, and hereafter to be raised, as aforesaid, and employed in our service within our kingdom of England, dominion of Wales, and town of Berwick-upon-Tweed, or which shall be employed abroad in conjunction with the troops of our allies: giving, and by these presents

---

[1] The Commission is entered on the Rolls, at the Rolls Chapel Office, and dated 24th of April, 1702.

granting, unto you full power and authority by yourself, commanders, captains, and other officers, them to exercise, array, and put in readiness, and, according to the provision of arms appointed for them, well and sufficiently cause to be weaponed and armed, and to take or cause to be taken, the musters of them, or any of them, by the Commissary-General of the Musters, or his deputies, or by such other officers as he shall assign for that purpose, as often as you shall see cause; and the said forces to divide into parties, regiments, troops, and companies, and with them, or any of them, respectively to resist all invasions which shall be made by our enemies, and to suppress all rebellions and insurrections which shall by levying war be made against us, and all enemies making such invasion and rebells, who shall, to levy war, and be found making resistance, to fight with, kill, and destroy, as also with full power and authority for us, and in our name, as occasion shall require, according to your discretion, by proclamation or otherwise, to tender our royal mercy and pardon to all such enemies and rebells as shall submit themselves to us, and desire to be received into our grace and pardon. And we do likewise give and grant unto you full power and authority to hold, or cause to be held, from time to time, as often as there shall be occasion, according to your discretion, one or more military or martial court or courts, in pursuance of and according to the purport and true meaning of an act of Parliament passed in the thirteenth year of the reign of our late dearest brother, King William the Third, of ever blessed memory, entitled an Act for Punishing of Officers and Soldiers that shall Mutiny or Desert in England or Ireland; and in the same court or courts to hear, examine, determine, and punish all Mutinies, Disobedience, Departure from Captains, Commanders, and Governors, according to the directions of the said Act, and to cause the sentence or sentences of the said courts to be put in execution, or to suspend the same, as you shall see cause; to have, hold, exercise, and enjoy the said office of captain-general, and to perform and execute the powers and authorities aforesaid, and all other matters and things which to your said office doth or may of right belong and appertain unto you, during our pleasure: willing and commanding all officers, soldiers, and persons whatsoever, any way concerned, to be obedient and assisting to you, our captain-general, in all things touching the due execution of this our commission, according to the purport and intent thereof. In witness, &c. And these our letters shall be your sufficient warrant and discharge in this behalf. Given under our signet, at our palace of Westminster, the fourteenth day of March, 170½, in the first year of our reign.

JOHN NICHOLAS.

To our trusty and welbeloved our Commissioners for
    executing the office of Keeper of our Privy Seal.

APPENDIX. 311

141.

Anne R.—Whereas we have thought fit that a detachment of our regiment of Foot Guards be formed into a battalion, be employed on board our fleet under the command of our right trusty and right entirely beloved cousin and councillor, James Duke of Ormond, General of our Horse; our will and pleasure is, that you cause the said battalion of Guards to march forthwith from their present quarters (according to the routes hereunto annexed) to Portsmouth, from whence they are to pass over to the Isle of Wight, where they are to encamp, and to follow such orders for their embarkation and otherwise, in reference to the present expedition, as they shall receive from the said Duke of Ormond; and the officers are to take care, &c. Given at our Court at St. James's, this 16th day of May, 1702, in the first year of our reign. By, &c.

WM. BLATHWAYT.

To the Earl of Romney, or to the officers in chief
   with the said regiments above mentioned.
Delivered to Col. Braddock, comm^g the
   Coldstream reg^t of Foot Guards.

Route for a detachment of four hundred men, with officers, of the Coldstream reg^t of Foot Guards, from London to Portsmouth:—Kingston and the Wick, Monday, May 25, 1702; Guilford and Godalmin, Tuesday, 26; Petersfield, Wednes., 27;—rest, Thurs., 28; Portsmouth, Friday, 29. WM. BLATHWAYT.

Route for a detachment of two hundred men, with officers, of the First regiment of Foot Guards, from London to Portsmouth:—Chertsey and Stains, Tuesday, May 26, 1702; Farnham, Wednes., 27;—rest, Thurs., 28; Petersfield, Friday, 29; Portsmouth, Saturday, 30.

WM. BLATHWAYT.

Note.—Returned to St. Helens and Chatham, and landed in Nov. 1702, and marched by routes to London.

142.

Anne R.—Right trusty and right entirely beloved cousin and councillor, wee greet you well. Whereas we have ordered several of our forces, viz. a battalion of our Foot Guards, the regiments of Foot and Marines, whereof our Lieut.-General Sir Henry Bellasyse, Lt.-Genl Churchill, Major-Genl Sir Charles Hara, Edward Fox, Esq., and the Lord Viscount Shannon, are Colonels, with a detachment of two hundred Dragoons, and officers proportionable, of Colonel William Lloyd's regiment, to repair to the Isle of Wight; and have likewise ordered the regiments whereof Brigadier William Seymour is Colonel, with five companies of Colonel Villiers's regiment of Marines, to be ready to embark at Plymouth on board such ships as shall be sent thither, as also five regiments of foot to come from our kingdom of Ireland, who are to serve on board our fleet and otherwise, under your command, for this summer's expedition; we do hereby signify our royal will and pleasure, that you take the said battalion of Foot Guards, regiments and companies of Foot and Marines, and detachment of Dragoons, under your command, and give them such orders from time to time, in reference to their embarkation and otherwise, during the present expedition, as our service shall require, in pursuance of such commission and instructions as you have received, or shall at any time receive, from us; for which this shall be your warrant. Given at St. James's, the 22d day of May, 1702, in the first year of our reign.

By her Majesty's command, WM. BLATHWAYT.

To our right trusty and right entirely beloved cousin and councillor, James Duke of Ormond, General of our Horse, and Commander-in-Chief of our Forces appointed for sea-service.

143.

Whitehall, 8th June, 1702.

My Lord,—His Royal Highness does think fit that, pursuant to her Majesty's orders dated 22d May last past, your Grace do give the necessary directions that the forces now in the Isle of Wight be forthwith embarked on board the ships appointed to receive them at Spithead.

I am, my Lord, your Grace's most ob^t and humble servant,
To the Duke of Ormond. WM. BLATHWAYT.

144.

Lieut.-Coll. Richd Holmes (Coldstream) humbly craves an allowance for his disbursments with a battalion of her Majesty's Foot Guards, from the 6th of July, 1702, to Colebrook, Stow, and Windsor, to the 19th day of August; and also from London to Bath, &c. from the 19th August to the 11th October following; viz.

	£.	s.	d.
For 3 waggons to carry the battalion's baggage, with their officers, and ammunition, &c. to Colebrook, Stow, and Windsor, as above, at 8d. p. mile	2	1	6
For candles, straw, and 2 guard-roomes, at Colebrook, Stow, and Windsor, during the Queen's stay at Windsor, from the 5th of July to the 24th August	5	16	6
For a lanthorne to relieve the centinells	0	5	0
For 3 waggons to carry the battalion's baggage, ammunition, and officers, from London to Bath, Marshfield, and Bradford, according to their sev^{ll} routs	9	18	4
	18	1	4

APPENDIX. 313

	£.	s.	d.
Brought forward	18	1	4
For fire, candles, and straw, for the sev[ll] guards at Bath, Marshfield, and Bradford, and upon the march, from the 19th August to the 11th October following	12	15	0
For 2 guard-chambers at Bath for the officers and battalion	4	2	6
For 3 carriages for the battalion's return, both from Bath, Marshfield, and Bradford, by sev[ll] routs	10	4	0
Totall is	45	2	10

RD. HOLMES, Major.

145.

The sum of £26 18s. 8d. to be paid to Lieut.-Colonel Henry Morryson of the Coldstream, for the contingent disbursements of a battalion of Foot Guards under his command, in their march from London on 20th March, 170¾, to Chichester, and from Chichester on the 17th May to Portsmouth, and back again, in two detachments, on the 18th and 20th August, to their quarters in London: and the sum of £26 16s. to Lieut.-Colonel Andrew Bissett of the Coldstream, for the con[t] disb[ts] of another battalion, under his command, on their march from London in August, 1703, to Bath; during their doing duty there; and from Bath, in October, back to London.

Dated St. Jameis, 16th December, 1703.

146.

The sum of £12 1s. 7d. to be paid to Lieut.-Colonel Charles Wakelyn, Quarter-Master to Coldstream, expended by him in providing centinel-boxes, and otherwise, for the service of the Coldstream regiment of Foot Guards.

To Captain William Stevenage £4 9s. 4d., disbursed by him in providing carriages on the march for a detachment of the Coldstream from London, on 18th March, 170¾, to Dover, and back again.

To Captain Allen £2 10s. 2d., for another detachment of the Coldstream on the march from London to Southampton.

Dated St. Jameis, 8th April, 1704.

147.

An Account of Money disbursed by Coll. Richard Holmes, Major of the Coldstream regiment of Foot Guards, for the carriages of the entire cloathing and all the accoutrements for the detachment of the said regiment, quartered in Portsmouth and the Isle of Wight, being 200 private sentinells, with serjeants, corporalls, and drummers. June, 1704.

	£.	s.	d.
For three waggons from London to Kingston, being 12 miles, at 8d. p. mile each	1	4	0
	1	4	0

314   APPENDIX.

	£.	s.	d.
Brought forward	1	4	0
From Kingston to Guilford, 18 miles	1	16	0
From Guilford to Haslemere, 12 miles	1	4	0
From Haslemere to Petersfield, 10 miles	1	0	0
From Petersfield to Portsmouth, 18 miles	1	16	0
For a hoy from Portsmouth to the Isle of Wight, to carry part of the cloathing	0	10	0
For a roome for the cloathing upon the march, and candles for the guard, being 6 nights	0	9	0
Totall	7	19	0

Rᴅ. Holmes, Major.

148.

Cock-pitt, July 7th, 1704.

My Lord;—The Comm^ee of Lords have met every day of late to consider of my Lord Gallway's proposalls, and they having given their opinions upon them, her Ma^ty has been pleased to order, that for the King of Portugall's assistance there be transported from Ireland to Lisbon 1500 recruits, and one reg^t of Foot and one reg^t of Dragoons, and from England one batallion of the Foot Guards, to consist of 600 men, and officers proportionable; these last are ordered to be ready by the 26th instant, and are designed to go by the way of Ireland, and take the troops from thence under one convoy. The Lords have still under their consideration the sending of one thousand English horse of about 14 hands high, they being judged fittest for that service, and very much wanted; but considering that the transports are with Sr Geo. Rooke at a great charge, and that it will be difficult to procure other ships for this transport, and that it will cost her Ma^ty about $\frac{m^1}{30}$ lib., for which there is no provision by the Parliament, I believe the Lords will rather incline to advise her Ma^ty to try to procure horses from Barbary; at least there will be no positive orders for sending any horses from hence, till it is known what can be had from Barbary. According to the liberty your Grace has given me, I shall trouble you now with a word out of my province. There is great reason to fear the Duke of Savoy will be lost, if nothing can be done for his assistance, or to divert the enemy in Italy; and in case of your success in bringing over Bavaria by force or treaty, it is apprehended the Emperor may press for assistance in Hungary against the malecontents. Your Grace is the best judge what measures to take in that case, but your goodness will pardon my own private thoughts, which are well meant, and with all submission; and they are, that nothing should divert your Grace from the thoughts of suc-

---

[1] £30,000.

couring Savoy one way or other, when the Emperor can spare any troops, and if the Emperor will not hearken to measures proposed for that purpose, I know not but it were better to make him apprehend that your Grace will march back again, if such troops as can be spared are not sent into Italy, and, if possible, with Prince Eugene at their head. If the empire be saved, 'tis by her Ma$^{ty's}$ troops under your Grace's conduct: this march was principally for his sake. Her Ma$^{ty's}$ fleet is in the Mediterranean, at a vast expence, for the support of the Confederates, and the Portugal expedition was undertaken for setling the Emperor's son on the throne of Spaine, when at the same time her Ma^{ty} has neither ships nor land forces in or near her own dominions, or can have them upon any emergency; all which being considered, her Ma^{ty} has a right to direct in the councills for the operations of the campagne, and it seems most resonable and fitt that the Emperor should comply with any proposalls your Grace should make for the service of the whole confederacy. It is pitty your Grace's glorious success should be any ways chequed, and there is no service in view that seems to be equivalent to the driving the French troops out of Italy, except that of clearing Bavaria of them, which we hope will speedily be the consequence of your victory of Donawert. I am, with the greatest respect and truth, my Lord, y^r Grace's most obedient and most humble servant,   C. HEDGES.

 Duke of Marlborough.

 Endorsed:—Mr. Secretary Hedges to the Duke of Marlborough, 7th July, 1704.   (Lansdowne MSS. 849. fol. 250.)

149.

 Anne R.—Our will and pleasure is, that you cause a detachment of six hundred private soldiers, with a competent number of commissioned and non-commissioned officers, to be forthwith made out of the several companies of our First and Coldstream reg^{ts} of Foot Guards now in England, proportionably, and to march according to the route hereunto annexed, to Portsmouth, where they are to embark on Wednesday, the 26th of this instant July, on board such ships as shall be appointed to carry them to Portugal, to be employed in our service there; and the officers, &c. Given at our Court at Windsor, this 10th day of July, 1704, in the third year of our reign.

     By, &c.   H. ST. JOHN.

To our trusty and right entirely beloved cousin and councillor, John Duke of Marlborough, Captain-General of
 our Forces, and Colonel of our First reg^t of Foot Guards.
And to our right trusty and welbeloved John Lord Cutts,
 Lieut.-Genl of our Forces, and Colonel of our Coldstream reg^t of Foot Guards; and to the officer-in-chief
 with those regiments and the detachment above mentioned respectively.

APPENDIX.

Route for a detachment of six hundred men and officers of the Foot Guards, from London to Portsmouth :—Kingston, Thursday, July 20, 1704; Guilford and Godalmin, Friday, 21; Petersfield, Saturday, 22; —rest, Sunday, 23; Portsmouth, Monday, 24.   H. St. John.

150.

Contingent Disbursements in the march of a detachment of six hundred men, besides officers, of the Foot Guards, from London to Portsmouth, that are going to Portugall. (Route dated 10th July, 1704.)

	£.	s.	d.
For 13 waggons for carrying downe to Portsmouth the armes, tents, kettles, field coullers, shoes, shirts, stockings, and severall other necessarys, provided extraordinary for the use of the soldiers in Portugall, being 73 miles, at 8*d*. a mile for each waggon	31	12	0
For ten waggons for the officers' baggage for ditto, they having made extraordinary provision of severall things on this occasion, which they could not furnish themselves in Portugall	24	6	8
For straw, candle, and other incident charges on their march	1	10	0
	57	8	8

(Richard) Russell, Commandant,
(Capt. and Lieut.-Col. 1st Foot Guards.)

151.

In future commissions, children will be restricted to two in any regiment at one time, and those to be the children of officers slain, or suffered extremely in the service; and when any regiment is ordered abroad, the children are to be removed into other regiments.

Dated 29th May, 1705.

152.

Extract of a Letter from Mr. St. John to Mr. Secretary Harley.

Whitehall, 3rd Nov. 1705.

Petition of Hugh Baxter.

" That by a warrant, dated the 7th August, 1703, under the hand of
" the late Sir William Matthews, who was Lieut.-Colonel to the Cold-
" stream reg^t of Foot Guards, I find the petitioner was appointed chy-
" rurgeon's mate of the said regiment, which I am informed was given
" him upon the refusal of the surgeon's mate to go abroad upon ser-
" vice, who afterwards, applying himself to my Lord Cutts upon his
" arrival from Holland, was restored, and is now abroad with the bat-
" talion of that regiment, and therefore the said Baxter was dismissed
" by his Lordship."

APPENDIX.   317

153.

Whitehall, 22d January, 170$\frac{3}{4}$.

Sir,—His Grace the Duke of Marlborough having given leave to Lt-Col. Moryson, with the detachment of the Coldstream regiment of Guards in Catalonia, to return to England, is pleased to order that you appoint another officer of the regiment to go over in his room with the first convoy bound for the Streights.

I am, Sir, your most humble servant,   H. St. John.

To Colonel Braddock, Coldstream Guards.

154.

Whitehall, 6th February, 170$\frac{5}{6}$.

Sir,—It appearing to his Grace the Duke of Marlborough, under the hands of two physicians, that Colonel Stevenage is labouring under a distemper which renders him unfit to serve with the detachment of the Coldstream regiment in Spain; his Grace does therefore think fit that you appoint the next officer in turn to go over thither in his stead.   I am, Sir, your most humble servant,

H. St. John.

To Colonel Braddock, Coldstream Guards.

155.

Anne R.—Whereas we have received information, that the battalion of our Foot Guards in Spain is reduced to three hundred private soldiers or thereabouts; our will and pleasure is, that you cause a detachment of three hundred and ten men to be made out of the severall companies of our First and Coldstream regiments of Foot Guards, now in England, proportionably; and putt on board such ships in the river of Thames as shall be appointed to receive them under the care of the officers of our said regiments who are now going to their commands in Spain; and for so doing this shall be your warrant. Given at our Court at St. James's, this 8th day of February, 170$\frac{5}{6}$, in the fourth year of our reign.   By her Majesties commands,

H. St. John.

To our right trusty, &c. John Duke of Marlborough, &c. and
our right trusty, &c. John Lord Cutts, &c.

" Memorand^m—This detachm^t is to embark upon notice from the
" Commissioners of Transportation that shipping is ready to receive
" them."

156.

Extract of a Lrē from Mr. St. John to the Comm^{rs} of Transports,
dated Whitehall, 12 Feb. 170$\frac{5}{6}$.

" An account of the detach^t of Foot Guards going to Spain, and of
" officers of other reg^{ts}.

"Coldstream reg^t of Foot Guards:—Lt.-Col. Scawen and 3 servants, "Ensign Bradbury and 1 servant, 140 private soldiers; total 146."

Extract of a Lr̃e from Mr. St. John to Mr. Burchett, 12 Feb. 170$\frac{6}{7}$.

"You are desired to give directions for the receiving on board the "convoy now bound for Lisbon, going to their commands in Spain, "&c.— Lt.-Col. Bissett, Lt.-Col. Wakelyn, Lt.-Col. Swan, of the "Foot Guards."

157.

Extract of a Letter from Mr. St. John to Col. Bissett, 18 Feb. 170$\frac{6}{7}$.

The three officers named to go on board the transports with the detach^t of 300 men of the Guards going to Spain, and not to go with the convoy to Lisbon.

Lt.-Col. Bissett commands the detachment of 300 recruits for the Guards going to Spain.—Dated 23d Feb. 170$\frac{6}{7}$.

The exact number of the detachment of Foot Guards going to Spain is agreed to be 338 soldiers, including officers and their servants.

To be taken on board to-morrow.—Dated 2d March, 170$\frac{6}{7}$.

158.

Two men a company to be allowed from 25th February last, to enable the two regiments of Guards to complete their arms, as well as to complete those in place of pikes which they would exchange for fire-arms.

Dated 16th March, 170$\frac{6}{7}$.

159.

The standards, as well as the banners of the kettle drums and trumpets of the troops of Horse Guards and Grenadier Guards, are to be altered upon the present occasion of the Union with Scotland; and new standards and banners are to be furnished out of the wardrobe under my Lord Chamberlain against the first day of May next.

Dated 18th April, 1707.

160.

Whitehall, 28th April, 1707.

Gentlemen,—In answer to your letter of the 26th instant, this is to acquaint you, that of the First regiment of ffoot Guards there are eleven comp^{as} in Holland; and of the other seventeen comp^{as} of that regiment, and the ffourteen comp^{as} of the Coldstream regiment, there is a detachment of six hundred men and officers in Spain formed into ten companys, so that there is remaining in England twenty-one companys of both regiments.

I am, Gentlemen, your most humble servant,   H. ST. JOHN.
To the principal officers of the Ordnance.

161.

Whitehall, 30th June, 1707.

Gentlemen,—In answer to your letter of the 13th instant, concerning the demand which the officers of the two regiments of Foot Guards make for powder, I am to acquaint you, that although by reason of the detachment of six hundred men which was made out of the 31 comp^{as} thereof in England and sent to Spain, the remainder of those companys might be computed to amount only to 21 full comp^{as}, yet the real number of companys in England are 17 of the 1st regiment, two whereof consist of 70 men, and the other fifteen of 50 men in each, and 14 of the Coldstream regiment of 50 men in each, all bearing fire-arms.

I am, Gentlemen, your most humble servant, H. St. John.
To the principal officers of the Ordnance.

162.

The 1st and Coldstream regiments of Foot Guards to recruit, to fill up the companies from whence the detachments were made that formed the batt^n in Spain.

Dated 15th Sept. 1707.

163.

Proposal of the Genl Officers relative to the Clothing of the Army. At a Meeting in the Great Room at the Horse Guards, on the 4th Feb. 170$\frac{7}{8}$, and another Meeting on the 7th Feb., it was agreed that the quantity and quality of clothing for the Foot should be, viz. :—

For the first year, — A good cloth coat, well lined, which may serve for the waistcoat the second year; a pair of good thick kersey breeches; a pair of good strong stockings; a pair of good strong shoes; a good shirt and a neckcloth; a good strong hat, well laced.

For the second year,—A good cloth coat, well lined, as for the first year; a waistcoat made of the former year's coat; a pair of strong kersey new breeches; a pair of good strong stockings; a pair of good strong shoes; a good shirt and a neckcloth; a good strong hat, well laced.

That all accoutrements, as swords, belts, *patrontashes*, and drum carriages, be made good as they are wanted.

That the recruits be supplied with a new waistcoat, and one shirt, and one neckcloth more than the old soldiers, who have some linen before hand.

That the serjeants and drums be clothed after the same manner, but every thing in its kind better.

Anne R.—Warrant approving and ordering recommendation of generall officers respecting clothing, and authorising a permanent Board for regulating clothing, dated Kensington, 14th January, 170⅞. Sealed patterns to be lodged in the office as a standard.

For this next campaign, 1708.

Foot.—A good full body'd cloth coat, well lined, which may serve for the waistcoat the second year; a waistcoat; a p^r of good kersey breeches; a p^r of good strong stockings; a p^r of good strong shoes; two good shirts and two neckcloths; a good strong hat, well laced.

For the second year.—A good cloth coat, well lined, as for the first year; a waistcoat made of the former year's coat; a pair of strong kersey new breeches; a pair of good strong stockings; a pair of good strong shoes; a good shirt and a neckcloth; a good strong hatt, well laced.

That the accoutrements, viz. swords, belts, cartridge boxes, and drum carriages, shall be provided out of the off-reckonings.

That the serjeants, corporals, and drums be clothed in the same manner, but every thing better in its kind.

164.

All brevet officers to do duty according to the posts they hold in their respective regiments.

Dated 2nd August, 1708.

165.

London Gaz. No. 4516. From 17 to 21 Feb. 170⅞.

Deserted out of Lt.-Col. Francis Scawen's comp^y, in her Majesty's Colds^m reg. of Foot Guards, Edward Evans, a black man, wears a black wig, about 5 foot 10 inches high, aged about 34 years, a pavier by trade. Thomas Tunnill, commonly called Islington Tom, about 5 foot 8 inches high, wears a bushy light brown wig, full face, with some small moles in his cheek; he was a labourer to the said Edward Evans, lived at Islington, and formerly drove hogs. John Keymoure, a dark brown man, his own lank brown hair, a full nose, thin face, a tinman by trade, born at the Devizes in Wiltshire, wrought lately with Mr. King in the Pall Mall St. James's, supposed to be gone to work at his trade in Bristol. Edward Lovelace, about 5 foot 10 inches high, a lusty well-set man, wears a brown wig, very full of pockholes in his face, born at Frome in Somersetshire, a clothier by trade, lately used the Sheers alehouse in Bell-Alley in Coleman Street, London, and wrought thereabouts. Whoever secures any of them, so that they may be delivered to Capt. Richard Green, giving notice at the Tilt-Yard Coffee-house, shall have 20s. reward for each; and if they will return to their colours in 14 days time after the date hereof, they shall be pardoned.

London Gaz. 4517, from 21 to 24 Feb. 170⅞.

Deserted out of Lt.-Col. Robert Bethell's comp^y, in her Majesty's

Colds. reg. of F. G^ds, comm^d by his Exc^y Genl Charles Churchill, Jonathan Shellvock, aged about 25 years, red-haired, wearing a brown wig, round visaged, stooping in the shoulders, born in Shropshire, 5 foot 7 inches high, and Jacob Harrison, aged 24 years, about 5 foot 6 inches high, pockholes in his face, wears his own short brown hair, born in Derbyshire. Whoever shall secure either of the two, and give notice to Mr. France at the Tilt-Yard Coffee-house, over-against Whitehall Gate, or to Mr. Man at Man's Coffee-house at Charing Cross, shall receive as a reward the sum of £5. for each; or if they will return to their colours in 10 days time, shall be kindly received and pardoned.

Lond. Gaz. 4549, from 13 to 16 June, 1709.

Deserted out of Lt.-Col. Turner's comp^y in the Colds. reg. of F. G^ds, comm^d by the Hon. Gen. Churchill, George Carey, about 5 foot 7 in., very well set, fair complexion, wearing his own hair pretty long, and turned at the ends, aged about 29, born in Kent, a glass-grinder by trade, and formerly worked with Mr. Gibbins in Hosier Lane. John King, a tall black man, about 5 foot 10 in., with a high nose, leaning a little to the right, wearing a dark brown wig, aged about 35, born in Worcestershire. Alcock Goolding, a well-set man, about 5 ft. 8 in. and a half, wearing his own sandy bushy hair, fair complexion, strait limbs, aged about 23, born within 6 or 7 miles of Colchester in Essex, a baker by trade. If they will return to their colours in 10 days, they shall be kindly received and pardoned; or whoever secures them and gives notice to Col. Turner at his house in Cleveland Court in St. James's, shall receive two guineas reward for each.

166.

The Colonels of the regiments in Flanders, by desire of his Grace the Duke of Marlborough, are to give directions to all the officers of their respective regiments, " to have red coats with black buttons and " button-holes, for their regimental clothing for the present year."—
Dated Whitehall, 16th March, 170⅞.

167.

Au Camp entre Quesnoy et Valenciennes, le 17e Sept. 1709.[1]

Ce fut le 11e de ce mois entre sept et huit heures du matin que l'Armée des Alliez attaqua la nôtre avec tant de furie que depuis plus d'un siecle il ne s'est vu une action plus sanglante que celle qui s'est faite ce jour-là, et qui sera mémorable à tous les siecles à venir. Les Anglois commencerent l'attaque par le Bois de Sart, que nous avions rempli d'Infanterie et parfaitement retranché. Mais on n'y fit pas toute la

---

[1] Camp Letters. State-Paper Office.

résistance qu'on auroit dû faire, puisque du succès de cette attaque dépendoit beaucoup celuy de la journée ; cependant peu de ceux qui le défendoient eschapperent, tant les ennemis estoient acharnés et hacheoient en pieces tout ce qui se rencontroit devant eux et même les morts lorsque leur fureur ne trouvoit pas des vivans à dévorer.

Les Hollandois ne furent pas si heureux à notre droite, parceque notre Infanterie y fit des merveilles, et ne fut forcée qu'après avoir défendu ses retranchements pendant cinq heures entieres par un feu des plus violens.

Il est constant aussi que les ennemis ont infiniment souffert de ce côté-là. Ils furent renversés par plusieurs reprises, et ce fut là où il se passa des actions héroïques de part et d'autre.

L'avantage du terrain, trois retranchements consécutifs, rien ne fut capable d'intimider nos terribles ennemis, et on les voyoit venir à corps découverts, non comme des hommes, mais comme des démons ; des décharges de vingt pieces de canon, portant à plomb tout à la fois dans leurs Bataillons, ne pouvoient les ébranler, quoyqu'elles renversassent des rangs tout entiers.

La valeur a esclaté de nostre costé autant qu'il a esté possible, les Généraux ne se sont pas espargnés, et ont donné bon exemple aux troupes par une opiniâtreté toute extraordinaire à ne vouloir jamais céder la victoire, et nous la crumes à nous lorsqu'un gros Corps de Cavalerie Ennemie dans le centre de leur Armée plia à Val deroute devant la Maison du Roy ; mais les Généraux ennemis s'étant mis à leur teste les ramenoyent bientost au combat, et avec tant de furie qu'ils enfoncerent peu après notre centre, dans le même tems que notre droite commençoit à succomber aux efforts de la gauche des ennemis, et que la nostre étoit chassée de ses retranchem^{ts} et des bois.

Alors la victoire se déclara contre nous, et il fallut céder à de si terribles efforts ; jamais on n'a vu nos Troupes plus animées à bien faire que ce jour-là, ni disposition mieux ordonnée ni mieux prise que celle que les Mareschaux de Boufflers et Villars avoient faite ; mais quand Dieu ne combat point avec les hommes, tout est inutile. Le Roi doit estre content de ses Troupes à cette action : il n'y a pas de doute que les ennemis y ont perdu leur meilleure Infanterie ; la nostre y a aussi extrêmement souffert, et nous comptons d'avoir laissé au moins sept mille morts sur le champ de bataille, et nous avons plus de dix mille blessez.

Nous ne pouvons pas encore pénétrer le véritable sujet pour quoy l'Ennemi n'a pas témoigné plus d'ardeur à nous poursuivre ; il paroît que ce ne peut estre que la perte de leur Infanterie. Nous avons fait assurément une des plus belles retraites qu'il se soit fait de mémoire d'homme, devant une Armée victorieuse ; mais il est sûr aussi que les Ennemis nous en ont donné tout le tems, et qu'ils ne nous ont poursuivi que par forme.

C'estoit cependant toute nôtre inquiétude, puisque, comme j'ay dit, lorsque les ennemis nous enfoncerent par le centre entre les deux bois, notre Armée fut séparée, la droite ne pouvant joindre la gauche, parceque les Ennemis se formerent d'abord jusqu'aux hayes des Tanieres, et c'estoit avec justice qu'on craignoit que la gauche ne fût enveloppée, parcequ'elle avoit esté poussée la premiere. Il n'estoit pas plus de deux heures et demie lorsque le combat finit, et les Ennemis avoient encore un beau reste de jour, et nous sceumes assez bien profiter du tems, puisqu'avant que le soleil fut bas nous avions passé Bavay, et par conséquent hors de danger.

Nous nous apperçumes alors que nôtre gauche n'estoit pas poursuivie plus que nous, et que les Ennemis s'estoient tout-à-fait contentés du champ de bataille : nous vismes cependant toute leur cavalerie sur les Hauteurs de Tanieres en forme de Croissant, et on ignoroit encore leur dessein vers les cinq heures ; mais après les avoir fait reconnoître, on eut avis qu'ils y faisoient halte : à la verité cette nouvelle nous fit beaucoup de plaisir, puisqu'elle nous donna le tems de respirer.

Les Ennemis n'ont fait d'autres prisonniers que les blessez qui n'ont pu suivre, et ceux qui sont restez par faiblesse à Bavay. Nous comptons Douze Cents Officiers blessez, parmi lesquels il y en a plusieurs de distinction. Le Ma͞al de Villars, qui a acquis beaucoup d'honneur pendant cette journée par sa valeur extraord^{re}, aura peine de se tirer d'affaire. Guiche, Albergotti, et plusieurs autres en reviendront. La Maison du Roy a perdu plusieurs Estandarts et Timbales ; mais il est sûr qu'elle a fait tout ce qu'on devoit attendre d'elle.

Les Eugene et Marlborough doivent estre bien contents de nous, puisque jusqu'à ce jour-là ils n'avoient jamais trouvé de résistance digne d'eux, et ils pourront dire à présent avec justice que rien ne doit tenir devant eux. Et qu'est-ce qui pourra arrester le cours rapide de ces deux fameux Héros, que nous ne pouvons cesser d'admirer, si une Armée de Cent Mille hommes des meilleures troupes, postée entre deux bois, retranchée triplement, faisant tous les devoirs que les plus braves gens peuvent faire, ne peut seulement les arrester une journée, ne direz-vous point avec moy qu'ils surpassent tous ceux des siecles passez ?

APPENDIX.

Liste de la perte de l'Infanterie des Hauts Alliez, tant tués que blessés, à la Bataille de Tanieres, l'onzième Septembre, 1709.

	Bataillons	Cols.		Lt. Cols.		Majs.		Capts.		Subalts.		Tot. d' Offrs.		Bas Offrs. & Comm.		Tot. des Morts & Blessés
		Morts	Blessés	Morts	Blessés	Morts	Blessés	Morts	Blessés	Morts	Blessés	Morts	Blessés	Morts	Blessés	
L'Armée de Son Alt. Monsgr. le Prince de Savoy.	50	4	7	5	10	3	9	20	67	52	161	84	254	1900	3177	5415
L'Armée de S. A. Mons. le Prince & Duc de Marlborough. — Anglois	*	4	2	4	3	–	3	13	26	13	62	34	95	541	1186	1856
Prussiens	18	2	4	1	1	1	6	2	17	9	33	15	61	294	833	1203
Hanovriens	12	–	1	1	2	–	4	2	12	10	44	13	63	285	1056	1417
Hollandois	30	6	6	5	11	5	14	42	116	85	242	143	389	2238	5692	8462
Somme	–	16	20	16	27	9	36	79	238	169	441	289	862	5258	11944	18353

List of the Officers of Her Majesty's Forces kill'd at the Battle of Tanieres.[1]

GUARDS.
Colonel Rivet.
Lieut.-Colonel Arundel.
Lieut.-Colonel Bethel.
Captain Phillips.
Captain Gould.
ORKNEY, FIRST BATT.
Lieutenant Higly.
ARGYLL.
Captain Eaton.
Captain Smith.
Captain Scott.
Captain Melvil.
Lieutenant Price.
Lieutenant Ledman.
WEBB.
Lieut.-Colonel Ramsey.

HOW.
Major Leslie.
LALO.
Brigadier Lalo.
Major Row.
Captain Fairly.
Captain Monro.
Captain Wemyss.
Lieutenant Ross.
SABINE.
Lieutenant Fullerton.
Lieutenant Barkley.
Lieutenant Parker.
TEMPLE.
Captain Twisden.
Lieutenant Aspin.
Ensign Soan.

PRESTON.
Colonel Cranstoun
Captain-Lieut. Shaw.
Lieutenant Cockburn.
Ensign Inglis.
ORRERY.
Captain Devine.
Lieutenant Gargrave.
Lieutenant Norton.
Quarter-Master Bishop.
MEREDYTH'S.
Ensign Jones.
PRENDERGAST.
Sir Thomas Prendergast.
LUMLEY'S HORSE.
Lieutenant Stirrup.

168.

It is her Majesty's pleasure, that a lieutenant with forty men and non-comm^d officers proportionally of the Foot Guards do march at three a clock this afternoon to the Piazzas in Covent Garden, and parade there, in order to be assisting the civil magistrates for pre-

---

* Nineteen Battalions; see Millner's Journal.
[1] Camp Letters. State-Paper Office. This list is also in the London Gazette No. 4595.

venting any mischief that may happen at the play-house in Covent Garden. Given at Whitehall, the 19th day of March, 17⁑.

G. GRANVILLE.

To Major-Gen¹ Tatton, or Major-Gen¹ Braddock, of her
Majesty's Foot Guards, and the officer commanding the
detacht. above mentioned.

169.

Whitehall, 9th August, 1711.

Gentlemen,—Her Majesty having thought fit that a field officer of the Foot Guards be always in waiting upon her Royal Person, in like manner as she is attended by an officer of the Horse Guards, I am commanded to acquaint you with her Majesty's pleasure herein, and that she expects a compliance therewith as soon as may be.

I am, gentlemen, your most humble servant,

G. GRANVILLE.

Officer-in-chief with the two regiments of Guards.

Windsor, August 15th, 1711.

Sir,—Her Majesty has commanded me to signify to you, that it is her Majesty's pleasure, a field-officer belonging to one of her regiments of Foot Guards do duty at her Palace, as was formerly practised in the reign of King Charles the Second, for the better preservation of good order and discipline near her royal person.

I am, Sir, your most humble servant,

Major-Gen¹ Holmes. G. GRANVILLE.

170.

Provision should be made in the Savoy Barracks for five hundred foot soldiers, and also a house for the officers who are to be constantly on duty there.—Dated 12th March, 17⁑.

171.

Anne R.—Our will and pleasure is, that you cause the fourteen companies of our Coldstream regiment of Foot Guards under your command to be disposed of in quarters as follows, vizt: In St. Andrew's Holborn, St. Giles's in the Fields, part of the Dutchy Liberty, Clerkenwell, Cripplegate, and St. Sepulchre's Without, where they are to remain until further orders. And the officers, &c. Given at our Court at St. James's, this 19th day of February, 17⁑, in the eleventh year of our reign. By her Majesty's command,

W. WYNDHAM.

To our trusty and welbeloved Charles Churchill, Esq.,
General of our Foot, and Colonel of our Coldstream
regiment of Foot Guards, or the Officer-in-chief with the
regiment.

172.

Five hundred men of the Foot Guards are to be lodged within the Savoy, as soon as barracks can be made for them; and in the mean time the barrack necessaries ordered, are to be delivered to an officer of the Coldstream to be made use of at Hampton Court and Kensington, where the soldiers are to be lodged until the conveniencies of the Savoy shall be fitted up.—Dated 10th April, 1713.

173.

The Contingent Bill of Captain John Parsons, Quar^r-Mas^r to her Majesty's Coldstream regim^t of Foot Guards, from 24th December, 1712, to 24th December, 1713.

	£.	s.	d.
Poundage of last contingent bill	2	3	10
For barges to carry beds, bolsters, blankets, ruggs, and sheets, for 500 men from the Tower to the Savoy and Hampton Court	8	0	0
Porters to load and unload the same	2	15	0
For a new wooden horse at the Tilt Yard, and painting	3	12	0
Fetching ammunition from the Tower severall times	4	0	0
Porters to load and unload the same	0	8	0
Two new centry-boxes in St. James's Park	6	0	0
For mending the centry-boxes in St. James's House and Park, and painting the same	9	7	6
Sending ammunition to Hampton Court, severall times, for the duty and exercise of the six companies there	1	18	0
For bringing the bedding from Hampton Court to the Savoy	5	0	0
Porters to load and unload the same	1	12	0
Sending ammunition to Windsor divers times	2	6	0
Carriage for officers' baggage to and from Windsor	3	4	0
Paid the smith for work at St. James's and Tilt Yard	4	2	0
Paid the glasier for mending windows at St. James's and Tilt Yard	3	11	0
For books, paper, pens and ink	3	6	8
For lanthorns, brooms, basketts and mopps	4	8	0
	£65	14	0

This is a reasonable bill, and ought to be allowed.

R^D. HOLMES, Major.

174.

James, Duke Marquis and Earl of Ormonde, &c. Captain Gen^{ll} of all her Maj^{ty's} Land fforces, &c.

Whereas I have received information that several soldiers of the regiment of Marines commanded by Maj.-Genl Wills, ordered to be disbanded, are assembled in a tumultuous manner at or near Rochester, in contempt of her Maj^{ty's} authority, and to the disturbance of the peace of her subjects; you are hereby directed and required forthwith to march with a detachment of six hundred men of the three regiments of Foot Guards, and officers proportionable, and a detachment of one hundred gentlemen of the four troops of Horse Guards, and threescore private men of the Horse Granadiers, and officers proportionable, (for which you are to apply to the R^t Honble the Earl of Arran or to Lieut.-General Compton); and you are to proceed towards Rochester according as you shall receive advice from Colonel Markham of the Lord Shannon's regiment, (with whom you are to keep a constant correspondence,) or otherwise, in order to suppress and appease the said mutineers and others that may joyn with them by force of arms, if it can not be done otherwise; and in case you shall find a further reinforcement either of foot, horse, or granadier guards may be wanting, for the performance of this service, you are hereby directed and empowered to send for as many more men of those corps as may be necessary; for which purpose the respective officers thereunto belonging are hereby required to observe and follow your orders; and as the speedy execution of this commission is of the greatest consequence, you are to lose no time in the complying with it. But as in case you shall receive advice that the mutineers are returned to their obedience, you are to proceed no further; so if you are obliged to come to action with them, you are to secure and bring back with you in safe custody as many prisoners as you shall take. For all which, this shall be to you and to all others concerned a sufficient warrant and direction. Given at Windsor, this 25th day of December, 1713.

ORMONDE.

By his Grace's command, HEN. WATKINS.

To Henry Withers, Esq. one of the Lieut.-Generals of her
  Maj$^{ty's}$ Forces, and Lieut.-Colonel of the First regt. of
  Foot Guards.

175.

" Order for the march of a detachm^t from the 1st, 2nd, and 3rd reg^{ts}
" of Foot Guards, to attend the Queen at Hampton Court and
" Windsor."

Anne R.—Our will and pleasure is, that you cause a detachm^t of 250 private soldiers, with commission and non-comm^n officers proportionable, of our Foot Guards, to march to Kingston and the Wick, Twittenham, Thistleworth, Hounslow, Hampton, the Molesey's, Dittons, Esher, Weybridge, Sunbury, Whitton, Teddington, and Walton, in order to attend our Royal Person at Hampton Court; and upon our removal from thence to Windsor, they are to march to Colebrook, Slough, Langford, Houghton, Burnham, ffernham, Cluworth, Iver, Datchet, Maidenhead, Stoke, and Old Windsor, to attend us at Windsor Castle; and the said detachment is to be relieved in the said duty by other detachments from London, from time to time, and as often as shall be necessary, during our stay at either of our said palaces, and afterwards to return to their former quarters. And the officers, &c. Given at Kensington, 7th July, 1714, in the 13th year of our reign. By her Ma$^{ty's}$ command,

F. GWYN.

It is her Majesty's pleasure that the detachments of the Guards in their march to and from Windsor do quarter at the Brentfords, Hounslow, Thistleworth, and Twittenham, as there shall be occasion.

F. GWYN.

To the Colonels of our 1st, 2nd, and 3rd reg^{ts} of Foot
Guards, or the officers-in-chief with the reg^{ts} and detachm^{ts} above men^d.

176.

By the Lords Justices—Harcourt C., W. Ebor., Shrewsbury, Buckingham P., Carlisle, Argyll, Abingdon, Scarborough, Orford, Townsend, Halifax.

We do hereby direct, that you cause the severall comp^s of Granadiers belonging to his Majesty's 1st, 2nd, and 3rd reg^{ts} of ffoot Guards, to march to Greenwich and to encamp in the Park there, in order to mount the King's guard upon his arrival at Greenwich, and to do duty on his Royal Person during his Majesty's continuance in that place; and you are also to cause the remainder of the said three regiments which shall not be upon duty on that day, (to which end the detachment now at the Tower will be relieved the day before by a detach^t of Lieut.-Gen^{ll} Webb's reg^t,) to line the streets from the place where the militia ends to the Palace at St. James's. And the officers, &c. Given at St. James's, 3rd September, 1714.

By, &c. F. GWYN.

To the Colonels of the three regiments of Foot Guards, and
to the officers-in-chief with the several companies of
Granadiers herein above mentioned respectively.

177.

George R.—Our will and pleasure is, that you cause a detachment to be made of seventy private men, with a commission officer, and non-commission officers proportionable, out of our three regiments of Foot Guards under your commands, to march to our Tower of London, to relieve the detachment of Lieut.-Generall Webb's[1] regiment

---

[1] Styled The King's "Own Regiment of Foot," under the command of Lieut.-Gen. John Richmond, alias Webb, (the present Eighth Foot.) The present Fourth Foot also called at this time the King's Own regiment of Foot.

of Foot now doing duty there, who are thereupon to march out to their former quarters; and you are likewise to cause them to be relieved from time to time, in such manner as heretofore, when they did the whole duty of that garrison, and to follow such orders as they shall receive from our Governor, Lieut.-Governor, or officer commanding in chief there, until further order. And the officer is to take care that the soldiers behave themselves civilly and duly pay their landlords; and all magistrates, justices of the peace, constables, and other our officers, are to be assisting unto you as there shall be occasion. Given at our Court at St. James's, this 27th day of September, 1714, in the first year of our reign.

By his Maj$^{ty's}$ command,   WM. PULTENEY.

To the Colonels of our three regiments of ffoot Guards,
and to the officers commanding in chief the said regiments respectively.

178.

George R.—Our will and pleasure is, that you cause the fourteen companies of our Coldstream regiment of Foot Guards under your command, to be disposed of in quarters as follows; viz. four companys in St. Andrew's Holborn, one in the Dutchy Liberty, one in St. Sepulchre's Without, one in Clerkenwell, three in Cripplegate, one in Whitechappell, two in Bishopsgate Without, and one in Shoreditch, where they are to remain untill further order. And the officers, &c. Given at our Court at St. James's, this 12th day of November, 1714, in the first year of our reign.

By his Maj$^{ty's}$ command,   WM. PULTENEY.

To our trusty and welbeloved William Cadogan, Esqr,
Lieut.-General of our Forces, and Colonel of our Coldstream regiment of ffoot Guards; or to the officer commanding in chief that regiment.

"Whitehall, 2nd February, 17$\frac{14}{15}$.

"It is his Maj$^{ty's}$ pleasure, that one of the four comp^s now in quar-
"ters in St. Andrew's Holborn, be removed to Spittlefield's Hamlett,
"where they are to remain untill further order.

"WM. PULTENEY."

"Whitehall, 7th February, 17$\frac{14}{15}$.

"It is his Maj$^{ty's}$ pleasure, that St. Katherine's, East Smithfield,
"and Wapping, Stepney, be added to the quarters of this regiment.

"WM. PULTENEY."

"Whitehall, 10th of August, 1715.

"It is his Maj$^{ty's}$ pleasure, that St. Mary-le-bone, Pancrass, and
"St. Mary Islington, be added to the quarters of this regiment,
"which is now augmented to 18 companys.   WM. PULTENEY."

179.

1715, June 10. The Guards were posted in different parts of London, to prevent persons wearing white roses.

Coldstream Orderly-room.

180.

George R.—Whereas we have thought fitt to add four companies to our Coldstream regiment of Foot Guards under your command, to consist of two serjeants, two corporals, two drummers, and forty private men in each company (including one for widows); these are to authorize you, by beat of drum or otherwise, to raise so many volunteers as shall be wanting to complete the said companies to the above numbers. And when you shall have listed twenty men fitt for service in any of the said companies, you are to give notice to two of our justices of the peace of the town or county wherein the same are, who are hereby authorized and required to view the said men, and certifie the day of their so doing, from which day the said twenty men, and the commission and non-commissioned officers of such company, are to enter into our pay. And all magistrates, justices of the peace, constables, and other our officers whom it may concern, are hereby required to be assisting unto you in providing quarters, impressing carriages, and otherwise, as there shall be occasion. Given at our Court at St. James's, this 23rd day of July, 1715, in the first year of our reign. By his Majesty's command,

WM. PULTENEY.

To our trusty and welbeloved William Cadogan, Esq. Lieut.-Genl of our Forces, and Colonel of our Coldstream regiment of Foot Guards, or to the officer or officers appointed by him to raise volunteers for the said regiment.

181.

Paid the following sums for a drummer's suit and surtout, &c^s. of the Coldstream regiment of his Majesty's Guards.[1] July, 1717.—

	£.	s.	d.
Scarlet cloath for the coat and breeches	3	7	6
Blue cloath for the waistcoat	0	18	0
Blue Genoa velvet to face the sleeves	1	4	0
Gold buttons to the coat	1	7	0
	6	16	6

---

[1] The colours and clothing of the drummers and hautbois of the three regiments of Guards were formerly supplied from the King's wardrobe, but in September 1716, £520 expended for that purpose, was allowed by Warrant upon the Contingencies, as set forth in the following bill :—

	£.	s.	d.
For the Colonel's Ensign	12	13	6
For 15 pair of colours, at £10. 10s. 6d. each pair	157	17	6
	170	11	0

APPENDIX.

	£.	s.	d.
Brought forward	6	16	6
Gold buttons to the waistcoat and breeches	1	5	0
Gold lace for the coat and waistcoat, and gold fringe for the sash	25	10	0
Blue serge to line the coat and skirts of the waistcoat	0	14	0
Gulix or garlick holland to line the body and sleeves of the waistcoat and the breeches through	0	6	0
Embroidering the badges on the breast and back of the coat	4	0	0
Leather for the pocketts	0	2	0
Making the suit	2	10	0
Two shirts and two neck cloths	1	0	0
A pair of hose	0	4	6
A pair of shoes	0	4	6
A pair of gloves	0	1	0
Mantua silk for the sash	0	15	0
A hat with gold lace	0	18	0
A cockade	0	2	6
Garters	0	0	6
A sword and belt	0	13	6
Scarlet cloath for the surtout	2	18	6
Blue cloath for facings and cape	0	6	0
Blue serge to line the surtout	0	10	6
Gold buttons to the coat	1	7	0
Gold lace do.	3	0	0
Making the surtout, with small materials	0	18	0
	54	3	0
To two drummers' suits and surtouts, &c^a. more, the like in all particulars as above, at £54 3s. each	108	6	0
Total	£162	9	0

Paid the following sums for suit, &c^a. for a hautbois of the Coldstream regiment of his Majesty's Guards. July, 1717.

	£.	s.	d.
Scarlet cloath for the coat and breeches	3	7	6
Blue cloath for the waistcoat and facing the coat sleeves	1	4	0
	4	11	6

	£.	s.	d.
Brought forward	170	11	0
For gilding with fine gold and painting four Major blazes, and eight numbers	5	0	0
For clothing of three drum-majors in rich liveries with surtout coats at £54. 3s. 0d. each livery	162	9	0
For clothing six hautboys at £30. 6s. 8d. each suit	182	0	0
	520	0	0

Report dated 9th November, 1717.   War-Office Records.

	£.	s.	d.
Brought forward	4	11	6
Blue serge to line the coat and skirts of the waistcoat	0	14	0
Gold lace for the coat and waistcoat	16	13	8
Gold buttons to the waistcoat, breeches, and coat	2	12	0
Gulix or garlick holland to line the body and sleeves of the waistcoat and breeches	0	6	0
Leather for the pockets	0	2	0
Making the suit	2	3	0
Two shirts and two neckcloths	1	0	0
A pair of hose	0	4	6
A pair of shoes	0	4	6
A pair of gloves	0	1	0
A hat with gold lace	0	18	0
A cockade	0	2	6
Garters	0	0	6
A sword and belt	0	13	6
	£30	6	8
To five hautbois' suits, &c^a. more, the like in all particulars as above, at £30. 6s. 8d. each	151	13	4
Total	182	0	0
Brought from the other side	162	9	0
This account is true. A. OUGHTON, Major.	£344	9	0

(S.)   Cadogan (Colonel).

"The like particulars were annexed to the warrants for the cloathing of the drums and hautbois of the 1st, 2nd, and 3d regiments of Foot Guards for cloathing for two years, from March, 172$\frac{2}{3}$, to March, 172$\frac{4}{5}$."

[Do. in every particular from 172$\frac{4}{5}$ to 1784, but in the establishment of the regiment for 1785 an allowance of £172. 4s. 6d. per annum for the state cloathing of the hautbois and drummers was added to the estimates on account of the pay, &c^a. of the Coldstream, which allowance still continues.]

182.

1717.—A party of drummers of the Guards were committed to the Marshalsea for beating a point of war before the Earl of Wexford's house on his acquittal of charges brought against him.—Coldstream Orderly-Room.

183.

It is his Majesty's pleasure that when and as often as you shall have due notice of a Ball to be held at the Theatre in the Haymarket,

APPENDIX. 333

you cause a detachment of one hundred private men, with a captain, and other commissioned and non-commissioned officers proportionable, to be made from the three regiments of Foot Guards under your command respectively, to march and do duty during the continuance of the said ball at the said theatre. And they are to take care that his Maj^{tys} peace be preserved, and, as far as possible, to prevent all rudeness or indecencies as well in words as in actions; nor are they to permit any persons to enter into the said theatre in habits that may tend to the drawing down reflections upon religion, or in ridicule of the same. And for your so doing, this shall be your warrant. Given at Whitehall, this 27th day of November, 1718.

By his Majesty's command,   Ro. Pringle.

To the Colonels of his Maj^{tys} three regiments of Foot Guards, or to the officer-in-chief with the said regiments and detachm^t respectively.

184.

The Contingent Bill of Coll. John Robinson, Major of his Majesty's Coldstream regiment of Foot Guards, for carriages, fire, and candle for the Battalion that marched into the West under his command. March the 9th, 171⅜.

	Miles.	£.	s.	d.
For 9 waggons, with 5 horses to each, from London to Chippenham in Wiltshire, by the way of Windsor	82	36	18	0
Ditto from Chippenham back again to London		36	18	0
For 1 waggon with 5 horses from Chippenham to Corsham, with a company detached there	3	0	3	0
Ditto back again from Corsham to Chippenham		0	3	0
For 1 waggon with 5 horses from Chippenham to Laycock, with a company detached there	3	0	3	0
Ditto back again from Laycock to Chippenham		0	3	0
For fire, candle, and straw for the several guards of the said battalion, from the 9th March, 171⅝, to the 9th May, 1719		10	2	6
For 1 waggon with 5 horses for the ammunition from London to Chippenham		4	2	0
Ditto back again from Chippenham to London		4	2	0
		£92	14	6

John Robinson (1st Major).

185.

It is their Excellencies the Lords Justices' directions that when a Quorum of them are together (any four of them being such) the Foot Guards, in whatever place or duty, do beat a march, rest their arms, and the officers salute them with their half-pikes in the same manner as when his Majesty is present in person; but with this difference, that they do not then drop their colours, or salute any of them at any time when single. Given at Whitehall, this 28th day of May, 1719.

By their Excell^{cies} command,   GEO. TREBY.

To the Colonels of his Majesty's three regiments of Foot
   Guards, or to the officers commanding those regiments.

186.

Extract.—" It is the Lords Justices' directions that, upon notice at any time from the Lord-mayor or Aldermen of the City of London of any riots in the said city, that you send sufficient detachments from St. James's and the Tilt Yard Guards to be aiding and assisting to suppress them." Dated Whitehall, June 4, 1719.

To the Colonels of his Majesty's three regiments of Foot
   Guards, or to the officers commanding those regiments.

187.

It is the Lords Justices' directions that you cause seven entire companys belonging to his Majesty's First reg^t of Foot Guards under your command, one of which to be grenadiers, to march on Tuesday morning next, (according to the route annexed) to Portsmouth, where they are to pass over to the Isle of Wight, and encamp there untill their embarkation under the care of the R^t Honble the Earl of Dunmore, who is to have the command of the three detachm^{ts} of the Guards. And in case the said companys, before their march, should, by sickness, desertion, or otherwise, want any men of their full complement, then you are to compleat them by draughts from the other companys of the regim^t. Wherein, &c. Given at Whitehall, this 23rd day of July, 1719.

By their Excell^{cys} command,

To the Duke of Marlborough.   GEO. TREBY.

" A like Order, of the same date, for the march of the Coldstream
" regiment of Foot Guards on Wednesday, according to the route an-
" nexed.

" Route for seven Comp^{as} of the Coldstream regiment of Foot Guards
                     from London to Portsmouth :—

" Kingston,   " To rest the Sundays if it happen on their march;
" Dorking,   " and in case they find themselves streightened in
" Godalmin,   " the towns thro' which they pass, then to enlarge
" Petersfield,   " their quarters with the adjacent villages.
" Fareham.   " From whence they are to march, and embark for
                          " the Isle of Wight, and encamp there.

" To the Lord Cadogan.   " GEO. TREBY."

A like Order, dated July 30, for the march of seven Comp^{as} of the Third Reg^t of Foot Guards to Southampton, and to pass over to the Isle of Wight, &c.

    To the Earl of Dunmore.

188.

The Contingent Bill of Sir Tristram Dillington, Major to his Majesty's Coldstream regiment of Foot Guards, for marching a battalion of the said regiment from London to the Isle of Wight. Order dated 23rd July, 1719.

	Miles.	£.	s.	d.
Fetching of tents, tent poles, pins, mallets, shovels, and pickaxes from the Tower		1	5	0
7 waggons for carrying the baggage of 7 companies from London to Kingston; one for ammunition, and one for the quarter-master, adjutant, and surgeon; in all 9 waggons	12	5	8	0
Ditto from Kingston to Darking, Godalmin, Petersfield, Fareham, and Stokes Bay	69	31	1	0
To the hoys for carrying 415 men from Stokes Bay to the Isle of Wight, at 6d. p. man		10	7	6
For boats to carry men and baggage on board and out of the hoys		2	2	0
From Cowes to the camp	4	1	16	0
To the hoys for carrying baggage, ammunition, and surgeon's chest		4	10	0
Fire and candle for the guard on their march		5	10	0
For 80 kettles, at 2s. 6d. each		10	0	0
For 392 flasks for water, at 2s. each		24	10	0
For 84 hatchets, at 2s. each		8	8	0
Lines for marking the ground in camp		0	12	0
7 camp colours for the battalion, at 15s. each		5	5	0
		110	14	6
Deduct in the articles for kettles, water-flasks, and hatchets		42	18	0
		£67	16	6

189.

One waggon only is allowed to two companies of a marching regiment, "but, out of respect to the regiments of Guards," one is allowed to each company. Dated 14th September, 1719.

190.

The Contingent Bill of Sir Tristram Dillington, Major of the Coldstream regiment of Foot Guards, in marching a battalion of the said regiment from the camp in the Isle of Wight, on the expedition to Vigo, and their return to London. Order dated Nov. 10th, 1719.

	Miles.	£.	s.	d.
For boats to bring the chevaux-de-frize on shore at Cowes		0	8	0
For a waggon to carry them to the camp		0	4	0
		£0	12	0

336   APPENDIX.

	£. s. d.
Brought forward	0 12 0
For seven waggons to carry the baggage of seven companies from the camp to Cowes; one for ammunition, and one for the quarter-master, adjutant, and surgeon's chest and baggage; in all 9 waggons . . 4 Miles	1 16 0
For boats to disembark the soldiers from on board the transports	1 15 6
For seven waggons to carry the baggage of seven comp^{as}; one for the qua^r-mast^r, adjutant, and surgeon, and one for the sick men, from Gosport to London 81	36 9 0
For fire and candle for the guard on their march .	5 10 0
	£46 2 6

191.

It is his Majesty's pleasure, that when and as often as you shall have due notice from Jno Jas. Heidegger, Esqr, of a Ball to be held at the King's Theatre in the Haymarket, you cause a detachm^t of one hundred private men, with non-commissioned officers proportionable, to be made from the three regiments of Foot Guards under your commands respectively, and march under the command of a lieutenant-colonel, captain, and ensign, to the said theatre, in order to do duty there during the continuance of the said ball, and to be aiding and assisting to the civil magistrates in the preservation of the peace, and prevent as much as possible all manner of drunkenness, rudeness, or indecencies, as well in words as in actions, by obliging those that are guilty of such misbehaviour to quit the place, and not to permit any person whatsoever to enter the said theatre in habits that may draw reflections upon the Church of England, or ridicule upon the same. And for so doing this shall be your warrant. Given at Whitehall, this 20th day of November, 1719. By his Maj^{tys} command,

GEO. TREBY.

To the Colonel of his Maj^{tys} three regiments of Foot Guards, or the officer-in-chief with the said regiments and detachment respectively.

192.

" Order for a Detachment of the Foot Guards to do duty at the King's
" Theatre in the Haymarket, every night an Opera is to be per-
" formed there."

It is his Majesty's pleasure, that when and as often as you shall have due notice from the directors of his Theatre in the Haymarket, of an Opera to be performed there, you cause a detachm^t of forty private men, and non-commission officers proportionable, to be made from the three regiments of Foot Guards under your commands respectively, and march under the command of a commission officer to the said theatre, in order to do duty there from time to time during the continuance of the said opera, and to be aiding and assisting to the civill magistrates in the preservation of the peace, and prevent as much as possible all manner of disorders that may happen there. Given at Whitehall, this 1st day of April, 1720.

By his Maj^{tys} command, GEO. TREBY.

To the Colonels of his Majesty's three regiments of Foot Guards, or to the officer-in-chief with the said regiments and detachment respectively.

193.

A State of his Majesty's Coldstream Reg^t of Foot Guards, as they appeared on Review, July 19, 1723.

Field offi^{rs} present, 2; capt^{ns}, 8; lieut^{ts}, 14; ensigns, 9; serj^{ts}, 49; corp^{ls}, 50; drum^{rs}, 36; effective private men, 858; men on duty, 40; sick, 41;—total, 939: wanting to complete, 15. Absent officers:—the lt.-col.; 1 major; 6 capt^{ns}; 6 l^{ts}; 7 ensigns. Memorandum. The above mentioned officers were absent either by leave or by sickness.—State-Paper Office.

194.

Return of the number of Ale-houses, Inns, Coffee-houses, and Brandy-shopps, belonging to the Burroughs of Southwark, liable to quarter soldiers, with the No. of Soldiers now quartered in each Parish, and Surplus Houses.—October 15th, 1723.

Parishes.		Number of Houses in each Parish.	Number of Soldiers' Quarters in each Parish.	Number of Surplus Houses.
St. George's		190	143	47
St. Saviour's		187	146	41
Christ Church		50	29	21
Lambeth		112	78	34
St. Olave's		193	107	86
St. Thomas's		15	11	4
Newington		76	57	19
7		823	571	252

Totall number of Houses . 823
,, of Men quartered . 571
,, Houses surplus . 252

Endorsed.—Return of the Coldstream Regiment Quartered in and about the Burrough of Southwark.—October 15th, 1723.

State-Paper Office.

195.

George R.—Warrant for regulating Clothing, dated St. James's, 20th Nov. 1729.

Size of the men for the Foot Guards to be 5 ft. 9 in.; marching reg^{ts} 5 ft. 8.

For a foot soldier:—A good full-bodied cloth coat, well lined, which may serve for the waistc^t the second year; a waistcoat; a p^r of good kersey breeches; a p^r of good strong shoes; two good shirts, and two good neckcloths; a good strong hat, well laced.

For the second year:—A good cloth coat, well lined, as the first year; a waistcoat made of the former year's coat; a pair of new kersey breeches; a pair of good strong stockings; a pair of good strong shoes; a good shirt, and a neckcloth; a good strong hat, well laced.

196.
13th June, 1735.

The officers (of the Coldstream) are to appear on Tuesday next, as at a Review, and to have on " twisted ramilyed wigs," according to the pattern which may be seen at the Tilt Yard to-morrow.

Coldstream Orderly-Room.

197.
18th June, 1735.

At the review by Lord Scarborough to-morrow, the men's pouches are to hang, as has been already shown them, with the fore-sling buckled under the sword-belt, which belt is to be on the outside of the coat, buckled tight, their coats pulled down so as to sit well and even, their hats to be well put on, and their hair tucked under, for no man will be suffered to wear a wig unless it is so like a head of hair as not to be perceived. Coldstream Orderly-Room.

198.

1735, October 29. The officers to mount all guards in their regimentals and gaiters during his Majesty's residence in town, and the serjeants to mount in their regimentals, the Tylt Yard guard as well as the King's. Coldstream Orderly-Room.

199.

1735. No soldier to pay above five shillings for a shirt, except it be ruffled at the bosom, and then sixpence more; two shillings for a pair of gaiters; five shillings for a pair of shoes; one shilling for a sword-scabbard; and sixpence for a bayonet-scabbard.

Coldstream Orderly-Room.

200.
11th April, 1736.

No centinel on any account to quit his arms, nor suffer any bench, chair, stone, or seat whatsoever, to be in his centry-box, nor drink or

APPENDIX. 339

smoke on his post, nor wear a night-cap when centry, but his hair under his hat, and every thing in good order.

Coldstream Orderly-Room.

201.

1737, July 6. At six o'clock to-morrow morning Colonel Pulteney will exercise the seven battalions, by the wave of the colours as usual, when the King sees them. The officers to appear in their new regimental clothes, gaiters, square-toed shoes, gorgets, sashes, buff-coloured gloves, regimental laced hats, cockades, the button worn on the left side, and twisted wigs according to the pattern. The men to appear perfecly clean and shaved, square-toed shoes, gaiters, their hats well cocked, and worn so low as to cover their foreheads, and raised behind, with their hair tucked well under and powdered, but none on their shoulders, the point of their hats pointing a little to the left, with cockades fixed under the loops as usual, their arms perfectly clean, the hilts of their swords and buckles of their accoutrements made as bright as possible. Coldstream Orderly-Room.

202.

1737, July 25th. The officers ordered with the detachment of the Coldstream to Hampton Court on Monday next to march in their blue frocks, regimental hats and wigs, and with their divisions, vizt. Lieut.-Colonels Parsons, Johnson, Needham; Captains Hodges, Corbett, Macro; Ensigns Lord Robert Manners, Rudyard, and Lord Robert Bertie. Coldstream Orderly-Room.

203.

1737, July 30th. Particular care to be taken that all the men for the Hampton Court party on Monday morning have good blue breeches on, because their clothes are to be looped up.

As often as any of the Royal Family pass by the encampment with guards or beef-eaters, all the men are to turn out between the bells of arms, with their swords on, hats well cock'd, &c., with their officers at their head. Coldstream Orderly-Room.

204.

1737, September 12th. It is his Majesty's commands, that none of the three regiments of Foot Guards take any notice of the Prince or Princess of Wales, or any of their family, till further orders.

Coldstream Orderly-Room.

205.

Order for Mourning for Her late Majesty.

1737, Nov. 26th. Every officer is to have a scarlet coat, buttoned to the waist with a mourning button, and faced with black cloth, no buttons on the sleeves or pockets, black cloth waistcoats and breeches, plain hats, no less than four inches in the brim, with crape hat-bands, an end appearing at each corner of the buttoned side of the hat, mourning swords and buckles; and to get crape for their sashes: to be all ready by Sunday se'nnight, the 4th of December; and the following officers must not fail to have theirs ready on any account whatever: Lieut.-Colonels Legge, Braddock, Needham; Captains Corbett, Milner, Williamson; Ensigns Stanhope, Gansell, and Rudyard.

Coldstream Orderly-Room.

206.

Dress of the Coldstream Guards in the year 1742.

Hat:—cocked very low, with white lace round the edge, and a small flat black cockade on the left side. The hair very full, and low down on the side of the face to cover the ear on both sides.

Coat:—scarlet, with pale-blue lappels, fastened back with twelve white loops and buttons; likewise one button on the shoulder to keep the lappels back. An edging of white lace round the outside of the lappels. The coat open down to the bottom of the waist, and then fastened with three buttons. The skirts of the coat cut large, coming round nearly to cover the thigh; four lace loops on the skirts, nearly in front of the thigh, with the points facing inward and outward, with four buttons in the middle of lace loops. The skirt turned back with pale-blue, edged with white lace, and hooked back. From the point at the extremity of the skirt, a button and loop of white lace. The whole length of skirt of coat to reach the knee. The sleeve scarlet, with a large pale-blue flap facing inward, and two white laces round it, and shewing blue between five buttons put on the sleeve outside the white lace, the buttons being on the scarlet. The sleeves very short, and the flap coming nearly up to the elbow.

Waistcoat:—scarlet, left open down to the waist, with six small buttons on the right side, the waistcoat cut long, and square at bottom, shewing on the thigh when the turnback of the coat is buttoned back. The bottom of the waistcoat edged with white lace.

Breeches:—pale-blue, with white gaiters coming above the knee, and fastened with a buff strap under the knee with a buckle, and a white strap under the shoe.

Pouch-belt:—buff, worn over the shoulder, yellow buckle, with black pouch to hang very long on the right side, nearly on the front of the thigh.

Waist-belt:—buff leather, with gilt buckle in front, and double frog on the left side to carry the sword and bayonet, the frog placed forward so as to allow the sword and bayonet to be carried nearly on the front of the thigh, to correspond with the pouch on the other side. A pricker and brush attached to pouch-belt, and hanging below the waist-belt. Gun-slings of buff.

The shirt worn full fronted, with white stock, shewing no collar.

[Description is taken from a book of coloured prints containing the uniforms of every cavalry and infantry regiment, published 1742.]

207.

1745, September 3rd. The men ordered not to pull off their hats when they pass an officer, or speak to them, but only to clap up their hands to their hats and bow as they pass by.

Coldstream Orderly-Room.

208.

1745, September 9. It is the General's (Folliott) positive order, that no Irishman nor Papist be entertained in any of the four battalions of Guards. (The other three battalions abroad.)

Coldstream Orderly-Room.

209.

1745, September 21. Instructions to officers recruiting: No Scotch, Irish, or vagabond, will be approved of.

Coldstream Orderly-Room.

210.

1745, October 9. When the Venetian Ambassador makes his public entry to-morrow at Kensington, the King's guard is to pay him the same compliment as his Majesty, both in going and returning from Court. Coldstream Orderly-Room.

211.

1745, October 25th. If the militia are reviewed to-morrow by his Majesty, the soldiers of the three regiments of Guards are to behave civilly, and not to laugh or make any game of them.

Coldstream Orderly-Room.

212.

It is his Majesty's pleasure that you cause two of the seven battalions belonging to three regiments of Foot Guards under your command, in London, to march from hence on Saturday next the 23rd instant, according to the route annexed, to Litchfield, there to remain until further order. Wherein, &c. Given at the War-Office, this 21st day of November, 1745.

By his Majesty's command,   WM. YONGE.

To the Field-Officer in Staff waiting for his Majesty's
    three regiments of Foot Guards.

Route for two battalions belonging to his Majesty's three regiments of Foot Guards, from London to Litchfield:—23rd November, Barnet and Whetstone; 24th, St. Albans; 25th, Dunstable, halt there the 26th; 27th, Fenny Stratford and Stony Stratford; 28th, Towcester; 29th, Daventry, halt there the 30th; 1st December, Coventry; 2nd, Coleshill; 3rd, Litchfield, there to remain until further order,

WM. YONGE.

It is his Majesty's pleasure that you cause the commission, non-commission officers, and private men, belonging to the two battalions of Foot Guards, ordered to the camp near Litchfield, remaining in London, to march forthwith from hence to Litchfield, there to join or follow the companies to which they belong. Wherein, &c. Given at the War-Office, this 23rd of November, 1745.

By his Majesty's command,

In the absence of the Secretary at War,   EDW. LLOYD.

To the Field-Officer in Staff waiting for
    the three regiments of Foot Guards.

Route of a Detachment belonging to his Majesty's three regiments of Foot Guards, from London to Litchfield (to halt every fourth day, &c.):—Barnet, St. Albans, Dunstable, Fenny Stratford, Towcester, Daventry, Coventry, Coleshill, Litchfield, there to join or follow the regiment.   In the absence of the Secretary at War,

EDW. LLOYD.

213.

It is his Majesty's pleasure that you cause the first battalion of the Second regiment of Foot Guards under your command in London, to march from hence to-morrow morning, being the 25th instant, according to the route annexed, to Nottingham, there to remain until further order. Wherein, &c. Given at the War-Office, this 24th day of November, 1745.   By his Majesty's command,

In the absence of the Secretary at War,   EDW. LLOYD.

To the Field-Officer in Staff waiting for his Majesty's
    three regiments of Foot Guards.

Route:—25th November, Barnet; 26th, St. Albans; 27th, Dunstable, halt there the 28th; 29th, Newport Pagnel; 30th, Northampton; 1st December, Harborough, halt there the 2nd; 3rd, Leicester; 4th, Loughborough; 5th, Nottingham, there to remain until further order.   In the absence of the Secretary at War,

EDW. LLOYD.

214.

It is his Majesty's pleasure that, notwithstanding any former order to the contrary, you cause the first battalion of the Second regiment of Foot Guards, upon their arrival under your command at Northamp-

ton, to march from thence on Sunday the 1st of December next, according to the route annexed, to Litchfield, there to remain until further order. Wherein, &c. Given at the War-Office, this 26th day of November, 1745. By his Majesty's command,
WM. YONGE.

To the Officer commanding in chief the first battalion of
the Second regiment of Foot Guards, upon their arrival
at Northampton.

Route for the first battalion of the Second regiment of Foot Guards from Northampton to Litchfield:—1st December, Daventry, halt there the 2nd; 3rd, Coventry; 4th, camp near Litchfield.
WM. YONGE.

215.

It is his Majesty's pleasure that you cause an officer, with a proper guard, to escort the baggage belonging to the first battalion of the Coldstream regiment of Foot Guards, from London, according to the route annexed, to Litchfield, where they are to join or follow the battalion. Wherein, &c. Given at the War-Office, this 26th day of November, 1745. By his Majesty's command,
WM. YONGE.

To the Field-Officer in Staff waiting for his Majesty's
three regiments of Foot Guards.

Route for an officer and the escort with the baggage belonging to the first battalion of the Coldstream regiment of Foot Guards, from London to Litchfield, (to rest every fourth day on their march, if there shall be occasion):—Barnet, St. Albans, Dunstable, Stony Stratford, Towcester, Daventry, Coventry, Coleshill, Litchfield, there to join or follow the battalion. WM. YONGE.

216.

$174\frac{5}{6}$, January 12th. It is Colonel Bockland's order, that all officers (on whatever guard soever) appear in white gaiters, and stiff-topt buff-colour'd gloves. Coldstream Orderly-Room.

217.

1746, June 24. A guard ordered to mount over the rebel prisoners at the Angel Inn, Piccadilly. Coldstream Orderly-Room.

218.

1746, August 15th. Detachments from the regiments of Guards, amounting to 1000 men, to attend the execution of the Earl of Kilmarnock and Lord Balmerino, on Monday next.
Coldstream Orderly-Room.

219.

Contingent Bill of the second battalion of the Coldstream regiment of Foot Guards, on the Expedition under the command of Major-General Fuller, for cash expended on account of the said battalion, repairing of arms, and to compleat camp necessaries lost and damaged in the said Expedition, 1746.

1746.		£.	s.	d.
Sep. 10.	Paid for barges to carry the battalion from Tower Wharf to Woolwich, to be embarked on board the transports	25	12	6
	Paid for carriage of camp necessaries, &c. to Whitehall	1	4	6
	Paid for hoys for carriage of camp necessaries, &c. to Woolwich	4	13	0
	Paid for camp lines at Plymouth	1	11	6
Oct. 31.	Paid for hoys to bring baggage from Deptford to Whitehall	3	3	0
	Paid for carriage of baggage to the store-room	0	16	0
	Paid for a covered barge to bring sick men from Deptford	2	5	0
	Paid for waterage for Serjeant-Major and Quar^r-Mas^r-Serjeant to attend the commanding officer	0	19	0
	Paid for making and mending barrells to put the powder and ball, received at Plymouth, and made into cartridges by Major-Genl Fuller's order, since opened to preserve	1	16	0
	For horses to Woolwich and back again, to examine the transports, by the Duke's order	0	12	0
		£42	12	6

Oct. Lost and damaged in a storm off Dungeness, October 23rd, viz.:

	£	s.	d.
To repairing arms	7	14	6
To 104 knapsacks at 2s. 6d. each	13	0	0
To 145 haversacks at 1s. each	7	5	0
To 33 hatchets at 2s. each	3	6	0
To 126 kettles with baggs at 3s. each	18	18	0
To 711 water-flasks with strings at 1s. 6d. each	53	6	6
	£146	2	6
Poundage of this bill	7	13	10
	£153	16	4

CHARLES RUSSELL, 2nd Major.

WM. EVELYN, Q^r-Mast^r.

220.

1746, November 27th. A detachment ordered to attend at the execution of the rebels, to-morrow.   Coldstream Orderly-Room.

221.

$174\frac{6}{7}$, 3rd February. No soldier will be permitted to wear a wig after the 25th of March next.

7th June, 1747. Ordered that the officers for the future do always mount guard with queue wigs, or their own hair done in the same manner.

21st Aug^t, 1747. Any men who cannot wear their hair, through age or infirmity, are to provide themselves with wigs made to turn up like the hair, which they are to wear on mounting days.
   Coldstream Orderly-Room.

222.

1747, April 7th. A detachment ordered to attend the execution of Lord Lovat, on the 9th instant.   Coldstream Orderly-Room.

223.

1747, June 15. All men whose hair is long enough to tuck up under their hats, to be done so for the future.   Coldstream Orderly-Room.

224.

1748, 25th May. It is Lord Dunbarton's order, that when a Quorum of Lords Justices are together, (any four of them being such,) the Foot Guards, on whatever duty, are to beat a march, rest their arms, and the officers salute with their spontoons, in the same manner as if his Majesty was present, with this difference, that the ensigns do not drop the colours.   Coldstream Orderly-Room.

225.

1749, February 27. Lord Albemarle orders, that all those men who have bad breeches be immediately furnished with red ones, made out of the remnants of last clothing.   Coldstream Orderly-Room.

226.

1749, March 10. The men ordered to be provided with brown cloth gaiters with black buttons, made in the same manner as the white ones. The brown gaiters to be worn only on detachments and outparties.   Coldstream Orderly-Room.

227.

1749, June 27. The officers to wear boots when the men wear brown gaiters.   Coldstream Orderly-Room.

228.

1749, July 4. Officers when on duty to wear buff-coloured waistcoats and breeches.   Coldstream Orderly-Room.

229.

Warrant regulating the Standards, Colours, Clothing, &c^a. and Rank or Number of Regiments of Cavalry and Infantry. Dated 1st July, 1751.

George R.—Our will and pleasure is, that the following regulations for the colours, cloathing, &c^a, of our marching regiments of Foot, and for the uniform cloathing of our cavalry, their standards, guidons, banners, &c^a, be duly observed and put in execution, at such times as these particulars are or shall be furnished, vizt:

Regulation for the colours, cloathing, &c^a, of the marching regiments of Foot.

No colonel to put his arms, crest, device, or livery, on any part of the appointments of the regiment under his command.

No part of the cloathing or ornaments of the regiments to be altered after the following regulations are put in execution, but by us, or our Captain-General's permission.

COLOURS.

The King's, or first colour of every regiment, is to be the great Union throughout.

The second colour to be the colour of the faceing of the regiment, with the Union in the upper canton; except those regiments which are faced with red or white, whose second colour is to be the red Cross of St. George in a white field, and the Union in the upper canton.

In the centre of each colour is to be painted or embroidered, in gold Roman characters, the number of the rank of the regiment within a wreath of roses and thistles, on the same stalk, except those regiments which are allowed to wear any royal devices, or ancient badges, on whose colours the rank of the regiment is to be painted towards the upper corner.

The size of the colours, and the length of the pike, to be the same as those of the royal regiments of Foot Guards.

The cords and tassels of all colours, to be crimson and gold mixed.

DRUMMERS' CLOATHING.

The drummers of all the royal regiments are allowed to wear the royal livery, vizt: red, lined, faced, and lapelled on the breast with blue, and laced with a royal lace.

The drummers of all the other regiments are to be cloathed with the colour of the faceing of their regiments, lined, faced, and lapelled on the breast with red, and laced in such manner as the colonel shall think fit for distinction sake, the lace however being of the colours of that on the soldiers' coats.

GRENADIERS' CAPS.

The front of the grenadiers' caps to be the same colour as the faceing

APPENDIX. 347

of the regiment, with the King's cypher embroidered, and crown over it; the little flap to the red, with the White Horse and motto over it, 'Nec aspera terrent;' the back part of the cap to be red; the turn-up to be the colour of the front, with the number of the regiment in the middle part behind. The royal regiments, and the six old corps, differ from the foregoing rule, as specified hereafter.

DRUMS.

The front or fore part of the drums to be painted with the colour of the faceing of the regiment, with the King's cypher and crown, and the number of the regiment under it.

BELLS OF ARMS.

The bells of arms to be painted in the same manner.

CAMP COLOURS.

The camp colours to be square, and of the colour of the faceing of the regiment, with the number of the regiment upon them.

Devices and Badges of the Royal Regiments, and of the Six Old Corps.

FIRST REGIMENT, OR, THE ROYAL REGIMENT.

In the centre of their colours, the King's cypher, within the circle of St. Andrew, and crown over it; in the three corners of the second colour, the Thistle and Crown. The distinction of the colours of the second battalion, is a flaming ray of gold descending from the upper corner of each colour towards the centre.

On the grenadier caps, the same device as in the centre of the colours, White Horse, and the King's motto over it, on the little flap.

The drums and bells of arms to have the same device painted on them, with the number or rank of the regiment under it.

SECOND REGIMENT, OR, THE QUEEN'S ROYAL REGIMENT.

In the centre of each colour, the Queen's cypher on a red ground, within the garter, and crown over it: in the three corners of the second colour, the Lamb, being the ancient badge of the regiment.

On the grenadier caps, the Queen's cypher and crown as in the colours, White Horse and motto, ' Nec aspera terrent,' on the flap.

The drums and bells of arms to have the Queen's cypher painted on them in the same manner, and the rank of the regiment underneath.

THIRD REGIMENT, OR, THE BUFFS.

In the centre of their colours, the Dragon, being the ancient badge, and the Rose and Crown in the three corners of their second colour.

On the grenadier caps, the Dragon; White Horse and King's motto on the flap.

The same badge of the Dragon to be painted on their drums and bells of arms, with the rank of the regiment underneath.

FOURTH REGIMENT, OR, THE KING'S OWN ROYAL REGIMENT.

In the centre of their colours the King's cypher on a red ground within the garter, and crown over it: in the three corners of their second colour the Lion of England, being their ancient badge.

On the grenadier caps the King's cypher, as on the colours, and crown over it; White Horse and motto on the flap.

The drums and bells of arms to have the King's cypher painted on them, in the same manner, and the rank of the regiment underneath.

FIFTH REGIMENT.

In the centre of their colours, St. George killing the Dragon, being their ancient badge, and in the three corners of their second colour the Rose and Crown.

On the grenadier caps, St. George killing the Dragon; the White Horse and motto, 'Nec aspera terrent,' over it on the flap.

The same badge of St. George and the Dragon to be painted on their drums, and bells of arms, with the rank of the regiment underneath.

SIXTH REGIMENT.

In the centre of their colours, the Antelope, being their ancient badge, and in the three corners of their second colour the Rose and Crown.

On the grenadier caps, the Antelope, as in the colours; White Horse and motto on the flap.

The same badge of the Antelope to be painted on their drums and bells of arms, with the rank of the regiment underneath.

SEVENTH REGIMENT, OR, THE ROYAL FUZILIERS.

In the centre of their colours, the Rose within the Garter and the Crown over it; the White Horse in the corners of the second colour.

On the grenadier caps, the Rose within the Garter, and Crown, as in the colours; White Horse and motto over it, 'Nec aspera terrent,' on the flap.

The same device of the Rose within the Garter, and Crown, on their drums and bells of arms, rank of the regiment underneath.

EIGHTH REGIMENT, OR, THE KING'S REGIMENT..

In the centre of their colours, the White Horse on a red ground within the Garter, and Crown over it: in the three corners of the second colour, the King's cypher and crown.

On the grenadier caps, the White Horse, as on the colours; the White Horse and motto, 'Nec aspera terrent,' on the flap.

The same device of the White Horse within the Garter, on the drums and bells of arms; rank of the regiment underneath.

EIGHTEENTH REGIMENT, OR, THE ROYAL IRISH.

In the centre of their colours, the Harp in a blue field, and the

APPENDIX. 349

Crown over it, and in the three corners of their second colour, the Lion of Nassau, King William the Third's arms.

On the grenadier caps, the Harp and Crown as on the colours, White horse and motto on the flap.

The Harp and Crown to be painted in the same manner on the drums and bells of arms, with the rank of the regiment underneath.

TWENTY-FIRST REGIMENT, OR, THE ROYAL NORTH BRITISH FUZILIERS.

In the centre of their colours, the Thistle within the circle of St. Andrew, and Crown over it; and in the three corners of the second colour, the King's cypher and crown.

On the grenadier caps, the Thistle, as on the colours; White Horse and motto over it, 'Nec aspera terrent,' on the flap.

On the drums and bells of arms, the Thistle and Crown to be painted, as on the colours, rank of the regiment underneath.

TWENTY-THIRD, OR, THE ROYAL WELCH FUZILIERS.

In the centre of their colours, the device of the Prince of Wales, vizt. Three Feathers issuing out of the Prince's coronet: in the three corners of the second colour, the badges of Edward the Black Prince, vizt. Rising Sun, Red Dragon, and the Three Feathers in the coronet; motto, 'Ich dien.'

On the grenadier caps, the Feathers as in the colours, White Horse and motto, 'Nec aspera terrent,' on the flap.

The same badge of the Three Feathers and motto, 'Ich dien,' on the drums and bells of arms; rank of the regiment underneath.

TWENTY-SEVENTH, OR, THE INNISKILLING REGIMENT.

Allowed to wear in the centre of their colours a Castle with three Turretts, St. George's colours flying, in a blue field, and the name 'Inniskilling' over it.

On the grenadier caps, the Castle and name, as on the colours: White Horse and King's motto on the flap.

The same badge of the Castle and name on the drums and bells of arms, rank of the regiment underneath.

FORTY-FIRST REGIMENT, OR, THE INVALIDS.

In the centre of their colours, the Rose and Thistle on a red ground within the Garter, and Crown over it: in the three corners of the second colour the King's cypher and crown.

On the grenadier caps, drums and bells of arms, the same device of the Rose and Thistle conjoined, within the Garter, and Crown, as on the colours.

HIGHLAND REGIMENT.

The grenadiers of the Highland regiment are allowed to wear bearskin fur caps, with the King's cypher and crown over it, on a red ground, in the turn-up or flap.

350   APPENDIX.

GENERAL VIEW OF THE FACEINGS OF THE SEVERAL MARCHING REGIMENTS OF FOOT.

Colour of the Facings.	Rank and Title of the Regiments.	Distinctions in the same colour.	Names of the present Colonels.
Blue	1st, or the Royal Regiment	. . .	Lieut.-Gen. St. Clair
	4th, or the King's Own Regt.	. . .	Col. Rich
	7th, or the Royal Fuziliers	. . .	Col. Mostyn
	8th, or the King's Regiment	. . .	Lieut.-Gen. Wolfe
	18th, or the Royal Irish	. . .	Col. Folliot
	21st or the Royal North British Fuziliers	. . .	Lieut.-Gen. Campbell
	23rd, or the Royal Welch Fuziliers	. . .	Lieut.-Gen. Huske
	41st, or the Invalids	. . .	Col. Wardour
Green	2nd, or the Queen's Rl. Regt.	Sea green	Major-Gen. Fowke
	5th Regiment	Gosling green	Lieutt.-Gen. Irvine
	11th Regiment	Full green	Col. Bockland
	19th Regiment	Yellowish grn.	Col. Lord G. Beauclerk
	24th Regt. (lined with white)	Willow green	Col. Earl of Ancram
	36th Regiment	. . .	Col. Lord R. Manners
	39th Regiment	. . .	Brigadier Richbell
	45th Regiment	Deep green	Col. Warburton
	49th Regiment	Full green	Col. Trelawny
Buff	3rd Regiment, or the Buffs	. . .	Col. Howard
	14th Regiment	. . .	Col. Herbert
	22nd Regiment	Pale buff	Brigadier O'Farrell
	27th, or the Inniskilling Regt.	. . .	Lieut.-Gen. Blakeney
	31st Regiment	. . .	Col. Holmes
	40th Regiment	. . .	Col. Cornwallis
	42nd Regiment	. . .	Col. Lord John Murray
	48th Regiment	. . .	Col. Earl of Home
White	17th Regiment	Greyish white	Lieut.-Gen. Wynyard
	32nd Regiment	. . .	Col. Leighton
	43rd Regiment	. . .	Col. Kennedy
	47th Regiment	. . .	Col. Lascelles
Red	33rd Regt. (white lining)	. . .	Lieut.-Gen. Johnson
Orange	35th Regiment	. . .	Lieut.-Gen. Otway
Yellow	6th Regiment	Deep yellow	Lieut.-Gen. Guise
	9th Regiment	. . .	Col. Waldegrave
	10th Regiment	Bright yellow	Col. Pole
	12th Regiment	. . .	Lieut.-Gen. Skelton
	13th Regiment	Philemot yelw.	Lieut.-Gen. Pulteney
	15th Regiment	. . .	Col. Jordan
	16th Regiment	. . .	Lieut.-Gen. Handasyde
	20th Regiment	Pale yellow	Col. Lord Visct. Bury
	25th Regiment	Deep yellow	Col. Earl of Panmure
	26th Regiment	Pale yellow	Lieut.-Gen. Anstruther
	28th Regiment	Bright yellow	Lieut.-Gen. Bragg
	29th Regiment	. . .	Col. Hopson
	30th Regiment	Pale yellow	Col. Earl of Loudon
	34th Regiment	Bright yellow	Col. Conway
	37th Regiment	. . .	Col. Dejean
	38th Regiment	. . .	Col. Duroure
	44th Regiment	. . .	Col. Sir P. Halket, Bart.
	46th Regiment	. . .	Col. Murray
Red with Blue Coats	Royal Regiment of Artillery	. . .	Col. Belford

ABSTRACT OF THE FOREGOING.

With Blue, 8 regiments; Green, 9 regiments; Buff, 8 regiments; Yellow, 18 regiments; White, 4 regiments; Red, 1 regiment; Orange, 1 regiment; Blue with Red, 1 regiment;—In all 50 regiments.

Regulation for the uniform cloathing of the cavalry, their standards, guidons, banners, housings, and holster-caps, drums, bells of arms, and camp colours.

STANDARDS AND GUIDONS.

The standards and guidons of the Dragoon Guards, and the standards of the regiments of Horse, to be of damask, embroidered and fringed with gold or silver; the guidons of the regiments of Dragoons to be of silk, the tassels and cords of the whole to be of crimson-silk and gold mixed; the size of the guidons and standards, and the length of the lance, to be the same as those of the Horse and Horse Grenadier Guards.

The King's or first standard, or guidon of each regiment, to be crimson with the Rose and Thistle conjoined, and Crown over them; in the centre, his Majesty's motto; ' Dieu et mon Droit,' underneath; the White Horse in a compartment, in the first and fourth corner; and the rank of the regiment, in gold or silver characters, on a ground of the same colour as the faceing of the regiment, in a compartment in the second and third corners.

The second and third standard, or guidon of each corps, to be of the colour of the faceing of the regiment, with the badge of the regiment in the centre, or the rank of the regiment in gold or silver Roman characters, on a crimson ground, within a wreath of Roses and Thistles on the same stalk, the motto of the regiment underneath; the White Horse on a red ground to be in the first and fourth compartments, and the Rose and Thistle conjoined upon a red ground in the second and third compartments.

The distinction of the third standard or guidon, to be a figure 3, on a circular ground of red, underneath the motto.

Those corps which have any particular badge, are to carry it in the centre of their second and third standard or guidon, with the rank of the regiment on a red ground, within a small wreath of Roses and Thistles, in the second and third corners.

BANNERS.

The banners of the kettle drums and trumpets to be the colour of the faceing of the regiment with the badge of the regiment, or its rank, in the centre of the banner of the kettle drums, as on the second standard; the King's cypher and crown to be on the banners of the trumpets, with the rank of the regiment in figures underneath.

DRUMS.

The drums of the Dragoon Guards and Dragoons to be of brass, the front or forepart to be painted with the colour of the facing of the regiment, upon which is to be the badge or rank of the regiment, as in the second guidon.

BELLS OF ARMS.

The bells of arms to be painted in the same manner as on the drums.

CAMP COLOURS.

The camp colours to be of the colour of the faceing of the regiment, with the rank of the regiment in the centre; those of the Horse to be square, and those of the Dragoon Guards, or Dragoons, to be swallow-tailed.

CLOTHING OF THE REGIMENTS; DISTINCTION OF THE SERJEANTS AND CORPORALS; CLOATHING OF THE KETTLE DRUMMERS, TRUMPETTERS, DRUMMERS, AND HAUTBOIS; DRUMMERS' CAPS.

The coats of the Dragoon Guards to be lapelled to the waist with the colour of the regiment, and lined with the same colour; slit sleeves, turned up with the colour of the lapell.

The coats of the Horse to be lapelled to the bottom with the colour of the regiment, and lined with the same colour (except the fourth regiment of Horse, whose facings are black, and the lining buff colour); small square cuffs of the colour of the lapell.

The coats of the Dragoons to be without lapells, double-breasted; slit sleeves, turned up with the colour of the facings of the regiments, the lining of the same colour.

The whole to have long pockets; the button-holes to be of a very narrow yellow or white lace, as hereafter specified, and set on two and two, or three and three, for distinction sake: the shoulder-knots of the dragoon regiments to be of yellow or white worsted, and worn on the right shoulder. The waistcoats and breeches to be of the colour of the facings, except those of the fourth regiment of Horse, which are buff colour.

The serjeants of the Dragoon Guards and Dragoons to be distinguished by a narrow gold or silver lace on the lapells, turn-up of the sleeves and pockets, and to have gold or silver shoulder-knots: the corporals of Horse, by a narrow gold or silver lace on the lapells, cuffs, pockets, and shoulder-straps; the corporals of Dragoon Guards and Dragoons by a narrow silver or gold lace on the turn-up of the sleeves and shoulder-strap, and to have yellow or white silk shoulder-knots.

The kettle drummers, trumpetters, drummers and hautbois coats to be of the colour of the facing of the regiment, lined and turned up with red, (except the royal regiments, which are allowed to wear the royal livery, viz. red, lined, and turned up with blue, blue waistcoats and breeches,) and laced with the same coloured lace as that on the housings and holster caps, red waistcoats and breeches. The drummers and hautbois of the Dragoon Guards, and the kettle drummers, and trumpetters of the Horse to have long hanging sleeves, fastened at the waist.

The caps of the drummers to be such as those of the Infantry, with the tassel hanging behind; the front to be of the colour of their facing, with the particular badge of the regiment embroidered on it, or a trophy of guidons and drums; the little flap to be red, with the White Horse and motto over it—' Nec aspera terrent;' the back part of the cap to be red likewise; the turn-up to be the colour of the front; and in the middle part of it behind, a drum, and the rank of the regiment.

HATS AND CAPS OF THE CAVALRY.

The hats to be laced with gold or silver lace, and to have black cockades.

The Royal North British Dragoons only, to wear caps instead of hats, which caps are to be of the same form as those of the Horse Grenadier Guards; the front blue, with the same badge as on the second guidon of the regiment; the flap red, with the White Horse and motto over it—' Nec aspera terrent ;' the back part to be red, and the turn-up blue, with a Thistle embroidered between the letters II. D., being the rank of the regiment. The watering or forage-caps of the Cavalry to be red, turned up with the colour of the facing, and the rank of the regiment on the little flap.

CLOAKS.

The cloaks to be red, lined as the coats, and the buttons set on at top, in the same manner, upon frogs, or loops of the same colours as the lace on the housings, the capes to be the colour of the facings.

HOUSINGS AND HOLSTER CAPS.

The housings and holster caps to be of the colour of the facing of the regiment, (except the First Regiment or King's Dragoon Guards, and the Royal Dragoons, whose housings are red, and the Fourth regiment of Horse, whose housings are buff colour,) laced with one broad white or yellow worsted, or mohair lace, with a stripe in the middle of one-third of the whole breadth, as hereafter specified. The rank of the regiment to be embroidered on the housings upon a red ground, within a wreath of roses and thistles, or the particular badge of the regiment, as on the second guidon or standard: the King's cypher with the Crown over it to be embroidered on the holster caps, and under the cypher the number or rank of the regiment.

UNIFORM OF THE OFFICERS, &c[a].

The clothing or uniform of the officers, to be made up in the same manner as those of the men, laced, lapelled, and turned up with the colour of the facing, and a narrow gold or silver lace or embroidery to the binding and button-holes, the buttons being set on in the same manner as on the men's coats; the waistcoats and breeches being likewise of the same colour as those of the men.

The housings and (holster) caps of the officers to be of the colour of the facing of the regiment, laced with one gold or silver lace, and a stripe of velvet in the middle, of the colour of that on the men's.

The standard belts to be the colour of the facing of the regiment, and laced as the housings.

Their sashes to be of crimson silk, and worn over the left shoulder.

Their sword-knots to be crimson and gold in stripes, as those of the Infantry.

QUARTER-MASTERS.

The Quarter-Masters to wear crimson sashes round ther waists.

SERJEANTS.

The Serjeants to wear pouches as the men do, and a worsted sash about their waist, of the colour of the facing of the regiment and of the stripes on the lace of the housings.

APPENDIX.

GENERAL VIEW OF THE DIFFERENCES AND DISTINCTIONS DRUMMERS' CLOATHING, HORSE

Colour of the several Facings.	Regiments. Ranks and Titles of the several corps of Dragoon Guards, Horse and Dragoons.	Cloathing of the Serjeants, Corporals, and Private Men.				Cloathing of the Drummers, Trumpeters, and Hautbois.		
		Colour of the Facings and Lapells.	Colour of the Button-holes and how the Buttons are set on.	Colour of Waist-coats and Breeches.	Hat Lace.	Colour, Facing, and Lining of the Coats.	Colr. of Waist-coats & Breeches.	Colours of the Lace on the Clothes of the Drummers, Trumpeters, &c.
Blue	1st, or King's Regiment of Dragn. Gds.	blue, with half lapells	yellow 2 & 2	blue	gold	red with blue	blue	royal lace, yellow and blue
	1st Horse	pale blue, lapelled	white. 2 and 2	pale blue	silver	pale blue w. red	red	white, with a red stripe
	1st or Royal Dragoons	blue, without lapells	yellw. 2 and 2	blue	gold	red with blue	blue	royal lace
	2nd or Royal North British Dragns.	ditto ditto	white. 2 and 2	blue	none	red with blue	blue	royal lace
	3rd or King's Own Regt. of Dragoons	light blue, ditto	yellw. 3 and 3	light blue	gold	red with blue	blue	royal lace
	5th, or Royal Irish Dns.	blue, ditto	white. 3 and 3	blue	silver	red with blue	blue	royal lace
Yellow	3rd Regt. of Horse, or the Carabineers	pale yellow, lapelled	white. 2 and 2	pale yelw	silver	pale yellow with red	red	white, with a red stripe
	6th, or the Inniskilling Dragoons	full yellow, without lapells	white. 2 and 2	full yelw	silver	full yellow with red	red	white, with a blue stripe
	8th Regt. of Dragoons	yellow, ditto	white. 3 and 3	yellow	silver	yellow with red	red	white, with a yellow stripe
	10th Regt. of Dragoons	deep yellow, ditto	white. 3, 4, & 5	deep yelw	silver	deep yellw. with red	red	white, with a green stripe
	14th Regt. of Dragoons	lemon colour, ditto	white. 3 and 3	lemon colr.	silver	lemon colr. with red	red	white, with red & green stripe
Buff and Black	2d, or Queen's Regt. of Dn. Guards	buff colr. with half lapells	yellw. 3 and 3	buff colr.	gold	red with blue	blue	royal lace, yellw. & blue
	4th Regt. of Horse	black, lapelled	yellw. 2 and 2	buff colr.	gold	buff colr. with red	red	white, with a black stripe
	9th Regt. of Dragoons	buff colr. wt. lapells	white. 2 and 2	buff colr.	silver	buff colr. with red	red	white, with a blue stripe
	11th Regt. of Dragoons	buff colour, do.	white. 3 and 3	buff colr.	silver	buff colr. with red	red	white, with a green stripe
White	3rd Regt. of Dn. Gds.	white, with half lapells	yellw. 2 and 2	white	gold	white with red	red	yellow, w. a red stripe
	7th, or the Queen's Rt. of Dragoons	white, without lapells	white. 3 and 3	white	silver	red with blue	blue	royal lace, yellow and blue
	12th Regt. of Dragoons	ditto, ditto	white. 2 and 2	white	silver	white with red	red	yellow, w. a green stripe
Green	2nd Regt. of Horse	full green, lapelled	yellw. 2 and 2	full grn.	gold	full green with red	red	white, with a red stripe
	4th Regt. of Dragoons	green, without lapells	white. 2 and 2	green	silver	green with red	red	white, with a blue stripe
	13th Regt. of Dragoons	light green, ditto	yellw. 3 and 3	light grn.	gold	light green with red	red	white, with a yellow stripe

Given at Our Court at Kensington, this 1st day of July, 1751.

APPENDIX.

OF THE SEVERAL CORPS OF CAVALRY, IN THE CLOATHING, FURNITURE, AND STANDARDS.

	Housings and Holster Caps.			Standards and Guidons.				
Colour of the Housings and Holster Caps.	Colours of the Lace on the Housings and Holster Caps.	Badge or Device on the Housings and Holster Caps.	Colour of the 2d and 3d Standard or Guidon.	Embroidery on the Three Standards.	Fringe on the Three Standards or Guidons.	Badge or Device on the Second and Third Standard or Guidon.	Motto on the Second and Third Standard or Guidon.
red	royal lace	King's Cypher within the Garter and Crown	blue	gold	gold	King's Cypher within the Garter	. . .
pale blue	white & red stripe	Rank of the Regiment I. H.	pale blue	gold & silver	gold & silver	Rank of the Regiment I. H.	. . .
red	royal lace	Crest of England within the Garter	blue	gold	gold	Crest of England within the Garter	. . .
blue	royal lace	Thistle within the circle of St. Andrew	blue	gold & silver	gold & silver	Thistle within the circle of St. Andrew	Nemo me impune lacessit.
light blue	royal lace	White Horse within the Garter	light blue	gold	gold	White Horse within the Garter	Nec aspera terrent.
blue	royal lace	Harp and Crown	blue	gold & silver	gold & silver	Harp and Crown	. . .
pale yelw	white & red stripe	Rank of the Regt. III. H.	pale yelw	gold	gold	Rank of the Regiment III H.	. . .
full yelw	white and blue stripe	Castle of Inniskilling within a wreath	full yelw	silver	silver & blue	Castle of Inniskilling	. . .
yellow	white and yellow stripe	Rank of the Regt. VIII. D.	yellow	silver	silver & yelw.	Rank of the Regt. VIII. D.	. . .
deep yelw	white and green stripe	Rank of the Regt. X. D.	deep yelw	silver	silvr & green	Rank of the Regiment x. D.	. . .
lemon colr.	white, red, and green stripe	Rank of the Regt. XIV. D.	lemon colr.	silver	silver and red	Rank of the Regt. XIV. D.	. . .
buff colr.	royal lace	Queen's Cypher within the Garter	buff colr.	gold	gold	Queen's Cypher within the Garter	. . .
buff colr.	white and black stripe	Rank of the Regt. IV. H.	black	gold	gold & silver	Rank of the Regt. IV. H.	. . .
buff colr.	white and blue stripe	Rank of the Regt. IX. D.	buff colr.	silver	silver & blue	Rank of the Regt. IX. D.	. . .
buff colr.	white and green stripe	Rank of the Regt. XI. D.	buff colr.	silver	silvr & green	Rank of the Regt. XI. D.	. . .
white	yellow and red stripe	Rank of the Regt. III. D. G.	white	gold & silver	gold & silver	Rank of the Regt. III. D. G.	. . .
white	royal lace	Queen's Cypher within the Garter	white	gold	gold	Queen's Cypher within the Garter	. . .
white	yellow and green stripe	Rank of the Regt. XII. D.	white	silver	silvr & green	Rank of the Regt. XII. D.	. . .
full grn.	white and red stripe	Rank of the Regt. II. H.	full grn.	gold	gold	Rank of the Regiment II. H.	Vestigia nulla retrorsum.
green	white and blue stripe	Rank of the Regt. IV. D.	green	silver	silver & blue	Rank of the Regt. IV. D.	. . .
light grn.	white and yellow stripe	Rank of the Regt. XIII. D.	light grn.	silver	silver & yelw.	Rank of the Regt. XIII. D.	. . .

in the twenty-fifth year of Our Reign.

By His Majesty's Command,

H. FOX.

230.

1754, November 7. After Midsummer, the drum-majors' clothes shall belong to the regiment, and no drum-major hereafter to pay for them.   Coldstream Orderly-Room.

231.

It is his Majesty's pleasure that you cause the 1st battalion of the Coldstream regiment of Foot Guards, under your command, to march from their present quarters in two divisions, according to the routes [1] annexed, to the Isle of Wight, where they are to encamp and remain until further order. Wherein, &c^a. Given at the War-Office, this 15th day of April, 1758.   By his Majesty's command,
                                BARRINGTON.

To the R^t Honble Lieut.-Genl Lord Tyrawley, or officer commanding the Coldstream regiment of Foot Guards.

Route for the 1st division of the First battalion of the Coldstream regiment of Foot Guards, consisting of four companies, viz. :—

Monday	May 15th, Esher and Cobham.
Tuesday	„ 16th, Godalmin.
Wednesday	„ 17th, Midhurst.
Thursday	„ 18th, Halt.
Friday	„ 19th, Chichester.
Saturday	„ 20th, Portsmouth.
Sunday	„ 21st, Halt.
Monday	„ 22d, Encamp in the Isle of Wight.

                                  BARRINGTON.

Route for the 2nd division of the First battalion of the Coldstream regiment of Foot Guards, consisting of five companies, viz. :—

Tuesday	May 16th, Kingston.
Wednesday	„ 17th, Guilford.
Thursday	„ 18th, Halt.
Friday	„ 19th, Petersfield.
Saturday	„ 20th, Portsmouth.
Sunday	„ 21st, Halt.
Monday	„ 22d, Encamp in the Isle of Wight.

                                    BARRINGTON.

232.

It is his Majesty's pleasure that you cause the first battalion of the First regiment of Foot Guards, under your command, to march on Tuesday next, the 9th instant, according to the route annexed, to the Isle of Wight, where they are to encamp, and remain until further

---

[1] Cancelled by Route, dated 6th May 1758.

APPENDIX.

order. Wherein the civil Magistrates, and all others concerned, are to be assisting in providing quarters, impressing carriages, and otherwise, as there shall be occasion. Given at the War-Office, this 6th day of May, 1758.   By his Majesty's command,
                                                                BARRINGTON.

To the officer commanding the First
  regiment of Foot Guards.

Route for the first battalion of the First regiment of Foot Guards:—
  Tuesday   . . May 9th, Esher Common.
  Wednesday .   ,, 10th, Ripley Common.
  Thursday .   ,, 11th, Godalmin Common.
  Friday   .   ,, 12th, Petersfield Common.
  Saturday .   ,, 13th, South Sea Common, near Portsmouth.
  Sunday   .   ,, 14th, Halt.
  Monday   .   ,, 15th, Embark and encamp in the Isle of Wight.
      To encamp each night on their march.

Like orders and routes of the same date, to Lieutenant-General Lord Tyrawley, or officer commanding the Coldstream regiment of Foot Guards.

And to Lieut^t-General the Earl of Rothes, or officer commanding the Third regiment of Foot Guards.

233.

It is his Majesty's pleasure, that you cause the 1st battalion of the Coldstream regiment of Foot Guards, under your command, to march immediately, according to the route annexed, in two divisions, to London, where they will receive orders for their being quartered. Wherein, &c. Given at the War-Office, this 8th day of October, 1758.   By his Majesty's command,
                                                                BARRINGTON.

To Major-General Boscawen, or officer commanding
  the forces in the Isle of Wight.

Route for the first battalion of the Coldstream regiment of Foot
                Guards from the Isle of Wight:—

Portsmouth,   The second division to march the day after
Petersfield,   the first, to halt the Sunday, and one other
Godalmin,   day that shall be found necessary.
Ripley and Cobham,
Kingston,
London.   BARRINGTON.

234.

The Contingent Bill of the 1st battalion of the Coldstream regiment of Foot Guards on service, from 9th May, 1758, to 20th October following:—

	£.	s.	d.
To 18 waggons to Portsmouth, 74 miles, at 1s. p. mile	66	12	0
To 18 do. from the camp at South Sea Common to place of embarkation for Isle of Wight, at 3s. 6d. p. waggon	3	3	0
Paid for water at South Sea Common for the battalion	1	1	0
To 18 waggons from the camp at Newport to Cowes, with the first expedition that went out, at 5s. p. waggon, being 5 miles	4	10	0
To do. from Cowes to Newport at the return of that expedition	4	10	0
To do. from Newport to Cowes with second expedition	4	10	0
To do. from Cowes to Newport at the return of that expedition	4	10	0
To do. from Newport camp to Cowes, with the battalion returning to London	4	10	0
To 18 waggons from Portsmouth to London, being 74 miles	66	12	0
To 1 do. to bring up the Major of Brigade's baggage, and 18 sick and wounded men of 1st reg^t of Foot Guards, who were left at the Isle of Wight, and came up with the Coldstream regiment	3	14	0
To 2 waggons to bring up sick of Coldstream battalion	7	8	0
To guard-rooms and straw	2	5	0
To cash paid Ensign Shutz, who was left behind at the Isle of Wight to take care of the sick in the hospital, for carriages to bring up the said sick	7	19	6
	181	4	6
Poundage	9	10	6
	190	15	0

JULIUS CÆSAR, Major.

235.

An Account of Losses sustained by commissioned officers and private men belonging to the 1st battalion of the Coldstream regiment of Foot Guards, upon the expedition to the coast of France, in the summer of 1758, as per return sworn to by the commanding officer, Colonel Julius Cæsar.

COMMISSIONED OFFICERS.

	£.	s.	d.		£.	s.	d.
4 Offrs horses at	15	0	0 each	60	0	0
2 Hats . . ,,	3	0	0 ,,	6	0	0
4 Sashes . . ,,	3	3	0 ,,	12	12	0
3 Gorgets . ,,	0	10	6 ,,	1	11	6
2 Fuzils . . ,,	6	6	0 ,,	12	12	0
4 Espontoons ,,	0	10	6 ,,	2	2	0
2 Swords . ,,	2	12	6 ,,	5	5	0

SERJEANTS.

	£.	s.	d.		£.	s.	d.
2 Coats . . ,,	4	4	0 ,,	8	8	0
2 Caps . . ,,	1	1	0 ,,	2	2	0
2 Waistcoats ,,	1	1	0 ,,	2	2	0
2 Breeches . ,,	0	10	0 ,,	1	0	0
5 Shirts . . ,,	0	7	0 ,,	1	15	0
2 Shoes . . ,,	0	5	6 ,,	0	11	0
26 Brown gaters . . ,,	0	2	8 ,,	3	9	4
4 Sashes . . ,,	0	10	0 ,,	2	0	0
1 Hanger . ,,	1	10	0 ,,	1	10	0
7 Swords . ,,	1	10	0 ,,	10	10	0
6 Belts to do. ,,	0	10	0 ,,	3	0	0

DRUMMERS.

	£.	s.	d.		£.	s.	d.
19 Brown gaters . . ,,	0	2	8 ,,	2	10	8
1 Hanger . ,,	0	5	2 ,,	0	5	2
1 Sword . . ,,	0	5	2 ,,	0	5	2

	£.	s.	d.		£.	s.	d.
40 Coats . . at	1	2	6 each	45	0	0
3 Hatts . . ,,	0	10	0 ,,	1	10	0
73 Caps . . ,,	0	7	0 ,,	25	11	0
41 Waistcoats ,,	0	7	0 ,,	14	7	0
40 Breeches . ,,	0	5	0 ,,	10	0	0
45 Shirts . . ,,	0	5	6 ,,	12	7	6
34 Shoes . . ,,	0	5	0 ,,	8	10	0
37 Stockings ,,	0	2	6 ,,	4	12	6
653 Brown gaters . . ,,	0	2	8 ,,	87	1	4
28 Hangers . ,,	0	5	2 ,,	7	4	8
65 Swords . ,,	0	5	2 ,,	16	15	10
65 Shoulder-belts . . ,,	0	11	0 ,,	35	15	0
69 Waistbelts ,,	0	4	6 ,,	15	10	6
84 Slings . . ,,	0	1	9 ,,	7	7	0
92 Pouches at 6d. & *						
				443	4	4

CAMP NECESSARIES.

	£.	s.	d.		£.	s.	d.
11 Bells of arms, standards, and pins . . at	2	10	0 each	27	10	0
149 Mallets . ,,	0	1	0 ,,	7	9	0
149 Hatchets . ,,	0	2	0 ,,	14	18	0
703 Knapsacks ,,	0	2	6 ,,	87	17	6
703 Haversacks,	0	1	0 ,,	35	3	0
703 Canteens . ,,	0	1	6 ,,	52	14	6
11 Camp colours . . ,,	0	15	0 ,,	8	5	0
9 Powder-bags . . ,,	0	7	0 ,,	3	3	0
141 Shoulder-belts . . ,,	0	11	0 ,,	77	11	0
464 Pouches & boxes . ,,	0	6	0 ,,	11	12	0
118 Waistbelts ,,	0	4	6 ,, †	26	1	0
56 Slings . . ,,	0	1	9 ,,	4	18	0
101 Pouch-boxes . ,,	0	0	6 ,,	2	10	6
				802	16	10
Poundage and fees				57	4	6
				860	1	4

THOS. FISHER, Agent.

---

* Left blank.   † Should be £26. 11s. 0d.

236.

1759, January 22nd. The brown gaiters to be immediately blackened, and tops put on them.—Coldstream Orderly-Room.

237.

It is his Majesty's pleasure that you cause the second battalions of the three regiments of Foot Guards, under your command, to march at such times, and to such place or places, as you shall think most convenient for their embarkation for Germany. Wherein, &c. Given at the War-Office, this 23rd day of July, 1760.

By his Majesty's command,

To Major-General Julius Cæsar. BARRINGTON.

238.

It is his Majesty's pleasure that you cause such men and horses as you shall think necessary, belonging to the 2nd battalion of the Coldstream regiment of Foot Guards, under your command, ordered to embark for Germany, to march to, and be quartered at, Dartford. Wherein, &c. Given, &c. 24th July, 1760.

By his Majesty's command,
In the absence of the Secretary at War,

To Major-General Cæsar. THOS. TYRWHITT.

239.

1761, June 21. Officers ordered to attend the exercising of two guns, attached to each battalion.—Coldstream Orderly-Room.

240.

It is his Majesty's pleasure that (notwithstanding any former order to the contrary) you cause the 2nd batt^n of the Coldstream regiment of Foot Guards, under your command, off Yarmouth, to disembark, and proceed by such routes, and in such divisions, as you shall think most convenient, to Sudbury, Lavenham, and such other place or places in the neighbourhood thereof as you shall judge best for his Majesty's service, acquainting this officer with their arrival at their destined quarters, where they are to be quartered, and remain until further order. Wherein, &c. Given at the War-Office, this 27th day of February, 1763.

By his Majesty's command,
In the absence of the Secretary at War, C. D'OYLY.

Lieut^t-Col. Craig, or officer commanding the 2nd batt^n of the
 Coldstream regiment of Foot Guards, off Yarmouth.

241.

It is his Majesty's pleasure that you cause the second battalion of the Coldstream regiment of Foot Guards, under your command, to

APPENDIX. 361

march from their present quarters according to the route annexed, acquainting this Office with the receipt of this order and the day of their arrival at their destined quarters, to London, where they are to be quartered and remain until further order. Wherein, &c. Given at the War-Office, this 28th day of February, 1763.

By his Majesty's command, W. ELLIS.

The officer commanding the second battalion of the Coldstream regiment of Foot Guards, at Sudbury.

Route for the second battalion of the Coldstream regiment of Foot Guards from Sudbury:

Thursday, 10th March	.	Bocking.
Friday, 11th	.	Chelmsford.
Saturday, 12th	.	Rumford and Ilford.
Sunday, 13th	.	London, and remain.

W. ELLIS.

242.

George R.—We are pleased to direct that for the future all captain-lieutenants of Cavalry and marching regiments in our service shall bear the rank of captain; and our will and pleasure is, that the said captain-lieutenants shall take rank on all occasions, as well in the army as in their respective regiments, from the date hereof, or from the date of such commissions of captain-lieutenant as we may hereafter be pleased to grant, whereof the generals, commanders-in-chief of our forces, and all other our officers whom it doth or may concern, are to take notice and govern themselves accordingly. Given at our Court at St. James's, this 25th day of May, 1772, in the twelfth year of our reign. By his Majesty's command,

BARRINGTON.

243.

Great George Street, 5th July, 1784.

Sir,—The report of a committee, appointed by the Board of General officers, to take into their consideration the present method of accoutring the Infantry, having been laid before the King, and the several alterations therein recommended been approved of by his Majesty, I have the honour to enclose to you the said report herewith, that you may take such measures for carrying the new regulations therein contained into execution, agreeably to his Majesty's pleasure signified to me upon the occasion, as may appear to you most expedient for that purpose. I have the honour to be, &c.

WM. FAWCETT, Adj.-Gen.

Right Hon.ble Sir George Yonge, Bart. &c. &c. &c.

Report of the Proceedings of a Committee of General Officers appointed by the Board, the 15th June, 1784.

The committee, in consequence of his Majesty's reference to the Board of General Officers, have taken the present method of accoutring the Infantry into their consideration, and have agreed to present the following observations.

In the first place, the Ordnance cartridge-box at present in use has been found to be exceedingly inconvenient; it is therefore submitted that it be laid aside, and a tin magazine in a slight leathern case, of the same price, (2*s.* 6*d.*) substituted in its place; but the committee conceive the expense of this article will not fall on the Colonel, on a presumption that it will be furnished by the Ordnance, in exchange for the present cartridge-box.

The powder-horns and bullet-bags of the Light Infantry, the committee is informed, were never used during the last war; it is therefore proposed to lay them aside.

The committee farther observe, that the matches and match-cases of the Grenadiers are become obsolete; also the Grenadiers' swords were never worn during the last war; it is therefore submitted that these articles be also laid aside.

Presuming these alterations may be approved of, the committee proposes that the following plan be adopted on any future delivery of a new set of accoutrements.

The committee is of opinion, that the whole battalion should be accoutred alike, with the addition of two articles for the Light Infantry, viz. the hatchet and priming-horn, and that it will be a great relief and convenience to the soldier, as well as tend greatly to the good appearance of the battalion, to wear the shoulder-belts of equal breadth, and have the ammunition (which is to consist of 56 rounds) divided so that he may be enabled to carry the pouch on the right side and the magazine on the left.

It is therefore proposed that the pouch be made as follows, viz. to hold 32 cartridges, 20 of which are to be in an upper tin box with five divisions, each containing 4 cartridges placed upright; the other 12 are to be stowed horizontally in a tin box underneath, with divisions made in it so as to fit the length of the cartridges.

The flap of the pouch to be plain, without any ornament, and the bottom part of it to be rounded at the corners.

The magazine to be carried occasionally, to contain 24 cartridges in a tin box of the length of two cartridges, with a partition in the middle, and of sufficient depth to contain 12 on each side, stowed horizontally; this magazine is fixed to the bayonet belt in such a manner as to be easily taken off or put on, it not being intended that it should be carried otherwise than on a march or in action.

The pouch and bayonet belts to be of buff leather, and the breadth of both of them to be two inches; the bayonet carriage to slip on and off the belt, with two loops.

The hatchet, and a small priming-horn, to hold about two ounces of powder, are considered as necessary appointments for the Light Infantry; but, being at present improperly fixed to the accoutrements, may be carried either with the knapsack, or in such other manner as the commanding officer shall think most convenient.

Pattern pouches and belts made according to the above directions may be deposited at the Clothing Board.

The committee, on conferring with different accoutrement makers, are satisfied, that provided the Ordnance furnishes the magazines, this alteration will not be attended with any increase of expense to the colonel.

On considering every part of the appointments of a soldier, the committee laments that a leathern cap, worn by some of the Light Infantry last war, had not been shown to the Board, and is induced, from the report of officers who have tried it, strongly to recommend it as most comfortable to the soldier, and considerably less expensive than the cap which was approved of.

The committee is likewise of opinion, that the black linen gaiter at present in use is extremely inconvenient and prejudicial to the soldier; and earnestly propose a black woollen cloth gaiter, with white metal buttons, without stiff tops, in its place.

F. CAVENDISH.
W. HOWE.
CORNWALLIS.

This report was this day read and considered in a meeting of the Board of General Officers, and unanimously approved.

Horse Guards, 25th June, 1784.   CHARLES GOULD.

[A warrant signed by the King, embodying all the preceding recommendations of the Board, dated 21st July, 1784, was accordingly issued, and directs that they be duly observed by the regiments of Foot Guards and marching regiments of Infantry, " in exact conformity to the new patterns approved by the King, and lodged in the Office of the Comptrollers of the Accompts of the Army."]

244.

George Rex.—Whereas we have been pleased to direct that our Coldstream regiment of Foot Guards under your command shall be forthwith augmented with two light-infantry companies, each to consist of 4 serjeants, 4 corporals, 2 drummers, and 71 private men, besides commissioned officers; These are to authorise you, by beat of drum or otherwise, to raise so many men in any county or part of our kingdom of Great Britain, as shall be wanted to complete the said augmentation. And all magistrates, justices of the peace, constables, and other our civil officers whom it may concern, are hereby required to be assisting unto you in providing quarters, impressing carriages, and otherwise as there shall be occasion. Given at our Court at St. James's, this 19th day of April, 1793, in the 33rd year of our reign.

By his Majesty's command,

GEORGE YONGE.

To our most dearly beloved son and councillor, Frederick Duke of York, General in our army, and Colonel of our Coldstream regiment of Foot Guards, or to the officer appointed by him to raise men for our said regiment.

[Placed on the establishment from 25th June, 1793.]

245.

Sir,—In consequence of your letter signifying his Majesty's pleasure that a table should be maintained at the public charge for the officers of the Foot Guards on duty at St. James's, and other guards connected therewith; I am commanded by the Lords Commissioners of his Majesty's Treasury to acquaint you, that they have agreed with Mr. Gorton for the execution of this service upon payment of five thousand five hundred pounds a year, to be paid quarterly, and to commence when the buildings now erecting at St. James's are ready, and also upon payment to him of the sum of five hundred and thirty-nine pounds fourteen shillings and three pence for the purchase of kitchen utensils, and other necessaries; and I am to desire you will lay the necessary warrants before his Majesty for payment of the above allowances to Mr. Gorton accordingly.

I am, Sir, your most obedient humble servant,

Treasury Chambers, 24th August, 1793.   CHARLES LONG.

To his Majesty's Secretary at War.

246.

Sir,—Having laid before the Lords Commissioners of his Majesty's Treasury a Memorial of William Gorton, the contractor for furnishing the table of his Majesty's Foot Guards at St. James's, praying to be allowed the additional sum of two thousand pounds per annum in consequence of four officers of the Horse Guards being added to the said table; I have received their Lordships' commands to acquaint you they approve of the increased allowance as proposed, and are pleased to desire you will lay warrants from time to time before his Majesty for payment thereof.

I am, Sir, your most obedient humble servant,

Treasury Chambers, 4th December, 1793.   CHARLES LONG.

To his Majesty's Secretary at War.

247.

St. James's, March 23rd, 1794.

Sir,—The officers of the Guards are extremely desirous of having their breakfasts at the Guard-Room St. James's, and have mentioned to me that they understand from General Stevens that Mr. Pitt had given directions accordingly: I shall therefore esteem it as a particular favor if you will have the goodness to acquaint me whether that be the case, in order that I may take the necessary measures for its being done. The different colonels of the guard assure me that they are at an expense of one guinea and a half every morning for their breakfasts at the coffee-house; I therefore hope the Board of Treasury will not think that sum too large a one to allow me on the occasion. I beg to mention my own doubts as to its being a sufficiency to defray the expense, as the officers of the Life Guards are also to be provided with breakfast, and all newspapers, gazettes, &c^a. If, however, at the end of the year it should appear that the necessary expenses have exceeded the allowance, I hope their Lordships will be pleased to indemnify me for the excess. I have the honor to be, Sir,

your most obedient humble servant,

To George Rose, Esq.   WM. GORTON.

248.

Sir,—The Lords Commissioners of his Majesty's Treasury having had under their consideration a letter from Mr. William Gorton, dated 23rd March last, relative to his furnishing breakfasts to the officers of the guard at St. James's, and requesting that an allowance may be made to him of one guinea and a half per diem for this service; I am commanded by their Lordships to transmit the same to you, and to acquaint you my Lords approve of Mr. Gorton's proposal, and desire you will lay warrants before his Majesty for payment of the said allowance from time to time, as the same shall become due, commencing from the 31st day of March last inclusive.

I am, Sir, your most obedient humble servant,

Treasury Chambers, 3rd June, 1794.   CHARLES LONG.

To his Majesty's Secretary at War.

249.

Regulations for the Table at St. James's.

1st. The guard table shall be supplied with two breakfasts and a dinner, daily, at the hours, and for the number of officers, undermentioned.

2d. The first breakfast for the eight officers of the Life and Foot Guards dismounting guard, to be on the table every morning precisely at nine o'clock.

3d. The second at eleven o'clock, for the same number of officers mounting guard, and the field-officer and adjutant in parade waiting of the Foot Guards.

4th. A dinner for thirteen officers to be provided, daily, and to be on the table punctually at seven o'clock, (according to a bill of fare, which shall be produced and signed by the contractor,) to consist of two regular courses, and a dessert, with port, sherry, and madeira wines, ale, porter, and table-beer.

5th. Claret shall not be introduced until the cloth is removed, nor any wine called for, on any account, after ten o'clock, at which hour tea and coffee shall be served.

6th. The dining-room to be closed at eleven o'clock; at which hour the officers are to be with their respective guards.

7th. The officers entitled to partake of the dinner are,

The officers of the Life Guards on duty	3
The officers of the Foot Guards on duty	5
The field-officers of the Foot Guards in brigade and parade waiting	2
The Silver-stick of the Life Guards	1
The adjutants of the Foot Guards in brigade and parade waiting	2
Total	13

8th. The field-officers in waiting of the Foot Guards, Silver-stick of the Life Guards, and adjutants in waiting of the Foot Guards, are to signify their intention of dining at St. James's to the captain of the King's Guard, before twelve o'clock; otherwise, that officer will have the privilege of filling up the vacant places, agreeable to ancient custom.

9th. The captain of the King's Guard, during the continuance of his duty, is to have the control of the table, and shall regularly sign the contractor's wine-book.

10th. It is, however, to be clearly understood, that as far as regards the conduct of individuals, he will (should circumstances require it) submit the case to the field-officer in brigade waiting, who, with the Silver-stick of the Life Guards, and the officers commanding battalions at St. James's, shall at all times form a committee to investigate and redress all references or complaints that may be made to them.

11th. The terms and conditions of the present and all future contracts for the supply of the table, shall be lodged in the Orderly-Room of the First or Grenadier regiment of Foot Guards, to be referred to as occasion may require.

Approved, (Signed) FREDERICK,
Colonel of the First or Grenadier Guards.

Allowances for the Table at St. James's.

	PER ANN.
In August, 1793,	£5500 0 0
December „ An additional sum of	2000 0 0
	£7500 0 0

APPENDIX. 367

| | Brought forward | £7500 | 0 | 0 |

3rd June, 1794. £1. 11s. 6d. a-day more, to provide the officers on duty with breakfast 574 17 6

£8074 17 6
In 1800, Allowed on account of the high duty on wine . 300 0 0

£8374 17 6
In 1801, £12 per cent., afterwards reduced to £10 per cent. on the annual sum 806 10 6

£9181 8 0
In 1816, A reduction was made in the grant of . . 3181 8 0

£6000 0 0

The allowance has always been subject to a deduction of one guinea per cent. for public fees on warrants being granted for the issue of the money.

250.

War-Office, 27th July, 1813.

Sir,—I have the honour to acquaint you, that in consideration of the meritorious services of the non-commissioned officers of the army, and with the view of extending encouragements and advantages to those ranks of the infantry, corresponding to the benefits which the appointment of troop serjeant-major offers in the cavalry; his Royal Highness the Prince Regent has been most graciously pleased, in the name and on the behalf of his Majesty, to order, that from the 25th June, 1813, inclusive, the pay of the serjeant-major in every regiment of infantry not subject to a limitation of service as to place, shall be increased to three shillings per diem.

His Royal Highness has also been pleased to order, that from the same date, one serjeant of the establishment in each company of the said regiments shall be designated " Colour-Serjeant," and that his pay shall be raised to two shillings and four-pence per diem.

The colour-serjeants are to be distinguished by an honourable badge; of which, however, and of the advantages attending it, they will, in case of misconduct, be liable to be deprived, at the discretion of the Colonel or Commanding-Officer of the regiment, or by the sentence of a court-martial. It is also intended, that the duty of attending the colours in the field shall at all times be performed by the colour-serjeants; but that these distinctions shall not be permitted to interfere with the regular performance of their regimental and company duties. I have the honour to be, Sir, &c.
Colonel of the . . . regiment of Foot. PALMERSTON.

" Mem.—The pay of the serjeant-major in each battalion of Foot

"Guards was increased, from the period above mentioned, by the nett addition of 6d. per diem, making his nett pay 3s. 2d. a-day; and the pay of the colour-serjeant per company in those battalions was also augmented by the same additional rate, making his nett pay 2s. 6d. per diem in all."

250.*

On the 24th of July, 1814, a circular letter was written, directed to the General Officers of the Foot Guards, by command of his Royal Highness the Duke of York, and signed by the Military Secretary, notifying his Royal Highness's intention to remove them from their regimental commissions. Field Officers and Captains of the Guards, who were General Officers, and "in the enjoyment of advantages peculiar to that branch of the service," were to receive as a compensation an increased rate of pay.

251.

London Gazette, No. 17045. Saturday, July 29th, 1815.

War-Office, July 29th, 1815.

The Prince Regent, as a mark of his royal approbation of the distinguished gallantry of the brigade of Foot Guards in the victory of Waterloo, has been pleased, in the name and on the behalf of his Majesty, to approve of all the ensigns of the three regiments of Foot Guards having the rank of lieutenants, and that such rank shall be attached to all the future appointments to ensigncies in the Foot Guards, in the same manner as the lieutenants of those regiments obtain the rank of captain.

His Royal Highness has also been pleased to approve of the 1st regiment of Foot Guards being made a regiment of Grenadiers, and styled "The 1st or Grenadier regiment of Foot Guards," in commemoration of their having defeated the grenadiers of the French Imperial Guards upon this memorable occasion.

252.

Cost of State caps, coats, belts, and swords, received by the band of the Coldstream Guards in the year 1815.[1]

	£.	s.	d.
22 plain jockey velvet caps, furnished by Mr. Cater	33	0	0
Gold lace, &c. for coats from Messrs. Hamburger	933	5	0
Cloth for 22 coats, from Messrs. Pearse	113	9	5
Making 22 coats	27	10	0
	1107	4	5

[1] Ordered to be discontinued by command of his Majesty King William IV. in 1832.

	Brought forward	£.1107	4	5
22 buff waist-belts at 16s. from Mr. Prosser		17	12	0
22 swords, at £2. 2s. do. do.		46	0	0
		63	12	0
	Total	£1170	16	5

253.

In 1793, the uniform of the Coldstream was a cocked hat, with the exception of the grenadier companies, who wore bear-skin caps, and the light infantry companies round hats, with bear-skin over the top in the form of a helmet; the light companies wore short coats, white cloth waistcoats and pantaloons, with black half-gaiters and shoes; the remainder of the regiment long coats, white waistcoats, breeches, long black cloth gaiters, and shoes.

Adjutant-General's Office, 1st February, 1796.

Sir,—I have the honor to acquaint you, for the information of the Clothing Board, that his Majesty has signified his royal pleasure, that the following alterations shall take place in the future clothings of the infantry of the line, viz.

The lappels are to be continued as at present, down to the waist; but to be made so as either to button over occasionally, or to clasp close with hooks and eyes all the way down to the bottom.

The cape is to stand up, instead of lying down, according to former regulations; an opening is to be left at the flap, on the outside of the pocket, so as to admit the hand into it, when the lappels are buttoned over. The pocket flaps of the light infantry companies are to be made oblique, or slashed, and the wings on the shoulders of the grenadier coats also are to remain as at present.

No alteration is to take place in the breadth of the lappels or cuffs of the sleeves, nor in the colours to the facings, or patterns of the laces, as worn by the different regiments according to his Majesty's former regulations.

For the further information of the Clothing Board, I send herewith two pattern coats, one for the battalion soldier, and one for the light infantry, made up according to his Majesty's orders as above, and to be deposited in the Office of the Army Comptrollers.

I am, &c.   WM. FAWCETT,
Thos. Fauquier, Esq., &c. &c.   Adjt.-Genl.

General Order.—Dated Adjutant-General's Office, 4th May, 1796. Regulates officers' ornament to their hats, swords, sword-knots, gorgets, &c.

About 1795 or 6, short coats for the men were adopted in lieu of long coats, universally. The cocked hat continued, with the exception of the grenadier and light infantry companies, up to 1800.

In 1801, cocked hats were discontinued, and a cap issued instead.

The cap was also substituted for the hat by the light companies. Up to 1831, caps have been worn by the battalion and light infantry, of various patterns.

The short coat, with the exception of the light companies, (who wore them till 1831,) was discontinued in 1820, when long ones were given. The white waistcoat, breeches, long black gaiters and shoes were still worn.

1823. Dark grey trowsers and laced half-boots were delivered in lieu of the white breeches, long black gaiters, and shoes. Feathers were worn by the regiment from 1793 to 1820. The grenadier companies had white, the light infantry green. Battalion companies were of various patterns during that time.

Since 1820, the regiment has worn hair plumes; grenadiers white, light infantry green; battalion companies white with red at the bottom; after that period all white.

In 1832, his Majesty ordered the regiment entire to wear bearskin caps with red feathers on the right side, and all distinction in dress between the battalion and flank companies ceased.

254.

From the following list of the non-commission officers who have been promoted and appointed to commissions for their good conduct in the regiment, it is evident that the well-known habits of discipline that distinguish the non-commissioned officers of the Foot Guards has not been overlooked. The perfect discipline which the Foot Guards have attained, the precision of their evolutions, and the admirable state of the dress and equipments of the men, have frequently called forth the approbation of foreigners. The non-commissioned officers of the Guards appear superior in their particular department to those of other nations. In France they may have equal or greater quickness, and are capable of being at once advanced to a higher grade. The German and Russian non-commissioned officers may be equally good disciplinarians, and may attend with as much care to the comforts and management of the soldier; but every thing taken into consideration it may be said, without evincing an undue degree of partiality, that the serjeants and corporals of our Foot Guards unite in their conduct and regimental arrangement the good qualities of the French, the Russian, and the German.

Mr. Alexander Hogg, Serjeant-Major and Deputy-Marshal in the Second regiment of Foot Guards, appointed Fort-Major and Adjutant of the garrison of Jersey, April, 1756.

War-Office, 17th September, 1756.

Sir,—The following serjeants of the Coldstream regiment of Foot Guards being appointed lieutenants in Major-General Stuart's regiment, viz. Serjeant Otley, Serjeant Collier, Serjeant Mackay; my Lord Barrington being out of town, I am commanded to acquaint you it is his Royal Highness's orders that the said Gentlemen be discharged from doing duty as serjeants.

     I am, Sir, your most obedient humble servant,
Commanding officer of the Coldstream   THOS. SHERWIN.
 regiment of Foot Guards.

   Like Letter.   War-Office, 21st September, 1756.
 Serjeant St. Clair of the Coldstream appointed lieutenant in Lord George Beauclerk's regiment.   (Signed BARRINGTON.)

   Like Letter.   War-Office, 1st October, 1756.
 Serjeant William Smith of the Coldstream appointed lieutenant in General Holmes's regiment.   (Signed BARRINGTON.)

Non-commissioned Officers of the Coldstream regiment of Guards who have received Commissions since the commencement of the War, from 1792.

Serjeant William Pitt, Ensign, 14th Foot.
 ,, Luke Robert Cook, Ensign, 103d Foot.
 ,, Alexander Millar, Ensign, 103d Foot.
Serj^t-Major George Young, Lieut. and Adjutant, 101st Foot.
Serjeant John Horner, Lieut. and Adjutant, Duke of Athol's Fencibles.
 ,, William Moore, Ensign, New South Wales Corps.
 ,, John Braybin, Ensign, New South Wales Corps.
 ,, Francis Starr, Quarter-Master, 14th Foot.
 ,, John Barber, Quarter-Master, 21st Foot.
 ,, William Cole, Ensign, South Devon Militia.
 ,, David Keith, Adjutant, Duke of Gordon's Fencibles.
Serj^t-Major John Holmes, Quarter-Master, Coldstream regiment of Foot Guards.
Serjeant Benjamin Vaughton, Ensign and Adjutant, Aberdeenshire Fencibles.
 ,, John Sellway, Quarter-Master, Light Infantry Battalion, Brigade of Foot Guards.
 ,, Thomas Williams, Quarter-Master, Coldstream Guards.
 ,, George Bird, Ensign, Invalids.
Serj^t-Major John Philips, Provost-Marshal, Army on the Continent.
 ,, Samuel Lunt, Quarter-Master, Coldstream Guards.
Serjeant William Hughes, Ensign, Invalids.
Serj^t-Major Edward Tomlin, Quarter-Master, 85th reg. of Foot.
Serjeant John Briggs, Quarter-Master, 58th reg. of Foot.
Serj^t-Major John Mc Gregor, Ensign, Invalids, in the Tower.
Serjeant Isaac Hilton, Ensign, Invalids, in the Tower.
Quar^r-Master-Serjeant Wm. Spinks, Ensign, Royal Garrison Battalion.
Serjeant John Prime, Ensign, Royal Garrison Battalion.
Serj^t-Major Henry Selway, Ensign and Adjutant, 16th Battⁿ, Army of Reserve.

372   APPENDIX.

Serjeant Thomas Owen, Ensign, Royal Garrison Battalion.
,,   John Martin, Adjutant, Duke of Clarence's Corps.
Serj^t-Major Joseph Jennings, Ensign and Adjutant, 51st Regiment.
Quar^r-Mas^r-Serj^t James Findlay, Quarter-Master, Coldstream Guards.
Serj^t-Major William Alpe, Provost-Marshal, Army on the Continent.
Serjeant John Barrett, Ensign and Adjutant, 54th Regiment.
,,   Daniel Gardner, Ensign, 7th Royal Veteran Battalion.
Serj^t-Major Matthew Semple, Adjutant, 28th Regiment.
Serjeant George Meadley, Ensign, 60th Regiment.
,,   Richard Welley, Quarter-Master, Royal West India Rangers.
,,   John Brokenshire, Ensign, 11th Royal Veteran Battalion.
,,   William Semple, Lieutenant, Royal Cornwall Militia.
,,   Thomas Harrison, Ensign, 8th Royal Veteran Battalion.
,,   William Edwards, Ensign, Royal York Rangers.
,,   William Elliott, Quarter-Master, South Devon Militia.
Serj^t-Major Michael Nevin, Adjutant, Holmesdale Volunteers.
Serjeant Samuel Wall, Adjutant, 1st Batt^n 36th Regiment.
,,   Thomas Mann, Ensign, 4th Royal Veteran Battalion.
Corporal Francis Laugharne, Ensign, Royal York Rangers.
Serjeant Wm H. Babbington, Ensign, Royal York Rangers.
,,   Joshua Fothergill, Adjutant, 88th Regiment.
,,   Thomas Clarke, Ensign, 31st Regiment.
Serj^t-Major John Deiterich, Adjutant, Foreign Depôt, Lymington.
Serjeant Benjamin Selway, Adjutant, Guildford Local Militia.
Corporal Anthony Bubb, Ensign, 61st Regiment.
Serjeant Thomas Randall, Quarter-Master, 2d Royal Veteran Batt^n.
,,   William Haywood, Ensign, 7th Royal Veteran Batt^n.
,,   Joseph Hilton, Ensign, Royal African Corps.
,,   Thomas Wheatley, Ensign, 3d Lancashire Militia.
Quar^r-Master-Serj^t Thomas Dwelly, Quar^r-Mas^r, Coldstream Guards.
Serjeant Richard Smith, Ensign, 13th Royal Veteran Batt^n.
,,   Hugh Burn, Adjutant, 27th Regiment.
,,   Henry Bishop, Ensign and Adjutant, 5th Regiment.
,,   John Birch, Ensign, 9th Royal Veteran Batt^n.
,,   Thomas Bush, Ensign, 2d Royal Veteran Batt^n.
,,   John Weyraugh, Ensign, 60th Regiment.
Serj^t-Major William White, Ensign and Adjutant, 50th Regiment.

255.

The Non-commissioned Officers' Fund was instituted some years ago for the support of themselves, their widows and children. Its origin is unknown, but there are proofs that it existed previous to 1797, as on the first of February in that year the rules and regulations of the fund were enrolled at the Quarter Sessions by the appellation of " The Benefit Society of Non-Commissioned Officers of his Majesty's Coldstream Regiment of Foot Guards." A serjeant's subscription was four-pence, a corporal's two-pence per week: the benefits were pensions for life after discharge, varying according to length of service; and a sum of money to the family on decease in the regiment. In June 1807, the rates of stoppages and pensions were augmented. In 1819, the amount of stoppages and other small allowances to the fund was augmented, to enable it to meet the increased demands of the pensioners, caused by reductions after the peace of 1814. In November, 1824, the general committee found the pensions granted too great for the stoppages. Therefore, after fixing annuities for the existing pensioners, they abolished the pension system. In lieu of which, they agreed to repay to each subscriber, on discharge, promotion, transfer to another corps, or to his widow, children, or next of kin, the whole amount of his contributions, with interest. The amended system was enrolled at the Sessions.

256.

The Nulli Secundus Club was instituted on the fourth of March, 1783, by the following officers of the Coldstream.

John Edward Freemantle.
Thomas B. Bosville.
Nathaniel Webb.
Francis Knight, Treasurer.
George Calvert.

The rules agreed on were, "That the Club should dine together once a month till the King's birth-day, (June 4th,) then adjourn till about the Queen's birth-day, (January, 1784,) and from that day dine together monthly till the King's birth-day, and then adjourn till the next year. The dinner to be provided at *five* shillings a head, and to be on table at five o'clock, and the bill brought up at nine." Each member was to pay, at the beginning of the year, his subscription to the treasurer, who was to be elected annually.

The number of members to be *fourteen*, elected by a ballot of at least six members; one black ball to exclude; and unless the whole Club were present, the candidate was not eligible, until he had been proposed one month. Any member " entering the holy state of matrimony" was to give a dinner.

The following are extracts from rules which were at various times subsequently enacted. In June, 1807, it was agreed to wear as a uniform, a dark blue coat, with ten silver engraved buttons, placed two and two, on each lapel; at top of the skirt, two buttons, with worked button-holes, and on each pocket-flap four buttons, two and two, white kerseymere waistcoat, and black breeches.

A member not appearing at the meetings dressed in strict conformity with this regulation, is fined a guinea.

Members, on marriage, become honorary, and occasion a vacancy for the election of a new member; they are exempted from the absentee forfeit, but pay the annual subscription.

When an officer leaves the Coldstream, he is no longer a member; but his company on a club-day, according to the rules, " will be thought an honour."

Any member who absents from a meeting, and omits the first opportunity to give a satisfactory reason to the members then present, is liable to forfeit a guinea. In 1788, it was resolved, " That all absentees should pay this fine towards the reckoning, except when absent on leave and military duty."

The chair to be taken by each member in turn, according to the treasurer's list, who also is to keep a roll of candidates, to be balloted for by seniority.

In 1795, it was agreed, that the dinner should be increased to seven shillings and sixpence a head. These, with some slight alterations, continued to be the rules of the Nulli Secundus for many years, the meetings of which were so regular, that even, before the enemy, they were not omitted.

In the treasurer's book is a minute of a meeting held March 24th, 1794, at Lord Cavan's quarters, Courtrai.

Present:

H. R. H. the Duke of York.	Lt.-Col. Morrison.
Colonel Morshead.	,, Calvert.
Earl of Cavan.	,, Hewgill.
Lt.-Col. Hon. Edward Finch.	,, De Visme.
,, Isaac Gascoyne.	Captain Wynyard.

Absent:

Captain Windsor, on piquet at Meugi.

Lieut-Col. Calcraft, with second battalion in England.

Lieut.-Col. Morrison elected treasurer.

Lieut.-Col. Fitzroy, Captain Buller, Captain Morris, Captain Dyke, elected members.

The meetings continued monthly from 1783 to 1815. On the 10th of April that year, Colonel Brand proposed that the third article of the original laws, respecting the annual subscription, should be expunged; and as some members had died, or quitted the regiment without paying their arrears, it was further proposed, that the members should not be called on for the subscription then due. This was adopted. From this period the meetings became less frequent, and only eleven took place up to 1827.

On the 14th of February, 1828, several members who were anxious to revive an institution by which those who had left the regiment might be still connected with it, met in Portman Street barracks, for the purpose of taking into consideration the existing rules of the Club, and of making certain propositions or amendments to them. These were submitted to a meeting, held at the Clarendon Hotel on the 18th of February, when the following were adopted and resolved on:—

"That the Club shall in future dine together on the days of muster, and on the twenty-ninth of May."

"That the dinner shall be ordered at fifteen shillings a head."

"That a certain rule, passed 27th June, 1814, H. R. H. the Duke of Cambridge in the chair, be revived, and that the agent do open an account in the name of the treasurer of this Club, to which he (the agent) be directed to pay the subscription of each member, viz. 15s. for each of the three yearly dinners, on the order of the presidents of the meetings. That the company present on each club-day shall determine upon the tavern at which they will next dine."

"That members shall be balloted for, and by six members at least; and that one black ball shall exclude."

"That the rule respecting the wedding dinners of members be annulled."

"That the uniform henceforth be a blue coat, with silver, or silver plated buttons of the Nulli Secundus Club pattern, with black velvet collar; fancy waistcoat; black trowsers, pantaloons, or breeches. That the fine of one guinea be required from a member improperly dressed, as heretofore."

"That married members be reckoned honorary, have a vote, and be exempted from the fine for absence from meetings."

"That a member on his marriage shall, therefore, make a vacancy for the election of a new member."

"That a married member who shall omit to notify to the tavern-keeper, two days at least before a meeting, whether he will or will not dine there, be fined a guinea."

"That a married man, three years in the Coldstream, and one year a candidate, may be elected honorary member by ballot."

"That the number of the members (which by a vote of 1825 had been increased to twenty-three) shall be fixed as in 1783, to fourteen."

"That all absentees be fined a guinea (as heretofore), to be deducted from the bill; King's leave, and military duty alone exempting."

"That members shall take the chair in turn, according to the treasurer's list; and that failing to do so, or to get a substitute, the defaulter shall be fined one guinea in addition to the fine for absence."

"That a member on quitting the Coldstream shall cease to be a member; but his company on club-days will be considered an honour."

"That all candidates, who have left the regiment since the last meeting, three years ago, but for whose election vacancies had oc-

"curred anterior to their resignation, be informed by the treasurer
"that the Club requests the pleasure of their company at their meet-
"ings: for inasmuch as these gentlemen would have been balloted
"for, if the Club had met regularly, according to their rules in 1825,
"1826, 1827, they are considered in the light of members of the
"Nulli, who have quitted the Coldstream."

From the period of his Majesty's accession to the throne, King William IVth has been graciously pleased to confer on the Club the signal honour of an invitation to an annual dinner.

SUCCESSION OF MEMBERS.

John Edward Freemantle,
Thomas B. Bosville, (treasurer six years)
Nathaniel Webb,
Francis Knight,
George Calvert, (treasurer five years)
Isaac Gascoyne
} Original Members.

1783. Gould
Vachell
Bridgeman
Hewgill
  (treasurer three years)
Fraser
Calcraft
N. Boscawen
1784. Fane
Sutton
Wyndham
Earl of Cavan
1785. Thoroton
Finch
Morshead
Lord Stopford
W. Boscawen
Morgan
1786. Maddocks
Parker
1788. Morrison
  (treasurer four years)
H. R. H. the Duke of York
1789. Spencer
1790. Lord Saye and Sele
Gregory
C. Hotham
1791. Earl of Aboyne
Eld
Wynyard
  (treasurer fifteen years)

Calvert
Windsor
Nugent
1794. G. Fitzroy
Buller
Morris
Lord Howard of Effingham
Dyke
1795. Fuller
Lord Forbes
Brand
1796. Brownrigg
Stanwix
1797. Vane
Brice
Earl of Cork
B. Hotham
Chester
1798. Wingfield
Armstrong
1799. Upton
1800. Peacocke
Bolton
Sir Gilbert Stirling
M. Wynyard
Lloyd
1801. Henry MacKinnon
Sir Wm. Sheridan
Lord Dunsany
Smith
J. Philips

1801.	Sir Richard Jackson	1819.	Chaplin
	Onslow		Armytage
	Cadogan		Maynard
	Ross	1820.	Cuyler
	Acland		Loftus
1805.	Conyers		Kortright
	Braddyll		Campbell
	Adams	1821.	Rous
1806.	H. R. H. the Duke of Cambridge		Whymper (treasurer seven years)
	Woodford	1822.	Buller
	Sir Wm. Pringle		Mildmay
	Dalling		Gooch
1808.	Hamilton		Drummond
	Sir Henry Bouverie	1823.	Girardot
1809.	Sutton		Shawe
1810.	Collyer		Salwey
	Barrow	1825.	G. Bentinck
	Buller		Powys
	Lord Aylmer		H. Bentinck
	Vachell		J. Forbes
1812.	Sullivan		W. Forbes
	Taylor		Macdonell
	Simpson (treasurer ten years)		Arbuthnot Sir Wm. Gomm
	Lascelles		O'Neill
1813.	Daniel Mac Kinnon		Waters
	W. C. Wynyard	1828.	Earl of Munster
1814.	Milman		Cornwall
	Raikes		Short
	Sandilands		Lord Graves
	Gore		Cowell
	Bowles		Hall
	Bayly		Dundass
1815.	Walpole		Murray
	Steele	1829.	Russell
	Walton		Broadhead
	Harvey		G. Bentinck
	Prince		Northey
	Dawkins		Rawdon
	Buller	1830.	Howden
	Talbot	1831.	Ashburnham
	Percival		Codrington
1818.	Lord Hotham		Hope
	G. Morgan		Lord Frederick Fitzclarence
	Rose		
	Bligh		Hobhouse
1819.	Wedderburn		Sir John Shelly
	Clifton		

257.

An establishment made and concluded upon by his Highness the Lord Protector and ye Councell, for the several forces in feild and guarrison in Scotland, to commence from Monday the three-and-twentieth day of July, one thousand six hundred fiftie-five, inclusive.

Thirteen regiments and one company of foot, consisting of 10640 soldiers, besides officers, for Scotland.

		By the Day.			By the Month.		
Feild and Staff Officers to a regiment of Foot, viz.	Colonell . . . . . £	0	12	0	16	16	0
	Lieutenant-Colonell . . .	0	7	0	19	16	0
	Major	0	5	0	7	0	0
	Preacher	0	6	8	9	6	8
	Chirurgeon 5s., and one Mate 2s. 6d.	0	7	6	10	10	0
	Quarter-Master and Provost Marshall united	0	4	0	5	12	0
	Gunsmith	0	2	6	3	10	0
	Drum-Major	0	1	6	2	2	0
	Sum . .	2	6	2	64	12	8
A private company, viz.	Captaine	0	8	0	11	4	0
	Lieutenant	0	4	0	5	12	0
	Ensigne	0	3	0	4	4	0
	Two Sergeantes, each 18d. . .	0	3	0	4	4	0
	Three Corporalles and two Drummers, each 12d.	0	5	0	7	0	0
	Eightie Soldiers, each 9d. . .	3	0	0	84	0	0
	Sum . .	4	3	0	116	4	0
	The pay of nine such companies more, to compleat a regiment of Foote	37	7	0	1,045	16	0
	In all for one regiment .	43	16	2	1,226	12	8
	The pay of twelve such regiments more	525	14	0	14,719	12	0
	The pay of three Captaines, three Lieutenantes, three Ensignes, six Sergeantes, nine Corporalles, six Drummers, and two hundred and fortie Soldiers, two of which companies to be added to one of the regimentes above mentioned for the keeping of Edinburgh and Lieth, amountes unto	12	9	0	348	12	0
	In all for 13 regimentes and one company	581	19	2	16,294	16	8

Extract.

The reducements made in this establishment are as followeth :—

The Wagoner of each regiment, each 3s.

The Quarter-Master and Provost-Martiall of each regiment united.

The regiments reduced to eight hundred soldiers besides officers.

The pay of each foote souldier of the *feild-forces* reduced from ten-pence to nine-pence p. diem.

The pay of each foote souldier of the *guarrisons* to be eight-pence p. diem.

State-Paper Office.

APPENDIX.

258.

The Establishment of the Forces in England and Scotland, commencing the 15th of October, 1655, with the allowances since made by his Highness the Lord Protector and Council. July 15th, 1657.

Extract.	Per Diem.			Per Mensem. (28 days.)		
	£.	s.	d.	£.	s.	d.
Commander-in-Chiefe of the Forces in Scotland	6	0	0	168	0	0
Major-General of the Foote in do.	0	10	0	14	0	0
One Adjutant for Scotland to have a troope of Horse, and to be allowed as Adjutant-Generall	0	2	0	2	16	0
That until a troope of Horse be provided for the Adjutant-General, he is to be allowed 12s. p. day.						
One Clerke to the Commander-in-Chiefe of the Forces in Scotland	0	5	0	7	0	0

Seaven regiments of Horse for Scotland, fouer companies of dragoons, and traine of artillery . . . .

Eleven regiments, and one company of Foote for Scotland, vizt.:—

		Per Diem.			Per Mensem. (28 days.)		
		£.	s.	d	£.	s.	d.
Feild and Staff officers to a regiment of Foote, viz.	Colonel	0	12	0	16	16	0
	Lieutenant-Colonel	0	7	0	9	16	0
	Major	0	5	0	7	0	0
	Preacher	0	6	8	9	6	0
	Chirurgeon 5s. and one mate 2s. 6d.	0	7	6	10	10	0
	Quarter-Master and Provost-Marshall, to be executed by one person	0	4	0	5	12	0
	Gunsmith	0	2	6	3	10	0
		2	4	8	62	10	8
A Colonel's company, viz.	Captain	0	8	0	11	4	0
	Lieutenant	0	4	0	5	12	0
	Ensign	0	3	0	4	4	0
	Two Serjeants each 18d.	0	3	0	4	4	0
	One Drummer	0	1	6	2	2	0
	Three Corporals and other Drummer, each at 12d.	0	4	0	5	12	0
	Seaventy-fouer souldiers, each at 9d.	2	15	6	77	14	0
		3	19	0	110	12	0
A private company, viz.	Captain	0	8	0	11	4	0
	Lieutenant	0	4	0	5	12	0
	Ensign	0	3	0	4	4	0
	Two Serjeants, each 18d.	0	3	0	4	4	0
	Three Corporals and two Drummers, each at 12d.	0	5	0	7	0	0
	Seaventy-fouer souldiers, each at 9d.	2	15	6	77	14	0
		3	18	6	109	18	0
The pay of eight such companies more, to compleate a regiment of Foote, att the same rates and numbers as are particularly mentioned in the private company		31	8	0	879	4	0
In all for one regiment		41	10	2	1,162	4	8
The pay of tenn such regiments more		415	1	8	11,622	6	8
In all for eleven regiments		456	11	10	12,784	11	4

State-Paper Office.

259.

An Establishment of the Forces in Scotland, commencing y̆e 21st of December, 1657, inclusive.

Eleven Regiments and one Company of Foote, consisting of 7770 souldiers, besides officers.

		By the Day.			By the Month.		
Feild and Staff Officers to a regiment of Foote, viz.	Colonell . . . . £	0	12	0	16	16	0
	Lieutenant-Colonell . . .	0	7	0	9	16	0
	Major	0	5	0	7	0	0
	Preacher	0	6	8	9	6	8
	Chirurgeon 4s., and one Mate 2s. 6d.	0	6	6	9	2	0
	Qr.-Master and Provost-Marshall, to be executed by one person	0	4	0	5	12	0
	Gunsmith	0	2	6	3	10	0
		2	3	8	61	2	8
One private company, viz.	Captaine	0	8	0	11	4	0
	Lieutenant	0	4	0	5	12	0
	Ensigne	0	3	0	4	4	0
	Two Serjeants, each 1s. 6d. .	0	3	0	4	4	0
	Three Corporalls above souldiers' pay 3d.	0	0	9	1	1	0
	One Drummer	0	1	0	1	8	0
	Seventy souldiers, the three Corporalls included, each at 9d.	2	12	6	73	10	0
		3	12	3	101	3	0
	The pay of nyne such companies more, to make up a regiment of 700 souldiers, besides officers	32	10	3	910	7	0
	In all for one regiment .	38	6	2	1,072	12	8
	The pay of ten such regiments more, and one company, according to the rates and numbers above expressed . . .	386	13	11	10,827	9	8
	In all for eleven regiments and one company	425	0	1	11,900	2	4

Extract.

The retrenchments made in this establishment are as followeth :—

A Drummer to the Colonell's company at 1s. 6d. p. diem, wholly reduced.
A Drummer in each of the other companies at 1s. p. diem, wholly reduced.
Three Corporalls in each company at 9d., reduced.
Four private Souldiers in each company at 9d., wholly reduced.
The pay of the Chirurgeon reduced one shilling p. diem.

State-Paper Office.

260.

Extracted from "an Establishment of the Forces in England and Wales as the same stood the 27th February, 16⅞⅞."

Twelve Regiments of Foot, consisting of 14,400 souldiers, besides officers, viz.:

		Per Diem.			Per Mensem.		
		£.	s.	d.	£.	s.	d.
Feild and Staff Officers to a regiment of Foot	Colonel as Colonel	0	12	0	16	16	0
	Lieutenant-Colonel as Lieutenant-Colonel	0	7	0	9	16	0
	Major as Major	0	5	0	7	0	0
	Preacher	0	6	8	9	6	8
	Surgeon 4s., and one Mate 2s. 6d.	0	6	6	9	2	0
	Quarter-Master and Provost-Marshal, to be executed by one person	0	4	0	5	12	0
		2	1	2	57	12	8
A company of Foot	Captain	0	8	0	11	4	0
	Lieutenant	0	4	0	5	12	0
	Ensigne	0	3	0	4	4	0
	Two Serjeants, each at 18d.	0	3	0	4	4	0
	Three Corporalls, each at 3d. p. diem above souldiers' pay	0	0	9	1	1	0
	One Drumm	0	1	0	1	8	0
	One hundred and twenty souldiers, each at 9d.	4	10	0	126	0	0
		5	9	9	153	13	0
	The pay of nine such company's more, to compleat a regiment of Foot consisting of 1200 souldiers, besides officers	49	7	9	1382	17	0
	In all for one regiment	56	18	8	1594	2	8

MS. Harleian. No. 6844. Brit. Mus.

261.

Charles R.—An Establishment for the new-raised Forces, to begin 26th January, 166¾.

(Extract.)

		Per Diem.			Per Mensem.			Per Annum.		
	Feild and Staff Officers of his Grace the Duke of Albemarle his Regiment of Foote.	£.	s.	d.	£.	s.	d.	£.	s.	d.
	Colonel as Colonel	0	12	0	16	16	0	219	0	0
	Lieutenant-Collonel as Lieutenant-Colonel	0	7	0	9	16	0	127	15	0
	Maior as Maior	0	5	0	7	0	0	91	5	0
	Chaplaine	0	6	8	9	6	8	121	13	4
	Chirurgion iiij^s and one Mate ij^s vj^d	0	6	6	9	2	0	118	12	6
	Quarter-Master and Marshall, to bee executed by one person	0	4	0	5	12	0	73	0	0
	Totall	2	1	2	57	12	8	751	5	10
The Duke of Albemarle his Regiment of Foote, consisting of 1000 Souldiers, besides Officers, vizt.	A Companie of Foote.									
	Captaine	0	8	0	11	4	0	146	0	0
	Lieutenant	0	4	0	5	12	0	73	0	0
	Ensigne	0	3	0	4	4	0	54	15	0
	Two Sarjeants at xviij^d	0	3	0	4	4	0	54	15	0
	Three Corporalls each at xij^d	0	3	0	4	4	0	54	15	0
	Three Drummers each at xij^d	0	3	0	4	4	0	54	15	0
	And one hundred souldiers each at x^d p. diem whilst they quarter in London, but to have but ix^d if they remove[1]	4	3	4	116	13	4	1520	16	8
	Totall	5	7	4	150	5	4	1958	16	8
	The pay of nine such companies to compleate the said regiment of Foote consisting of 1000 souldiers besides officers (the said nine companies only having two Drumms each) amounts to	47	17	0	1339	16	0	17465	5	0
	In all for the said last mentioned regiment	55	5	6	1547	14	0	20175	7	6
	"One Adjutant to Our G̃rall's regiment of Foot" from June 1661	0	4	0	5	12	0	72	16	0

State-Paper Office.

[The Establishment from January 166¾ is precisely the same numbers and rates, and the Adjutant included among the Field and Staff Officers.]—State-Paper Office.

[1] Pay of the Guards to be *eightpence* a day when not in attendance on the King, from May . . 1671.—Extract from King's Warrant, dated 12th May, 1671.

262.

The Establishment of the Lord Generall's Regiment of His Majesties Foot Guards, to commence the 26th of September, 1668.

Consisting of 960 Soldiers, besides Officers, in twelve companies.

Feild and Staff Officers.	Per Diem.			Per Mensem.			Per Annum.		
	£.	s.	d.	£.	s.	d.	£.	s.	d.
Generall as Colonell	0	12	0	16	16	0	218	8	0
Lieutenant-Colonell as Lieutenant-Colonell	0	7	0	9	16	0	127	8	0
Major as Major	0	5	0	7	0	0	91	0	0
Chaplain	0	6	8	9	6	8	121	6	8
Adjutant	0	4	0	5	12	0	72	16	0
Chirurgeon 4s. and one Mate 2s. 6d.	0	6	6	9	2	0	118	6	0
Quarter-Master and Marshal, to be executed by one person	0	4	0	5	12	0	72	16	0
	2	5	2	63	4	8	822	0	8
The Lord Generall's Company as Colonell.									
Generall as Captain	0	8	0	11	4	0	145	12	0
Lieutenant	0	4	0	5	12	0	72	16	0
Ensign	0	3	0	4	4	0	54	12	0
Two Serjeants, each 18d.	0	3	0	4	4	0	54	12	0
Three Corporals, each 12d.	0	3	0	4	4	0	54	12	0
Two Drummers, each 12d.	0	2	0	2	16	0	36	8	0
Eightie Soldiers, each 10d.	3	6	8	93	6	8	1213	6	8
	4	9	8	125	10	8	1631	18	8
The Lieutenant-Colonell's Company	4	9	8	125	10	8	1631	18	8
Ten companies more as that of the Lieutenant-Colonell to compleat the said regiment	44	16	8	1255	6	8	16319	6	8
Fire and Candles for the four Courts of Guard kept by this regiment	0	9	0	12	12	0	163	16	0
In all for this regiment	56	10	2	1589	4	8	20569	0	8

State-Paper Office.

263.

Establishment of the Coldstream Guards, to commence from the first of January, 16$\frac{72}{80}$; consisting of 720 Soldiers, besides Officers, in twelve companies of sixty in each company.

	Per Diem.			Per Annum.		
Field and Staff Officers.	£.	s.	d.	£.	s.	d.
Colonel as Colonel	0	12	0	219	0	0
Lieutenant-Colonel as Lieutenant-Colonel	0	7	0	127	15	0
Major as Major	0	5	0	91	5	0
Chaplain	0	6	8	121	13	4
Adjutant	0	4	0	73	0	0
Chirurgeon 4s., and one Mate 2s. 6d.	0	6	6	118	12	6
Quarter-Master and Marshal, to be executed by one person	0	4	0	73	0	0
	2	5	2	824	5	10
The Colonel's Company.						
Colonel as Captain	0	8	0	146	0	0
Lieutenant	0	4	0	73	0	0
Ensign	0	3	0	54	15	0
Two Serjeants, each 18d.	0	3	0	54	15	0
Three Corporals, each 12d.	0	3	0	54	15	0
Two Drummers, each 12d.	0	2	0	36	10	0
Drum-Major	0	1	6	27	7	6
Sixty Soldiers, each 10d.	2	10	0	912	10	0
	3	14	6	1,359	12	6
The Lieutenant-Colonel's Company.						
Lieutenant-Colonel as Captain	0	8	0	146	0	0
Lieutenant	0	4	0	73	0	0
Ensign	0	3	0	54	15	0
Two Serjeants, each 18d.	0	3	0	54	15	0
Three Corporals, each 12d.	0	3	0	54	15	0
Two Drummers, each 12d.	0	2	0	36	10	0
Sixty Soldiers, each 10d.	2	10	0	912	10	0
	3	13	0	1,332	5	0
The pay of ten companies more to complete this regiment, at the rates and numbers expressed in the Lieutenant-Colonel's company	36	10	0	13,322	10	0
Fire and Candle for the several Courts of Guards kept by this regiment	0	9	0	164	5	0
Total for this regiment	46	11	8	17,002	18	4

MS. Harleian No. 6425. Brit. Mus.

264.

Establishment of the Coldstream Guards, from the first of January, 168¾; consisting of 770 Men, besides Officers, in twelve companies of sixty in each, and the addition of a Granadier company of fifty granadiers.

Field and Staff Officers.	Per Diem. £.	s.	d.	Per Annum. £.	s.	d.
Colonel as Colonel	0	12	0	219	0	0
Lieutenant-Colonel as Lieutenant-Colonel	0	7	0	127	15	0
Major as Major	0	5	0	91	5	0
Chaplain	0	6	8	121	13	4
Adjutant	0	4	0	73	0	0
Chirurgeon 4s., and one Mate 2s. 6d.	0	6	6	118	12	6
Quarter-Master and Marshal, to be executed by one person	0	4	0	73	0	0
Drum-Major	0	1	6	27	7	6
	2	6	8	851	13	4
One Company.						
Captain	0	8	0	146	0	0
Lieutenant	0	4	0	73	0	0
Ensign	0	3	0	54	15	0
Two Serjeants, each 18d.	0	3	0	54	15	0
Three Corporals, each 12d.	0	3	0	54	15	0
Two Drummers, each 12d.	0	2	0	36	10	0
Sixty Soldiers, each 10d.	2	10	0	912	10	0
	3	13	0	1,332	5	0
Eleven Companies more, at the same numbers and rates	40	3	0	14,654	15	0
One Company of Granadiers belonging to the Regiment.						
Captain	0	8	0	146	0	0
Two Lieutenants, each 4s.	0	8	0	146	0	0
Three Serjeants, each 18d.	0	4	6	182	2	6
Three Corporals, each 12d.	0	3	0	54	15	0
Two Drummers, each 12d.	0	2	0	36	10	0
Fifty Granadiers, each 8d.[1]	1	13	4	608	6	8
	2	18	10	1,073	14	2
Fire and Candle for the several Courts of Guards kept by this regiment	0	9	0	164	5	0
Total for this regiment, with the Granadiers	49	10	6	18,076	12	6

"Memo.—That as any of the companies of the two regiments of
"Guards are or shall be garrisoned or quartered in other places than

---

[1] Charles R.—Whereas we have thought fit to establish two companies of Granadiers on ffoot, consisting of fifty in each company, besides officers, to be

" the cities of London and Westminster and borough of Southwark,
" and thereabouts, the pay of the private soldiers of those companies
" so absent from about London shall then be but 8*d.* a day during such
" time as they shall so remain in other places as aforesaid." [1]

The regulation of the weekly subsistance for his Majesty's regiments of Foot Guards, and for compleating the musters, is to be in the manner following:

        To be paid, 4*s.* a week to a private soldier.
                ,,   5*s.* a week to a drummer or corporal.
                ,,   7*s.* a week to a serjeant.
                ,,   10*s.* 6*d.* an ensign.
                ,,   14*s.* a week to a lieutenant.

And all off-reckonings and pay of ye severall officers are to be compleatly satisfied and cleared according to the establishment and muster-rolls before ye end of the succeeding musters, and general officers, reformed officers, and pensioners, be quarterly paid, so that one quarter be still paid before the second becomes due.—War-Office.

---

added to our two regiments of ffoot Guards, and finding it necessary that for such time as the said companies of Granadiers shall be garrisoned or quartered within our citties of London, Westminster, and borough of Southwark, or thereabouts, they be allowed the same pay as the other private soldiers of the same regiments to which they belong, We do therefore hereby make and put this our establishment to commence from the first day of April, 1684, notwithstanding any former directions to the contrary, viz.

Fifty Granadiers belonging to our First regiment of Guards, each 10*d.* per diem=£2 1*s.* 8*d.*   £760 8*s.* 4*d.* per annum.

Fifty Granadiers belonging to our Coldstream regiment of Guards, each 10*d.* per diem=£2 1*s.* 8*d.*   £760 8*s.* 4*d.* per annum.

[1] This distinction of pay continued till the Revolution, from which time it was ten-pence a day, wherever stationed.

APPENDIX. 387

265.

Establishment of the Coldstream Guards, from the first of May, 1689.

Consisting of fourteen Companies of eighty men: in all 1120, besides Officers.

Field and Staff Officers.	Per Diem.			Per Annum.		
	£.	s.	d.	£.	s.	d.
Colonel as Colonel	0	12	0	219	0	0
Lieutenant-Colonel as Lieutenant-Colonel	0	7	0	127	15	0
Major as Major	0	5	0	91	5	0
Chaplain	0	6	8	121	13	4
Two Adjutants, each 4s.	0	8	0	146	0	0
Chirurgeon 4s., and two Mates, each 2s. 6d.	0	9	0	164	5	0
Quarter-Master	0	4	0	73	0	0
Solicitor to this Regiment[1]	0	4	0	73	0	0
Drum-Major	0	1	6	27	7	6
	2	17	2	1,043	5	10
One Company.						
Captain	0	8	0	146	0	0
Lieutenant	0	4	0	73	0	0
Ensign	0	3	0	54	15	0
Three Serjeants, each 18d.	0	4	6	82	2	6
Three Corporals, each 12d.	0	3	0	54	15	0
Two Drummers, each 12d.	0	2	0	36	10	0
Eighty Private Soldiers, each 10d.	3	6	8	1,216	13	4
	4	11	2	1,663	15	10
Eleven Companies more, at the same numbers and rates	50	2	10	18,301	14	2
One Company of Granadiers.						
Captain	0	8	0	146	0	0
Two Lieutenants, each 4s.	0	8	0	146	0	0
Three Serjeants, each 18d.	0	4	6	82	2	6
Three Corporals, each 12d.	0	3	0	54	15	0
Two Drummers, each 12d.	0	2	0	36	10	0
Eighty Granadiers, each 10d.	3	6	8	1,216	13	4
	4	12	2	1,682	0	10
Another Company of Granadiers, the same	4	12	2	1,682	0	10
Total	66	15	6	24,372	17	6

MS. Harleian. No. 4847. Brit. Mus.

Mem.

Fire and Candle for Guards included in a separate estimate from this period.

---

[1] The Solicitor performed the duties of Regimental Agent.

The Pay of the Officers of the Coldstream was increased from the first of January, 16$\frac{90}{91}$, as shown in the Warrant annexed.

William R.—Whereas we have thought fit to make the following additional allowance of pay to the Officers of our Coldstream regiment of Foot Guards, Our will and pleasure is, that the same do commence from the first day of January, 16$\frac{90}{91}$ inclusive, in the first year of our reign. Given at our Court at Whitehall, the 15th day of April, 1691, in the third year of our reign.

	Per Diem.			Per Annum.		
	£.	s.	d.	£.	s.	d.
To the Colonel as Colonel	0	8	0	146	0	0
To the Lieutenant-Colonel as Lieutenant-Colonel	0	5	0	91	5	0
To the Major as Major	0	3	0	54	15	0
To fourteen Captains at 6s. each	4	4	0	1533	0	0
To sixteen Lieutenants at 3s. each	2	8	0	876	0	0
To twelve Ensigns at 2s. each	1	4	0	438	0	0
Total	8	12	0	3139	0	0

MS. Harleian. No. 7437. Brit. Mus.

(Examined)   WILLIAM BLATHWAYT,
                     (Secretary at War.)

A similar Warrant increasing the Pay of the Officers of the First Foot Guards: dated the 10th day of January, 169$\frac{8}{9}$.

APPENDIX.

266.
COLDSTREAM REGIMENT OF FOOT GUARDS. 1695.

Foot.	Comps.	Com^d. Off^{rs}.	Non-com^d. Off^{rs}.	Private men.	Together.	Pay per Annum.	Servants allowed.	Servants pay per Annum.
Second Reg^t. of Guards.	14	51	112	1120	1283	£. s. d. 27,511 17 6	74	£. s. d. 1125 8 4

Com. Off^{rs}.	Non-com^d. Off^{rs}.	Private men.	Servants allowed.	THE SECOND OR COLDSTREAM REGIMENT OF GUARDS.	Personal pay per Ann. of each Officer with his servants, & each private man.			Pay per Annum.		
					£.	s.	d.	£.	s.	d.
1	.	6	6	Colonel, 20s.; 3 servants, each 10d.; as Captain, 14s.; 3 servants, 10d.	711	15	0	711	15	0
1	.	3	3	Lieutenant-Colonel, 12s.; as Captain, 14s.; 3 servants, each 10d.	520	2	6	520	2	6
1	.	3	3	Major, 8s.; as Captain, 14s.; 3 servants, each 10d.	447	2	6	447	2	6
1	.	.	.	Chaplain, 6s. 8d.	121	13	4	121	13	4
1	.	.	.	Chyrurgeon, 4s.	73	0	0	73	0	0
2	.	.	.	Chyrurgeons Mates, each 2s. 6d.	45	12	6	91	5	0
2	.	.	.	Adjutants, each 4s.	73	0	0	146	0	0
1	.	1	1	Quarter-Master, 4s.; & one servant, 10d.	88	4	2	88	4	2
1	.	.	.	Solicitor, 4s.	73	0	0	73	0	0
1	.	.	.	Drumm-Major, 18d.	27	7	6	27	7	6
11	.	33	33	Captains, more, each 14s.; and 3 servants at 10d.	301	2	6	3,312	7	6
16	.	16	16	Lieutenants, each 7s.; and one servant, 10d.	142	19	2	2,287	6	8
12	.	12	12	Ensigns, each 5s.; & one servant, 10d.	106	9	2	1,277	10	0
.	42	.	.	Serjeants, each 18d.	27	7	6	1,149	15	0
.	42	.	.	Corporalls, each 12d.	18	5	0	766	10	0
.	28	.	.	Drummers, each 12d.	18	5	0	511	0	0
.	.	1046	.	Private men, each 10d.	15	4	2	15,907	18	4
51	112	1120	74					27,511	17	6

Throughout the Army, the Collonels, Lieutenant-Collonels, and Majors, are also paid as Captains. And they, as well as all other commission officers, have addiconall pay for their servants;[1] of which the Establishments take no notice.

---

[1] Extract from "Instructions to the Commissary-General of Musters," dated Whitehall, 4th December, 1660.
Article 4. "That no Captain shall muster above two servants, a Lieutenant "but one, and an Ensign but one, and those serviceable, and none else any."

In respect to the number of private men, viz. The Establishment setts forth, the whole number of private men to be 1120: whereas, in truth, as appears by this state, there is but 1046 effective men; the remaining 74 being only a fictitious number, and their pay amounting to £1125. 8s. 4d. per annum, distributed amongst the officers, as is particularly herein sett downe.

By which method there is in the whole army 5747 private men lesse; and their pay, amounting to £107,545. 10s. 10d. per annum, the officers receive amongst them over and above their own personall pay.

MS. Harleian. No. 1308. Brit. Mus.

Extract from a King's Warrant, dated Whitehall, 10th November, 1677.

The pay of men under fictitious names as servants to officers to be discontinued; and in future the Colonels of the two regiments of Foot Guards to be allowed to muster six servants a-piece, the Captains three a-piece, and the Lieutenants and Ensigns one soldier a-piece as servants, the Quarter-Masters one servant in the Colonel's company, or other company he appoints.

Extract from a Letter, dated Whitehall, 23rd February, 1679.
All servants are to appear at muster in proper arms, &c.

Extract from Report of a Committee of the House of Commons, 1746.
1699. Three servants from each company of Foot deducted, which had been esteemed part of their personal pay.———Till about the end of James's reign, officers' servants were obliged to appear at musters in the ranks, clothed and accoutred.

APPENDIX.

An Abstract of the Amount of ye Off-reckonings for the Coldstream Regiment of Foot Guards for the year 1695.[1]

[Extract.]

	The full amount of the off-reckonings.	The deduction of 12 pence in the pound.	The deduction of one day's pay for the Hospitall. (Chelsea.)	To the officers for the off-reckonings of their servants.	The deduction of 2 pence in the pound for agency.	Neat off-reckonings to be paid to the clothiers yearly.
The Second or Coldstream Reg.	6101 11 8	973 0 7	53 6 4	294 6 11½	. . 0 *	4780 17 9½

For the full off-reckonings of 42 serjeants at 3s. 6d., 42 corporalls and 28 drummers at 2s., and 1120 men at 1s. 10d. each per week, for 52 weeks and 1 day, amounts to . . .	. . .	6101 11 8
Whereof poundage for their whole pay being £19,460 11s. 8d. is . . .	973 0 7	
One day's pay for the Hospitall (Chelsea) . .	53 6 4	
		1026 6 11
Remains to be issued to the agent . . .	. .	5075 4 9
To be by him applyed, viz.—		
To the off-reckonings of 74 servants, at 1s. 10d. each per week, for 52 weeks and 1 day, amounts to .	. . .	353 14 0½
Deduct poundage of the full pay of the servants, £1125 8s. 4d. is . . .	56 5 5	
One day's pay for the Hospitall (Chelsea) . .	3 1 8	
		59 7 1
Remains to the officers for their servants . . .	. .	294 6 11½
And for the contractors for cloathing . . .	. .	4780 17 9½
		5075 4 9

Thus, for the Second Regiment of Foot Guards, (call'd the Coldstream Regiment) consisting of 14 companies, of 80 men in each, besides officers . . 4780 17 9½

Note.—The Establishment allows pay for an agent to this and the First Regiment of Foot Guards: soe no agency is there charged, as is in all the other regiments on the English establishment.

MS. Harleian. No. 1308. Brit. Mus.

---

[1] The King's Warrant establishing new regulations in regard to the Off-reckonings, to take effect from 1st January, 169⅘, is dated Camp at Becelaer, 17th June (O. S.) 1695.—War-Office.

267.

Establishment of the Coldstream, from the twenty-sixth of March, 1699; consisting of fourteen companies of forty private men in each; in all 560, besides officers.

Field and Staff Officers.	£	s.	d.	Per Diem. £	s.	d.	Per Annum. £	s.	d.
Colonel as Colonel	1	.	.	1	1	8	395	8	4
In lieu of his servants	.	1	8						
Lieutenant-Colonel as Lieutenant-Colonel	.	.	.	0	12	0	219	0	0
Major as Major	.	.	.	0	8	0	146	0	0
Chaplain	.	.	.	0	6	8	121	13	4
Chirurgeon 4s., and one Mate 2s. 6d.	.	.	.	0	6	6	118	12	6
Adjutant	.	.	.	0	4	0	73	0	0
Quarter-Master	.	.	.	0	4	0	73	0	0
Solicitor to this regiment	.	.	.	0	4	0	73	0	0
Drum-Major	.	.	.	0	1	6	27	7	6
Deputy-Marshal	.	.	.	0	1	0	18	5	0
				3	9	4	1,265	6	8

One Company.

	£	s.	d.	£	s.	d.	£	s.	d.
Captain	.	14	.	0	15	8	285	18	4
In lieu of his servants	.	1	8						
Lieutenant	.	7	.	0	7	10	142	19	2
In lieu of his servant	.	.	10						
Ensign	.	5	.	0	5	10	106	9	2
In lieu of his servant	.	.	10						
Two Serjeants, each 18d.	.	.	.	0	3	0	54	15	0
Two Corporals, each 12d.	.	.	.	0	2	0	36	10	0
Two Drummers, each 12d.	.	.	.	0	2	0	36	10	0
Forty private men, each 10d.	.	.	.	1	13	4	608	6	8
				3	9	8	1,271	8	4
Eleven Companies more, at the same numbers and rates				38	6	4	13,985	11	8

1st Company of Granadiers.

	£	s.	d.	£	s.	d.	£	s.	d.
Captain	.	14	.	0	15	8	285	18	4
In lieu of his servants	.	1	8						
Two Lieutenants, each 7s.	.	14	.	0	15	8	285	18	4
In lieu of their servants, each 10d.	.	1	8						
Two Serjeants, each 18d.	.	.	.	0	3	0	54	15	0
Two Corporals, each 12d.	.	.	.	0	2	0	36	10	0
Two Drummers, each 12d.	.	.	.	0	2	0	36	10	0
Forty Granadiers, each 10d.	.	.	.	1	13	4	608	6	8
				3	11	8	1,307	18	4
2nd Company of Granadiers, the same				3	11	8	1,307	18	4
Total for 365 days				52	8	8	19,138	3	4

War-Office.

[In the establishments, from 25th April, 1700, to 24th June, 1713, the pay of the regulated number of non-effective men was allowed to the officers as before, and the allowance in lieu of servants withdrawn.]

268.

Establishment of the Coldstream from the twenty-fourth of June, 1713; consisting of fourteen companies of forty private men in each; in all, 694, officers included.

Field and Staff Officers.	£	s.	d.	Per Day. £	s.	d.	For 184 Days. £	s.	d.
Colonel as Colonel	1	.	.	1	2	6	207	0	0
In lieu of his servants	.	2	6						
Lieutenant-Colonel as Lieutenant-Colonel	.	.	.	0	12	0	110	8	0
Major as Major [1]	.	.	.	0	8	0	73	12	0
Chaplain	.	.	.	0	6	8	61	6	8
Chirurgeon 4s., and one Mate 2s. 6d.	.	.	.	0	6	6	59	16	0
One Adjutant	.	.	.	0	4	0	36	16	0
Quarter-Master	.	.	.	0	4	0	36	16	0
Solicitor to this regiment	.	.	.	0	4	0	36	16	0
Drum-Major	.	.	.	0	1	6	13	16	0
Deputy-Marshal	.	.	.	0	1	0	9	4	0
				3	10	2	645	10	8
One Company.									
Captain	.	14	.	0	16	6	151	16	0
In lieu of his servants	.	2	6						
Lieutenant	.	7	.	0	7	10	72	1	4
In lieu of his servant	.	.	10						
Ensign	.	5	.	0	5	10	53	13	4
In lieu of his servant	.	.	10						
Two Serjeants, each 18d.	.	.	.	0	3	0	27	12	0
Two Corporals, each 12d.	.	.	.	0	2	0	18	8	0
Two Drummers, each 12d.	.	.	.	0	2	0	18	8	0
Forty private men, each 10d.	.	.	.	1	13	4	306	13	4
				3	10	6	648	12	0
Eleven Companies more, at the same numbers and rates				38	15	6	7134	12	0
1st Company of Granadiers.									
Captain	.	14	.	0	16	6	151	16	0
In lieu of his servants	.	2	6						
Two Lieutenants, each 7s.	.	14	.	0	15	8	144	2	8
In lieu of their servants, each 10d.	.	1	8						
Two Serjeants, each 18d.	.	.	.	0	3	0	27	12	0
Two Corporals, each 12d.	.	.	.	0	2	0	18	8	0
Two Drummers, each 12d.	.	.	.	0	2	0	18	8	0
Forty Granadiers, each 10d.	.	.	.	1	13	4	306	13	4
				3	12	6	667	0	0
2nd Company of Granadiers, the same				3	12	6	667	0	0
Total for 184 days				53	1	2	9762	14	8

War-Office.

---

[1] A second Major to the regiment was appointed 25th April, 1711, but omitted in the establishment.

269.

Establishment and Rates of Pay of the Coldstream Guards, from 25th May, 1797; consisting of 20 companies of 95 private men in each: in all, 2214 men, officers included.

	Per Diem.			For 365 Days.		
Field and Staff Officers.	£.	s.	d.	£.	s.	d.
Colonel as Colonel, £1; and in lieu of his servants, 2s. 6d.	1	2	6	410	12	6
Lieutenant-Colonel as Lieutenant-Colonel	0	12	0	219	0	0
Two Majors as Majors, each 8s. 0d.	0	16	0	292	0	0
Two Adjutants . 4 0	0	8	0	146	0	0
Quarter-Master . 4 8 } Allowance . 1 0 }	0	5	8	103	8	4
Surgeon	0	15	0	273	15	0
Three Assistant Surgeons, } 5 0 each }	0	15	0	273	15	0
Solicitor	0	4	0	73	0	0
Drum-major	0	1	6	27	7	6
Deputy Marshall	0	1	0	18	5	0
Allowance in lieu of the Chaplain's pay[1]	0	6	8	121	13	4
	5	7	4	1,958	16	8
One Company.						
Captain, 14s.; in lieu of his servants, 2s. 6d.	0	16	6	301	2	6
Lieutenant, 7s.; in lieu of his servant, 10d.	0	7	10	142	19	2
Ensign, 5s.; in lieu of his servant, 10d.	0	5	10	106	9	2
Five Serjeants, each . 1s. 10d. } 2 4¾ Additional pay . 6¾ }	0	11	11¾	218	12	6¾
Five Corporals, each . 1 2 } 1 8¼ Additional pay . 6¼ }	0	8	5¼	155	19	8¼
Two Drummers, each . 1 0 } 1 5¾ Additional pay . 0 5¾ }	0	2	11½	53	19	9¼
Ninety-five privates, each . 0 10 } 1 4 Additional pay . 6 }	6	6	8	2,311	13	4
	9	0	2½	3,288	16	0½
Allowance to the widows . 1 8 } „ to the Colonel, and for } 1 7¾ clothing lost by deserters, &c. } Allowance to the Captain for Re- } 1 1½ cruiting, &c. } Allowance to the agent . 0 6¾ }	0	5	0	91	5	0
	9	5	2½	3,380	1	0½
Fifteen Companies more . .	138	18	1½	50,700	15	7½
	148	3	4	54,080	16	8

[1] The regimental chaplain was discontinued from 25th December, 1796, but pay allowed till a vacancy occurred.

Establishment and Rates of Pay of the Coldstream Guards, from 25th May, 1797; consisting of 20 companies of 95 private men in each: in all, 2214 men, officers included.—*Continued.*

					Per Diem.			For 365 Days.		
					£.	s.	d.	£.	s.	d.
Brought forward					148	3	4	54,080	16	8
One Company of Grenadiers.										
Captain, 14*s.*; in lieu of his servants, 2*s.* 6*d.*					0	16	6	301	2	6
Two Lieutenants, each 7*s.*; in lieu of their servants, 1*s.* 8*d.*					0	15	8	285	18	4
	s.	*d.*	*s.*	*d.*						
Five Serjeants, each	1	10	2	4¾	0	11	11¾	218	12	4¾
Additional pay	0	6¾								
Five Corporals, each	1	2	1	8¼	0	8	5¼	153	19	8¼
Additional pay	0	6¼								
Two Drummers, each	1	0	1	5¾	0	2	11½	53	19	9½
Additional pay	0	5¾								
Two Fifers, each	1	0	1	5¾	0	2	11½	53	19	9½
Additional pay	0	5¾								
Ninety-five private men, each	0	10	1	4	6	6	8	2,311	13	4
Additional pay	0	6								
					9	5	2	3,379	5	10
Allowances to widows, &c., as before					0	5	0	91	5	0
					9	10	2	3,470	10	10
One Company more of Grenadiers					9	10	2	3,470	10	10
One Company of Light Infantry.										
Captain, 14*s.*; in lieu of his servants, 2*s.* 6*d.*					0	16	6	301	2	6
Two Lieutenants, each 7*s.*; in lieu of their servants, 1*s.* 8*d.*					0	15	8	285	18	4
	s.	*d.*	*s.*	*d.*						
Five Serjeants, each	1	10	2	6¾	0	11	11¾	218	12	4¾
Additional pay	0	6¾								
Five Corporals, each	1	2	1	8¼	0	8	5¼	153	19	8¼
Additional pay	0	6¼								
Two Drummers, each	1	0	1	5¾	0	2	11½	53	19	9½
Additional pay	0	5¾								
Ninety-five private men, each	0	10	1	4	6	6	8	2,311	13	4
Additional pay	0	6								
					9	2	2½	3,325	6	0½
Allowances to widows, &c., as before					0	5	0	91	5	0
					9	7	2½	3,416	11	0½
One Company more of Light Infantry					9	7	2½	3,416	11	0½
Total for this Regiment					191	5	5	69,813	17	1
Allowance for clothing Drummers and Hautbois					.	.	.	172	4	6

War-Office.

[The preceding rates were subject to the following stoppages, on account of the off-reckonings for clothing, poundage, agency, and Chelsea Hospital, viz.:

From the pay of each	Serjeant	6*d.*	a day,	leaving	1*s.*	10¾*d.*	a day	net pay
"	Corporal	3½	"	"	1	4¾	"	"
"	Drummer	3½	"	"	1	2¼	"	"
"	Private	3	"	"	1	1	"	"

270.

Establishment and Rates of Pay of the Coldstream Guards, from 25th June, 1806; consisting of 20 companies of 123 privates in each: in all, 2887 men, officers included.

Field and Staff Officers.	Each.		Per Diem.			For 365 Days.		
	s.	d.	£.	s.	d.	£.	s.	d.
Colonel £1.14s., and in lieu of his servants 5s.	.	.	1	19	0	711	15	0
Lieut.-Col. £1. 6s. ditto 2s. 6d.	.	.	1	8	6	520	2	6
Two Majors, each £1. 2s., ditto each 2s. 6d.	1	4	6	2	9	0	894	5	0
Surgeon-Major	.	.	.	1	0	0	365	0	0
Battalion Surgeon	.	.	.	0	12	0	219	0	0
Four Assistant-Surgeons, each 7s. 6d.	.	7	6	1	10	0	547	10	0
Two Adjutants, each 10s.	.	10	.	1	0	0	365	0	0
Two Quarter-Masters, each 4s. 8d., allowance 1s. 10d. each	.	6	6	0	13	0	237	5	0
Solicitor	.	.	.	0	4	0	73	0	0
Deputy-Marshal	.	.	.	0	1	0	18	5	0
Two Serjeant-Majors, each 1s. 10d., additional pay 1s. 4d.	.	3	2	0	6	4	115	11	8
Two Quarter-Master Serjeants, each 1s. 10d., additional pay 1s. 4d.	.	3	2	0	6	4	115	11	8
Two Armourers, as Serjeants, each 1s. 10d., additional pay 8d.	.	2	6	0	5	0	91	5	0
Drum-Major	.	.	.	0	1	6	27	7	6
			11	15	8	4,300	18	4

One Company.

Captain 14s., and in lieu of his servants 2s. 6d.	.	.	.	0	16	6	301	2	6
Two Lieutenants, each 7s., and in lieu of their servants each 10d.	.	7	10	0	15	8	285	18	4
Ensign 5s., and in lieu of his servant 10d.	.	.	.	0	5	10	106	9	2
Seven Serjts., each 1s. 10d., additional pay 8d.	.	2	6	0	17	6	319	7	6
Seven Corporals, each 1s. 2d., addl. pay 6½d.	.	1	8½	0	11	11½	218	4	9¼
Two Drummers, each 1s., additional pay 5¾d.	.	1	5¾	0	2	11½	53	19	9¼
One hundred and twenty-three Privates, each 10d., additional pay 6d.	.	1	4	8	4	0	2,993	0	0
				11	14	5	4,278	2	1
Allowance to the widows	.	.	.	0	1	8	30	8	4
Ditto to the Colonel and for clothing lost by deserters	.	.	.	0	1	7¾	30	0	8¾
Allowance to the Captain for recruiting, &c.	.	.	.	0	1	1½	20	10	7½
Ditto to the Agent	.	.	.	0	0	6½	10	5	3¼
Total for one Company				11	19	5	4,369	7	1
Fifteen Companies more of the like numbers and rates				179	11	3	65,540	6	3
				191	10	8	69,909	13	4

Establishment and Rates of Pay of the Coldstream Guards, from 25th June, 1806; consisting of 20 companies of 123 privates in each: in all, 2887 men, officers included.—*Continued.*

	Each.		Per Diem.			For 365 Days.		
	s.	*d.*	£.	*s.*	*d.*	£.	*s.*	*d.*
Brought forward			191	10	8	69,909	13	4
One Company of Grenadiers.								
Captain 14*s.*, and in lieu of his servant 2*s.* 6*d.*	.	.		16	6	301	2	6
Three Lieut. each 7*s.*, ditto each servant 10*d.*	7	10	1	3	6	428	17	6
Seven Serjs., each 1*s.* 10*d.*, additional pay 8*d.*	2	6	0	17	6	319	7	6
Seven Corporals, each 1*s.* 2*d.*, do. do. 6½*d.*	1	8½	0	11	11½	218	4	9½
Two Drummers, each 1*s.*, do. do. 5¾*d.*	1	5¾	0	2	11½	53	19	9½
Two Fifers, each 1*s.*, do. do. 5¾*d.*	1	5¾	0	2	11½	53	19	9½
One hundred and twenty-three privates, each 10*d.*, additional pay 6*d.*	1	4	8	4	0	2,993	0	0
			11	19	4½	4,368	11	10½
Allowance to the widows, to the Colonel, Captain, and Agent, as detailed above	. . .		0	5	0	91	5	0
Total for one Company of Grenadiers	. . .		12	4	4½	4,459	16	10½
One Compy. of Grenadiers more of the like numbers and rates	. . .		12	4	4½	4,459	16	10½
			24	8	9	8,919	13	9
One Company of Light Infantry.								
Captain 14*s.*, and in lieu of his servants 2*s.* 6*d.*	.	.	0	16	6	301	2	6
Three Lieuts., each 7*s.*, ditto each servant 10*d.*	7	10	1	3	6	428	17	6
Seven Serjs., each 1*s.* 10*d.*, additional pay 8*d.*	2	6	0	17	6	319	7	6
Seven Corporals, each 1*s.* 2*d.*, do. do. 6½*d.*	1	8½	0	11	11½	218	4	9½
Two Drummers, each 1*s.*, do. do. 5¾*d.*	1	5¾	0	2	11½	53	19	9½
One hundred and twenty-three privates, each 10*d.*, additional pay 6*d.*	1	4	8	4	0	2,993	0	0
			11	16	5	4,314	12	1
Allowance to the widows, to the Col., Capt., and Agent			0	5	0	91	5	0
Total for one Company of Light Infantry			12	1	5	4,405	17	1
One Company of Light Infantry more of the like numbers and rates			12	1	5	4,405	17	1
Total for the two Light Infantry Companies			24	2	10	8,811	14	2
,, two Grenadier Companies			24	8	9	8,919	13	9
,, sixteen Battalion Companies			191	10	8	69,909	13	4
,, Field and Staff Officers			11	15	8	4,300	18	4
Allowance for the clothing of Drummers and Hautbois			.	.	.	172	4	6
,, to three Field Officers removed from their companies, each £75			.	.	.	225	0	0
Allowance for great-coats to the non-commissioned officers and privates, at the rate of 3*s.* per man per annum			.	.	.	418	13	0
Total for this Regiment			251	17	11	92,757	17	1

Additional pay to corporals and privates, at 1*d.* a day after seven, and 2*d.* after fourteen years' service, commencing from 25th June, 1806.

War-Office.

[The preceding rates were subject to the following stoppages, on account of the off-reckonings for clothing, poundage, agency, and Chelsea Hospital, viz., from the pay of each Staff Serjeant and Serjeant 6*d.* a day, corporal and drummer 3½*d.*, and privates 3*d.*]

398   APPENDIX.

271.
ESTABLISHMENT.

(Compiled from Official Documents in the Sate-Paper Office, British Museum, and War-Office.)

From	To	No. of Comps.	Field Offrs Col., Lt.-Col., Maj.	Captains.	Capt.-Lt. & Lts.	Ensigns.	Adjutant.	Qr.-Master and Prov.-Marsh.	Surgeon.	Mates.	Chaplain.	Solicitor.	Drum-Major.	Gunsmith.	Serjeants.	Corporals.	Drummers.	Privates.	Total.	Servants.	
July 1650	Aug 1650	10	3	7	10	10	.	2	1	1	1	.	1	1	20	30	20	1000	1107	.	Drafted from the regts. in garr. at Newcastle and Berwick.
Aug 1650	Dec 1652	10	3	7	10	10	.	2	1	1	1	.	1	1	20	30	20	1200	1307	.	Raised to the same establishment as the other regts.in Scotland. A waggon-master also added.
Jan 1652/3	22 July 1655	10	3	7	10	10	.	2	1	1	1	.	1	1	20	30	20	1000	1107	.	Reduced 20 men each company.
23 July 1655	14 Oct 1655	10	3	7	10	10	.	1	1	1	1	.	1	1	20	30	20	800	906	.	The waggon-master and 20 men per comp. reduced, and quarter-master and provost-marshal "united in one person."
15 Oct. 1655	20 Dec 1657	10	3	7	10	10	.	1	1	1	1	.	1	1	20	30	20	740	845	.	The drum-major and 6 privates in each comp. reduced.
21 Dec 1657	Nov 1659	10	3	7	10	10	.	1	1	1	1	.	.	1	20	.	10	700	765	.	The corporals,1 drummer, and 4 privates in each comp. reduced: 3 privates per comp. to act as corporals, with 3d. a day extra.
Dec 1659	25 Jan 1660/1	10	3	7	10	10	.	1	1	1	1	.	.	.	20	.	10	1200	1264	40	The private men increased by General Monck at Coldstream. Servants allowed by regulation, dated Whitehall, Dec. 4, 1660; capts. 2, lieuts. and ensigns 1 each.
26 Jan 1660/1	Feb 1663/4	10	3	7	10	10	1	1	1	1	1	.	.	.	20	30	21	1000	1106	42	Placed on the establishment as a regiment of Guards. Regimental adj. appointed in June 1661.
Mar 1663/4	10 May 1667	10	3	7	10	10	1	1	1	1	1	.	.	.	20	30	21	1000 500	1606	42	"500 men added for sea-service."
11 May 1667	12 June 1667	12	3	9	12	12	1	1	1	1	1	.	.	.	24	36	25	1200	1326	50	Two additional companies added.
13 June 1667	25 Sep 1668	12	3	9	12	12	1	1	1	1	1	.	.	.	36	36	25	1800	1938	50	An augmentation of 1 serj. and 50 privates to each company.
26 Sept 1668	3 May 1672	12	3	9	12	12	1	1	1	1	1	.	.	.	24	36	24	960	1085	50	1 serj. and 70 privates in each company, and the extra drummer in the Colonel's comp. reduced.
4 May 1672	15 Nov 1672	3 9	3	9	12	12	1	1	1	1	1	.	.	.	6 27	9 27	6 18	240 882	1256	50	The establishment of the 3 comps. at sea remain the same, but to have 20 supernumeraries in each; the 9 comps. in and about London augmented 1 serj. and 18 privates each.
16 Nov 1672	6 Mar 1673/4	11 1	3	9	12	12	1	1	1	1	1	.	.	.	33 3	33 3	22 2	880 100	1117	50	The 11 companies in and about London reduced to 80 privates a comp. The company ordered on foreign service augmented to 100.

APPENDIX. 399

ESTABLISHMENT.—Continued.

From	To	No. of Comps.	Col., Lt.-Col., Maj.	Field Offrs	Captains.	Capt.-Lt. & Lts.	Ensigns.	Adjutant.	Qr.-Master and Prov.-Marsh.	Surgeon.	Mates.	Chaplain.	Solicitor.	Drum-Major.	Gunsmith.	Serjeants.	Corporals.	Drummers.	Privates.	Total.	Servants.	
7 Mar 1673	31 Mar 1674	11	3	1	9	12	12	1	1	1	1	1	.	.	.	22 3	33 3	22 2	770 100	996	50	1 serj. and 10 privates of each of the 11 companies disbanded.
1 Apr 1674	10 Jan 1675	12	3		9	12	12	1	1	1	1	1	.	.	.	24	36	24	720	845	50	The regt. reduced to 60 privates a company.
11 Jan 1675	15 Jan 1678	12	3		9	12	12	1	1	1	1	1	.	.	.	36	36	24	1200	1337	64	An augmentation of 1 serj. and 40 privates each company. The colonel allowed 6 servants, field-officers and capts. 3 each, lieuts., ensigns, and the quarter-master 1 each: warrant dated Nov. 10, 1677.
16 Jan 1678	Apr 1679	20 1	3		17 1	20 2	20 .	2	2	1	2	1	.	.	.	60 3	60 3	40 .	2000 100	2228 109	105 5	8 new comps. added. A grenadier comp. formed in April 1678: warrant to raise it, dated March 30.
May 1679	31 Dec 1679	12	3		9	12	12	1	1	1	1	1	.	.	.	24	36	24	720	845	64	All the new-raised comps. disbanded; and the old comps. reduced to former establishment.
1 Jan 1680	31 Dec 1683	12	3		9	12	12	1	1	1	1	1	.	1	.	24	36	24	720	846	64	A drum-major replaced on the establishment.
1 Jan 1684	12 June 1685	12 1	3		9 1	12 2	12 .	1	1	1	1	1	.	1	.	24 3	36 3	24 2	720 50	907	69	A grenadier comp. added from 1st January.
13 June 1685	15 July 1685	12 1	3		9 1	12 2	12 .	1	1	1	1	1	.	1	.	36 3	36 3	24 2	1200 100	1449	69	Recruited to 3 serjeants and 100 privates each company.
16 July 1685	24 July 1685	12 1	3		9 1	12 2	12 .	1	1	1	1	1	.	1	.	36 3	36 3	24 2	960 80	1189	69	20 privates in each comp. reduced.
25 July 1685	31 Dec 1685	12 1	3		9 1	12 2	12 .	1	1	1	1	1	.	1	.	24 3	36 3	24 2	720 60	917	69	12 serjts. and 260 privates disbanded.
1 Jan 1686	31 Aug 1688	12 1	3		9 1	12 2	12 .	1	1	1	1	1	.	1	.	36 3	36 3	24 2	960 80	1189	69	20 privates a comp., and 1 serj. to each battalion comp., added.
1 Sept 1688	30 Apr 1689	16 1	3		13 1	16 2	16 .	2	1	1	2	1	.	1	.	48 3	48 3	32 2	1280 80	1555	89	Four new comps. added from Sept. 1, and an additional adj. and surgeon's mate from Nov. 1.
1 May 1689	17 July 1698	12 2	3		9 2	12 4	12 .	2	1	1	2	1	1	1	.	36 6	36 6	24 4	960 160	1283	74	Three comps. transferred; and a 2d. grenadier comp. formed. The solicitor, who was previously paid through another channel, placed on the establishment.

APPENDIX.
ESTABLISHMENT.—Continued.

From	To	No. of Comps.	Field Offrs Cl., Lt. Cl., 1st&2dMaj.	Captains.	Capt.-Lt. & Lts.	Ensigns.	Adjutant.	Qr.-Master and Prov.-Marsh.	Surgeon.	Mates.	Chaplain.	Solicitor.	Drum-Major.	Dep.-Marshal.	Serjeants.	Corporals.	Drummers.	Privates.	Total.	Servants.	
18 July 1698	25 Mar 1699	14	3	11	16	12	1	1	1	1	1	1	1	.	42	42	28	980	1141	58	An adjutant, a surgeon's-mate, and 10 men a comp. reduced. Two servants only allowed to each captain of a company.
26 Mar 1699	24 June 1700	14	3	11	16	12	1	1	1	1	1	1	1	1	28	28	28	560	694	None	A further reduction of 1 serj., 1 corp., and 30 privates in every company. Servants to officers discontinued. A deputy-marshal placed on the establishment.
25 June 1700	31 May 1702	12 2	3	9 2	12 4	12 .	1	1	1	1	1	1	1	1	24 6	24 6	24 4	600 120	858	58	The battalion comps. augmented 10 men a comp., and the two grenadier comps. 1 serj., 1 corp., and 20 privates each. Servants re-allowed.
1 June 1702	31 Mar 1705	14	3	11	16	12	1	1	1	1	1	1	1	1	42	42	28	840	1002	58	1 serjeant, 1 corporal, and 10 privates added to each of the battalion companies.
1 Apr 1705	24 Apr 1711	14	3	11	16	12	2	1	1	1	1	1	1	1	42	42	28	980	1143	74	An augmentation of a 2d adjutant, and 10 privates to all the comps. Three servants again allowed to captains of comps., from Dec. 25, 1705.
25 Apr 1711	24 Oct 1712	14	4	10	16	12	2	1	1	1	1	1	1	1	42	42	28	980	1143	74	A 2d major appointed, retaining his company.
25 Oct. 1712	24 May 1713	14	4	10	16	12	2	1	1	1	1	1	1	1	42	42	28	840	1003	74	10 privates a comp. reduced.
25 May 1713	21 July 1715	14	4	10	16	12	1	1	1	1	1	1	1	1	28	28	28	560	694	.	A further reduction of an adj., 1 serj., 1 corp., and 20 privates each comp. Servants finally discontinued.
22 July 1715	25 Sept 1715	18	4	14	20	16	1	1	1	1		1	1	1	36	36	36	720	890	.	Four new comps. added.
26 Sept 1715	24 Aug 1716	18	4	14	20	16	2	1	1	2	1	1	1	1	54	54	36	1260	1468	.	An augmentation of a 2d adjutant, a mate, 1 serj., 1 corp., & 30 privates to each company.
25 Aug 1716	23 Nov 1717	18	4	14	20	16	2	1	1	2	1	1	1	1	54	54	36	1170	1378	.	Ordered " to muster 65 privates per comp. from Aug. 25."
24 Nov 1717	24 Jan 1722/3	18	4	14	20	16	2	1	1	2	1	1	1	1	36	54	36	882	1072	.	The establishment to be reduced, and to consist of 2 serjeants, 3 corporals, 2 drummers, and 49 privates each company.
25 Jan. 1722/3	24 Dec 1725	18	4	14	20	16	2	1	1	2	1	1	1	1	54	54	36	1026	1234	.	1 serjeant and 8 privates added to each company. A provost-marshal to the three regiments of Foot Guards, at 3s. per diem. established from Dec. 25, 1724.

APPENDIX. 401

ESTABLISHMENT.—Continued.

From	To	No. of Comps.	Field Offrs Cl., Lt. Cl., 1st&2dMaj	Captains.	Capt.-Lt. & Lrs.	Ensigns.	Adjutant.	Qr.-Master and Prov.-Marsh.	Surgeon.	Mates.	Chaplain.	Solicitor.	Drum-Major.	Dep.-Marshal.	Serjeants.	Corporals.	Drummers.	Privates.	Total.	
25 Dec 1725	31 Jan 1726	18	4	14	20	16	2	1	1	2	1	1	1	1	54	54	36	1008	1216	1 private per company reduced.
1 Feb. 1726	24 Nov 1729	18	4	14	20	16	2	1	1	2	1	1	1	1	54	54	36	1080	1288	Augmented four privates each company.
25 Nov 1729	24 Feb 1733	18	4	14	20	16	2	1	1	2	1	1	1	1	54	54	36	900	1108	Reduced 10 privates each company.
25 Feb 1733	24 Feb 1734	18	4	14	20	16	2	1	1	2	1	1	1	1	54	54	36	1080	1288	Augmented 10 privates each company.
25 Feb 1734	14 Jan 1734	18	4	14	20	16	2	1	1	2	1	1	1	1	54	54	36	1260	1468	Ditto; making each comp. 70 privates.
15 Jan 1734	24 June 1739	18	4	14	20	16	2	1	1	2	1	1	1	1	54	54	36	1080	1288	Reduced 10 privates per company.
25 June 1739	27 May 1742	18	4	14	20	16	2	1	1	2	1	1	1	1	54	54	36	1278	1486	Augmented 11 privates each company.
28 May 1742	23 Sept 1745	9 9	2 2	7 7	10 10	8 8	1 1	1 1	1 .	1 2	1 .	. 1	1 .	. .	27 27	27 27	18 18	639 639	745 743	1st batt. on foreign service; 2d batt. at home. An additional qr.-master and surgeon's mate appointed.
24 Sept 1745	3 Oct 1745	18	4	14	20	16	2	2	1	3	1	1	1	1	54	54	36	1278	1488	Both battalions at home.
4 Oct. 1745	24 Dec 1746	18	4	14	20	16	2	2	1	3	1	1	1	1	72	72	36	1800	2046	1 serj., 1 corp., and 29 privates added to each company.
25 Dec 1746	24 Dec 1748	18	4	14	20	16	2	2	1	3	1	1	1	1	72	72	36	1620	1866	Reduced 10 men a comp.; each to consist of 4 serjs., 4 corps., 2 drummers, and 90 privates.
25 Dec 1748	15 Feb 1748	18	4	14	20	16	2	2	1	3	1	1	1	1	54	54	36	1080	1290	1 serj., 1 corp., and 30 privates per comp. reduced.
16 Feb 1748	31 Mar 1755	18	4	14	20	16	2	1	1	2	1	1	1	1	36	54	36	864	1054	A further reduction of the youngest qr.-master, and surgeon's-mate; and 1 serj. and 12 privates a company.
1 Apr 1755	24 Dec 1758	18	4	14	20	16	2	1	1	2	1	1	1	1	54	54	36	1260	1468	Augmented 1 serj. and 22 privates each company.
25 Dec 1758	10 July 1759	18	4	14	20	16	2	1	1	2	1	1	1	1	54	54	40	1260	1472	4 fifers added to the two grenadier companies.
11 July 1759	24 Oct 1759	18	4	14	20	16	2	1	1	2	1	1	1	1	54	72	40	1440	1670	Augmented 1 corp. and 10 privates each company.
25 Oct 1759	7 Mar 1760	18	4	14	20	16	2	1	1	2	1	1	1	1	72	72	40	1620	1868	A further augmentation of 1 serj. and 10 privates a comp.

APPENDIX.

ESTABLISHMENT.—*Continued.*

From	To	No. of Comps.	Field Offrs Cl., Lt.-Cl., 1st&2dMaj.	Captains.	Capt.-Lt. & Lts.	Ensigns.	Adjutants.	Quart.-Masters.	Surgeon-Major.	Mates & Ass. Sus.	Chaplain.	Solicitor.	Drum-Major.	Dep. Marshal.	Serj.-Majors.	Qu.-Mr. Serjs.	ArmorerSerjs.	Serjeants.	Corporals.	Drmurs.&Fifers.	Privates.	Total.	
8 Mar 1760	24 Mar 1763	18	4	14	20	16	2	1	1	3	1	1	1	.	.	.		72	72	40	1800	2049	10 men a company added; making each to consist of 100 privates. An additional surgeon's mate from Aug. 1, 1760.
25 Mar 1763	24 Mar 1778	18	4	14	20	16	2	1	1	2	1	1	1	1	.	.	.	54	54	40	846	1058	A surgeon's mate, and 1 serj., 1 corp., and 53 privates in each comp. reduced.—12 serjeants, 11 corporals, 4 drummers, 2 fifers, and 270 privates, drafted, in March 1776, to the brigade of Guards, for service in North America, and the like number recruited.
25 Mar 1787	24 June 1783	18	4	14	20	16	2	1	1	2	1	1	1	1	.	.	.	60	61	40	1080	1305	6 serjeants and 7 corporals added; and 13 privates to each company.
25 June 1783	23 Sept 1787	18	4	14	20	16	2	1	1	2	1	1	1	1	.	.	.	54	54	40	846	1058	The same number reduced.
24 Sept 1787	8 Nov 1787	18	4	14	20	16	2	1	1	2	1	1	1	1	.	.	.	54	72	40	1026	1256	An augmentation of 1 corporal and 10 privates to each company.
9 Nov 1787	7 May 1790	18	4	14	20	16	2	1	1	2	1	1	1	1	.	.	.	54	54	40	846	1058	A reduction of the same number.
10 May 1790	Oct. 1790	18	4	14	20	16	2	1	1	2	1	1	1	1	.	.	.	54	72	40	1026	1256	1 corporal and 10 privates added to each company.
8 Oct. 1790	9 Nov 1790	18	4	14	20	16	2	2	1	2	1	1	1	1	.	.	.	72	72	40	1206	1455	A further augmentation of 1 serj. and 10 privates to each company. A 2d qr.-master added from Oct. 15, the 1st battalion being under orders for foreign service.
10 Nov 1790	23 Feb 1792	18	4	14	20	16	2	1	1	2	1	1	1	1	.	.	.	54	54	40	846	1058	The 2d qr.-master, 1 serj., 1 corporal, and 20 privates per company reduced.
24 Feb 1792	24 Dec 1792	18	4	14	20	16	2	1	·1	2	1	1	1	1	.	.	.	54	54	40	792	1004	A reduction of 3 privates a company.
25 Dec 1792	23 Jan. 1793	18	4	14	20	16	2	1	1	2	1	1	1	1	.	.	.	54	54	40	972	1184	10 privates a company added.
24 Jan. 1793	24 June 1793	18	4	14	20	16	2	1	1	2	1	1	1	1	.	.	.	72	72	40	1278	1526	1 serj., 1 corp., and 17 privates added to each company.
25 June 1793	6 Aug 1793	20	4	16	24	16	2	1	1	2	1	1	1	1	.	.	.	80	80	44	1420	1694	Two light infantry comps. consisting of 2 capts., 4 lieuts., 8 serjts, 8 corps., 4 drummers, and 142 privates added.
7 Aug 1793	2 July 1798	20	4	16	24	16	2	1	1	3	1	1	1	1	.	.	.	100	100	44	1900	2215	A surgeon's mate, 1 serj., 1 corp., and 24 privates a company added. Regimental chaplain abolished from December 25th, 1796.

APPENDIX.

ESTABLISHMENT.—Continued.

From	To	No. of Comps.	Field Offrs (Cl, Lt.-Cl., 1st&2dMaj.)	Captains	Capt.-Lt. & Lrs.	Ensigns	Adjutants	Qnart.-Masters	Surgeon-Major and Surgeons	Mates & Asst. Sus	Chaplain	Solicitor	Drum-Major	Dep. Marshal	Serjt.-Majors	Qu.-Mr. Serjs	Armorer Serjs	Serjeants	Corporals	Drumrs. & Fifers	Privates	Total	Notes
3 July 1798	24 Nov 1799	20	4	16	24	16	2	2	1	3	.	1	1	1	.	.	.	120	120	44	2280	2635	A 2d qr.-master appointed, and 1 serj., 1 corp., and 19 privates added to each company.
25 Nov 1799	24 Nov 1801	20	4	16	44	16	2	2	1	3	.	1	1	1	.	.	.	140	160	44	2840	3275	1 lieut., 1 serj., 2 corps., and 28 privates added to each company; making them each to consist of 142 privates.
25 Nov 1801	24 Apr 1802	20	4	16	44	16	2	2	1	3	.	1	1	1	.	.	.	140	160	44	2340	2775	25 privates a company reduced.
25 Apr 1802	24 May 1802	20	4	16	44	16	2	2	1	3	.	1	1	1	.	.	.	120	140	44	2140	2535	1 serj. 1 corp., and 20 privates reduced in each company.
25 May 1802	24 June 1802	20	4	16	44	16	2	2	1	3	.	1	1	1	.	.	.	100	100	44	1900	2235	1 serj., 2 corps., and 12 privates a company reduced.
25 Jun 1802	24 Dec 1802	20	4	16	24	16	2	2	2	4	.	1	1	1	2	2	2	60	80	44	1420	1683	A reduction of the additional lieut., 2 serjts., 1 corp., and 24 privates a company. A surgeon, an assistant-surgeon, and 2 armorer-serjts. added. The 2 serjeant-majors & qr.-master-serjts. placed on the establishment; they previously received an allowance of 6d. a day each out of the non-effective money, in addition to their pay as serjeants.
25 Dec 1802	24 Mar 1803	20	4	16	24	16	2	2	2	4	.	1	1	1	2	2	2	80	80	44	1420	1703	1 serjt. a comp. added.
25 Mar 1803	24 May 1803	20	4	16	24	16	2	2	2	4	.	1	1	1	2	2	2	80	80	44	1620	1903	10 privates a comp. added.
25 May 1803	24 June 1803	20	4	20	24	16	2	2	2	4	.	1	1	1	2	2	2	80	80	44	1620	1907	The field-officers relinquished their comps. and four capts. added.
25 Jun 1803	24 Oct 1803	20	4	20	24	16	2	2	2	4	.	1	1	1	2	2	2	100	100	44	1900	2227	1 serjt., 1 corp., and 14 privates, added to each company.
25 Oct 1803	24 Oct 1805	20	4	20	44	16	2	2	2	4	.	1	1	1	2	2	2	120	120	44	2280	2667	An addl. lieut., serj., corp. and 19 privates added to each company.
25 Oct 1805	24 Dec 1805	20	4	20	44	16	2	2	2	4	.	1	1	1	2	2	2	140	140	44	2660	3087	1 serjt., 1 corp., and 19 privates added to each company.
25 Dec 1805	24 Dec 1809	20	4	20	44	16	2	2	2	4	.	1	1	1	2	2	2	140	140	44	2460	2887	10 privates, a company reduced.

APPENDIX.

ESTABLISHMENT.—Continued.

From	To	No. of Comps.	Field Offrs Cl., Lt. Cl., 1st&2dMaj.	Captains.	Lieutenants.	Ensigns.	Adjutants.	Qr.-Masters.	Surgeon - Major, & Bn. Surgeons.	Assist.-Surgs.	Chaplain.	Solicitor.	Drum-Maj.	Dep.-Marsh.	Serg.-Majs.	Qr-Mr-Serjs.	Armr. Serjts.	Sch.Mr.Serj.	Serjeants.	Corporals.	Drums. & Fifers.	Privates.	Total.	
25 Dec 1809	25 Dec 1811	20	4	20	44	16	2	2	2	4	.	1	2	1	2	2	2	.	140	140	43	2260	2687	10 privates a comp. reduced; a 2d drum-maj. added from Sept.25,1810, and 1 drummer discontinued.
25 Dec 1811	24 Dec 1813	20	4	20	44	16	2	2	2	4	.	1	2	1	2	2	2	2	140	140	43	2260	2689	2 school-master serjts. added.
25 Dec 1813	24 Sept 1814	20 2	4	20 2	44 2	16 4	2	2	3	4	.	1	2	1	2	2	2	2	160 16	160 16	43 4	2460 246	3220	Augmentation of a 2d bat. surg.; 1 serj.,1 corp., and 10 privates a comp.: and two addl. comps. added.
25 Sept 1814	24 Dec 1815	20	4	20	28	32	2	2	3	4	.	1	2	1	2	2	2	2	120	120	43	2280	2670	The two addl. comps. reduced, and 16 lieuts.; 2 serjts., 2 corps., and 9 privates, a comp. also reduced: 16 ens^s. added.
25 Dec 1815	24 Mar 1817	20	4	20	28	32	2	2	3	4	.	1	2	1	2	2	2	2	100	100	43	1900	2250	1 serj., 1 corp., and 19 privates a comp. reduced.
25 Mar 1817	24 Dec 1818	20	4	20	28	32	2	2	3	4	.	1	2	1	2	2	2	2	80	100	43	1700	2030	1 serj. and 10 privates in each company reduced.
25 Dec 1818	24 Aug 1821	20	4	20	24	16	2	2	3	2	.	1	2	1	2	2	2	2	80	80	43	1520	1808	4 lieuts., 16 ens., 2 assist-surgs.; 1 corp., and 9 privates a comp. reduced.
25 Aug 1821	24 Dec 1828	16	4	16	20	12	2	2	3	2	.	1	2	1	2	2	2	2	64	64	35	1344	1580	Four comps. reduced; the privates in each remaining comp. increased from 76 to 84.
25 Dec 1828	31 Mar 1833	16	4	16	20	12	2	2	3	2	.	1	2	.	2	2	2	2	64	64	35	1344	1579	The dep.-marshal[1] discontinued on the establishment as an effective man. One bat.-surg. ordered to be reduced in July, 1830; continued as a supernumerary.

[1] The allowance of 1s. a day to be paid as usual to the staff-serjeant who holds the appointment.

272.

Statement showing the variations in the Pay of the Army, from 1684; extracted from official documents for the Right Honourable Sir Henry Hardinge, when Secretary at War, by Mr. Croomes of the War-Office.

The earliest establishment of the Forces in the War-Office commences from the first of January, 168¾.

OFFICERS.—The subsistence of the army was issued periodically in advance;[1] but the arrears, amounting to one quarter of the gross pay, were reserved until the accounts of the regiments had been cleared.

In consideration of the subsistence being issued in advance, the gross pay of the officers was subject to a deduction of one shilling in every twenty shillings, called poundage, under a warrant of King Charles the 2nd, dated 16th March, 168¾.[2]

---

[1] Charles R.—Whereas by agreement in August, 1662, betwixt the officers of our guards and garrisons and Sir Stephen Fox, then Paymaster-General of our Forces, there hath been a deduction of twelve pence out of every twenty shillings drawn from the pay of all our said Forces, to enable the said Paymaster to advance their pay by weekly subsistence, and within a short time after the end of every muster to complete the full pay thereof both to officers and soldiers, which agreement hath proved of great advantage to our service in the constant payment of our said forces, and hath since been humbly resigned up unto us, by the said Sir Stephen Fox, with the deduction thereunto belonging; and we, thinking it absolutely necessary that our Forces be constantly paid by way of advance, as they have hitherto been; and having referred it to the care of the Commissioners of our Treasury to see it punctually observed, we do hereby direct, that the same deduction of twelve pence out of every twenty shillings shall be, as formerly, drawn out of the pay of our said Forces; whereof one-third shall be applied for Exchequer fees, and to the Paymaster of our Forces for the time being, and the other two-thirds shall remain in the said Paymaster's hands upon accompt, to be disposed of either towards the erecting, building, and maintaining our Royal Hospital at Chelsea, for aged, maimed, and infirm land soldiers, or towards the payment of the establishment of our Forces, as we shall from time to time direct, by the Commissioners of our Treasury, who are hereby appointed to take and examine the accompts of the said building, and of all monies expended towards the said hospital; and the said Paymaster is hereby authorised and directed to apply out of the said deduction what is necessary for the said hospital for three years, to commence from the end of December, 1682, and to be accomptable for the same to the Commissioners of our Treasury, so as what shall be undisposed of towards the use of the said hospital be applied to the lessening the charge upon the establishment of our said forces. Given at our Court at Newmarket, the 17th day of March, 168¾, in the thirty-sixth year of our reign. By his Majesty's command.

A Warrant, dated 17th June, 1684, directs a further deduction of one day's pay " from our Guards and Garrisons every year, and two
" days every Leap-year, towards the building and maintaining the
" said Hospital."

[2] The first warrants for deducting the poundage and hospital are dated in 168¾, and annexed to the establishment of that year.

A further deduction of one day's gross pay annually, called Hospital Money, was likewise made, under a warrant of 17th June, 1684. These contributions were made applicable to the maintenance of Chelsea Hospital, and appropriated to other military and civil disbursements on account of the army.

The gross pay was likewise subject, from the earliest date, to a deduction of 2d. in the pound, as an allowance to the regimental agent.

When the accounts of a regiment were cleared, deductions for the poundage and hospital were made by the Paymaster-General from the arrears in his hands; the balance was issued to the agent, who, after deducting his agency, paid the residue to the officers, under the title of net arrears.

SOLDIERS.—The pay of the non-commissioned officers and privates was liable to the like deductions, and was divided into subsistence and off-reckonings.

The subsistence was issued net periodically, but the off-reckonings were reserved, and applied to the following purposes.

First.—The poundage and hospital money on the gross pay were deducted by the Paymaster-General, in the same manner, and for the same objects as from the arrears of the officers.

Secondly.— One halfpenny per week was reserved by the regimental agent for the Surgeon as medicine-money.

Thirdly.—One halfpenny per week was also reserved for the officer acting as Paymaster.

Fourthly.—Two-pence in the pound on the gross pay was retained by the agent as his allowance, and the residue, being the net off-reckonings, became the property of the Colonel; out of which he was bound to provide clothing, under his Majesty's regulations, framed from time to time by boards of general officers.

In the cavalry was included, as a component part of the pay of every officer and man, an allowance of 9d. per diem, being for the subsistence of his horse; which 9d. was subject to similar deductions of poundage, hospital and agency, and also to a further deduction of one halfpenny per diem, to cover the cost of shoeing, &c.

The pay of the man and horse was, until 1783, subject likewise to a deduction of one penny per diem, as an allowance to the riding-master for the period during which the horses were at grass; which period varied from sixteen to twenty weeks in each year. For the purpose of defraying the recruiting and other charges, the pay of a fixed number of men, termed "non-effective men," was included in the numbers borne on the establishment of each corps; the charge for which non-effectives was admitted in the accounts of each troop or company.

From the first Parliamentary sanction of a standing army in England, in 1689, to the year 1771, the only alterations made in the pay of the several ranks of officers and men of the army, and in the allowances borne upon the regimental establishments, were—

APPENDIX. 407

First.—In 1691, the following officers of Foot Guards were allowed an augmentation of pay, to take retrospective effect from 1st January, 16$\frac{89}{90}$, in consideration of their constant and chargeable attendance upon his Majesty's royal person in London and elsewhere, viz.

	s.				s.	s.
Colonel	8	a day, increasing his pay from	12 to 20
Lt.-Colonel	5	,,	,,	,,	7 ,, 12
Major	3	,,	,,	,,	5 ,, 8
Captain	6	,,	,,	,,	8 ,, 14
Lieutenant	3	,,	,,	,,	4 ,, 7
Ensign	2	,,	,,	,,	3 ,, 5

In January, 1701, the staff-officers of the Guards petitioned for a similar augmentation of pay. This petition was reported upon by the Paymaster-General, (Lord Ranelagh,) and the Secretary at War, (Mr. Blathwayt,) who submitted the following addition to the pay of the—

	s.	d.			s.	d.	s.
Chaplain	3	4,	increasing his pay from	6	8 to 10
Chirurgeon	2	0	,,	,,	4	0 ,, 6
Adjutant	2	0	,,	,,	4	0 ,, 6
Quarter-Master	2	0	,,	,,	4	0 ,, 6
Solicitor	2	0	,,	,,	4	0 ,, 6

if his Majesty should think fit to grant the prayer of the petition. The increase was not, however, extended to those ranks.

Secondly.—The grant of an allowance in 1713 and 1714, varying from 8d. to 4s. 6d. a day, in addition to the pay of the officers, in lieu of non-effective but paid soldier servants, who thenceforward either became effective, or ceased to be borne on the establishment. This allowance was not extended to Quarter-Masters of Infantry until 1718.

Thirdly.—In 1718, the following allowances were first borne on the establishment of each regiment of Cavalry and Infantry, viz. the pay of two warrant-men in every troop or company for the widows of officers.

Queen Anne, in 1707, directed (Warrants, dated 6th January, 170$\frac{6}{7}$, and 23rd Aug^t, 1708), that two men per troop or company should be kept non-effective in every regiment then serving in Spain, and their pay applied to the payment of pensions to the widows of the officers killed at the battle of Almanza. A board of General Officers, held at Whitehall in 1712, recommended in their report of the 16th October, that this practice should be adopted in every regiment, in order that a fund might thereby be created, for the purpose of allowing, under his Majesty's regulations, pensions to the widows of officers of the army generally.

This was acceded to; but in 1718, (Warrants, dated 9th April, 1717, and 15th May, 1717,) the practice of keeping two men of the establishment of each troop and company non-effective, was discontinued; but an allowance for this object, equivalent to such pay, was thenceforward borne on the regimental establishment, which continued until

1783, when a distinct vote was first taken for the charge of such pensions.

1718.— The pay of one warrant-man in every troop or company to the Colonels for clothing lost by deserters.

This continues to the present day; but by the clothing warrant of the 26th May, 1827, was increased from 6d. to 1s. for each warrant-man to the Colonel of every Infantry regiment, in consequence of an arrangement then adopted for the discontinuance of his former allowance of off-reckonings for certain fictitious ranks, and of his contribution in aid of the expense of great-coats.

1718.—The pay of one warrant or contingent man per troop or company to the Captain.

This allowance was for the purpose of covering the expenses and losses which the Captains of troops or companies might incur by burials of deceased soldiers, by men dying in their debt, and by desertions, &c.; and the present contingent allowance, which varies according to the number of privates borne on the establishment of each troop or company, has been substituted for the pay of the warrant-man since Mr. Burke's Act of 1783.

1718.—The pay of one warrant-man per troop or company to the agent.[1]

This continues to the present time, except that in the Cavalry the charge was reduced from 2s. to 1s. 6d. per diem for each warrant-man, when the subsistence of the horse was discontinued as a charge on the regimental establishment in 1810.

The warrant of the 15th July, 1717, under which these allowances to the Colonels, Captains, and agents, were first borne upon the establishment of every regiment in 1718, shows that they were substituted in each case for the pay of a certain number of non-effective men, whose pay had previously been provided on the establishment for similar purposes, and that the change took place with the sole view of making the nominal numbers of the establishment more nearly correspond with the actual effectives.

Fourthly.—In 1721, an addition[2] of 3d. per diem to the pay of the serjeants, corporals, drummers, and privates of Dragoons in Great Britain, to commence from the 25th December, 1720, " as a benefit " to the landlords, to prevent the frequent complaints made by them " of the great burthen the Dragoons had always been to them. The

---

[1] By a regulation of 1830, the agency was fixed at the following rates; 1¼d. in the pound upon the total amount (except clothing) borne upon the establishment, and in the Cavalry a daily allowance of 1s. per troop, if the regimental establishment shall consist of 600 rank and file and upwards, and of 11d. per troop, if below that establishment, and in the Infantry a daily allowance of 6d. for each company.

[2] This addition was not liable to the deduction for poundage and Chelsea Hospital.

APPENDIX. 409

" whole of the said addition to be paid to the landlords over and above
" what was paid for the subsistence of men and horses in former
" years."

In 1727 an increase [1] of 4*d*. per diem to the pay of the serjeants, and 2*d*. per diem to the pay of the corporals of the Foot Guards.

In 1771, by a regulation dated in May, the deductions for poundage and hospital money from the pay of the non-commissioned officers and privates of the regular Cavalry and Infantry, were ordered to be continued by the Paymaster-General, but the amount thereof was directed to be returned to them under the name of Necessary Money. This regulation, although it made an addition to the income of the soldier, did not in any degree affect the establishment of the regiment, as it only reduced the amount of saving to the public, by the amount of the deduction of poundage and hospital money returned to the soldier.

By the Pay-Office Act of 1783, commonly called Mr. Burke's Act, (from the enactments of which, however, the Household Troops [2] were excepted,) it was directed, that the deductions for poundage and hospital should be discontinued, and the net residue of the pay of the officer should be borne on the regimental establishment, and that the pay only of the non-commissioned officers and men, exclusive of the off-reckonings before explained, should likewise be borne on the regimental establishment. That the pay of non-effective men provided for the purpose of recruiting each troop or company should cease, and that in lieu of the emoluments which the captains had formerly derived out of the fund created by the said pay, an allow^{ce} of £20 per annum to each Captain should thenceforth be borne upon the regimental establishment, (this allowance to each Captain was so borne upon the establishment until 1824, when it was discontinued in regiments of Infantry, and in lieu thereof an addition of 1*s*. 1*d*. per diem was made to his pay, thereby augmenting it from 10*s*. 6*d*. to 11*s*. 7*d*. per diem,) under the title of Non-effective Allowance; and that the actual expense of recruiting and other contingencies should be charged in the regimental accounts, and be defrayed by the public; that the pay of the contingent men should likewise cease, and that an allowance in lieu thereof, varying according to the strength of each troop or company borne on the establishment, should be granted to each Captain, in order to cover his expenses and losses by deaths and desertions; and also, that fixed annual rates, varying according to the strength of the establishment, should be granted to the surgeon, to the officer acting as Paymaster, and in Cavalry regiments to the riding-master.

---

[1] This addition was not liable to the deduction for poundage and Chelsea Hospital.

[2] The establishments of the Life Guards and Horse Guards for the year 1831 have been prepared upon the same principle as other regiments of cavalry, and are in future to come under the enactments of the Act of 1783.

The establishment, as reformed in 1783, continued without alteration until 1797, the following allowances, which were granted in the interval, not having affected the regimental establishments.

In 1792 a further allowance was made to the non-commissioned officers and men, called a new allowance for necessaries; and in the same year an additional allowance of $1\frac{1}{2}d.$ per diem, called Bread Money, was also granted to them on home-service.

In 1795 the several allowances of old necessary money, (granted in 1771, as before explained,) and new necessary money and bread money, (granted in 1792,) were consolidated, and fixed at $2\frac{1}{2}d.$ per diem for each man; and by the Secretary-at-War's letter of 1st May, 1795, a further allowance was granted to the non-commissioned officers and men, to cover the extra price of bread and meat. The extra price of bread was, in that year, about $1d.$ per diem, and of meat about $\frac{1}{2}d.$ per diem per man.

Thus the private of infantry received as pay $6d.$ per diem, and as allowances $4d.$ per diem, out of which he was liable to a deduction for the cost of his mess, not exceeding $3s.$ per week, or $5\frac{1}{7}d.$ per diem.

In 1797 these allowances, having been found insufficient, were increased by an addition of $2d.$ per diem; and the whole, so consolidated and augmented, were added to the pay of $6d.$, and from this period borne on the establishment of the regiment at $1s.$ per diem, as the personal pay of the soldier; but at the same time the stoppage for his mess was increased from a sum not exceeding $3s.$ per week to a sum not exceeding $4s.$ per week, or $6\frac{6}{7}d.$ per diem, on "home service," and he was made liable to a stoppage on "foreign service" of $6d.$ per diem, when supplied with rations at the public expense, and of $3\frac{1}{2}d.$ per diem when not so supplied.

In 1797, the distinction which had so long existed between subsistence and arrears was discontinued for the officers of the army, (except in the Life Guards,[1] Horse Guards, and Foot Guards,) upon the appointment of a Commissioned Paymaster, instead of an acting one for every regiment, and the adoption of a new system of regimental accounts. The daily pay of the Field-Officers and Captains was simplified by excluding the minute fractions into which it had unavoidably been divided, in consequence of the former deductions from their gross pay; and the pay of the subalterns was increased by discontinuing the deductions for poundage and hospital. A further increase of $1s.$ per diem was also granted to subalterns of infantry not holding another commission.

In 1800, the small-beer, which had previously been supplied in kind to the soldier on home service, when in barracks, or billeted in settled quarters, was discontinued, and a contingent allowance of $1d.$

---

[1] This distinction ceased in the Life Guards and Horse Guards from 1st January, 1831.

per diem, in lieu thereof, was granted; but he was then made liable to a stoppage for his mess, not exceeding 4s. 7d. a week, or 7$\frac{6}{7}$d. per diem.

In 1803, the Field-Officers ceased to hold troops or companies, and additional Captains were appointed to those troops or companies; but the non-effective allowance of £20 per annum was continued to each of the three Field-Officers so removed, and is still allowed to the Colonel, Lieut.-Colonel, and first Major.

In 1804,[1] the medical officers of the army were placed upon a new footing; their pay was increased, and they were also allowed additional pay after certain periods of service.

In 1806, the pay of the regimental officers, and of the non-commissioned officers of infantry generally, was increased; and at the same time Captains, with the Brevet rank of Field-Officer, were allowed 2s. a day additional pay; Lieutenants of seven years standing as such, were allowed 1s. a day additional pay; but the difference between the former and the increased pay and allowance was not in any case to be received by an officer holding more than one military commission[2] or appointment. The privates of the Life Guards and Royal Horse Guards, and corporals and privates of every other regiment of Cavalry, were at the same time allowed additional pay at 1d. per diem after ten years' service, and at 2d. per diem after seventeen years' service; and the corporals and privates of the Foot Guards, and of every other regiment of Infantry, were allowed additional pay at 1d. per diem, after seven years' service, and at 2d. per diem after fourteen years' service; this additional pay, both for Cavalry and Infantry, after the second period of service, still exists; but the grant of additional pay after the first period of service was discontinued by his Majesty's Warrant of 24th December, 1822, for all men enlisted after the 25th January, 1823.

The claims to additional pay, admitted service in the East and West Indies to reckon in the proportion of two years' service in those climates, as three years of active service elsewhere.

By his Majesty's warrant and regulations of the 14th November, 1829, this distinction of climate was cancelled, and the claim of 2d. a day additional pay only commences after seventeen years, and fourteen years' service actually completed.—War-Office, June, 1830.

---

[1] By warrant of 29th July, 1830, the rates of additional pay of medical officers were again altered.

[2] By the Staff Pay Warrant of 30th July, 1830, this distinction between old and new rates of regimental pay of officers holding staff, garrison, or other military situations was abolished, and fixed deductions were to be made for the several ranks of regimental officers from the future issue of their staff pay.

273.

STATIONS.[1]

(Extracted from various official sources; but from 1670, principally from the Marching Route Books in the War-Office.)

Date	No. of Comps.	Station	Date	No. of Comps.	Station
19 July, 1650	10	At Newcastle and Berwick.	10 May 1652	10	Before Dunotter.
24 ,, ,,	10	Mordington.	26 ,, ,,	10	Dunotter Castle.
25 ,, ,,	10	Cooperspath.	June ,, ,,	10	Highlands.
26 ,, ,,	10	Dunbar.	,, ,, ,,	10	Lochaber.
27 ,, ,,	10	Haddington.	July ,, ,,	1	Bray of Mar and Ruthven Castle, (Capt. Powell's compy.)
28 ,, ,,	10	Musselburgh.			
29 ,, ,,	10	Arthur's Hill.	,, ,, ,,	9	Bashenough.
Aug. ,, ,,	10	Pencland Hills and Musselburgh.	,, ,, ,,	9	Loch Tamer.
			Aug. to Dec.	1	Bray of Mar and Ruthven Castle, (Capt. Powell's compy.)
18 ,, ,,	10	Do. and Collington.			
24 ,, ,,	10	Redhall.	Jan. 1653	9	Edinburgh.
29 ,, ,,	10	Musselburgh.	10/13 } Oct.1653	9	Linlithgow and Dunbarton.
30 ,, ,,	10	Haddington.			
1 Sept. ,,	10	Dunbar.	. Oct. ,,	1	Ruthven Castle.
3 ,, ,,	10	Do. (BATTIE).	Jan. 1653	9	Highlands.
6 ,, ,,	10	Edinburgh.	May 1654	10	Stirling.
14 ,, ,,	10	Towards Stirling.	,, ,,	10	Glasgow, Kilsith, Cardross, &c.
21 ,, ,,	10	Edinburgh.	June ,,	10	Stirling.
11 Oct. ,,	10	Glasgow.	8 ,, ,,	10	St. Johnstone's.
16 ,, ,,	10	Edinburgh.	9 ,, ,,	10	From St. Johnstone's towards the foot of Lough Tay.
8 Nov. ,,	10	Haddington.			
28 ,, ,,	10	Glasgow.	12 ,, ,,	10	Ruthven in Badgenoth [Badenoch], Cluney, and Glenroy.
Dec. ,,	10	Edinburgh.			
,, ,,	10	Hume Castle.	23 ,, ,,	10	Loughloughee.
,, ,,	10	Blackness Castle.	24 ,, ,,	10	Glenmoriston.
Feb. 1651	10	Edinburgh.	25 ,, ,,	10	Glenquoish.
4 ,, ,,	10	Linlithgow.	26 ,, ,,	10	Glensinnick in Kintale.
8 ,, ,,	10	Edinburgh.	27 ,, ,,	10	Eoghel.
,, ,,	10	Tantallon Castle.	30 ,, ,,	10	Glenteugh and Browling.
March 1651	10	Tiviotdale and Kelso.	3 July ,,	10	Duneene, near Inverness.
April ,,	10	Edinburgh.	6 ,, ,,	10	Fallow, near Inverness.
18 ,, ,,	10	Hamilton.	13 ,, ,,	10	Glendowert.
19 ,, ,,	10	Glasgow.	14 ,, ,,	10	Glenloughee.
2 May ,,	10	Edinburgh.	16 to 20 ,,	10	From Strathfillan towards Glenlyon.
June ,,	10	Do.			
29 ,, ,,	10	Linlithgow.	21 ,, ,,	10	Near Weemys.
30 ,, ,,	10	Torwood.	23 ,, ,,	10	Near St. Johnstone's.
7 July ,,	10	Glasgow and Kilsith.	Aug. ,,	10	Lence.
14 ,, ,,	10	Linlithgow.	2 ,, ,,	10	Stirling to Callander.
16 ,, ,,	10	Callender House.	7 ,, ,,	10	Balquidder.
20 ,, ,,	10	Queen's Ferry, Fifeshire.	10 ,, ,,	10	Stanbar to Glen Catron, (called Devil's Den.)
21 ,, ,,	10	Linlithgow.			
3 Aug. ,,	10	Towards Stirling.	12 ,, ,,	10	Foot of Glen Catron.
11 ,, ,,	10	Stirling.	13 ,, ,,	10	Aberfoyle.
16 ,, ,,	10	Do. and Stirling Castle.	21 ,, ,,	10	Do.
21 ,, ,,	9	Dumblaine.	Sept. ,,	10	Stirling.
,, ,,	1	Stirling.	,, ,,	10	Dalkeith and Edinburgh.
22 ,, ,,	9	Blackford.	Oct. ,,	10	Do. Do.
25 ,, ,,	9	St. Johnstone's.	Jan. ,,	10	Do. Do.
26 ,, ,,	9	Before Dundee.	17 Mar. 1654	2	Berwick.
1 Sept. ,,	9	Dundee.	From this period to Oct. 1659	10	The regiment was quartered in Edinburgh and the garrisons in the vicinity.
Oct. ,,	10	Do.			
Nov. ,,	10	Do.			
,, ,,	10	Aberdeen.	Nov. ,,	10	Berwick.
Dec. ,,	10	Do.	8 Dec. ,,	10	Coldstream.
Jan. 1652	10	Do.	1 Jan. 1660	10	Crosses the river Tweed.
24 ,, ,,	10	Dundee.	2 ,, ,,	10	Wooller.
Jan. to May 1652.	10	Do.	3 ,, ,,	10	Village between Wooller and Morpeth.

---

[1] The object in stating the movements of the regiment so minutely, is to show that a perfect trace of its services has been made, and that no material circumstance has escaped notice.

APPENDIX.

STATIONS.—*Continued.*

Date	No. of Comps.	Station	Date	No. of Comps.	Station
4 Jan. 16 59/60	10	Morpeth.	Feb. 1670/1	12	In London and Southwark.
5 ,, ,,	10	Newcastle.	16 Aug. 1671	12	City of London.
6 and 7 ,,	10	(Halt.)	6 Mar. 1671½	1	Bertye's company, 100 men, to march to Deal and embark.
8 ,, ,,	10	Durham.			
9 ,, ,,	10	North Allerton.	12 ,, ,,		Ditto to Portsmouth, and embark in such ships as the Duke of York shall appoint; 21 of the men on board the St. Michael.
10 ,, ,,	10	Boroughbridge.			
11 ,, ,,	10	York.			
12 to 15 ,,	10	(Halt.)			
16 ,, ,,	10	Ferrybridge.			
17 ,, ,,	10	Bawtry.	6 ,, ,,	1	Huitson's company, 100 men, to march to Gravesend, and embark. 31 men to go on board the Victory, Capt. Kempthorne.
18 ,, ,,	10	Mansfield.			
19 to 22 ,,	10	Nottingham, and halted.			
23 ,, ,,	10	Leicester.			
24 ,, ,,	10	Harborough.			
25 ,, ,,	10	Northampton.	18 ,, ,,		The two regiments of Guards to do duty in the Tower as they may be required.
26 ,, ,,	10	Stony Stratford.			
27 ,, ,,	10	Dunstable.			
28 ,, ,,	10	St. Albans.	27 Mar. 1672	10	In London.
29,30,31 } 1 Feb. } ,,	10	(Halt.)	22 April, ,,	1	Coke's company (100 men) to embark as the Duke of York shall think fit.
2 ,, ,,	10	Barnet.			
3 ,, ,,	10	London.	22 ,, ,,	.	Ten men from the Coldstream to march to Deptford, and embark on board the Dartmouth, Captain Sadlington.
14 Feb. 1661	10	Do.			
1662	10	Do.			
1663	10	Do.			
May, 1664	10	A draft of 50 men from the Lord General's regiment sent on board the ships bound for Guinea.	May, ,,	.	31 men from the Coldstream embarked on board the Princess, Captain Munden, on 8th instant.
,, ,,	.	A draft of 50 men for sea-service.	8 ,, ,,	.	Lieuts. Francis and Lascelles, and Ensigns Meade and Cotton, 4 serjeants, 1 corporal, and 199 privates, to embark on the 9th instant at the Tower, and go on board the fleet in the river.
,, ,,	10	London.			
Mar. 1665	10	300 men from the regiments of Guards, under Capt. Bennet, embarked on board the fleet in the Downes, on the 28th instant.			
			14 ,, ,,	3	To go to Gravesend by water to join Prince Rupert: if gone, two companies to proceed to Rochester.
,, ,,	10	London.			
1666	10	London, and a proportion on board the fleet under the Duke of Albemarle.	18 ,, ,,	3	Ditto ordered to return to their quarters in London.
May, 1667	12	London, Sheerness, &c. with the Duke of Albemarle.	19 May & 2 June, ,,	.	The men from on board the fleet to return to London.
1668	12	London.	1 Nov. ,,	.	18 soldiers out of each of the 12 companies of the Coldstream here in town to embark on board such ships as the Duke of York shall appoint.
1669	12	London.			
21 Feb. 1669/70	.	One commissioned officer, one serjeant or corporal, and 50 privates of the Coldstream regiment to embark in the ships going to the Straits, to join Sir Thomas Allen.			
			5 ,, ,,	1	Captain Huitson's company to march to Canterbury, and go for France, with the battalion formed for the service of the French King.
24 Mar. ,,	12	Quartered in London and Westminster.			
3 May, 1670	2	companies of the Coldstream to march to the borough of Southwark. (Captain Coke's and Bertye's.)	24 ,, ,,	11	In London.
				1	At Canterbury: going on service.
6 June, ,,	2	Captains Mutlow and Huitson's companies to relieve the two companies in the Borough, which are to return to their quarters in London.	May, 1673 to Sept. ,,	6	In London.
				5	On board the fleet.
				1	In the service of the King of France.
13 July, ,,	.	Eight soldiers from the Coldstream to march on 14th instant to Deptford, and embark on board the London, Captain Tinker.	2 Mar. 1673/4	11	In London.
			,, ,, ,,	1	In the service of the King of France. (Ordered to return home: landed 14th April.)
20 Oct. ,,	.	A serjeant and 12 musketeers of the Coldstream to embark on board the St. Andrew, Capt. Tinker, now at Woolwich.	12 May, 1674	12	In London, in the usual parishes.
			6 June, ,,	2	To march to Windsor and encamp.
			6 Nov. ,,	2	To march to Rochester. (Maj.

APPENDIX.
STATIONS.—Continued.

Date	No. of Comps.	Description	Date	No. of Comps.	Description
		Winter's and Captain Mutlowe's.) [1]			"to march up to the quarters of the regiment in London and Westminster."
6 Nov. 1674	10	Earl of Craven's, Lt.-Col. Sir James Smyth's, Capts. Mansfield's, Clarke's, Kirkbye's, Coke's, Huitson's, Sander's, Miller's, and Wythe's, in London.	20 Mar. 1678	.	The men under Capt. Mutlowe returned from Virginia to disembark on 23rd of March at Gravesend, and quarter there.
26 Feb. 1674¾	2	Sir James Smyth's and Mansfield's to Rochester, to relieve the two now there.	25 ,, ,,	.	Ditto to march from Gravesend to London, and join the regiment.
Mar. ,,	10	London.	28 Apr. ,,	2	OKeover's and Eastland's comps. to march from Rochester to the quarters of the regt. in and about London.
24 June, 1675	2	Earl Craven's and Clarke's to relieve the two companies at Rochester.	30 ,, ,,	4	Sinclair's comp. to embark on 1st May at the Tower Wharf, and go in boats to Greenwich, where they are to be put on board the ships for Ostend.
11 Aug. ,,	4	Southwark, (Mansfield's, Huitson's, Coke's, & Wythe's,) to assist the deputy-lieuts. in the suppression of riots.			Brett's comp. to embark at Dover for Ostend forthwith. Newport's and Sullyard's comps. to embark at Rochester for Ostend forthwith.
1 Nov. ,,	2	Coke's & Kirkbye's to relieve the two comps. at Rochester.			
8 Feb. 1675⅚	1	Lambeth, (Wythe's,) to aid in suppressing the great tumults of disorderly persons of the trades of hatters, weavers, &c.	13 June, ,,	1	Talmash's company to return from Guernsey to Portsmouth.
24 ,, ,,	2	Huitson's and Saunders's to relieve the two companies at Rochester.	22 ,, ,,	1	Ditto to march from Portsmouth to London.
20 June, 1676	2	Miller's & Wythe's to relieve the two comps. at Rochester.	26 ,, ,,	8	Comps. of the Coldstream to march to Hounslow Heath on Friday the 28th instant, and encamp.
Oct. ,,	10	London.			
4 ,, ,,	.	A detachment of 1 Captain, 1 Lieut., 1 Ensign, 2 serjeants, and 84 men, under Mutlowe, to embark for Virginia.	29 July, ,,	.	80 men to reinforce the comps. in Flanders, to embark under Captain Tonge at the Tower Wharf, for Ostend.
25 ,, ,,	2	Earl Craven's and Graham's to relieve the two companies at Rochester; "and the said reliefs are to be made every 4 months till further order."	4 Aug. ,,	8	Companies of the Coldstream at Brussells.
			10 ,, ,,	3	To march to Maidenhead on Wednesday the 14th instant, to attend the King whilst holding his Court there, and afterwards return to London.
1677	12	London and Rochester.			
Jan. 1677⅚	12	London and Rochester.			
23 ,, ,,	8	The new companies, as raised, to be quartered at Rochester, Dartford, and Erith.	14 Dec. ,,	8	The batt. of the Coldstream, on arrival from Flanders, to disembark at the Tower, and quarter in the Hamlets in the Tower.
2 Feb. ,,	1	Talmash's to embark at Harwich for Guernsey.			
6 ,, ,,	2	Parry's and Sullyard's to relieve Howard's company of the King's regt. of Guards at Rochester.	Jan. 1678⅚	5	Companies of the Coldstream landed at Dover to proceed to London.
7 ,, ,,	2	To Maidstone (Sinclair's and Brett's), and "to compleat their levies in those parts."	5 June, 1679	2	Companies of the Coldstream to march to Windsor to attend the King during his stay there.
20 ,, ,,	2	Price's and Street's from Rochester to London.	27 ,, ,,	2	Mansfield's and Mutlowe's comps. to march to Windsor on the 28th instant to attend the King, ditto
26 ,, ,,	1	Brett's from Maidstone to Dover, on Saturday or Monday next.			
,, ,, ,,	1	OKeover's to quarter at Maidstone, "and perfect his levies there."	12 Apr. 1680	2	Lord Craven's and Captain Street's comps. to march to Windsor to attend the King, ditto.
27 ,, ,,	4	To embark at the Tower for Flanders, on Thursday the 28th instant. (Wythe's, Miller's, Price's, and Clarke's.)	2 June, ,,	.	A detachment of 1 Captain, 2 Lieuts., 1 Ens., 4 serjeants, 6 corporals, 2 drummers, and 120 privates, ordered to embark at the Tower Wharf and
1 Mar. ,,	2	Sinclair's and Parry's comps.			

[1] "Dover is to be manned by one of the six companies of those two regiments of Guards quartered in and about Rochester."—State-Paper Office.

APPENDIX.

STATIONS.—*Continued.*

Date	No. of Comps.	Description
		proceed to Portsmouth, and transport themselves to Tangiers.
6 Sept. 1680	2	Lord Craven's and Street's to march from Windsor to Westminster.
Feb. 1680	12	The Coldstream quartered about Spital Fields.
Mar. ,,	.	A detachment of the Coldstream to march on the 11th instant to Oxford to attend the King.
,, ,,	3	Companies of the Coldstream to occupy the King's Mews on the 18th instant.
Apr. 1681	.	The detachment of the Coldstream arrived from Oxford: marched into the King's Mews on the 5th instant.
18 Apr. 1682	2	Companies of the Coldstream to march to Windsor, and quarter at Maidenhead.
Apr. 1683	6	Companies of the Coldstream on duty in the Mews.
,, ,,	2	Ditto at Maidenhead.
,, ,,	2	Ditto at Winchester.
,, ,,	2	Ditto at Tilbury, &c.
1 Sept. ,,	6	Ditto at the Mews, Tilt-Yard, St. James's, and Arlington-Gate Guards.
,, ,,	2	Markham's and Pope's at Winchester.
,, ,,	2	At Tilbury Fort.
27 Sept. ,,	2	Capts. Markham's and Pope's companies to march to Westminster.
30 Oct. ,,	2	Lord Craven's and Captain Markham's comps. to march to Tilbury Fort on the 1st November, to relieve Miller's and Heneage Finch's, who are to return to London.
19 Dec. ,,	2	Lord Craven's and Captain Markham's comps. to return from Tilbury Fort to London.
22 Feb. 1683	2	Huitson's & Kendall's comps. to march to Newmarket, and from Newmarket, on the 21st March, on their return to Westminster.
1 Apr. 1684	2	Ditto to march on the 3rd instant to Windsor.
12 ,, ,,	.	The detachment of the two regts. of Guards from Tangiers to disembark in the river, and to be quartered at Lambeth.
21 May, ,,	1	Cotton's comp. to march on 26th instant to Oakingham.
10 July, ,,	1	Ditto from Oakingham to Maidenhead.
16 Aug. ,,	2	Huitson's & Kendall's comps. to march on 26th instant to Hurley Pitts and Twyford, near Winchester.
,, ,,	1	Cotton's comp. to march on the 26th inst. from Maidenhead to London.
Sept. ,,	2	Huitson's & Kendall's comps. to march on the 25th instant from Winchester to London.
Oct. 1684	2	Cotton's & Markham's comps. to march on the 3rd instant to Newmarket, and from Newmarket on the 24th inst., on their return to London.
19 June, 1685	7	One batt. of the Coldstream to march on the 20th instant to Marlborough, and receive further orders from the Earl of Feversham.
13 July, ,,	.	The Coldstream to be quartered from Chancery Lane to Bishopsgate Street, at Islington, Holloway, &c.
Aug. ,,	4	Lord Craven's, Capts. Wakelyn's, Cholmondley's, and Rupert's comps. to march on the 3rd instant, and encamp at Windsor.
17 ,, ,,	.	One officer and 60 men of the Coldstream to attend Mr. Pepys, Secretary to the Admiralty.
20 ,, ,,	.	Some companies of the Coldstream to march to Hounslow Heath and back on 20th Aug.
24 ,, ,,	.	Some companies of ditto to march on the 26th instant from Windsor to Maidenhead.
4 Oct. ,,	.	Ditto to march on Tuesday next from Maidenhead to London.
6 Nov. ,,	.	The Coldstream to be quartered from Chancery Lane to Ludgate, Bishopsgate Street, &c.
Apr. 1686	.	100 men, with officers in proportion, of the Coldstream, to march on 1st May to New Hall, Essex, and encamp, to attend the King during his stay, and afterwards return to their former quarters.
May, ,,	3	Companies to march on 13th inst. to Maidenhead, &c., to attend the King at Windsor.
,, ,,	7	One batt. of the Coldstream, with a comp. of Grenadiers, to march on the 27th May to Hounslow Heath, & encamp.
24 June, ,,	7	The batt. of the Coldstream at Hounslow camp to be relieved, and march to London.
Aug. ,,	4	Companies of the Coldstream to march on 10th August to Maidenhead, to attend the King at Windsor.
,, ,,	.	The three batts. of the two regiments of Foot Guards at Hounslow to decamp on 10th August, and return to their former quarters in London.
Sept. ,,	.	The comps. of the Coldstream attending the court at Windsor to march on the 1st October to London.
May, 1687	3	Companies of the Coldstream to march on 16th May to Maidenhead, to attend the King at Windsor.

APPENDIX.

STATIONS.—Continued.

Date	No. of Comps.	Description	Date	No. of Comps.	Description
June, 1687	.	One batt. of the Coldstream to march on 8th June from London to the camp at Hounslow.	8 Mar. 168⅞	17	The two batts. of the Coldstream to embark forthwith for Holland: (arrived at Helvoetsluys 21st March.)
July, ,,	2 / 4	Companies of the Coldstream to march from London on 4th July to Hounslow and Windsor: to Colnbrook, Slough, & Datchet, on the 6th July, to relieve the 1st regiment of Guards.	1 May, 1689	.	Three comps. are to be drawn out of the Coldstream in Holland, 2 whereof to be incorporated into the First Foot Guards, and the other comp. as the King shall direct.
18 July, ,,	.	The batt. of the Coldstream attending at Windsor, on being relieved, to march and encamp at Hounslow.	Oct. ,,	.	The regt. in winter-quarters at Ghent.
			11 Jan. 16⁸⁹⁄₉₀	7	Comps. of the Coldstm. lately ordered to be raised to march to Colchester.
Aug. ,,	.	The batt. encamped at Hounslow to march on 5th August to London.	29 Mar. 1690		The batt. to march as follows:
			,, ,,	2	From Colchester to Colnbrook.
,, ,,	3	From London to Windsor.	,, ,,	3	Do. to Windsor, Eton, and Slough.
,, ,,	2	Companies to march on 31st August from Windsor, to attend the King at Oxford.	,, ,,	2	Do. to Staines and Egham.
			Apr. ,,	7	1st batt. quitted their winter-quarters at Ghent.
Oct. ,,	3	Companies to march on 11th Oct. from Windsor to London.	24 May, ,,	7	The 2nd batt. to march to the Tower.
June, 1688	7	One batt. of the Coldstream to march on 27th June to Hounslow Heath, and encamp.	1 Aug. ,,	7	Do. from the Tower to their former quarters.
			15 ,, ,,	7	Do. to quarter in the several Quarters in the city, Fleet St., Aldersgate St., and Holborn, &c.
Aug. ,,	3	Companies of the Coldstream to march on 7th August from London to Maidenhead, to attend the King at Windsor.	15 Nov. ,,	3	Companies to remove into quarters in Moor Fields, Shoreditch, &c.
3 Nov. ,, [1]	.	One batt. of the Coldstream to march with all possible speed to Portsmouth.	30 ,, ,,	1	From London to Tilbury Fort, and returned on the 6th of Dec.
22 ,, ,,	5	To rest at the Wallops, near Salisbury, and villages adjacent.	3 June, 1691	7	The batt. of the Coldstream under Lieut.-Col. Selwyn to march from London to Portsmouth.
,, ,, ,,	.	The batt. of the Coldstream that arrived first at Salisbury to march on Friday the 23rd Nov. to Stockbridge, next day to Winchester, and from thence to Kingston, in Surrey.	28 Sept. ,,	1	From Portsmouth to Bishop's Waltham.
			,, ,,	2	From do. to Chichester.
			,, ,,	1	From do. to Midhurst.
,, ,, ,,	5	Companies at the Wallops to march to Kingston.	13 Oct. ,,	1	From Bishop's Waltham to Southampton.
,, ,, ,,	5	From Andover to Kingston. The batt. of the Coldstream to march on 25th Nov. from Winchester to Uxbridge, and arrive there on the 29th.	,, ,,	3	From Portsmouth to Winchester, and the whole batt. to return to Portsmouth at such time as the Lt.-Governor shall direct.
,, ,, ,,	5	Comps. to march from Basingstoke on 25th November to Maidenhead, and arrive there on the 27th.	27 ,, ,,	3	From Winchester to London.
			,, ,,	1	From Midhurst to London.
			11 Nov. ,,	.	The Coldstream battalion to be quartered in Fleet Street, Aldersgate St., Holborn, &c.
Dec. ,,	17	In London: head-quarters at Whitehall.	4 Jan. 169¼	3	The companies at Portsmouth to march to London.
,, ,,	.	The regiment to march on 19th Dec. from London to Rochester.	6 ,, ,,	1	Lt.-Col. Skelton's company to embark on Tuesday the 12th inst. at Greenwich for Mardyke or Williamstadt.
21 ,, ,,	17	Rochester, Maidstone, and Dover.			
31 ,, ,,	3	To march from Dover to Milton and Sittingbourne.	Oct. 1692	8	1st battalion, winter-quarters Ghent.
29 Jan. 168⅞	.	The quarters of the regiment enlarged to Feversham, where 2 companies are to return.	,, ,,	6	2nd battalion in London.
			29 Apr. 1693	.	A detachment of 40 men of the Coldstream to embark for

[1] At this time William landed at Torbay, and James with the forces he could collect marched to oppose him: the route of the Coldstream was as detailed above.

APPENDIX. 417

STATIONS.—*Continued.*

	No. of Comps.			No. of Comps.	
		Flanders, to recruit the batt. there.			march on 26th inst. to Slough, Datchet, and Eton, to attend the King, and afterwards return to London.
8 Aug. 1693	.	Do. of 100 men, do. do.			
6 Oct. ,,	8	1st batt. of the Coldstream in winter-quarters at Ghent.	3 May, 1699	.	240 men from the 2 regiments of Guards to march on 4th inst. to Slough, Datchet, and Eton, do. do.
21 Feb. 169¾	6	Of the Coldstream to be quartered in Clerkenwell, Holborn, St. Giles's, and Gray's Inn Lane, &c.	7 June ,,	.	A detachment of 120 men from the 1st and Coldstream, under Lt.-Col. John Seymour, to march to Windsor, and remain during the stay of the Prince and Princess of Denmark: from 25th June to 11th Nov.
May, 1694	.	Lieut.-Col. John Hope, Capt. John Wilson, Harry Lawrence, and Ensign John Miller, with a detachment of the Coldstream, marched on 15th May to Portsmouth, and embarked, on board the fleet for Cameret Bay.			
Aug. ,,	.	The officers before named, and 4 serjeants, 6 corporals, 3 drummers, 138 private men, disembarked on 2nd Aug. at Portsmouth, from on board the fleet, and marched to London.	15 ,, ,,	.	30 men from the 1st and Coldstream to march to Upnor Castle.
			1 Nov. ,,	.	The detachment of the 1st and Coldstream at Slough, Datchet, & Eton, to return to London.
			27 Apr. 1700	.	A detachment of 300 men to march to Kingston, the Dittons, Hampton Court, and places adjacent, to attend the King, and to be relieved from time to time.
1 Oct. ,,	8	1st batt. of the Coldstream in winter-quarters at Ghent.			
21 Jan. 169⅘	.	Detachments from the regiments of Guards ordered to attend the King at Richmond.			
10 Oct. 1695	.	Do. of 180 men to Newmarket, and to return.	7 Feb. 170½	.	A detachment of the Guards to march to the Tower.
13 Nov. ,,	.	A detachment of 320 men from the regiments of Guards in London, to march in two divisions to Windsor and Eton, to attend the King.	27 Mar. 1702	2	Of the Coldstream to be quartered in St. Ann's, Westminster.
				2	St. Clement's Danes, and St. Mary's, Savoy.
Mar. 1696	8	The 1st batt. of the Coldstream arrived in the river 8th March from Flanders, and returned 6th April following.		8	St. Giles's in the Fields, and St. Andrew's, Holborn.
				2	St. Sepulchre's Without, and Clerkenwell.
17 Sept. ,,	8	1st batt. of the Coldstream winter-quarters at Ghent.	6 Apr. ,,	.	A detachment of 100 men from 1st and Coldstream to march to Windsor, "to attend the "Queen as often as she shall "repair there, and return "from time to time."
,, ,, ,,	6	2nd battalion in London.			
May, 1697	.	A detachment of 108 men from the Coldstream to embark for Flanders, to recruit the batt. there.	16 May, ,,	.	The detachments at the Tower and Hampton Court to join their regiments.
19 Oct. ,,	8	1st batt. of the Coldstream, on arrival from Flanders, to march to Deptford, Greenwich, &c.	,, ,, ,,	.	A detachment of 400 men of the Coldstream to march on 25th instant, and 200 of the 1st Foot Guards on the 26th, to Portsmouth, and pass over to the Isle of Wight.
14 ,, ,,	8	The 1st battalion quartered at Deptford, Greenwich, and Woolwich.			
,, ,, ,,	6	2nd battalion in London.			
17 Nov. ,,	8	1st batt. of the Coldstream at Deptford, Greenwich, and Woolwich, to march to the Tower of London.	8 June, 1702	.	The forces in the Isle of Wight to embark forthwith on the expedition under the Duke of Ormond.
16 Mar. 169⅞	.	A detachment of 200 men from the 1st and Coldstream Gds. to march to Windsor to attend the King, and return to London.	6 July ,,	.	260 men of the Guards, under Lieut.-Col. Holmes of the Coldstream, to march to Slough and Eton, on 8th inst., to attend the Queen: returned to London 19th August.
29 ,, 1698	7	A battalion of the Coldstream, under Colonel Matthews, to march on 30th inst. to Newmarket, to attend the King, and afterwards return to London: returned 22nd April.	Aug. ,,	.	60 men of the Coldstream, and 120 of the 1st Guards, under Lt.-Col. Holmes of the Coldstream, to march on 19th Aug. from London to Marshfield, to attend the Queen at
25 Dec. ,,	.	A detachment of 200 men of the 1st and Coldstream to			

APPENDIX.

STATIONS.—Continued.

Date	No. of Comps.	Description	Date	No. of Comps.	Description
5 and 14 Nov. 1702	.	Bath: returned to London 11th October. The batt. of the two regiments (1st and Coldstream) arrived from Vigo at St. Helens and Chatham to march to London.	9 Aug. 1703	.	their march from Portsmouth on 18th August. 180 men of the two regiments of Guards, under Lieut.-Col. Bissett of the Coldstream, to march to Bath to attend the Queen: returned 27th Oct.
25 Jan. 170⅔	.	A detachment of 80 men of the two regiments of Foot Guards to march to Windsor to attend the Queen and return.	10 ,, ,,	.	The detachment of the two regiments at Portsmouth to march on 16th inst., under Lieut.-Col. Ashton of First Guards, on their return to London.
Mar. ,,	.	Detachments of the two regiments of Guards to march as follows: 200 men, under Lt.-Col. Morryson of the Coldstream, to march on 20th inst. to Chichester, Havant, Fareham, and Titchfield; 70 men, under Lt.-Col. Ashton of First Guards, on 22d inst. to Midhurst; 70, under Capt. Filbridge, of First Guards, on 22d inst. to Arundel; 60 to Shoreham and Brighton; 80, under Capt. Stevenage of Coldstream, on 18th inst. to Dover Castle; 60, under Capt. Phillips of the Coldstream, on 18th inst. to Tilbury Fort, and back on 21st; and 60 on 18th to Sheerness.	,, ,, ,,	.	The detachment at Dover to return to London.
			Nov. ,,	.	60 men of the two regiments to march on the 3d instant from London to Farnham, as a guard over the French prisoners.
			,, ,,	.	60 men of the two regiments, under Captain Allen of the Coldstream, to march on the 1st November from London to Southampton.
			25 Dec. ,,	.	150 of the two regiments of Guards, under Lieut.-Col. Rivett of the Coldstream, to march on 27th instant from London to Winchester and Portsmouth, to attend the King of Spain.
Apr. 1703	.	70 men of the Guards from Midhurst to Portsmouth, 60 from Shoreham and Brighton to Portsmouth, 70 from Arundel to Portsmouth.	,, ,,	.	100 men of the two regiments, under Capt. Bodenham of First Guards, to march on the 26th instant from London to Chichester and Portsmouth, to attend the King of Spain.
2 ,, ,,		Quarters of the Coldstream regiment:—			
	2	St. Anne's, Westminster.			
	2	St. Clement's Danes, and St. Mary, Savoy.	,, ,,	.	50 men of the two regiments, under Capt. Peachey of First Guards, to march on 27th instant from London to Petersfield and Portsmouth to attend the King of Spain.
	8	St. Giles's in the Fields, and St. Andrew's, Holborn.			
	2	St. Sepulchre's Without, and Clerkenwell.			
27 ,, ,,	.	80 men from the two regts. of Guards to march to Windsor to attend the Queen, and afterwards return to their quarters in London.	11 Jan. 170¾	.	60 men of the two regiments to pass over to the Isle of Wight to attend the King of Spain.
			22 ,, ,,	.	A further detachment to go from Portsmouth to the Isle of Wight, to attend the King of Spain.
May ,,	.	The detachment of 200 men, under Lt.-Col. Morryson of the Coldstream, at Chichester and places adjacent, to march on 17th May on their return to London.	15 May, 1704	.	80 men of the two regiments to Windsor, to attend the Queen, and return to London.
17 ,, ,,	.	Detachment of 210 of the two regts. to Colnbrook, Slough, Eton, &c., to attend the Queen, and return.	27 ,, ,,	.	210 men of the two regiments, under Lieut.-Col. Stevenage of the Coldstream, to march to Windsor on the 1st June, to attend the Queen, and afterwards return to London. Returned 11th October.
4 Aug. ,,	.	The detachment of the two regiments of Guards at Portsmouth to be completed to 400 men.			
,, ,, ,,	.	A detachment of 400 men of the two regiments under Lt.-Col. Morryson of the Coldstream, to march on 7th Aug. to Portsmouth, and embark on board the fleet: ordered back to London, and began	2 June ,,	.	320 men of the two regiments, under Lieut.-Col. Salisbury of the Coldstream, to march on the 10th inst. from Portsmouth to London.
			20 ,, ,,	.	40 men of the Guards in the Isle of Wight to join their regiments in London.

APPENDIX.

STATIONS.—*Continued.*

Date	No. of Comps.	Description	Date	No. of Comps.	Description
20 June, 1704	.	60 men of the two regiments, from Farnham to London, under Capt. Bodenham of the First Guards, on the 29th instant.	Apr. 1707	.	28 men of the Coldstream and 3 drummers, drafted to recruit the battalion of the First Guards serving in Holland.
10 July, ,,	.	600 men of the two regiments, under Lieut.-Col. Russell of First Guards, to march from London to Portsmouth, and embark on the 26th instant for Portugal.	8 May, ,,		"Quarters of the fifty men in "each of the 14 companies "of the Coldstream in England."
Mar. 1705	.	8 men a company, drafted from the several companies of the two regiments of Guards in England, to recruit the battalion of First Foot Guards in Holland.		2	Islington.
				2	St. Clement's Danes, and St. Mary's, Savoy.
				8	St. Giles's in the Fields, and St. Andrew's, Holborn.
				2	St. Sepulchre's Without, and Clerkenwell.
2 April, ,,	.	A detachment of 200 men from the two regiments, under Lt.-Col. D'Avenant of the First regiment, to march on the 5th instant from London to Newmarket, to attend the Queen: returned to London on 25th April.	10 June, ,,	.	210 men of the First and Coldstream to march on Tuesday, 11th instant, to Windsor, to attend the Queen, and return.
			12 Aug. ,,	.	40 men of the First and Coldstream to Tilbury Fort, and 40 to Sheerness, to relieve the companies now there.
9 ,, ,,	.	120 men of the two regiments to march to the Tower of London.	20 Sept. ,,	.	200 men of the two regiments, under Colonel Hobart of the Coldstream, to Newmarket, to attend the Queen, and return to London.
,, ,, ,,	.	60 men of the First and Coldstream regiments to march on the 23rd April from London to Farnham.	26 ,, ,,	.	The detachments of 40 men each, at Tilbury and Sheerness, to return to Town.
10 May ,,		Quarters of the Coldstream:	14 Mar. 170⅞	.	A batt., making up 520 privates of the First and Coldstream Guards, to march on 15th instant from London to York.
	2	With their additional men, in St. Ann's, Westminster.			
	2	With ditto, in St. Clement's Danes and St. Mary's, Savoy.	3 Apr. 1708	.	The batt. of the two regiments of Guards at York to march on the 12th instant to Nottingham.
	8	With ditto, in St. Giles's in the Fields, and St. Andrew's, Holborn.			
	2	With ditto, in St. Sepulchre's Without and Clerkenwell.	8 ,, ,,	.	Ditto from Nottingham on the 21st instant, and arrive at Colchester the 5th May, to embark at Harwich for Ostend.
30 ,, ,,	2	The companies quartered in St. Ann's, Westminster, to march to Islington and remain.			
12 July, ,,	.	The detachment of the two regiments at Farnham to return to London.	29 ,, ,,	.	A detachment of 124 men from the two regiments, under Lt.-Col. Wheeler of First Guards, to march from London to Colchester, and join the batt.
23 Aug. ,,	.	210 men of the two regiments, under Lieut.-Col. Newton of First Guards, to march on 24th instant from Windsor to Winchester, to attend the Queen, and return.	. May, ,,	.	The batt. embarked on board the Anglesea and Nonsuch men-of-war at Harwich, and landed at Ostend on 22nd May.
8 Feb. 170⅝	.	310 men of the two regiments to go, on the 3rd March, on board the transports at Gravesend, and proceed to Spain to recruit the battalion there, now reduced to about 300 men.	20 June, ,,	.	A detachment of 200 men, with officers in proportion, from the First and Coldstream Guards, to march on 25th instant to Windsor, to attend the Queen, and return.
21 May, 1706	.	210 men of the two regiments to march on the 22nd instant to Windsor, to attend the Queen, and return.	22 Sept. ,,	.	200 men of the two regts. to Newmarket, to attend the Queen, and return to London.
21 Sept. ,,	.	200 men of the two regiments, under Lieut.-Col. Rivett of the Coldstream, to march to Newmarket, to attend the Queen, and return.	4 Oct. ,,	.	200 men of two regiments, to Windsor, to attend the Queen, and return.
			Apr. 1709	.	A detachment of the Coldstream sent to join the companies in Flanders.

APPENDIX.

STATIONS.—*Continued.*

	No. of Comps.			No. of Comps.	
May, 1709	8	Companies of the Coldstream quartered in London.			Quarters of the Coldstream: (8 companies.)
	6	Serving in Flanders.	6 Dec. 1711	2½	St. Giles's in the Fields.
17 June, ,,	.	It is Her Majesty's pleasure, that the recruits raised for the First and Coldstream Guards be quartered in the usual quarters in the room of those detached for Flanders.		2½	St. Andrew's, Holborn.
				1	Clerkenwell.
				1	Cripplegate.
				1	The Dutchy Liberty and St. Sepulchre's.
			13 Mar. 17$\frac{11}{12}$	.	A detachment of 200 men from the First and Coldstream to go in hoys to Harwich, and embark to join their regiments in Flanders.
25 ,, ,,	.	210 men of the two regiments to march to Windsor to attend the Queen.			
31 Oct. ,,	.	The batt. of the Foot Guards attending the Queen at Windsor, to march to London.	16 July, 1712	.	A detachment of 240 men of the First and Coldstream, "with commissioned & non-commissioned officers proportionable," to march to Windsor to attend the Queen during her stay there.
11 Apr. 1710	8	The companies of the Coldstream in England to be disposed of as follows:—St. Giles's in the Fields; St. Andrew's, Holborn; St. Clement's Danes; St. Giles's, Cripplegate; St. Sepulchre's; Islington; and St. James's, Clerkenwell.			
			22 Dec. ,,	1	The comp. of the Coldstream at Islington to remove, and quarter in the parish of St. Andrew's, Holborn.
			19 Feb. 17$\frac{12}{13}$		Quarters of the Coldstream:
,, ,,	.	131 men of the Coldstream, drafted from the eight comps. in England, to complete the six companies in Flanders.		14	St. Andrew's, Holborn; St. Giles's in the Fields; part of the Duchy Liberty; Clerkenwell; Cripplegate; and St. Sepulchre's Without.
26 Sept. ,,	.	210 men of the two regiments to march to Hampton and places adjacent, to attend the Queen, and return to London.	24 Mar. 1713	6	The batt. of the Coldstream arrived from Ghent at Gravesend, to proceed to London on 27th instant.
Mar. 17$\frac{10}{11}$	.	120 men of the Coldstream, drafted from the companies in England, to recruit the companies in Flanders.			
			,, ,,	6	Companies of the Coldstream quartered in the Savoy from 28th March to 30th April.
19 ,, ,,	.	A lieut. and 40 men of the First and Coldstream Guards to parade in Covent Garden, "to prevent any mischief that may happen at the playhouse in Covent Garden."	May, ,,	6	Ditto in barracks at Hampton Court from 1st May to 31st July.
			29 July, ,,	14	Quarters of the Coldstream the same as ordered on 19th February last.
25 Apr. 1711	2	Comps. of the Coldstream to proceed from London to Harwich, to embark for Flanders.	1 Aug. ,,	.	A detachment of 240 men of the First and Coldstream, with commissioned and non-commissioned officers, to march to attend the Queen at Hampton Court and Windsor, and afterwards return to their quarters in London.
10 May, ,,	2	Ditto to return from Harwich forthwith to their former quarters in London.			
22 June, 1711	.	A detachment of 200 men from the First & Coldstream regiments, "with officers proportionable," to march to Windsor to attend the Queen during her stay.			
			3 Sept. ,,	.	The detachment of the First and Coldstream to march from Windsor (as soon as relieved by the first battalion of the Third Foot Guards,) to their former quarters in London; at the same time a detachment of 70 men, from the 1st & Coldstream "with officers proportionable," to relieve the detachment of said Third regt. of Guards in the duty of the Tower.
4 July, ,,	8	Quarters of the Coldstream: St. Giles's in the Fields; St. Andrew's, Holborn; St. Clement's Danes; St. Giles's, Cripplegate; St. Sepulchre's; & St. James's, Clerkenwell. At Avesne le Sec: encamped.			
6 Sept. 1711	6	The detachment of the First and Coldstream attending the Queen at Windsor to march to attend Her Majesty at Hampton Court during her stay, and afterwards return to their quarters in London.			
18 Oct. ,,	.				
			,, ,,	6	"Companies of the Coldstream, which came from Hampton Court, &c., in the Savoy, from 5th Sept. to 6th Oct."

APPENDIX. 421

STATIONS.—*Continued.*

Date	No. of Comps.	Description	Date	No. of Comps.	Description
23 Sept. 1713	14	Quarters of the Coldstream: St. Andrew's, Holborn; the Dutchy Liberty; Clerkenwell; Cripplegate; St. Sepulchre's Without; Norton Falgate; and Shoreditch.			to do duty in the Tower, and relieve a detachment of Webb's regiment.
21 Oct. ,,		Quarters enlarged to the parish of Stepney.	12 Nov. 1714		Quarters of the Coldstream: (14 companies.)
31 ,, ,,		A detachment of 263 men, including officers, of the Coldstream regt. of Foot Guards, to march on Monday 2nd of Nov. to Old Windsor and places adjacent, to attend the Queen, & afterwards return (upon their being relieved) to their former quarters in London. (Relieved 30th of Nov. by First Foot Guards.)		4	St. Andrew's, Holborn.
				1	The Dutchy Liberty.
				1	St. Sepulchre's Without.
				1	Clerkenwell.
				3	Cripplegate.
				1	White Chappell.
				2	Bishopsgate Without.
				1	Shoreditch.
			17 June, 1715		Quarters of the Coldstream: (14 companies.)
				3	St. Andrew's, Holborn.
				2	Clerkenwell.
				1	The Dutchy Liberty.
				1	St. Sepulchre's Without.
25 Dec. ,,		A detachment of 600 men of the three regiments of Foot Guards, with officers proportionable, (and other troops,) to march to Rochester to aid in quelling the mutinous conduct of Wills's marines.		2	Cripplegate Without.
				5	White Chappell; St. Katherine's; Bishopsgate Without; Shoreditch; St. John's, Wapping; & Spitalfields Hamlet.
			10 Aug. ,,		St. Marylebone, Pancras, and St. Mary's, Islington, to be added to the quarters of the Coldstream, which is now augmented to eighteen companies.
19 Jan. 171¾		A detachment of 263 men, including officers, of the Coldstream regt. of Foot Guards, to march on Monday the 25th of January to Old Windsor and places adjacent, to attend the Queen, and afterwards return to their former quarters in London.	. July, ,,	14	The Coldstream encamped in Hyde Park from 23rd July.
			16 Sept. ,,		A detachment of 200 men, with commissioned and non-commissioned officers in proportion, from the 3 regiments of Foot Guards, to march to Greenwich and Woolwich, to attend his Majesty during his stay.
13 Feb. ,,		In case of the Queen's return to Hampton Court, on the way to London, to be quartered during her stay near Hampton, &c.			
,, ,, ,,		3 commissioned officers, 3 serjeants, and 50 private men, of the Coldstream, to march from London to Bristol, and embark for Kinsale.	19 ,, ,,		Quarters of the Coldstream:— (18 companies.)
				3	St. Andrew's, Holborn.
				1	The Dutchy Liberty.
				3	St. Giles's, Cripplegate.
21 June, 1714		Quarters of the Coldstream: (13 companies.)		1	St. Sepulchre's.
				1	Clerkenwell.
	4	St. Andrew's, Holborn.		2	St. Mary's, White Chappell; & Trinity, Minories.
	1	The Dutchy Liberty.			
	1	St. Sepulchre's Without.		1	Spitalfields Hamlet.
	1	Clerkenwell.		2	St. Leonard's, Shoreditch; & Norton Falgate.
	3	Cripplegate.			
	1	White Chappell.		1	The Liberty of East Smithfield.
	2	Bishopsgate Without.		1	St. Katherine's Precinct.
4 July, ,,		St. Pancras & St. Mary le Bone to be added to the quarters in St. Andrew's, Holborn.		1	St. John's, Wapping.
				1	St. Mary's, Islington.
7 ,, ,,		A detachment of the 3 regts. of Guards to march to Hampton Court and Windsor, to attend the Queen, and afterwards return to London.	7 Oct. ,,	14	The Coldstream encamped in Hyde Park " to hut."
			1 Dec. ,,		Quarters of the Coldstream:
				12	In the Tower Hamlets.
				6	In Finsbury Division: (according to an Act passed last session, "during the present exigency of affairs.")
3 Sept. ,,		The 8 comps. of grenadiers of the three regts. of Guards to march to Greenwich, to mount the King's Guard upon his arrival.	. ,, ,,	14	The Coldstream " decamped from Hyde Park on 10th December."
27 ,, ,,		A detachment of 70 men, with officers proportionable, out of the 3 regts. of Foot Guards,	31 Mar. 1716		Quarters of the Coldstream:
				12	In the Tower Hamlets.
				6	In Finsbury Division.

VOL. II. 2 E

APPENDIX.
STATIONS.—Continued.

Date	No. of Comps.		Description	Date	No. of Comps.		Description
June, 1716	18		The Coldstream encamped in Hyde Park from 14th June.				Seymour's[2] regt. of Foot in the duty of the Castle.
23 July, ,,		.	A detachment of 400 private soldiers, with commissioned and non-commissioned officers in proportion, of the 3 regiments of Foot Guards, to march to Hampton Court, & encamp there, to attend his Royal Highness the Prince of Wales (Guardian of the Kingdom), and the said detachment to be relieved in said duty by other detachments from the camp in Hyde Park, as often as necessary.	14 Nov. 1717		.	A detachment of 4 serjents, 4 corporals, 2 drummers, & 54 private men, from the 3 regts. of Foot Guards, under the command of a commissioned officer, to march to Hampton Town and places adjacent, to do the usual duty at Hampton Palace.
				18 Jan. 17$\frac{17}{18}$		.	One serjeant and two privates of the Coldstream to march from London to Warwick for a deserter from that regt., & return with him to London.
6 Oct. ,,		.	The detachment from the 3 regiments of Foot Guards now doing duty at Hampton Court, to quarter in Kingston, the Wick, Hampton Town, Twickenham, & Ditton, untill further orders.	31 ,, ,,		.	A detachment of one man a company, from the 3 regts. of Foot Guards, with non-commissioned officers proportionable, under the command of a subaltern officer, to march to Windsor to relieve the detachment now there in the duty of the Castle.
8 ,, ,,			Quarters of the Coldstream:				
	12		In the Tower Hamlets.				
	6		In Finsbury division.	12 June, 1718			Quarters of the Coldstream:— (18 companies.)
,, ,,		18	The Coldstream "decamped from Hyde Park on 12th Oct."		3		St. Andrew's, Holborn.
14 Jan. 17$\frac{16}{17}$		.	A detachment of 170 private men, with commissioned and non-commissioned officers in proportion, from the 3 regiments of Foot Guards, to march to Greenwich, to mount the King's Guard upon his Majesty's arrival there.		2		Clerkenwell.
					1		St. Sepulchre's.
					2		Cripplegate.
					1		Islington.
					1		Shoreditch & Norton Falgate.
					1		Spitalfields.
					1		White Chapel.
					1		Stepney.
16 July,[1] 1717		.	A detachment of 400 private soldiers, with commissioned and non-commissioned officers "proportionable," of the 3 regiments of Foot Guards, to march to Hampton Town, Kingston, and places adjacent, to attend the King during his stay there, and the said detachment is to be relieved by other detachments from the three regiments of Guards in and about London, as often as shall be necessary.		1		East Smithfield & St. Katherine's.
					1		Wapping and St. Katherine's.
					2		Radcliffe.
					1		Shadwell.
				11 Aug. ,,		.	A detachment of 400 private soldiers, with commissioned and non-commissioned officers in proportion, out of the 3 regiments of Foot Guards, to attend the King at Hampton Court, and to be relieved as often as necessary.
9 Aug. ,,		.	The detachment of the 3 regts. of Foot Guards at Kingston to march to Windsor, until the assizes at Kingston are over, and then return there again.	29 Oct. ,,		.	A detachment of 64 private men out of the 3 regiments of Foot Guards, with commissioned and non-commissioned officers proportionable, to proceed on 1st Nov. from London to Sheerness, to relieve part of Sabine's[3] regiment in the duty of that garrison.
6 Nov. ,,		.	A detachment of one man a company, with non-commissioned officers proportionable, to be made from the 3 regiments of Foot Guards, to march under the command of a subaltern officer to Windsor, to relieve two companies of	,, ,, ,,		.	Do. 50 men, do., to Tilbury Fort, to relieve ditto.
				,, ,, ,,		.	28 men more added to the above detachments.
				,, ,, ,,	7		A detachment of 350 men from

[1] The King at this time signed the marching warrants or routes occasionally only, and soon after discontinued to do so, when they were issued by the Secretary-at-War in the King's name.

[2] Present 4th Foot, or King's Own.   [3] Present 23rd Foot, or Welch Fusiliers.

APPENDIX. 423

STATIONS.—*Continued.*

Date	No. of Comps.	Description	Date	No. of Comps.	Description
		the 3 regts. of Foot Guards, with a proportionate number of officers and non-commissioned officers, to march on 1st Nov., under the command of Lt.-Col. Townsend, from London to Portsmouth, to relieve Wills's[1] regiment in garrison.	14 Mar. 17$\frac{18}{19}$	.	The detachment of the three regiments of Foot Guards now at Windsor, to march to London as soon as relieved.
6 Nov. 1718	.	A detachment of 30 men from the 3 regts. of Foot Guards to proceed from London to Rochester and Stroud, and relieve each other in the duty of Upnor Castle.	26 ,, ,,	.	The quarters of the Coldstream regiment at Chippenham to be enlarged with the adjacent villages, (Cosham and Laycock.)
,, ,, ,,	.	30 men from the 3 regiments of Foot Guards from London to Greenwich, as a guard over the powder-magazine.	2 Apr. 1719		Quarters of the Coldstream:— (18 companies.)
				3	St. Andrew's, Holborn.
				2	Clerkenwell.
20 ,, ,,	.	The detachments of the three regts. of Guards at Sheerness, &c., on being relieved, to return to London.		1	St. Sepulchre's.
				2	Cripplegate.
				1	Islington.
				1	Shoreditch & Norton Falgate.
				1	Spitalfields.
				1	White Chapel.
17 Jan. 17$\frac{18}{19}$	.	A detachment of 30 serjeants, corporals, and drummers, to be made from the 3 regts. of Foot Guards, to march from London to Portsmouth to relieve the like detachment of non-commissioned offrs. now there, in the duty of that garrison, and to be relieved by other detachments from London as often as necessary.		1	Stepney.
				1	East Smithfield & St. Katherine's.
				2	Radcliffe.
				1	Shadwell.
				1	Wapping and St. Catherine's.
				.	7th of May, the parishes of Pancras and St. Mary le Bone to be added to the quarters of the Coldstream.
			28 Apr. ,,	9	The battalion of the Coldstream to march forthwith from Chippenham and places adjacent, to London.
5 Feb. ,,	.	A detachment of one man a company from 3 regiments of Foot Guards, to march under the command of a commissioned officer to Hampton Town and places adjacent, & do the usual duty at the Palace of Hampton Court; the said detachment to be relieved as often as necessary.	18 May ,,	.	"That as the young Princesses "are suddenly to remove to "Kensington, the same guard "is to be kept of the several "troops of Horse and Grenadier Guards, and Foot "Guards, during their Royal Highnesses' residence "there, as when his Majesty "is in the said Palace in person; and that both there and "at such other of his Majesty's palaces where their "(Royal) Highnesses shall "reside during his Majesty's "absence, the officers of the "Guards who shall be upon "duty are to observe such "orders as they shall receive from the Countess "Dowager of Portland, Governess to their Royal "Highnesses."
6 Mar. ,,	9	One of the batts. of the Coldstream, under Col. Robinson, to march forthwith to Newbury, Speenhamland, and Hungerford.
8 ,, ,,	9	The batt. of the Coldstream under marching orders for Newbury, Speenhamland, & Hungerford, upon their arrival at those places to proceed directly to Chippenham and the adjacent places, there to remain until further orders, taking care in their march that they rest but one night in a place, the Sunday excepted.
			10 June ,,	.	A detachment of 40 private men, with non-commissioned officers in proportion, from the three regiments of Foot Guards, to march under the command of a subaltern to Windsor, to do duty at the Castle: to be relieved as often as necessary.
14 ,, ,,	7	The detachment of the three regiments of Foot Guards now at Portsmouth, under Lt.-Col. Townsend, to march from thence to London as soon as relieved.
			19 ,, ,,	.	A detachment of 240 private soldiers, with commissioned

[1] Present 3rd Foot, or Buffs.

APPENDIX.

STATIONS.—*Continued.*

Date	No. of Comps.	Description	Date	No. of Comps.	Description
		and non-commissioned officers proportionable, of the three regiments of Foot Guards, to march from London to Old Windsor and places adjacent, to attend as a guard upon the persons of their Royal Highnesses the young Princesses during their stay at Windsor, and afterwards return to their quarters in London.			officers proportionable, from the three regiments of Foot Guards, under the command of a Lieut.-Colonel, Captain, and Ensign, to attend and do duty at the King's Theatre in the Haymarket, every night a ball is to be held there.
			25 Nov. 1719	18	Quarters of the Coldstream: the same as expressed in the order dated 2nd April, 1719.
			18 Mar. 17$\frac{19}{20}$	18	Ditto, ditto.
23 July, 1719	7	Seven companies (one of which to be granadiers) of the Coldstream Guards, to march on Wednesday morning next to Portsmouth, and pass over to the Isle of Wight and encamp there until their embarkation, under the command of the Earl of Dunmore. (Embarked 5th, and sailed 21st September.)	28 ,,	1720	. The parishes of Pancras, St. Marylebone, and Paddington, to be added to the quarters of the Coldstream.
			1 April ,,	.	A detachment of 40 private men, and non-commissioned officers proportionable, from the three regiments of Foot Guards, under the command of a commissioned officer, to do duty at the King's Theatre in the Haymarket, every night an opera is to be performed there.
28 ,, ,,	.	A detachment of 100 men, with commissioned and non-commissioned officers proportionable, from the three regiments of Foot Guards, to march on Thursday next, 30th of July, to Spitalfields Market, to assist in the preservation of the peace, as well as to prevent any disorders that may happen during the time the weavers shall stand in the pillory there, and afterwards return to their former quarters.	11 May ,,	.	A detachment of 50 private men, with non-commissioned officers proportionable, from the three regiments of Foot Guards, to march immediately under the command of two commissioned officers to the Tower, to reinforce the garrison now there.
			,, ,, ,,	.	A detachment to be made daily of 100 private men, with commissioned officers proportionable, out of the three regiments of Foot Guards, and march to the Tower to do the usual duty of the place: to be relieved as heretofore, and to follow such orders as they shall receive from the Governor or Lieut.-Governor, or officer commanding in chief there.
11 Aug. ,,	.	A detachment of 100 privates, with commissioned and non-commissioned officers in proportion, of the three regiments of Foot Guards, to march forthwith from London to Southampton, where they are to pass over to the Isle of Wight, to complete the companies of the Foot Guards there; and in case there are more than sufficient, the remainder then are to return to London.	19 ,, ,,	.	A detachment of 40 men from the three regiments of Foot Guards, to march from London to Windsor under the command of two commissioned officers, and to be there on Monday next, and remain during the installation of the Right Honorable the Earl of Sunderland, and afterwards return to London.
15 Sept. ,,	.	A corporal and one private of the Coldstream to march from London to Portsmouth, and join the battalion on board the fleet; the corporal to return to London.			
(20) Nov. ,,	7	"Route for seven companies "of his Majesty's Coldstream "regiment of Foot Guards, "from Portsmouth to London: — Fareham, Petersfield, Godalmin, Dorking, "Kingston, London, where "they are to join, &c. "Geo. Treby," (Secretary at War.)	20 June, ,,	.	Same order as on the 18th of May, 1719, for the Horse and Foot Guards to do duty at the residences of the young Princesses during the King's absence at Hanover.
20 ,, ,,	.	A detachment of 100 private men, with non-commissioned	4 Nov. ,,	.	A detachment of 30 private men, with non-commissioned officers proportionable, from the three regiments of Foot Guards, under the command

APPENDIX.

STATIONS.—*Continued.*

Date	No. of Comps.	Description	Date	No. of Comps.	Description
		of an ensign, to proceed from London to Rochester, to be aiding and assisting in obliging all ships and persons to perform quarantine, pursuant to the several proclamations relating to the infection at Marseilles and other places abroad.			from Hyde Park on Saturday next the 24th inst., and be disposed of in quarters in Westminster and the liberties thereof.
31 Jan. 17 20/21	·	As often as you have due notice of a rehearsal of an opera at the King's Theatre, Haymarket, a detachment of a serjeant and 12 men from the 3 regiments of Foot Guards to attend.	June, 1723	18	The Coldstream encamped in Hyde Park.
			11 ,, ,,	·	Order renewed for the Horse and Foot Guards to do duty at the Palaces of St. James's, Kensington, &c., when the young Princesses are residing there, during the King's absence.
25 Mar. 1721	18	Quarters of the Coldstream, the same as expressed in the order of 2nd of April, 1719.	22 ,, ,,	·	A detachment of 40 private men from the 3 regts. of Foot Guards, under a subaltern & non-commissioned offrs. proportionable, to march to Windsor, to relieve a detachment of Clayton's regiment.
11 Sept. ,,	·	A detachment of 70 men, with commissioned and non-commissioned officers proportionable, out of the 3 regts. of Foot Guards, to march to the Tower of London, to relieve the detachment there.	,, ,, ,,	·	A detachment of 24 men from the 3 regts. (as before) to march to Hampton Court, to relieve ditto.
4 Dec. ,,	·	A detachment of 30 men, with a commissioned & non-commissioned officers proportionable, of the 3 regiments of Foot Guards, to march from London to Hampton Court.	24 ,, ,,	·	A detachment of 240 private men, with commissioned & non-commissioned offrs. proportionable, from the three regiments of Foot Guards, to march to the Tower of London: to be relieved from time to time by other detachments from the camp in Hyde Park.
28 ,, ,,	·	A serjeant and a corporal of the Coldstream to march to Boston, to bring from thence twelve recruits.			
24 Mar. 17 21/22	18	Quarters of the Coldstream, the same as expressed in the order of 2nd of April, 1719, with the exception of 1 company drawn from St. Andrew's, Holborn, and added to Whitechapel.	13 July, 1723	·	The detachments of the three regiments of Foot Guards at Windsor and Hampton Court to march to the camp in Hyde Park, and join their regts.
			22 ,, ,,	·	Detachments (as before) to march to Hampton & Windsor.
31 ,, 1722	·	A serjeant of the Coldstream to march to Loughborough, to bring up from thence eight recruits.	19 Sept. ,,	18	The Coldstream to decamp from Hyde Park on Monday the last day of September, & be disposed of as follows: In the barracks in the Savoy.
June, ,,	18	The Coldstream encamped in Hyde Park.		9	
28 July, ,,	·	The sick men of the 3 regts. of Foot Guards to return into the same quarters as before their encampment in Hyde Park.		9	In St. Olave's parish, St. Saviour's, St. Thomas's, St. George's, in Newington, Lambeth, Christ Church, & in the Clink.
9 Nov. ,,	·	A detachment of 40 men, with commissioned and non-commissioned officers proportionable, from the 3 regts. of Foot Guards, to march to Windsor.	20 June, 1724	·	The detachments of the three regiments of Foot Guards at Windsor & Hampton Court to march to London.
			2 July, ,,	·	The 3 regts. of Foot Guards to be reviewed in Hyde Park to-morrow morning the 3rd inst. by the King.
17 ,, ,,	·	A detachment of 24 men, with commissioned and non-commissioned officers in proportion, from the 3 regts. of Foot Guards, to march to Hampton Court.	7 ,, ,,	·	Detachments, (as before,) to march to Windsor & Hampton Court.
21 ,, ,,	·	Both the preceding detachments ordered to return to the camp in Hyde Park.	21 ,, ,,	·	A detachment of 50 men, & 2 commissioned with non-commissioned offrs. proportionable, from the 3 regiments of Foot Guards, to march to
23 ,, ,,	18	The Coldstream to decamp			

426   APPENDIX.

STATIONS.—Continued.

	No. of Comps.			No. of Comps.	
11 Aug. 1724	.	Windsor, and remain until the Installation is over. A detachment of 100 private men, with commissioned and non-commissioned offrs. proportionable, from each of the 3 regts. of Foot Guards, to march on Wednesday the 12th inst. to Old and New Windsor to attend the King.			Highness Prince William and his Grace the Duke of Montagu, Great Master of the Order of the Bath during the procession, installation, and dining, of the several Knights of the Bath.
3 Sept. ,,	.	80 men, with commissioned and non-commissioned offrs. proportionable, of the detachment at Windsor, to be quartered at Maidenhead.	15 June, 1725	.	A detachment of 100 men, with commissioned and non-commissioned officers in proportion, from the three regts. of Foot Guards, under the command of a lt.-col., captain, ens., adjt., and serjt.-major, to march to the Theatre Royal in the Haymarket, on Thursday next the 17th inst., and follow the orders of Prince William and the Duke of Montagu during the ball to be held at that theatre on that night.
2 Oct. ,,	.	A detachment of 40 private men, as before, to march to Windsor.			
7 ,, ,,		Quarters of the Coldstream :— (18 companies) :			
	4	St. Giles's in the Fields.			
	3	St. Andrew's, Holborn.			
	1	The Dutchy liberty.	6 Aug. ,,	.	A detachment of 64 men from the 3 regts. of Foot Guards, under a lieut. and ensign, to march to Barnet, and remain, and be assisting in seizing & securing the deer-stealers who infest his Majesty's chase of Enfield, and carry away the deer.
	1	Pancrass and Marylebone.			
	1	St. Sepulchre's.			
	2	Clerkenwell.			
	2	St. Giles's, Cripplegate.			
	1	Shoreditch & Norton Falgate.			
	1	Spital Fields.			
	1	White Chapel.			
	1	East Smithfield and St. Catherine's.	14 Oct. ,,	18	Quarters of the Coldstream : in the city and liberties of Westminster.
6 Nov. ,,	.	A serjt., corporal, drummer, and 20 privates of the Coldstream, now quartered in the Dutchy liberty, to remove to Saffron-hill liberty.	1 Feb. 172⅚	.	The detachment of the three regiments of Foot Guards at Barnet to return to London.
15 Jan. 172¼	.	Guards to be furnished for the masquerades, balls, and operas, at the King's Theatre in the Haymarket, as often as due notice is given, consisting of 100 men, with non-commissioned offrs. proportionable, from the 3 regts. of Foot Guards, under the command of a lieut.-col., capt., ensign, adjt., & serjt.-majr., to be aiding and assisting in the preservation of the peace, and preventing all manner of profaneness, rudeness, drunkenness, or indecencies, and not to permit any person whatsoever to enter the said theatre in habits worn by the clergy.	15 ,, ,,	.	A detachment of 100 men, with the usual officers, to attend at the King's Theatre, Haymarket, as often as a ball is held there ; and as the same is intended only for the diversion and amusement of the best of company, it is his Majesty's pleasure that they should prevent all rudeness, drunkenness, and indecencies ; and upon all such occasions to direct the serjt.-major to oblige the musicians and butlers to retire in good time.
			26 Mar. 1726	.	A detachment of 40 men, with commissioned and non-commissioned officers proportionable, from the 3 regts. of Foot Guards, to march to Kingston on Tuesday morning next, and be a guard over the criminals to be tried at the assizes there.
10 June, 1725	.	Order renewed : the Horse and Foot Guards to keep the same guard at St. James's, Kensington, &c., when the young Princesses are residing there, as when his Majesty is present.			
15 ,, ,,		Four battalions to be formed from the three regiments of Foot Guards, and march on Thursday next, the 17th inst., to Old Palace Yard, and follow the orders of his Royal	13 June, ,,	.	A detachment of 50 men, and 2 commissioned officers, with non-commissioned officers proportionable, from the 3 regiments of Foot Guards, to march on Tuesday morning next to Windsor, and remain

APPENDIX. 427

STATIONS.—*Continued.*

	No. of Comps.			No. of Comps.	
		until the Installation is over, and then return.	10 Oct. 1728		Quarters of the Coldstream:
22 Oct. 1726		Quarters of the Coldstream:		9	In the City and Liberties of Westminster.
	9	In the barracks in the Savoy.		8	In Holborn division.
	9	In the barracks in the Tower.		1	In Clerkenwell Green.
17 July, 1727	.	The detachments of the three regiments of Foot Guards at Windsor and Hampton Court to march on Tuesday next the 18th instant to London, and join their regiments.	12 June, 1729	.	A detachment of 4 serjts., 4 corporals, 2 drummers, & 70 private men, with officers proportionable, from the Coldstream, to march on Sunday next the 15th inst. to the Tower of London, to relieve the companies of 1st Foot Guards, " to be re- " viewed the next day by " Sir Charles Wills, their " colonel, in Hyde Park, " when they will return, and " the Coldstream march out " to their former quarters."
22 ,, ,,	.	A detachment of 40 men to march to Windsor, and 24 men to Hampton Court, with the usual officers, from the three regts. of Foot Guards.			
25 ,, ,,	.	A detachment of 400 private men, with commissioned and non-commissioned officers proportionable, from the 3 regiments of Foot Guards, to march early on Thursday morning, the 27th instant, to Hyde Park, in order to form a line for the King to review the several troops of Horse Guards and Horse Grenadier Guards.	10 July, ,,	1	The quarters of one company of the Coldstream to be enlarged with Great and Little Chelsea, Brompton, & places adjacent.
			16 Oct. ,,		Quarters of the Coldstream:
				9	In the Tower of London.
				9	In the barracks in the Savoy.
28 Sept. ,,		Quarters of the Coldstream:	15 May, 1730	.	A detachment of 400 men from the three regts. of Foot Guards, with commissioned and non-commissioned officers proportionable, to march early on Wednesday morning next, the 20th inst., to Hyde Park, to form a line for the King to review the several troops of Horse Guards and Horse Grenadier Guards.
	9	In Holborn division.			
	9	In the Borough of Southwark, in the usual parishes.			
12 Oct. ,,	.	Guards to be furnished for the masquerades, balls, and operas, as in the order dated 15th of February, 172⅔.			
1 Dec. ,,	3	The three companies of the Coldstream, quartered in the parishes of Rotherhithe, Bermondsey, and Newington, to be removed into the parishes of St. Sepulchre's, Clerkenwell, and St. Giles's Cripplegate.	2 June, ,,	.	A detachment of 100 men, as usual, from the 3 regts. of Foot Guards to march the day after they have been reviewed by the King, to Old & New Windsor, and places adjacent, to attend upon their Majesties during their residence at the Castle.
30 ,, ,,	1	One of the companies now quartered in St. Giles's in the Fields to remove into Clerkenwell, St. Sepulchre's, and St. Giles's Cripplegate.	23 ,, ,,	.	A detachment of 100 men, as usual, to Windsor, to attend their Majesties.
6 May, 1728		12 comps. of the Coldstream to be disposed of as follows:	5 Sept. ,,	.	A detachment of 2 serjts., 2 corporals, and 24 private soldiers (12 of whom are to be grenadiers) from the three regiments of Foot Guards, to march Monday next the 7th inst. to the Plantation Office near the Cockpit, there to follow the orders of Alured Popple, Esq., Secretary to the Lords Commissioners of Trade and Plantations.
	1	St. John's, Wapping; and Stepney.			
	2	Clerkenwell and Islington.			
	2	St. Giles's, Cripplegate.			
	3	Shoreditch, Norton Falgate, and Spital Fields.			
	2	Whitechapel.			
	1	East Smithfield and St. Catherine's.			
	1	Bermondsey and Newington.			
3 Sept. ,,	.	A detachment of 100 privates, with commissioned and non-commissioned officers proportionable, from the 3 regts. of Foot Guards, to march on Thursday the 5th inst., to Old and New Windsor, to attend the King and Queen at Windsor Castle.	8 ,, ,,	.	A similar detachment ordered on the same duty on Wednesday the 9th inst. Also two serjts. and 12 grenadiers ordered in addition.
			22 ,, ,,	.	A detachment of 100 private

APPENDIX

STATIONS.—*Continued*

Date	No. of Comps.	Description
9 Oct. 1730	.	men, as usual, from the three regts., to march to Windsor to attend their Majesties. A detachment of 40 private men, as usual, from the three regiments of Foot Guards, to march to Windsor to do duty at the Castle.
13 ,, ,,	.	"It is his Majesty's pleasure "that you cause George "Ramsey, a grenadier be-"longing to the Earl of Albe-"marle's company in the "Coldstream regiment of "Foot Guards, to be quar-"tered at Bath, in order to "use the waters there for "the recovery of his limbs. "By his Majesty's command, "WILLIAM STRICKLAND." Quarters of the Coldstream:
20 ,, ,,	9	In Southwark, Bermondsey, St. Olave's, St. Saviour's, St. Thomas's, St. George's parishes, Newington, the Clink, Christ Church, and Lambeth.
	8	In the City and Liberties of Westminster.
	1	In Great and Little Chelsea.
1 June, 1731	.	The detachment of the three regiments of Foot Guards at Hampton Court to march to London and join their regiments.
2 ,, ,,	.	A detachment of 400 men, as usual, from the three regts. of Foot Guards, to march early on Wednesday next, the 9th inst., to Hyde Park, to form a line for the King to review the Horse Guards & Horse Grenadier Guards.
29 ,, ,,	9	One batt. of the Coldstream (the 1st battalion) to march from their present quarters, the first day to Dartford and the next to Rochester, Stroud, and Chatham, and remain till further orders.
5 Aug. ,,	9	The batt. of the Coldstream to return from Rochester, Chatham, and Stroud, to London.
21 Oct. ,,		Quarters of the Coldstream: (18 companies.)
	8	In Holborn division.
	2	Clerkenwell.
	1	St. Sepulchre's and Glasshouse Yard.
	2	St. Giles's, Cripplegate.
	5	In the Tower division.
15 June, 1732	18	The quarters of the Coldstream are the same as in the order dated 21st of October last.
24 ,, ,,	.	Four batts. to be made from the 3 regts. of Foot Guards, and march on Friday the 30th inst., by 5 o'clock in the morning, to Old Palace Yard, and follow orders from his Royal Highness the Duke, and his Grace the Duke of Montagu, Great Master of the order of the Bath, during the procession, installation, and dining of the several knights of the Bath. They are to take care to see that the coaches of the nobility, gentry, and others, that go through King Street to the Abbey, do go round Tothill Street, and return through St. James's Park, by way of Buckingham House, to St. James's. Quarters of the Coldstream:
3 Oct. 1732	16	In the City and Liberties of Westminster.
	1	In Kensington and the Gravel Pits.
	1	In Great and Little Chelsea, and Walham Green.
4 Apr. 1733	18	Quarters the same as on the 3rd of October last.
5 May, ,,	.	A detachment of 40 private men, as usual, from the three regts., to march to Windsor, to do the duty of the Castle.
9 June, ,,	.	A detachment of 24 men, as usual, from the 3 regts., to Hampton Court, to do the usual duty there.
11 July, ,,	.	A detachment of the Coldstream, consisting of 3 capts., 6 subalterns, an adjt., a serjt.-maj., and 300 privates, with non-commissioned officers, & drummers in proportion, to march in 2 divisions on Sunday and Monday next, to Hampton Court, and encamp.
5 Sept. ,,	.	A detachment of 40 private men, as usual, from the three regiments to Windsor. Quarters of the Coldstream:
8 Oct. ,,	9	In the Tower of London.
	9	In the barracks in the Savoy.
22 Apr. 1734	18	Quarters the same as on the 8th October last.
18 June, ,,	.	The detachments of the three regts. at Windsor and Hampton Court to march Wednesday next and join their regts., in order to be reviewed on the 22nd inst. by the King in Hyde Park, afterwards like detachments to return.
26 ,, ,,	.	A detachment of 400 private men, as usual, from the three regiments of Foot Guards, to march early Saturday 29th inst. to Hyde Park, to form a line for the King to review the Horse Guards and Horse Grenadier Guards. Quarters of the Coldstream:
17 Oct. ,,	9	In Southwark, and the same

APPENDIX. 429

STATIONS.—*Continued.*

Date	No. of Comps.	Description	Date	No. of Comps.	Description
		parishes as expressed in the order of 20th of October, 1730.			tains, 6 subalterns, an adjutant, a surgeon, serjeant-major, and 300 privates, with non-commissioned officers in proportion, to march on Monday, 1st August, to Hampton Court, and encamp; to relieve a like detachment of the First Foot Guards, now there.
	5	In the Tower Division.			
	4	In Finsbury Division.			
21 Oct. 1734	.	Rotherhithe to be added to the quarters.			
31 „ „	.	Fulham and Parson's Green ditto.			
19 Mar. 173⅝	18	Quarters the same as on the 17th of October last.	17 Oct. 1737		The change of quarters of the Coldstream to take place on the 25th instant, as follows:
23 June, 1735	.	A detachment of 52 private men, as usual, from the three regts. of Guards, to march to Windsor to do the usual duty at the Castle.		9	In Southwark, in the usual parishes.
				9	In the Lower Liberty of Westminster.
11 Sept. „	.	A detachment of 28 men from the three regiments of Foot Guards, as usual, to march to Hampton Court.	25 Mar. 1738	18	Quarters the same as ordered on the 17th of October last.
13 Oct. „		Quarters of the Coldstream: the change to take place on 25th instant. (18 companies):—	15 June, „	.	The detachments of the three regiments of Foot Guards at Windsor and Hampton Court to march to London to join their regiments, in order to be reviewed by the King in Hyde Park, and afterwards similar detachments to return.
	8	In Holborn division, and St. Andrew's, Holborn.			
	1	In Finsbury division.			
	8	In the City and Liberties of Westminster.	20 „ „	.	A detachment of 400 private men as usual from the three regiments of Foot Guards to march early on Saturday morning next, 24th inst., to Hyde Park, to form a line for the King to review the Horse Guards and Horse Grenadier Guards.
	1	At Kensington, the Gravel Pits, and Hammersmith.			
1 Apr. 1736	.	A detachment of 40 private men, as usual, from the three regiments of Foot Guards, to march to Windsor to do the duty of the Castle.			
31 Mar. „	18	Quarters the same as expressed in the order of 13th October last.	2 Oct. „		The Coldstream to change quarters on 25th instant: (18 companies.)
2 Aug. „	.	Serjeant Smith, the quartermaster serjeant of the Coldstream Guards, to attend always at regimental court-martials.		8	In Holborn division, and St. Andrew's, Holborn.
				5	In the Finsbury division.
28 Sept. 1736		Quarters of the Coldstream: the change to take place on 25th October.		5	In the Tower division.
			25 Oct. „	.	A detachment of 40 private men, as usual, from the three regiments of Foot Guards to march to Windsor to do the usual duty of the Castle.
	9	The first battalion in the barracks in the Savoy.			
	9	The second battalion in the barracks in the Tower.	29 Mar. 1739	18	The Coldstream to remain in the quarters ordered on 2nd October last.
25 Mar. 1737	18	Same quarters as ordered on the 28th of September last.	11 June, „	.	The detachments of the three regiments of Foot Guards at Windsor and Hampton Court to join their regiments in London, in order to be reviewed on Saturday next by the King in Hyde Park, and afterwards similar detachments to return.
25 May, „	.	A detachment of 40 private men, as usual, from the three regiments of Foot Guards to march to Windsor to do the duty of the Castle.			
8 July, „	.	The detachments of the three regiments of Foot Guards at Windsor and Hampton Court to march to London to join their regiments, in order to be reviewed by the King in Hyde Park, and afterwards similar detachments to return to Windsor and Hampton Court.	19 „ „	.	A detachment of 400 private men from the three regiments of Foot Guards to march early on Saturday morning next, the 23d inst., to Hyde Park, to form a line for the King to review the Horse Guards and Horse Grenadier Guards.
25 July, „	.	A detachment of the Coldstream, consisting of 3 cap-			

STATIONS.—Continued.

Date	No. of Comps.	Description	Date	No. of Comps.	Description
19 July, 1739[1]	.	A detachment of 40 private men, as usual, of the three regiments of Foot Guards to march to Windsor to do the duty of the Castle.	. May, 1742	9	The first battalion of the Coldstream embarked on 26th May at Woolwich, and landed at Ostend.
22 Oct. ,,		Quarters of the Coldstream from 25th inst.:—(18 companies.)	18 June, ,,	9	The second battalion of the Coldstream with four staff officers to be quartered in the city and liberties of Westminster.
	8	In the Upper Liberty of Westminster.	13 Oct. ,,		Quarters of the second battalion of the Coldstream:
	1	Kensington and the Gravel Pits.		4	With 2 staff officers in the Upper Liberty of Westminster.
	8	In Holborn division, and St. Andrew's, Holborn.		5	With 3 staff officers in Holborn division & St. Andrew's, Holborn; not to extend to the outskirts, of Hampstead, Highgate, or Kentish Town; nor beyond Tottenham Court Turnpike, St. Mary-le-bone Church, nor to any of the adjacent outskirts thereto belonging.
	1	In St. Sepulchre's Without, and Glass-House-Yard liberty.			
21 Dec. ,,	.	120 corporals or privates, good sober men, and qualified by their writing to be made serjeants, to be drafted in equal proportions out of the three regts. of Guards, and delivered over to the colonels of the six regiments of marines ordered to be raised.			
			8 Apr. 1743	9	The second battalion of the Coldstream to remain in the quarters ordered in the warrant of 13th October last.
27 May, 1740	.	The same guard of the several troops of Horse Guards and regiments of Foot Guards to be kept during the residence of his Royal Highness the Duke, and their Royal Highnesses the Princesses Amelia, Carolina, and Louisa, at St. James's, or any other palace, as when his Majesty is present.	23 ,, ,,	.	All the recruits raised for the first battalion of the Coldstream, and first battalion of the Third Foot Guards, to march to Gravesend, and remain till they can embark on board the transports for Flanders.
			18 May, ,,	.	A detachment equal to a battalion from the First and Coldstream Guards under a field officer, and officers in proportion, to hold themselves immediately in readiness to march on the first notice to Barnet, or Highgate, or such other place as shall be found necessary, to suppress the mutiny in Lord Sempill's regiment of Highlanders which are ordered to embark for foreign service.
. June, ,,	18	The Coldstream encamped at Hounslow from 18th June to 14th October.			
10 Oct. ,,	.	The battalions of the three regiments of Foot Guards encamped near Hounslow to march to London and be disposed of in the same quarters as ordered in the warrants dated 22nd October, 1739.			
21 ,, ,,		The Coldstream to change quarters on 25th inst.			
	9	In the Tower of London.	15 July, ,,	.	A guard from the three regiments of Foot Guards to escort three deserters from Lord Sempill's regiment of Highlanders to the Tower, there to be present at the execution of the two corporals and private man belonging to the said regiment on Monday next, the 18th instant.
	9	In the barracks in the Savoy.			
8 ,, 1741		Quarters of the Coldstream from 25th instant:			
	9	In Southwark, in the usual parishes, & five staff officers.			
	8	In the Lower Liberty of Westminster, and 5 staff officers.			
	1	{ 40 men in ditto. 42 men in Great and Little Chelsea & Walham Green. }			
16 Apr. 1742	18	The quarters of the Coldstream the same as ordered in the warrant dated 8th October last.	4 Oct. ,,	9	The quarters of the 2nd battalion of the Coldstream to be in the barracks in the Savoy from the 25th instant.

[1] The Windsor and Hampton Court parties continued to be sent and relieved two or three times a year, or " as often as necessary," till the year 1798, when Windsor became the station of an entire battalion.

APPENDIX. 431

STATIONS.—*Continued.*

Date	No. of Comps.	Description
. Oct. 1743	9	The 1st battalion at Brussels, in winter-quarters.
. Feb. 1744	9	The 2nd battalion marched on 29th February, from the Parade, St. James's Park, to Rochester and Sittingbourne, and returned to the Savoy barracks on the 20th March.
14 Aug. 1744	.	A detachment of 1 captain, 3 subalterns, and 100 private men, with non-commissioned officers in proportion, to be made from the 4 battalions of the 3 regiments of Foot Guards at home, and to be at Vauxhall to-morrow, the 14th inst., to escort 150 prisoners of war, as far as Guilford, on their way to Porchester Castle.
4 Oct.	,,	A serjt. and 16 private men from the 4 battalions at home of the 3 regiments of Foot Guards, to be at Holborn Bars to morrow morning, the 5th inst., to assist in safely conveying the prisoners ordered for execution to Tyburn, and in preventing the rescue of the said prisoners.
,, ,,	9	The 2nd battalion of the Coldstream to remove to the Tower of London, on the 25th instant.
. ,, ,,	9	The 1st battalion, winter-quarters at Ghent.
19 ,, ,,	.	A sufficient detachment from the 4 battalions at home of the 3 regiments of Foot Guards to receive from a vessel off the Tower upwards of 50 prisoners of war, and escort them as far as Guilford, on their way to Porchester Castle.
20 ,, ,,	.	The same detachment also to receive from the keeper of the Savoy, Henry Gray, an impressed man, and a notorious gambler belonging to Lieut.-General Philip's regiment, and convey him with the prisoners of war to Guilford, on his way to Portsmouth to embark for Newfoundland.
29 Jan. 1744	.	A detachment of the Guards from St. James's, to consist of 1 serjt. and 15 men, to escort .... Dogan, just now convicted of high treason, from Westminster Hall to Newgate, it being apprehended that some attempt may be made to rescue him.
1 Feb. ,,	.	A detachment of 150 men, including commissioned and non-commissioned officers, to be made from the 4 batts. of the 3 regiments of the Foot Guards at home, and march to Windsor, there to remain, to be a guard upon the Duke de Belleisle, marshal of France.
18 Feb. 1745	.	A detachment of 2 officers and 60 men from the 3 regiments of Foot Guards to march to-morrow to Greenwich, and conduct the Marshal Belleisle from the place of his landing to his quarters: as soon as he is gone, the party to return to the Tower.
22 ,, ,,	.	The detachment of Guards, as soon as replaced in the duty upon Marshal Belleisle at Windsor, and other duties of the Castle, to march to London to join their regiments.
. July, ,,	.	A battalion formed out of the 4 battalions of the 3 regts. of Foot Guards at home, embarked 24th July, in the river, for Ostend.
21 Sept. ,,		The 2 battalions of the Coldstream Guards to be disposed of in quarters as follows:
	4	Of the 1st battalion, in Finsbury division, which quarters are not to extend further than Islington Church.
	5	Of the 1st battalion, together with 17 staff officers, in the Tower division.
	9	Second battalion in Southwark, that is to say, Rotherhithe, St. John's Bermondsey, St. Olave's, St. Thomas's, St. Saviour's, Clink Liberty, St. George's Newington, Christ Church, and Lambeth parishes.
23 ,, ,,	9	The 1st battalion of the Coldstream disembarked at the Tower, &c. on 23rd September, from Flanders.
26 ,, ,,	.	The Coldstream to encamp in Hyde Park forthwith.
3 Oct. ,,	.	A detachment of 2 capts., 8 subalterns, and 400 private men, with non-commissioned officers in proportion, to be made from the three regts. of Foot Guards, and march to the Tower of London to relieve the 2nd batt. of the 3rd Guards in the duty of that garrison.
19 ,, ,,	.	"It is his Majesty's pleasure "that you cause the batt. of "Foot Guards (coming from "Ostend), upon their land- "ing at Yarmouth, to march "to London and join the 3 "regts. of Guards to which "they belong." Like order should the batt. land at Dover or Harwich.

APPENDIX.
STATIONS.—Continued.

Date	No. of Comps.		Date	No. of Comps.	
Oct. 1745	.	The batt. of the 3 regts. of Guards, "which served at Ostend," arrived in the river and landed on the 25th October.			regiment, and other our forces, in the duty of that garrison.
„ „	9	On the 25th October, the 2nd batt. of the Coldstream relieved the 2nd batt. of the 3rd Guards at the Savoy barracks; ordered to quarter in the Tower Hamlets.	21 Dec. 1745		The two battalions of the Coldstream to be disposed of as follows, from 26th instant:
				4	Of the first battalion in Finsbury division, which quarters are not to extend beyond Islington Church.
21 Nov. „	.	Two of the 7 batts. belonging the regts. of Foot Guards in London (the 1st batt. of the 1st and 3rd regts.) to march from hence on Saturday next, the 23rd inst., to Litchfield.		5	Of the first battalion, together with 17 staff officers, in the Tower division.
				9	Of the second battalion, in Southwark: parishes as before.
23 „ „	.	The commissioned and non-commissioned officers & private men belonging to the 2 batts. of Foot Guards, ordered to the camp near Litchfield, remaining in London, to march forthwith and join the companies to which they belong.	25 „ „	.	The quarter-masters to provide billets for the first battalions of each of the three regiments of Guards (on their march from Litchfield), and meet them to-morrow morning at Highgate, to deliver the billets to them.
24 „ „	9	The 1st batt. of the Coldstream Guards, in London, to march from hence to-morrow morning the 25th inst. to Nottingham.	„ „ „	.	A corporal from each company of the second battalion of the Coldstream to go to Highgate to-morrow morning, to receive the men lent to the first battalion, and go with them to the quarters of their respective companies.
26 „ „	9	Notwithstanding any former order to the contrary, the 1st battalion of the Coldstream Guards on their arrival at Northampton to march from thence on Sunday the 1st of Dec. next to Litchfield.	25 Jan. 174⅚	.	A quarter-master with a quarter-master-serjeant of each regiment of Guards to go to Highgate on Tuesday next, to meet Colonel Lambton with the detachment on their march from Carlisle, and deliver billets to the men, who are to march from thence to their quarters.
„ „ „	.	An officer with a proper guard to escort the baggage belonging to the first battalion of the Coldstream regiment of Foot Guards, from London to Litchfield, where they are to join, or follow the batt.	11 June, 1746	.	A sufficient detachment from the three regiments of Foot Guards to be at Southwark on Saturday, the 14th instant, to escort about 400 French prisoners to Porchester Castle.
29 „ „	.	Major-General Bragg's regiment to march from the camp near Dartford, to the Tower of London, to replace the detachment from the three regiments of Foot Guards in the duty of that garrison.	26 Aug. „	9	The second battalion of the Coldstream, under Colonel Chas. Russell, to hold themselves in readiness to go on service. Embarked on 10th Sept. at the Tower wharf, for the transports in the river, on a secret expedition. Sailed from Plymouth 10th October, and returned on the 19th: reached the Downs 24th October, and proceeded to the river to disembark.
30 „ „	.	A drum-major and a corporal of the Coldstream Guards to march from London to Berkeley.			
6 Dec. „	.	Four of the five companies of Grenadiers belonging to the four battalions of Foot Gds. doing duty in London, to march to St. Albans.—(Order cancelled.)			
21 „ „	.	A detachment of one captain, six subalterns, and 400 private men, with non-commissioned officers in proportion, from the three regiments of Foot Guards, to march on Monday next to the Tower, to replace Maj.-Gen. Bragg's	13 Sept. „	.	An officer, 4 serjeants, 4 corporals, 1 drummer, and 54 private men, belonging to the First and Coldstream regiments of Foot Guards, to be quartered at Greenwich, to do the duty at the magazine.
			18 „ „	.	The preceding detachment to

APPENDIX.

STATIONS.—*Continued.*

	No. of Comps.			No. of Comps.	
		march from Greenwich to Gravesend, and cross the river to Tilbury Fort, to do the duty of that place.	12 May, 1747	.	A detachment consisting of 1 captain, 5 subalterns, 12 serjeants, 12 corporals, 6 drummers, and 222 private men, to be made from the four battalions of the three regiments of Foot Guards doing duty at home, to relieve the third battalion of First Foot Guards in the duty of the Tower.
19 Sept. 1746	9	The first battalion of the Coldstream, with 11 staff officers, together with 279 men belonging to the second battalion (on service), to be quartered in Holborn division from the 25th instant; which quarters are not to extend beyond Pancras, Tottenham Court, Mary-le-bone, or Kentish Town.	12 June, ,,	3	Of the first battalion of the Coldstream doing duty at home, to be quartered in the parishes of St. Luke, St. Sepulchre's, and Islington, till further orders.
26 Oct. ,,	.	The two battalions of Guards, (third battalion of the First, and second battalion of the Coldstream,) upon their being disembarked at Gravesend, to march to London.	18 Sept. ,,	9	First battalion of the Coldstream, with 14 staff officers, to be quartered from 23rd instant in Southwark.
27 ,, ,,	.	An officer and 110 men belonging to the three regiments of Foot Guards, to march from London to Tilbury Fort, to relieve the detachment there, which is to return to London.	,, ,, ,,	9	The second battalion of the Coldstream at Bois-le-Duc.
28 ,, ,,		Quarters of the Coldstream from 31st instant:—	12 Oct. ,,		A detachment of 1 officer and 60 men, with non-commissioned officers in proportion, from the four battalions of the Foot Guards at home, to escort about 50 recruits and deserters from the Savoy to Portsmouth, for the 12 independent companies ordered on an expedition.
	9	With 11 staff officers, in Holborn division.			
	9	With 6 staff officers, in Finsbury and the Tower divisions; which quarters are not to extend beyond Islington Church, Radcliff, Stepney Church, Limehouse, Bethnal Green, Bow-bridge, nor so far as Hackney.	15 Nov. ,,	.	It being apprehended that an attempt will be made to rescue Thomas Puryour, alias Blacktooth, and Thos. Fuller, two smugglers, who are to be executed to-morrow at Tyburn, a sufficient detachment is to be made from the four battalions of Foot Guards at home, to assist in escorting them to Tyburn, and during the execution.
24 Nov. ,,	.	An officer, 6 serjeants, 6 corporals, and 55 private men, from the three regiments of Foot Guards, to relieve the detachment of Guards now at Tilbury Fort.			
26 ,, ,,	.	A sufficient detachment to be made from the three regiments of Foot Guards, and be at the new gaol in Southwark on Friday next, the 28th instant, to assist in guarding the condemned rebel prisoners to Kennington Common, and likewise be assisting during their execution.	18 Apr. 1748	.	A draft of 128 men to be made from the battalions of the First and Coldstream Guards at home; namely, 57 from the First regiment, and 71 from the Coldstream; which men are to leave their arms and accoutrements with their companies, and are to march with a proper number of commissioned and non-commissioned officers to Harwich, and embark for HelvoetSluys.
14 Apr. 1747	.	The detachment of the 3 regts. of Foot Guards at Tilbury Fort to return to London.	25 May, ,,	.	The Horse and Foot Guards to do the same duty at the palaces during the residence of the Princesses, as when his Majesty is present in person.
5 May, ,,	9	The second battalion of the Coldstream to embark on Saturday, the 9th instant, at the Tower wharf, on board the lighters appointed to convey them to the transports at Gravesend.	15 Sept. ,,	9	The first battalion of the Coldstream, with 14 staff officers, to be quartered from the 23rd instant in the Lower Liberty of Westminster.
,, ,,	9	The second battalion of the Coldstream anchored in the harbour of Flushing on the 12th instant.	18 Dec. ,,	.	A sufficient detachment from the four battalions of Foot Guards doing duty at home,

APPENDIX.

STATIONS.—*Continued.*

Date	No. of Comps.		Date	No. of Comps.	
		to receive one Bevern (formerly a soldier in the Guards, but last an officer in the Independent companies in the Netherlands, from which he deserted to the French) from the keeper of the Savoy, and escort him by way of Harwich to Williamstadt, where they are to deliver him over to Lieut.-Gen. Huske, and follow his orders.			order dated 15th Feb. $172\frac{5}{6}$) from the 3 regts. of Guards are to attend to preserve order, and oblige the musicians and butlers to retire in good time.
21 Dec. 1748		The second battalion of the Coldstream (on arrival from Flanders), with 16 staff officers, to be disposed of in quarters, viz.	25 Apr. 1750	.	"Twelve deserters, in the "Savoy, whom no merchant-"ship would take on board, "as they were so mutinous "last year when they em-"barked, that it was neces-"sary to land them at Ports-"mouth, being ordered to "Plymouth to embark on "board H.M S. Rainbow for "Nova Scotia, a sufficient "detachment is to be made "from the 3 regts. of Guards "to escort them as far as "Exeter."
	8	In the Tower division.			
	1	In the parish of St. Luke's, Middlesex.			
" "	.	Part of the battalion sailed on 16th December from Williamstadt: dispersed in a gale, and landed on the 20th at Yarmouth.	6 Sept. "	9	Of the Coldstream, with 16 staff officers, to be quartered from the 24th instant in the Upper Liberty of Westminster.
25 " "		All the men belonging to his Majesty's three regiments of Foot Guards disembarked at Yarmouth, to march to London, where they are to join the several companies to which they belong.		6	With 10 staff officers, in the Holborn division; which quarters are not to extend beyond St. Pancras Church, Tottenham Court, Kentish Town, or Paddington Church, nor include the Rolls Liberty.
29 Jan. $174\frac{8}{9}$	.	That part of the Coldstream regiment of Guards on board the transports, under Colonel Hedworth Lambton, arrived in the Downs from Williamstadt, to be immediately disembarked and march to London.		3	With 6 staff officers, in the parishes of Clerkenwell, St. Sepulchre's, Glass-House-Yard, St. Luke's, and Islington, not to extend beyond the church.
8 Sept. "	9	Of the Coldstream, with 15 staff officers, to be quartered from 23rd instant in Southwark; not to extend above half a mile beyond Rotherhithe Church, nor above half a mile beyond Vauxhall turnpike.	6 Dec. "	.	The sick men of the Coldstream to be quartered at Highgate, as the commanding officer and surgeon shall think proper, for their recovery.
	9	In the Tower of London.	3 Sept. 1751	9	Of the 1st batt. of the Coldstream, from 23rd inst., in the Savoy barracks.
17 Oct. "	.	Sixteen criminals being ordered for execution to-morrow, the 18th instant, and it being apprehended that it may not be safe to conduct them to the place of execution without a guard, a sufficient detachment is to be made from the three regiments of Foot Guards to assist in safely conducting the said malefactors to Tyburn, and remain till they shall have suffered according to their respective sentences.		9	With 16 staff officers of the 2nd battalion, in the Lower Liberty of Westminster.
			27 Aug. 1752		The Coldstream to be quartered as follows, from the 25th of September next:
				8	With 14 staff officers of the 1st battalion, in the Tower Hamlets.
				1	With 4 staff officers, in Finsbury division.
				9	With 16 staff officers of the 2nd battalion, in Southwark.
23 Oct. 1749	.	As often as notice is given by Mr. Robert Arthur of a ball to be held at the King's Theatre, Haymarket, a detachment of 100 men (with the officers mentioned in the	10 Feb. 1753		Order for quartering eight companies of the Coldstream:
				5	With 9 staff officers in that part of the Tower Hamlets not occupied by the comps. of the 1st Foot Guards, not to extend beyond Mile-end

APPENDIX.   435

STATIONS.—*Continued.*

Date	No. of Comps.	Description	Date	No. of Comps.	Description
		Old Town, or Limehouse Church.			time at Highgate, Finchley, Hornsey, and Stoke Newington.
	3	With five staff officers, in the parishes of Clerkenwell, St. Sepulchre's, Glasshouse Yard, St. Luke's, and Islington. [This change was in consequence of 5 comps. of the 1st batt. First Guards being removed from the Tower to quarters in the Tower Hamlets; part of the barracks in the Tower being about to be taken down and rebuilt.]	20 Oct. 1755	.	The 1st batts. of the 3 regts. of Guards ordered to take the field.
			12 Mar. 1756	.	A detachment, consisting of 4 capts., 4 lieuts., 4 ensigns, 12 serjeants, 12 corporals, 8 drummers, and 348 private men, under Col. Hudson, to be made from the 4 batts. of the 3 regts. of Guards, not under orders, to take the field, and begin their march on Tuesday next the 16th inst. to Dover Castle, and receive directions from the engineer for carrying on the works.
31 Aug. 1753	5	Of the 1st battalion Coldstream, in the Tower of London, from the 25th of September next.			
	4	With 8 staff officers, in that part of the Tower Hamlets most contiguous to the Tower, not to extend beyond Whitechapel Church, St. George's Church, nor Old Gravel Lane.	21 ,, ,,	.	A detachment of 1 captain, 3 subalterns, and 120 men, with non-commissioned officers in proportion, from the 3 regts. of Foot Guards, to escort a convoy of artillery stores from the Tower to Portsmouth, and afterwards return to London.
	9	Of the 2nd batt., with 16 staff officers, in the Upper Liberty of Westminster, which quarters are not to extend beyond Kensington Church.	3 Apr. ,,	.	A detachment of 1 capt. & 3 subalterns, 7 serjts., 7 corporals, 4 drummers, and 130 private men, to be made from the first brigade of Guards, and escort on Tuesday next the 6th inst. from St. George's Fields a convoy of gunpowder and artillery stores to Portsmouth, and afterwards return to London.
27 ,, 1754		Quarters of the Coldstream from 25th September:			
	6	Of the 1st batt., with 10 staff officers, in Holborn division.			
	3	With 6 staff officers, in Finsbury division.			
	9	Of the 2nd batt., in the Savoy barracks.			
4 Jan. 1755	.	As often as notice is given by Mr. Benjamin May of a ball to be held at the King's Theatre, the usual detachment from the 3 regts. to attend, as directed in the order dated 15th of Feb. 1722/3.	,, ,, ,,	.	On the delivery of the stores at Portsmouth, 1 subaltern, 2 serjts., 2 corporals, 1 drummer, and 30 men of the detachment to receive the two field-pieces and detachment of artillery belonging to the Royal Fusiliers, and escort them from thence to Woolwich.
2 Apr. ,,		"Whereas we have thought "fit to order each company "in our three regts. of Foot "Guards to be forthwith aug"mented; our will & plea"sure therefore is, that you "cause the Coldstream "Guards to be disposed of "in quarters as follows:"	12 ,, ,,	.	The detachment of the Foot Guards at Dover Castle to return to London.
	9	In the Savoy barracks.	12 May, ,,	9	The 2nd batt. of the Coldstream to remove from their quarters in the Tower Hamlets, &c., and to be "in can"tonment in the New Horse "Guards" from 14th May.
	6	With 10 staff officers, in Holborn division.			
	3	With 6 staff officers, in Finsbury division.	8 June, ,,	.	A detachment of 1 lieut., 1 ensign, and 60 private men, with non-commissioned officers in proportion, from the 3 batts. of Guards doing duty at the west end of the town (the first brigade and Tower batt. being excepted) to escort the waggons of powder and ammunition for the Hessian batts. to Farnham, and
12 Aug. ,,	9	Of the 1st battalion Coldstream, from the 25th inst., with 16 staff officers, to be quartered in the Lower Liberty of Westminster.			
	7	Of the 2nd batt., with 12 staff offrs., in the Tower Hamlets.			
	2	With 4 staff officers, in Finsbury division. The sick men to be quartered from time to			

APPENDIX.
STATIONS.—*Continued.*

Date	No. of Comps.	Description	Date	No. of Comps.	Description
10 July, 1756	.	afterwards return to London. A detachment from the first batts. of the three regts. of Guards, forming the first brigade, to encamp in Hyde Park from 12th July, with six field guns for practice: to be relieved from time to time.			& cross to the Isle of Wight, where they are to encamp. [Embarked 26th May, and sailed 1st June for the coast of France: returned to Cowes, and landed 5th July. Re-embarked 23rd July, and sailed for the French coast 1st August: returned to Weymouth Roads 19th Aug. Sailed 31st Aug., and landed in the Bay of St. Lunaire 4th September; embarked in the Bay of St. Cas the 11th; returned to Cowes; landed 19th September, & encamped at Newport.]
23 Oct. ,,	.	Do to march to-morrow the 24th inst. from the camp in Hyde Park to their respective quarters in London.			
20 Nov. ,,		Order for quartering the first batt. of the Coldstream:			
	6	With 10 staff officers, in the Upper Liberty of Westm^r.	18 May, 1758	.	Field-Marshal Lord Ligonier orders that the battalions of Guards doing duty at the west end of the town, do for the future mount " by batt."
	3	To remain in their present quarters, namely, one comp. Covent Garden & St. Mary's, one comp. Drury Lane, St. Martin's, Long Acre, & New Street, one company Drury Lane, St. Clement's, Holywell, and Sheer Lane.	29 Sept. ,,	9	The 1st battalion of the Coldstream (on arrival from Portsmouth) in Upper Westminster, whose quarters are not to extend beyond Kensington Church.
,, ,, . ,,	9	The 2nd batt. " in cantonment in the New Horse " Guards."		9	The 2nd batt. to remove from the Horse Guards to the Tower on 16th October.
29 Apr. 1757	.	Riots and disturbances having taken place in the Dock-Yard at Woolwich, the 3 batts. of Guards in cantonment to assemble, and a detachment made therefrom of 300 men, with commissioned and non-commissioned officers in proportion, commanded by a field officer, & march immediately to Woolwich to assist in suppressing any disturbance, and securing the rioters.	8 Oct. ,,	9	The 1st batt. to cross from the Isle of Wight to Portsmouth, and march to their quarters in London.
			25 Nov. ,,	.	The staff officers of the Coldstream having been omitted in the King's order of the 29th of Sept. last for quartering the regt., it is his Majesty's pleasure that the 32 staff officers belonging to the said regt. be quartered in Upper Westminster.
5 Aug. ,,	.	A detachment, under Captain Thornton, of 1st Foot Guards, consisting of 1 lieutenant, 1 ensign, & 40 men, with non-commissioned officers in proportion, to be made from the first brigade of Foot Guards, and be at the Tower on the 6th inst. to escort powder & ammunition to Andover, so as to arrive on the 11th, the detachment to encamp every night on their march, and after the performance of this duty to return to London.	16 Dec. 1758	.	The men belonging to the 1st regt., Coldstream, and Third Guards, lately prisoners in France, (when disembarked) to march from Dover to London, and join their regts.
			9 Jan. 1759	.	Serjeant Neale of the Coldstream to conduct the recovered men from Newport in the Isle of Wight to London, where they are to join their regiments.
			13 ,, ,,	.	The soldiers belonging to the 3 regts. of Guards who were taken prisoners at St. Cas, and lately arrived from St. Maloes, and disembarked at Portsmouth, to march to London and join their regiments.
31 Oct. ,,	9	The 1st battalion of the Coldstream in quarters, as before: the men who are to change to assemble to-morrow at the alarm-posts of their companies, and move into their quarters.	31 July, ,,	.	An augmentation having taken place in the Coldstream regt., the quarters are to be for the 1st and 2nd battalions the same as expressed in the order dated 29th Sept. last.
-	9	The second battalion remain in the Horse Guards.			
5 May, 1758	9	The 1st battalion of the Coldstream to march on Tuesday the 9th inst. to Portsmouth,	23 Oct. ,,	.	A further augmentation hav-

APPENDIX.

STATIONS.—*Continued*.

Date	No. of Comps.	Description	Date	No. of Comps.	Description
8 Dec. 1759	.	ing taken place in the Coldstream, the quarters of the regiment are to be for both battalions the same as in the order dated 29th Sept. 1758. It having been represented that the quarters of the 2nd battalion in the Tower are not sufficient to contain the men, they are to be enlarged with the Tower Hamlets, so that they do not extend beyond Ratcliff Cross.	15 Sept. 1762	.	not to extend beyond Stepney Church; and the remaining part of the battalion in the Tower of London. A detachment of 6 officers and 224 men, from each of the 4 battalions of Guards at home, to march on 20th inst., under Major-Gen. Hudson, and encamp near Windsor, to attend at the Installation of Knights of the Garter.
5 Apr. 1760	.	Another augmentation having taken place in the Coldstream, the quarters of the regiment are to be:—the 1st battalion in Upper Westminster, and 2nd battalion in the Tower and the Tower Hamlets, according to a former order.	23 Dec. ,,	9	The 2nd battalion of the Coldstream, on their arrival from Germany, to be quartered (with 24 staff officers) in the Tower Hamlets, not extending beyond Stepney.
23 July, ,,	.	The 2nd battalions of the 3 regiments of Foot Guards to march to such places as shall be convenient for their embarkation for Germany.	,, ,,	9	The 2nd battalion of the Coldstream mustered at Vreden on 31st December, 1762.
24 ,, ,,	.	Such men and horses of the 2nd battalion of the Coldstream ordered to embark for Germany, to march to and be quartered at Dartford.	27 Feb. 1763	9	The 2nd battalion of the Coldstream, under the command of Lieut.-Col. Craig, off Yarmouth, to disembark, and march to Sudbury, Lavenham, and places adjacent. (The batt. landed at Yarmouth the 26th February.)
. Aug. ,,	9	The 2nd battalion of the Coldstream joined the army under Prince Ferdinand near the village of Buhne, 25th Aug.	28 ,, ,,	9	The 2nd battalion of the Coldstream to march from Sudbury, &c., on the 10th of March, and arrive at their quarters in London on the 13th.
11 Dec. ,,	9	Do. ordered into winter-quarters at Paderborn.	3 Aug. ,,	9	The 1st battalion of the Coldstream, with 20 staff officers, to be quartered in Holborn and Finsbury divisions.
28 Mar. 1761	.	A detachment of 574 men from the 3 regts. of Guards to join the battalions in Germany. (Embarked 3rd of April at the Tower Wharf, in lighters appointed to take them to the transports at Gravesend.)	,, ,,	9	The 2nd battalion, with 20 staff officers, in the borough of Southwark.
			,, ,, 1764	9	The 1st battalion of the Coldstream, with 25 staff officers, to be quartered in Upper Westminster.
12 Aug. ,,	9	The 1st battalion of the Coldstream to be quartered as follows, from 25th instant:— 40 men per company, with 20 staff officers, in Holborn and Finsbury division, and the remainder in the Savoy barracks.		9	The 2nd batt., with 25 staff officers, in the Tower Hamlets.
			2 ,, 1765	9	The 1st battalion of the Coldstream to remain in their present quarters.
				9	The 2nd battalion to remove to the Tower of London.
30 Mar. 1762	.	The 400 drafts from the three regts. of Guards destined to recruit their respective battalions in Germany to march with all possible expedition to Gravesend for embarkation. ("To embark on Saturday, 3rd April, on board "bilanders, and proceed to "the transports at Graves-"end.")	20 ,, 1766	9	The 1st battalion of the Coldstream to remove to the Savoy barracks.
				9	The 2nd batt. to be quartered, namely: 6 companies, with 34 staff officers, in Holborn division ; and 3 companies, with 16 staff officers, in Finsbury division.
			24 July, 1767	9	The 1st battalion of the Coldstream, and 25 staff officers, to be quartered in Southwark.
6 Aug. ,,	9	The 1st battalion of the Coldstream to be quartered as follows, from 25th instant:—40 men per company, with 20 staff officers, in the Tower Hamlets, whose quarters are		9	The 2nd battalion, with 25 staff officers, in Upper Westminster.
			16 June, 1768	8	The grenadier companies of the 3 regts. of Guards formed

APPENDIX.
STATIONS.—*Continued.*

	No. of Comps.			No. of Comps.	
		into a battalion, to march on Monday the 27th instant to Richmond and Petersham, in order to their being reviewed by the King on Tuesday the 28th instant, and afterwards return to their quarters.	24 July, 1770	9	Church, Spitalfields; and St. Leonard's, Shoreditch; to aid in suppressing any tumults or riots in that neighbourhood. The 1st battalion of the Coldstream, namely, 6 companies, with 17 staff officers, to be quartered in Holborn division; and 3 comps., and 8 staff officers, in Finsbury division.
16 June, 1768	16	The Coldstream to march on Monday the 27th instant from their present quarters: viz. one battalion to Mitcham, Streatham, Wimbledon, Merton, Upper and Lower Tooting; and the other battalion to Wandsworth, Clapham, & Clapham Common, in order to their being reviewed by the King on the 28th instant, with the other regiments of Guards, and afterwards return to their quarters in London.		9	2nd batt., with 25 staff officers, in the borough of Southwark, not to extend half a mile beyond Rotherhithe church, and half a mile beyond Vauxhall turnpike.
			21 Aug. 1771	9	The 1st battalion of the Coldstream, with 25 staff officers, to be quartered in Upper Westminster.
10 Aug. ,,	9	The 1st battalion of the Coldstream, with 50 staff officers, to be quartered in the Tower Hamlets.		9	2nd batt., with 25 staff officers, in the Tower Hamlets.
			24 July, 1772	9	The 1st battalion of the Coldstream, with 50 staff officers, to be quartered in Upper Westminster.
5 Oct. ,,	9	2nd battalion, Savoy barracks.		9	2nd batt., Tower of London.
	.	The eight companies of grenadiers belonging to the three regts. of Foot Guards to march from their present quarters on Friday the 7th instant, viz. 4 comps. to Wandsworth and Wimbledon, and 4 to Putney and Putney Bowling Green; and, after being reviewed by the King, to return to their quarters.	11 Aug. 1773	9	The 1st battalion of the Coldstream to remove to the Savoy barracks.
				9	2nd batt., viz., 6 comps., with 34 staff officers, to be quartered in Holborn division, & 3 comps., with 16 staff officers, in Finsbury division.
17 June, 1769	18	The Coldstream to march from their present quarters on Friday the 23rd instant, viz.: 5 companies of one battalion to Kingston; and 4 to Wimbledon, Merton, Upper & Lower Tooting, and Mitcham; and 6 comps. of the other batt. to Putney, Putney Bowling Green, Roehampton, & Fulham, and 3 comps. to Wandsworth, in order to be reviewed by the King, and afterwards return to London.	25 July, 1774	9	The 1st battalion of the Coldstream, with 25 staff officers, in the borough of Southwark.
				9	2nd batt., with 25 staff officers, in Upper Westminster.
			26 ,, 1775	9	The 1st battalion of the Coldstream, with 50 staff officers, in the Tower Hamlets.
				9	2nd battalion, Savoy barracks.
			17 Feb. 1776	9	The 1st battalion of the Coldstream, with 50 staff officers, in the Tower Hamlets.
				9	2nd battalion, Savoy barracks.
24 July, ,,	9	The 1st battalion of the Coldstream to remove to the Tower of London.	3 Mar. ,,	.	Such parties of the 2nd batt. of the Coldstream as shall be necessary on account of the late fire in the Savoy barracks, to be quartered in Upper and Lower Westminster.
	9	The 2nd batt., with 50 staff officers, to be quartered in Lower Westminster, not to extend beyond the Cheshire Cheese, in Chelsea.	4 ,, ,,	.	Notwithstanding any former order, the 2nd batt. of the Coldstream to be quartered as follows:
1 Oct. ,,	.	A detachment from the first batt. of the Coldstream in the Tower, consisting of 1 lieut., 1 ensign, and 60 private men, with a proper number of non-commissioned officers, to march on Monday the 2nd of October, and be quartered in the parishes of St. Matthew, Bethnal Green; Christ		2	Holborn and Finsbury divisions.
				2	Southwark.
				5	Upper and Lower Westminster.
			12 ,, ,,	.	The detachment of ten comps. drawn from the 3 regts. of Guards, under orders for North America, to march

APPENDIX.

STATIONS.—*Continued.*

Date	No. of Comps.	Entry	Date	No. of Comps.	Entry
30 Mar. 1776	.	from their present quarters on Friday the 15th inst. to Putney, Fulham, Parson's Green, Walham Green, Hammersmith, Turnham Green, the Tootings, Mitcham, and Merton, Clapham, Clapham Common, Wandsworth, Wimbledon, Roehampton, Richmond, Sheen, Mortlake, and Barnes. The detachment from the 3 regts. of Guards under the command of Colonel Mathew to march from their present quarters on Monday 1st of April, viz., 5 companies to Chichester, and 5 to Guilford and Godalmin, where they are to remain till the transports are ready to carry them to North America, when they will proceed to Portsmouth, and embark.	19 Mar. 1779	.	The detachment from the 3 regts. of Guards destined for North America to march on Monday the 22nd inst. to Petersfield, and embark as soon as the transports are ready, at Portsmouth.
11 Apr. ,,	.	That part of the detachment under the command of Col. Mathew at Godalmin, &c. to march on Saturday the 13th inst., viz. 2 comps. to Petersfield, and 3 to Fareham and places adjacent, till ordered to embark.	27 ,, ,,	.	On the arrival of the transports at Spithead, the detachment from the Foot Guards destined for North America to march from Petersfield to Portsmouth, and embark.
31 July, ,,	9	The 1st batt. of the Coldstream to remove to the Tower of London on Monday the 26th August.	5 Aug. 1779	9	The 1st battalion of the Coldstream, with 50 staff officers, to be quartered from the 25th inst. in Upper Westminster.
	9	2nd batt. with 50 staff officers to be quartered in Lower Westminster.		9	The 2nd batt. in the Tower of London.
Mar. 1777	.	A detachment from the three regts. of Guards embarked in the river to join the brigade serving in America.	. June, 1780	.	The 1st batt. of the Coldstream encamped in St. James's Park from 12th June to 15th August. [Four other batts. of the Guards also encamped from 10th June to 15th August.]
13 Aug. ,,		The Coldstream to change quarters on 25th instant.	4 Aug. ,,	9	The 1st batt. of the Coldstream from the 15th inst. in Somerset House barracks.
	9	The 1st batt., namely, 6 companies, with 17 staff officers, in Holborn division; and 3 comps., with 8 staff officers, in Finsbury division.		9	The 2nd batt., viz., 6 comps., with 34 staff officers, in Holborn division, and 3 comps., with 16 staff officers, in Finsbury division.
	9	2nd batt., with 25 staff officers, in the borough of Southwark.	1 Jan. 1781	.	The detachment from the 3 regts. of Foot Guards to recruit the brigade in North America, to march on Tuesday the 2nd inst. to Petersfield, and, on the arrival of the transports at Spithead, proceed to Portsmouth, and embark.
27 Mar. 1778	.	The non-commissioned officers and private men of the augmentation to each of the battalions of the Coldstream to be quartered as follows; 124 men of the 1st batt. in Holborn and Finsbury divisions, 123 men of the 2nd batt. in Southwark.	4 ,, ,,	.	In case the detachment of the Foot Guards for North America should not have left Petersfield before the 11th inst., it is to march on that day to Portsmouth and Portsmouth Common, and remain till the transports are ready.
23 July, ,,	9	The 1st batt. of the Coldstream, with 25 staff officers, to be quartered, from the 25th August next, in Upper Westminster.	27 July, ,,	9	The 1st battalion of the Coldstream, with 25 staff officers, from the 25th August next, in the borough of Southwark.
	9	The 2nd batt., with 25 staff officers, in the Tower Hamlets.		9	The 2nd batt., with 25 staff officers, in Upper Westminster.
			31 July, 1782	9	The 1st battalion of the Coldstream, with 50 staff officers, from Monday the 26th August, in the Tower Hamlets.
				9	The 2nd batt. in Somerset House barracks.
			25 Jan. 1783	.	The detachment of the brigade of Guards on board his Majesty's ship Adamant, on arrival at Dover or Deal,

APPENDIX.

STATIONS.—*Continued.*

Date	No. of Comps.	Description	Date	No. of Comps.	Description
7 July, 1783	.	to disembark and march to London, and join their respective battalions. The detachment of the brigade of Guards lately arrived at Spithead from North America, on board his Majesty's ship Jason, to be disembarked at Portsmouth and march to London, and join their respective regts.	1 Aug. 1788	9	The first battalion of the Coldstream, with 4 staff officers, in the borough of Southwark.
				9	The second battalion, with 4 staff officers, in Upper Westminster.
30 ,, ,,	9	The 1st battalion of the Coldstream to remove on the 25th August to the Tower of London.	7 Aug. 1789	9	The first battalion of the Coldstream, with 8 staff officers, in the Tower Hamlets.
	9	The 2nd batt., with 16 staff officers, to be quartered in Lower Westminster.		9	The second battalion in the barracks at Knightsbridge.
			28 July, 1790	9	The first battalion of the Coldstream in the Tower of London.
4 Aug. 1784	9	From the 25th inst., the 1st batt. of the Coldstream, viz., 6 companies, with 5 staff officers, in Holborn division, and 3 comps., with 3 staff officers, in Finsbury division. The 2nd batt., with 8 staff officers, in the borough of Southwark.		9	The second battalion, with 8 staff officers, in Lower Westminster.
			29 July, 1791	9	The first battalion of the Coldstream, viz. 4 companies in Holborn division, and 4 companies in Finsbury division.
				9	The second battalion, with 4 staff officers, in the borough of Southwark.
27 July, 1785	9	The first battalion of the Coldstream, with 6 staff officers, from the 25th August in Upper Westminster.			The grenadier company of the first battalion of the Coldstream in the Liberty of the Savoy, parcel of the Dutchy of Lancaster.
2 Aug. 1786	9	The second battalion, with 2 staff officers, in the Tower Hamlets.	25 July, 1792	9	The first battalion of the Coldstream, with 4 staff officers, in Upper Westminster.
	9	The first battalion of the Coldstream, with 8 staff officers, from 25th instant in Upper Westminster.		9	The second battalion, with 4 staff officers, in the Tower Hamlets.
20 July, 1787		The second battalion in the Tower of London.	23 Feb. 1793	.	The battalions of the regiments of Foot Guards under the command of Major-Gen. Lake, ordered on foreign service, to march and embark on board the vessels provided for their reception.
	9	The first battalion of the Coldstream in Somerset House barracks.
	9	The second battalion, viz. 5 comps. with 5 staff officers, in Holborn division, and 3 companies with 5 staff officers in Finsbury division.		8	The first battalion of the Coldstream embarked on the 25th February at Greenwich for Holland.
		The grenadier company of the second battalion to be quartered in the Liberty of the Savoy, parcel of his Majesty's Dutchy of Lancaster.		1	The grenadier company of the first battalion, with the grenadier companies of the two battalions of the other regiments of Guards, formed into a separate battalion, embarked at the same time.
6 June, 1788		The Coldstream Guards, together with such men of the Royal Artillery as may be attached thereto, to march, on Monday the 9th instant, to the following places, and Wednesday the 11th they are to return to their quarters in London ;	6 Mar. 1793	9	The 2nd batt. of the Coldstream, with 7 staff officers, to remove from the Tower Hamlets to Upper Westminster.
			19 Apr. ,,	.	A light infantry company to be added to each batt. of the Coldstream from 25th June.
	9	The first battalion, Richmond (head-quarters), Kew, Petersham, East Sheen, Mortlake, Barnes ;	. July, ,,	1	The light infantry company of 1st battalion Coldstream embarked for the Continent on 9th instant.
	9	The second battalion, Putney (head-quarters), Roehampton, Fulham, Wandsworth, Wimbledon, Merton, and Tooting.	21 Aug. ,,	10	The 2nd batt. of the Coldstream, viz. 400 men, in that part of the Tower Hamlets most contiguous to the

APPENDIX.

STATIONS.—Continued.

Date	No. of Comps.	Description	Date	No. of Comps.	Description
30 Oct. 1793	.	Tower of London, and the remainder in the Tower of London. The detachment from the regts. of Foot Guards destined for the Continent, to march on Saturday the 2nd of Nov. to Greenwich, and embark for Ostend.			Windsor to march on Monday the 29th inst. to London, and join their regiments.
. Nov. „	10	The first battalion in winter quarters at Menin.	27 June, 1795	8	The 2nd battalion of the Coldstream (eight batt. comps.) to march from their present quarters on Wednesday the 1st July to Warley Common, and encamp.
	10	The second battalion in the Tower and Tower Hamlets.		2	The grenadier comp. of 2nd batt. in Westminster, and the light infantry comp. at Windsor.
. Mar. 1794	.	A draft for the 3 first batts. of the Guards, consisting of 21 serjts., & 766 rank and file, embarked 1st of March at Greenwich for Flanders.	1 July, „	10	The 1st battalion of the Coldstream removed to Knightsbridge barracks and Upper and Lower Westminster.
3 July, „	.	The detachments from the 3 regts. of Foot Guards destined for the Continent to march on Saturday the 5th inst. to Greenwich,& embark.	14 Oct. „	10	The 1st battalion of the Coldstream to remain in Knightsbridge barracks, and in the quarters now occupied by them in Upper and Lower Westminster, where "6 officers" are also to be quartered.
	1	The light infantry company of the 2nd battalion of the Coldstream marched on Saturday the 5th July to Greenwich, and embarked for Flanders.		10	The 2nd battalion, with 4 staff officers (on arrival from Warley), in the borough of Southwark.
23 July, „	9	The 2nd battalion of the Coldstream in Knightsbridge barracks, and in those parts of Upper and Lower Westminster most contiguous thereto.	16 „ „	8	The 2nd battalion of the Coldstream at Warley camp, to march on Tuesday the 20th inst. to London.
25 Mar. 1795	10	The 1st battalion of the Coldstream (on arrival), viz. 7 comps., with 8 staff officers, in Holborn division, and 3 comps., with 5 staff officers, in Finsbury division, together with such men of the 2nd batt. as cannot be accommodated in Knightsbridge barracks.		2	(The flank comps. of the 2nd batt. in Westminster.)
			27 July, 1796	10	The 1st battalion of the Coldstream, with 6 staff officers, in the Tower Hamlets and the Tower Liberty not to extend beyond Stepney Church.
	10	The remainder of the 2nd batt. to continue in Knightsbridge barracks.		10	The 2nd battalion, with 5 staff officers, in Lower Westminster.
„ „ „	1	One comp. of the Coldstream to be quartered in the Liberty of the Savoy, parcel of the Dutchy of Lancaster.	23 Aug. „	.	Notwithstanding the warrant of the 27th July last, 302 men of the 1st batt. of the Coldstream are to be quartered in Holborn and Finsbury divisions, viz. 199 in the former, and 103 in the latter division.
. Apr. „	11	The 1st battalion of the Coldstream, and light company of the 2nd battalion, embarked for England near Bremen Lehe on the 14th April, and disembarked at Greenwich on the 9th of May, and marched to their quarters in London.	2 Aug. 1797		Quarters of the Coldstream from 25th instant:
				10	As many men of the 1st batt. in the Tower of London as it can contain, and the remainder in that part of the Tower Hamlets & the Tower Liberty most contiguous to the Tower.
23 May, „	8	The light infantry battalion formed from the brigade of Guards (including the two comps. of the Coldstream) to march in two divisions on the 25th and 26th inst. to Windsor.		10	The 2nd batt., with 11 staff officers, to remain in their present quarters in Lower Westminster.
27 June, „	.	Four of the light infantry comps. (including that of the 1st batt. of Coldstream) of the brigade of Guards at	24 Apr. 1798	.	The 7 light infantry comps. of the brigade of Guards in London to march on the 26th of April, viz. 4 comps. to Sittingbourn and Milton, and 3 to Rochester. The comp.

APPENDIX.

STATIONS—*Continued*.

Date	No. of Comps.	Description	Date	No. of Comps.	Description
		of the 3rd battalion of the 1st Guards at Winchester to East and West Malling.			ver 5th of April, and marched to London.
7 May, 1798	1	The grenadier company of the Coldstream Guards now stationed in the Tower to be quartered in that part of Lower Westminster, lately occupied by Col. Calcraft's light infantry company.	5 Apr. 1799	.	130 men (including 1 commissioned officer, 2 staff officers, and 6 serjts.) of the Coldstream, on their arrival at Dover from the Continent, to be quartered in Lower Westminster.
,, ,,	.	The 8 light infantry comps. of the brigade of Guards (including the Coldstream) embarked at Margate on 13th of May. The four comps. belonging to the Coldstream and Third regiments disembarked at Ostend on the 19th, and surrendered prisoners of war on the 20th May.	6 June ,,	.	The remainder of the men of the light infantry comps. of the regts. of Foot Guards, on arrival from the Continent, to be quartered, viz. 3 officers, and 30 non-commissioned officers and privates, in Holborn division, and 1 officer & 77 men in Finsbury division.
9 June, ,,	8	The battalion companies of the first batt. of the Coldstream to march from their present quarters to-morrow the 10th instant, by way of Kingston, Guilford, and Liphook, to Hilsea barracks. (A forced march.) [The batt. consisting of one major (Col. Andrew Cowell), 3 captains & lieuts.-cols., 7 lieutenants & captains, 6 ensigns, 1 quartermaster, 2 surgeons, 33 serjts., 9 drummers, and 600 rank & file, embarked on the 12th June at Portsmouth on board H.M.Ss. Queen Charlotte and Repulse for Waterford: arrived 16 June.]	29 ,, ,,	8	The 1st battalion of the Coldstream from Ireland, disembarked at Southampton, marched to Shirley Common, & encamped the 2nd of July.
			2 July, ,,	8	The grenadier battalion, under Col. Henry Wynyard, of the brigade of Foot Guards (including the two grenadier comps. of the Coldstream) to march from London, in 3 divisions, on the 4th, 5th, & 6th inst., to Shirley camp, near Southampton.
,, ,,	8	The 2nd battalion of the Coldstream removed to the Tower.	15 ,, ,,	.	The 1st & 2nd brigades of the forces, composed of 4 batts. of the Foot Guards, including the 1st batt. and grenadier comps. of the Coldstream, to march, in two divisions, on the 17th and 18th inst. from Shirley camp to Barham Downs, and encamp every night on the march: arrived 27th & 28th inst.
11 ,, ,,	8	The grenadier batt. of the brigade of Guards to be quartered in Lower Westminster.			
13 ,, ,,	.	Such part of the 2nd batt. of the Coldstream as cannot be accommodated with quarters in the Tower of London, to be quartered in that part of the Tower Hamlets & Tower Liberty most contiguous to the Tower.	24 ,, ,,	.	A detachment of the Coldstream, consisting of 1 subaltern, 5 serjts., 1 corporal, & 113 privates, to march on 25th inst. from London to Barham Downs.
			8 Aug. ,,	.	A detachment of the Coldstream to march with the clothing of the 1st batt. to Dover, & afterwards return to their quarters in London.
15 Aug. ,,	8	The 2nd battalion of the Coldstream to be quartered in the borough of Southwark.	,, ,,	8	The battalion comps. of 1st batt. of Coldstream embarked for Holland on 12th August.
8 Dec. ,,	.	The detachment of the Coldstream, consisting of 3 offrs., 15 serjts., and 348 rank and file, intended for Ireland, to march on Monday the 10th of Dec. to Gosport, and follow the orders of Gen. Sir William Pitt. Embarked 7th January, 1799.	,, ,,	2	The grenadier comps. of both batts. embarked with the grenadier batt. at the same time: landed 27th August.
. Apr. 1799	2	The light infantry comps. of the Coldstream, late prisoners of war at Lisle, landed at Do-	14 ,, ,,	8 2	The second battalion of the Coldstream and the two light infantry comps. to be quartered as follows, viz. as many of the second battalion in the barracks in Portman Street[1]

---

[1] These barracks were first occupied by the 1st batt. of the 3rd Foot Guards in Aug. 1797.

APPENDIX. 443

STATIONS.—*Continued.*

No. of Comps.			No. of Comps.		
		as can be accommodated, and the remainder of the battalion, with 6 staff officers, in that part of Upper Westminster most contiguous to the said barracks. The two light infantry companies to remain in their present quarters in Lower Westminster.	6 Aug. 1800	8	marched with the grenadier and light infantry battalions. The second battalion of the Coldstream (as many men as can be accommodated) in the Tower of London, and the remainder in that part of the Tower Hamlets and the Tower Liberty most contiguous.
11 Oct. 1799	8	The light infantry battalion of the brigade of Guards to march to-morrow, the 12th instant, to Greenwich, and embark on board the vessels provided for their reception.	„ „	8	The first battalion of the Coldstream marched from Kinsale to Monkstown, and embarked on 18th August: sailed on the 20th from Cove of Cork with the expedition under Sir James Pulteney.
15 „ „	8	The light infantry battalion of Foot Guards, on arrival off Gravesend, to disembark and return to London.	27 „ „	8	The grenadier battalion (8 companies including 2 of the Coldstream) of the brigade of Guards at Swinley camp, to march from thence in three divisions on the 1st, 2nd, and 3rd of September to Colchester barracks.
28 „ „	.	Such parts of the regiments of Guards as may arrive from Holland at Harwich, Yarmouth, Deal, or in the Isle of Thanet, to disembark and march to their quarters in London.	„ „	8	The light infantry battalion (8 companies including 2 of the Coldstream) of the brigade of Guards at Swinley camp, to march in three divisions on the 1st of Sept. to Colchester barracks.
. „ „		The first battalion of the Coldstream arrived from Holland, and disembarked at Yarmouth 31st October.	1 Sept. „	8	The first battalion of the Coldstream in Vigo Bay, by returns of this date. (Destined against Cadiz.)
	8	The grenadier battalion from the brigade of Guards, including two companies of the Coldstream, disembarked at Ramsgate.	1 Oct. „	8	The first battalion of the Coldstream in Gibraltar Bay, by returns of this date.
30 „ „	8	The first battalion of the Coldstream, with the two grenadier and two light infantry companies, as also five staff officers, to be quartered in Upper Westminster.	1 Dec. „	8	Ditto Malta, ditto.
	4		1 Jan. 1801	8	Ditto Egypt, ditto.
			. Mar. „	8	Ditto landed in Aboukir Bay on 8th March.
„ „	8	The second battalion to remain in Portman-street barracks.	18 May „	.	Such detachments from the Coldstream & Third Guards as may be directed by the Adjutant-General, to proceed from London, on the 21st instant, to Portsmouth, in such conveyance as may be provided to expedite their arrival with as little loss of time as possible.
8 Mar. 1800	8	The first battalion of the Coldstream (leaving their flank companies) to march in three divisions, on Thursday the 13th instant, to Portsmouth and Gosport, where they are to embark on board the vessels provided to convey them to Ireland: embarked 18th and 19th, and disembarked at Cork on 26th of March.	20 „ „		The second battalion of the Coldstream to remove from the Tower. (8 companies.)
27 May, „	4	Part of the second battalion of the Coldstream, viz. 4 companies, with staff officers, to be quartered in Holborn division.		4	And four companies, with 4 staff officers, to be quartered in Holborn division.
				3	Three companies in Finsbury division.
7 June, „		The brigade of Guards intended for Swinley camp to march, Monday the 9th inst., to Hounslow and encamp, and proceed on the 10th to Swinley camp. The flank companies of the Coldstream (the grenadiers and light infantry of each battalion)		1	One company in the Liberty of the Savoy, parcel of the Dutchy of Lancaster.
			„ „ „	4	The flank companies of both the battalions of the Coldstream at Colchester barracks.
	4		7 July, „	8	The grenadier battalion (eight companies including two of the Coldstream) of the bri-

APPENDIX.
STATIONS.—Continued.

Date	No. of Comps.	Description	Date	No. of Comps.	Description
		gade of Guards, and the 3rd battalion of First Guards, to march on Saturday the 11th instant from Colchester to Chelmsford barracks.		3	val of the 1st batt.) and to be quartered, viz. 3 comps., with staff officers, in Finsbury division, four comps., with 4 staff officers, in Holborn division, and a detachment of about 60 men in the Liberty of the Savoy, parcel of the Dutchy of Lancaster.
7 July, 1801	8	The light infantry battalion (eight companies including two of the Coldstream) of the brigade of Guards to march from Colchester, on Friday the 10th instant, to Chatham, and encamp within the lines.		4	
				1	
18 „ „	8	The grenadier battalion (eight companies including two of the Coldstream) of the brigade of Guards to march from Chelmsford, on Monday the 20th of July, to Chatham, and encamp.	18 Dec. 1801	4	The flank comps. of both the batts. at Chatham barracks.
			„ „	8	The 1st battalion of the Coldstream from Egypt disembarked at Portsmouth, in several divisions, and marched to Winchester barracks.
29 „ „	8	As many men of the second battalion of the Coldstream to remove from their present quarters as can be accommodated in the Knightsbridge barracks, and the remainder, with 4 staff officers, to be quartered in that part of Lower Westminster most contiguous.	28 „ „	.	The remaining part of the 1st batt. of the Coldstream off Portsmouth, to disembark and march to Winchester barracks.
			5 Jan. 1802	8	The 1st battalion of the Coldstream to march on Friday 8th inst., in 2 divisions, from Winchester to Knightsbridge barracks.
. Aug. „	4	The flank companies of both batts. at Chatham barracks.	23 Apr. „	4	The flank comps. of the 1st and 2nd batts. of the Coldstream to march on Tuesday the 27th inst. from Chatham to London, and join the regt.
5 Sept. „	8	The second battalion of the Coldstream to march from London on Monday the 7th instant, in three divisions, to Chelmsford barracks.	11 Aug. „	10	The 1st batt. of the Coldstream are to remove from Knightsbridge barracks and be quartered, with 6 staff officers, in the borough of Southwark.
21 Oct. „	8	The second battalion of the Coldstream to march from Chelmsford on Friday the 23rd instant, in 4 divisions, to London, or in the neighbourhood, where they are to be quartered.	21 „ „	10	The 2nd batt. of the Coldstream to march on Wednesday the 25th inst., in 2 divisions, from Holborn and Finsbury to Windsor barracks, New Windsor, and Clewer, &c., and relieve the 1st batt. of the First Guards.
. „ „	8	The second battalion Coldstream in Knightsbridge barracks.	. Oct. „	.	A detachment from the 2nd batt. at Windsor are to be quartered at Kew.
11 Dec. „	.	An escort from the Coldstream to proceed to Chatham with the clothing of the four flank companies of the regiment in Chatham barracks, and afterwards return to London.	14 Feb. 1803	10	As many men of the 1st batt. of the Coldstream from the borough of Southwark to the barracks in Portman Street as can be accommodated, and the remainder, with 6 staff officers, in that part of Upper Westminster most contiguous.
18 Dec. „	8	On the arrival of the 1st batt. of the Coldstream in London, such part as cannot be accommodated in Knightsbridge barracks to be quartered, with 4 staff officers, near the barracks, and in Upper and Lower Westminster.	19 „ „	10	The 2nd batt. of the Coldstream to march from Windsor and Kew on the 26th inst. to Knightsbridge barracks, and such other quarters as may be directed.
„ „ „		The 2d batt. of the Coldstream to remove from Knightsbridge barracks (on the arri-	23 Mar.[1] „		A detachment from the Cold-

---

[1] In March, 1803, Sir James Pulteney, Bart. (then Secretary at War,) permitted the Quarter-Master-General to take the entire direction of the movement of the troops, and changes of quarters: henceforth all applications for routes were and continue to be made to his department, the Secretary at War, or his deputy, signing (as the law requires) each route sent.

APPENDIX.

STATIONS.—*Continued.*

Date	No. of Comps.	Description	Date	No. of Comps.	Description
		stream of 2 subts., 3 serjts., 3 corpls., 1 drummer, and 60 privates, to march to Purfleet, to be relieved as often as necessary.			comps. of the 2nd batt. of the Coldstream,) and 52 musicians of the First and Coldstream, to march on Friday the 19th inst. to Windsor barracks and town, to attend an Installation.
23 June, 1803	10	The 1st battalion of the Coldstream to march from London on Monday the 27th inst. to Chelmsford barracks. The batt. encamped in Sept. at Widford, and returned to Chelmsford barracks in October.	24 Apr. 1805	.	The 4 flank comps. from the 2nd brigade of Guards, (including the 2 of the 1st batt. of Coldstream,) to march on Friday 26th inst. from Windsor to Chatham barracks, and join their battalions.
3 Aug. ,,	10	The 2nd batt. of the Coldstream to be quartered, viz., 6 comps. in Upper Westminster, and 4 comps. in Lower Westminster.	,, ,, ,,	.	The six flank companies of the 3rd brigade of Guards, (including the two of 2d batt. of Coldstream,) to march Friday the 26th inst. from Windsor to London, and join their battalions.
9 Dec. ,,	.	A detachment of 2 captains, 6 subalterns, 12 serjeants, 12 corpls., and 270 private men, to march to-morrow to Chelmsford to join the 1st battalion.	25 May, ,,	10	The 1st battalion of the Coldstream to march on the 27th inst., from Chatham to London, in two divisions, and arrive on the 29th inst.
. Feb. 1804	10	The 2nd battalion of the Coldstream removed from Upper and Lower Westminster to Portman Street barracks.	14 June, ,,	10	The 1st battalion of the Coldstream to march on 17th inst. from London to Chatham barracks, in two divisions, and arrive on the 19th inst.
20 July, ,,	.	The brigade of Guards at Chelmsford (including the 1st batt. of the Coldstream) to march on Tuesday the 24th inst. and proceed to Coxheath, and encamp.	. Aug. ,,	10	The 2d battalion of the Coldstream to remove from Lower Westminster to Portman Street barracks.
. Aug. ,,	10	2nd batt. of the Coldstream to remove from Portman Street to Knightsbridge barracks.	29 ,, ,,	.	The 2d brigade of Guards at Chatham (including the 1st batt. of the Coldstream) to march to-morrow the 30th inst. to Deal, to replace the 1st brigade of Guards now there.
. Nov. ,,	10	The 1st battalion of the Coldstream at Coxheath marched to Chatham barracks on the 1st and 2nd November.			
31 Jan. 1805	.	A detachment of one captain, 4 subalterns, 8 serjeants, 8 corporals, and 125 privates of the Coldstream, to march to-morrow from Knightsbridge to Chatham barracks, and join the 1st battalion.	5 Oct. ,,	10	The 1st battalion of the Coldstream to march, Wednesday the 9th inst., from Deal to Dover Castle, and the barracks: [marched to Ramsgate, and embarked on the 23d inst. for Cuxhaven, and proceeded to Bremen.]
,, ,, ,,	.	One subaltern, two serjeants, 2 corporals, and 85 privates of the 1st batt., to march from Chatham to Knightsbridge barracks, and join the 2nd battalion.	. Feb. 1806	10	The 2d battalion of the Coldstream to remove from Portman Street to Knightsbridge barracks.
13 Feb. ,,	10	The 2nd battalion of the Coldstream to remove from Knightsbridge barracks to quarters in Lower Westminster.	. ,, ,,	10	The 1st battalion of the Coldstream disembarked on the 23d inst. at Ramsgate, from the Elbe, and marched to Deal.
11 April, ,,	.	The four flank comps. from the 2nd brigade of Guards at Chatham, including the two of 1st batt. Coldstream, to march on Tuesday the 16th inst. to Windsor barracks and town, to attend at an Installation.	20 Aug. ,,	10	The 2d battalion of the Coldstream to remove to the barracks in the Savoy Square, and quarters in Lower Westminster.
			. ,, ,,	10	The 1st battalion of the Coldstream removed from Deal to Chatham barracks.
17 ,, ,,	.	The 6 flank comps. from the 3rd brigade of Guards in London, (including the two	18 Feb. 1807	10	The 2d battalion of the Coldstream to remove to Portman Street barracks, and that part of Holborn most contiguous.

APPENDIX.
STATIONS.—Continued.

Date	No. of Comps.	Description	Date	No. of Comps.	Description
25 July, 1807	10	The 1st battalion of the Coldstream, consisting of 41 commissioned officers, 73 serjts., 22 drummers, and 1191 rank and file, embarked at Chatham and Sheerness for Copenhagen.			Chatham, and arrived in London on 21st instant.
11 Aug. „	10	The 2d battalion of the Coldstream to remove to Knightsbridge barracks, and that part of Upper Westminster most contiguous.	10 Oct. 1809	10	The 1st battalion of the Coldstream, Badajos.
			30 Dec. „	10	The 1st battalion of the Coldstream, Vizeu.
			23 Feb. 1810	10	The 2nd battalion of the Coldstream to remove to Portman Street barracks, & that part of Holborn most contiguous.
1 Sept. „	10	The 1st battalion of the Coldstream before Copenhagen.	6 Mar. „	2	That part of the 2nd batt. of the Coldstream, under orders for foreign service (Cadiz), to march on Wednesday the 7th inst. for Portsmouth, & follow the orders of the officer commanding there.
13 Nov. „	10	The 1st battalion of the Coldstream disembarked at Chatham, and occupied the barracks.			
11 Feb. 1808	10	The 2d battalion of the Coldstream to remove to the barracks in the Savoy Square, and quarters in Lower Westminster.	7 „ „	8	The 2nd battalion of the Coldstream to move from Portman Street barracks, Holborn and Finsbury quarters, to Lower Westminster.
17 Aug. „	10	The 2d battalion of the Coldstream to remove to Portman Street barracks, and that part of Holborn most contiguous.	27 Apr. „	10	The 1st battalion of the Coldstream at Villa Cova in Portugal.
26 Dec. „	10	The 1st battalion of the Coldstream to march from Chatham to Canterbury in 3 divisions on the 27th inst., and follow the orders of the officer commanding at that place.	5 Aug. „	8	The 2nd battalion of the Coldstream to occupy the barracks in Savoy Square and Queen's Guard House, and that part of Lower Westminster most contiguous to the Bird-Cage Walk.
. „ „	10	The 1st battalion of the Coldstream left Canterbury, and embarked at Ramsgate for the Peninsula on 29th Dec.	. „ „	2	Comps. of the 2nd battalion of the Coldstream at Cadiz.
			18 Nov. „	10	The 1st battalion of the Coldstream at Cartaxo.
2 Jan. 1809	10	The 1st battalion, at Spithead, sailed 16th inst. (Light company at Waterford).	22 Feb. 1811	8	The 2nd battalion of the Coldstream to remove to Knightsbridge barracks, & that part of Westminster the most contiguous.
10 Feb. „	10	Ditto at Cove of Cork, and sailed 25th inst.			
17 „ „	10	The 2nd battalion of the Coldstream to remove to Knightsbridge barracks, & that part of Upper Westminster most contiguous.	19 Mar. „	10	The 1st battalion of the Coldstream in camp near Sarzedas.
			. May, „	.	Two officers, 3 serjeants, and 98 rank and file, of the two companies of the 2nd batt. at Cadiz, ordered to join the 1st batt. at St. Olaia: the remainder embarked 4th May for England.
. Mar. „	.	The brigade of Guards (including the 1st batt. Coldstream) disembarked on 13th March at Lisbon, & marched into Belem barracks.			
. July, „	2	The flank comps. of the 2nd batt. of the Coldstream, consisting of 9 officers, 18 non-commissioned officers, and 240 rank and file, embarked on 16th inst. at Chatham for Walcheren; these comps. formed part of the grenadier and light infantry batts. of the brigade of Guards.	24 „ „	.	The detachmt. of Foot Guards (from Cadiz), on arrival at Haslemere, to be quartered and march from thence on 27th inst. to London: arrived 30th May.
			7 Aug. „	10	The 2d batt. of the Coldstream to remove from Knightsbridge barracks to the Tower, and Holborn and Finsbury divisions.
11 Aug. „	8	The 2nd battalion of the Coldstream to remove to the barracks in the Savoy Square, and quarters in Lower Westminster.	17 Feb. 1812	10	The 2d battalion of the Coldstream to remove from the Tower, Holborn, & Finsbury, to Lower Westminster.
			20 „ „	10	The 1st battalion of the Coldstream at Abrantes.
18 Sept. „	2	The flank comps. of the 2nd batt. of the Coldstream, from Walcheren, disembarked at	5 Sept. „	10	The 2d battalion of the Coldstream to remove from Lower

APPENDIX.

STATIONS.—*Continued.*

Date	No. of Comps.	Description	Date	No. of Comps.	Description
		Westminster to Portman St. barracks, and that part of Holborn most contiguous.			barracks to Lower Westminster.
20 Sept. 1812	10	The 1st battalion of the Coldstream in camp before Burgos.	. Nov. 1815	10	The 2nd battalion of the Coldstream from the Bois de Boulogne to Paris.
25 Dec. ,,	10	The 1st battalion of the Coldstream at Mongualda.	. Feb. 1816	10	Ditto, from Paris to Cambray.
24 Feb. 1813	10	The 2d battalion of the Coldstream to remove from Portman St. barracks to Knightsbridge barracks, and that part of Westminster most contiguous.	. Mar. ,,	10	The 1st battalion of the Coldstream from Lower Westminster to Knightsbridge barracks.
			6 Aug. ,,	10	The 1st batt. of the Coldstream to remove from Knightsbridge barracks to the Tower on the 26th instant.
25 May, ,,	10	The 1st battalion of the Coldstream at Bragança.	. ,, ,,	10	The 2d battalion of the Coldstream in camp near Cambray.
. Aug. ,,	10	The 2d batt. of the Coldstream to remove from Knightsbridge barracks to the Savoy barracks, and Lower Westminster.	18 Feb. 1817	10	The 1st battalion of the Coldstream to march from the Tower to Windsor on the 25th and 26th instant.
			. ,, ,,	10	The 2d battalion of the Coldstream at Cambray.
. Nov. ,,	6	Companies of the 2d batt. embarked 24th Nov. at Greenwich, and a detachment on 10th Dec. at Ramsgate, for Holland.	8 Aug. ,,	10	The 1st battalion of the Coldstream to march from Windsor to Lower Westminster on the 25th instant.
25 Dec. ,,	10	The 1st battalion of the Coldstream in camp near Bidart.	. ,, ,,	10	The 2d battalion of the Coldstream at Cambray.
. Feb. 1814	10	Ditto, in camp near Bayonne.	7 Feb. 1818	10	The 1st battalion of the Coldstream to remove from Lower Westminster to Portman St. barracks on the 25th instant.
15 ,, ,,	6	The 2nd battalion of the Coldstream, and the 2 additional companies, to remove on the 25th instant from the Savoy barracks, & occupy the Magazine and Queen's Guard barracks; the remainder to be quartered in Lower Westminster.	. ,, ,,	10	The 2d battalion of the Coldstream at Cambray.
			. Aug. ,,	10	The 1st battalion of the Coldstream to remove from Portman St. barracks to Knightsbridge barracks.
	6	Of ditto, at Steinbergen.	. ,, ,,	10	The 2d battalion of the Coldstream at Cambray.
. July, ,,	10	The 1st batt. of the Coldstream, (consisting of 63 serjeants, 69 corporals, 19 drummers, & 691 privates,) disembarked at Portsmouth on the 28th inst., marched to London, and arrived in Portman St. barracks on the 4th of August.	28 Nov. ,,	10	The 2d battalion of the Coldstream, on arrival from Cambray, to march from Dover to Chatham, from 25th to 28th instant.
			11 Feb. 1819	10	The 1st batt. of the Coldstream to march from Knightsbridge barracks to Windsor on the 25th instant.
. Aug. ,,	6	Companies of the 2nd batt. of the Coldstream at Brussels.	,, ,, ,,	10	The 2d battalion of the Coldstream to march from Chatham to the Tower on the 24th and 25th instant.
8 ,, ,,	4	Companies of the 2nd batt. of the Coldstream, (consisting of 29 serjeants, 29 corporals, 10 drummers, & 312 private men,) to march on the 9th inst. from London to Chatham: proceeded to Ramsgate, & embarked on the 27th inst. for Ostend, to join the six companies at Brussels.	10 Aug. ,,	10	The 1st battalion of the Coldstream to march from Windsor to quarters in Holborn division, &c., on the 26th inst.
			,, ,, ,,	10	The 2d battalion of the Coldstream to remove from the Tower to quarters in Westminster on the 25th instant.
. Mar. 1815	10	The 1st battalion of the Coldstream to remove from Portman St. barracks to Knightsbridge barracks.	11 Feb. 1820	10	The 1st battalion of the Coldstream to march from Holborn to Windsor, and proceed to Portsmouth from 15th to 21st instant.
,, ,,	10	The 2d battalion of the Coldstream at Brussels.			
. July, ,,	10	The 2d battalion of the Coldstream in the Bois de Boulogne, Paris.	,, ,,	10	The 2nd battalion of the Coldstream to remove from Westminster to Portman Street barracks on the 15th instant.
. Aug. ,,	10	The 1st battalion of the Coldstream from Knightsbridge			

APPENDIX.

STATIONS.—Continued.

Date	No. of Comps.	Description	Date	No. of Comps.	Description
17 June, 1820	10	The 1st battalion of the Coldstream to march from Portsmouth to Windsor, from 19th to 23rd instant.			stream to remove from Lower Westminster to Portman-Street barracks and adjacent quarters on the 25th inst.
25 Aug. ,,	10	The 1st battalion of the Coldstream to march from Windsor to the Tower on the 26th instant.	17 Aug. 1822	8	The 1st battalion of the Coldstream to remove from Knightsbridge barracks to the King's Mews on the 20th inst.
,, ,, ,,	10	The 2nd battalion of the Coldstream to remove from Portman St. barracks to Knightsbridge barracks on the 26th instant.	7 Feb. 1823	8	The 1st battalion of the Coldstream to remove from the King's Mews to the Tower on the 25th inst.
. Feb. 1821	10	The 1st battalion of the Coldstream to remove from the Tower to Westminster on the 26th instant.		8	The 2nd battalion from Portman Street to Knightsbridge barracks on the 25th inst.
,, ,, ,,	10	The 2d batt. of the Coldstream to march from Knightsbridge barracks to Windsor on the 26th instant.	21 July, ,,	8	The 1st battalion of the Coldstream to march from London to Liverpool, from 25th of July to 2nd of August, and embark for Dublin.
12 July, ,,	10	The 2d battalion of the Coldstream to march from Windsor to Westminster on the 17th inst.	12 Aug. ,,	8	The 2d batt. of the Coldstream to remove from Knightsbridge barracks to Westminster, &c. on the 13th inst.
11 Aug. ,,	10	The 2d battalion of the Coldstream to march from Westminster to Hounslow camp on the 13th inst.: on their return quartered in the King's Mews.	16 Feb. 1824	8	The 2nd battalion of the Coldstream to remove from Westminster to the Tower on the 25th inst.
21 ,, ,,	8	The 1st battalion of the Coldstream to remove from Westminster to the King's Mews on the 25th inst.	10 Aug. ,,	8	The 1st battalion of the Coldstream, on arrival from Dublin and Liverpool at Paddington by the canal boats, to march into Knightsbridge barracks on the 13th inst.
6 Sept. ,,	8	The 1st battalion of the Coldstream to remove on the 7th inst. from the King's Mews to Portman Street, quartering in the Upper Liberty of Westminster such men as cannot be accommodated in the barracks.	,, ,, ,,	8	The 2nd battalion of the Coldstream to remove from the Tower to the King's Mews on the 13th inst.
			23 Feb. 1825	8	The 1st battalion of the Coldstream to remove from Knightsbridge barracks to Westminster on the 25th inst.
,, ,, ,,	8	The 2d battalion of the Coldstream to break up camp at Hounslow Heath to-morrow the 7th inst., and march to the barracks in the King's Mews.	,, ,, ,,	8	The 2nd battalion of the Coldstream to remove from the King's Mews to Portman-Street barracks on the 25th inst.
5 Feb. 1822	8	The 1st battalion of the Coldstream to remove from Portman Street to Knightsbridge barracks on the 25th inst.	21 July ,,	8	The 1st battalion of the Coldstream to march from Knightsbridge to Windsor on the 25th inst.
,, ,,	8	The 2nd battalion to march in two divisions from the King's Mews to Chatham on the 25th and 26th inst.	6 Aug. ,,	8	The 2nd battalion from Portman Street to Lower Westminster, and to occupy part of the Armoury, the Kensington and Magazine barracks.
22 Apr. ,,	4	Of the 2d battalion of the Coldstream to march from Chatham to Windsor, from the 24th to the 27th April.	20 Feb. 1826	8	The 1st battalion of the Coldstream to march from Windsor to the King's Mews and Holborn on the 25th inst.
17 May, ,,	4	The left wing of the 2nd batt. of the Coldstream to march from Chatham to Windsor barracks, from 22nd to 25th inst.		8	The 2nd battalion to remove from Westminster to Knightsbridge barracks on the 25th inst.
2 July ,,	8	The 2nd battalion of the Coldstream to march from Windsor to Lower Westminster on the 5th inst.	1 May, ,,	8	The 2nd battalion of the Coldstream to proceed by canal-boats from Paddington to Manchester on the 13th inst.
24 ,, ,,	8	The 2nd battalion of the Cold-	. May, ,,	8	The 1st battalion to remove to Knightsbridge barracks.

APPENDIX. 449

STATIONS.—Continued.

Date	No. of Comps.	Description	Date	No. of Comps.	Description
. July, 1826	8	The 2nd battalion of the Coldstream to march on the 24th inst. from Manchester to Liverpool, & embark for Dublin.			stream landed at Bristol from Ireland, to march to Portman Street barracks from the 20th of August to 1st of September.
7 Aug. ,,	8	The 1st batt. of the Coldstream to remove from Knightsbridge barracks to the Tower on the 25th inst.	24 Aug. 1830	8	The 2nd battalion to remove from Portman Street to Buckingham House, half the Armoury and Holborn quarters, on the 1st of September.
22 Dec. ,,	8	The 1st batt. of the Coldstream to remove from the Tower to Westminster, &c. on the 21st, 22nd, and 26th inst.	Nov. ,,	8	The 2nd battalion removed to the King's Mews.
. ,, ,,	8	The 1st batt. of the Coldstream to remove from Westminster, &c., to the Tower on the 29th inst.	1 Mar. 1831	8	The 1st battalion of the Coldstream to march from Portman Street to Windsor on the 1st inst.
26 Feb. 1827	8	The 1st battalion of the Coldstream to remove from the Tower to Portman Street barracks on the 26th inst.	,, ,,	8	The 2nd battalion to remove from the King's Mews to Portman Street barracks on the 1st inst.
1 Aug. ,,	8	The 1st battalion of the Coldstream to remove from Portman Street to the King's Mews on the 1st inst.	25 July, ,,	8	The 1st battalion of the Coldstream to march from Windsor to the Tower of London on the 2nd and 3rd of August.
. ,, ,,	8	The 2nd battalion of the Coldstream, on arrival from Dublin, to proceed by canal-boats to London, and occupy the barracks in Portman Street.	30 ,, ,,	1	Company of the second battalion of the Coldstream to march from London to Islip, from 30th of July to 2d of August.
7 Apr. 1828	8	The 1st battalion of the Coldstream to remove from the King's Mews to Westminster on the 15th inst.		7	Ditto from Portman Street to Windsor on the 2nd August.
	8	The 2nd battalion of the Coldstream to remove from Portman Street to the King's Mews on the 15th inst.	1 Sept. ,,	7	The second battalion of the Coldstream to march from Windsor to Lower Westminster on the 5th and 6th inst.
16 Aug. ,,	8	The 1st battalion of the Coldstream to remove from Westminster to Knightsbridge barracks on the 16th inst.	5 ,, ,,	1	The company of the second battalion of the Coldstream at Islip to march from thence to Windsor from 6th to 8th of September.
. ,, ,,	8	The 2nd battalion of the Coldstream to march from the King's Mews to Windsor.	7 ,, ,,	7	The 2nd batt. of the Coldstream to march from Lower Westminster to Windsor barracks on the 9th and 10th inst.
29 Sept. ,,	8	The 1st batt. of the Coldstream to march from Knightsbridge to Manchester from 1st to 16th of October.	21 Oct. ,,	4	The head-quarters and one wing of the second battalion of the Coldstream to march from Windsor to Brighton barracks from the 24th to the 27th instant.
18 Feb. 1829	3	The 2nd battalion of the Coldstream to march from Windsor to the Tower of London on the 25th inst.	7 Feb. 1832	1	Of the second battalion of the Coldstream to march from Windsor to Islip on the 8th, 9th, and 10th instant.
21 July, ,,	8	The 1st battalion of the Coldstream to march from Manchester on the 23rd and 24th inst. to Liverpool and embark for Dublin.	25 ,, ,,	1	A company of the first battalion of the Coldstream to march from the Tower on the 27th instant to Croydon barracks.
5 Aug. ,,	8	The 2nd battalion of the Coldstream to remove from the Tower to Westminster on the 5th inst.	,, ,, ,,	3	Of the second battalion of the Coldstream to march from Brighton to the Tower of London from the 27th of Feb. to the 1st of March.
23 Feb. 1830	8	The 2nd battalion of the Coldstream to remove from Westminster to Knightsbridge barracks.	,, ,, ,,	1	Of the second battalion of the Coldstream to march from Brighton to the Tower from the 1st to the 5th of March.
. July, ,,	8	The 2nd batt. of the Coldstream to remove from Knightsbridge to Portman Street barracks on the 27th July.	,, ,, ,,	8	The first battalion of the Coldstream to remove from the Tower to the Armoury in the
24 Aug. ,,	8	The 1st battalion of the Cold-			

APPENDIX.

STATIONS.—*Continued.*

	No. of Comps.			No. of Comps.	
25 Feb. 1832	3	Bird-Cage Walk, barracks at the Magazine, Buckingham House, Recruit-houses, and King's Mews, on the 1st of March. Of the second battalion of the Coldstream to march from Windsor to the Tower on the 1st of March.	23 July, 1832	8	on the 9th and 10th instant to Bristol, & embark for Dublin. The first battalion of the Coldstream to move on Wednesday, the 1st of August, from the Mews barracks, Buckingham House, Recruit-houses, &c. to Knightsbridge barracks, the Kensington and Magazine barracks.
,, ,, ,,	1	Of the second battalion of the Coldstream to march from Islip to the Tower of London from the 3rd to the 7th of March.	4 Aug. ,,	2	The flank companies of the first battalion of the Coldstream to march, on Thursday the 9th instant, from Knightsbridge to Twickenham; and on Friday the 10th, to Windsor, and encamp.
9 Apr. ,,	1	The company of the 1st battalion of the Coldstream at Croydon to march on the 11th instant to London and join the regiment.	10 ,, ,,	2	Ditto to march on the 14th instant from the camp at Windsor to Twickenham, and on the 15th to Knightsbridge barracks.
5 July, ,,	8	The second battalion of the Coldstream to march from the Tower in two divisions			

In January, 1833, the regiment continued in the quarters last ordered. The first battalion, Knightsbridge barracks, &c. The second battalion, Dublin.

APPENDIX.

274.
Officers of Colonel Monck's Regiment. 1650, 1651.

Colonel: George Monck. Lieutenant-Colonel: William Gough. Major: Abraham Holmes. Captains: ——— Gardiner ——— Hughes James Rose ——— Hart Ethelbert Morgan Francis Nichols John Robins William Powell.	Lieutenants: Thomas Parker. Ralph Walton.	Ensigns: Francis Norris John Wells.

275.
Officers of Colonel Monck's Regiment re-appointed and approved by Parliament, on Saturday, 30th July, 1659.

Colonel: George Monck. Lieutenant-Colonel: William Gough. Major: . . . .[1] Captains: Ethelbert Morgan Francis Nichols George Parker Benjamin Groome George Walton Roger Hachman William Downes.	Lieutenants: Capt.-Lieut. Rob. Winter Joseph Fellow Robert Carter John Painter Thomas Mansfield John Wells Nicholas Parker James Wilson Augustine Richards Christopher Browne.	Ensigns: William Brangman John Rooke John Saunders James Hubbard Thomas Goodwin John Clarke Robert Burrowes Roger Lawrence John Harrison William Underhill.

Chaplain, John Price.
Surgeon, Nicholas Priddy.
Quarter-Master and Marshal, Henry Dennis.

Journal of the House of Commons.

276.
Officers of George Duke of Albemarle's Regiment, re-appointed and approved at the Restoration of Charles II. 18th August, 1660.

Colonel: George Monck, Duke of Albemarle, &c. Lieutenant-Colonel: Ethelbert Morgan. Major: Francis Nichols. Captains: John Miller (Adjutant-General) William Downes Robert Winter Thomas Mansfield John Collins John Peters John Mutlow.	Lieutenants: Cap.-Lieut. John Paynter Thomas Goodwin John Saunders Robert Cooper William Underhill James Hubbard John Rook John Harrison William Brangman Thomas Feiges.	Ensigns: Ralph Butcher Richard Rowcastle John Cobb Edward Basenet Michael Adderses John Clarke Daniel Court Thomas Figgs William Mac Kerith John Balder (Waller).

Chaplain, John Price.
Chyrurgeon, Nicholas Priddy.
Quarter-Master and Marshal, Richard Collins.

Mercurius Publicus.

---

[1] Major Abraham Holmes, appointed on the same day Lieutenant-Colonel of Colonel Roger Sawrey's regiment of Foot.

277.

Officers of the Duke of Albemarle's regiment of Foot Guards in 1661.

Colonel:	Lieutenants:	Ensigns:
George Duke of Albemarle.		
Lieutenant-Colonel:	Capt.-Lieut. John Clarke	John Waller
Ethelbert Morgan.	John Painter	John Huitson
Major:		
Francis Nicholls.	John Saunders	John Cobb
Captains:		
John Miller	Robert Cooper	Edward Basnett
William Downes	Richard Rowcastle	Michael Aldersey
Robert Winter	Samuel Hubbord	Ralph Butcher
Thomas Mansfield	William Dyke	Daniel Court
John Peters	William Brangman	William Mac Kerith
John Mutlow	Thomas Figges	John Baker (Cornet)
Samuel Clarke.	John Harrison.	Thomas Fiege.

Quarter-Master and Marshal, Richard Collins.

State-Paper Office.

278.

Renewal of the Commissions of the Officers of the Coldstream Guards, at the Accession of James the Second.

Colonel:	Date.	Lieutenants:	Date.	Ensigns:	Date.
Wm. Earl of Craven.	9 Feb. 1684/5	Cap.-Lt. H. Cope	9 Feb. 1684/5	George Wythe	18 Feb. 1684/5
Lieut.-Col.:					
Ed. Sackville.	9 Feb. ,,	Edm. Stuckley	10 ,, ,,	Wm. Wakefield	10 ,, ,,
Major:					
John Huitson.	9 Feb. ,,	Henry Wharton	11 ,, ,,	Henry Winde	11 ,, ,,
Captains:					
John Miller	9 Feb. ,,	John Drake	12 ,, ,,	Adrian Moor	12 ,, ,,
Anth. Markham	10 ,, ,,	Robert Wilkins	13 ,, ,,	Fran. Marshall	13 ,, ,,
James Kendall	11 ,, ,,	William Gibbons	14 ,, ,,	Wm. Mathew	14 ,, ,,
William Wakelyn	12 ,, ,,	Ed. Braddock	15 ,, ,,	Gamal. Chetwin	15 ,, ,,
W. Cholmondley	13 ,, ,,	John Clarke	16 ,, ,,	John Shepheard	16 ,, ,,
Charles Cotton	14 ,, ,,	William Hewitt	17 ,, ,,	Charles Wakelyn	17 ,, ,,
Richard Pope	15 ,, ,,	William Rigg	18 ,, ,,	Bozoom Symons	. . .
Heneage Finch	16 ,, ,,	Edward Jones	19 ,, ,,	John Wybert	19 ,, ,,
J. Bridgeman, Gren'. Comp.	17 ,, ,,	{ 1st, E. Shenton { 2nd, J. Ward	21 ,, ,, 21 ,, ,,		
Dudley Rupert.	18 ,, ,,	John Hope.	20 ,, ,,	Charles Stanley.	20 ,, ,,

Adjutant, Lieut. Robert Wilkins . | 9 Feb. 1684/5.
Surgeon, Joseph Troutbeck . | 9 ,, ,,
Quarter-Master, Mathew Ingram . | 9 ,, ,,
Chaplain, Dr. John Price . | 9 ,, ,,

War-Office.

APPENDIX. 453

279.

(On the first leaf is written, "This did belong to King James; I had it from Coll. Grahame.")

The Coldstream regiment of Foot Guards. November, 1687.

Colonel:	Lieutenants:	Ensigns:
William Earl of Craven.	Capt.-Lieut. John Hope	Henry Wind
Lieut.-Colonel:		
Edward Sackvill.	Edmond Steukly	William Matthews
Major:		
John Huitson.	Henry Wharton	John Wyberd
Captains:		
John Miller	John Drake	Adrian Moor
Anthony Markham	Robert Wilkins	Thomas Sackvill
William Wakelin	Edward Bradock	Francis Savage
William Cholmondly	John Clark	John Shephard
Charles Cotton	William Hewitt	Charles Wakelin
Richard Pope	William Rigg	William Clark
Heneage Finch	Edward Jones	Joseph Massey
James Bridgeman (Granadiers)	{ Edward Shenton, 1st { James Ward, 2nd	
Henry Cope	William Wakefield	William Latham
Thomas Bellasyse.	William Gibbon.	Henry Bellasyse.

Staff Officers
{ Dr. John Price, Chaplain.
{ Robert Wilkins, Adjutant.
{ John Brown, Chirurgeon.
{ Matthew Ingram, Quarter-Master.

MS. Harleian. No. 4847. Brit. Mus.

280.

Officers of the Coldstream at the Accession of Queen Anne, 1702.

	Dates of Commissions		Dates of Commissions
Colonel, John Lord Cutts	3 Oct. 1694	Lieut. Roger James	23 Apr. 1697
Lt.-Col., Wm. Matthew	26 Feb. 169¾	,, Butler Ramsden	. Dec. 1699
Major, William Matthew	,, ,, ,,	,, Daniel Woollett	. . .
Capt. Edward Braddock	. . . 1690	,, John Wyvell, Adj.	. . .
,, Francis Chantrell	20 Dec. 1691	,, Arthur Cecil	. . .
,, Henry Edgeworth	1 May, 1693	,, Cornelius Swan	. . .
,, Richard Holmes	8 Mar. 169¾	,, . . .	. . .
,, Thomas Pearce	14 Oct. 1694	Ens. John Miller	1 Sept. 1688
,, Henry Morryson	22 Dec. ,,	,, John Selwyn	31 Dec. ,,
,, Edmond Rivett	1 Jan. 169⅝	,, Richard Gore	23 Oct. 1690
,, Richard Cole	. . .	,, William Windress	1 Jan. 169¼
,, Charles Salisbury	23 Apr. 1697	,, James Allen	26 Apr. 169¼
,, John Hobart	30 Jan. 170⁰	,, Anthony Vernatti	20 Sept. 1695
,, Thomas Moor	25 ,, 170⁰	,, Washington Shirley	. . .
Capt.-Lt. Andrew Bissett	1 ,, 169⅝	,, Thomas Talmash	. . .
Lieut. Charles Wakelyn, Quarter-Master	. Sept. 1688	,, William Bradbury	17 July, 1698
		,, ―― Bearce	. . .
,, William Otter	31 Dec. 1688	,, ―― Stanhope	. . .
,, John Wilson	6 July, 1689	,, John Duncombe	14 Apr. 1702
,, Magn. Kempenfelt	1 May, 1692	Adjut., John Wyvell	1 May, 1693
,, William Stevenage	,, ,, ,,	Qr-Master, Ch. Wakelyn	15 July, 1695
,, Hy (Edw.) Rowles	,, ,, ,,	Surgeon, Jac. D'Abbadie	. . .
,, Francis Scawen	11 Oct. 1694	Chaplain, Dr. John King	31 Dec. 1688
,, Jonathan Atkins	20 Sept. 1695	Solicitor, John Acton.	2 Apr. 1695

War-Office.

281.

Renewal of the Commissions of the Officers of the Coldstream Guards, at the Accession of George the First.—(All dated the 11th January, 17$\frac{14}{15}$.)

	Dates of Commissions		Dates of Commissions		Dates of Commissions
Colonel:		Lieutenants:		Ensigns:	
Hon. W. Cadogan	11 Oct. 1714	Capt.-Lt. John Folliot	12 Nov. 1713	Richard Holmes	30 Oct. 1711
Lieut.-Colonel:					
Maj.-Gen. Ed. Braddock	10 Jan. 170$\frac{8}{9}$	Sir Winwood Mowat, Bt.	11 July, 1712	Ed. Braddock	11 ,, 1710
First Major:					
Richard Holmes	10 ,, 170$\frac{3}{4}$	Cha. Whynyates	25 June, 1713	Walter Corbett	5 Aug. 1712
2nd Major:					
Henry Morryson	25 April, 1711	Henry Morryson	16 Nov. 1713	George Matthew	16 Nov. 1713
Captains:					
Andrew Bissett	. . 1697	Thomas Hunt	20 Mar. 171$\frac{2}{3}$	Gabriel Reeve	22 July, 1713
John Hobart	30 Jan. 170$\frac{8}{9}$	John Warren	. Sept. 1713	James Hussey	27 June, 1712
Cornelius Swann	1 Oct. 1706	{ William Price Thos. Hamilton }	25 Mar. 1710 30 Oct. 1711	} Grenadier company	
John Robinson	. . 1709	{ Wm. Hanmer Edw. Thomas }	13 May, 1709 1 Oct. 1709	} Grenadier company	
Sir Tristram Dillington, Bt.	Oct. 1709	John Parsons	24 April, 1708	Edward Eaton	1 Oct. 1709
Thomas Smith	10 Feb. 170$\frac{5}{6}$	Edward Shorte	30 Nov. 1710	John Keating	. . 1710
John Boys	10 Nov. 1713	Thomas Serjeant	,, May, 1713	Henry Cox	29 Aug. 1710
James Shorte	12 ,, 1713	Richard Green	24 April, 1707	William Sotheby	21 July, 1711
Thomas Cæsar	12 ,, 1713	Edward Borrett	20 Oct. 1706	Francis Wheeler	30 Mar. 1710
John Chudleigh	20 Mar. 171$\frac{2}{3}$	Obediah Stocker	1 ,, 1709	Richard Legg	3 Nov. 1710

		Dates of Commissions
Adjutant	Lieut. Sir Winwood Mowat, Bart.	16th Nov. 1713
Quarter-Master	Lieut. John Parsons	30th ,, 1710
Surgeon	Ambrose Dickens	. May, 1713
Chaplain	Dr. John King	31st Dec. 1688

War-Office.

APPENDIX. 455

282.

Renewal of the Commissions of the Officers of the Coldstream Guards at the Accession of George the Second.

(All dated 20th June, 1727.)

	Dates of Commissions		Dates of Commissions		Dates of Commissions
Colonel:		**Lieutenants:**		**Ensigns:**	
Richard Earl of Scarborough	18 June, 1722	Capt.-Lt. John Parsons	8 July, 1721	Bezaleel Brownsmith	13 Mar. 172¾
Lieut.-Colonel:					
Sir Adolphus Oughton, Bt.	12 Aug. 1717	Humph. Fishe	5 Oct. 1723	Francis Townsend	28 Apr. 1725
First Major:					
John Robinson	12 Aug. 1717	Henry Carey	. . 1715	Tho. Hapgood	24 May, 1723
Second Major:					
John Folliott	8 July, 1721	Hedworth Lambton	11 Feb. 172¾	Sir Henry Heron, Bart.	28 July, 1715
Captains:					
James Short	12 Nov. 1713	Gabriel Reeve	12 May, 1727	Rich. Walford	14 Sept. 1715
John Chudleigh	20 Mar. 171¾	Peter Darcey	15 Aug. 1715	Thomas Venner	20 Apr. 1717
Henry Pulteney	22 July, 1715	{ Ed. Braddock / John Hodges	1 Aug. 1716 / 14 Mar. 172?	} Grenadier Company.	
William Leigh	22 July, 1715	Edward Eaton	15 Aug. 1715	Ld. Charles Hay	18 May, 1722
John Huske	22 July, 1715	Thomas Noel	24 May, 1723	Tho. Macroe	14 Mar. 172?
George Churchill	28 Sept. 1715	Peter Burjaud	8 Feb. 172¾	James Hayman	23 Mar. 172?
William Anne Earl of Albemarle	25 Aug. 1717	{ Ed. Thomas / Wm. Sotheby	1 Oct. 1709 / 20 May, 1721	} Grenadier Company.	
William Hanmer	20 Dec. 1717	Richard Legg	15 Aug. 1715	Tho. Hockenhall	24 Mar. 171?
Geo. Chudleigh	3 Jan. 171?	George Scroope	13 Mar. 172¾	Fenwick Williamson	12 May, 1727
Hon. Ch. Howard	21 Apr. 1719	Samuel Needham	21 Aug. 1717	Rob. Williamson	15 May, 1718
Wm. Douglass	3 May, 1720	Wm. Lethieullier	24 May, 1723	Rob. or Jas. Wilson	2 Sept. 1726
Wm. Vachell	28 May, 1720	Edward Borrett	20 Oct. 1706	Thomas Corbett	20 Apr. 1717
Anth. Lowther	8 July, 1721	John Vernon	8 July, 1721	Charles Bodens	15 Jan. 172¾
Wm. Congreve	30 Mar. 1725	Obediah Stocker	1 Oct. 1709	Courthorpe Clayton	16 Feb. 172?

	Dates of Commissions
Adjutant, Samuel Needham	28 February, 172?
,, Thomas Hapgood	24 May, 1723
Quarter-Master, Edward Eaton	24 May, 1723
Surgeon, George Putland	1 December, 1726
Chaplain, Rev. Henry Pyniot	6 May, 1727
Solicitor, Robert Mitchenor	16 February, 172?.

War-Office.

456   APPENDIX.

283.
Coldstream Regiment of Foot Guards. July, 1739.

	Dates of their present Commissions.	Dates of their first Commissions.		Dates of their present Commissions.	Dates of their first Commissions.
Colonel: Rich. Earl of Scarborough	18 June, 1722	. .	Lieutenants: Robert Milner	17 Jan. 1728/9	Ensign 13 May, 1709
Lieut.-Colonel: John Folliot	30 Oct. 1734	Ensign 20 Mar. 1703	William Kellett	8 May, 1730	Lieutenant 24 Mar. 172 5/6
First Major: John Huske	5 July, 1739	Ensign 20 Aug. 1707	Hon. B. Noel	20 Mar. 1730/1	. .
Second Major: Geo. Churchill	5 July, 1739	Lieutenant 12 Jan. 1707	R. Williamson	10 Apr. 1733	Ensign 15 May, 1718
Captains: William Hanmer	20 Dec. 1717	Captain 15 May, 1709	John Dives	25 Apr. 1734	Ensign 20 June, 1727
Geo. Chudleigh	3 Jan. 1717/8	Ensign 8 Mar. 1703/4	John Twisleton	8 July, 1734	Ensign 23 Aug. 1711
Wm. Douglass	9 June, 1720	Ensign 1 Oct. 1708	Thomas Macro	30 Oct. 1734	Ensign 14 Mar. 1721
Anth. Lowther	8 July, 1721	Ensign 16 Oct. 1704	Tho. Hapgood, (Adjutant)	10 Feb. 1735/6	Ensign 24 May, 1723
John Johnson	1 Mar. 1727/8	Ensign . 1706	Fran. Townshend	25 Aug. 1737	Ensign 28 Apr. 1725
John Parsons	6 Oct. 1729	Captain 24 Apr. 1708	Wm. A'Court	21 Jan. 1737/8	Ensign 26 Dec. 1726
Hon. J. Lumley	31 Jan. 1731/2	Ensign 24 Oct. 1721	D. Urquhart	30 Dec. 1738	Lieutenant 2 Oct. 1731
Richard Legg	30 Oct. 1734	Ensign 3 Nov. 1710	Charles Perry	31 Dec. 1738	Ensign 4 Nov. 1721
Ed. Braddock	10 Feb. 1735/6	Ensign 11 Oct. 1710	Chas. Churchill	3 Jan. 1738/9	Cornet 6 May, 1722
S. Needham, (Adjutant)	30 June, 1737	Ensign 5 Mar. 1707	Henry Newton	4 Jan. 1738/9	Ensign 10 Oct. 1727
Wm. Sotheby	25 Aug. 1737	Ensign 21 July, 1711	Julius Cæsar	24 May 1739	Ensign 18 Jan. 1730/1
John Hodges	15 Dec. 1738	Ensign 20 Apr. 1717	John Lambton	9 July 1739	Ensign 12 Oct. 1732
M. Bockland	15 Dec. 1738	Cornet . Dec. 1715	Ensigns: Wm. Gansell	11 Feb. 1733/4	
Aug. Earl of Berkeley	9 July, 1739	Ensign 30 Oct. 1734	Charles Craig Lord R. Manners John Robinson John Clavering	25 Apr. 1734 26 July, 1735 8 Jan. 1735/6 10 Feb. 1735/6	.
Capt.-Lieut.			Benj. Rudyard	5 July, 1737	.
Hedw. Lambton, (Qr.-Mr.)	9 July, 1739	Ensign 11 June, 1710	Lord R. Bertie Chas. Vernon	9 July, 1737 25 Aug. 1737	. .
Lieutenants:			G. Visct. Bury	1 Feb. 1737/8	.
W. Lethieullier	24 May, 1723	. .	Hon. T. Southwell	1 May, 1738	.
Thomas Corbett	20 Jan. 1727/8	Ensign 20 Apr. 1717	Wm. Farrell George Bodens	2 May, 1738 24 May, 1739	. .
Sir H. Heron, Bt.	3 Oct. 1728	Ensign 28 July, 1715	Thomas Burton Charles Wilmer William Evelyn	9 July, 1739 17 July, 1739 17 July, 1739	. . .

	Dates of Commissions.
Adjutant Samuel Needham	28 Feb. 1729
Adjutant Thomas Hapgood	24 May, 1723
Quarter-Master Hedworth Lambton .	4 July, 1733
Surgeon William Ellis	14 Mar. 1731/2
Chaplain Rev. Henry Pyniot	6 May, 1727
Solicitor Robert Mitchenor	16 Feb. 1729

War-Office.

284.
Coldstream Regiment of Foot Guards. February, 1754.*

	Dates of Commissions		Dates of Commissions
Colonel:		**Lieutenants:**	
William Anne Earl of Albemarle	5 Oct. 1744	Henry Lister	29 Mar. 1748
		Sir William Wiseman, Bt.	5 Apr. 1748
Lieut.-Colonel:		Thomas Clarke	15 May, 1749
Hedworth Lambton	12 May, 1753	Richard Henry Roper	27 Nov. ,,
First Major:		Charles Rainsford	29 Jan. 17$\frac{50}{51}$
Hon. Bennet Noel	,, ,, ,,	Robert Orme	24 Apr. 1751
		John Mackay	29 ,, ,,
Second Major:		William Wright	30 ,, ,,
Julius Cæsar	,, ,, ,,	Henry Clinton	1 Nov. ,,
		Edward Mathew	17 Dec. ,,
Captains:			
Lord Robert Bertie	11 Apr. 1744	Harry Trelawny	4 Mar. 1752
Charles Perry	27 May, 1745	William Gwyn	16 ,, ,,
Hon. Joseph Yorke	,, ,, ,,	Lord Frederick Cavendish	17 ,, ,,
William A'Court	7 Aug. ,,	James Craig	23 Dec. ,,
John Lambton	24 Jan. 174$\frac{8}{9}$	Thomas D'Avenant	12 June, 1753
Hon. John Barrington	15 Feb. 174$\frac{8}{9}$	**Ensigns:**	
John Thomas	28 Nov. 1749	John Thornton	14 Jan. 174$\frac{7}{8}$
Henry Vane (afterwards Earl of Darlington)	6 Feb. 17$\frac{49}{50}$	William Winch	29 Mar. 1748
William Gansell	29 Jan. 1750	Lewis Buckeridge	30 Apr. ,,
Charles Craig	17 Dec. 1751	Anthony George Martyn	23 July, ,,
Robert Dingley	4 Mar. 1752	George Scott	21 Dec. 1749
John Robinson	15 ,, ,,	Hon. Wilmot Vaughan	30 Jan. 17$\frac{50}{51}$
John Clavering	7 June, 1753	Timothy Caswell	16 Mar. ,,
Cadwallader Blayney	8 ,, ,,	Richard Hussey	24 Apr. 1751
		Lord George Lennox	17 Dec. ,,
Captain-Lieutenant:		Thomas Northey	22 Apr. 1752
Charles Vernon	10 ,, ,,	Lucius Ferdinand Carey	23 Dec. ,,
		Wadham Wyndham	13 Jan. 1753
Lieutenants:		Thomas Osbert Mordaunt	27 ,, ,,
William Evelyn	16 Apr. 1744	William Charles Sloper	13 June, ,,
George Bodens	1 May, 1745	Thomas Calcraft	18 ,, ,,
William Alexander Sorrel	29 ,, ,,	Henry Delaval	2 Feb. 1754
Francis Craig	28 June, 1746		

	Dates of Commissions.
Chaplain, John Jefferys	11 May, 1742
Adjutants, { William Alexander Sorrel	28 Oct. 1746
{ Thomas D'Avenant	21 Dec. 1749
Quarter-Master, William Wright	30 April, 1751
Surgeon, Peter Triquet	19 Jan. 174$\frac{5}{6}$
Solicitor, Gilbert Elliot	2 June, 1744
Agent, Mr. Adair, Pall Mall	
	War-Office.

* From this year, Army-Lists were annually published by the War-Office.

285.—COLDSTREAM

NAMES.	Ensign.	Lieutenant.	Capt.-Lieut.	Captain.
George Monck, afterwards Duke of Albemarle	•	•	•	•
William Gough	•	•	•	•
Abraham Holmes	•	•	•	•
. . . Gardiner	•	•	•	July 1650
5 . . . Hughes	•	•	•	July 1650
James Rose	•	•	•	July 1650
. . Hart	•	•	•	July 1650
Ethelbert Morgan	•	•	•	July 1650
Francis Nichols	•	•	•	July 1650
10 John Robins	•	•	•	July 1650
William Powell	•	July 1650	•	. . 1651
Thomas Parker	•	July 1650	•	•
Ralph Walton	•	July 1650	•	•
Francis Norris	. July 1650	•	•	•
15 George Parker	. . 165 .	•	•	Prior to July 1659
Benjamin Groome	. . 165 .	•	•	Prior to July 1659
George Walton	. . 165 .	•	•	Prior to July 1659
Roger Hackman	. . 165 .	•	•	Prior to July 1659
William Downes	. . 165 .	•	•	Prior to July 1659
20 Robert Winter	. . 165 .	•	Prior to July 1659	. Oct. 1659
Joseph Fellow	. . 165 .	Prior to July 1659	•	•
Robert Carter	. . 165 .	Prior to July 1659	•	•
John Wells	17 Nov. 1651	Prior to July 1659	•	•
John Painter	. . 165 .	Prior to July 1659	Prior to Aug. 1660	•
25 James Wilson	. . 165 .	Prior to July 1659	•	•
Augustine Richards	. . 165 .	Prior to July 1659	•	•
Christopher Browne	. . 165 .	Prior to July 1659	•	•
Nicholas Parker	. . 165 .	Prior to July 1659	•	•
Thomas Mansfield	. . 165 .	Prior to July 1659	•	. Oct. 1659
30 Roger Lawrence	Prior to July 1659	•	•	•
Robert Burrowes	Prior to July 1659	•	•	•
William Brangman	Prior to July 1659	. Oct. 1659	•	•
John Rooke	Prior to July 1659	. Oct. 1659	•	•
James '(Samuel)' Hubbard	Prior to July 1659	. Oct. 1659	•	•
35 Thomas Goodwin	Prior to July 1659	: Oct. 1659	•	•
John Harrison	Prior to July 1659	. Oct. 1659	•	•
William Underhill	Prior to July 1659	. Oct. 1659	•	•
John Clarke	Prior to July 1659	. Oct. 1659	. . 1661	21 July 1665
John Saunders	Prior to July 1659	. Oct. 1659	. . 1665	. . 1673
40 John Collins	•	•	•	. Oct. 1659
John Miller, (Adj.-Gen.)	•	•	•	. . 1659
John Peters	•	•	•	. . 1660
John Mutlowe	•	•	•	. . 1660
Robert Cooper	•	. . 1660	•	•
45 Thomas Feiges, or Figges	•	. . 1660	•	•
Ralph Butcher	. . 1660	•	•	•
Richard Rowcastle	. . 1660	. . 1661	•	•
John Cobb	. . 1660	•	•	•
Edward Basnett	. . 1660	•	•	•
50 Michael Adderses, or Aldersey	. . 1660	•	•	•
Daniel Court	. . 1660	•	•	•
Thomas Figg or Fiege	. . 1660	•	•	•
William Mackerith	. . 1660	5 Aug. 1665	•	•
John Balder, or Waller	. . 1660	•	•	•
55 Samuel Clarke	•	•	•	. . 1661
William Dyke	•	. . 1661	•	•

ROLL.

2nd Major.	1st Major.	Lieut.-Col.	Colonel.	Remarks.
.	.	.	July 1650	Died 3rd January, 16$\frac{69}{70}$.
.	.	July 1650	.	Removed by Monck in October, 1659.
.	July 1650	.	.	{ Appointed Lt.-Col. of Col. Roger Sawrey's regt. of Foot in 1659.
.	.	.	.	Out of the regt. before 1659.
.	.	.	.	5 Out of the regt. before 1659.
.	.	.	.	Slain in Scotland, July, 1651.
.	.	.	.	Killed at Dundee, 1st Sept., 1651.
.	.	. Oct. 1659	.	Retired in July, 1665.
.	. Oct. 1659	.	.	{ Appointed "Surveyor of the Ordnance in the Tower" in June, 1660. Successor to his majority appointed in March, 166$\frac{1}{4}$.
.	.	.	.	10 Died at Aberdeen in December, 1651.
.	.	.	.	{ Killed by a party of Highlanders, 6th December, 1652.
.	.	.	.	Died in Scotland, 1651.
.	.	.	.	Died in Scotland, 1651.
.	.	.	.	{ Died of his wounds received at Dundee, in September, 1651.
.	.	.	.	15 Removed by Monck in October, 1659.
.	.	.	.	Resigned in October, 1659.
.	.	.	.	Resigned in October, 1659.
.	.	.	.	Removed by Monck in October, 1659.
.	.	.	.	Retired in August, 1665.
.	. . 1673	.	.	20 Retired in 1676.
.	.	.	.	Out of the regiment before August, 1660.
.	.	.	.	Removed by Monck in October, 1659.
.	.	.	.	Removed by Monck, Do. Do.
.	.	.	.	Out of the regiment, 1665.
.	.	.	.	25 Removed by Monck in October, 1659.
.	.	.	.	Superseded by Monck, Do. Do.
.	.	.	.	Superseded by Monck, Do. Do.
.	.	.	.	Out of the regiment before August, 1660.
.	. . 1676	.	.	Retired 1681.
.	.	.	.	30 Superseded by Monck in October, 1659.
.	.	.	.	Out of the regiment before August, 1660.
.	.	.	.	Out of the regiment in August, 1665.
.	.	.	.	Out of the regiment in 1661.
.	.	.	.	Out of the regiment in 1665.
.	.	.	.	35 Out of the regiment in 1661.
.	.	.	.	Out of the regiment in 1665.
.	.	.	.	Out of the regiment in 1661.
.	.	.	.	Out of the regiment in 1679.
.	.	.	.	Out of the regiment in 1671.
.	.	.	.	40 Out of the regiment in 1661.
.	21 July 1665	.	.	Retired in 1673.
.	.	.	.	Out of the regiment in 1673.
.	.	.	.	{ Deputy Governor of Portsmouth from March, 1680, to April, 1681. Left the regiment in 1680.
.	.	.	.	Out of the regiment in 1666.
.	.	.	.	45 Out of the regiment in 1666.
.	.	.	.	Out of the regiment in 1666.
.	.	.	.	Out of the regiment in 1665.
.	.	.	.	Out of the regiment in 1665.
.	.	.	.	Out of the regiment in 1665.
.	.	.	.	50 Out of the regiment in 1665.
.	.	.	.	Out of the regiment in 1667.
.	.	.	.	Out of the regiment in 1665.
.	.	. .	.	Out of the regiment in 1670.
.	.	.	.	Out of the regiment in 1665.
.	.	.	.	55 { Removed to the King's regiment of Foot Guards, 1666.
.	.	.	.	Out of the regiment in 1666.

APPENDIX.

COLDSTREAM

NAMES.	Ensign.	Lieutenant.	Capt.-Lieut.	Captain.
John Huitson	. . 1661	.	21 July 1665	. . 1669
John Baker, (Cornet)	. . 1661	.	.	.
Sir James Smith, Kt., M.P.	.	.	.	.
60 Robert Cox	6 July 1663	.	.	.
Anthony Vincent	23 Jan. 166¾	.	.	.
Ralph Edgerton	.	Prior to 1665	.	.
Thomas Fleetwood	.	24 May 1665	.	.
Henry Hooker	.	1 Aug. 1665	.	.
65 . . Halliday	1 Aug. 1665	.	.	.
Richard Eangley	5 Aug. 1665	.	.	.
John Stringer	5 Aug. 1665	24 Dec. 1666	.	.
John Hinton	.	.	.	17 Aug. 1665
Alban Lovell	16 Sept. 1665	.	.	.
70 Nicholas Travers	14 Oct. 1665	.	.	.
John Peryn	24 Dec. 1666	.	.	.
Sir Robert Holmes, Knt.	.	.	.	. Apr. 1667
Robert Coke	.	.	.	. Apr. 1667
William Earl of Craven	.	.	.	.
75 Charles Bertye	.	.	.	Prior to 1670
Richard Kirkbye	.	.	.	Prior to 1670
John Miller	.	Prior to 1671	.	. . 1673
Robert Wythe	.	Prior to Feb. 1671	.	Prior to Mar. 1673
Daniel Francis	.	Prior to May 1672	.	.
80 George Lascelles	.	Prior to May 1672	.	.
Roger Kirkbye	Prior to Mar. 167¾	.	.	.
Richard Meade	Prior to May 1672	.	.	.
Charles Cotton	Prior to May 1672	.	.	Prior to May 1683
Richard Aston	.	Prior to Apr. 1674	.	.
85 Henry Wharton	.	Prior to Sep. 1674	.	.
David Le Grosse	Prior to 1674	. . 167 .	.	.
Henry Cope	Prior to June 1675	. . 167 .	Prior to 1684	30 July 1686
John Hope	Prior to June 1675	. . 167 .	30 July 1686	12 April 1688
William Rigg	Prior to June 1675	. . 167 .	.	.
90 John Clarke	Prior to 1676	28 Oct. 1678	.	.
James Graham	.	.	.	Prior to Oct. 1676
John Tonge	.	Prior to Oct. 1676	.	.
Thomas Seymour	Prior to Oct. 1676	. . 1679	.	.
Edward Jones	Prior to 1677	22 Dec. 1678	Prior to 1695	.
95 Ingoldsby Daniell	.	.	.	1677

APPENDIX. 461

ROLL.—_Continued._

2nd Major.	1st Major.	Lieut.-Col.	Colonel.		REMARKS.
.	. . 1682	.	.		Lt.-Col. to Sir Charles Wheeler's new raised regt. from 1st March, 167$\frac{7}{8}$, to Mar. 1679; retaining his company in the Coldstream. Resigned his commission to King James at Rochester, 21st December, 1688. (Dead in April, 1689.)
.	.	.	.		Out of the regiment in 1665.
.	11 Mar. 166$\frac{1}{2}$	21 July 1665	.		Appointed Colonel of the Orange regt. of City Trained Bands, May, 1681, and retired.
.	.	.	.	60	Out of the regiment in 1668.
.	.	.	.		Out of the regiment in 1665.
.	.	.	.		Adjutant of the Coldstream from 1st Aug. 1665, to 1679. Out of the regiment in 1680.
.	.	.	.		Out of the regiment in 1670.
.	.	.	.		Out of the regiment in 1670.
.	.	.	.	65	Out of the regiment in 1670.
.	.	.	.		Out of the regiment in 1670.
.	.	.	.		Out of the regiment in 1670.
.	.	.	.		Out of the regiment before 1670.
.	.	.	.		Out of the regiment before 1680.
.	.	.	.	70	Out of the regiment before 1680.
.	.	.	.		Out of the regiment before 1682.
.	.	.	.		Also a Captain, Royal Navy. Retired prior to 1670. Appointed Governor of the Isle of Wight.
.	.	.	.		Out of the regiment in 1678.
.	.	.	6 Jan. 16$\frac{69}{70}$		Lieut.-General 18th June, 1685. Resigned 1st May, 1689.
.	.	.	.	75	Out of the regiment in 1673.
.	.	.	.		Out of the regiment before 1678.
.	.	.	.		Fell from his horse 30th July, 1688, and died the next day.
.	.	.	.		Left the regiment in 1684.
.	.	.	.		Out of the regiment in 1678.
.	.	.	.	80	Out of the regiment in 1678.
.	.	.	.		Out of the regiment in 1678.
.	.	.	.		Out of the regiment in 1678.
.	.	.	.		Out of the regiment in April, 1693.
.	.	.	.		Out of the regiment in 1678.
.	.	.	.	85	Left the regiment in December, 1688.
.	.	.	.		Promoted to Captain in "The Admiral's regiment," July, 1678.
.	.	.	.		Resigned his commission in April, 1688.
. .	.	.	.		Major to Sir Lyonel Walden's new raised regt. from 1st March, 167$\frac{7}{8}$, to Mar. 1679, retaining his Ensigncy in Sir James Smith's company of the Coldstream. Out of the regiment in 1697.
.	.	.	.		Captain of the new raised company of the Coldstream Grenadiers from 1st March, 167$\frac{7}{8}$, to April, 1679, (then reduced,) retaining his Lieutenancy in Capt. Street's company. Out of the regiment in 1688.
.	.	.	.	90	Out of the regiment in 1688.
.	.	.	.		Lt.-Col. to Edward Lord Morpeth's new raised regt. from 1st March, 167$\frac{7}{8}$, retaining his company in the Coldstream. Left the Coldstream in January, 167$\frac{8}{9}$.
.	.	.	.		Out of the regiment 1682.
.	.	.	.		Left the regiment . . . 1684.
.	.	.	.		Adjutant to second battalion Coldstream Guards from 1st Jan. 16$\frac{88}{89}$, to 31st December, 1696. Wounded at Namur, 8th July, 1695. Retired 1st Jan. 169$\frac{6}{7}$, on his full pay as Capt.-Lieut. and the half of his pay as Adjutant to the second battalion, on account of his long services.
.	.	.	.	95	Out of the regiment 1682.

COLDSTREAM

	NAMES.	Ensign.	Lieutenant.	Capt.-Lieut.	Captain.
	John Street	.	.	.	. . 1677
	Herbert Price	.	.	.	. . 1677
	Francis Newport	.	.	.	16 Jan. 167$\frac{7}{8}$
	Thomas Talmash, or Tollemache	.	.	.	16 Jan. 167$\frac{7}{8}$
100	Simon Parry	.	.	.	16 Jan. 167$\frac{7}{8}$
	Humphrey OKeover	.	.	.	16 Jan. 167$\frac{7}{8}$
	Robert Brett	.	.	.	16 Jan. 167$\frac{7}{8}$
	Thomas Sulyard	.	.	.	16 Jan. 167$\frac{7}{8}$
	Robert Sinclair	.	.	.	16 Jan. 167$\frac{7}{8}$
105	James Eastland	.	.	.	16 Jan. 167$\frac{7}{8}$
	Thomas Troutbeck	Prior to Feb. 167$\frac{7}{8}$	.	.	.
	Ronald Graham	.	Prior to Feb. 167$\frac{7}{8}$	.	.
	. . . Sandys	.	Prior to Apr. 1678	.	.
	. . . Dallison	.	Prior to Apr. 1678	.	.
110	David Oglevie	.	.	.	. June 1678
	William Wakefield	28 Oct. 1678	22 Oct. 1687	.	.
	John Wybert	22 Dec. 1678	.	.	.
	Anthony Markham	.	.	.	20th Jan. 167$\frac{8}{9}$
	Matthew Ingram	.	Prior to 1679	.	.
115	Allen Cotton	Prior to 1681	.	.	.
	Edward Sackville	.	.	.	.
	James Kendall	.	.	.	Prior to 1682
	William Wakelyn	.	.	.	Prior to 1682
	William Cholmondley	.	.	.	Prior to 1682
120	Richard Pope, (Major)	.	.	.	Prior to 1683
	Heneage Finch	.	.	.	Prior to 1683
	John Drake	Prior to 1683	. . 1684	.	29 Sept. 1688
	Edward Shenton, (Lieut. Grenadier company)	Prior to 1683	. . 1688	.	. . 1691
	James Bridgeman, (Capt. Grenadier company)	.	Prior to 1683	.	1 April 1684

*. This is the first appointment of the kind in the

ROLL.—*Continued.*

2nd Major.	1st Major.	Lieut.-Col.	Colonel.		REMARKS.
.	.	.	.		Dismissed the service in July, 1683, for false musters of his company.
.	.	.	.		From First Foot Guards. Out of the Coldstream, August, 1678.
.	.	.	.		Out of the regt. 1679. Company reduced.
.	.	.	1 May 1689		Lt.-Col. to Lord Allington's new-raised regiment from 1st March, 167⅞, to March, 1679, retaining his company in the Coldstream. Reduced in April following. Entered the Dutch service. Appointed Col. of the present Fifth Foot in Holland in 1688, and Colonel of the Coldstream, 1st of May, 1689: Governor of Portsmouth, December, 1688: Major-General, 20th of December, 1690: Lieut.-General, 23rd January, 169¾. Mortally wounded at Cameret Bay, 8th June, 1694, and died on the 12th, at Plymouth.
.	.	.	.	100	Out of the regt. in 1679. Company reduced.
.	.	.	.		Out of the regt. in 1679. Company reduced.
.	.	.	.		Out of the regt. in 1679. Company reduced.
.	.	.	.		Out of the regt. in 1679. Company reduced.
.	.	.	.		Out of the regt. in 1679. Company reduced.
.	.	.	.	105	Out of the regiment in June, 1678.
.	.	.	.		Out of the regiment . . . 1679.
.	.	.	.		Captain of a company in Edward Lord Morpeth's regiment, from 1st Sept. 1678, to March, 1679, retaining his lieutenancy in Capt. Talmash's company. Out of the regiment in 1679.
.	.	.	.		Out of the regiment in 1679.
.	.	.	.		Out of the regiment in 1679.
.	.	.	.	110	Out of the regt. in 1679: company reduced.
.	.	.	.		Out of the regiment in 1689.
.	.	.	.		Out of the regiment in 1688.
.	.	.	.		Left the regiment in Jan. 168⅞.
.	.	.	.		Regimental Quarter-Master from Dec., 1679, to June, 1695. Appointed "Aide-de-Camp* or Adjutant" to the Earl of Craven, 20th June, 1685. Out of the regiment 1695.
.	.	.	.	115	"Son-in-law and Ensign to Captain John Street" of the Coldstream. Left the regiment December, 1684.
.	.	. Jan. 168½	.		From First Foot Guards. Governor of Tangiers from Oct., 1680, to July following. Appointed "Colonel of Foot," 12th June, 1685; Brigadier of the forces, 3rd July, 1685; and Major-General, 7th Nov., 1688. Resigned his commissions to King James at Rochester, 19th Dec., 1688.
.	.	.	.		Out of the regiment, Feb., 168⅞.
.	.	.	.		Out of the regiment in 1692.
.	.	.	.		Out of the regiment in 1690.
.	.	.	.	120	Died in London, May, 1689. (Will dated 7th May, and proved 27th May, 1689, in the Prerogative Court of Canterbury.)
.	.	.	.		Out of the regiment in 1689.
.	.	.	.		Left the regiment in 1689. (Died 15th Dec., 1716).
.	.	.	.		Died on service in Flanders, 1693.
.	. . 1688	. . 1691	.		Adjutant to the Coldstream from 1683 to 31st March, 1684. Died in Flanders in July, 1692. (His will proved in the Prerogative Court of Canterbury, Nov., 1693.)

Coldstream: it was signed by the Earl of Craven.

COLDSTREAM

NAMES.	Ensign.	Lieutenant.	Capt.-Lieut.	Captain.
125 Dudley Rupert	.	.	.	. . 1684
Robert Wilkins, Lieut.-Colonel	.	Prior to Oct. 1684; 25 Feb. 170$\frac{4}{5}$	Aug. 1688	. . 1688
James Ward, (Lieut. of Grenadier company)	.	Prior to Oct. 1684	.	.
Edmond Stuckley	.	Prior to Oct. 1684	.	.
William Gibbons	.	Prior to Oct. 1684	.	.
130 Edward Braddock	.	Prior to Oct. 1684	.	. . 1690
William Hewitt	.	Prior to Oct. 1684	.	.
Bozoon Symons	Prior to Oct. 1684	.	.	.
William Mathew	Prior to Oct. 1684	1 Dec. 1687	.	. . 1691
Henry Winde	Prior to Oct. 1684	12 April 1688	.	.
135 George Wythe	Prior to Oct. 1684	.	.	.
Adrian Moor	Prior to Oct. 1684	26 Sept. 1688	.	.
Francis Marshall	Prior to Oct. 1684	.	.	.
Gamaliel Chetwyn	Prior to Oct. 1684	.	.	.
Charles Wakelyn	Prior to Oct. 1684	. Sept. 1688	2 Nov. 1702	4 May 1705
140 John Shepheard	16 Feb. 168$\frac{4}{5}$	.	.	.
Charles Stanley	20 Feb. 168$\frac{4}{5}$	.	.	.
Thomas Bellasyse	.	.	.	21 Feb. 168$\frac{6}{7}$
Thomas Sackville	29 March 168$\frac{6}{7}$	.	.	.
Francis Savage	. . 1687	.	.	.
145 William Clark	. . 1687	.	.	.
Joseph Massey	. . 1687	30 Sept. 1688	.	.
William Latham	4 May 1687	.	.	.
Henry Bellasyse	26 Oct. 1687	.	.	.
Jeremiah Macawliffe	1 Dec. 1687	.	.	.
150 Roger Baker	4 Feb. 168$\frac{7}{8}$	1 Oct. 1688	.	.
John Burgis	.	.	12 April 1688	. Aug. 1688
William Otter	12 April 1688	31 Dec. 1688	.	.
William Errington	12 April 1688	.	.	.
John Miller	1 Sept. 1688	.	.	.
155 John Hanford	24 Sept. 1688	.	.	.
Henry Lawrence, (Lieut. of Grenadier company)	25 Sept. 1688	1 Jan. 16$\frac{88}{89}$	.	.
Roger Hungate	25 Sept. 1688	.	.	.
Thomas Shirley	25 Sept. 1688	.	.	.
Gabriel Thorne	25 Sept. 1688	.	.	.
160 Francis Napier	.	.	.	26 Sept. 1688
Arthur Rolleston	26 Sept. 1688	Prior to Sept. 1693	.	.
George Wingfield	.	.	.	27 Sept. 1688
Charles Huddleston	27 Sept. 1688	.	.	.
Francis Edwards	.	.	.	28 Sept. 1688
165 Bartholomew Brayn	28 Sept. 1688	.	.	.
Charles Filkes	2 Oct. 1688	.	.	.
Henry Fox	3 Oct. 1688	.	.	.
Thomas King	.	.	.	31 Dec. 1688
Thomas Farrington	.	.	.	31 Dec. 1688

APPENDIX. 465

ROLL.—*Continued.*

2nd Major.	1st Major.	Lieut.-Col.	Colonel.	REMARKS.
.	.	.	.	125 { "Natural son to Prince Rupert." Killed at the siege of Buda, $\frac{2}{13}$ July, 1686. (A volunteer).
.	.	.	.	{ Adjutant to the Coldstream from 1st April, 1684, to 17th Oct., 1688. Left the regiment April, 1697, and re-appointed Lieutenant in Lieut.-Col. Hobart's company. Resigned in Sept. 1713.
.	.	.	.	Out of the regiment in 1689.
.	.	.	.	Out of the regiment in 1689.
.	.	.	.	Out of the regiment in 1689.
.	1 Oct. 1702	10 Jan. 170$\frac{3}{4}$	.	130 { Appointed Brigadier 1st Jan., 170$\frac{5}{6}$, and Major-General 1st Jan., 170$\frac{9}{10}$. Retired in Sept., 1715. (Died 15th June, 1725.)
.	.	.	.	Out of the regiment in 1690.
.	.	.	.	Out of the regiment Feb., 168$\frac{4}{5}$.
.	26 Feb. 169$\frac{4}{5}$	1 Oct. 1702	.	{ Adjutant from 18th Oct., 1688, to Oct., 1690. Appointed Governor of the Leeward Islands in Jan., 170$\frac{2}{3}$. (" Knighted " at St. James's 23rd March, 170$\frac{2}{3}$. Died " in March, 170$\frac{4}{5}$.")
.	.	.	.	Out of the regiment in 1690.
.	.	.	.	135 Out of the regiment in Oct., 1687.
.	.	.	.	Out of the regiment in 1689.
.	.	.	.	Out of the regiment in Oct., 1687.
.	.	.	.	Out of the regiment in Oct., 1687.
.	.	.	.	{ Wounded at Landen in July, 1693. Quarter-Master from 15th July, 1695, to May, 1705. Died in Spain, Aug., 1706.
.	.	.	.	140 Out of the regiment in 1688.
.	.	.	.	Out of the regiment in 1687.
.	.	.	.	Left the regiment in Dec., 1688.
.	.	.	.	Left the regiment in 1688.
.	.	.	.	Out of the regiment in 1689.
.	.	.	.	145 Out of the regiment in 1689.
.	.	.	.	Out of the regiment in 1689.
.	.	.	.	Out of the regiment in 1688.
.	.	.	.	Left the regiment in Dec., 1688.
.	.	.	.	Out of the regiment in 1689.
.	.	.	.	150 Out of the regiment in 1689.
.	.	.	.	Out of the regiment in 1691.
.	.	.	.	{ Appointed Adjutant to the Royal Horse Guards 25th March, 1706.
.	.	.	.	Out of the regiment 1689.
.	.	.	.	{ Wounded at Namur 8th July, 1695. Out of the regiment in July, 1704.
.	.	.	.	155 Out of the regiment in 1688.
.	.	.	.	Out of the regiment in 1695.
.	.	.	.	Out of the regiment in 1689.
.	.	.	.	Out of the regiment in 1689.
.	.	.	.	{ "Son-in-law and Ensign" to Col. Huitson of the Coldstream. Surrendered his commission to King James at Rochester, 21st Dec., 1688.
.	.	.	.	160 Out of the regiment in 1688.
.	.	.	.	Out of the regiment in 1695.
.	.	.	.	Out of the regiment in 1689.
.	.	.	.	Out of the regiment in 1689.
.	.	.	.	{ From Lieutenant in First Foot Guards. Out of the regiment in 1697.
.	.	.	.	165 Out of the regiment in 1690.
.	.	.	.	{ Promoted Lieutenant in the First Foot Guards Jan., 169$\frac{3}{4}$.
.	.	.	.	Out of the regiment in 1690.
.	.	.	.	Removed to First Foot Guards in 1689.
.	.	.	.	{ Appointed Colonel of a new-raised regiment, 16th Feb.. 169$\frac{2}{3}$; subsequently disbanded.

COLDSTREAM

NAMES.	Ensign.	Lieutenant.	Capt.-Lieut.	Captain.
170 David Taylor				31 Dec. 1688
Henry Morryson		31 Dec. 1688		22 Dec. 1694
Andrew Bissett, (Lieut. of the Grenadier company)		31 Dec. 1688	1 Jan. 169$\frac{5}{7}$	. . 1702
John Selwyn	31 Dec. 1688			
William Selwyn				. . 1688
175 Magnus Camperfield, or Kempenfelt	1 Jan. 168$\frac{8}{9}$	1 May 1692		
William Bewerton	1 Mar. 168$\frac{8}{9}$			
John Wilson		6 July 1689		
Thomas Clent, (Captain of the Grenadier company)				Prior to ... 168?
William Seymour, (Sir William)				
180 Richard Gore	23 Oct. 1690	13 Oct. 1702		
Edward Morryson	11 Dec. 1690			
Richard Cole		1 June 1691		. . 1697
William Watkins		12 July 1691		
Francis Chanterell				20 Dec. 1691
185 Paul Wentworth		1 Jan. 169$\frac{1}{4}$		
William Windress	1 Jan. 169$\frac{1}{2}$	. . 1702		
Piercy Collyear	Prior to 1692			
John Skelton				. . 1691
William Stevenage		1 May 1692		11 May 1704
190 Henry (or Edward) Rowles		1 May 1692		
Thomas Holmes	1 May 1692			
Daniel Woollett	1 May 1692	Prior to 1702		
Henry Withers				
. . Markham		Prior to 1693		
195 . . O'Brien		Prior to 1693		
. . La Ferrelle	Prior to ... 1693			
William Hill	Prior to ... 1693	15 July 1695		
Henry Edgeworth				1 May 1693
Richard Holmes			1 May 1693	8 Mar. 169$\frac{3}{4}$
200 Russel Allsop		28 Feb. 169$\frac{3}{4}$		
James Allen	26 April 1694			

APPENDIX.

ROLL.—*Continued.*

2nd Major.	1st Major.	Lieut.-Col.	Colonel.		REMARKS.
.	.	.	.	170	From Lieutenant in First Foot Guards. Out of the regiment in Oct., 1694.
25 Apr. 1711	.	.	.		Taken prisoner at Namur July, 1695. Appointed Brevet-Colonel 19th Oct., 1704; Brigadier-General 1st Jan., 170$\frac{9}{10}$; and Col. of the Eighth Foot 5th Aug., 1715.
.	.	.	.		Wounded at Landen 19th July, 1693. Appointed Brevet-Colonel 20th Oct., 1704, in Spain; Brigadier-Gen. 1st Jan., 170$\frac{9}{10}$; and Col. of Thirtieth Foot 24th Aug., 1717.
.	.	.	.		Resigned in Sept., 1705, in favor of his brother, Henry Selwyn.
.	.	.	.		Appointed Colonel of the Second Foot 18th Dec., 1691.
.	.	.	.	175	Entered the Coldstream as a volunteer 7th Oct., 1686. Appointed Quarter-Master 1st Jan., 168$\frac{8}{9}$; and Adjutant 1st Nov., 1690. Promoted to a company in Fourth Foot; commission dated 1st May, 1702.
.	.	.	.		Out of the regiment in 1699.
.	.	.	.		Left the regiment in 1702.
.	.	.	.		Dead in Jan., 170$\frac{0}{1}$.
.	.	1691	10 Aug. 1692	.	Wounded at Landen 19th July, 1693. Appointed Colonel of Lord Cutts's late regiment 3rd of October, 1694, and afterwards Colonel of the 24th and 4th regiments of Foot.
.	.	.	.	180	Appointed "Additional Adjutant" 3rd April, 1705. Resigned in March, 1710.
.	.	.	.		Out of the regiment in 1695.
.	.	.	.		Left the regiment in May, 1704.
.	.	.	.		Out of the regiment in 1695.
.	.	.	.		From Captain of a company in the 2d Foot. Out of the regiment in May, 1705.
.	.	.	.	185	Killed in the trenches before Namur, 23rd July, 1695.
.	.	.	.		Left the regiment on promotion in Feb. 170$\frac{4}{5}$.
.	.	.	.		Out of the regiment in 1694.
.	.	.	.		"Major of Brigade to the Foot Guards in Flanders," from 1st June, 1692, to 31st of Oct. 1695. Out of the regt. in 1697.
.	.	.	.		Appointed Adjutant to second battalion 1st March, 169$\frac{8}{9}$, and Regimental Quarter-Master, 1st April, 1703. Out of the regiment in April, 1709.
.	.	.	.	190	Out of the regiment in April, 1704.
.	.	.	.		Killed at Namur 8th July, 1695.
.	.	.	.		Left the regiment in March, 1705.
.	10 Aug. 1692	.	.		Appointed Major of First Foot Guards 26th February, 169$\frac{4}{5}$.
.	.	.	.		Wounded at Landen 19th July, 1693, and at Namur, 8th July, 1695. Out of the regiment in 1696.
.	.	.	.	195	Wounded at Landen 19th July, 1693, and died of his wounds.
.	.	.	.		Wounded at Landen 19th July, 1693. Out of the regiment in 1694.
.	.	.	.		Wounded at Landen 19th July, 1693, and at Namur 8th July, 1695. Out of the regiment 1697.
.	.	.	.		Wounded at Namur 8th July, 1695. Left the regiment in April, 1703.
.	10 Jan. 170$\frac{2}{3}$	28 Sept. 1715	.		Appointed Brevet-Col. 10th January, 170$\frac{3}{4}$; Brigadier-General, 1st January, 170$\frac{9}{10}$; and Major-General, 1st January, 170$\frac{9}{10}$. Retired in Aug. 1717. (Died 7th May, 1723.)
.	.	.	.	200	Out of the regiment in 1697.
.	.	.	.		Appointed Quarter Master 1702. Out of the regiment in April, 1704.

APPENDIX.

COLDSTREAM

NAMES.	Ensign.	Lieutenant.	Capt.-Lieut.	Captain.
John Whitehall	17 July 1694	.	.	.
John Lord Cutts	.	.	.	.
Francis Scawen	.	11 Oct. 1694	.	3 Feb. 170¾
205 Thomas Pearce, (Captain of the Grenadiers)	.	.	.	14 Oct. 1694
William Matthew	.	.	.	.
Jonathan Atkins	Prior to . . 1695	20 Sept. 1695	.	.
Benjamin Weston	.	6 May 1695	.	.
John Wyvell	15 July 1695	Prior to 1702	.	.
210 Arthur Cecill	20 Sept. 1695	Prior to 1702	.	.
Anthony Vernatti	20 Sept. 1695	.	.	.
Edmond Rivett, (Captain of the Grenadiers)	.	.	.	1 Jan. 169⅚
Henry Cartwrighte	.	Prior to 1697	.	.
Charles Salisbury	.	.	.	23 April 1697
215 Roger James	.	23 April 1697	2 Oct. 1706	.
Washington Shirley	. . 1697	.	.	.
Thomas Talmash, or Tollemache	. . 1697	7 Sept. 1702	.	.
William Bradbury	17 July 1698	.	.	.
Butler Ramsden, (Lt. of the Grenadier company)	.	. Dec. 1699	.	.
220 John Hobart	.	.	.	30 Jan. 170⁰⁄₁
Thomas Moor	.	.	.	25 Jan. 170½
Cornelius Swan	.	Prior to 1702	4 May 1705	1 Oct. 1706
. . . Bearce	Prior to . . 1702	.	.	.
. . . Stanhope	Prior to . . 1702	11 Dec. 1703	.	.
225 John Duncombe	14 April 1702	.	.	.
William Mathew	1 May 1702	4 May 1705	.	.
Sampson Brady	.	1 July 1702	.	.
John Phillips	.	16 July 1702	.	.
Gervaise Robinson	2 Nov. 1702	.	.	.
230 Sir Richard Vernon, Bt.	.	10 Nov. 1702	.	.
John Hill	.	.	.	. April 1703
Gabriel Hale	.	.	.	. April 1703
Edward Matthew	. . 1702	.	.	.

ROLL.—*Continued.*

2nd Major.	1st Major.	Lieut.-Col.	Colonel.	REMARKS.
.	.	.	.	"Quitted the regiment in July, 1698."
.	.	.	3 Oct. 1694	Appointed Governor of the Isle of Wight, 1693; Major-General, 1st June, 1696; & Lieut.-General, 1st June, 170$\frac{3}{4}$. Wounded at Namur, 20th August, 1695. Died 26th January, 170$\frac{8}{9}$, at Dublin.
.	.	.	.	Appointed Quarter-Master, 11th May, 1704. Surrendered prisoner of war at Almanza, 26th of April, 1707. (N.S.) Dead in February, 17$\frac{10}{11}$.
.	.	.	.	205 Wounded and taken prisoner at Namur, 8th July, 1695. Wounded at Vigo, 12th October, 1702. Appointed Colonel of a new-raised regiment for service in Ireland, 10th April, 1703, and Colonel of the Fifth Foot, 5th of February, 170$\frac{3}{4}$.
.	.	26 Feb. 169$\frac{4}{5}$	.	From Major of First Foot Guards. Wounded at Namur, 8th July, 1695. Out of the regiment in September, 1702.
.	.	.	.	Taken prisoner at Namur, 8th July, 1695. "Killed on a party in Spain, August, "1706."
.	.	.	.	Killed at Namur, 8th July, 1695.
.	.	.	.	Appointed Ensign from Adjutant of the regiment. Wounded at Namur, 8th July, 1695. Out of the regt. in Dec. 1703.
.	.	.	.	210 Out of the regiment in December, 1703.
.	.	.	.	Out of the regiment in December, 1704.
.	.	.	.	Killed at Malplaquet, 11th September, 1709. (N.S.)
.	.	.	.	"Quitted in December, 1699."
.	.	.	.	Out of the regiment in October, 1704.
.	.	.	.	215 Wounded at Gibraltar, . . . February, 170$\frac{4}{5}$, and Barcelona, . . . April, 1706, and taken prisoner. Resigned in May, 1709, "being disabled from wounds received in Spain."
.	.	.	.	Left the regiment in March, 170$\frac{3}{4}$.
.	.	.	.	Left the regiment on promotion in Nov. 1703.
.	.	.	.	Surrendered prisoner of war at Almanza, 27th April, 1707. (N.S.) Died in France, April, 1709.
.	.	.	.	Killed at Vigo, 12th October, 1702.
.	.	.	.	220 From Lieut.-Col. on half-pay of Brudenell's late regiment. Appointed Brevet-Col. 25th March, 1705, and Brigadier 1st Jan. 170$\frac{9}{10}$. Retired in June, 1716.
.	.	.	.	Appointed Col. of the late Col. Allen's regt. 1st. Jan. 170$\frac{7}{8}$. Subsequently disbanded.
.	.	.	.	From Col. William Seymour's (late Cutts's) regiment. Surrendered prisoner of war at Almanza, 27th April, 1707. (N.S.) Appointed Brevet-Colonel 15th November, 1711. Out of the regiment in June, 1715.
.	.	.	.	Out of the regiment in 1703.
.	.	.	.	Left the regiment in December, 1707.
.	.	.	.	225 Promoted Lieutenant in the First Foot Guards, 1703.
.	.	.	.	Regimental Quarter-Master from 24th April, 1708, to 29th Nov. 1710. Resigned in Nov. 1710.
.	.	.	.	Dead in October, 1710.
.	.	.	.	Killed at Malplaquet, 11th Sept. 1709. N. S.
.	.	.	.	Left the regiment in 1703.
.	.	.	.	230 Left the regiment 1703.
.	.	.	.	Appointed Colonel of the Eleventh Foot 8th May, 1705.
.	.	.	.	Out of the regiment in February, 170$\frac{3}{4}$.
.	.	.	.	Left the regiment in April, 1704.

COLDSTREA

NAMES.	Ensign.	Lieutenant.	Capt.-Lieut.	Captain.
. . . Wood	.	. Nov. 1703	.	.
235 Francis Williamson	.	9 Dec. 1703	.	.
Sir James Holford, Bt.	20 Dec. 1703	1 Jan. 170$\frac{7}{8}$	.	28 April 170
Samuel Masham, afterwards Lord Masham	.	.	.	10 Jan. 170
Obediah Stocker	27 Jan. 170$\frac{3}{4}$	1 Oct. 1709	7 Oct. 1729	.
Abednego Matthew	7 Feb. 170$\frac{3}{4}$	.	.	.
240 John Folliott	20 Mar. 170$\frac{3}{4}$	24 June 1706	12 Nov. 1713	23 Nov. 171
Edward Thomas, Lieut. of Grenadier company	5 April 1704	1 Oct. 1709	.	.
. . . Montague	. April 1704	. . 170$\frac{5}{6}$	.	.
Thomas Smith	.	25 April 1704	.	10 Feb. 170
William Stevenage	6 May 1704	.	.	.
245 Richard Spencer	.	11 May 1704	.	.
Jonathan Ashley	24 July 1704	. . 1710	.	.
Charles Churchhill	.	.	.	25 Oct. 170
Richard Green	18 Dec. 1704	24 April 1707	.	.
Michael Acton	.	24 Feb. 170$\frac{4}{5}$	.	.
250 Randyll Emily	.	25 Mar. 1705	.	.
Thomas Brushfield	.	25 Mar. 1705	.	.
Edmond Turner	.	.	.	8 May 170
James Short	.	30 July 1705	26 July 1710	12 Nov. 171
Villiers Charnock	24 Aug. 1705	.	.	.
255 Henry Selwyn	14 Sept. 1705	10 Oct. 1710	.	.
Henry Morryson	7 Oct. 1705	16 Nov. 1713	.	.
John Arundel	.	.	.	15 Mar. 170
John Robinson	.	25 Mar. 1706	7 May 1709	. . 170
Jefferey Saunders	.	21 April 1706	.	.
260 William Cope	.	25 April 1706	.	.
John Hughes	26 Aug. 1706	.	.	.
Edward Borrett	.	20 Oct. 1706	.	.
Charles Churchill, General	.	.	.	.
John Moody	.	14 Mar. 170$\frac{6}{7}$	.	.
265 Robert Bethell	.	12 April 1707	.	13 Apr. 170
John Chudleigh	24 April 1707	27 April 1710	.	20 Mar. 17
Richard Molesworth, afterwards Visc. Molesworth	.	.	.	5 May 170
Sir Winwood Mowat, Bt.	19 Aug. 1707	11 July 1712	.	.
William Scroggs	20 Oct. 1707	.	.	.

ROLL.—*Continued.*

2nd Major.	1st Major.	Lieut.-Col.	Colonel.	REMARKS.
.	.	.	.	Left the regiment in April, 1706.
.	.	.	.	235 Out of the regiment in April, 1706.
.	.	.	.	Appointed "Aid-de-camp to Lieut.-Gen. William Seymour in present intended Expedition," dated 10th July, 1708. "Died 12th November, 1713, and buried at Chelsea on Tuesday 17th November."
.	.	.	.	Appointed "Brevet-Colonel of Foot" 20th Oct. 1704, and "Colonel of a regiment of Horse," late Viscount Windsor's, in April, 1707; subsequently disbanded.
.	.	.	.	Died 10th of April, 1730.
.	.	.	.	Out of the regiment in 1707.
8 July 1721	3 Aug. 1733	30 Oct. 1734	.	240 First Adjutant of the Coldstream from 25th March, 1710, to 15th Nov., 1713, and again from 30th July, 1715, to 27th Feb., 172$\frac{0}{1}$. Appointed Lieutenant-Governor of Pendennis Castle June, 1729; Governor of Carlisle 9th July, 1739; and Lieutenant-Colonel of the First Foot Guards 1st April, 1743.
.	.	.	.	Dead in January, 172$\frac{7}{8}$.
.	.	.	.	Left the regiment in April, 1707.
.	.	.	.	Resigned in May, 1720.
.	.	.	.	Out of the regiment in 1709.
.	.	.	.	245 Left the regiment in July, 1705.
.	.	.	.	Dead in July, 1712.
.	.	.	.	"Leave to come home from Gibraltar," dated 10th April, 1705, "to serve in Flanders." Left the regiment in March, 170$\frac{5}{6}$. Brevet-Colonel dated 1st January, 170$\frac{6}{7}$.
.	.	.	.	Out of the regiment in July, 1715.
.	.	.	.	Out of the regiment in March 170$\frac{5}{6}$.
.	.	.	.	250 Out of the regiment in January, 170$\frac{7}{8}$.
.	.	.	.	Appointed Adjutant 4th May, 1705. Left the regiment in March, 1710.
.	.	.	.	Resigned in February, 170$\frac{9}{10}$.
.	.	.	.	Retired from the Service 25th August, 1737, and "allowed to receive his pay, 16*s*. 6*d*. a day, during his life."
.	.	.	.	Out of the regiment in January, 170$\frac{7}{8}$.
.	.	.	.	255 Left the regiment in June, 1713.
.	.	.	.	Promoted to Captain of a company in the 8th Foot 21st August, 1717.
.	.	.	.	Killed at Malplaquet 11th Sept., 1709. N.S.
28 Sept. 1715	12 Aug. 1717	3 Aug. 1733	.	Died 21st October, 1734.
.	.	.	.	Out of the regiment in October, 1706.
.	.	.	.	260 Dead in June, 1706.
.	.	.	.	Resigned in February, 170$\frac{8}{9}$.
.	.	.	.	Promoted Captain of an Independent company of Invalids 28th January, 172$\frac{8}{9}$.
.	.	.	25 Feb. 170$\frac{6}{7}$	From Colonel of 3rd regiment of Foot. Resigned Sept., 1714.
.	.	.	.	"Employed with Brigadier George Macartney, in present intended Expedition," dated 22nd March, 170$\frac{8}{9}$. Second Adjutant in the Coldstream from 27th June, 1712, to 6th March, 17$\frac{12}{13}$. Appointed Lieutenant-Governor of Placentia in March, 1713.
.	.	.	.	265 Killed at Malplaquet 11th Sept. 1709. N.S.
.	.	.	.	Died 5th October, 1729.
.	.	.	.	From Lieutenant First Foot Guards. Appointed Colonel of "Colonel Moor's late regiment" of foot, subsequently disbanded, dated 9th July, 1710.
.	.	.	.	First Adjutant to the Coldstream, from 16th Nov., 1713, to 29th July, 1715. Left the regiment in July, 1715.
.	.	.	.	Left the regiment in April, 1709.

APPENDIX.

COLDSTREAM

NAMES.	Ensign.	Lieutenant.	Capt.-Lieut.	Captain.
270 Charles Selwyn	.	2 Jan. 170⅞	.	.
Nathaniel Farewell	31 Jan. 170⅞	.	.	.
Michael Reau	.	13 April 1708	.	.
John Parsons	.	24 April 1708	8 July 1721	6 Oct. 1729
John Uthwayt	. Feb. 170⅝	.	.	.
275 Edward Short	5 April 1709	30 Nov. 1710	.	.
Henry Green	27 April 1709	.	.	.
Ralph Bagnall	.	28 April 1709	.	.
William Hanmer, (Lieut. of Grenadier company)	.	13 May 1709	12 Aug. 1717	20 Dec. 1717
Thomas Hamilton, (Lt. of Grenadier company)	. . 1709	30 Oct. 1711	.	.
280 Edward Eaton	1 Oct. 1709	15 Aug. 1715	2 Oct. 1731	3 Apr. 1733
Sir James Abercrombie	.	.	. .	. . 1710
Sir Tristram Dillington, Bt., M.P.	.	.	.	. . 1710
John Keating	. . 1710	.	.	.
William Price, (Lieut. of the Grenadier company)	.	25 Mar. 1710	.	.
285 Francis Wheeler	30 Mar. 1710	1 Aug. 1716	.	.
John Hatton	27 Apr. 1710	.	.	.
Thomas Norton	.	.	.	9 July 1710
Henry Cox	29 Aug. 1710	15 Aug. 1715	.	.
Edward Braddock, (Lt. of Grenadier company)	11 Oct. 1710	1 Aug. 1716	30 Oct. 1734	10 Feb. 173⅝
290 Richard Legg	3 Nov. 1710	15 Aug. 1715	5 Apr. 1733	30 Oct. 1734
William Corbett	30 Nov. 1710	.	.	.
Edward Henry, Lord Quarendon	.	.	.	12 Feb. 17¹⁰⁄₁₁
William Southeby, (Lt. of Grenadier company)	21 July 1711	20 May 1721	.	25 Aug. 1737
Richard Holmes	30 Oct. 1711	15 Aug. 1715	.	.
295 Cornelius Swan	. . Apr. 1712	.	.	.
James Hussey	27 June 1712	.	.	.
Walter Corbett	5 Aug. 1712	.	.	.
William Birbero	{ . . 1712 / 14 Oct. 1721 }	.	.	.
Thomas Serjeant	.	. May 1713	.	.
300 Charles Whynyates	.	25 June 1713	.	.
Gabriel Reeve	22 July 1713	12 May 1727	.	.

* Walter Corbett, No. 297, appears to be the same

ROLL.—Continued.

2nd Major.	1st Major.	Lieut.-Col.	Colonel.		REMARKS.
.	.	.	.	270	Promoted to Major of Col. John Selwyn's regiment (Third Foot) 13th March, 1710⁄11.
.	.	.	.		Left the regiment in July, 1711.
.	.	.	.		Resigned in April, 1710.
.	.	.	.		Second Adjutant Coldstream from April, 1710, to Nov. following, and Quarter-Master from 30th Nov., 1710, to 23d May, 1723. Appointed Colonel of the Forty-first Foot 4th March, 1752.
.	.	.	.		Second Adjutant of the Coldstream from 16th December, 1710, to 26th June, 1712. Left the regiment in June, 1712.
.	.	.	.	275	Dead in May, 1727.
.	.	.	.		Resigned in August, 1710.
.	.	.	.		Left the regiment in 1710.
.	.	.	.		Appointed Colonel of a regiment of Marines "to be forthwith raised." Commission dated 25th December, 1740.
.	.	.	.		Left the regiment in July, 1716.
.	.	.	.	280	Qr.-Master Coldstream, from 24th May, 1723, to 3d July, 1733. Died 4th Jan. 1737.
.	.	.	.		From Captain of a company in the Royals. Appointed Town-Major of Dunkirk 24th Oct., 1712. Retired in Nov. 1713. "Leave "to sell his company in the Coldstream "to enable him to purchase the First "Lieutenant-Colonelcy in the Royal re- "giment of Foot."
12 Aug. 1717	.	.	.		Wounded at Malplaquet. Governor of Hurst Castle. Died 4th July, 1721.
.	.	.	.		Left the regiment in July, 1715.
. .	.	.	.		Resigned in September, 1715.
. .	.	.	.	285	Resigned in November, 1720.
.	.	.	.		Dead in April, 1712.
.	.	.	.		Left the regiment in March, 1713⁄14.
.	.	.	.		Dead in July, 1716.
2 Apr. 1743	27 May 1745	21 Nov. 1745	.		"Fought a duel with sword and pistol "with Colonel Waller in Hyde Park, 26th "May, 1718." Appointed Colonel of Fourteenth Foot 17th February, 1753, and "General and Commander of the Forces "in an expedition to North America 24th "Sept., 1754." Wounded at Fort du Quesne, on the Ohio, 9th July, 1755, "of "which he died the fourth day."
.	.	.	.	290	Died 7th June, 1753.
.	.	.	.		Out of the regiment or his company in 1712.*
.	.	.	.		Died 21st October, 1713.
.	.	.	.		Retired in April, 1744.
.	.	.	.		Promoted to Major of Thirty-eighth Foot 16th April, 1719.
.	.	.	.	295	Left the regiment in July, 1713.
.	.	.	.		Dead in April, 1725.
.	.	.	.		Left the regiment in April, 1717.
.	.	.	.		Second Adjutant to the Coldstream from 7th March, 1712⁄13, to 24th May, 1713. Reduced: reappointed Adjutant 24th Oct., 1715, and to an Ensigncy in Oct. 1721. Resigned Adjutancy 23rd May, 1723. Died in August, 1726.
.	.	.	.		Resigned in November, 1716.
.	.	.	.	300	Left the regiment in August, 1715.
.	.	.	.		Died 22nd April, 1734.

person re-appointed to another company.

COLDSTREAM

NAMES.	Ensign.	Lieutenant.	Capt.-Lieut.	Captain.
John Warren	.	. Sept. 1713	.	.
John Boys	.	.	.	10 Nov. 1713
Thomas Cæsar	.	.	.	12 Nov. 1713
305 George Matthew	16 Nov. 1713	.	.	.
Thomas Hunt	.	20 Mar. 17$\frac{13}{14}$	.	.
Jefferey Gibbons, Lt.-Col.	.	.	.	1 Apr. 1714
William Cadogan, afterwards Earl of Cadogan	.	.	.	.
Edward Montagu, Lord Hinchinbrook, (Captain of Grenadier company)	.	.	.	11 June 1715
310 Hon. Charles Cadogan	.	.	.	11 June 1715
Robert Morgan	20 July 1715	.	.	.
Nathaniel Blackistone	20 July 1715	20 Apr. 1717	.	.
Henry Pulteney, (Captain of Grenadier company)	.	.	.	22 July 1715
William Leigh	.	.	.	22 July 1715
315 John Cope	.	.	.	22 July 1715
John Huske	.	.	.	22 July 1715
John Smith	.	23 July 1715	.	.
Sir Harry Heron, Bt.	28 July 1715	3 Oct. 1728	.	.
James Gendrault	.	30 July 1715	.	.
320 Hon. Charles Howard, M.P.	10 Aug. 1715	.	.	21 Apr. 1719
Peter Darcey	.	15 Aug. 1715	.	.
John Price	15 Aug. 1715	.	.	.
George Bellamy	15 Aug. 1715	.	.	.
Richard Walford	14 Sept. 1715	.	.	.
325 Jasper Tryce	14 Sept. 1715	.	.	.
Francis Pilliord	14 Sept. 1715	16 Apr. 1719	.	.
John Wynne, (Lieut. of the Grenadier company)	.	22 Sept. 1715	.	.
John Griffiths	.	27 Sept. 1715	.	.
Sir Adolphus Oughton, Bt. M.P.	.	.	.	.
330 George Churchill	.	.	.	28 Sept. 1715
William Cæsar Strang	5 Dec. 1715	1 Feb. 17$\frac{17}{18}$	.	.
Richard Waller	.. . 1715	.	.	.
Henry Carey	.	.. . 1715	.	.
Hon. William Fitzmaurice, afterwards Earl of Kerry	.	.	.	23 June 1716
335 Hon. Charles Leslie	1 Aug. 1716	.	.	.
Peter Darcey	1 Aug. 1716	.	.	.

APPENDIX. 475

ROLL.—*Continued.*

2nd Major.	1st Major.	Lieut.-Col.	Colonel.		REMARKS.
.	.	.	.		Resigned in September, 1715.
.	.	.	.		{ "From the Pension List." Retired in June, 1715.
.	.	.	.		Resigned in September, 1721.
.	.	.	.	305	Left the regiment in August, 1715.
.	.	.	.		Left the regiment in July, 1717.
.	.	.	.		Out of the regiment in December, 1714.
.	.	.	11 Oct. 1714		{ Late Colonel of Fifth Dragoon Guards. Governor of Isle of Wight Sept. 1715; Lieut.-Gen. 1st Jan. 170$\frac{8}{9}$; Gen. 12th July, 1717. Appointed Col. of the First Foot Guards, 18th June, 1722.
.	.	.	.		{ Appointed A.D.C. to the King 25th Dec., 1715. Promoted to Lieut.-Col. of Twelfth Foot 22nd Nov., 1716, and Colonel of the Thirty-seventh Foot 11th Dec., 1717.
.	.	.	.	310	{ Promoted Colonel of the Fourth Foot, by purchase, 21st April, 1719.
.	.	.	. .		{ Appointed Cornet in Third Dragoon Gds. 19th March, 17$\frac{12}{13}$.
.	.	.	.		Resigned in Feb., 172$\frac{2}{3}$.
3 Aug. 1733	30 Oct. 1734	.	.		{ From First Foot Guards. Appointed Col. of Thirteenth Foot 5th July, 1739.
.	.	.	.		Died 12th January, 173$\frac{3}{4}$.
.	.	.	.	315	{ Promoted to Lieutenant-Colonel of First troop of Horse Grenadier Guards, 27th April, 1720.
30 Oct. 1734	5 July 1739	.	.		{ From First Foot Guards. Appointed Governor of Hurst Castle 8th July, 1721, and Colonel of the Thirty-second Foot 25th December, 1740.
.	.	.	.		Resigned in March, 172$\frac{2}{3}$.
.	.	.	.		Retired 26th November, 1741.
.	.	.	.		{ To a company in the Twentieth Foot in October, 1723.
.	.	.	.	320	{ Promoted to Captain of a company in the Sixteenth Foot 20th June, 1717. From Wynn's Dragoons to Captain of a company in the Coldstream in April, 1719. Appointed Deputy-Governor of Carlisle in March, 1725; A.D.C. to the King 23rd of April, 1734; and Colonel of the Nineteenth Foot 1st November, 1738.
.	.	.	.		Dead in January, 172$\frac{2}{3}$.
.	.	.	.		Dead in November, 1720.
.	.	.	.		Resigned in May, 1718.
.	.	.	.		Dead in May, 1733.
.	.	.	. .	325	Left the regiment in December, 1717.
.	.	.	.		Resigned in Feb., 172$\frac{2}{3}$.
.	.	.	.		Left the regiment in April, 1717.
. .	.	.	.		Resigned in Feb., 17$\frac{14}{15}$.
.	28 Sept. 1715	12 Aug. 1717	.		{ From First Foot Guards. Appointed Col. of the Eighth Dragoons 7th Aug., 1733.
5 July 1739	25 Dec. 1740	1 Apr. 1743	.	330	{ From Captain of a company in the Fifteenth Foot. Appointed Colonel of a regiment of Marines 20th Sept., 1745.
.	.	.	.		Resigned in May, 1725.
.	.	.	.		{ Exchanged to First Foot Guards with Ensign Peter Darcey, 1st Aug., 1716.
.	.	.	.		{ Exchanged to half-pay of Montague's regiment of Foot, 8th July, 1734, with Lieut. John Twisleton.
.	.	.	.		{ Left the regiment in Jan., 17$\frac{14}{15}$. (Appointed Governor of Ross Castle.)
.	.	.	.	335	{ Promoted to Lieutenant in Third Foot Guards 16th Feb., 172$\frac{3}{4}$.
.	.	.	.		{ "Exchanged from First Foot Guards with Ensign Richard Waller." Out of the regiment in Dec., 1717.

APPENDIX.

COLDSTREAM

NAMES.	Ensign.	Lieutenant.	Capt.-Lieut.	Captain.
Henry Lord Herbert	.	.	23 Nov. 1716	12 Aug. 1717
John Sawbridge	.	24 Nov. 1716	.	.
Thomas Venner	20 Apr. 1717	.	.	.
340 Thomas Corbet	20 Apr. 1717	20 Jan. 172⅞	5 May 1740	25 Apr. 1741
John Hodges, (Lieut. of the Grenadier company)	20 Apr. 1717	14 Mar. 172⁰/₁	.	15 Dec. 1738
Henry Hildyard	.	19 July 1717	.	.
Edward Rich	19 July 1717	.	.	.
Martin Madan	.	12 Aug. 1717	.	.
345 Samuel Needham	.	21 Aug. 1717	10 Feb. 173⅜	30 June 1737
William Anne Viscount Bury, afterwards Earl of Albemarle, (Captain of the Grenadier company)	.	.	.	25 Aug. 1717
George Furnese	19 Dec. 1717	25 Nov. 1720	.	.
Anthony Lowther	.	.	20 Dec. 1717	8 July 1721
George Chudleigh	.	.	.	3 Jan. 171⅞
350 Henry Vachell	3 Jan. 171⅞	.	.	.
Thomas Hockenhall	24 Mar. 171⅞	.	.	.
Robert Williamson	15 May 1718	10 Apr. 1733	.	.
George Scroope	16 Apr. 1719	13 Mar. 172¾	.	.
Stephen Cornwallis	19 Mar. 17¹⁹⁄₂₀	.	.	.
355 William Vachell	.	.	.	28 May 1720
William Douglas	.	.	.	9 June 1720
Lord James Hay	25 Nov. 1720	.	.	.
. . . Mordaunt	25 Nov. 1720	.	.	.
Hon. Charles Fielding	.	24 Jan. 172⁰/₁	.	7 Nov. 1739
360 Thomas Macro	14 Mar. 172⁰/₁	30 Oct. 1734	.	.
Hon. Thomas Noel	20 May 1721	24 May 1723	.	.
John Vernon	.	8 July 1721	.	.
William Cole	.	.	.	11 Sept. 1721
Samuel Gumley	.	11 Sept. 1721	.	.
365 Hon. John Lumley, M.P. (Captain of Grenadier company)	24 Oct. 1721	.	.	31 Jan. 173¼

APPENDIX.

ROLL.—Continued.

2nd Major.	1st Major.	Lieut.-Col.	Colonel.		REMARKS.
.	.	.	.		Appointed Colonel of first troop of Horse Guards 20th Sept., 1721.
.	.	.	.		Resigned in March, 172¾.
.	.	.	.		Dead in Jan., 173¾.
.	.	.	.	340	Wounded at Fontenoy 11th May, 1745, N. S. Died 24th Jan., 17⁴⁹⁄₅₀.
.	.	.	.		Resigned in Aug., 1745.
.	.	.	.		Resigned in Jan., 172⁹⁄₁₀.
.	.	.	.		Left the regiment in Jan., 171⁷⁄₁₈.
.	.	.	.		Promoted to Captain of a troop in First Dragoon Guards 20th May, 1721.
.	.	.	.	345	Appointed Quarter-Master to the battalion of the Coldstream on the expedition to Vigo, 19th July, 1719. First Adjutant to the Coldstream from 28th Feb., 172⁹⁄₁₀, to 15th March, 174⁹⁄₁₀. Surveyor of the barracks in the Savoy, and of all guard-rooms belonging to the Foot Guards in and out of London, dated 22nd December, 1727. Wounded at Fontenoy, 11th May, 1745, N. S., and died of his wounds.
.	.	.	5 Oct. 1744		Appointed Aid-de-camp to the King 31st March, 1727; Colonel of Twenty-ninth Foot from 22nd Nov., 1731, to 7th May, 1733; and Colonel of the third troop of Horse Guards from 8th May, 1733, to 4th Oct., 1744. Lieutenant and Governor-General of Virginia in Sept., 1737. Returned to the Coldstream as Colonel Oct., 1744. Wounded at Fontenoy. Died at Paris 22nd Dec., 1754.
.	.	.	.		Promoted to Captain of a troop in First Dragoon Guards 11th Sept., 1721.
.	.	.	.		Appointed Colonel of a regiment of Marines "to be forthwith raised." Commission dated 19th Nov., 1739.
.	.	.	.		From First Foot Gds. Died 4th Sept., 1739.
.	.	.	.	350	Resigned in April, 1722.
.	.	.	.		Dead in Oct., 1732.
.	.	.	.		Promoted to Capt. of an Independent comp. of Invalids at Plymouth, 5th March, 174⅔.
.	.	.	.		Placed on half-pay 31st Dec. 1738, "being unable to serve."
.	.	.	.		Promoted to Captain "of a troop of Dragoons in Ireland," 15th Jan. 172¾.
.	.	.	.	355	From Fifth Foot; exchanged to half-pay of Magny's Dragoons 1st March, 172⅔, with Lieut.-Col. John Johnson.
29 Dec. 1740	27 Apr. 1743	.	.		From Croft's Dragoons. Appointed Col. of Thirty-second Foot 27th May, 1745.
.	.	.	.		Resigned 17th May, 1722.
.	.	.	.		Dead in Oct., 1721.
.	.	.	.		Promoted out of the regt. Appointed to a comp. in the Coldstream from Pembroke's Horse (First Dragoon Gds.) Retired 23rd Jan., 174⅘. (Died 6th Feb. following.)
.	.	.	.	360	Exchanged to Captain of a company in Tenth Foot with Captain John Thomas, 12th July, 1739.
.	.	.	.		"Succeeded by his brother, the Hon. Bennet Noel," 20 March, 173¾.
.	.	.	.		From the half-pay. Replaced on half-pay 8th May, 1730.
.	.	.	.		From First Dragoon Guards. Died 23rd March, 172¾.
.	.	.	.		Resigned on promotion in May, 1723.
.	.	.	.	365	Promoted to a troop in Seventh Dragoons 29th May, 1723, and re-appointed to a company of Grenadiers in the Coldstream. Died 16th Oct., 1739.

COLDSTREAM

NAMES.	Ensign.	Lieutenant.	Capt.-Lieut.	Captain.
Arthur Younge	19 Apr. 1722	.	.	.
Lord Charles Hay	18 May 1722	.	.	.
Richard Earl of Scarborough	.	.	.	.
Charles Bodens	15 Jan. 172$\frac{2}{3}$	26 Jan. 1735	.	.
370 Hedworth Lambton	.	11 Feb. 172$\frac{2}{3}$	9 July 1739	7 Nov. 1739
Bezaleel Brownsmith	13 Mar. 172$\frac{2}{3}$	.	.	.
William Lethieullier	.	24 May 1723	7 Nov. 1739	26 Apr. 1740
Thomas Hapgood	24 May 1723	10 Feb. 173$\frac{5}{6}$	.	.
Humphrey Fish	.	5 Oct. 1723	.	.
375 Peter Burjaud	.	8 Feb. 172$\frac{3}{4}$	.	.
Joseph Moxon	7 May 1724	.	.	.
Courthorpe Clayton	16 Feb. 172$\frac{4}{5}$	.	.	.
Philip Henry Shrimpton	2 Mar. 172$\frac{4}{5}$	.	.	.
William Congreve	.	.	.	30 Mar. 1725
380 Francis Townsend	28 Apr. 1725	25 Aug. 1737	.	.
James Hayman	23 Mar. 172$\frac{5}{6}$	.	.	.
Robert or James Wilson	2 Sept. 1726	.	.	.
Fenwick Williamson	12 May 1727	.	.	.
Henry Newton, (Lieut. of Grenadier company)	10 Oct. 1727	4 Jan. 173$\frac{8}{9}$	.	.
385 Count Henry de Nassau D'Auverquerque, Earl of Grantham	17 Nov. 1727	2 Oct. 1731	.	.
John Dives	25 Jan. 172$\frac{7}{8}$	25 Apr. 1734	.	.
John Johnson, (Lt.-Col.)	.	.	.	1 Mar. 172$\frac{7}{8}$
Hon. Benjamin Bathurst	28 Nov. 1728	.	.	.
Robert Milner	.	17 Jan. 172$\frac{8}{9}$	.	.
390 James Ramsay	.	25 Jan. 172$\frac{8}{9}$	.	.
Lord Vere Bertie	19 Mar. 172$\frac{8}{9}$	.	.	.
Thomas Bludworth	.	25 Dec. 1729	.	.
Gilbert Talbot	.	.	23 Apr. 1730	.
William Kellett	.	8 May 1730	.	9 Feb. 174$\frac{0}{1}$
395 Henry Cleland	11 June 1730	.	.	.
William Cooke	.	10 Dec. 1730	.	.
Julius Cæsar, (Captain of the Grenadier company)	18 Jan. 173$\frac{0}{1}$	24 May 1739	27 May 1745	17 Sept. 1746
Hon. Bennet Noel	.	20 Mar. 173$\frac{0}{1}$	10 Feb. 174$\frac{0}{1}$	10 May 1742
John Lamb	22 Mar. 173$\frac{0}{1}$	.	.	.
400 Lord Anne Hamilton	4 Apr. 1731	.	.	.

APPENDIX. 479

ROLL.—*Continued*.

2nd Major.	1st Major.	Lieut.-Col.	Colonel.		REMARKS.
.	.	.	.		Resigned in March, 172¾.
.	.	.	.		Promoted in Ninth Dragoons Oct., 1727.
.	.	.	18 June 1722		{ From first troop of Grenadier Guards. Died 29th Jan., 17 38/30.
.	.	.	.		Resigned in May, 1739.
1 Dec. 1747	17 Dec. 1751	12 May 1753	.	370	{ From Third regiment of Foot. Quarter-Master to the Coldstream from 4th July, 1733, to 12th Feb., 174½. Appointed Col. of Fifty-second Foot 20th Dec., 1755.
.	.	.	.		Dead in March, 172⅝.
.	.	.	.		{ Retired in March, 1752, "on Major's half-pay in Fraser's regiment."
.	.	.	.		{ Second Adjutant to the Coldstream from 24th May, 1723, to — Feb., 174½, the date of his death.
.	.	.	.		{ From Ensign in First Foot Guards. Out of the regiment in Oct., 1728.
.	.	.	.	375	{ Exchanged to a company in Thirtieth Foot with Capt. Wm. Cooke, 10th Dec., 1730.
.	.	.	.		Dead in Feb., 172¼.
.	.	.	.		{ Appointed Cornet in the Royal regiment of Horse Guards, 17th Nov., 1727.
.	.	.	.		Removed to First Foot Gds. 23d March, 172⅝.
.	.	.	.		{ From half-pay of Pocock's regiment. Retired 10th Feb., 173⅔, "on an allowance of 16s. 6d. a day, being incapable from age and long services."
.	.	.	.	380	{ Wounded at Fontenoy 11th of May, 1745, N. S., and died the same day.
.	.	.	.		Dead in May, 1730.
.	.	.	.		Dead in April, 1731.
.	.	.	.		Dead in Dec., 1735.
.	.	.	.		Placed on half-pay in Oct., 1751.
.	.	.	.	385	{ Appointed Lord Chamberlain to the Queen in June, 1727. Promoted to Capt.-Lieut. in First Foot Guards 5th July, 1735.
.	.	.	.		Retired in Nov., 1741.
.	.	.	.		{ Exchanged from Lieut.-Col. on half-pay of Magny's Dragoons, with Lieut.-Colonel William Vachell. Appointed Colonel of Thirty-third Foot 7th Nov., 1739.
.	.	.	.		Retired in March, 1739.
.	.	.	.		From Twelfth Foot. Died 14th Oct., 1739.
.	.	.	.	390	{ From half-pay of Clayton's regiment. Promoted to Capt. of an Independent comp. at Albany, New York, 30th Dec. 1738.
.	.	.	.		Retired in July, 1737.
.	.	.	.		{ From half-pay of Tyrawley's Fuziliers. Resigned in Jan., 173⅝.
.	.	.	.		{ From Captain of a company in Third regiment of Foot. Dead in Sept., 1731.
.	.	.	.		{ From Lieutenant in the Royal Fuziliers. Wounded at Fontenoy 11th May, 1745, N. S., and died of his wounds.
.	.	.	.	395	Out of the regiment in Feb., 173⅔.
.	.	.	.		{ Exchanged from Thirtieth Foot with Capt. Burjaud. Promoted to Major of Colonel James Oglethorpe's new-raised regiment of Foot 30th Nov. 1737.
12 May 1753	25 Dec. 1755	12 Apr. 1762	.		{ Wounded at Fontenoy 11th May, 1745, N.S. Appointed Major-Gen. 24th June, 1759. Fell from his horse, and died 7th August, 1762, in Germany.
7 Dec. 1751	12 May 1753	22 Dec. 1755	.		{ Succeeded his brother, the Hon. Captain Thomas Noel, as Lieutenant-Major-General, 26th Jan., 1758. Appointed Colonel of Forty-third Foot 12th April, 1762.
.	.	.	.		Dead in April, 1738.
.	.	.	.	400	Resigned in May, 1733.

COLDSTREAM

NAMES.	Ensign.	Lieutenant.	Capt.-Lieut.	Captain.
Theodorus Hoste	2 Oct. 1731	.	.	.
John Lambton	12 Oct. 1732	9 July 1739	.	24 Jan. $174\frac{5}{6}$
Hugh Cholmley	10 Apr. 1733	.	.	.
James Grant, or James Colquhon	21 May 1733	.	.	.
405 Hon. George Stanhope	22 May 1733	.	.	.
Alexander Earl of Balcarras	.	.	.	27 Aug. 1733
William Gansell	11 Feb. $173\frac{3}{4}$	7 Nov. 1739	28 Nov. 1749	29 Jan. $175\frac{0}{1}$
Charles Craig	25 Apr. 1734	10 May 1740	30 Jan. $175\frac{0}{1}$	17 Dec. 1751
Robert Halls	7 May 1734	.	.	.
410 John Twisleton	.	8 July 1734	.	.
Augustus Viscount Dursley, afterwards Earl of Berkeley	30 Oct. 1734	.	30 June 1737	9 July 1739
Lord Robert Manners	26 July 1735	10 May 1740	.	.
John Robinson	8 Jan. $173\frac{5}{6}$	25 Apr. 1741	.	15 Mar. 1752
John Clavering, (Captain of Grenadier company)	10 Feb. $173\frac{5}{6}$	27 Nov. 1741	23 Dec. 1752	7 June 1753
415 Benjamin Rudyard	5 July 1737	13 Feb. $174\frac{1}{2}$	.	.
Lord Robert Bertie	9 July 1737	13 Feb. $174\frac{1}{2}$	.	11 Apr. 1744
Charles Vernon	25 Aug. 1737	7 Apr. 1744	10 June 1753	27 Aug. 1754
William A'Court	.	21 Jan. $173\frac{7}{8}$	.	7 Aug. 1745
George Viscount Bury	1 Feb. $173\frac{7}{8}$	.	14 Apr. 1743	27 May 1745
420 Hon. Thomas Southwell	1 May 1738	.	.	.
William Farrell	2 May 1738	22 Apr. 1742	.	.
Maurice Bockland, M.P.	.	.	.	15 Dec. 1738
Duncan Urquhart	.	30 Dec. 1738	.	.
Charles Perry	.	31 Dec. 1738	.	27 May 1745
425 Charles Churchill	.	3 Jan. $173\frac{8}{9}$	.	.
George Bodens	24 May 1739	1 May 1745	1 Jan. 1756	1 June 1756
Thomas Burton	9 July 1739	29 May 1745	.	.
John Thomas	.	12 July 1739	17 Feb. $174\frac{7}{8}$	28 Nov. 1749
Charles Willmer	17 July 1739	.	.	.

APPENDIX.

ROLL.—Continued.

2nd Major.	1st Major.	Lieut.-Col.	Colonel.		REMARKS.
.	.	.	.		Promoted to Lieutenant in the Royal Horse Guards 7th May, 1734.
.	.	.	.		Quarter-Master to the Coldstream from 13th Feb., 1744, to 23rd Jan., 1744. Appointed Colonel of Sixty-eighth Foot 28th April, 1758.
.	.	.	.		Died 29th August, 1737.
.	.	.	.		Promoted to Captain in Moyle's regiment, (Thirty-sixth Foot,) 22nd Jan., 1737.
.	.	.	.	405	Promoted to Captain of a company in Twelfth Foot 5th January, 1738.
.	.	.	.		Died 26th July, 1736.
.	.	.	.		Adjutant of the Coldstream from 13th Feb., 1744, to 20th December, 1749. Appointed Colonel of Fifty-fifth Foot 20th Aug., 1762.
.	.	.	.		Died 30th March, 1761, on service in Germany.
.	.	.	.		From Ensign Third Foot Guards. Resigned in July, 1739.
.	.	.	.	410	Exchanged from Lieutenant on half-pay of Montague's regiment of Foot, with Captain Henry Carey. Left the regiment in April, 1744.
.	.	.	.		Resigned 7th April, 1742.
.	.	.	.		Promoted to a company in the First Foot Guards, 22nd April, 1742.
.	.	.	.		Retired in January, 1759.
.	.	.	.		Appointed Colonel of Fifty-second Foot, 1st April, 1762.
.	.	.	.	415	Promoted to Captain of a company in the Nineteenth Foot, 15th May, 1749; vice Captain Thomas Clarke, who exchanged.
.	.	.	.		Wounded at Fontenoy 11th May, 1745, N.S. Appointed A.D.C. to the King 4th March, 1752, and Colonel of the Seventh Foot 20th August, 1754.
.	.	.	.		Retired in August, 1762.
29 Dec. 1755	12 Apr. 1762	20 Aug. 1762	.		From Cornet in the Fourth Dragoons. Superseded 23rd December, 1763.
.	.	.	.		Promoted to Captain-Lieutenant in the Royal Dragoons, 25th April, 1741, and returned to the Coldstream in April, 1743. Appointed A.D.C. to the Duke of Cumberland in February, 1745, and to the King 24th April, 1746. Colonel of the Twentieth Foot 1st November, 1749.
.	.	.	.	420	Retired in November, 1741.
.	.	.	.		Retired in March, 1746.
27 May 1745	21 Nov. 1745	.	.		From Captain of a troop in First Dragoon Guards. Appointed Colonel of the Eleventh Foot 1st December, 1747.
.	.	.	.		Died 11th January, 1744.
.	.	.	.		From Second regiment of Foot. Appointed Colonel of Fifty-seventh Foot (present Fifty-fifth), dated 25th December, 1755.
.	.	.	.	425	From Lieutenant in Tenth Dragoons. Resigned in June, 1745.
.	.	.	.		Retired in January, 1763.
.	.	.	.		From Quarter-Master Sixth Dragoons. Wounded at Fontenoy 11th May, 1745, N.S. Retired in April, 1748.
2 Apr. 1762	20 Aug. 1762	23 Dec. 1763	.		From Captain in Tenth regiment of Foot, vice Captain Thomas Macro, who exchanged. Appointed Lieutenant-Governor of Fort St. Philip, Minorca, 21st November, 1777.
.	.	.	.		Retired in November, 1741.

COLDSTREAM

NAMES.	Ensign.	Lieutenant.	Capt.-Lieut.	Captain.
430 William Evelyn	17 July 1739	16 Apr. 1744	27 Aug. 1754	24 Mar. 1755
His Royal Highness William Duke of Cumberland	.	.	.	.
Lord John Sackville	.	.	.	1 May 1740
Hon. Shaw Cathcart	13 Nov. 1740	.	.	.
Palmes Robinson	14 Nov. 1740	27 June 1746	.	.
435 Richard Williamson	15 Nov. 1740	.	.	.
Hon. John Bateman	16 Nov. 1740	.	.	.
John Salter	16 Mar. 1740	.	.	.
. . . Vanbrugh	24 Apr. 1741	.	.	.
Robert Dingley	.	25 Apr. 1741	17 Dec. 1751	4 Mar. 1752
440 Hon. Joseph Yorke	25 Apr. 1741	.	.	27 May 1745
William Campbell	.	26 Nov. 1741	.	.
Robert Shaftoe	26 Nov. 1741	24 Jan. 1744½	.	.
William Alexander Sorell	27 Nov. 1741	29 May 1745	4 June 1756	8 Apr. 1758
. . . Southwell	28 Nov. 1741	.	.	.
445 George Viscount Lempster	11 Feb. 1741½	.	.	.
. . . Whitworth	13 Feb. 1741½	.	.	.
Abednigo Matthew	14 Feb. 1741½	26 Mar. 1746	.	.
Charles Duke of Marlborough	.	.	.	.
Francis Craig, (Captain of the Grenadier Company)	22 Apr. 1742	28 June 1746	.	28 Apr. 1758
450 John Mostyn	.	.	2 Sept. 1742	2 Apr. 1743
Westrow Hulse	24 Apr. 1743	.	.	.
Henry Kingscote	16 Apr. 1744	.	.	.
Henry Campbell	.	11 May 1744	.	.
Hon. William Keppel	26 June 1744	25 June 1745	.	.
455 John Nicholson	22 Aug. 1744	.	.	.
Martin Price	21 Nov. 1744	.	.	.
Henry Lister	9 Mar. 1744¾	29 Mar. 1748	.	4 May 1758
Robert Molesworth	11 Apr. 1745	.	.	.
George Needham	1 May 1745	28 Nov. 1749	.	.

OLL.—Continued.

2nd Major.	1st Major.	Lieut.-Col.	Colonel.		Remarks.
Aug. 1762	23 Dec. 1763	.	.	430	Appointed "Quarter-Master to the batt. under orders for foreign service," 28th May, 1742. Appointed Colonel Twenty-ninth Foot 3rd November, 1769.
.	.	.	30 Apr. 1740		Appointed Colonel of First Foot Guards, 18th February, 174½. (Wounded at Dettingen 27th June, 1743, N.S.)
.	.	.	.		From Captain of a company in the Thirty-seventh Foot. Removed from the service in September, 1746.
.	.	.	.		Killed at Fontenoy 11th May, 1745, N.S.
.	.	.	.		"Retired on half-pay of Sir Andrew Agnew's regt. of Marines, in the place of Lieut. Bulkeley," in November, 1749.
.	.	.	.	435	Resigned in September, 1745.
.	.	.	.		Retired 10th February, 174¼.
.	.	.	.		Adjutant to the Coldstream from 16th March, 1749, to 5th April, 1743. Appointed Ensign and Adjutant to the First Foot Guards 6th April, 1743.
.	.	.	.		Wounded at Fontenoy 11th May, 1745, N.S., and died the same day.
.	.	.	.		From Lieutenant in Third regiment of Foot. Died 16th October, 1755.
.	.	.	.	440	Promoted to Lieut. in First Foot Guards 24th April, 1743, and to a company in the Coldstream May, 1745. Appointed A.D.C. to the King 1st November, 1749, and Colonel of the Ninth Foot 18th March, 1755.
.	.	.	.		From Cornet in the Royal Horse Guards. Resigned in May, 1744.
.	.	.	.		Resigned in December, 1750.
Jan. 1769	3 Nov. 1769	.	.		Adjutant of the Coldstream from 28th October, 1746, to 7th April, 1758. Major-General 25th May, 1772. Appointed Col. of Forty-eighth Foot 15th Dec., 1773.
.	.	.	.		Retired in November, 1744.
.	.	.	.	445	Promoted to Captain of a company in the Thirty-first Foot 30th April, 1743.
.	.	.	.		Left the regiment in March, 174¾.
.	.	.	.		Retired in March, 1752.
.	.	.	18 Feb. 174¼		From second troop of Horse Guards. Resigned the Colonelcy of the Coldstream in March, 1744.
Nov. 1769	15 Dec. 1773	.	.		Appointed Lieutenant-Colonel of First Foot Guards 8th September, 1775.
.	.	.	.	450	From Captain of a company in the Thirty-first Foot. Wounded at Fontenoy 11th May, 1745, N.S. Appointed A.D.C. to the King 3rd December, 1747, and Colonel of Seventh Foot 26th January, 1759.
.	.	.	.		Promoted to Captain of a troop in the Sixth Dragoons April, 1745.
.	.	.	.		Promoted to Lieutenant in Third Foot Guards 13th October, 1746.
.	.	.	.		From Lieut. Seventh Dragoons Guards. Dead in August, 1747.
.	.	.	.		Promoted to Captain-Lieutenant in First Foot Guards 28th April, 1751.
.	.	.	.	455	Left the regiment in October, 1748.
.	.	.	.		From Cornet in Fourth Dragoons. Resigned in July, 1748.
Dec. 1773	8 Sept. 1775	21 Nov. 1777	.		Died at Twickenham 17th November, 1785.
.	.	.	.		Killed at Fontenoy 11th May, 1745, N.S.
.	.	.	.		From Ensign in Fourth Foot. Quarter-Master to the Coldstream from 24th Jan. 174⅝, to 29th April, 1751. Exchanged to Forty-sixth Foot 30th April, 1751, with Captain William Wright.

APPENDIX.

COLDSTREAM

NAMES.	Ensign.	Lieutenant.	Capt.-Lieut.	Captain.
460 Charles Rainsford	1 May 1745	29 June 1750	5 Mar. 1761	5 May 1761
Sacheverel Poole	1 May 1745	.	.	.
Thomas Gray	29 May 1745	26 Dec. 1750	.	.
Richard Hicks	29 May 1745	.	.	.
Daniel Webb	29 May 1745	.	.	.
465 William Wiseman, afterwards Sir William .. Bart.	12 Sept. 1745	5 Apr. 1748	.	30 Jan. 1759
Robert Orme	16 Sept. 1745	24 Apr. 1751	.	.
Charles Russell	.	.	.	.
Edward Mathew	24 Jan. 1745/6	17 Dec. 1751	29 Mar. 1762	14 Apr. 1762
Richard Ottley	26 Mar. 1746	.	.	.
470 John Lawrence	27 June 1746	.	.	.
Harry Trelawney	28 June 1746	4 Mar. 1752	.	21 Aug. 1762
Heritage Lenton	24 Aug. 1746	.	.	.
Hon. John Barrington	.	.	17 Sept. 1746	15 Feb. 1747/8
... Hales	13 Oct. 1746	.	.	.
475 William Gwynn	27 Nov. 1746	16 Mar. 1752	20 Aug. 1752	23 Sept. 1763
James Craig	26 Feb. 1746/7	23 Dec. 1752	23 Sept. 1763	23 Dec. 1763
Thomas D'Avenant	16 Aug. 1747	12 June 1753	23 Dec. 1763	4 May 1767
Hon. Thomas Cecil	.	27 Aug. 1747	.	.
John Thornton	14 Jan. 1747/8	24 July 1754	4 May 1767	11 Jan. 1769
480 William Wynch	29 Mar. 1748	27 Aug. 1754	.	.
Lewis Buckeridge	30 Apr. 1748	14 July 1755	.	.
Anthony George Martin	23 July 1748	13 Jan. 1756	11 Jan. 1769	3 Nov. 1769
Robert Gunning	1 Nov. 1748	.	.	.
Thomas Clarke	.	15 May 1749	.	4 Mar. 1761
485 Richard Henry Roper	.	27 Nov. 1749	.	.
George Scott	21 Dec. 1749	12 June 1756	.	.
Henry Vane, afterwards Earl of Darlington	.	.	.	6 Feb. 1759/60

APPENDIX. 485

ROLL.—*Continued.*

2nd Major.	1st Major.	Lieut.-Col.	Colonel.	REMARKS.
21 Nov. 1777	.	.	.	460 {From Cornet in Third Dragoons. Adjutant from 8th April, 1758, to 4th May, 1761. Appointed Colonel of Ninety-ninth Foot 2d June, 1780: (Subsequently disbanded.)
.	.	.	.	{Promoted to Captain in Twenty-third Fuziliers 5th August, 1746.
.	.	.	.	{Killed (run through the body) in a duel with Lord Viscount Lempster, in Mary-le-bone Fields, 24th February, 1752.
.	.	.	.	{Adjutant of the Coldstream from 18th of April, 1743, to 27th of October, 1746. Promoted to Lieutenant of an Independent Company at Tilbury Fort 17th November, 1746.
.	.	.	.	Resigned in February, 1744/7.
.	.	.	.	465 Died 25th May, 1774.
.	.	.	.	{From Ensign in Thirty-fourth Foot. Resigned in October, 1756.
21 Nov. 1745	1 Dec. 1747	.	.	{From Captain of a company in the First Foot Guards. Appointed Colonel of the Thirty-fourth Foot 17th December, 1751.
.	.	.	.	{A.D.C. to the King. Brigadier General, commanding the Brigade of Guards in North America. Major-General 19th February, 1779. Appointed Colonel of the Sixty-second Foot 17th November, 1779.
.	.	.	.	Retired in January, 1754/5.
.	.	.	.	470 Left the Coldstream in January, 1747/8.
.	.	5 May 1780	23 Nov. 1785	.	{From Ensign in the Third regiment of Foot (carried the colours during the Rebellion in 1745). Wounded at the heights of Freehold, North America, 28th June, 1778. Retired 25th May, 1789.
.	.	.	.	Retired in June, 1751.
.	.	.	.	{From Lieutenant Third Foot Guards. Appointed A.D.C. to the King in June, 1756, and Colonel of the Sixty-fourth Foot 21st April, 1758.
.	.	.	.	{From Ensign Fourteenth Foot. Dead in August, 1747.
.	.	.	.	475 Retired 31st May, 1774.
.	.	.	.	Retired on 16s. 6d. a day, 15th of May, 1767.
.	.	.	.	{From Ensign Eighth regiment of Foot. Adjutant of the Coldstream from 21st December, 1749, to 18th August, 1763. Retired 31st January, 1776.
.	.	.	.	Resigned in April, 1751.
.	.	.	.	{From Ensign in the First Foot or Royals. Retired 29th December, 1778.
.	.	.	.	480 Died in February, 1762, in Germany.
.	.	.	.	Died 20th June, 1760.
7 June 1780	23 Nov. 1785	26 May 1789	.	{Major-General 20th November, 1782. Appointed Colonel of Fifty-first Foot 2d December, 1795.
.	.	.	.	Retired in March, 1759.
3 Sept. 1775	21 Nov. 1777	.	.	{Exchanged from Captain of a company in Nineteenth Foot, with Lieutenant and Captain Benjamin Rudyard. Appointed Colonel of Thirty-first Foot 3rd of May, 1780.
.	.	.	.	485 {From Third regiment of foot. Retired in July, 1754.
.	.	.	.	{Promoted to Major of Eighty-ninth Foot 13th October, 1759. (Subsequently disbanded.)
.	.	.	.	{From Lieutenant and Captain First Foot Guards. Resigned in May, 1758.

VOL. II.   2 I

APPENDIX.

COLDSTREAM

NAMES.	Ensign.	Lieutenant.	Capt.-Lieut.	Captain.
John Dalling	26 Dec. 1750	.	.	.
Charles Palmer	26 Jan. 1750	.	.	.
490 Hon. Wilmot Vaughan	30 Jan. 1750	.	.	.
Timothy Caswell	16 Mar. 1751	25 Oct. 1756	.	.
Richard Hussey	24 Apr. 1751	2 May 1758	.	.
John Mackay	.	29 Apr. 1751	.	.
William Wright	.	30 Apr. 1751	5 May 1761	29 Mar. 1762
495 William Smith	17 June 1751	.	.	.
Henry Clinton	.	1 Nov. 1751	.	.
Charles Duke of Richmond	16 Dec. 1751	.	.	.
Lord George Henry Lennox	17 Dec. 1751	.	.	.
James Forrester (Major)	.	.	4 Mar. 1752	.
500 Lord Frederick Cavendish	.	17 Mar. 1752	.	.
Thomas Northey	22 Apr. 1752	.	.	.
Hon. Lucius Ferdinand Carey	23 Dec. 1752	.	.	.
Wadham Wyndham	13 Jan. 1753	3 May 1758	.	2 July 1771
Thomas Osbert Mordaunt	27 Jan. 1753	.	.	.
505 Hon. Cadwallader Blayney (Major)	.	.	.	8 June 1753
William Charles Sloper	13 June 1753	4 May 1758	.	.
Thomas Calcraft	18 June 1753	.	.	.
Henry Delaval	2 Feb. 1754	.	.	.
George Augustus Wyvill	24 July 1754	30 Jan. 1759	.	.
510 William Schutz	28 Aug. 1754	11 Mar. 1760	15 Dec. 1773	3 June 1774
Hon. Henry St. John	31 Dec. 1754	.	.	.
Hon. Martin Sandys	.	.	25 Mar. 1755	3 Nov. 1755
James Lord Tyrawley, Lieutenant-General	.	.	.	.
George Spencer, Marquis of Blandford	14 July 1755	.	.	.
515 Henry Townshend	2 Oct. 1755	.	.	.
Charles Morgan	4 Oct. 1755	30 June 1760	.	.
Ruvigny de Cosne	.	.	4 Nov. 1755	29 Dec. 1755

ROLL.—*Continued.*

2nd Major.	1st Major.	Lieut.-Col.	Colonel.		REMARKS.
.	.	.	.		From Ensign in Twentieth Foot. Promoted to Captain of a company in Fourth Foot 27th January, 1753.
.	.	.	.		Resigned in January, 1753.
.	.	.	.	490	Resigned in December, 1754.
.	.	.	.		Retired 11th August, 1762.
.	.	.	.		From half-pay of Jordan's regiment of Marines. Exchanged to Eighty-fifth Foot 3rd March, 1761. (Subsequently disbanded.)
.	.	.	.		From Captain on half-pay of Loudon's regiment. Promoted to Major in Fifth Foot 2nd January, 1756.
.	.	.	.		From Captain of a company in Forty-sixth Foot, in exchange with Captain George Needham. Quarter-Master from 30th of April, 1751, to 4th May, 1761. Retired 3rd April, 1772.
.	.	.	.	495	From Ensign Third regiment of Foot. Resigned in February, 1754.
.	.	.	.		From Capt.-Lieut. in the New York companies. Promoted to Captain of a company in the First Foot Guards 6th May, 1758.
.	.	.	.		Promoted to Captain of a company in the Twentieth Foot 18th June, 1753.
.	.	.	.		Promoted to Captain of a company in the twenty-fifth Foot 23rd March, 1756.
.	.	.	.		From Major of the Royal regiment of Foot. Promoted to Captain of a company in the Third Foot Guards 23rd Dec. 1752.
.	.	.	.	500	From Ensign First Foot Guards. Promoted to Lieut.-Col. of Twenty-ninth Foot 18th June, 1755.
.	.	.	.		Promoted to Captain of a company in Thirty-first Foot 3rd of September, 1756.
.	.	.	.		Promoted to Capt.-Lieut. in the Fourteenth Foot 14th October, 1755.
.	.	.	.		Retired 13th December, 1778.
.	.	.	.		Promoted to Capt.-Lieut. in Tenth Dragoons 25th December, 1755.
.	.	.	.	505	" From half-pay, late of Pepperell's regiment." Appointed Colonel of Ninety-first Foot 2nd March, 1761. (Subsequently disbanded.)
.	.	.	.		Retired 19th May, 1772.
.	.	.	.		From Ensign in the Nineteenth Foot. Promoted to Captain of a company in the Seventh Foot 8th November, 1755.
.	.	.	.		Promoted to Captain of a company in Thirty-fourth Foot 2nd of September, 1757.
.	.	.	.		From Ensign Twenty-fourth Foot. Wounded 21st September, 1762, at Brucker Muhl. Resigned 1st December, 1768.
.	.	.	.	510	Retired 21st October, 1782.
.	.	.	.		Promoted to Captain of a company in the Eighteenth Foot 12th January, 1758.
3 Dec. 1763	.	.	.		From Lieut. Third Foot Guards. Died 26th December, 1768.
.	.	.	8 April 1755		From Colonel of Third Dragoons. Appointed Governor of Portsmouth 1st of May, 1759. General, 7th March, 1761. Died at Twickenham 13th July, 1773.
.	.	.	.		Promoted to Captain of a company in the Twentieth Foot 7th of June, 1756.
.	.	..	.	515	Promoted to Captain of a company in the Fifth Foot 8th May, 1758.
.	.	.	.		Retired 24th February, 1767.
.	.	.	.		From Captain Twelfth Foot. Retired 22nd September, 1763.

APPENDIX.

COLDSTREAM

NAMES.	Ensign.	Lieutenant.	Capt.-Lieut.	Captain.
Charles O'Hara	.	14 Jan. 1756	3 Nov. 1769	15 Dec. 1773
Thomas Bishopp	13 Jan. 1756	4 Mar. 1761	3 June 1774	8 Sept. 1775
520 Spencer Compton	21 Jan. 1756	.	.	.
Matthew Smith	23 Jan. 1756	5 Mar. 1761	8 Sept. 1775	1 May 1777
John Lambton	12 June 1756	20 Feb. 1762	.	.
Henry Dilkes	21 June 1756	19 May 1761	.	.
George Banks	6 Sept. 1756	29 Mar. 1762	.	.
525 John Hall	8 Nov. 1756	.	.	.
William Woseley	2 Sept. 1757	.	.	.
John Twisleton	3 Sept. 1757	11 Aug. 1762	.	.
George Morgan	1 Mar. 1758	23 Aug. 1762	.	26 May 1775
Robert Eden	8 May 1758	23 Sept. 1762	.	.
530 James Birch	9 May 1758	23 Sept. 1763	.	.
John Burgoyne	.	.	10 May 1758	.
William Bowyer	10 May 1758	23 Dec. 1763	.	.
Lewis George Dive	11 May 1758	25 Feb. 1767	.	.
John Edmunds	23 May 1758	.	.	.
535 Henry Leheup	30 Jan. 1759	.	.	.
Henry Thomas	11 Mar. 1760	.	.	.
Richard Byron	10 May 1760	4 May 1767	.	.
Richard Clive	30 June 1760	.	.	.
Charles Cooper	.	3 Mar. 1761	.	4 Mar. 1773
540 John Wrottesley	4 Mar. 1761	.	.	.
George Stuart Bourne	5 Mar. 1761	15 July 1768	.	.
Edmond Stevens	19 May 1761	2 Dec. 1768	.	.
Alexander Macdonald	20 May 1761	.	.	.
William Bosville	24 Dec. 1761	11 Jan. 1769	.	.
545 Thomas Lord Howard, afterwards Earl of Effingham	20 Feb. 1762	.	.	.
Edward Hawke	29 Mar. 1762	.	.	.
Sir Thomas Spencer Wilson, Bart.	.	.	14 Apr. 1762	20 Aug. 1762
Vincent Corbet	11 May 1762	3 Nov. 1769	.	.

APPENDIX.

ROLL.—*Continued.*

2nd Major.	1st Major.	Lieut.-Col.	Colonel.		REMARKS.
.	.	.	.		From Cornet in Third Dragoons. Appointed Quarter-Master-General to the troops in Portugal 10th February, 1762. Brigadier-General, commanding the brigade of Guards in North America, from January to October, 1781. Wounded at Guilford 15th March, 1781. Surrendered prisoner of war at York Town 19th Oct. following. Major-General, 19th October, 1781. Appointed Colonel of Twenty-second Foot 18th April, 1782.
.	.	.	.		Retired 14th May, 1783.
.	.	.	.	520	Promoted to Captain of a company in Thirty-first Foot, 2nd September, 1757.
.	.	.	.		Retired 14th March 1779.
.	.	.	.		From Twelfth Foot. Adjutant from 24th August, 1761, to 11th January, 1764. Exchanged to a company in the Seventy-ninth regiment (subsequently disbanded) with Captain de la Douespe, 12th Jan. 1764.
.	.	.	.		Died in October, 1772.
.	.	.	.		Retired 29th August, 1771.
.	.	.	.	525	From First Troop of Horse Guards. Died in May, 1758.
.	.	.	.		Resigned 19th May, 1761.
.	.	.	.		Killed in action at Brucken Muhl 21st September, 1762.
26 May 1789	.	.	.		From Ensign in Sixth Foot. Adjutant from 19th August, 1763, to 7th March, 1774. Surrendered prisoner at York Town 19th October, 1781. Major-General 28th Apr. 1790. Retired 31st January, 1793.
.	.	.	.		From "Lieutenant Fire-worker." Retired 14th July, 1768.
.	.	.	.	530	Retired 26th April, 1770.
.	.	.	.		From Captain of a troop in Eleventh Dragoons. Appointed "Lieutenant-Colonel Commandant" of Sixteenth Dragoons, commission dated 4th August, 1759.
.	.	.	.		Exchanged to a company in Seventh Foot 4th October, 1765.
.	.	.	.		Resigned 5th June, 1773.
.	.	.	.		Promoted to Capt. in Ninety-fourth Foot 10th Jan. 1760. (Subsequently disbanded.)
.	.	.	.	535	Retired 23rd December, 1761.
.	.	.	.		Died 9th November, 1762.
.	.	.	.		Retired 1st February, 1776.
.	.	.	.		Killed in action at Brucken Muhl 21st September, 1762.
.	.	.	.		From Captain in Eighty-fifth Foot. Retired 25th May, 1775.
.	.	.	.	540	Promoted to Captain in Eighty-fifth Foot 12th April, 1762.
.	.	.	.		Died at New York in December, 1776.
.	.	.	.		From Cornet in First Dragoons. Adjutant from 12th January, 1764, to 14th May, 1778. Promoted to a company in First Foot Guards 15th May, 1778.
.	.	.	.		Resigned 19th June, 1768.
.	.	.	.		Retired 24th June, 1777.
.	.	.	.	545	Promoted to Captain in Sixty-eighth Foot 1st August, 1766.
.	.	.	.		Promoted to Captain in Fifth Foot 13th September, 1765.
.	.	.	.		From Captain in Eighth Foot. Appointed Colonel of Fiftieth Foot 30th April, 1777.
.	.	.	.		Retired 22nd April, 1771.

APPENDIX.

COLDSTREAM

NAMES.	Ensign.	Lieutenant.	Capt.-Lieut.	Captain.
James Hamilton	24 Aug. 1762	27 Apr. 1770	28 Oct. 1779	20 Nov. 1779
550 Thomas Reynolds, afterwards Lord Ducie	.	.	.	25 Aug. 1762
Lord Spencer Hamilton	.	25 Aug. 1762	.	1 Feb. 1776
Heneage Lloyd	23 Sept. 1762	23 Apr. 1771	.	.
James Hutton	10 Nov. 1762	.	.	.
Glynn Wynn	.	.	.	8 Jan. 1763
555 Henry Bristowe	28 Jan. 1763	2 July 1771	.	.
Charles Jacob Sheffield	31 Jan. 1763	30 Aug. 1771	.	.
George Tate	23 Sept. 1763	20 May 1772	.	.
Hon. George Damer	23 Dec. 1763	.	.	.
Henry De la Douespe	.	12 Jan. 1764	1 May 1777	21 Nov. 1777
560 Lowther Pennington	4 July 1764	20 Oct. 1772	.	14 Dec. 1778
James O'Hara	2 Oct. 1765	.	.	.
John Swinnerton Dyer, afterwards Sir John Dyer, Bart.	.	4 Oct. 1765	21 Nov. 1777	.
John Byde	1 Aug. 1766	4 Mar. 1773	.	30 Dec. 1778
Thomas Slaughter Stanwix	26 Sept. 1766	6 June 1773	.	22 Feb. 1779
565 Hon. John Fitzwilliam	24 Feb. 1767	15 Dec. 1773	.	.
Sir William Murray, Bart.	4 May 1767	.	.	.
John Duroure	20 June 1768	3 June 1774	.	15 Mar. 1779
Lobert Lovelace	15 July 1768	6 May 1775	5 May 1780	7 June 1780
John Sutton	2 Dec. 1768	26 May 1775	7 June 1780	26 April 1782
570 William Augustus Spencer Boscawen	11 Jan. 1769	8 Sept. 1775	.	1 Feb. 1781
William H. Monckton	10 April 1769	.	.	.
Charles Viscount Petersham	3 Nov. 1769	.	.	.
John Delap Halliday	24 Nov. 1769	.	.	.
William Langley	5 Jan. 1770	14 Sept. 1775	.	.
575 William Tomkins	27 Apr. 1770	2 Feb. 1776	.	.
Thomas Willett Saltren	13 Sept. 1770	4 Feb. 1776	26 April 1782	.
William Morshead	23 Apr. 1771	8 Feb. 1776	5 Feb. 1783	11 July 1785
John Bagnall	2 July 1771	.	.	.
Nicholas Eveleigh	30 Aug. 1771	.	.	.
580 Richard Grenville	.	.	.	4 April 1772
George Turnpenny Symes	20 May 1772	.	.	.
Thomas Thoroton	20 Oct. 1772	13 June, 1776	.	22 Oct. 1782
Charles Trelawney	4 Mar. 1773	17 Jan. 1777	11 July 1785	23 Nov. 1785
Richard Bennett Lloyd	26 Mar. 1773	.	.	.

APPENDIX.

ROLL.—*Continued.*

2nd Major.	1st Major.	Lieut.-Col.	Colonel.	Remarks.
.	.	.	.	Retired 1st February, 1781.
.	.	.	.	550 { From Captain in Third Dragoons. Resigned 1st July, 1771.
.	.	.	.	{ From Ensign in Third Foot Guards. Retired 12th January, 1790.
.	.	.	.	{ From Cornet in Sixth Dragoons. Died 22nd December, 1776.
.	.	.	.	Retired 25th September, 1766.
.	.	.	.	{ From Captain in Ninetieth Foot. Retired 3rd March, 1773.
.	.	.	.	555 { From Lieutenant in One hundred & eighth Foot. Retired 3rd February, 1776.
.	.	.	.	Retired 13th November, 1775.
.	.	.	.	Retired 12th June, 1776.
.	.	.	.	Resigned 3rd July, 1764.
.	.	.	.	{ Exchanged from Captain of a company in Seventy-ninth Foot, with Captain John Lambton. Retired 21st February, 1779.
1 Feb. 1793	1 Apr. 1795	.	.	560 { Major-Gen. 20th December, 1793. Appointed Colonel of One hundred and Thirty-first Foot 23rd June, 1795. (Subsequently disbanded.)
.	.	.	.	Retired 23rd November, 1769.
.	.	.	.	{ Exchanged from Captain of a company in Seventh Foot. Appointed Capt.-Lieutenant in First Foot Guards, 14th May, 1778.
.	.	.	.	"Retired on his pay, 29th November, 1790."
1 Apr. 1795	23 June 1795	2 Dec. 1795	.	{ Major-Gen. 20th December, 1793. Lieut.-Gen. 26th June, 1799. Appointed Colonel Commandant of Sixtieth Foot 9th May, 1800.
.	.	.	.	565 Retired 5th May, 1775.
.	.	.	.	Resigned 9th April, 1769.
.	.	.	.	Retired 15th December, 1789.
.	.	.	.	Retired 31st January, 1781.
.	.	.	.	Retired 23rd March, 1790.
.	.	.	.	570 Retired 26th October, 1790.
.	.	.	.	Resigned 4th January, 1770.
.	.	.	.	{ Promoted to Captain in Twenty-ninth Foot 26th July, 1773.
.	.	.	.	Retired 12th September, 1770.
.	.	.	.	Retired 20th June, 1781.
.	.	.	.	575 { From Ensign in Eleventh Foot. Retired 24th March, 1778.
.	.	.	.	{ From Ensign in Third regiment of Foot. Adjutant of the Coldstream from 8th Mar. 1774, to 8th July, 1779. "Adjutant-Gen. to the Expedition" under Major-General Meadows in February, 1781. In the action with the French fleet in Porto Praya Bay, Island of St. Jago, 16th April, 1781, and at the capture of the Dutch East Indiamen in Saldanha Bay, on 9th July, 1781. Died in 1782.
23 June 1795	2 Dec. 1795	.	.	{ Major-General 26th February, 1795. Appointed Colonel Commandant of Sixtieth Foot 30th December, 1797.
.	.	.	.	Retired 16th October, 1774.
.	.	.	.	Retired 25th March, 1773.
23 Nov. 1785	.	.	.	580 { From Captain in Twenty-fourth Foot. Aidde-camp to the King, 19th February, 1779. Major-General, 20th November, 1782. Appointed Colonel of Twenty-third Foot 21st April, 1786.
.	.	.	.	Died 18th June, 1774.
.	.	.	.	Retired 14th June, 1791.
.	.	.	.	Retired 13th May, 1790.
.	.	.	.	Retired 13th September, 1775.

APPENDIX.

COLDSTREAM

NAMES.	Ensign.	Lieutenant.	Capt.-Lieut.	Captain.
585 Nicholas Boscawen	6 June 1773	20 Jan. 1777	21 Apr. 1786	.
John Earl of Waldegrave, General	.	.	.	.
John Byron	26 July 1773	1 May 1777	.	.
Hon. William Maynard	15 Dec. 1773	25 June 1777	.	.
Hon. Chapel Norton	.	.	.	1 June 1774
590 William Viscount Cantilupe, afterwards Earl of Delawar	3 June 1774	21 Nov. 1777	20 Nov. 1779	5 May 1780
William Lord Dunglass	20 July 1774	25 Mar. 1778	.	.
Hon. Henry Astley Bennett	17 Oct. 1774	15 May 1778	.	.
George Calvert	6 May 1775	14 Dec. 1778	.	.
Thomas Bosville	26 May 1775	30 Dec. 1778	.	26 May 1789
595 Wilmot Vaughan	8 Sept. 1775	.	.	.
William Hodgson	14 Sept. 1775	22 Feb. 1779	.	.
George Gibson	14 Nov. 1775	15 Mar. 1779	.	.
William Schutz	20 Nov. 1775	28 Oct. 1779	.	.
Bertie Greathead	2 Feb. 1776	.	.	.
600 George Mathew	4 Feb. 1776	20 Nov. 1779	.	.
George Eld	30 Mar. 1776	5 May 1780	.	16 Dec. 1789
John Baker	15 July 1776	7 June 1780	.	.
Henry Greville	17 Jan. 1777	12 Feb. 1781	.	24 Mar. 1790
Edward Morrison	20 Jan. 1777	15 Sept. 1780	.	13 Jan. 1790
605 Washington Shirley	1 May 1777	8 Feb. 1781	.	.
William Wemyss	25 June 1777	.	.	.
Charles Gould, afterwards Sir Charles Morgan, Bart.	21 Nov. 1777	22 Mar. 1781	.	14 May 1790
Hon. Charles Wyndham	25 Mar. 1778	.	.	.
George Viscount Chewton	.	.	16 May 1778	.
610 Thomas Grenville	18 May 1778	.	.	.
Hon. William Wyndham	14 Dec. 1778	18 Apr. 1781	.	.
Francis Delap Halliday	22 Jan. 1779	.	.	.
John Edwards Freemantle	15 Mar. 1779	21 June 1781	13 Oct. 1790	30 Nov. 1790
Andrew Cowell	16 Mar. 1779	25 June 1781	.	27 Oct. 1790
615 Richard Earl of Cavan	2 Apr. 1779	27 July 1781	30 Nov. 1790	23 Aug. 1793
John Francis Cradock	9 July 1779	12 Dec. 1781	.	. .

ROLL.—Continued.

2nd Major.	1st Major.	Lieut.-Col.	Colonel.		REMARKS.
.	.	.	.	585	Retired 12th October, 1790.
.	.	.	15 July 1773		{ From Colonel of Second Dragoon Guards. Died 15th October, 1784.
.	.	.	.		{ From Ensign in Sixty-eighth Foot. Adjutant from 30th July, 1778, to 20th June, 1779. Retired 14th September, 1780.
.	.	.	.		{ Wounded at Guilford, North America, 15th March, 1781, and died of his wounds 17th April following.
21 Apr. 1786	26 May 1789	.	.		{ From Major of the First regiment of Foot. Major-Gen. 28th Sept., 1787. Appointed Col. of Eighty-first Foot 25th March, 1795.
.	.	.	.	590	Died at Lisbon in January, 1783.
.	.	.	.		{ Wounded at Guilford 15th March, 1781, and died of his wounds in Dec. following.
.	.	.	.		{ Exchanged to Captain-Lieutenant of Sixteenth Dragoons 24th January, 1780.
.	.	.	.		Retired 17th April, 1788.
.	.	.	.		{ Adjutant from 21st June, 1779, to 21st June, 1782. Killed at Lincelles 18th Aug., 1793.
.	.	.	.	595	Resigned 19th November, 1775.
.	.	.	.		{ From Ensign in Fourth Foot. Died in February, 1781.
.	.	.	.		{ Adjutant from 9th July, 1779, to 31st Aug., 1781. Retired 11th December, 1781.
.	.	.	.		{ Wounded at Guilford 15th, and died of his wounds 21st March, 1781.
.	.	.	.		Retired 21st January, 1779.
.	.	.	.	600	Retired 24th June, 1781.
.	.	.	.		{ Prisoner of war at York Town 19th Oct., 1781. Killed in action near Furnes 24th August, 1793.
.	.	.	.		{ Exchanged to a company in Twenty-fourth Foot 12th December, 1787.
.	.	.	.		{ Prisoner of war at York Town 19th Oct., 1781. Exchanged to Lieutenant-Colonel of Fourth Dragoon Guards 6th Oct., 1790.
2 Dec. 1795	30 Dec. 1797	9 May 1800	.		{ Major-General 1st Jan., 1798. Appointed Colonel of "Prince of Wales's, or Leicester Fencible Infantry," 19th Nov., 1800.
.	.	.	.	605	Retired 26th July, 1781.
.	.	.	.		Retired 1st April, 1779.
.	.	.	.		{ Prisoner of war at York Town 19th Oct., 1781. Retired 4th December, 1792.
.	.	.	.		{ Promoted to Lieutenant in Ninetieth Foot 26th November, 1779.
.	.	.	.		{ From Lieut. and Captain in Third Foot Guards. Appointed Lieut.-Col. of Eighty-seventh Foot 4th Oct. 1779. (Subsequently disbanded.)
.	.	.	.	610	{ Promoted to Lieutenant in Eighty-sixth Foot 30th September, 1779.
.	.	.	.		Retired 17th August, 1784.
.	.	.	.		Retired 16th November, 1779.
.	.	.	.		{ Adjutant from 1st Sept., 1781, to 12th Oct., 1790. Retired 21st January, 1794.
30 Dec. 1797	9 May 1800	19 Nov. 1800	.		{ Major-General 18th June, 1798. Removed from the Coldstream 25th July, 1814, being a General Officer.
9 May 1800	19 Nov. 1800	.	.	615	{ Wounded before Valenciennes 3rd June, 1793. Major-Gen. 18th June, 1798. Appointed Col.-Commandant of Sixty-eighth Foot, 18th June, 1801.
.	.	.	.		{ From Cornet in Fourth regiment of Horse (7th Dragoon Guards). Promoted to Major of Twelfth Dragoons 25th June, 1785.

COLDSTREAM

NAMES.	Ensign.	Lieutenant.	Capt.-Lieut.	Captain.
William Bulkeley	17 Nov. 1779	13 Dec. 1781	.	.
John Henry Fraser	24 Nov. 1779	26 April 1782	.	25 April 1792
Isaac Gascoyne	19 Jan. 1780	18 Aug. 1784	.	5 Dec. 1792
620 Wastel Briscoe	.	24 Jan. 1780	.	.
Hon. Thomas Parker	24 Feb. 1780	22 Oct. 1782	.	.
Nicholas Price	17 Mar. 1780	.	.	.
John Bridgeman	5 May 1780	.	.	.
Nathaniel Webb	28 June 1780	11 July 1785	.	.
625 Charles Howard Bulkeley	15 Sept. 1780	23 Feb. 1785	.	25 April 1793
William Lord Cathcart	.	.	.	2 Feb. 1781
John Calcraft	12 Feb. 1781	13 July 1785	.	25 April 1793
Thomas Cole	14 Mar. 1781	24 Aug. 1785	.	.
Hon. James Forbes, afterwards Lord Forbes	13 June 1781	21 April 1786	23 Aug. 1793	28 Aug. 1793
630 Richard Vachell	26 July 1781	18 April 1788	.	.
James George Viscount Stopford, afterwards Earl of Courtown	8 Dec. 1781	17 Sept. 1788	.	.
Edward Webber	12 Dec. 1781	.	.	.
William De Visme	19 Jan. 1782	26 May 1789	18 Nov. 1793	19 May 1794
Henry Levett Hall	6 Mar. 1782	16 Dec. 1789	.	.
635 Edwin Hewgill	19 Mar. 1782	13 Jan. 1790	.	22 Jan. 1794
Wentworth Serle	26 April 1782	24 Mar. 1790	19 May 1794	1 April 1795
Roger Morris	22 Oct. 1782	14 May 1790	.	22 Dec. 1794
Hon. Henry Brodrick	.	.	18 Dec. 1782	5 Feb. 1783
Hon. Edward Finch	.	5 Feb. 1783	.	3 Oct. 1792
640 George Quarme	7 Mar. 1783	.	.	.
Joseph Maddocks	30 April 1783	13 Oct. 1790	.	.
Hon. Thomas Fane	.	.	.	15 May 1783
Beaumont Hotham	18 Aug. 1784	20 Oct. 1790	23 June 1795	23 June 1795
His Royal Highness Prince Frederick, Duke of York	.	.	.	.
645 Solomon Henry Durell	10 Nov. 1784	.	.	.
John Spencer	2 March 1785	.	.	.

ROLL.—Continued.

2nd Major.	1st Major.	Lieut.-Col.	Colonel.		REMARKS.
.	.	.	.		From Cornet in Sixteenth Dragoons. Retired 22nd February, 1785.
.	.	.	.		Exchanged to Lieut.-Colonel of Eleventh Foot 17th May, 1796.
.	.	.	.		From Ensign in Twentieth Foot. Wounded at Lincelles 18th Aug. 1793. Exchanged to Lieutenant-Col. of Thirty-fourth Foot 24th January, 1799.
.	.	.	.	620	From Captain-Lieutenant in Sixteenth Dragoons. Retired 12th July, 1785.
.	.	.	.		Retired 19th October, 1790.
.	.	.	.		Retired 6th March, 1783.
.	.	.	.		Resigned 9th November, 1784.
.	.	.	.		Adjutant from 22nd June, 1782, to 4th Sept., 1787. Retired 23rd November, 1790.
.	.	.	.	625	From Cornet in Tenth Dragoons. Retired 20th November, 1799.
.	.	.	.		From Major of Thirty-eighth Foot. Exchanged to Lieutenant-Col. of Twenty-ninth Foot 6th October, 1789.
18 June, 1801	4 Aug. 1808	.	.		Surrendered prisoner at Ostend 20th May, 1798. Major-Gen. 29th April, 1802. Lt.-Gen. 25th April, 1808. Removed from the Coldstream 25th July, 1814, being a General Officer.
.	.	.	.		Retired 16th September, 1788.
.	.	.	.		Major-General 29th April, 1802. Appointed Colonel of Third Garrison Battalion 19th July, 1807.
.	.	.	.	630	Exchanged to a company in Twenty-third Foot 19th February, 1790.
.	.	.	.		Retired 3rd May, 1791.
.	.	.	.		From Ensign in Sixty-first Foot. Promoted to Captain in First regiment of Foot 11th April, 1783.
.	.	.	.		Retired 17th January, 1799.
.	.	.	.		Exchanged to a company in Sixty-fourth Foot 1st December, 1790.
.	.	.	.	635	From Lieutenant in West Suffolk Militia. Adjutant from 5th Sept., 1787, to 21st Jan., 1794. Military Secretary to H.R.H. the Duke of York, in Flanders. Exchanged to Lieut.-Col. of Nineteenth Foot 10th May, 1800.
.	.	.	.		Exchanged to Lieutenant-Col. of Eighty-eighth Foot 21st June, 1795.
.	.	.	.		Killed in action at Bergen, 19th September, 1799.
.	.	.	.		From Major of Fifty-fifth Foot. Died at Lisbon 16th June, 1785.
19 Nov. 1800	18 June 1801	.	.		From Lieutenant in Eighty-seventh Foot. Major-Gen. 1st Jan. 1801; Lieut.-Gen. 25th April, 1808. Appointed Colonel of Fifty-fourth Foot 3rd August, 1808.
.	.	.	.	640	From Cornet in First troop of Horse Guards. Retired 5th April, 1785.
.	.	.	.		Exchanged to a company in Forty-first Foot 15th October, 1790.
.	.	.	.		From Major of Second Foot. Retired 24th December, 1793.
.	.	.	.		Retired 4th September, 1799.
.	.	.	27 Oct. 1784		Appointed Colonel of First Foot Guards 5th September, 1805.
.	.	.	.	645	Promoted to Lieutenant in Sixtieth Foot 21st June, 1789.
.	.	.	.		Promoted to Captain of an Independent company 24th January, 1791

496 APPENDIX.

COLDSTREAM

NAMES.	Ensign.	Lieutenant.	Capt.-Lieut.	Captain.
Arthur Brice	6 April 1785	27 Oct. 1790	2 Dec. 1795	13 July 1797
Hon. Gregory William Twisleton, afterwards Lord Saye and Sele	11 July 1785	24 Nov. 1790	.	.
Charles Hotham	13 July 1785	30 Nov. 1790	.	.
650 Richard Gregory	24 Aug. 1785	4 May 1791	.	.
Thomas Jones	.	.	23 Nov. 1785	21 April 1786
Kenneth Alexander Howard	21 April 1786	25 April 1793	30 Dec. 1797	25 July 1799
James Lord Torphichen	.	12 Dec. 1787	28 Aug. 1793	18 Nov. 1793
Hon. Henry Windsor	18 April 1788	25 April 1792	.	.
655 Hon. John Thomas Capel	17 Sept. 1788	.	.	.
Charles Lennox	.	.	.	26 March 1789
William Buller	26 May 1789	3 Oct. 1792	.	.
George Lord Strathaven	.	.	.	15 June 1789
William Walter Vane	21 July 1789	5 Dec. 1792	13 July 1797	30 Dec. 1797
660 Lord Henry Fitz-gerald	.	.	.	6 Oct. 1789
George Dashwood	16 Dec. 1789	.	.	.
Thomas Armstrong	13 Jan. 1790	25 April 1793	25 July 1799	23 Sept. 1799
Harry Calvert	.	19 Feb. 1790	.	25 Dec. 1793
Richard Hulse	24 March 1790	25 April 1793	23 Sept. 1799	9 May 1800
665 Harry Chester	14 May 1790	25 April 1793	.	18 Jan. 1799
George Nugent	.	.	.	6 Oct. 1790
Sir John Shelly, Bart.	13 Oct. 1790	7 Aug. 1793	.	.
William Wynyard	.	15 Oct. 1790	1 April 1795	23 June 1795
Hon. Samuel Ongley	20 Oct. 1790	23 Aug. 1793	.	.
670 Henry Bayly	27 Oct. 1790	28 Aug. 1793	.	5 Sept. 1799
Hilton Jolliffe	24 Nov. 1790	25 Dec. 1793	.	21 Nov. 1799
Francis Gerard Lake	30 Nov. 1790	.	.	.
Hon. George Pomeroy	.	1 Dec. 1790	.	.

ROLL.—*Continued.*

2nd Major.	1st Major.	Lieut.-Col.	Colonel.		REMARKS.
.	.	.	.		Adjutant from 22nd Jan., 1794, to 1st December, 1795. Wounded and taken prisoner on 14th March, 1801, in Egypt, and died of his wounds.
.	.	.	.		Retired 6th February, 1794.
.	.	.	.		Retired 20th February, 1794.
.	.	.	.	650	Retired 6th August, 1793.
.	.	.	.		From Major of the 102nd Foot. Retired 25th March, 1789.
4 Aug. 1808	.	.	.		Wounded in action at St. Amand 8th May, 1793. Adjutant from 11th Dec., 1793, to 29th Dec., 1797. Major-Gen. 25th July, 1810. Removed from the Coldstream 25th July, 1814, being a General Officer.
.	.	.	.		Exchanged from Captain in Twenty-fourth Foot. Retired 21st December, 1794.
.	.	.	.		Promoted to Major of 111th Foot 30th May, 1794.
.	.	.	.	655	Removed to Captain of an Independent company 24th January, 1791.
.	.	.	.		From Captain in Thirty-fifth Foot. Exchanged to Lieutenant-Colonel of Thirty-fifth Foot 15th June, 1789.
.	.	.	.		Exchanged to a company in Eighty-second Foot 29th July, 1795.
.	.	.	.		Retired 24th April, 1792.
.	.	.	.		From Lieutenant in Sixty-second Foot. Retired 24th December, 1802.
.	.	.	.	660	Exchanged from Lieut.-Col. of Twenty-ninth Foot. Retired 2nd Oct. 1792.
.	.	.	.		Retired 11th December, 1792.
.	.	.	.		Surrendered prisoner at Ostend 20th May, 1798. Retired 11th May, 1808.
.	.	.	.		Exchanged from a company in Twenty-third Foot. Brevet-Major 1st July, 1793. Exchanged to Lieutenant-Colonel of Sixty-third Foot 27th January, 1799.
.	.	.	.		Major-General 1st January, 1812. Died in Spain 7th September, 1812.
.	.	.	.	665	Adjutant from 9th December, 1795, to 17th Jan., 1799. Major-General 1st Jan., 1812. Removed from the Coldstream 25th July, 1814, being a General Officer.
.	.	.	.		Exchanged from Lieut.-Col. of Fourth Dragoon Guards. Appointed Col. of Eighty-fifth Foot 18th November, 1793.
.	.	.	.		Retired 24th December, 1793.
.	.	.	.		Exchanged from a company in Forty-first Foot. Adjutant from 15th Oct., 1790, to 10th Dec. 1793. Appointed Deputy-Adjutant-General on the Continent in Dec., 1793. Col. of the Royal West-India Rangers, dated 25th October, 1806.
.	.	.	.		Exchanged to Captain of an Independent company 9th October, 1793.
.	.	.	.	670	From Ensign of late Eighty-fifth Foot. Wounded at Lincelles 18th August, 1793. Major-General 1st January, 1812. Removed from the Coldstream 25th July, 1814, being a General Officer.
.	.	.	.		Retired 15th August, 1804.
.	.	.	.		From Ensign in Thirty-fifth Foot. Promoted to Captain of an Independent company 5th February, 1793.
.	.	.	.		Exchanged from a company in Sixty-fourth Foot. Exchanged to Captain of an Independent company 12th February, 1794.

498   APPENDIX.

COLDSTREAM

NAMES.	Ensign.	Lieutenant.	Capt.-Lieut.	Captain.
Hon. William Fitzroy	26 Jan. 1791	25 Dec. 1793	19 Nov. 1800	14 May 1801
675 Lord William Bentinck	27 Jan. 1791	.	.	.
George Hart Dyke	4 May 1791	25 Dec. 1793	14 May 1801	18 June 1801
Lord Charles Henry Somerset	.	.	.	15 June 1791
John Henry Lord Templetown	25 April 1792	.	.	.
Joseph Fuller	1 Aug. 1792	22 Jan. 1794	18 June 1801	25 May 1803
680 William Lemon	3 Oct. 1792	7 Feb. 1794	.	.
John Carter Atherley	5 Dec. 1792	21 Feb. 1794	.	.
Hon. Camden Grey Mac Lellan	12 Dec. 1792	19 May 1794	.	.
Thomas Stibbert	23 Jan. 1793	5 Nov. 1794	.	25 June 1803
Hon. George Frederick Fitzroy, afterwards Lord Southampton	.	.	.	1 Feb. 1793
685 John Peniston Milbanke	8 Feb. 1793	11 Mar. 1795	.	.
Hon. John Wingfield Stratford	25 April 1793	13 Mar. 1795	.	10 July 1801
William Cosby	.	26 April 1793	.	.
George Wynyard	.	26 April 1793	.	.
Sir William Sheridan	26 April 1793	1 April 1795	.	25 June 1803
690 Hon. Henry Brand	27 April 1793	23 June 1795	.	25 Oct. 1806
William Stackpoole	28 April 1793	.	.	.
Hon. Edward Plunkett, afterwards Lord Dunsany	18 Sept. 1793	11 Nov. 1795	.	16 Aug. 1804
Henry Mac Kinnon	.	9 Oct. 1793	.	18 Oct. 1799
Warren Marmaduke Peacocke	.	6 Nov. 1793	9 May 1800	19 Nov. 1800
695 Hon. Arthur Percy Upton	6 Nov. 1793	2 Dec. 1795	.	.
John S. Stuart, afterwards J. Stuart Wortley	.	3 Dec. 1793	.	.
Hon. Robert Fitzroy	25 Dec. 1793	.	.	.

APPENDIX. 499

ROLL.—*Continued.*

2nd Major.	1st Major.	Lieut.-Col.	Colonel.		REMARKS.
.	.	.	.		From Ensign in Twenty-ninth Foot. Exchanged to half-pay of Eighth-fifth Foot with Lord Aylmer, 9th June, 1803.
.	.	.	.	675	Promoted to Captain-Lieutenant in Second Dragoons 1st August, 1792.
.	.	.	.		Retired 7th March, 1810.
.	.	.	.		From Captain in Seventy-seventh Foot. Appointed Colonel of One hundred and third Foot 19th May, 1794.
.	.	.	.		Retired 22nd January, 1793.
.	.	.	.		Major-General 4th June, 1813. Removed from the Coldstream 25th July, 1814, being a General Officer.
.	.	.	.	680	Exchanged to a company in Eighty-second Foot 28th March, 1794.
.	.	.	.		From Ensign in Fifty-first Foot. Died 22nd Jan. 1795, on service in Holland.
.	.	.	.		From Ensign in Second Foot. Dismissed the service 9th April, 1803.
.	.	.	.		From Ensign in First regiment of Foot. Wounded 28th July, 1809, at Talavera. Retired 27th June, 1810.
.	.	.	.		From Major of the Fifty-first Foot. Appointed Colonel of Thirty-fourth Foot 13th July, 1797.
.	.	.	.	685	Exchanged to a company in Seventeenth Foot 31st May, 1798.
.	.	.	.		Retired 22nd June, 1808.
.	.	.	.		From Captain on half-pay of an Independent company. Exchanged to Captain of an Independent company 3rd December, 1793.
.	.	.	.		From Captain-Lieutenant in Thirty-third Foot. Exchanged to Captain of an Independent company 6th Nov. 1793.
.	.	.	.		From Cornet in Thirteenth Dragoons. Wounded at Talavera 28th July, 1809, and taken prisoner of war on 6th August following. Major-General 4th June, 1814. Removed from the Coldstream 25th July, 1814, being a General Officer.
.	.	25 July 1814	.	690	Removed from the Coldstream on promotion to the rank of Major-General, 19th July, 1821.
.	.	.	.		Promoted to Lieutenant of Ninety-seventh Independent company 12th April, 1794.
.	.	.	.		Promoted to a company in Sixteenth Foot 28th October, 1795. Removed to Fortieth Foot 11th November following, and exchanged into the Coldstream, same date, with Capt. George Bruhl. Wounded 8th March, 1801, at landing in Aboukir Bay. Retired 21st December, 1808.
.	.	.	.		Exchanged from Captain of an Independent company. Major-General 1st Jan. 1812. Killed at Ciudad Rodrigo 19th January, 1812.
.	.	.	.		Exchanged from Captain of an Independent company. Major-General 4th June, 1811. Removed from the Coldstream 25th July, 1814, being a General Officer.
.	.	.	.	695	Promoted to Major of Thirteenth Foot 7th May, 1807.
.	.	.	.		Exchanged from Captain of an Independent company. Died 14th January, 1797.
.	.	.	.	.	Promoted to Captain of a company in Whitelocke's regiment, dated 1st July, 1795.

APPENDIX.

COLDSTREAM

NAMES.	Ensign.	Lieutenant.	Capt.-Lieut.	Captain.
Willoughby Bean	7 Feb. 1794	27 Jan. 1797	.	.
John Ross	.	12 Feb. 1794	.	25 Dec. 1802
700 George Bruhl	.	28 Mar. 1794	.	.
Richard Boulton	11 April 1794	13 July 1797	.	.
Robert French	23 May 1794	.	.	.
John Allen Lloyd	30 May 1794	30 Dec. 1797	.	.
Richard Downes Jackson	9 July 1794	31 May 1798	.	4 Aug. 1808
705 Montagu J. Wynyard	10 Dec. 1794	25 July 1799	.	28 July 1809
Henry Edward Bunbury	14 Jan. 1795	.	.	.
Sir John Gordon, Bart.	1 April 1795	23 Sept. 1799	.	.
George Morgan	17 April 1795	.	.	.
Lancelot Holland	14 May 1795	.	.	.
710 Sir Gilbert Stirling, Bart.	15 May 1795	18 Jan. 1799	.	12 May 1808
Robert Brownrigg	.	.	.	21 June 1795
James Philips	.	29 July 1795	.	23 July 1807
Charles Philips	18 Sept. 1795	10 Oct. 1799	.	.
Charles Viscount Petersham	2 Dec. 1795	.	.	.
715 Lord Charles Bentinck	20 Jan. 1796	.	.	.
George Sedley	20 Jan. 1796	25 Nov. 1799	.	.
Richard Beadon	11 May 1796	25 Nov. 1799	.	.
Edmond Viscount Dungarvon, afterwards Earl of Cork	.	.	.	17 May 1796
John Thompson	11 Aug. 1796	25 Nov. 1799	.	.
720 Isaac Hartman	6 Dec. 1796	25 Nov. 1799	.	.
Matthew Richard Onslow	1 Feb. 1797	25 Nov. 1799	.	.
Hon. Alexander Murray	13 July 1797	25 Nov. 1799	.	.
John Frederick	19 Sept. 1797	25 Nov. 1799	.	.
Hon. Alexander Duncan	30 Dec. 1797	25 Nov. 1799	.	.
725 George Smyth	2 Mar. 1798	5 Dec. 1799	.	23 June 1808
H. John Conyers	27 June 1798	5 Dec. 1799	.	.

APPENDIX.

ROLL.—*Continued.*

2nd Major.	1st Major.	Lieut.-Col.	Colonel.		REMARKS.
					From Ensign in Forty-eighth Foot. Surrendered prisoner of war at Ostend, 20th May, 1798. Placed on half-pay of the regiment from 25th December, 1802, by exchange with Captain O'Neill.
.					Exchanged from Captain of an Independent company. Brevet-Major 29th April, 1802. Killed 27th July, 1809, at Talavera.
.				700	Exchanged from Captain in Eighty-second Foot. Exchanged 11th November, 1795, to a company in Fortieth Foot with Capt. Plunkett.
.					Exchanged to half-pay of the regiment 25th Dec. 1802, with Captain Collier.
.					Retired 5th December, 1796.
.					Placed on half-pay of the regiment from 25th December, 1802, by exchange with Captain Bouverie.
.	25 July 1814	.	.		Promoted to Captain of a company in Seventeenth Foot, 24th May, 1798. Exchanged into the Coldstream 31st May following with Captain Milbanke. Appointed Colonel of the Royal Staff Corps, 18th January, 1820.
.	.	.	.	705	Adjutant from 21st November, 1799, to 13th April, 1808. Exchanged to Lieut.-Col. of the Second Garrison Battalion, 8th August, 1811, with Lieut.-Col. James Macdonell.
.	.	.	.		Promoted to Capt. of a troop in Sixteenth Dragoons, 16th August, 1797.
.	.	.	.		Superceded 14th November, 1805.
.	.	.	.		Retired 20th November, 1799.
.	.	.	.		Retired 10th August, 1796.
.	.	.	.	710	Adjutant from 18th January, 1799, to 25th May, 1803. Wounded 28th July, 1809, at Talavera. Retired 29th January, 1812.
.	.	.	.		Exchanged from Lieut.-Colonel of Eighty-eighth Foot. Appointed Colonel-Commandant of Sixtieth Foot, 25th July, 1799.
.	.	.	.		Exchanged from Captain in Eighty-second Foot. Brevet-Major, 1st January, 1805. Retired 2nd June, 1813.
.	.	.	.		Retired 31st May, 1809.
.	.	.	.		Promoted to Captain-Lieutenant in Tenth Dragoons, 21st November, 1799.
.	.	.	.	715	Promoted to Lieutenant in Forty-fourth Foot, 28th February, 1798.
.	.	.	.		Retired 28th October, 1802.
.	.	.	.		Wounded 8th March, 1801, at landing in Aboukir Bay, and on the 13th in action near Alexandria. Exchanged to a company in Third Foot 24th Sept. 1803.
.	.	.	.		Exchanged from Lieut.-Col. of Eleventh Foot. Exchanged with Lt.-Col. Pringle to the Fourth Foot 17th Sept. 1802.
.	.	.	.		From Cornet in Twelfth Dragoons. Died 22nd March, 1808.
.	.	.	.	720	Retired 29th May, 1800.
.	.	.	.		Exchanged to Captain of a company in Sixty-sixth Foot 13th June, 1805.
.	.	.	.		Placed on half-pay from 25th May, 1802, at the reduction.
.	.	.	.		Wounded 8th March, 1801, at landing in Aboukir Bay, and died 18th April following.
.	.	.	.		Died 27th November, 1802, in the Mediterranean.
.	.	.	.	725	Retired 2nd October, 1811.
.	.	.	.		Retired 16th April, 1806.

COLDSTREAM

NAMES.	Ensign.	Lieutenant.	Capt.-Lieut.	Captain.
John Leveson Gower	.	.	.	17 June 1799
Francis Cunynghame	.	.	.	24 Jan. 1799
John Levington Campbell	6 June 1799	{ 9 May 1800 / 30 Nov. 1803 }	.	.
730 Henry Lord Grey de Ruthyn	25 July 1799	30 May 1800	.	.
Hon. John Bruce Richard O'Neill	10 Oct. 1799	8 May 1800	.	11 July 1816
Henry Frederick Bouverie	23 Oct. 1799	19 Nov. 1800	.	28 June 1810
John Hamilton	21 Nov. 1799	{ 13 May 1801 / 1 Dec. 1803 }	.	30 Jan. 1812
Edward Dalling	.	6 Dec. 1799	.	.
735 Thomas Braddyll	.	7 Dec. 1799	.	22 Dec. 1808
Frederick Adam	.	8 Dec. 1799	.	.
Hon. Henry Cadogan	.	9 Dec. 1799	.	.
George Collier	10 Dec. 1799	{ 14 May 1801 / 25 Dec. 1802 }	.	3 Oct. 1811
Charles Fane	.	11 Dec. 1799	.	.
740 B ... Jenkinson	11 Dec. 1799	.	.	.
John Lyons Nixon	.	19 Dec. 1799	.	.
Thomas Roberts	19 Dec. 1799	18 June 1801	.	.
Alexander Woodford	.	20 Dec. 1799	.	8 Mar. 1810

* Extract of a letter from the Commander-in-Chief to the Secretary at War, dated Horse Guards, last promotion are to be made out as Majors only, like the line, and not as First and Second Major,

APPENDIX.

ROLL.—*Continued.*

2nd Major.	1st Major.	Lieut.-Col.	Colonel.		REMARKS.
.	.	.	.		Exchanged from Lieutenant-Col. of Sixty-third Foot. Exchanged to Lieutenant-Col. of Thirty-first Foot 17th Oct., 1799, vice Lieutenant-Colonel Hepburn.
.	.	.	.		Exchanged from Lieutenant-Colonel of Thirty-fourth Foot. Wounded 19th September, 1799, in action at Bergen. Retired 9th July, 1801.
.	.	.	.		Placed on half-pay from 25th Dec. 1802, on reduction. Re-appointed to the Coldstream from Captain in the Ninety-second Foot 30th Nov., 1803. Exchanged to Captain in Twenty-first Foot 1st Dec. 1804, with Sir John Lowther Johnstone.
.	.	.	.	730	Placed on half-pay, from 14th Jan. 1802, on reduction.
.	.	.	.		Appointed Captain of a troop in Eighteenth Dragoons 28th April, 1804. Exchanged from Lieutenant-Colonel of Nineteenth Dragoons, 11th July, 1816, with Lieutenant-Colonel Wyndham. Removed from the Coldstream 27th May, 1825, on promotion to Major-General.
18 Jan. 1820	25 July 1821*	.	.		From Cornet in Second Dragoon Guards. ... Wounded 28th July, 1809, at Talavera. (Staff.) Removed 27th May, 1825, on promotion to Major-General.
.	27 May 1825	.	.		Placed on half-pay from 25th Dec. 1802, on reduction. From half-pay of the regiment, 1st Dec. 1803. Retired 15th May, 1829.
.	.	.	.		From Captain-Lieutenant in Thirty-seventh Foot. Brevet-Major, 25th Oct. 1809. Died 31st July, 1811, in Portugal.
.	.	.	.	735	From Captain in Seventeenth Foot. Retired 6th November, 1811.
.	.	.	.		From Captain-Lieutenant in Ninth Foot. Appointed Major of the Fifth Battalion of Reserve, 9th July, 1803.
.	.	.	.		From Captain in Sixtieth Foot. Promoted to Major of Fifty-third Foot 8th Dec. 1804.
.	.	.	.		From Cornet in the Fourteenth Dragoons. Placed on half-pay at the reduction, 25th Dec. 1802. Exchanged from half-pay of the regiment with Captain Boulton 25th Dec. 1802. Wounded 28th July, 1809, at Talavera, and on 14th April, 1814, before Bayonne. Died of his wounds 10th May following.
.	.	.	.		From Captain in the Ninth Foot. Adjutant from 26th May, 1803, to 17th April, 1805. Brevet-Major 1st Jan. 1805. Promoted to Major of Eighth Foot 18th April, 1805.
.	.	.	.	740	Killed 13th March, 1801, in action near Alexandria.
.	.	.	.		From Captain in the Ninth Foot. Exchanged to a company in Twenty-eighth Foot 5th Nov. 1803.
.	.	.	.		Placed on half-pay of the regiment from 25th Dec. 1802, on reduction.
5 July 1814	18 Jan. 1820	25 July 1821	.		From Captain-Lieutenant in Ninth Foot. Removed 27th May, 1825, on promotion to Major-General.

8th September, 1821. The Commissions of the Majors of the three regiments of Guards at the is heretofore.

APPENDIX.

COLDSTREAM

NAMES.	Ensign.	Lieutenant.	Capt.-Lieut.	Captain.
William James Myers	.	11 Jan. 1800	.	.
745 Lucius Frederick Adams	.	12 Jan. 1800	.	31 Jan. 1812
George I. B. Warren	16 Jan. 1800	29 Jan. 1801	.	.
Richard Beckett	23 Jan. 1800	16 July 1801	.	.
Thomas William Brotherton	24 Jan. 1800	17 July 1801	.	.
Charles Parker	7 Mar. 1800	27 Jan. 1803	.	.
750 William Mallett Dansey	8 Mar. 1800	29 Oct. 1802	.	.
George Lord Delvin, afterwards Marquis of Westmeath	9 Mar. 1800	24 Sept. 1803	.	.
Muine Walrond	.	21 Mar. 1800	.	.
James Richard Lewis Lloyd	22 Mar. 1800	.	.	.
Hon. Edward Acheson	8 May 1800	17 June 1802	.	25 July 1814
755 Francis Manners Sutton	9 May 1800	3 Dec. 1803	.	25 Dec. 1813
Wroth Palmer Acland	.	.	.	10 May 1800
Richard Toulmin North	10 July 1800	.	.	.
Francis Miles Milman	3 Dec. 1800	28 April 1804	.	25 Dec. 1813
Sir John Lowther Johnstone, Bart.	17 Dec. 1800	1 Dec. 1804	.	.
760 Charles Maitland Christie	5 Mar. 1801	16 Aug. 1804	.	.
Frederick Morshead	13 May 1801	.	.	.
George Heneage Finch	14 May 1801	29 Dec. 1804	.	.
Thomas Gore	3 Sept. 1801	4 July 1805	.	25 Dec. 1813
Henry W. Vachell	15 Oct. 1801	28 Nov. 1805	.	.
765 Thomas Wood	28 April 1802	27 Mar. 1806	.	.

APPENDIX. 505

ROLL.—*Continued.*

Jun. Major.	Sen. Major.	Lieut.-Col.	Colonel.		REMARKS.
.	.	.	.		From Captain on half-pay (unattached). Wounded 8th March, 1801, at landing in Aboukir Bay. Promoted to Major of Fifteenth Foot 6th May, 1802.
.	.	.	.	745	From Captain-Lieutenant in Twentieth Foot. Brevet-Major 4th June, 1811. Retired 13th May, 1817.
.	.	.	.		From Cornet in the Fifteenth Dragoons. Promoted to Captain in Sixtieth Foot 22nd Jan. 1801, and re-appointed to the Coldstream 29th ditto. Killed 8th March, 1801, at landing in Aboukir Bay.
.	.	.	.		Killed 28th July, 1809, at Talavera. (Staff.)
.	.	.	.		Placed on half-pay of the regiment from 25th Dec. 1802, on reduction.
.	.	.	.		Retired 24th Dec. 1806.
.	.	.	.	750	Placed on half-pay of the regiment from 25th Dec. 1802, on reduction.
.	.	.	.		Promoted to Captain in Third Foot, 17th Sept. 1803, and exchanged with Captain Beadon 24th of Sept. following. Exchanged to Eighty-eighth Foot, with Captain Gore, 4th July, 1805, and placed on half-pay.
.	.	.	.		From Captain in the Sixtieth Foot, and placed on half-pay of that regiment, from 25th Nov. 1802, on reduction.
.	.	.	.		Suspended 9th April, 1803, by the sentence of a court-martial. Appointed Cornet in Seventeenth Dragoons 5th May, 1803.
.	.	.	.		Placed on half-pay from 25th Dec. 1802, on reduction. Appointed to a company in the Coldstream 25th July, 1814, from Major of Sixty-seventh Foot. Placed on half-pay from 25th Dec. 1823. "No successor to be appointed."
.	.	.	.	755	Retired 31st July, 1822.
.	.	.	.		Exchanged from Lieut.-Col. of Nineteenth Foot, with Lieutenant-Colonel Hewgill. Major-General 25th July, 1810. Lieutenant-General 4th June, 1814. Removed from the Coldstream 25th July, 1814, being a General Officer.
.	.	.	.		Promoted to Capt. in Hompesch's Mounted Riflemen 8th Sept. 1802.
22 July 1830	.	.	.		Wounded 28th July, 1809, at Talavera, and taken prisoner on 6th August following. Effective in Jan. 1833.
.	.	.	.		Promoted to Lieutenant in the York Hussars 23rd July, 1802. Exchanged to the Coldstream from Captain in Twenty-first Foot 1st Dec. 1804, with Captain John L. Campbell. Retired 26th March, 1806.
.	.	.	.	760	Wounded 28th July, 1809, at Talavera, and taken prisoner on 6th August following. Retired 20th June, 1810.
.	.	.	.		Resigned 23rd May, 1804.
.	.	.	.		Placed on half-pay of the Royal York Rangers from 28th Feb. 1805.
.	.	.	.		Promoted to Captain of a company in Eighty-eighth Foot 27th June, 1805, and exchanged to the Coldstream with Lord Delvin 4th July, 1805. Retired 19th Feb. 1823.
.	.	.	.		Died at Penzance 29th August, 1813.
.	.	.	.	765	Wounded 28th July, 1809, at Talavera. Retired 16th Jan. 1811.

APPENDIX.

COLDSTREAM

NAMES.	Ensign.	Lieutenant.	Capt.-Lieut.	Captain.
William Henry Pringle	.	.	.	17 Sept. 1802
Richard Oriel Singer	{ 24 Dec. 1802 } { 3 Sept. 1803 }	.	.	.
William Wharton Rawlins	24 Feb. 1803	.	.	.
Hon. George Pelham	5 May 1803	17 April 1806	.	.
770 Herbert Taylor	.	.	.	25 May 1803
Edward Jenkinson	26 May 1803	29 May 1806	.	.
Matthew Lord Aylmer	.	.	.	9 June 1803
Charles Doyle	28 July 1803	.	.	.
Thomas Thoroton	28 July 1803	6 Nov. 1806	.	.
775 Thomas Barrow	12 Aug. 1803	25 Dec. 1806	.	2 June 1814
George Thomas Baldwin	1 Oct. 1803	14 May 1807	.	.
Henry Frederick Cooke	.	5 Nov. 1803	.	7 Nov. 1811
Sir Henry Sullivan, Bart.	.	2 Dec. 1803	.	24 Sept. 1812
William Clinton Wynyard	3 Dec. 1803	23 July 1807	.	.
780 William Fairfield	5 Dec. 1803	.	.	.
George Bryan	6 Dec. 1803	24 July 1807	.	.
Hon. William George Crofton	7 Dec. 1803	10 Mar. 1808	.	.
Daniel MacKinnon	16 Jan. 1804	25 Mar. 1808	.	25 July 1814
Newton Dickenson	3 Feb. 1804	12 May 1808	.	.
785 Hon. John Walpole	18 Feb. 1804	23 June 1808	.	25 July 1814
Matthew Fortescue	3 Mar. 1804	4 Aug. 1808	.	.
Henry Dawkins	10 Mar. 1804	25 Aug. 1808	.	25 July 1814
Thomas Steele	17 Mar. 1804	1 June 1809	.	18 Jan. 1820
William Lord Alvanley	31 Mar. 1804	22 Dec. 1808	.	.
790 Hon. Charles Vere Ferrars Townshend	28 April 1804	.	.	.
Edward Harvey	24 May 1804	17 Aug. 1809	.	.
William Burroughs	26 July 1804	28 Sept. 1809	.	.
Francis James	7 Sept. 1804	.	.	.

APPENDIX. 507

ROLL.—*Continued.*

Jun. Major.	Sen. Major.	Lieut.-Col.	Colonel.		REMARKS.
.	.	.	.		{ Exchanged from Lieut.-Colonel of Fourth Foot. Exchanged to Lieutenant-Colonel of First Foot 1st Dec. 1808.
.	.	.	.		{ Placed on half-pay from date of appointment. Re-appointed from half-pay of the regiment 3rd Sept. 1803. Retired 4th Dec. 1803.
.	.	.	.		Retired 19th Dec. 1804.
.	.	.	.		Retired 26th June, 1810.
.	.	.	.	770	{ Appointed from Lieutenant-Colonel on half-pay of the Ninth West India regiment. Major-General 4th June, 1813. Removed from the Coldstream 25th July, 1814, being a general officer.
.	.	.	.		{ Wounded 28th July, 1809, at Talavera, and died of his wounds on 24th August following.
.	.	.	.		{ Exchanged from Lieutenant-Colonel on half-pay of the Eighty-fifth Foot, with Lieut.-Col. the Hon. William Fitzroy. Major-General 4th June, 1813. Removed from the Coldstream 25th July, 1814, being a general officer.
.	.	.	.		{ Promoted to Captain in the First Garrison Battalion 13th March, 1806.
.	.	.	.		Resigned 6th March, 1811.
.	.	.	.	775	{ Brevet-Major 21st Sept. 1813. Placed on half-pay of the regt. from 15th June, 1830.
.	.	.	.		Retired 9th March, 1808.
.	.	.	.		{ Exchanged from Captain in the 28th Foot. Exchanged to "Staff in North America" with Lt.-Col. H. Loftus, 23rd July, 1812.
.	.	.	.		{ Appointed from Capt. in Sixty-sixth Foot. Killed before Bayonne 14th April, 1814.
.	.	.	.		Died in Sloane Street, 27th April, 1814.
.	.	.	.	780	{ Promoted to Captain in Sixtieth Foot 25th July, 1806.
.	.	.	.		{ Adjutant from 1st May, 1805, to 30th Sept. 1809. Wounded 27th July, 1809, at Talavera, and died of his wounds 30th September following.
.	.	.	.		{ From Lieutenant in the Royal Fusiliers. Wounded 18th Oct. 1812, before Burgos. Killed 14th April, 1814, before Bayonne.
22 June 1826	16 May 1829	22 July 1830	.		{ Wounded 18th June, 1815, at Waterloo. Effective in January, 1833.
.	.	.	.		Retired 31st January, 1810.
.	.	.	.	785	{ Wounded 18th October, 1812, before Burgos. Retired 27th April, 1825.
.	.	.	.		Retired 18th July, 1810.
.	.	.	.		{ Adjutant from 14th April, 1808, to 22nd April, 1810. Wounded 14th April, 1814, before Bayonne. (Staff.) Exchanged to half-pay, unattached, with Lieutenant-Colonel Chaplin, 31st August, 1826.
.	.	.	.		{ Brevet Lieutenant-Colonel 29th December, 1814. Exchanged to half-pay, unattached, 1st June, 1829.
.	.	.	.		{ Exchanged to Captain in Fiftieth Foot 16th August, 1810.
.	.	.	.	790	Resigned 6th September, 1804.
.	.	.	.		{ Wounded 5th May, 1811, at Fuentes d'Honor. Killed 18th October, 1812, before Burgos.
.	.	.	.		{ Adjutant from 23rd April, 1810, to 3rd June, 1812. Wounded 14th April, 1814, before Bayonne, and died of his wounds 26th April following.
.	.	.	.		{ Promoted to Captain in Eighty-first Foot 3rd March, 1808.

APPENDIX.

COLDSTREAM

NAMES.	Ensign.	Lieutenant.	Capt.-Lieut.	Captain.
George Bowles	20 Dec. 1804	1 Feb. 1810	.	27 May 1825
795 John Boswell	21 Dec. 1804	8 Mar. 1810	.	.
Hon. Francis Hay Drummond	22 Dec. 1804	21 June 1810	.	.
Lord Alexander Gordon	.	28 Feb. 1805	.	.
Thomas Sowerby	28 Feb. 1805	27 June 1810	.	14 May 1817
Harry Parker	18 Apr. 1805	.	.	.
800 Edward Lascelles	25 Apr. 1805	28 June 1810	.	.
Hon. Edward Boscawen, afterwards Earl of Falmouth	1 May 1805	.	.	.
Patrick Sandilands	2 May 1805	19 July 1810	.	.
William Henley Raikes	.	13 June 1805	.	3 June 1813
His Royal Highness Adolphus Frederick, Duke of Cambridge	.	.	.	.
805 Richard Greville	12 Sept. 1805	.	.	.
John Freemantle	17 Oct. 1805	2 Aug. 1810	.	1 Aug. 1822
John Prince	31 Oct. 1805	29 Oct. 1810	.	.
George Frederick Augustus Lord Kilcoursie	6 Feb. 1806	13 Dec. 1810	.	.
James Vigors Harvey	10 Apr. 1806	17 Jan. 1811	.	.
810 Charles Gregory	1 May 1806	.	.	.
Peter Gaussen	2 May 1806	.	.	.
William Lovelace Walton	8 May 1806	7 Mar. 1811	.	20 Feb. 1823
William Lockwood	21 Aug. 1806	5 Sept. 1811	.	.
Edward Noel Long	4 Dec. 1806	.	.	.
815 Hon. John Ashburnham	1 Jan. 1807	.	.	.
Hon. John Wingfield	16 Apr. 1807	.	.	.
Paulet St. John Mildmay	14 May 1807	3 Oct. 1811	.	.
Alexander Wedderburn	17 Sept. 1807	7 Nov. 1811	.	17 Apr. 1823
Charles White	7 Apr. 1808	30 Jan. 1812	.	.
820 Thomas Bligh	21 April 1808	13 Feb. 1812	.	.
Charles Shawe	26 May 1808	23 April 1812	.	28 April 1825
Lord William Fitzgerald	4 Aug. 1808	.	.	.
George Henry Macartney Greville	8 Sept. 1808	24 Sept. 1812	.	.
Michael Watts	20 Oct. 1808	.	.	.
825 Charles Antonio Ferdinand Bentinck	16 Nov. 1808	24 Sept. 1812	.	27 May 1825

APPENDIX.

ROLL.—Continued.

Jun. Major.	Sen. Major.	Lieut.-Col.	Colonel.	Remarks.
.	.	.	.	Brevet-Major 18th June, 1815, and Brevet-Lieutenant-Colonel 14th June, 1821. Effective in January, 1833.
.	.	.	.	795 Retired 12th December, 1810.
.	.	.	.	Drowned 28th October, 1810, in Scotland.
.	.	.	.	From Captain in Fifth Foot. Appointed Captain in Fifty-ninth Foot, 29th May, 1806.
.	.	.	.	Retired 16th April, 1823.
.	.	.	.	Killed 28th July, 1809, at Talavera.
.	.	.	.	800 Adjutant from 3rd December, 1812, to 30th September, 1815. Died 30th September, 1815, at Barrington Park, Gloucestershire.
.	.	.	.	Resigned 16th November, 1808.
.	.	.	.	Wounded 28th July, 1809, at Talavera. Brevet-Major 21st January, 1819. Promoted to a company in Third Foot Guards 30th August, 1821.
27 May 1825	.	.	.	Exchanged from Captain in Sixty-sixth Foot. Retired 21st June, 1826.
.	.	.	5 Sept. 1805	Effective in January, 1833.
.	.	.	.	805 Retired 7th May, 1806.
.	.	.	.	Adjutant from 16th November, 1809, to 2nd December, 1812. Brevet-Major 21st June, 1813. Brevet Lieutenant-Colonel 21st March, 1814. Effective in Jan. 1833.
.	.	.	.	Adjutant from 26th October, 1815, to 2nd January, 1818. Died 2nd January, 1818, in Hanover Street, London.
.	.	.	.	Retired 24th March, 1813.
.	.	.	.	From Lieutenant in Fourth Foot. Wounded 14th April, 1814, before Bayonne. Exchanged to half-pay of the regiment 6th May, 1819.
.	.	.	.	810 Promoted to Captain in Second Ceylon Regiment 4th August, 1808.
.	.	.	.	Died 8th October, 1808, at Dartford.
.	.	.	.	Effective in January, 1833.
.	.	.	.	Resigned 7th October, 1812.
.	.	.	.	Drowned 9th March, 1809, on passage to Portugal.
.	.	.	.	815 From Lieutenant in the Royal Fusiliers. Supposed to be drowned on his passage from Portugal to England, in Dec. 1809.
.	.	.	.	Died at Coimbra, 4th May, 1811.
.	.	.	.	Gentleman Cadet from R. M. C. Retired 22nd April, 1812.
.	.	.	.	Adjutant from 8th January, 1818, to 16th April, 1823. Brevet-Major 21st January, 1819. Effective in January, 1833.
.	.	.	.	Retired 15th August, 1821.
.	.	.	.	820 Retired 14th May, 1823.
.	.	.	.	Wounded 9th March, 1814, at Bergen-op-Zoom. Effective in January, 1833.
.	.	.	.	Resigned 7th September, 1808.
.	.	.	.	From Ensign in Ninth Foot. Exchanged to Captain in the Royal Fusiliers 23rd September, 1813.
.	.	.	.	Killed 5th March, 1811, at Barrosa.
.	.	.	.	825 Gentleman Cadet from R.M.C. Wounded 5th March, 1811, at Barrosa. Adjutant from 4th June, 1812, to 2nd February, 1820. Brevet-Major 18th June, 1815. Effective in January, 1833.

APPENDIX.

COLDSTREAM

NAMES.	Ensign.	Lieutenant.	Capt.-Lieut.	Captain.
John Talbot	17 Nov. 1808	26 Nov. 1812	.	.
Frederick William Buller	.	.	.	1 Dec. 1808
George Harvey Percival	16 Mar. 1809	25 Mar. 1813	.	.
William Stothert	23 Mar. 1809	2 June 1813	.	.
830 Walter George Baynes	6 April 1809	1 June 1813	.	.
John Stepney Cowell	18 May 1809	9 Sept. 1813	.	15 June 1830
Wentworth Noel Burgess	1 June 1809	.	.	.
William Ainslie	25 Aug. 1809	.	.	.
John Mills	21 Dec. 1809	10 Jan. 1814	.	.
835 James Bradshaw	4 Jan. 1810	.	.	.
Francis Love Beckford	25 Jan. 1810	.	.	.
Samuel Bates Ferris	1 Mar. 1810	.	.	.
John Charles Buckeridge	29 Mar. 1810	.	.	.
John Lucie Bluckman	5 April 1810	10 Jan. 1814	.	.
840 William Grimstead	21 June 1810	25 Dec. 1813	.	.
Beaumont Hotham, afterwards Lord Hotham	27 June 1810	{ 25 Dec. 1813 10 Nov. 1825 }	.	.
Hon. John Rous, afterwards Earl of Stradbroke	28 June 1810	4 May 1814	.	.
Windham Anstruther	5 July 1810	17 Mar. 1814	.	.
Charles Shirley	19 July 1810	5 May 1814	.	.
845 Charles Mackenzie Fraser	.	16 Aug. 1810	.	.
John Harcourt Powell	20 Sept. 1810	.	.	.
John Drummond	22 Nov. 1810	26 May 1814	.	22 June 1826
Hon. Robert Moore	21 Mar. 1811	2 June 1814	.	1 Apr. 1824
Charles Andrew Girardot	4 April 1811	1 Sept. 1814	.	27 July 1826
850 Thomas Chaplin	18 April 1811	6 Oct. 1814	.	31 Aug. 1826
Edward Clifton	25 April 1811	6 July 1815	.	.
Henry Salwey	13 June 1811	20 July 1815	.	15 Feb. 1827
George Gould Morgan	4 July 1811	26 Oct. 1815	.	.
James Macdonell	.	.	.	8 Aug. 1811

* See note to No. 732

APPENDIX. 511

ROLL —*Continued.*

Jun. Major.	Sen. Major.	Lieut.-Col.	Colonel.	REMARKS.
.	.	.	.	Wounded 5th March, 1811, at Barrosa. Retired 24th October, 1821.
.	.	.	.	Exchanged from Lieutenant-Colonel of the First Foot. Major-General 4th June, 1813. Removed from the Coldstream 25th July, 1814, being a General Officer.
.	.	.	.	Gentleman Cadet from R.M.C. Died 11th November, 1815.
.	.	.	.	Taken prisoner 5th May, 1811, at Fuentes d'Honor. Retired 13th December, 1815.
.	.	.	.	830 Retired 4th October, 1820.
.	.	.	.	Brevet-Major 17th February, 1820. Retired 21st June, 1832.
.	.	.	.	From Ensign in Fifty-second Foot. Killed before Burgos 19th October, 1812.
.	.	.	.	Died in Dover Street, London, 24 Mar. 1810.
.	.	.	.	Resigned 31st August, 1814.
.	.	.	.	835 Resigned 16th December, 1812.
.	.	.	.	Resigned 29th December, 1813.
.	.	.	.	Retired 12th June, 1811.
.	.	.	.	Killed before Burgos 7th October, 1812.
.	.	.	.	Killed at Waterloo, 18th June, 1815.
.	.	.	.	840 Gentlemen Cadet from R.M.C. Exchanged to Captain in Royal York Rangers 28th May, 1818.
.	.	.	.	Gentleman Cadet from R.M.C. Wounded 22nd July, 1812, at Salamanca. Brevet-Major 21st Jan. 1819. Exchanged to half-pay of the regiment 14th Oct. 1819, and from ditto 10th Nov. 1825. Promoted to Lieutenant-Colonel on half-pay unattached, 24th December, 1825.
.	.	.	.	Exchanged to Captain in Ninety-third Foot 6th November, 1817.
.	.	.	.	Wounded 10th November, 1813, in the Pyrenees. Retired 26th February, 1817.
.	.	.	.	Exchanged to half-pay of the regiment, 4th November, 1819.
.	.	.	.	845 Exchanged from Captain in Fiftieth Foot. Wounded before Burgos in September, 1812. Retired 16th March, 1814.
.	.	.	.	Retired 4th March, 1812.
.	.	.	.	Exchanged to half-pay unattached, 13th April, 1832.
.	.	.	.	Wounded at Waterloo, 18th June, 1815. Placed on half-pay of the regiment, from the date of his promotion, to Captain and Lieutenant-Colonel of a company.
.	.	.	.	Promoted to Lieutenant-Colonel half-pay unattached, 11th July, 1826. Exchanged from ditto, 27th July following.
.	.	.	.	850 Gentleman-Cadet from R.M.C. Wounded 31st Aug., 1813, at the assault of St. Sebastian. Promoted to Lieut.-Col. half-pay unattached, 15th Aug. 1826. Exchanged from ditto 31st August following. Effective in January, 1833.
.	.	.	.	Retired 27th October, 1819.
.	.	.	.	Promoted to Lieut.-Col. half-pay unattached 30th Decem., 1826. Exchanged from ditto 15th Feb. following. Exchanged to ditto 6th August, 1829.
.	.	.	.	Exchanged to half-pay of the regiment 25th February, 1819.
25 July 1821*	.	27 May 1825	.	Exchanged from Lt.-Col. of Second Garrison Battalion with Lt.-Col. M. I. Wynyard.—Removed from the Coldstream, on promotion to Major-Gen. 22nd July, 1830.

of this Roll, page 502.

COLDSTREAM

NAMES.	Ensign.	Lieutenant.	Capt.-Lieut.	Captain.
855 Frederick Vachell	19 Sept. 1811	.	.	.
Thomas Slingsby Duncombe	17 Oct. 1811	23 Nov. 1815	.	.
Francis Eyre	26 Dec. 1811	.	.	.
Henry Shirley	30 Jan. 1812	.	.	.
Hon. James Forbes	13 Feb. 1812	14 Dec. 1815	.	22 July 1830
860 William Pitt	5 Mar. 1812	.	.	.
Thomas Powys	30 April 1812	{ 22 Jan. 1818 / 4 Nov. 1819 }	.	.
Henry Loftus	.	.	.	23 July 1812
Henry Gooch	23 July 1812	28 Oct. 1819	.	26 Nov. 1832
Augustus Cuyler	15 Oct. 1812	27 Feb. 1817	.	.
865 Mark Beaufoy	12 Nov. 1812	{ 15 May 1817 / 14 Oct. 1819 }	.	.
William Kortright	26 Nov. 1812	{ 6 Nov. 1817 / 25 Feb. 1819 }	.	.
Henry Armytage	27 Nov. 1812	{ 28 May 1818 / 6 May 1819 }	.	4 Dec. 1828
Hon. William Rufus Rous	17 Dec. 1812	18 Nov. 1819	.	.
Henry John William Bentinck	25 Mar. 1813	18 Jan. 1820	.	16 May 1829
870 Francis Manby Shawe	6 May 1813	5 Oct. 1820	.	.
Humphry St. John Mildmay	9 Sept. 1813	16 Aug. 1821	.	.
Edward Sumner	.	23 Sept. 1813	.	.
Frederick Thomas Buller	30 Dec. 1813	6 Sept. 1821	.	4 June 1829
Henry Frederick Griffiths	25 Jan. 1814	.	.	.
875 James Frederick Buller	26 Jan. 1814	.	.	.
Hon. John Montagu	27 Jan. 1814	25 Oct. 1821	.	13 Aug. 1829
George Richard Buckley	17 Feb. 1814	.	.	.

ROLL.—Continued.

Jun. Major.	Sen. Major.	Lieut.-Col.	Colonel.		REMARKS.
.	.	.	.	855	From Ensign in Fifty-second Foot. Wounded 14th April, 1814, before Bayonne, and died of his wounds, 13th May following.
.	.	.	.		Resigned 17th November, 1819.
.	.	.	.		Retired 31st May, 1815.
.	.	.	.		Gentleman Cadet from Royal Military Coll. Retired 5th May, 1813.
.	.	.	.		Cadet from Royal Military Coll. Effective in January, 1833.
.	.	.	.	860	Wounded 14th April, 1814, before Bayonne, and died of his wounds 24th April following.
.	.	.	.		Placed on half-pay of the regt. on reduction from 25th December 1818: exchanged from ditto 4th November, 1819. Exchanged to half-pay unattached 30th April 1829.
.	.	.	.		Exchanged from the "Staff in North America" with Lieut.-Col. H. F. Cooke. Died 11th July, 1823, at Stifkey, Norfolk.
.	.	.	.		Gentleman Cadet from Royal Military Coll. Effective in January, 1833.
.	.	.	.		From Ensign in Sixty-ninth Foot. Promoted to Lieut.-Colonel half-pay unattached 10th June 1826.
.	.	.	.	865	Placed on half-pay of the regt. on reduction from 25th December, 1818: exchanged from ditto, 14th October, 1819. Adjutant from 17th April, 1823, to 9th February, 1825. Retired 9th February, 1825.
.	.	.	.		From Ensign in Sixty-eighth Foot. Promoted to Captain in Ninety-third Foot 11th September, 1817, and exchanged from ditto 6th Nov. following. Placed on half-pay of the regt. on reduction, from 25th December 1818; exchanged from ditto 25th February, 1819. Exchanged to ditto 10th November, 1825, with Lord Hotham.
.	.	.	.		Promoted to Captain in the Royal York Rangers, 5th March 1818, and exchanged from ditto 28th May following. Placed on half-pay of the regt. on reduction from 25th December, 1818; exchanged from ditto 6th May, 1819. Promoted to Lieut.-Colonel half-pay unattached 21st Nov. 1828; exchanged from ditto 4th December following. Effective in January, 1833.
.	.	.	.		Cadet from R. M. C. Exchanged to Captain in Fifty-fifth Foot 19th February, 1823.
.	.	.	.		Adjutant from 3rd February, 1820, to 15th May, 1829. Effective in January, 1833.
.	.	.	.	870	Exchanged to half-pay unattached 13th April, 1826.
.	.	.	.		Exchanged to Captain in Thirty-fifth Foot 25th December, 1823.
.	.	.	.		Exchanged from Captain in the Royal Fusileers. Wounded at Waterloo 18th June, and died of his wounds 26th June, 1815.
.	.	.	.		Exchanged to Lieut.-Col. half-pay unattached 3d February, 1832.
.	.	.	.		From the Stafford Militia. Wounded at Waterloo 18th June, 1815. Died in the Tower of London 19th January, 1821.
.	.	.	.	875	Died 4th January, 1816, in Paris.
.	.	.	.		Wounded at Waterloo, 18th June, 1815. Retired 26th January, 1832.
.	.	.	.		Died 15th August, 1815, in Paris.

APPENDIX.

COLDSTREAM

NAMES.	Ensign.	Lieutenant.	Capt.-Lieut.	Captain.
James Hervey	15 Mar. 1814	.	.	.
Henry Vane	16 Mar. 1814	1 Aug. 1822	.	.
880 Francis James Douglas	17 Mar. 1814	.	.	.
Robert Bowen	24 Mar. 1814	19 Feb. 1823	.	27 Jan. 1832
Frederick Fitz-Clarence, afterwards Lord Frederick Fitz-Clarence	12 May 1814	.	.	.
Alexander Gordon	19 May 1814	.	.	.
Hon. Walter Forbes	2 June 1814	20 Feb. 1823	.	.
885 Hon. Alexander Abercromby	.	.	.	25 July 1814
Sir Colin Campbell	.	.	.	25 July 1814
Sir Robert Arbuthnot	.	.	.	25 July 1814
Hon. Hercules Robert Pakenham	.	.	.	25 July 1814
Sir William Maynard Gomm	.	.	.	25 July 1814
890 Henry Wyndham	.	.	.	25 July 1814
Charles Short	13 Oct. 1814	17 Apr. 1823	.	21 Sept. 1830
William Leedes Serjeantson	17 Nov. 1814	15 May 1823	.	.
Richard Beamish	22 Dec. 1814	.	.	.
Joseph Henry Lord Wallscourt	5 Jan. 1815	.	.	.
895 Jasper Taylor Hall	{ 1 June 1815 / 15 Apr. 1819 }	25 Dec. 1823	.	.
John Simon Jenkinson	{ 6 July 1815 / 28 Oct. 1819 }	.	.	.
William Henry Cornwall	{ 10 Aug. 1815 / 5 Oct. 1820 }	9 Dec. 1824	.	10 Feb. 1832
Henry Murray	{ 21 Sept. 1815 / 31 May 1821 }	21 Apr. 1825	.	.

APPENDIX. 515

ROLL.—*Continued.*

Jun. Major.	Sen. Major.	Lieut.-Col.	Colonel.		REMARKS.
•	•	•	•		Exchanged to half-pay of the regiment 15th April, 1819.
•	•	•	•		Wounded at Waterloo, 18th June, 1815. Died at Sidmouth 9th August, 1829.
•	•	•	•	880	Thrown from his horse in St. James's Park, and died 29th May, 1821, of the injuries he received.
•	•	•	•		Promoted to Captain in Fifty-fifth Foot 30th Jan., 1823. Exchanged from ditto 19th Feb. following. Effective in Jan., 1833.
•	•	•	•		Promoted to Captain in the Cape Corps of Infantry 23rd February, 1820.
•	•	•	•		Killed at Cambray, 1st April, 1818, in a duel with a French officer.
•	•	•	•		Retired 20th April, 1825.
•	•	•	•	885	From Lieut.-Col. of the Twenty-eight Foot. Placed on half-pay of the regiment on reduction from 25th October, 1821.
•	•	•	•		From Major of Sixty-third Foot, and Assistant Quarter-Master General. Removed from the Coldstream on promotion to Major General 27th May, 1825.
•	•	•	•		From the Portuguese Service. Exchanged to Lieutenant-Colonel half-pay unattached, 27th July, 1826.
•	•	•	•		From Lieut.-Col. of Twenty-sixth Foot. Exchanged to Lieutenant-Colonel half-pay unattached, 15th May, 1817.
6 May 1829	22 July 1830	•	•		From Major of the Ninth Foot. Effective in January, 1833.
•	•	•	•	890	From Lieutenant-Colonel of Dillon's regiment. Exchanged to Lieut.-Col. of the Nineteenth Dragoons 11th July, 1816.
•	•	•	•		Gentleman Cadet from R.M.C. Effective in January, 1833.
•	•	•	•		Exchanged to Captain half-pay unattached 9th December, 1824.
•	•	•	•		Gentleman Cadet from M.R.C. Placed on half-pay of the regiment on reduction, from 25th December, 1818.
•	•	•	•		Died 11th October, 1816.
•	•	•	•	895	Placed on half-pay of the regiment on reduction from 25th Dec., 1818. Exchanged from ditto 15th April, 1819. Promoted to Captain in Thirty-fifth Foot 13th Nov., 1823, and exchanged from ditto 25th Dec. following. Promoted to Major half-pay unattached 1st August, 1826.
•	•	•	•		Placed on half-pay of the regiment on reduction from 25th Dec., 1818. Re-appointed from ditto 28th October, 1829. Retired 16th January, 1822.
•	•	•	•		Placed on half-pay of the regiment on reduction from 25th Dec., 1818. Re-appointed from ditto 5th Oct., 1820. Promoted to Captain half-pay unattached 6th Nov., 1824, and exchanged from ditto 9th Dec., following. Adjutant from 10th Jan., 1828, to 9th Feb., 1832. Effective in January, 1833.
•	•	•	•		From Page of Honour to the Prince Regent. Placed on half-pay of the regiment on reduction from 25th Dec., 1818. Re-appointed from ditto 31st May, 1821. Exchanged to Captain half-pay unattached 5th October, 1826.

APPENDIX.

COLDSTREAM

NAMES.	Ensign.	Lieutenant.	Capt.-Lieut.	Captain.
Edward John Duke	26 Oct. 1815	.	.	.
900 Joseph Sydney Tharp	23 Nov. 1815	.	.	.
Hon. Percy Ashburnham	28 Dec. 1815	.	.	.
Charles Loftus	25 Jan. 1816	.	.	.
Hon. George Charles Grantley Berkeley	{ 7 Nov. 1816 16 Aug. 1821 }	.	.	.
Hon. Arthur Charles Legge	27 Feb. 1817	.	.	.
905 John Waters	.	.	.	15 May 1817
Thomas Kingscote	15 May 1817	.	.	.
Brinckman Broadhead	{ 17 Sept. 1817 13 Sept. 1821 }	28 Apr. 1825	.	20 Apr. 1832
John Blenkinsopp Coulson	22 Jan. 1818	.	.	.
Charles Ricketts	5 March 1818	.	.	.
910 John Arthur Douglas Bloomfield	9 April 1818	.	.	.
Thomas Butler	20 Aug. 1818	.	.	.
Hon. Henry Dundass	18 Nov. 1819	1 Apr. 1824	.	.
Frederick William Culling Smith	18 Jan. 1820	.	.	.
Hon. William Thomas Graves, afterwards Lord Graves	8 June 1820	10 Feb. 1825	.	.
915 Arthur Richard Wellesley	25 Jan. 1821	.	.	.
Charles Murray Hay	1 Nov. 1821	24 Dec. 1825	.	22 June 1832
William Harcourt	20 Dec. 1821	.	.	.
George Bentinck	17 Jan. 1822	13 Apr. 1826	.	.
William Brook Northey	1 Aug. 1822	20 Apr. 1826	.	.
920 John Dawson Rawdon	29 Jan. 1823	10 June 1826	.	.
Hon. Thomas Ashburnham	30 Jan. 1823	22 June 1826	.	.
Hon. Henry St. Clair Erskine	20 Feb. 1823	11 July 1826	.	.
William John Codrington	24 April 1823	20 July 1826	.	.
Ely Duodecimus Wigram	29 May 1823	1 Aug. 1826	.	.
925 St. John Dent	19 June 1823	15 Aug. 1826	.	.

APPENDIX. 517

ROLL.—*Continued.*

Jun. Major.	Sen. Major.	Lieut.-Col.	Colonel.		REMARKS.
.	.	.	.		Exchanged to Ensign in Forty-sixth Foot 20th August, 1818.
.	.	.	.	900	Placed on half-pay of the regiment on reduction, from 25th December, 1818.
.	.	.	.		Cadet from R. M. C. Placed on half pay of the regiment on reduction, from 25th December, 1818.
.	.	.	.		Placed on half-pay of the regiment on reduction, from 25th December, 1818.
.	.	.	.		Placed on half-pay of the regiment on reduction, from 25th Dec., 1818. Re-appointed from ditto 16th August, 1821. Exchanged to Ensign in Sixty-first Foot 19th June, 1823.
.	.	.	.		From Ensign in Twenty-eight Foot. Placed on half-pay of the regiment on reduction, from 25th December, 1818.
.	.	.	.	905	From half-pay Portuguese Service. Exchanged to Lieutenant-Colonel half-pay unattached 15th February, 1827.
.	.	.	.		Placed on half-pay of the regiment on reduction, from 25th December, 1818.
.	.	.	.		Placed on half-pay of the regiment on reduction from 25th December, 1818. Re-appointed from ditto 13th September, 1821. Effective in January, 1833.
.	.	.	.		Placed on half-pay of the regiment on reduction, from 25th December, 1818.
.	.	.	.		Placed on half-pay of the regiment on reduction, from 25th December, 1818.
.	.	.	.	910	From Page of Honour to the Prince Regent. Placed on half-pay of the regiment on reduction, from 25th December, 1818.
.	.	.	.		Exchanged from Ensign in the Forty-sixth Foot. Placed on half-pay of the regiment on reduction, from 25th December, 1818.
.	.	.	.		Promoted to Major unattached 11th July, 1826.
.	.	.	.		From Cornet in Second Dragoon Guards. Promoted to Captain of a troop in the Royal Horse Guards 2nd January, 1823.
.	.	.	.		From Page of Honour to the King. Retired 15th March, 1830.
.	.	.	.	915	From Page of Honour to the King. Appointed Cornet in the Royal Horse Guards 20th December, 1821.
.	.	.	.		From Ensign in the Forty-third Foot. Effective in January, 1833.
.	.	.	.		From Cornet in the Fifth Dragoon Guards. Promoted to Captain half-pay unattached 19th May, 1825.
.	.	.	.		Promoted to Captain half-pay unattached 8th April, 1826. Exchanged from ditto 13th April following. Exchanged to ditto 31st December, 1830.
.	.	.	.		Adjutant from 10th Feb., 1825, to 9th Jan., 1828. Placed on half-pay of the regiment as Lieut. and Capt. from 25th May, 1828.
.	.	.	.	920	From Ensign in Seventy-ninth Foot. Effective in January, 1833.
.	.	.	.		Effective in January, 1833.
.	.	.	.		From Ensign in Eighty-fifth Foot. Died 24th May, 1829, in London.
.	.	.	.		From Ensign in the Forty-third Foot. Effective in January, 1833.
.	.	.	.		Effective in January, 1833.
.	.	.	.	925	From Ensign in the Sixty-first Foot. Retired 2nd August, 1830.

518　　　　　　　　　　APPENDIX.

COLDSTREAM

NAMES.	Ensign.	Lieutenant.	Capt.-Lieut.	Captain.
Hon. Henry Sutton Fane	27 Nov. 1823	.	.	.
Hon. James Hope	8 April 1824	30 Dec. 1826	.	.
Willoughby Cotton	6 Nov. 1824	21 Nov. 1828	.	.
Hon. Arthur Upton	10 Feb. 1825	16 May 1829	.	.
930 Frederick Paget	24 Feb. 1825	4 June 1829	.	.
Boyd Pollen Manningham	21 April 1825	.	.	.
Hon. Edward Bootle Wilbraham	28 April 1825	13 Aug. 1829	.	.
Lord Montagu William Graham	19 May 1825	16 March 1830	.	.
George Fitz Clarence, afterwards Earl of Munster	.	.	.	6 July 1825
935 Francis Russell	.	.	.	7 July 1825
Hon. Charles Howard	22 Oct. 1825	.	.	.
John Henry Pringle	24 Dec. 1825	15 June 1830	.	.
John Christie Clitherow	8 Apr. 1826	22 July 1830	.	.
Gordon Drummond	10 June 1826	3 Aug. 1830	.	.
940 Lord Frederick Paulet	11 June 1826	21 Sep. 1830	.	.
Christopher Wilmot Horton	29 June 1826	27 Jan. 1832	.	.
Hugh Forbes	11 July 1826	.	.	.
John Forbes	1 Aug. 1826	10 Feb. 1832	.	.
Montagu George Burgoyne	2 Aug. 1826	20 Apr. 1832	.	.
945 Edward Isaac Hobhouse	15 Aug. 1826	22 June 1832	.	.
Robert Vansittart	21 Sept. 1826	26 Nov. 1832	.	.
William Stewart	.	5 Oct. 1826	.	.
Charles Ash Windham	30 Dec. 1826	.	.	.
Charles Philip Wilbraham	21 Nov. 1828	.	.	.
950 George Knox	.	30 Apr. 1829	.	.
John Frederick Gore Langton	16 May 1829	.	.	.
James Loftus Elrington	4 June 1829	.	.	.
Henry Daniell	13 Aug. 1829	.	.	.
Charles Atticus Monck	1 Oct. 1829	.	.	.
955 Frederick Halkett	11 June 1830	.	.	.
Hastings Dent	15 June 1830	.	.	.
Charles Whitley Deans Dundas	3 Aug. 1830	.	.	.
Richard Samuel Hulse	21 Sep. 1830	.	.	.
Edward Harvey	.	31 Dec. 1830	.	.
960 Duncan Macdonell Chisholm	24 May 1831	.	.	.
Stephen Rowley Conroy	27 Jan. 1832	.	.	.
Hon. Frederick William Child Villiers	10 Feb. 1832	.	.	.
Henry Brand	20 Apr. 1832	.	.	.
George Herbert	22 June 1832	.	.	.

APPENDIX.   519

ROLL.—*Continued.*

Jun. Major.	Sen. Major.	Lieut.-Col.	Colonel.	REMARKS.
			.	{ From Ensign in the Ninety-third Foot. Promoted to Captain, half-pay unattached, 22nd October, 1825.
			.	{ Adjutant from 16th May, 1829. Effective in January, 1833.
			.	{ From Ensign in the Sixty-second Foot Effective in January, 1833.
			.	Effective in January, 1833.
			.	930 { From Ensign in the Thirty-sixth Foot. (Late Page of Honour to the King.) Effective in January, 1833.
			.	Retired 20th September, 1826.
			.	Effective in January, 1833.
-			.	Effective in January, 1833.
			.	{ Appointed from Lieutenant-Colonel on half-pay unattached. Exchanged to ditto, 4th December, 1828.
			.	935 { From Captain and Brevet Lieut.-Colonel, on half-pay of the Twelfth Dragoons. Died 24th November, 1832, in London.
			.	{ From Ensign in the Seventieth Foot. Retired 30th September, 1829.
			.	Effective in January, 1833.
			.	{ From Second Lieutenant in the Rifle Brigade. Effective in January, 1833.
			.	Effective in January, 1833.
			.	940 { From Page of Honour to the King. Effective in January, 1833.
			.	{ Adjutant from 10th February, 1832. Effective in January, 1833.
			.	{ Promoted to Captain, half-pay unattached, 24th May, 1831.
			.	{ From Ensign in the Fifty-third Foot. Effective in January, 1833.
.	.	.	.	Effective in January, 1833.
.	.	.	.	945 Effective in January, 1833.
.	.	.	.	Effective in January, 1833.
.	.	.	.	{ Exchanged from Captain on half-pay unattached. Effective in January, 1833.
.	.	.	.	{ Gentleman Cadet from R.M.C. Effective in January, 1833.
.	.	.	.	Effective in January, 1833.
.	.	.	.	950 { Exchanged from Captain on half-pay unattached. Effective in January, 1833.
.	.	.	.	Effective in January, 1833.
.	.	.	.	Effective in January, 1833.
.	.	.	.	Effective in January, 1833.
.	.	.	.	Effective in January, 1833.
.	.	.	.	955 Effective in January, 1833.
.	.	.	.	Effective in January, 1833.
.	.	.	.	{ From Ensign in the Forty-second Foot. Effective in January, 1833.
.	.	.	.	Effective in January, 1833.
.	.	.	.	{ Exchanged from Captain on half-pay unattached. Effective in January, 1833.
.	.	.	.	960 Effective in January, 1833.
.	.	.	.	Effective in January, 1833.
.	.	.	.	Effective in January, 1833.
.	.	.	.	Effective in January, 1833.
.	.	.	.	Effective in January, 1833.

APPENDIX.
STAFF OFFICERS.

ADJUTANTS.	Second Adjutant.	First Adjutant.	REMARKS.
John Miller	.	.	Adjutant-General to Monck, 1659. Promoted to Major of the regiment, 21st July, 1665.
. . .	.	. June 1661	A regimental Adjutant appointed.
Ralph Edgerton	.	1 Aug. 1665	Out of the regiment in 1680.
James Bridgeman	.	Prior to 1683	Promoted to a company in the Coldstream 1st April, 1684.
5 Robert Wilkins	.	1 Apr. 1684	Ditto in October, 1688.
William Mathew	.	18 Oct. 1688	Promoted in the regiment Oct. 1690.
Edward Jones (2nd Battalion)	1 Jan. 1688/9	.	Retired on his pay 1st January, 1696.
Magnus Kempenfelt	.	1 Nov. 1690	From Quarter-Master. Resigned the Adjutantcy April, 1693.
John Wyvell	.	1 May, 1693	Left the regiment in December, 1703.
10 William Stevenage (2nd Battalion)	1 Mar. 1696	.	Appointed regimental Quarter-Master 1st April, 1703.
Richard Gore	3 Apr. 1705	.	Resigned in March, 1710.
Thomas Brushfield	.	4 May 1705	Left the regiment in March, 1710.
John Folliott	.	25 Mar. 1710	Resigned the Adjutantcy in Nov. 1713.
John Parsons	. Apr. 1710	.	Appointed regimental Quarter-Master 30th November, 1710.
15 John Uthwayt	16 Dec. 1710	.	Left the regiment in June, 1712.
John Moody	27 June, 1712	.	Appointed Lieutenant-Governor of Placentia in March, 1713.
William Birbero	7 Mar. 1712/3	.	Reduced as jun. Adjut. 24th May, 1713.
Sir Winwood Mowatt, Bart.	.	16 Nov. 1713	Left the regiment in July, 1715.
John Folliott (Lieut. Col.)	.	30 July, 1715	Re-appointed. Resigned the Adjutantcy 27th February, 1720.
20 William Birbero	24 Oct. 1715	.	Re-appointed. Resigned the Adjutantcy 23rd May, 1723.
Samuel Needham	.	28 Feb. 1720	Resigned the Adjutantcy 15th Mar.1740.
Thomas Hapgood	24 May, 1723	16 Mar. 1740	Died in February, 1744.
	Junior Adjutant.	Senior Adjutant.	
John Salter	16 Mar. 1740	13 Feb. 1744	Appointed Adjutant in the First Foot Guards 6th April, 1743.
William Gansell	13 Feb. 1744	7 Apr. 1743	Promoted to Captain-Lieutenant in the regiment 28th November, 1749.
25 Richard Hicks	18 Apr. 1743	. .	Resigned the Adjutantcy 27th Oct. 1746.
William Alexander Sorrell	28 Oct. 1746	28 Nov. 1749	Promoted to a company in the Coldstream 8th April, 1758.
Thomas D'Avenant	21 Dec. 1749	8 Apr. 1758	Resigned the Adjutantcy 18th Aug. 1763.
Charles Rainsford	8 Apr. 1758	.	Promoted to a company in the Coldstream 5th May, 1761.
John Lambton	24 Aug. 1761	19 Aug. 1763	Exchanged to a company in the Seventy-ninth Foot 11th Jan. 1764.
30 George Morgan	19 Aug. 1763	12 Jan. 1764	Sold the Adjutantcy 8th March, 1774.
Edmond Stevens	12 Jan. 1764	8 Mar. 1774	Promoted to a company in the First Foot Guards 15th May, 1778.

STAFF OFFICERS.—*Continued.*

ADJUTANTS.	Junior Adjutant.	Senior Adjutant.	REMARKS.
Thomas Willett Saltren	8 Mar. 1774	30 July, 1778	Sold the Adjutancy 9th July, 1779.
John Byron	30 July, 1778	.	Resigned the Adjutancy 20th June, 1779.
Thomas Bosville	21 June, 1779	9 July, 1779	Resigned the Adjutancy 21st June, 1782.
35 George Gibson	9 July, 1779	.	Sold the Adjutancy 1st Sept. 1781.
John Edwards Freemantle	1 Sept. 1781	22 June, 1782	Promoted to Captain-Lieutenant in the Coldstream 13th Oct. 1790.
Nathaniel Webb	22 June, 1782	.	Sold the Adjutancy 5th Sept. 1787.
Edwin Hewgill	5 Sept. 1787	14 Oct. 1790	Promoted to a company in the Coldstream 22nd January, 1794.
William Wynyard	15 Oct. 1790	.	Appointed Deputy-Adjutant-General on the Continent in Dec., 1793.
40 Kenneth Alexander Howard	11 Dec. 1793	22 Jan. 1794	Promoted to Captain-Lieutenant in the Coldstream 30th Dec., 1797.
Arthur Brice	22 Jan. 1794	.	Promoted to Captain-Lieutenant in the Coldstream 2nd Dec., 1795.
Harry Chester	9 Dec. 1795	30 Dec. 1797	Promoted to a company in the regiment 18th January, 1799.
Hon. Arthur Percy Upton	30 Dec. 1797	18 Jan. 1799	Appointed A.D.C. in November, 1799.
Sir Gilbert Stirling, Bart.	18 Jan. 1799	21 Nov. 1799	Resigned the Adjutancy 25th May, 1803.
45 Montagu J. Wynyard	21 Nov. 1799	26 May, 1803	Resigned the Adjutancy 13th April, 1808.
Charles Fane	26 May, 1803	.	Promoted to Major in the Eighth Foot 18th April, 1805.
George Bryan	1 May, 1805	14 Apr. 1808	Died of his wounds at Talavera 30th September, 1809.
Henry Dawkins	14 Apr. 1808	1 Oct. 1809	Appointed Major of Brigade in April, 1810.
John Freemantle	16 Nov. 1809	23 Apr. 1810	Resigned the Adjutancy 2nd December, 1812.
50 William Burroughs	23 Apr. 1810	.	Resigned the Adjutancy 3rd June, 1812.
Charles Antonio Ferdinand Bentinck	4 June, 1812	3 Dec. 1812	Resigned the Adjutancy 2nd February, 1820.
Edward Lascelles	3 Dec. 1812	.	Died 30th September, 1815.
John Prince	26 Oct. 1815	.	Died 2nd January, 1818.
Alexander Wedderburn	8 Jan. 1818	3 Feb. 1820	Promoted to a company in the regiment 17th April, 1823.
55 Henry John William Bentinck	3 Feb. 1820	17 Apr. 1823	Promoted to a company in the regiment 16th May, 1829.
Mark Beaufoy	17 Apr. 1823	.	Resigned the Adjutancy 9th February, 1825.
William Brook Northey	10 Feb. 1825	.	Resigned the Adjutancy 9th January, 1828.
William Henry Cornwall	10 Jan. 1828	16 May, 1829	Promoted to a company in the regiment 10th February, 1832.
Hon. James Hope	16 May, 1829	10 Feb. 1832	Effective in January, 1833.
60 Christopher Wilmot Horton	10 Feb. 1832	.	Effective in January, 1833.

APPENDIX.
STAFF OFFICERS.—*Continued.*

QUARTER-MASTERS.	Appointed.	REMARKS.
Henry Dennis	Prior to July 1659	Removed by Monck in October, 1659.
Richard Collins	. . 1660	. . .
Richard Washbourne	Prior to June 1675	Out of the regiment in December, 1679.
Matthew Ingram	Dec. 1679	Ditto in 1695.
5 Magnus Kempenfelt	1 Jan. 1688⅔	With the regiment in Flanders. Appointed Adjut. of the Coldstream 1st November, 1690.
William Bissett	1 Nov. 1690	Appointed to the batt. in Flanders. Promoted to Capt.-Lt. in the Fourth Foot 1st July, 1695.
Charles Wakelyn	15 July 1695	Promoted to a company in the Coldstream 4th May, 1705.
James Allen	. . 1702	Left the regiment in April, 1704.
William Stevenage	1 April 1703	Promoted to a company in the Coldstream 11th May, 1704.
10 Francis Scawen	11 May 1704	Promoted to a company in ditto 3rd Feb., 170¾.
William Swan	3 April 1705	Left the regiment in April, 1708.
William Matthew	24 April 1708	Resigned in November, 1710.
John Parsons	30 Nov. 1710	Resigned the Quar.-Mastership 23rd May, 1723.
Samuel Needham	19 July 1719	Appointed to the battalion going on the expedition to Vigo.
15 Edward Eaton	24 May 1723	Promoted to a company in the Coldstream 3rd April, 1733.
Hedworth Lambton	4 July 1733	Resigned the Quarter-Mastership 12th Feb., 174¼.
John Lambton	13 Feb. 174¼	Promoted to a company in the Coldstream 24th January, 174⅔.
William Evelyn	28 May 1742	Appointed to the first battalion under orders for foreign service.
George Needham	24 Jan. 174⅔	Exchanged to the Forty-sixth Foot 30th Apr., 1751.
20 William Wright	30 April 1751	Exchanged from the Forty-sixth Foot. Promoted Capt.-Lt. in the Coldstream 5th May, 1761.
William Hodenett	29 June 1761	From Serjeant-Major of the Coldstream. Died 2nd November, 1772.
Henry Harman	22 Dec. 1772	From Serjeant-Major, ditto. Placed on the Retired List 18th July, 1805.
Samuel Lunt	21 Jan. 1793	From Serjt.-Major ditto. Appointed Lieut. in Col. Poole's corps of Waggoners 27th Feb., 1794.
Thomas Williams	13 Mar. 1794	From Serjeant ditto. Placed on half-pay from 25th December, 1795.
25 John Holmes	25 Mar. 1798	From Serjeant-Major ditto. Placed on the Retired List 26th November, 1812.
James Findlay	18 July 1805	From Quarter-Master-Serjeant ditto. Promoted to Lieutenant in the Seventh Veteran battalion 10th April, 1806.
Edward Tomlin	17 April 1806	From Lieutenant in Twenty-fourth Foot. Died 7th October, 1812.
Thomas Dwelly	15 Oct. 1812	From Quarter-Master-Serjeant of the Coldstream. Effective in January, 1833.
Benjamin Selway	26 Nov. 1812	From Ensign and Adjutant of the Surry Local Militia. Effective in January, 1833.

APPENDIX. 523

STAFF OFFICERS.—*Continued*.

SURGEONS.	Assistant-Surgeon.	Surgeon.	Senior Surg. or Surg.-Maj.	REMARKS.
Nicholas Priddy	.	Prior to July, 1659	.	. . . . .
John Daniel Shambub	.	13 Dec. 1665	.	. . . . .
Joseph Troutbeck	.	Prior to 1671	.	. . . . .
John Brown	.	26 Mar. 1686	.	vice Troutbeck.
5 .... Baptist	.	4 Oct. 1695	.	. . . . .
Jacob D'Abbadie	.	Prior to 1702	.	. . . . .
John Wilson	.	25 Oct. 1707	.	Dead in May, 1713.
Ambrose Dickens	.	. May, 1713	.	Resigned 12th Dec.,1717.
John Harris, Junior	.	13 Dec. 1717	.	Left the Coldstream in November, 1726.
10 George Putland	.	1 Dec. 1726	.	Ditto March, 173¾.
William Ellis	.	14 Mar. 173¾	.	Retired 18th Jan., 174⅚.
Peter Triquet	.	19 Jan. 174⅚	.	Retired 7th May, 1780.
Francis Knight	.	8 May, 1780	.	Appointed Inspector-General of Army Hospitals 27th Dec., 1801.
George Rose	.	8 July, 1795	.	Wounded 8th March, 1801, on landing in Aboukir Bay, and died of his wounds March 11.
15 Bailie Robertson	25 Dec.*1796	.	.	Died 7th August, 1798.
John Fullelove	25 Dec. 1796	.	.	Appointed Surgeon to the light-infantry battalion of the brigade of Guards April 20, 1799.
George Edward Lawrence	} 25 Dec. 1796	.	.	Resigned 9th Oct., 1799.
James Thomas	25 Dec. 1796	.	.	Resigned 3rd April, 1798.
John Treadwell Simpson	} 4 April, 1798	.	11 Mar.† 1802	Appointed Surgeon to the light-infantry battalion of the brigade of Guards, 23d Jan., 1800. Re-appointed to the Coldstream March 11, 1802, from Surgeon of the Invalids at the Tower, by exchange with Surgeon Gilham. Retired 23rd February, 1825, on half-pay.
20 William Palmer	8 Aug. 1798	.	.	Resigned March 14, 1799.
John Allen Gilham	15 Mar. 1799	19 May, 1801	4 Mar. 1802	Exchanged with Surgeon Simpson to the Invalids at the Tower, 11th March, 1802.

* Previously to this, "Surgeon's Mates" were attached to the regiment; they were not commissioned by the King, but appointed by warrants from the Colonels.

† Extract of a letter from the Commander-in-Chief to the Secretary-at-War, dated Horse Guards, 18th April, 1804:—" The Senior Surgeons of the regiments of Guards are to have the " appellation of 'Surgeon-Major.' "

STAFF OFFICERS.—*Continued.*

SURGEONS.	Assistant-Surgeon.	Surgeon.	Senior Surgeon or Surg.-Major.	REMARKS.
John Burnall	20 April, 1799	4 Mar. 1802	. .	Appointed Apothecary to the Forces 15th August, 1805.
Peter M'Gregor	21 Nov. 1799	.	.	Appointed Surgeon to the Royal Military Asylum Feb. 9, 1804.
Charles Tyce	21 Jan. 1800	.	.	Resigned 22nd Oct., 1800.
25 Henry Robert Ince	26 June, 1800	.	.	Exchanged to Assistant-Surgeon on half-pay of the Invalids at the Tower, 29th Oct., 1802.
Henry Fearon	23 Oct. 1800	.	.	From Hospital Mate. On retired full pay from January, 1802.
Charles Coombe	19 May, 1801	15 Aug. 1805	.	Placed on half-pay from 26th November, 1812.
John Gordon M'Kenzie	11 Mar. 1802	.	.	Died 21st February, 1808.
John Crake	29 Oct. 1802	.	. .	Exchanged from Assistant-Surgeon on half-pay of the Invalids at the Tower. Promoted to Surgeon of Sixty-seventh Foot 22nd December, 1808.
30 Thomas Rose	31 Mar. 1804	26 Nov. 1812	.	Appointed Surgeon in Sixty-fourth Foot 30th April, 1818.
William Whymper (Sir William)	14 Nov. 1805	25 Dec. 1813	24 Feb. 1825	Effective in Jan., 1833.
Charles Herbert	3 Mar. 1808	.	.	Resigned 24th Oct., 1810.
Thomas Clarke	20 April, 1809	.	.	Resigned 3rd Oct., 1810.
James Owen	4 Oct. 1810	.	.	Superseded 20th Feb., 1811.
35 Edward Nixon	25 Oct. 1810	.	.	Resigned 28th April, 1813.
Thomas Maynard	21 Feb. 1811	28 May, 1818	.	Effective in Jan., 1833.
George Smith	17 Dec. 1812	24 Feb. 1825	.	Effective in Jan., 1833.
Septimus Worrell	29 April, 1813	.	.	Exchanged to half-pay of the regiment 23rd August, 1821.
William Hunter	{ 10 Feb. 1814 21 Feb. 1825 }	.	.	Placed on half-pay of the regiment from 25th Dec., 1818. Re-appointed 24th Feb., 1825. Effective in Jan., 1833.
40 Sherrington Gilder	{ 28 May, 1818 23 Aug. 1821 }	.	.	Placed on half-pay of the regiment from 25th Dec., 1818. Exchanged from ditto, 23rd Aug., 1821. Exchanged to half-pay of the First Foot Guards June 20, 1822.
Frederick Gilder	20 June, 1822	.	.	Exchanged from half-pay of the First Foot Guards. Effective in January, 1833.

STAFF OFFICERS.—*Continued.*

CHAPLAINS.	Appointed.	REMARKS.
John Price, D.D.	Prior to July, 1659	Resigned December, 1688.
John King, D.D.	31 Dec. 1688	Out in May, 1727.
Henry Pyniot, M.A.	6 May, 1727	Resigned 10th May, 1742.
John Jefferies, M.A.	11 May, 1742	Out in May, 1759.
5 John Loftie, M.A.	26 May, 1759	Retired 13th August, 1772.
Frederick Dodsworth, M.A.	14 Aug. 1772	Retired 30th July, 1778.
George Routh, M.A.	31 July, 1778	Retired 12th June, 1792.
George Trevelyan, M.A.	13 June, 1792	Exchanged to the Eleventh Dragoons 6th May, 1795.
John Gamble, M.A.	6 May, 1795	Exchanged from the Eleventh Dragoons. Appointed Chaplain-General to the Forces 21st September, 1796.

SOLICITORS.		
Russel Allsop	. 1689	Out in 1695.
John Acton	2 Apr. 1695	Out in 1710.
John Merrill	. Feb. 1710	Out in October, 1714.
William Burroughs	. Oct. 1714	Out in June, 1722.
5 Robert Mitchenor	25 June, 1722	Out in May, 1725.
James Adams	29 May, 1725	Out in February, 1725.
Robert Mitchenor	16 Feb. 1725	Died 1st June, 1744.
Gilbert Elliot	2 June, 1744	Died 30th March, 1765.
Justice Willis	12 Apr. 1765	Died 19th March, 1772.
10 Justice Willis, Junior	20 Mar. 1772	Died 24th June, 1792.
Thomas Lowten	27 June, 1792	Died 2nd January, 1814.
John Wilkinson	24 Feb. 1814	Died 10th December, 1823.
William George Carter	29 Jan. 1824	Effective in January, 1833.

NOTE.—It was the practice, up to the reign of Queen Anne, to grant fresh commissions to officers who exchanged, or were removed from one company to another. When a regiment was on foreign service, the Commander of the Forces filled up all vacancies without the knowledge or control of the Government at home: this privilege continued till the Peace in 1748; and it is in many instances become extremely difficult, and frequently impossible, to ascertain the names of the officers appointed abroad, or the dates of their commissions on promotion.   War-Office, January, 1833.

INDEX.

Abensberg, battle of, ii, 122
Abercrombie, Lieut.-Col., ii, 18, 51,53,67—defeats the French, 68—expedition under, 74—moves to Mandora, 78—his death, 81
Aboukir Castle, surrender of, ii, 78
Abrantes, arrangements of the British army on quitting the place, ii, 114
Adams, Samuel, declared a rebel, i, 432
Adjutants, first commissioned to the Guards, i, 108
Adolphus, Prince, (since Duke of Cambridge) wounded, ii, 45
Aire, taken, i, 329
Aix-la-Chapelle, treaty of peace signed at, i, 390
Alava, Gen., anecdote of, ii, 215
Albemarle, Duchess of, some account of, i, 129, 130
Albemarle, Duke, engages the Dutch off Dunkirk, i, 117—victory gained by, 118—his determination, 119—his person described, 128—his death, 129—his son succeeds him, 130—his funeral, 132—inscription on his coffin, 138—appoints Anthony Vincent his ensign, ii, 253—his order respecting matchlocks, 253
Albemarle, William Anne, (second Earl of,) Col. of the Coldstream, wounded, i, 359—his death, 393—some account of him, *ib.*

Albuera, battle of, ii, 163
Albuquerque, Duke del, retreat of, ii, 121—barricades the bridge of Zuozo, 130
Alexandria, battle of, ii, 81—capitulation of, 84
Alkmaar, forces of General Brune at, ii, 69—battle of, 71—capitulation of the town, *ib.*
Allen, Sir Thomas, fleet under, i, 140
Almanza, battle of, i, 308—English forces at, 309—loss at, 312
Almarez, bridge of, carried by General Hill, ii, 172
Almeida, invested, ii, 158—escape of General Brennier from, 162
Alured, Colonel, surprises a party of Charles's friends, i, 42
Alva, French retire behind the, ii, 146
America, preparations for reducing the British Colonies in, i, 430—proclamation of George III., 432—declared independent, ii, 21
Amiens, treaty of, ii, 87
Anderlecht, Confederates assemble at, i, 209
André, Major, taken as a spy and hanged, ii, 9
Anhalt, Prince of, i, 412
Anne, Queen, alienated from Marlborough, i, 337—death of, 341
Anson, Lord, sails for the Bay of Biscay, i, 394

Antwerp, intended attack on, ii, 124
Arapiles, village of, struggle for its occupation, ii, 175
Argyle, taken prisoner, i, 180
Arlington, Lord, letters of, ii, 254, 255
Armstrong, Lieut.-Col., battalion under, ii, 90
Army, English, in Scotland, force of, i, 37 — marches into the Highlands, 53
Army of Portugal, under Massena, ii, 132
Army, Scotch, defeated at Dunbar, i, 23—statement respecting, 36
Arnold, the American General, ii, 9—takes New London, 17
Arran, Earl of, his regiment, i, 109
Arzobispo, arrival of the Allies at, ii, 121
Aschaff, a small river, i, 354
Asgill, Captain, imprisonment of, ii, 19
Assessments, mode of levying, i, 7
Ath, invested by the French, i, 268 —taken, 270—council of war at, ii, 50
Athlone, Lord, bombards Givet, i, 262
Austerlitz, battle of, ii, 92
Austria, unites with Russia against France, ii, 184
Austria, Emperor of, accedes to the treaty of Petersburg, ii, 90

Bacon, Serjeant, reprimanded, i, 428
Badajoz, invested by Beresford, ii, 158, 163—blockade of, 164— capitulation of, 171—prisoners taken in, ib.—loss of the Allies at, ib.
Baird, Sir David, Indian army under, ii, 85—forms a junction with Sir John Moore at Mayorga, 102
Bandaris, town of, burnt, i, 120
Barcellar, General, ii, 138, 145
Barcelona, projected expedition to, i, 290—taken, 293—invested by the French, 296
Barri, wood of, i, 367

Barrosa, battle of, ii, 156
Bavaria, Elector of, army under, i, 228
Bayonets, provided for the two regiments of Guards, i, 184—their introduction into the French army, ib.—first adopted in the English army, 185—used instead of pikes, 222, 223
Bayonne, blockaded by the Allies, ii, 200—desperate sortie from, 202
Beaumont, advance of King William to, i, 212
Bell, Mr., his observations on the regalia of Scotland quoted, i, 34, 49
Beresford, Major-Gen., appointed commander-in-chief of the Portuguese levies, ii, 104—invests Badajoz, 158, 163—enters Bourdeaux, 201
Bergen-op-Zoom, siege of, i, 389 Guards embark for, ii, 34—battle of, 70—failure of the attack on, 205
Berwick, re-taken from the Scots, i, 7—arrival of Major-General Lambert at, 47
Berwick, Duke of, taken prisoner, i, 232—stratagem of, 310
Besieux, British encamp at, i, 338
Beverwick, position of the French at, ii, 72
Bidassoa, forded by the Allies, ii, 190
Birch, Colonel, his address to the soldiers, i, 100
Bissett, Lieut.-Col., i, 295—memorial of, 313
Blackness, surrenders to General Monck, i, 35
Bligh, Lieut.-Gen., command entrusted to, i, 396—marches for Guildo, 399
Blucher, Marshal, retires on Wavre, ii, 212
Bois-le-Duc, quarters of the British at, i, 390
Boniface, gallantry of, i, 116
Bonnet, General, reinforces the French at Tordesillas, ii, 173
Boston, arrival of Generals Howe, Burgoyne, and Clinton at, i, 432

INDEX.

Bosville, Lieut.-Col., killed, ii, 43
Bouchain, siege of, i, 336
Boufflers, Marshal, marches to Tournay, i, 246—taken prisoner, 259—liberated, *ib.*—encamps at Parck, 263—army under, 264—repasses the Sambre, *ib.*—opposes the investment of Mons, 321—dispatch of, 324—prepares the defence of Landau, 360
Bouge, village of, affair near, i, 247
Bourdeaux, entry of the Allies into, ii, 201
Bowes, Major-Gen., killed, ii, 172
Brabant, army of, i, 265—takes the field, 267
Braddock, Col. Edward, his battalion of Guards, i, 388—embarks for Flushing, 389
Braga, arrival of the British at, ii, 112
Brakel, British camp at, i, 417
Brandenburg, Elector of, besieges Keyserswaert, i, 203—takes the fortress of Bonn, 203
Brandywine, battle of, i, 445
Bremen, retreat of the British to, ii, 62—arrival of the Coldstream at, 91
Brennier, General, escapes from Almeida, ii, 162
Brest, expedition against, i, 242
Brice, Lt.-Col., his death, ii, 79
Bridgeman, Col. James, i, 216
Brodrick's History of the late War in the Netherlands, i, 312
Broghill, Lord, entertainment given to, i, 66
Broglio, Duke, commands the French forces, i, 404 — reinforced, 409
Brooks, Nathan, his Army-List, i, 169
Brown, Corporal, extracts from his Journal, ii, 39, 43, 51
Brucken Muhl, battle of, i, 425
Bruges, submits to the French, i, 373
Brunswick, proceedings of the Royalists at, i, 441
Brussels, council of war held at, i, 262, 364 — forces under the Duke of Wellington at, ii, 209
Buckingham, Duke of, his Memoirs, i, 144, 154

Buhne, village of, i, 407
Buonaparte, Prince Jerome, column commanded by, ii, 215
Buonaparte, Joseph, proclaimed King of Spain, ii, 100—enters Seville, 130—quits Madrid and unites with Marmont, 177—joins Suchet, 178—commands the army at Vittoria, 186—defeated, 187
Buonaparte, sails from Toulon for Egypt, ii, 74—his losses with the Turks and Mamelukes, 75—total overthrow of his power in Egypt, 85—his selfish policy, *ib.*—made President of the Cisalpine Republic, 87—First Consul for life, *ib.*—crowned at Paris, 89—his threatened invasion of England, 87, 90—crosses the Rhine, 91—induces Ferdinand to cede his claims to the Spanish throne, 100—imperial decree of, *ib.*—returns to Paris and determines to place his brother Joseph on the Spanish throne, 101—his proclamation at Madrid, 102—gains the battle of Abensberg, 122—defeats the Arch-Duke Charles at Eckmuhl, 123—energy of, 125—his objects in invading Spain and Portugal, 151—his expedition to Russia, 176—his loss there, 184 — concentrates his force, 184—his abdication, 202—escapes from Elba, 208—quits Paris, and heads the troops, 209 — proclamation of, *ib.* — defeats the Prussians at St. Amand, 211 — his objects at the battle of Waterloo, 222
Burgos, siege of, ii, 178—loss of the Allies during it, 179—siege raised, 180
Burgoyne, General, i, 432—takes the command of the Northern army, 448
Burke's Extinct Peerage, quoted, i, 130
Burnet, Bishop, quoted, i, 10, 283, 284, 291, 293, 300, 308
Burrard, Major-Gen., his brigade of guards, ii, 67
Busaco, battle of, ii, 136

Cadiz, expedition against, i, 279 force of the Allies at, ii, 132

Cadogan, Earl of, appointed Colonel of the Coldstream, i, 343—services of, 349

Cæsar, Col., marches to Dol, near St. Maloes, i, 395—three battalions under his command, 407—his death, 422

Calcraft, Colonel of the Coldstream, ii, 64

Callender House, surrenders to Cromwell, i, 38

Cambacères, his communication to Buonaparte, ii, 88

Cambridge, Duke of, appointed Colonel of the Coldstream, ii, 90

Campbell, Brigadier-Gen., ii, 102

Campbell's Lives of the Admirals, i, 118, 142, 146

Capilio, town of, i, 302

Cardonnel, Mr., his letter respecting the battle of Malplaquet, i, 327—extract of a letter from him, 328

Carleton, General, succeeds Sir Henry Clinton, ii, 21

Carleton's Memoirs, quoted, i, 187, 290, 291, 293, 301, 311

Carlisle, surrenders to Charles Edward, son of the Pretender, i, 376

Cartaxo, arrival of the Guards at, ii, 141

Carteret, Lord, quoted, i, 359

Castries, Marshal de, i, 418

Catawba, forded by the British, ii, 11

Cateau, heights of, occupied by the British, ii, 52

Cathcart, Lord, force under, ii, 90—expedition under, against the Danes, 95

Catinat, Marshal, invests Ath, i, 268

Cavan, Earl of, appointed to the command of the brigade of Guards, ii, 82

Chamberlayne's account of the Foot Guards, i, 274

Chanclos, Lieut.-Gen., capitulation of, i, 374

Charlemont, Lord, i, 292

Charleroi, attempt on, i, 225—siege of, 235, 236

Charles II., war between, and the Parliament, i, 14—his escape after the battle of Worcester, 39—meditates the invasion of England, 69—his reception in London, 107—his arrival at Bath, 112—reviews his Foot and Life Guards, 123—proclaimed King, 94—his triumphal entry into London, 95—reviews his troops, 96—his order respecting the precedency of regiments, 148—at variance with Lewis XIVth, 156—two companies of the Coldstream Guards attend him to Oxford, 163—reviews his troops on Putney Heath, 170—his death, 172

Charles II., king of Spain, his death, i, 277—commission of, appointing Monck Captain-General of the Forces, ii, 239—his order as to the regulations to be observed by the troops, 250

Charles IV. abdicates the throne of Spain, ii, 99—cedes his claims in favour of Napoleon, 100

Charles Edward, eldest son of the Pretender, attempt of, i, 374—his person described, *ib.*—lands in Scotland, 375—his successes over the King's troops, *ib.*—encamps at Dalkeith, 376—reaches Derby and proclaims his father King, *ib.*—his arrival at Manchester, 377—retreat of, 378—enters Preston, *ib.*—continues to retire, 382—reinforced at Perth, *ib.*—want of discipline in his troops, 383—retraces his steps to Culloden, *ib.*—completely defeated, 384—escapes to France, *ib.*—his romantic adventures, *ib.*—anecdote of him, 385

Charles, Prince, enthusiastic reception of, i, 293—his misunderstanding with Lord Peterborough, 296—deserts Galway, 306

Charles, Prince of Lorraine, his success in Bavaria, i, 355—crosses the Rhine and enters France, 361—army under, 362

Chateaurenard, attacked by Sir G. Rooke, i, 284

Chatham, Lord, expedition under, ii, 123—sufferings of his army, 124
Cherbourg, British fleet before, i, 396, 397 — army disembark and enter the town, *ib.*—conduct of the soldiery at, *ib.*—troops re-embark, 398
Churchill, Col. John, i, 147—brigade commanded by, 160
Churchill, Gen. Charles, appointed Colonel of the Coldstream, i, 305—his resignation, 343—some account of him, *ib.*
Ciudad-Rodrigo, capitulates to Marshal Massena, ii, 133 — blockaded by Lord Wellington, 164—capture of, 169
Clarendon, extracts from, i, 5, 15, 192
Clarges, Ann, married to the Duke of Albemarle, i, 129
Clarke, Mr. Wm., his letters to Mr. Lenthall, i, 40, 54, 61
Clarke, Rev. T. S., his Life of James II, i, 69, 99, 117, 136, 154, 164, 197, 198
Clausel, General, command of the French army devolves on, ii, 177—retreats to Valladolid, 177
Clephane, Col., gallantry of, ii, 72
Clerk, Major, i, 30
Cleves, Castle of, surrenders, i, 408
Clinton, Major-Gen., i, 432—joins the army 436—remonstrance of, 441—appointed Commander-in-Chief in America, ii, 2—dispatch of, 3—proceeds to New York, 4 —dispatches from, 15—puts to sea to relieve Lord Cornwallis, 20—returns to New York, *ib.*—defeats the French at Arapiles, 175
Clothing, committee for supplying the army with, ii, 60
Coimbra, reception of the Guards at, ii, 108—arrival of Sir Arthur Wellesley at, 109—head-quarters of Massena at, 139
Coldstream Guards, owe their origin to General Monck, i, 1—five companies drafted from Hesilrige's regiment and five companies from Fenwick's, 4—placed on the establishment of the Commonwealth, *ib.*—enter Scotland with Cromwell, 10—sketch of Monck's life, 12—present at the taking of Collington House, 22—storming of Redhall, *ib.*—assist in the defeat of the Scots army at Dunbar, 23—engaged in the reduction of Derlton House, 32—Edinburgh Castle, 33 — Tantallon Castle, 34 — Blackness, 35 —encamp near Redhall, 37 — present at the taking of Callender House, 38—beleaguerment of Stirling Castle, 39—which capitulates, 40—the regiment proceeds to Dundee, 41—storming of that place, 43—illness of Monck, 44—Montrose, Aberdeen, &c. taken, *ib.*—winter quarters of the army, 45—siege of Dunotter Castle, 48—which surrenders, *ib.*—the regiment marches into the Highlands, 53 — command devolves on Col. Morgan, 55—Col. Monck appointed General of the Fleet, 57—the Dutch defeated, *ib.*—medals, &c. voted to the officers, 58—war re-commences in the Highlands, 59—Monck resumes his command of the troops in Scotland, 60--enters Stirling, 61—Loch Tay island, &c. taken, *ib.*—Morgan defeats Middleton, 62—Monck's headquarters at Dalkeith, 63—two companies strengthen the garrison at Berwick, 64—letter from Monck and the officers of his regiment, 69—names of the officers in Monck's regiments read to the House, 70—Monck determines to support the Parliament, 72 — secures several strongholds in Scotland, *ib.* — letters detailing his proceedings, 73—officers sent by Monck to treat with the Committee of Safety, 80—names of officers who abandoned him, 81—his army assembles at Coldstream, 82—his march from Coldstream, 85—

gives the command of his own regiment to Captain Morgan, *ib.* —the Coldstreamers enter London, 88 — Parliament orders Monck to restore order in the city, 93—the regiment encamped at Blackheath to receive Charles II., 94—Monck created Duke of Albemarle, 95—the troops reviewed by the King, 96— the Coldstream constituted his household troops, 98 — adjutants first commissioned in the Guards, 108 — reviewed by Charles II., 110—Capt. Holmes reduces the New Netherlands, 114—a detachment from the Lord General's regiment goes on board the fleet destined to act against the Dutch, 116—Albemarle in conjunction with Prince Rupert commands the fleet, 117 —defeats the Dutch, 118—precedency of regiments, 121— death of Albemarle, 129—his funeral, 130—Earl Craven succeeds to the command of the regiment, 137—a detachment embarks for the Mediterranean, 139—two companies drafted into Monmouth's regiment, 141 — engagement between the English and Dutch fleets, *ib.*—the Coldstreamers disembark, and return to their quarters, 142— a company embarks at Dover, and forms part of a regiment to remain in the service of Lewis XIV., *ibid.*—detachments from the Coldstream embark, and the fleet sails, *ib.*—precedency of regiments, 143—six companies go on board the fleet under Prince Rupert, *ibid.*—battalion under the command of Captain Skelton returns to London, 146 —Monmouth's letter to Craven on the rank of regiments, 148— the Coldstream reviewed by the King, 150—drafts from the regiment to serve in Virginia, 155— first introduction of grenadiers, 156—the regiment augmented, 157 — four companies embark for Ostend, 158—services of a brigade in Flanders, 160 —its return to London, 161 reduction in the regiment, *ib.*— quartered at Somerset-house, *ibid.* — a detachment sails for Tangiers, 162—two companies attend Charles II. to Oxford, 163—King's Mews fitted up as a barrack, 164 — Col. Edward Sackville appointed lieutenant-colonel, 166—pedestrian feat of Captain Wakelin of the Coldstream, 167—change in the arms of the regiment, *ib.*—return of the battalion from Tangiers, 168—Another Grenadier company added to the regiment, *ib.* —change in the appointments of Infantry officers, 169—reviewed by the King on Putney Heath, 170—their dress on the coronation of James II., 173—list of the officers of the, under Earl Craven, 175—first battalion leaves town for Marlborough, 179—reduction in the regiment, 181—bayonets provided for it, 184—reviewed at Hounslow, 186—rank of Lieut.-Col. granted to Captains, 190—four additional companies added to, 191—the regiment ordered into Kent, on the arrival of William in London, 197 — Lord Craven succeeded by Col. Talmash, 201—some account of Lord Craven, *ib.*— with the Allies under Prince Waldeck, 202—proceed to the relief of Walcourt, 203—billeted at Ghent, 204 — battle of Fleurus, 206—join the army under Prince Waldeck, 207— quartered in Brussels, *ibid.*— the King takes the command, 208—rank of Captains given to Lieutenants, 211 — command given to Col. James Bridgeman, 216—reviewed at Genappe, 217 — battle of Steenkirk, 218 — officers killed there, 220—sent to occupy Dixmuyde, 224—at Parck Camp, 228—battle of Landen, 232 — reinforcements sent from England, 236—siege of Charleroi, 236—investment of Hüy, 240—straw huts of the regiment destroyed by fire, 241—death of Lieut.-Gen. Talmash, 242—Lord Cutts becomes Colonel, *ib.*— expedition against Brest, *ib.*—Lord Cutts arrives at the camp at Templeux with six battalions, 246—which suffer severely in an assault near Bouge, 247 — Lord Cutts appointed Brigadier, 249 — siege of Namur, 252—the Guards proceed to Ghent, 260—arrive at Gravesend, 262—return to Flanders, *ibid.* — Lord Cutts appointed Major-General; 263—two battalions proceed with King William to Wavre, *ibid.* — leave Ghent for the villages between Brussels and Halle, 267—siege of Ath, 269 — return of the Guards to England, 272—disembark at Harwich, 273 — Chamberlayne's account of the regiment, 274 — Third Guards on the establishment, 275—expedition to Cadiz, 279—disposition of the Guards, July 1st, 1702, 280—gallant conduct of Col. Pierce, 282—attack on Fort Matagorda, *ib.*—troops re-embark, after blowing up St. Catherine's, 283—Confederates attack Chateaurenard in the Harbour of Vigo, 284—Rodendella taken, *ib.*—a battalion ordered to proceed to Portugal with Lord Galway, 286—lands at Lisbon, *ib.*—goes to the relief of Gibraltar, 287—the enemy retire, after seven months' siege, 289—expedition to Barcelona, 290—attack on Montjuich, 291— Barcelona taken, 292 — garrison remains with Prince Charles, 293—Lord Peterborough proceeds to Valencia, 294—detachments embark for Spain, 295—Philip attempts to recover Barcelona, 296 — Barcelona invested, 297—Lord Donnegal arrives with four regiments from Gerona, *ib.*—conflict at Montjuich, 299—death of Lord Donnegal, *ib.*—French raise the siege, 300 — troops sail for Valencia, 301—Earl of Galway takes Ciudad Rodrigo, *ib.*—cruelty to a party of the Coldstream, 302—Gen. Charles Churchill appointed Colonel on the death of Lord Cutts, 305—new colours given to the regiment, 307—use of pikes discontinued, *ib.* — sufferings of the troops at the battle of Almanza, 313 — a battalion ordered to Scotland, 314—countermanded at York, and sent to Colchester, *ib.*—embarks for Flanders, 315 —battle of Oudenarde, 317—capitulation of Lisle, 318 — quartered at Brussels, 319 — surrender of Tournay, 321 — battle of Malplaquet, 322—loss of the Allies, 325—capitulation of Mons, 328—army goes into winter-quarters, 329—two additional companies sent to Harwich, 330 — detachment countermanded, from the difficulty of providing for the Tower duty, 333 — Second-Major first appointed to the regiment, 333—Ormond succeeds Marlborough in the command of the army, 338 — which encamps at Besieux, *ib.* — suspension of hostilities, 339—troops arrive from Ghent at Gravesend, 340—Earl of Cadogan succeeds General Churchill, 343—four additional companies raised, 345—the regiment reviewed by the Prince of Wales, *ib.*—seven companies embark for Corunna, 336—Vigo taken, *ib.*—rates paid for commissions, *ibid.* — Duke of Grafton purchases Col. John Russell's commission, 348—the Earl of Scarborough appointed Colonel, *ib.*—services of Cadogan, 349 — troops attend the Coronation of George II., 350 the Duke of Cumberland succeeds as Colonel, 351—who is succeeded by the Duke of Marlborough, *ibid.* — first battalions embark at Deptford and Woolwich for Flanders, 353—move towards the Rhine, 353—George II. joins the Confederates in Germany, 354—battle of Dettingen, 356—Allies arrive at Hanau, 359—treaty of Worms, 360 — the Duke of Cumberland appointed Commander-in-Chief of the Confederate forces, 364—investment of Tournay, 365—battle of Fontenoy, 366—Ghent taken by surprise, 373—Bruges, Oudenarde, Ostend, &c. submit to the French, *ib.*—arrival of the Guards in England, 376—troops proceed to the North to oppose the young Pretender, 377—battle of Culloden, 384—intended expedition under Admiral Lestock and Gen. Sinclair, 387—second battalion proceeds to Flushing, 389—employed at the siege of Bergen-op-Zoom, *ib.*—in quarters at Bois-le-Duc, 390—Serjeants discontinue wearing ruffles, *ib.*—Guards return to England on the treaty of Aix-la-Chapelle, 391—receive new colours, *ib.*—use of wooden ramrods, 393—expedition destined for the coast of France, 394—troops march for Dol, 395—enter Cherbourg, 397—re-embark, 398—land to the westward of St. Maloes, *ib.*—defeated at St. Cas, 400—return to London, 402—the three battalions of Guards, under the command of Major-Gen. Julius Cæsar, join the Allies near the village of Buhne, 407—Hereditary Prince surprises Zierenberg, 408—surrender of Cleves, *ib.* — attempt to surprise the French camp, *ib.*—Allies move by Genderick, 409—Duderstadt taken and retaken, 411 — brigade of Guards joins the advance, *ib.*—enemy defeated by Prince Ferdinand at Kirchdenkern, *ib.* — troops cross the Rhine, 415—in camp at Brakel, 417—battle of Gravenstein, 418 — concentrate at Holtzhausen and Weimar, 420 — castle of Waldeck capitulates, 421—attack on Melsungen, 423—battle of Brucken Muhl, 424—the Guards embark at Williamstadt, and arrive at Yarmouth, 427—Waldegrave succeeds Lord Tyrawley as Colonel of the regiment, 430—forces raised to reduce the American Colonies, 431 — Generals Howe, Burgoyne, and Clinton, arrive at Boston, 432—battalion under Colonel Mathew embarks for America, 433—arrives at Staten Island, 434—disembarks near Utrecht, 435—operations of the army near Flat Bush, 436—the enemy compelled to retreat from Long Island, 438—British take possession of New York, *ibid.* — reinforced by foreign troops in English pay, 439—Fort Washington and Fort Lee carried by assault, 440 — Lord Cornwallis further reinforced, *ibid.* — moves forward to Prince Town, 441—Gen. Clinton and Sir Peter Parker take possession of Rhode Island, *ib.*—the Guards formed into two battalions, 442 —proceed to Amboy, 444—Sir William Howe determines to quit the Jerseys, *ib.*—success of Gen. Knyphausen at Chad's Ford, 445—battle of Brandywine, *ib.*—inactivity of Howe, 446—Washington attacks the British at Germantown, 447—Fort of Mud Island abandoned, *ib.*—Howe retires to Philadelphia, 448—battle of Freehold Court House, ii, 3—Guards embark for Virginia, 5 — surrender of Fort La Fayette, *ib.* — troops embark for Newhaven, *ib.*—town taken, *ib.* —army marches through Fairfield, 6—shipping, stores, &c. burnt, *ib.*—troops re-embark, *ib.* —land at Norwalk, and Greenfield, *ib.*—both places destroyed, —English return to New York, *ib.*—Guards form part of the garrison during the winter, *ib.* — Clinton embarks at Sandy Hook to reduce South Carolina, *ib.*—Lord Stirling attempts to take Staten Island, *ib.* — Young's House taken, 7—army crosses the Catawba, 11 — Guards distinguish themselves, *ibid.* — attack on the enemy's lines at Guildford Court House, 12 — British move towards Wilmington, 15 — Cornwallis reaches Petersburg, crosses the Roanoke, Meherren, and Nottaway rivers, 15 — army reinforced through Hanover county, *ib.* — Cornwallis defeats La Fayette, *ib.*—Crosses James River, and concentrates in York Town, 16—that place invested, 17—Cornwallis surrenders, 19—Carleton succeeds in command, 21 — Returns of the officers who served in America, 22—Lord Waldegrave succeeded as Colonel by Frederick Duke of York, 30—first battalions embark for Holland, 34—march to Orcq, *ib.*—attack the French near St. Amand, 35 — Condé blockaded, 39—investment of Valenciennes, *ib.*—carried by the Duke of York, *ib.*—surrender of Condé, 40—defeat of the French at Lincelles, 43—siege of Dunkirk, 45—troops move towards Menin, *ib.*—defeat the French at Lannoy, 47—occupy St. Peter's barracks at Ghent, 48—Return of officers of the first battalion on the Continent, *ib.* — reinforcements sent from England, 49—success of the two columns under the Duke of York, 51—siege of Landrecy, 52—French driven from Cæsar's Camp, and defeated near Cateau, *ib.*—the enemy compelled to evacuate Lannoy, 53 — Allies repulsed near Fleurus, 59 — retreat to Romaux, *ib.*—light companies at home embark for the Continent, *ibid.* — army crosses the Maese, 60 — Walmoden succeeds in command, 61—spirited affair at Rhenen, *ib.*—troops retreat to Deventer, *ib.*—to Bremen, 62—embark at Bremenlee, 63—land at Greenwich, and march to London, *ib.* — light companies sent to Ostend, 64 — first battalions proceed to Ireland, 66 — expedition to Holland, 67—two brigades of Guards embark, *ib.*—land near the Helder Point, *ib.*—Dutch fleet surrenders, 68—French and Batavians repulsed, *ib.* — battle of Alkmaar, *ib.*—battle of Bergen, 71—first battalion lands at Yarmouth, 73 — joins the expedition under Abercrombie, 74—attack on the French lines, 77—battle of Alexandria, 78—arrival of reinforcements, 82—Cavan appointed to command the brigade of Guards, *ib.* — Marabout capitulates, 83—surrender of Alexandria, 84—army returns to England, 86—peace of Amiens, 87—war with France, *ib.*—first battalions, under Finch, proceed to Chelmsford, *ib.*—march for Cox-Heath Camp, 89 — in quarters at Chatham, *ibid.* — reviewed at Wimbledon, *ib.*—Duke of York succeeds in command of the First Guards, *ibid.* — Duke of Cambridge appointed Colonel of the regiment, 90 — treaty of Petersburgh, *ib.*—first battalion embarks under Lord Cathcart, *ib.* — lands at Cuxhaven and marches to Bremen, 91—battle of Austerlitz, 92 — expedition returns to England, *ib.*—officers address the Duke of York, 94—Duke's reply, *ib.*—investment of Copenhagen, 97—troops re-embark, 99—go into barracks at Chatham, *ib.*—second brigade embarks at Ramsgate, 102—fleet sails for Cadiz, 103—proceeds to the Tagus, *ib.*—nine companies of the first battalion land at Lisbon, 104—march through Saccavem and Batalha to Lyria,

105—proceed to Coimbra, 108—Wellington advances against Oporto, 109—the Guards halt at Scavessade Rio, 110—return to Oporto, 112—march through Coimbra, Thomar, and concentrate at Abrantes, 113—advance to Talavera de la Reyna, 120—suffer severely for want of provisions, 116—battle of Talavera, 118—Allies cross the Tagus at Arzobispo, 121—fall back to Zaraicejo, 121—flank companies of the second battalion embark at Flushing, 124—British army crosses the Tagus, 126—Eleven companies proceed to Cadiz, 132—Capture of Ciudad Rodrigo, 133—battle of Busaco, 136—army retires to the lines of Torres Vedras, 139—pursues Massena towards Santarem, 141—head-quarters at Cartaxo, *ib.*—passage of the Tagus, *ib.*—British army reinforced, 143—skirmish at Pombal, 144—French defeated at Sabugal, 148—Guards at Almadilla and Puebla, 155—battle of Barrosa, 157—Siege of Badajoz, 158—Almeida invested, *ib.*—battle of Fuentes d'Honor, 159—first division march to Penamacor, 163—battle of Albuera, *ib.*—Blockade of Badajoz, 164—troops encamp at St. Oloia, *ib.*—head-quarters at Fuente Guinaldo, *ib.*—Graham succeeds Spencer,*ib.*—Blockade of Ciudad Rodrigo, *ib.*—army retreats on the advance of Marmont, 165—goes into winter-quarters,*ib.*—arrives at Lagoisa, Valdozares, and afterwards at Pinhel, *ib.*—Return of officers of the first battalion for the year 1811, 166—siege and capture of Ciudad Rodrigo, 170—army marches for the South, *ib.*—siege of Badajoz, 171—troops cantoned between the Agueda and Coa, *ib.*—Bridge of Almarez carried, 172—Capture of the forts in Salamanca,*ib.*—battle of Salamanca, 174—Wellington moves to Madrid, 177—first division leaves Madrid for the Escurial, 178—entry into Valladolid, *ib.*—siege of Burgos, *ib.*—head-quarters at Freynada, 181—return of officers of the first battalion for the year 1812, 182—affair at Osma, 185—battle of Vittoria, 187—Graham defeats Joseph Buonaparte at Tolosa, *ib.*—siege of St. Sebastian, 188—which capitulates, 189—surrender of Pampeluna, 191—battle of Nivelle, 194—troops return to their quarters at St. Jean de Luz, 196—return of the officers of the first battalion for the year 1813, 198—Bayonne blockaded, 200—battle of Orthez, *ib.*—battle of Toulouse, 201—sortie from Bayonne, in which the Coldstream suffer severely, 202—troops encamp at Bourdeaux, 203—return to England,*ib.*--officers of the 1st battalion from January to July 1814, 204—six companies of the second battalion embark for Holland, 205—inspected at Steenbergen, *ib.*—failure of the attack on Bergen-op-Zoom,*ib.*—troops go into winter-quarters at Brussels, 206—return of officers who embarked for Holland, 24th Nov. 1813, 207—escape of Napoleon from Elba, 208—reinforcements sent to Belgium, 209—position of the Allies, *ib.*—Napoleon heads the Northern army, *ib.*—his proclamation, *ib.*—British march to Quatre Bras, 211—their bravery at the battle of Waterloo, 213—their obstinate defence of the Chateau of Hugomont, 214, 215, 216, 217, 218—list of killed and wounded at Waterloo, 220—their dress in 1742, 340—order respecting their clothing, 352—list of non-commissioned officers who have received commissions since the commencement of the war from 1792, 371—rates of pay, 394—stations of the regiment from 1650 to the present time, 412—roll of the regiment, 458

Collington House, taken, i, 12
Colour-serjeants, first introduced, ii, 188
Colours, new, given to the Guards, i, 391—captured at Preston, &c. removed from Westminster-Hall, i, 94
Commissions, rates paid for, i, 346 practice of selling, 347
Concord, magazines destroyed at, i, 431
Condé, surrender of, ii, 40
Conti, Prince of, carries the village of Neerwinden, i, 232
Conway, General, takes the castle of Waldeck, i, 421
Cooke, Major-Gen., ii, 205
Coote, General, his expedition to Ostend, ii. 64— surrender of, 65—brigade of, 81—mission of, 82
Copenhagen, officers of the Coldstream at, ii, 96—capitulates to the British, 97—remarks on that event, 98
Cornwallis, Lord, reinforced, i, 440 — defeats Lord Stirling and General Maxwell, 444—at the battle of Brandywine, 445—fords the Catawba, ii, 11—attacks the Americans at Guildford Court House, 12 — and defeats them, 13 —his army reinforced, 15—marches through Hanover County to Williamsburg, ibid. — defeats Lafayette, 16 — fortifies York Town and Gloucester, 16—besieged in York Town, 18— capitulates to Washington, 19 —character of, 90
Corunna, projected capture of, i, 336—battle of, ii, 102
Cosmo III., his description of Oxford's Horse and review of the Guards, i, 124—visits the Earl of Albemarle, 127
Court-martial at Stirling, i, 63
Court-martial extraordinary, i, 46
Coxe's Memoirs of John Duke of Marlborough, i, 156, 248
Cox-Heath, corps encamped at, ii, 89
Cradock, Lieut.-Gen., force under, ii, 104—resigns his command to Sir Arthur Wellesley, 105
Crauford, Gen., light brigade of, ii, 120 — retreats behind the Coa, ii, 134—defeats Ney, 137— crosses the Agueda and invests Ciudad Rodrigo, 169
Crauford, Lord, remarks of, i, 367—his orders at Fontenoy, 369—conducts the retreat, 372
Craven, Earl, succeeds to the Coldstream, i, 137—letter from Monmouth to, 147—2nd reg. of Coldstream Guards under his command, 175—letter of the Prince of Orange to, 193—deprived of his regiment, 201— some account of him, ib.
Crequi, Marquis de, i, 232
Cromwell, his army enters Scotland, 10 — proceeds thither in person, 19—destroys the Scotch army at Dunbar, 23—proclamation of, 24—entertained by the city, 60—his reported death, 35 —proclaimed Lord Protector, at Edinburgh, 66—his death, 67 —his son proclaimed Lord Protector, ib.—his letter to the Parliament, detailing the battle of Dunbar ii, 229—his letter respecting the medal struck in memory of the battle of Dunbar, 234 — commission from, appointing John Wells ensign, 235
Crowdjye, Colonel, gallant charge of, ii, 81
Cuesta, General, defeated, ii, 116 —abandons the sick and wounded of the Allied army, 120—retires to Deleytosa, 121
Culloden, battle of, i, 384
Cumberland, Duke of, succeeded by the Duke of Marlborough as Colonel of the Coldstream, i, 351—sails for Holland, 353— joins the army, 354—wounded, 359—appointed Commander-in-Chief, 362—proceeds to Brussels, 364—reaches Halle, 365— his bravery at Fontenoy, 370— arrives in London, 376—commands the troops destined to oppose Prince Charles Edward,

377 — reaches Preston in pursuit of the rebels, 379—arrives at Edinburgh with his forces, 382—lands at the Hague, 389
Cutts, Lord, becomes Colonel of the Coldstream, i, 242 — appointed brigadier of the Guards, 249—wounded, 256—his death, 305—some account of him, *ib.*

D'Abrantes, Duke, defeated, ii, 101
Daendels, General, Dutch fleet under, ii, 67
D'Aguillon, Duke, force under, i, 400
Dalhousie, Earl of, reinforces the Allies, ii, 180
Dalkeith, list of the rebel army at, i, 376
Dalrymple's account of Monmouth's appointment as Lord General of the army, i, 153—his statement of the troops in Flanders, 159
Dampierre, General, attacks the Prussians, ii, 35—his death, 36
Daniel, Père, his " Histoire de la Milice Françoise," i, 184
Darley, Serjeant-Major, his extraordinary valour, ii, 36—letter of Capt. Hewgill respecting, *ib.*
Dartmouth, Lord, circular letter of, i, 432
Daubigney's Club, letter of Col. Lennox to the members of, ii, 31
Dauphin, reviews the French at Gemblours, i, 238
D'Auvergne's " History of the Campaign in Flanders," i, 207, 210, 213, 217, 220, 221, 224, 229, 233, 235, 241, 249, 251, 260
Davies, Lieut.-Col., ii, 173
Dean, Captain, troop of, i, 80
Deane, General, killed, i, 57
Debt, arrest for, i, 428
Denmark, prohibits commerce with Great Britain, ii, 95
Derlton House, surrender of, i, 32
De Ruyter, Admiral, i, 141
Dettingen, battle of, i, 356

Deventer, retreat of the British to, ii, 62
De Witt, chain-shot invented by, i, 117—his fleet attacks Sheerness, 122
D'Humieres, Marshal, defeated, i, 203
Dieghem, head-quarters of the Allies at, i, 227
Dilkes, Brigadier-General, ii, 157, 158
Dixmuyde, occupation of, i, 224, 226—defence of, 250
Dog, calamity averted by, i, 299 —fidelity of one, 399
Dol, near St. Maloes, i, 395
Domestic Intelligence, quoted, i, 162
Donnegal, Lord, arrives before Barcelona with four regiments, i, 297—killed at Montjuich, 299
Donop, Col., his corps of Chasseurs, i, 436—unsuccessful attempt of, 447
Douglas, Lieut.-Gen., his death, i, 211
Douro, passage of the, ii, 111
D'Oyley, Major-Gen., brigade of Guards under, ii, 67
Drummer, tried and shot, i, 36
Drummer's suit, expense of, ii, 330
Duas Casas, river, ii, 160
Dublin, regiment of Guards raised for duty in, i, 113
Dublin Journal, quoted, i, 389, 390
Duderstadt, entry of the French into, i, 411—the town re-taken, *ib.*
Dumbarton Castle, capitulates, i, 47
Dunbar, list of the Scotch army at, i, 23—prisoners taken at, 26 —Cromwell's account of the battle of, 229—medal in memory of the victory, 234
Duncan, Lord, fleet under, ii, 67
Dundee, surrenders to General Monck, i, 43
Dunkirk, defeat of the Spaniards at, i, 117—expedition prepared at, 261
Dunotter Castle, surrenders to Col. Morgan, i, 48—answer of the governor of, 50

INDEX. 539

Dupont, surrender of his army, ii, 100
Durand, Col., Court-Martial on, i, 376
D'Urban, General, defeats the French, ii, 177
Dury, Major-General, commands the Guards, i, 397—wounded at St. Cas, 400
Dutch, abandon their intention to invade England, i, 145—engagement with, 146—peace concluded with the, *ib.*
Dutch fleet, defeated, i, 115, 118 —vessels burnt, 120—attacks Sheerness, 122—successes over, 140—engagement with, 141—action with off the North Foreland, 57—surrenders to Admiral Mitchell, ii, 68

Edinburgh Castle, capitulates to General Monck, i, 33
Edward, Prince, (afterwards Duke of York,) anecdote of his valour, i, 400
Elba, escape of Napoleon from, ii, 208
Eld, Lieut.-Col., killed, ii, 44
Ellembergh, Maj.-Gen., executed, i, 260
Elley, Col., ii, 212
Ellis, Alexander, Court-Martial on, ii, 263
Ellis Correspondence, quoted, i, 131, 187
England, threatened invasion of, ii, 87, 90
Ensigns, distinctions in, i, 177
Entick's Late War, quoted, i, 395, 397
Erskine, Sir W., left in command of the troops, ii, 48—success of, 51
Escurial, occupied by the Allies, ii, 178
Eugene, Prince, moves from Tournay, i, 328 — rejoins the army between Douai and Valenciennes, 334—marches from Quesnoy to Hartre, 339
Evelyn's Memoirs, alluded to, i, 94, 111, 115, 123, 158, 181
Exclusion Bill, thrown out, i, 169
Executions for high treason, i, 111

Fagel, General, i, 336—invests Quesnoy, 338
Fairfax, Sir Thomas, letter from, i, 6
Fairfield, destroyed by the British, ii, 6
Falckenberg, operations on the heights of, i, 422
Famars, camp of, ii, 39
Fenwick, Col., letter of thanks to, i, 4 — appointed Governor of Berwick, 7 — stations of his corps, 8—killed, 117
Ferdinand, Prince, i, 404, 406, 409—at Kirchdenkern, 412
Finch, Hon. Captain John, his death, i, 444
Finch, Hon. Col. Edward, accidentally wounded, ii, 64 — appointed Major-General, 87, 88—arrives in Elsinore Roads, 95
Flanders, Allies assemble in, i, 159—return of a battalion of the Coldstream Guards from, 161—British winter-quarters in, 353 —invaded by the French, 361
Fleurus, battle of, 206—Allies repulsed near, 59
Flushing, armament for the occupation of, ii, 123—capitulation of, 124
Fontenoy, battle of, i, 366—loss of the English at, 372—of the French, *ib.*—French account of, *ib.*
Fox, Henry, extract of a letter from, i, 393
Fox, Major-Gen., ii, 54, 55
Foy, Gen., retires on Bayonne, ii, 187, 217, Extract from his Narrative of the War in the Peninsula, 224
Foz d'Aronse, retreat of the French at, ii, 146
France, events that led to the Revolution in, i, 33—war declared against by England, 34, 199—alliance against, 202—peace concluded with, 272—declares war against Great Britain, 361—injudicious descents on the coast of, 401
Freehold Court House, battle of, ii, 3

Freytag, Marshal, ii, 44—wounded, 45
Fuentes d'Honor, battle of, ii, 160
Fulda, passage of the, i, 420
Fuller, Lieut.-Col., ii, 113

Gage, Gen., retaliation of, i, 431
Galway, Lord, assumes the command in Portugal, i, 286 — crosses the Tagus at Fuenta d'Uenna, 304—joined at Veles by Lieut.-Gen. Wyndham, 304 —his conduct censured, 312
Gambier, Admiral, ii, 95
Gansell, Major-Gen., rescue of, i, 428
Gantelop, punishment of, i, 20
Garth, Colonel, ii, 4, 5
Gawen, Lieut. Alexander, brought prisoner to London, i, 200
Gemblours, arrival of the Allies at, i, 210
Genappe, the Allies proceed to, i, 217
Genderick, operations of the Allies at, i, 409
George I., ascends the throne, i, 341—his public entry into the City, 342—embarks at Gravesend, 345—his death, 349
George II., coronation of, i, 350 —supports the cause of the Allies in the Netherlands, 352— sails for Holland, 353—joins the army, 354—his bravery at the battle of Dettingen, 356—proceeds to Hanover, 359—his army reinforced, ib.—takes up his quarters at Mentz, 360—his arrival in London, ib.
George III., his speech from the throne, i, 428 — reviews the troops, 433, ii, 34, 89
George, Prince of Hesse-Cassel, i, 355
German Town, attacked by Washington, i, 447
Germany, Confederates assemble in, i, 354—continuation of the war in, 404—overthrow of the French power in, ii, 191
Gerpynes, arrival of the Allies on the plains of, i, 211
Ghent, encampment of the Allies near, i, 239, 362—taken by surprise, 373
Gibraltar, surrenders to Sir G. Rooke, i, 286
Ginckel, Gen., troops under, i, 361
Ginkel, Gen., (afterwards Earl of Athlone,) subdues the Royals, i, 200
Givet, bombardment of, i, 262
Glebe, British troops land at, ii, 4
Glencairn, Earl of, his arrest, i, 65
Gloucester, Duke of, his death, ii, 89
Godfrey, Mr., Deputy Governor of the Bank of England, killed, i, 249
Gordon, Lieut.-Col., Court-Martial on, ii, 10—his duel with Col. Thomas, ib.
Gorsuch, Col., wounded, i, 316— his death, 318
Grafton, Duke of, purchases Col. John Russell's commission, i, 348
Graham, Lieut.-Gen., force under, ii, 132—his situation at Barrosa, 156—defeats the enemy, 157—dispatch of, ib.—succeeds Sir Brent Spencer, 164—entrusted with the siege of Ciudad Rodrigo, 169—crosses the Douro, 185—repulses the French at Osma, ib.—defeats them at Vittoria, 187—invests St. Sebastian, 188—and takes it, 190 —succeeded as second in command by Sir John Hope, 191— his attack on Bergen-op-Zoom, 205
Grammont, Duke de, crosses the Maine with his troops, i, 356
Granby, Lord, crosses the river Lahn, i, 412—his valour, 420
Grandwal, Chevalier de, hanged for high treason, i, 223
Granger's "Biographical History of England," i, 129
Granville, Mr., his letter to Mr. Secretary St. John, i, 330
Granville, Sir John, brings a letter from Charles to the Parliament, i, 94
Grasse, Count de, dispatches from, ii, 17

INDEX.   541

Gravenstein, battle of, i, 418
Green, the American General, ii, 15
Grenadier Guards, formation of, i, 106
Grenadiers, first introduced into the army, i, 156—four companies embark for Ostend, 157—generally adopted in regiments of infantry, 157—four additional companies proceed to Ostend, 158
Grose's " Military Antiquities," quoted, i, 99, 102, 108, 158, 180, 199, 275, 372. ii, 63
Grouchy, Marshal, force under, ii, 210, 212
Guarda, retreat of Massena from, ii, 147
Guildford Court House, the Americans defeated at, ii, 13
Gumble's "Life of Gen. Monck," quoted, i, 10, 83, 89, 90, 95

Hall, Lieut.-Colonel, ii, 8, 11—killed, 12
Hall, Serjeant, his letter respecting the battle of Malplaquet, i, 325
Hanau, arrival of the Allies at, i, 359
Hancock, John, declared a rebel, i, 432
Harleian MS., extracts from, i, 37, 73, 76, 109, 116, 123, 138, 180, 220
Harman, Sir John, i, 117
Harrison, Major-General, sent to Cumberland to oppose the Scotch, i, 37
Harwich, two additional companies of the Coldstream sent to, i, 331—they are recalled, 332
Hautbois, expense of a suit for, ii, 331
Hawley, Gen., defeated by the rebels, i, 382
Heath's triumphs of Charles, i, 95
Heister, Lieut.-Gen. de, posted at Flat Bush, i, 436, 437
Helder Point, arrival of the troops at, ii, 68—4000 Russians land at, 71
Hendtschoote, battle of, ii, 45

Herman, Gen., made prisoner, ii, 70
Hesilrige, Sir Arthur, companies drafted from his regiment, i, 4 —his personal valour, 5—appointed Governor of Newcastle, 6—defeats Langdale, ib.—particulars respecting, ib. — complains of the non-payment of assessments, 7—stations of his corps, 8—his letter respecting the prisoners taken at Dunbar, 26—report of, 70, 71
Hesse Darmstadt, Prince of, express from, i, 286—makes a sortie, 287—sails with the fleet for Altea Bay, 290—lands near Barcelona, ib.—killed, 292
Heure, river, passage of the, i, 212
Hewgill, Capt., his letter to Serjeant-Major Coleman, ii, 36
Hill, Gen., wounded, ii, 117—his corps in the vicinity of Abrantes, 128—at the battle of Busaco, 136—crosses the Tagus, 141—at Alentejo, 164—brilliant exploit of, at Arroyo de Molinos, 165—carries the bridge of Almarez, 172—returns to Estremadura, 181—at the battle of Vittoria, 186—moves to Helleté, 199
Hillinger, Gen., capitulation of of, ii, 92
Hinton, Major John, gallantry of, i, 117
History of Illustrious Persons, i, 22
Holland, British forces in, in 1702, i, 278—expedition to, ii, 67
Holmes, Capt., reduces the New Netherlands, i, 114—returns to England, ib.—vessels burnt by, 120—successes of, 140
Holtzhausen, encampment of the Allies at, i, 420
Home, Lieut.-Col., ii, 216, 217
Hook, Col., mission of, i, 313
Hope, Brigadier-General, ii, 84—succeeds Graham as second in command, 191—blockades Bayonne, 200—wounded and taken prisoner, 202
Houchard, charges against, ii, 45

guillotined, 46—remarks on his condemnation, *ib.*
Houghton, Gen., crosses the Tagus, ii, 144
Hounslow, review at, i, 186
House of Brunswick, conspicuous for courage, ii, 33
Howe, Gen., his arrival at Boston, i, 432—his conduct condemned, 442—attempts to bring Washington to action, 443—returns to Amboy, 444—supineness of, 446—winters at Philadelphia, 448
Hugomont, Chateau of, ii, 212, 213 — obstinately defended by the British, 214, 215, 216
Huitson, Capt., his company of the Coldstream, i, 146—resigns his commission, 197
Hume, extracts from, i, 8, 180
Hutchinson, Lord, general orders given by, ii, 82
Hüy, Castle of, taken, i, 229, 240
Hyde Park, Guards encamp in, i, 344, 349

Imperial Guards, at the battle of Waterloo, ii, 224
Ingoldsby, defeats Lambert, i, 93 — charge entrusted to, 367—tried by a Court-Martial, 368
Ireland, present patriots of, i, 386 —Guards sent to repress disturbances in, 66
Isla, opposite Cadiz, abandoned by the French, ii, 177
Italy, army of, its achievements, ii, 75

Jacobins, declaration of, ii, 55
James II., his accession to the throne, i, 173—deserted by his friends, 192—quits London, *ib.* —follies of, 193 — orders the troops from London, *ib.* — escapes to France, 198—his death, 277
Jones, Col., report of, i, 4
Jourdan, Gen., repulses the Allies, ii, 59—Major-Gen. under Joseph Buonaparte, 186

Kingdom's Intelligencer, i, 112

King's Mews, fitted up as a barrack, i, 164
King's Own regiment of Infantry, i, 125
King's Theatre, Guards ordered to do duty at, ii, 336
Klein Ostein, village of, i, 355
Knobelsdorf, the Prussian General, ii, 35
Knyphausen, Gen., gallant affair of, i, 445—at New York, ii, 7, 8—destroys Springfield, 10
Konigseck, Count, reaches Halle, i, 365

Lafayette, anecdote of, i, 446—defeated by Lord Cornwallis, ii, 16
Lake, Major-Gen., brigade of, ii, 18, 34—ordered to assist the Dutch, 41
Lambert, Major-Gen., arrives at Leith, i, 47—his journey to Scotland, i, 79—forces under, 82—his escape from the Tower, 93—re-taken, and again committed, *ib.*
Lancaster, British prisoners sent to, ii, 19
Landen, battle of, i, 232
Landrecy, siege of, ii, 52
Langdale, Sir Marmaduke, organises an army in Scotland, i, 6—defeated, *ib.*
Lannoy, evacuated by the French, ii, 53
La Pena, Gen., joins Gen. Graham at Tarifa, ii, 155
Laws, Mr. T., letters from, i, 336
Le Breton, Col., defends Burgos, ii, 180
Leicester, arrival of the Coldstreamers at, i, 87
Leigh, Col., battalion under, ii, 34
Leinster, Duke of, arrives at Ostend with fifteen regiments, i, 224
Le Marchant, General, killed, ii, 175
Lennox, Lieut.-Col., his misunderstanding with the Duke of York, ii, 30—his duel with him, 32—remarks on his conduct in the affair, 33
Lenthall, Mr., letters to, i, 40, 54 —arrested, 72

Leon, Isle of, return of the Guards at, ii, 130

Lerida, surrender of, i, 313

Leslie, Major-Gen., his proceedings in Virginia, ii, 11 — receives orders to join Lord Cornwallis, *ib.*

Lestock and Sinclair, secret expedition under, i, 387

Lewis XIV., concentrates his army round Mons, i, 215—superintends the siege of Namur, 216—prepares an expedition at Dunkirk, 261 — sends re-inforcements to Spain, 308—attempts to restore the Pretender, 314—his advances to obtain peace, 319

Lewis XV., heads the army, i, 361 — arrives at the camp before Tournay, 365

Lewis XVI., murder of, ii, 33

Lewis XVIII., his flight from Paris, ii, 208

Lexington, disasters at, i, 431

Liege, arrival of the Allies at, i, 229

Lieut.-Colonel, rank of, granted to Captains of companies, i, 190

Life Guards, officers in the, i, 104

Ligonier, Sir John, i, 367

Lilburn, Colonel, appointed commander of the forces in Scotland, i, 59

Lincelles, Dutch troops driven from, ii, 41

Lisbon, Sir John Moore's letter on the defence of, ii, 150—Lord Wellington's opinion on the subject, 153

Lisle, surrender of, i, 318

Lisle, Lord, eldest son of the Earl of Leicester, i, 17

Litchfield, arrival of the Guards at, i, 378

Lobsters, regiment of, i, 5

Loch Tay, &c., captured, i, 61

London, great fire of, i, 120— alarm in, 122—troops in, declare for the Parliament, 82— entry of Gen. Monck into, 88— Gen. Monck ordered to restore order in, 90—triumphal entry of Charles II. into, 95—troops ordered out of, 193 — great alarm in, at the success of Charles Edward, 377

London Gazette, quoted, i, 373, 376, 380, 390, 406, 420

Long Island, patent for, i, 113— battle of, 437—retreat of the Americans from, 438

Long Parliament, revived, i, 68

Lottum, Count, i, 322

Loudon, Earl of, his orders to the army, i, 433

Ludlow, Lieut-Gen., memoirs of, i, 42, 43, 71

Ludlow, Maj.-Gen., thanks to, ii, 82

Lumley, Gen., left in command of the army, i, 340

Luxembourg, Duke of, reconnoitres the position of the Allies, i, 209, 212—advantage gained by, 213—encamps at Falay, 227 —takes the Castle of Hüy, 229 —marches to Soignies, 235— his death, 241

Macdonell, Lieut.-Col., ii, 214—directions to, 215—bravery of, 216, 217

Mack, Gen., capitulates at Ulm, ii, 92

MacKinnon, Col. Henry, ii, 113 —his humanity, 120—removes the sick and wounded to Elvas, 121—present at the battle of Busaco, 137—his gallantry at Fuentes d'Honor, 161—killed, 169

MacKinnon, Lieut.-Col., repulses Kellerman, ii, 211—moves to the support of Hugomont, 217

Macpherson, Lieut.-Col., ii, 10

Mac Pherson's "Secret History of Great Britain," quoted, i, 99, 102

Madrid, entry of Napoleon into, ii, 102—quitted by King Joseph, and entry of the Allies into, 177

Maestricht, taken, i, 145

Malplaquet, battle of, i, 322—loss of the Allies at, 325—that of the French, *ib.*

Manchester, arrival of Prince Charles Edward at, i, 377

544 INDEX.

Marabout, capitulates to the British, ii, 83
Markham, Capt. Anthony, i, 178
Marlborough, Duke of, lands at Rotterdam, i, 202—enters Brussels, 319—besieges Mons, 327—moves from Tournay, 328—returns to England, 329—proceeds to the Hague, 334—' Ne plus ultra' of, 335—termination of his military career, 337—attempts to vindicate his conduct, *ib.*—succeeded by the Duke of Ormond, 338—his death, 362
Marlborough, Lieut.-Gen., Duke of, i, 394—his march to St. Servan and Solidone, 395—manifesto of, *ib.*—sent to command the British on the Continent, 396
Marmont, his operations at Salamanca, ii, 162, 164—marches to the relief of Ciudad Rodrigo, 165—retires to Salamanca, 171—advances to St. Christoval, 172—crosses the Tormes, 173—retreats behind the Douro, 173 attempts to cut off Wellington's communication with Salamanca and Ciudad Rodrigo, 174—wounded 177—retreat of the army under, to Valladolid, *ib.*
Massachusetts, National Congress of, i, 431
Massena, Marshal, forces under, ii, 90—defeated by the Archduke Charles, 92—Ciudad Rodrigo, capitulates to, 133—proclamation of, *ib.*—his army enters Portugal, 135—establishes his head-quarters at Coimbra, 139—pursues the Allies, *ib.*—retreats to Thomar, 141—his army reinforced, *ib.*—retires from Pombal, 144—through Condeixa and Cazal Nova to Miranda de Corvo, 145—reaches Celerico, 147—retreats to, from Guarda, *ib.*—enters Spain, 148—justification of, 149—conduct of his troops, 154—retires on Salamanca, 158—recalled to France, 162—succeeded by Marshal Ragusa, *ib.*

Massey, Col., wounded, i, 35
Matagorda Fort, attack on, i, 282
Matchlocks, discontinued by the Guards, i, 167
Mathew, Col. Edward, embarks for America, i, 433—enters Virginia, ii, 4—communication made to, 7
Maxwell, Gen., defeated, i, 444
Mehaigne, arrival of the Allies at, i, 216
Menin, British encamp at, ii, 42
Menou, Gen., army under, before Alexandria, ii, 80—retreat of, 82—truce requested by, 84—his conduct censured, 85
Mentz, arrival of the Confederate forces at, i, 360
Mercurius Publicus, extracts from, i, 100, 103, 109, 110
Meriden, camp at, i, 380
Middleton, Lieut.-Gen., lands in Scotland, i, 58—defeated, 62—killed by a fall from his horse, 192
Miller, Serjeant-Major, docquet of a grant of arms and crest to, i, 116
Miranda de Corvo, reduced to ruins, ii, 146
Mitchell, Admiral, Dutch fleet surrenders to, ii, 68
Moira, Lord, joins the Duke of York, ii, 59
Moncall, Col., wounded, i, 288
Monck, General, originates the Coldstream Guards, i, 1—his return from Ireland, *ib.*—command entrusted to, 4—his regiment enters Scotland with Cromwell, 10—sketch of his life, 12—born at Potteridge, in Devonshire, *ib.*—pedigree of, *ib.*—goes with the expedition to Cadiz at the age of seventeen, 14—appointed Ensign, *ib.*—Captain in Lord Goring's regiment, *ib.*—made Governor of Dublin, *ib.*—arrested by the King's orders, 15—rejoins his regiment, *ib.*—taken prisoner, *ib.*—sent to the Tower, 16—his " Observations upon Military and Political Affairs, *ib.*"—pro-

ceeds to Ireland, 17 — his regiment enters Scotland with Cromwell, 19 — commands the Fleet, 57 — thanks of Parliament voted to him, 59 — resumes his command of the troops in Scotland, 60 — captures Loch Tay, &c. 61—his head-quarters at Dalkeith, 63 —contemplated assassination of, 64 — his declaration, 72—proceedings of, 73 — marches to Lithgowe, 74 — expostulations with, 79—deserted by his officers, 80—his regiment retained by the King, 98—his army assembles at Coldstream, 82 — troops who accompany him to London, 83—letter from, 84—commences his march from Coldstream, 85—gives the command of his regiment to Capt. Morgan, *ib.* — Commissioners meet the army near Leicester, *ib.*—his entry into London, 88 —ordered by Parliament to restore tranquillity in the City, 90—thanks of the House voted him, 91—appointed General of the Fleet, 92—his regiment encamps at Blackheath in readiness to receive the King, 94—created Duke of Albemarle, 95 — his letter to Lord Henry Cromwell, ii, 235 — to Lord Fleetwood, on the posture of affairs, 236—his order respecting Snaphance muskets, 238 —appoints James Pembruge Lieutenant, 239 — Commission of Charles II., constituting him Captain-General of the Forces, 239—(*See* Earl of Albemarle.)

Monmouth, Duke of, joins the French in Flanders, i, 140—completion of his regiment, 141 — his letter on the precedency of regiments, 147—authorised to issue orders for the removal of quarters, 152—on his appointment as Lord General, 153,—his commission taken from him, 155—lands in Dorsetshire, 179 — proclaimed King, *ib.*— taken prisoner, 180—beheaded, 181—his letter to Lord Craven, ii, 271

Mons, surrender of, i, 208 — French army before, 215—attempt to surprise, 217

Montague, Edward, appointed General of the Fleet, i, 93

Montbrun, Gen., summons Coimbra, ii, 145

Montjuich, attack on, i, 291, 298, 299

Moore, Sir John, sent to reinforce the army of Portugal, ii, 102—killed at Corunna, 103—his letter on the defence of Lisbon, ii, 150

Morgan, Col. Thomas, his letter detailing the surrender of Dunotter Castle, i, 48 — his address to the soldiers, 100—defeats Middleton, 62

Moryson, Brigadier Henry, i, 333

Muckle Meg, a famous piece of ordnance, described, i, 33

Mud Island, fort of, abandoned, i, 447

Mulhausen, operations near, i, 417

Munster, siege of, i, 415

Murray, Col. Sir James, his letter respecting the bravery of the Coldstream at St. Amand, ii, 37—brigade under, 110

Musters, extract of a regulation for, i, 188

Mutiny Bill, passed, i, 200

Mutlow, Capt., his regiment returns to England, i, 159

Muy, Chevalier de, i, 405

Namur, invested by Marshal Boufflers, i, 216—its surrender, 217—invested by the Elector of Bavaria, 246—siege of, 249—capitulation of, 251, 258

Necker, folly or treachery of, ii, 33

Neerwinden, village of, conflict at, i, 230, 231—carried by the Prince of Conti, 232

Newcastle, discontent at, i, 82

Newhaven, success of the British at, ii, 5

New London, taken by General Arnold, ii, 17

546 INDEX.

New York, occupation of, by the British, i, 438
Ney, Marshal, attacks General Crauford, ii, 134—defeated, 137—retreats through Condeixa, 145—attempts to force the British position at Quatre Bras, 211
Nicholas, Colonel, 113
Nimeguen, treaty of, i, 161
Nivelle, position of the French on the, ii, 191
Noailles, Duke de, remains in the Palatinate, i, 354—preparations of, 356—remains at Hochstadt, 358—retires from Heidelberg, 359—regiment of, 371
Normandy, attack on the coast of i, 243
North, Lord, rejection of his "Conciliatory Proposition," i, 432
Norton, Lieut.-Col., marches for Young's House, ii, 7—and takes it, 8
Nulli Secundus Club, instituted, ii, 30—regulations of the, 373—succession of members, 376

Ocana, loss of the Spanish at, ii, 126
Officers, commissioned, Committee for nominating, i, 70
——— of infantry, change in their appointments, i, 168
——— trust reposed in them, i, 69
——— who deserted General Monck, i, 80
Oglevy, Captain, his letter to Colonel Morgan, i, 50
O'Hara, Brigadier-Gen., gallantry of, ii, 14
O Key, Col., his regiment, i, 20—describes the storming of Dundee, 43
O'Moran, seized as a spy and sent to Paris, ii, 44
O'Neil, pacification with, i, 18
Oporto, insurrection at, ii, 100—capitulates to Marshal Soult, 105—attacked by Sir Arthur Wellesley, 110
Orange, Prince of, directs the siege of Landrecy, ii, 52—drives the enemy from Charleroi, 54—situation of, 62—his intention to attack Lisle, 209—stationed at Nivelle, 211
Ormond, Duke of, succeeds Marlborough in the command of the army, i, 338—reviews the guards, ib. publishes a suspension of hostilities, 339—returns to England, 340—sails from Cadiz, to assist the Pretender, 345—his fleet dispersed by a storm, 346
Orthez, battle of, ii, 200
Osma, the French repulsed at, ii, 185
Ostend, army sent to, i, 157, 158—submits to the French, 373—expedition to, under General Coote, ii, 64—non-success of, 65
Oudenarde, battle of, i, 317—submits to the French, 373
Oudenbourg, troops encamp at, i, 224
Oughtred, the mathematician, his death, i, 94
Overton, Col., lands in Tarbat Bay, i, 54—committed to the Tower, 64—declares for Parliament, 86
Oxford Blues, first raised, i, 102, 124

Pack, Gen., failure of, ii, 175
Pakenham, Major-Gen., defeats the French, ii, 175
Pampeluna, garrison of, surrenders, ii, 191
Parck Camp, list of the Confederate army at, i, 228
Paris, treaty of, 202
Parke, Serj., reprimanded, i, 428
Patriotic Fund, letter to, ii, 87
Patriotism, true, where to be found, i, 385
Pay of the Coldstream Guards, ii, 396—variations in it, 405
Pearson, Col., his letter on General Monck's proceedings, i, 77
Peck, a village near Tournay, ii, 47
Peers, new creation of, i, 337
Pennington, Col., gallantry of, ii, 8—his duel with Captain Talmash, ib. commands the Guards at St. Amand, 35
Perrin, Lieut.-Col. James, ii, 34
Peterborough, Earl of, sails for

Lisbon, i, 289—lands near Barcelona, 290—takes the Fort of Montjuich, 291 — gallantry of, 292—proceeds with a small force to Valencia, 294—his misunderstanding with Prince Charles, 296—marches for Valencia, 301 — hears of the cruelty of the Spaniards, 303—leaves Spain for Savoy, 304

Petersburgh, treaty of, ii, 90

Peyman, Gen., requests passports for the King's nieces, ii, 97

Philadelphia, General Congress at, i, 432—occupation of, by the British, 446—evacuated, ii, 2

Philip, attempts the recovery of Barcelona, i, 296 — joins the French army, 298

Philippon, Gen., escape of, ii, 171

Pichegru, Gen., repulsed, ii, 55—passes the Waal, and attacks the Allies, 60

Picton, General, division under, ii, 145

Pierce, Col., his gallant conduct, i, 282

Pikes, use of, discontinued, i, 307

Pitt, Mr., declared an enemy to the human race, ii, 55

Pombal, skirmish at, ii, 144

Pont-à-Vendin, French lines forced at, i, 328

Pontechin, village of, carried by the Allies, ii, 55

Pontevedra, taken, i, 336

Portugal, evacuated by the French, ii, 101, 148—desolation produced by the invading army, 154

Powell, Capt., murdered, i, 55

Pretender, enters the Frith of Forth, i, 314—his flight, 345—received as King of Madrid, *ib.* conspiracy for placing him on the throne, 349

Price's "History of the Restoration," i, 86

Pride, Col., regiment of, i, 20

Prince George, transport, accident to the, ii, 103

Prince Regent, declares his intention of joining the Allies, ii, 208

Proby, Lord, thanks the Guards for their conduct in the attack on Bergen-op-Zoom, ii, 206

Prynne, Wm., Esq., the celebrated antiquary, i, 100

Puebla, arrival of the Guards at, ii, 155, 163

Putney Heath, review on, i, 170

Quarters, appointed for the English, Scots, and Irish forces, i, 193

Quesnoy, surrenders to the British, i, 338

Quiberon, expedition to, i, 389

Ragusa, Marshal, succeeds Massena in the command of the army of Portugal, ii, 162

Ramrods, iron ones, substituted for wooden, i, 393

Rawdon, Lord, acts as second to the Duke of York, ii, 32

Regiments, English, in Scotland, force of, i, 60—marched out of London, 88 — precedency of, 121, 142, 147—order of the King relative to, 148

Regnier's "State of Egypt," quoted, ii, 82

Reresby, Sir J., memoirs of, i, 197

Rhenen, the French repulsed at, ii, 61

Rhode Island, seizure of government stores in, i, 431

Rivers, Lord, army under, i, 223

Rodendella, carried by assault, i, 284

Roize, General, killed, ii, 82

Rooke, Sir George, attacks Chateaurenard in the Harbour of Vigo, i, 284—Gibraltar surrenders to him, 286

Roswell Castle, surrenders to General Monck, i, 33

Round Tower, Gibraltar, attacked by the French, i, 288

Royal regiment of Guards, i, 105 —revolt of, 199—compelled to surrender, 200

Rupert, Prince, i, 118—his fleet attacks the Dutch, 144—intrepidity of, 145

Rushworth's Historical Collections, quoted, i, 18, 32

Ryley, Mr., Norrey King of Arms, i, 25

Sabugal, defeat of the French at, ii, 148
Sackville, Col., appointed Lieut.-Col. of the Coldstream Guards, i, 166
St. Amand, severe struggle near, ii, 35—account of the affair, 37
St. Cas, defeat of the British at, i, 400—French account of, 40
St. Catherine's Fort, Cadiz, blown up, i, 283
St. Christoval, the Allies occupy the heights of, ii, 172
St. Denis, village of, fortified, i, 254—battle of, 160
St. George, Chevalier, lands in Scotland, i, 344
St. Germain, Count de, i. 404
St. Jean de Luz, head-quarters of the Allies at, ii, 195
St. Jean Pied de Port, blockaded by the Spaniards, ii, 199
St. John, Mr., letter of Mr. Granville to, i, 330
St. Maloes, expedition for, i, 394, 398
St. Quintin Linneck, i, 235
St. Sebastian, siege of, ii, 188
Salamanca, capture of the forts in, ii, 173—battle of, 174
Saltoun, Lord, bravery of the corps under, ii, 214, 215, 216, 218
Sandford's History of the Coronation of James II., i, 173
Sandwich, Lord, his death, i, 141
Sarré, village of, carried by the Allies, ii, 193
Savoy, fitted up for soldiers, i, 162—used as barracks, ii, 326
Saxe, Marshal, military talents of, i, 365—his command at Fontenoy, 370, 372
Scarborough, Earl of, appointed Colonel of the Coldstream, i, 348
Schorel, village of, taken, ii, 70
Scotland, army raised for invading, i, 1—army organised in, to invade England, 6
Scott, Colonel, battalion under, i, 341
Scott, Major, takes Dumfries, i, 44
Scout, The, a periodical paper, i, 63

Second-Major, appointed to the Coldstream, i, 333
Sedgemore, battle at, i, 179—allowance granted to the wounded at, 182
Segur, Lieut.-General de, taken prisoner, i, 409
Selingenstadt, bridge at, i, 356, 357
Serjeants, discontinue wearing ruffles, i, 390
Seville, entry of Joseph Buonaparte into, ii, 130—affair at, 177
Sheerness, attacked by the Dutch, i, 122
Shepherd's dog, fidelity of, i, 399
Sherbrooke, Major-General, force under, ii, 103
Shovel, Sir Cloudesley, sails for Lisbon, i, 289
Shrimpton, Major-General, i, 311
Silveira, General, retakes Chaves, ii, 105
Skelton, Captain, his battalion returns to London, i, 146
Skinner, Dr. Thomas, his Life of General Monck, i, 14, 16, 86, 87
Smith, Jeremiah, adjutant of Horse, i, 86
Smith, Colonel, exhaustion of his men, i, 431
Smith, Sir James, appointed Major of the Coldstream Guards, i, 109—proceeds to Exeter, 110
Smollett, quoted, i, 337, 338
Soldier, British, his superiority, ii, 63
Solmes, Count de, and James II., i, 196
Somerset-House, the residence of the Queen Mother, i, 161
Soubise, Marshal, raises the siege of Munster, i, 415
Soult, defeats the Spanish near Monterry, ii, 104—carries Oporto, 105—his loss there, 111 critical situation of his army, 112—forces the passes between Salamanca and Placentia, 120— passes the Sierra Morena, 130 marches to the relief of Badajoz, 163—returns to Seville, 164 —again advances to support Badajoz, 171—in Granada, 178— ordered to join the grand army in Germany, 185 resumes the

command in the South of France and defeated, 188 — concentrates in front of Bayonne, 195 —repulsed in his attacks on the left of the Allies, 196

Spain, hostilities re-commence with, i, 345—amount of French forces in, 185

Spaniards, barbarity of the, i, 302

Spencer, Colonel, ii, 81—crosses the Tagus, 164

Sporcken, General, corps of, i, 405, 406, 414, 418

Spragg, Sir Edward, defeats the Dutch, i, 123 — engages the Dutch, 144, 145—drowned, 146

Springfield, destroyed, ii, 10

Stainville, General, i, 421

Stair, Earl of, sent ambassador to Holland, i, 352—commander-in-chief of the Confederates, 353—moves towards the Rhine, 354 —encourages the troops, 358

Standards and guidons, order respecting, ii, 351

Stanhope, Colonel, battery taken by, ii, 51

Stedman's History of the American War, i, 431, 441

Steenkirk, battle of, i, 218—officers killed and wounded at, 220

Stewart, Lieut.-Col., killed, ii, 14

Stirling Castle, i, 39—capitulates to General Monck, 40

Stirling, Lord, defeated, i, 444—his attempt on Staten Island, ii, 6

Stoney Point, fortifications at, ii, 5

Stopford, Colonel, Wellington's communication to, ii, 129 — wounded, 202

Straw huts of the Coldstream, burnt, i, 241

Sulivan, Gen., taken prisoner, i, 437

Sun, eclipse of, i, 300

Swords, used instead of espontoons, ii, 30

Symonds, Mr., his journey to Edinburgh, ii, 234

Talavera, battle of, ii, 117

Talmash, Captain, killed in a duel, ii, 8

Talmash, Colonel, appointed to the Coldstream, i, 201—his troops encamp at Oudenbourg, 218—conducts the infantry in their retreat from Landen, 234, 235—dies of his wounds, 242—some account of him, *ib.*

Tangiers, importance of its occupation, i, 162 — return of the troops from, 168

Tantallon Castle, surrenders to General Monck, i, 34

Tarifa, junction of the confederates at, ii, 155

Tarleton, Lieut.-Col., ii, 12

Templeux, camp at, i, 246

Tessé, Marshal de, threatens Tortosa, i, 297—censured, 300

Third Foot Guards, account of, i, 274

Thomas, Col., killed in a duel, ii, 10

Torbay, Prince of Orange lands at, i, 191

Tordesillas, position of the French army at, ii, 173

Tormes, forded by the Allies, ii, 172, 174—the French army cross the, 176

Torres Vedras, retreat of the Allies to, ii, 139—defeat of the French at, 153

Toulouse, battle of, ii, 201

Tournay, capitulation of, i, 321—investment of, 365—surrenders to the French, 373

Trained City Bands, i, 98, 345

Trant, Col., position of, ii, 108—his well-planned attack near Togal, 135—sufferings of his troops, 138—retreats behind the Vouga, *ib.*—surprises the enemy at Coimbra, 140—firm conduct of, 145—ordered to watch Marmont, 170

Tryon, Lieut.-Gen., takes Newhaven, ii, 5

Turcoin, conflict at, ii, 54

Tyrawley, Lord, succeeds to the command of the Coldstream, i, 394—returns to London, 402 —his death, 430

Utrecht, treaty of, 340

Val, battle of, i, 389

Valenciennes, invested by the

550 INDEX.

British, ii, 39—the town capitulates, 40

Valladolid, retreat of the French to, ii, 177—evacuated by them, 185

Van Trump, Admiral, killed, i, 58

Van Trump, Admiral, his advantages over the British and French Fleets, i, 145

Vase, presented to the Duke of York, ii, 94

Vauban, the celebrated engineer, i, 243

Vaudemont, Prince, army under, i, 246, 251—reinforced, 253—heads the Guards, 254—detachment under, 264

Vaux, village of, plundered, ii, 51

Venner, infatuation of, i, 98

Vermy, convent of, i, 334

Vernon, Colonel, anecdote related by, i, 399

Victor, Marshal, French troops under, ii, 116

Vienna, entered by the French, ii, 92

Vigo, taken by the British, i, 336, 350—expedition against, ii, 74

Villars, Marshal, opposes the investment of Mons, i, 321—wounded, 323—intrepidity of, 324—reconnoitres the position of the Allies, 329

Villeroy, Marshal, his march to Brussels, i, 252—encamps between Senoff and Arkiennes, 253—moves towards Perwys, 257—his march to Montigny, 258—arrives at Valenciennes, 262—reviews his troops, 264

Vimeira, battle of, ii, 101

Virginia, regiment formed for service in, i, 155—returns to England, 159—proceedings in, ii, 11

Vittoria, battle of, ii, 186

Vizeu, arrival of the Guards at, ii, 126—French army concentrated at, 135

Vlie, vessels burnt in, i, 120

Voltaire, his 'Age of Lewis XIV.,' i, 308, 321, 358, 359, 365, 369, 371, 372

Voorthuizen, retreat of the English to, ii, 61

VVemmel, junction of the Allied forces at, i, 235

Wakelin, Captain, walks round St. James's Park five times in two hours, i, 167

Walcheren, expedition to, ii, 123, 125—evacuation of, 126

Walcourt, attack of the French on, i, 203

Waldeck, castle of, capitulates, i, 421

Waldeck, Prince, commands the allied army, i, 202—defeats the French at Walcourt, 203—retreats from Fleurus, 207—reinforced by the Coldstream, ib. proceeds to the Hague, 214—his conference with the Duke of Cumberland, 366—attacks Fontenoy, 367, 370

Waldegrave, Earl of, appointed to the command of the Coldstream, i, 430—his death, 30—succeeded by Frederick Duke of York, ib.—some account of him, ib.

Waller, Sir William, i, 5

Walmoden, General, ii, 45—command of the army devolves upon him, 61

War-Office Records, i, 394

Warren, Lieut.-Colonel Harry, i, 15

Washington Fort, carried, i, 440

Washington, George, elected commander-in-chief of the American forces, i, 433 — defective state of his army, 436—superintends the passage of the troops from Long Island to New York, 438—retreat of, 440—his judgment, 443—crosses the Delaware, 444—defeated at Brandywine, 445 — re-organises his troops, 446— attacks German Town, 447—quits his position at Skippack Creek, ib.—strong position of, 448—his arrival at Freehold Court House, ii, 3—defeated at Guildford Court House, 13 — joined by the French from Rhode Island, 17—determines to attack Lord Cornwallis, ib.—lays siege to York Town, ib.—Lord Cornwallis capitulates to him, 19

Waterloo, battle of, ii, 213—policy of Wellington at, 222

Wavre, allied army at, i, 263
Welaw, sufferings of the troops at, ii, 61
Wellesley, Sir Arthur, sails from Cork, ii, 101 — defeats the French at Vimeira, *ib.*—appointed commander of the forces in Portugal, 105—his aides-decamp, *ib.*—arrives at Coimbra, 109—attacks Oporto, 110—arrives at Braga, 112—determines to commence operations in Spain, 115—returns to Oropesa, 120—crosses the Tagus at Arzobispo, 121—created Viscount Wellington, 126—his communication to Col. Stopford, 129—moves from Vizeu to Celerico, 132—proclamation issued by, 134—retires to the lines of Torres Vedras, 139—his army reinforced, 143—detained for want of provisions, 147—drives Massena from Guarda, *ib.*—policy of, 152—his opinion on the defence of Lisbon, 153—visits the troops in the Alentejo, 158—returns to Villa Formosa, *ib.*—recrosses the Tagus, 164—blockades Ciudad Rodrigo, *ib.*—retreats on the approach of Marmont, *ib.*—takes Ciudad Rodrigo, 169—besieges and captures Badajoz, 171—moves for the north, *ib.*—fords the Tormes, 172—captures the forts in, 173 — establishes his head-quarters at Rueda, *ib.*—attempt to cut off his communication with Salamanca and Ciudad Rodrigo, 174—his generalship at the battle of Salamanca, *ib.*—dispatch of, 176 — moves by Cuellar, through Segovia, to Madrid, 177 —enters Valladolid, 178—lays siege to Burgos, *ib.* — retires on Ciudad Rodrigo, 181 — reaches Salamanca, 185—gains the battle of Vittoria, 187—besieges St. Sebastian, 188—and takes it, 190—resolves to pass into France, 192—his humane proclamation, *ib.*—his triumphs, *ib.*—defeats Soult at Orthez, 200—marches on Bordeaux, 201

—gains the battle of Toulouse. *ib.* — forces under, at Brussels, 209 — falls back on Waterloo, 212 — characteristic trait of, 215—his policy at the battle of Waterloo, 222, 223
Wentworth, Lord, appointed Col. of the royal regiment of Guards, i, 106—killed, 250
Wesel, invested, i, 408
Westminster Hall, colours hung up in, i, 25—ordered to be removed from, 94
———— Journal, quoted, i, 373, 374, 376, 380, 388, 389
Whitehall, new buildings at, first occupied by the Coldstream, i, 394
Widows of officers, petition the House for relief, i, 45
William, Prince of Orange, lands at Torbay, i, 191—his letter to the Earl of Craven, 193—his arrival in London, 198—attempts to shake his throne, 200—projects an alliance against France, 202—proceeds to Holland to take the command in Flanders, 207—reviews his army, 208—quits Halle and embarks for England, 209—returns to the Hague, *ib.*—crosses the Heure with his troops, 212—advances with the army to Fleury, *ib.*—crosses the river below Ath, 213 leaves the camp for Loo, *ib.*—returns to England, 214—embarks for the Hague, 215—moves towards the Mehaigne, 216—reviews the troops, 217—present at the battle of Steenkirk, 219—retreats to Halle, *ib.* —returns to England, 225—rejoins the army at the Hague, 226—advances on Liege, 229—present at the battle of Landen, 232—his intrepidity, 233—retreat of, *ib.*—moves to Louvain, 235—returns to England, 236—proceeds to Holland, 237 —reviews the troops, *ib.*—arrives with the allied forces at Arseele, 245—his departure for Namur, 246—his head-quarters at the Chateau de la Falize, 246

—his satisfaction at the conduct of the Guards, 248—lands at Margate, 260—joins the army in Holland, 263— moves towards Gemblours, 265—strength of the army under him, 269—assembles a council of war, 270— his army reinforced, 271—quits the army and proceeds to Hague, *ib.* — concludes peace with France, 272— his triumphant entry into London, 274—his death, 277

Williamsburg, arrival of Lord Cornwallis at, ii, 15

Williamson, Secretary, i, 150, 153, 154

Wilson, Sir Robert, on Egypt, ii, 83

Wimbledon Common, review on, i, 433

Winchelsea, Earl of, acts as second to Lieut.-Col. Lennox, ii, 32

Winter, severe, ii, 6—in America, 62

Wirtemburg, Prince of, attacks the French at Steenkirk, i, 218

Woodford, Lieut.-Col., maintains the village of Arapiles against the French, ii, 176

Woodford, Col., companies under, ii, 217, 218

Worcester, battle of, i, 39

Worms, treaty of, i, 360

Wrestling-match in St. James's Park, i, 166

Wutgenau, Lieut.-Gen., i, 412

Wyndham, Lieut.-Gen., captures Requena, i, 301 — joins Lord Galway, 304

Wyndham, Sir Wm., extract of a letter from, i, 313

Xavier, Prince, takes Gottingen, i, 406, 409, 418—retreat of, 421

York, Frederick Duke of, succeeds to the command of the Coldstream on the death of Lord Waldegrave, ii, 30—his misunderstanding with Lieut.-Col. Lennox, and duel with him, 32—general order of, 38—invests Valenciennes, 39—and takes the town, 40—separates from the Austrians and marches to Dunkirk, 41, 44—abandons the siege, 45—quits the army for London, 48—success of, 51—Drives the enemy from Cæsar's Camp, 52 defeats the French near Tournay, 53—his address to the troops relative to the sanguinary proclamation of the French, 56—retreats through Tournay, 59—crosses the Maese and encamps at Wichen, 60—returns to England, 61—resumes his command of the army in Holland, 69—carries the village of Schorel, 70—takes Alkmaar, 71—succeeds to the command of the 1st regiment of Guards, 89—which he resigns, 93—vase presented to, 94—his address on accepting it, *ib.* — his partiality to the Coldstream, 95

York, Duke of, i, 115—fleet of, 141

York Town, invested by the Americans, ii, 17

Young's House, American post at, ii, 7—taken by the British, 8

Zadora, Valley of, ii, 186

Zastrow, Major-Gen., i, 371

Zierenberg, surprised, i, 408

THE END.

PRINTED BY A. J. VALPY,
RED LION COURT, FLEET STREET.

www.ingramcontent.com/pod-product-compliance
Lightning Source LLC
Chambersburg PA
CBHW051106230426
43667CB00014B/2455